CHILD WORKERS IN ENGLAND, 1780–1820

Child Workers in England, 1780–1820
Parish Apprentices and the Making of the Early Industrial Labour Force

KATRINA HONEYMAN
University of Leeds, UK

ASHGATE

© Katrina Honeyman 2007

All rights reserved. No part of this publication may be reproduced, stored in a retrieval system or transmitted in any form or by any means, electronic, mechanical, photocopying, recording or otherwise without the prior permission of the publisher.

Katrina Honeyman has asserted her moral right under the Copyright, Designs and Patents Act, 1988, to be identified as the author of this work.

Published by
Ashgate Publishing Limited
Gower House
Croft Road
Aldershot
Hampshire GU11 3HR
England

Ashgate Publishing Company
Suite 420
101 Cherry Street
Burlington, VT 05401-4405
USA

Ashgate website: http://www.ashgate.com

British Library Cataloguing in Publication Data
Honeyman, Katrina
 Child workers in England, 1780–1820 : parish apprentices and the making of the early industrial labour force. –
 (Studies in labour history)
 1. Child labor – England – History – 18th century 2. Child labor – England – History – 19th century 3. Apprentices – England – History – 18th century 4. Apprentices – England – History – 19th century
 I. Title
 331.3'1'0942'09033

Library of Congress Cataloging-in-Publication Data
Honeyman, Katrina.
 Child workers in England, 1780–1820 : parish apprentices and the making of the early industrial labour force / by Katrina Honeyman.
  p. cm. – (Studies in labour history)
 Includes bibliographical references.
 ISBN-13: 978-0-7546-6272-3 (alk. paper) 1. Child labor–England–History–18th century. 2. Child labor–England–History–19th century. I. Title.
 HD6250.E542H66 2007
 331.3'18–dc22
                                                                                            2007005525

ISBN 978-0-7546-6272-3

Printed and bound in Great Britain by MPG Books Ltd, Bodmin, Cornwall.

Contents

List of Tables		*vii*
General Editor's Preface		*ix*
Acknowledgements		*xi*
List of Abbreviations		*xiii*
1	Industrial Change in England 1780–1820	1
2	The Poor Law and the Parish Apprentice	15
3	Factory Apprenticeship: Structure, Process and Legislation	33
4	The Supply and Distribution of Parish Apprentices	55
5	Textile Enterprise and the Parish Apprentice	91
6	The Costs and Benefits of Parish Apprenticeship	113
7	Parish Factory Apprenticeship and the Nature of Work	129
8	The Making of a Gendered Labour Force?	151
9	The Exploitation of Little Children	175
10	The Voices of the Children	199
11	The Protection of Parish Apprentices	215
12	The Neglect of Parish Apprentices	239
13	Conclusion	261
Appendix		*265*
Bibliography		*293*
Index		*325*

List of Tables

3.1	Age of Child Apprentices to William Toplis, Cuckney, 1786–1805	46
4.1	St Clement Danes Parish Factory Apprentices	59
4.2	St Giles in the Fields Parish Factory Apprentices	61
4.3	St Luke, Chelsea Parish Factory Apprentices	63
4.4	St Pancras Parish Factory Apprentices	64
4.5	St Martin in the Fields Parish Factory Apprentices	65
4.6	St Mary at Lambeth Parish Factory Apprentices	69
4.7	St George the Martyr Southwark Parish Factory Apprentices	71
4.8	St Leonard, Shoreditch Parish Factory Apprentices	73
4.9	St George, Hanover Square Parish Factory Apprentices	74
4.10	St James, Piccadilly Parish Factory Apprentices	75
4.11	St Pauls, Covent Garden Parish Factory Apprentices	75
4.12	St Mary Newington (Southwark) Parish Factory Apprentices	76
4.13	St Anne, Soho Parish Factory Apprentices	76
4.14	St Botolph Aldergate Parish Factory Apprentices	76
4.15	St Botolph Without Aldergate Parish Factory Apprentices	77
4.16	St Margaret and St John the Evangelist, Westminster Parish Factory Apprentices	77
4.17	Birmingham Factory Apprentices	84
4.18	Bristol Factory Apprentices	86
5.1	The Distribution of Parish Apprentices in Early Textile Production	92
5.2	Chronology of Factory Parish Apprenticeship	100
5.3	The Estimated Proportion of Parish Apprentices in a Sample of Textile Factories	105
8.1	Parish Factory Apprenticeship by Gender	154
11.1	Indicators of Parish Protection of Apprentices	217
11.2	Indicators of Parish Negligence of Apprentices	220
12.1	Conditions in Early Textile Factories	240
12.2	Reports on Firms Visited Under the 1802 Act	244

Studies in Labour History
General Editor's Preface

This series of books provides reassessments of broad themes in labour history, along with more detailed studies arising from the latest research in the field. Most books are single-authored but there are also volumes of essays, centred on key themes and issues, usually emerging from major conferences organized by the British Society for the Study of Labour History. Every author approaches their task with the needs of both specialist and non-specialist readerships in mind, for labour history is a fertile area of historical scholarship, stimulating wide-ranging interest, debate and further research, within both social and political history and beyond.

When this series was first launched (with Chris Wrigley as its general editor) in 1998, labour history was emerging, reinvigorated, from a period of considerable introspection and external criticism. The assumptions and ideologies underpinning much labour history had been challenged by postmodernist, anti-Marxist and, especially, feminist thinking. There was also a strong feeling that often it had emphasized institutional histories of organized labour, at the expense of histories of work generally, and of workers' social relations beyond their workplaces – especially gender and wider familial relationships. The Society for the Study of Labour History was concerned to consolidate and build upon this process of review and renewal through the publication of more substantial works than its journal *Labour History Review* could accommodate, and also to emphasize that though it was a British body, its focus and remit extended to international, transnational and comparative perspectives.

Arguably, the extent to which labour history was narrowly institutionalized has been exaggerated. This series therefore includes studies of labour organizations, including international ones, where there is a need for modern reassessment. However, it is also its objective to maintain the breadth of labour history's gaze beyond conventionally organized workers, sometimes to workplace experiences in general, sometimes to industrial relations, and naturally to workers' lives beyond the immediate realm of work.

Malcolm Chase
Society for the Study of Labour History
University of Leeds

Acknowledgements

Early research from which this, a rather different book than initially envisaged, has emerged was conducted with Gill Cookson and supported financially by the Pasold Research Fund. Gill has remained interested in the progress of this work and I thank her for this and for her enduring friendship. Subsequently the research has been facilitated by periods of research leave from the School of History at the University of Leeds. The final stage of the writing process was supported by an AHRC Research leave award, for which I am extremely grateful.

The process of archival investigation was made enjoyable and productive by dedicated teams at libraries and record offices across England. I thank those at Birmingham City Archives; Bristol Record Office; Camden Local Studies and Archives Centre, especially Richard Knight; Croydon Local Studies Library and Archives Service, especially Chris Bennett; Derbyshire Record Office, especially Paul Beattie; Doncaster Archives; Essex Record Office; Guildhall Library; Haringey Archives Service, especially Jeff Gerhardt; Herefordshire Record Office; Hertfordshire Archives; Hull City Archives; Islington Local History Centre; Keighley Library; Lancashire Record Office; London Metropolitan Archives; Manchester City Archives; National Archives; Nottinghamshire Archives; Oxfordshire Record Office; Shropshire Archives; Southwark Local History Library, especially Stephen Humphries; Staffordshire Record Office; Warwickshire County Record Office; Westminster Archives Centre, especially Alison Kenny; the branches of the West Yorkshire Archives Service at Bradford, Halifax, Huddersfield, Leeds, and Wakefield; and the Worcestershire Record Office. I am privileged to have on my doorstep one of the finest collections of eighteenth-century documents and textile business records in the land. The Brotherton Library at the University of Leeds and its Special Collections provided many valuable sources for this work and I thank those whose efforts maintain these records for all to use.

My debt to the community of scholars is huge. I benefited greatly from audiences at seminars and conferences, especially at the universities of Cambridge, Leeds, Manchester and Oxford to whom early versions of parts of this work were delivered; at the Economic History Society Conference in Durham; and at the stimulating ESRC First Labour Market seminar, so imaginatively and ably organised by Jane Humphries and Leonard Schwarz. Among those individuals who advised me at various stages of the research and who read drafts of this work, I would particularly like to thank Linda Clarke, Nigel Goose, Jane Humphries, Joanna Innes, Peter King, Peter Kirby, Alysa Levene, and Leonard Schwarz. For their combined expertise, generous observations, and encouragement I will always be grateful. In addition, Chris Aspin advised on early water mills; Sheila Gallagher pointed me to valuable sources on Southwark apprentices; Dominic Johnson of the Nottinghamshire Family History Society provided valuable material; Michael Quinn offered me important insights into the writings of Jeremy Bentham; and Denis Warwick kindly shared with me his unrivalled knowledge of the history of Burley-in-Wharfedale. Thanks to them all. I also recognise the importance of a congenial and lively working environment, and this has been provided over the last seven years by colleagues and students in the School of History and elsewhere in the University of Leeds, especially Malcolm Chase, Simon Dixon, Kate Dossett, Shane Doyle, John Gooch, William Gould, Simon Hall, Sarah Irwin, Emilia Jamroziak, Robert Jones, Jill Liddington, and Nicola Reader.

I am blessed with wonderful family and friends who have sustained me through a sometimes daunting project. Among those to whom I owe so much are numerous Honeymans, especially Andy, Ben, Danny, Gill, and Will; Susan Wale and Geoff Newis; Pam Bird and Mike Bird; John Barber, Amanda Cottrell, Gill Cracknell, Jane Durham, Neil Price, Liz Rodgers, David Rodgers and Elizabeth Silva. I now look forward to spending more time with them all. It is a great sadness that both my parents died during the time I was writing this book. They are sorely missed but remembered with much love.

Katrina Honeyman
Leeds, January 2007

List of Abbreviations

BCA	Birmingham City Archives
BRO	Bristol Record Office
CLSAC	Camden Local Studies and Archives Centre
CRO	Croydon Record Office
DRO	Derbyshire Record Office
DA	Doncaster Archives
ERO	Essex Record Office, Chelmsford
GL	Guildhall Library
HAS	Haringey Archives Service
HRO	Herefordshire Record Office
HALS	Hertfordshire Archives and Local Studies
HCA	Hull City Archives
ILHC	Islington Local History Centre
KL	Keighley Library
LRO	Lancashire Record Office
LMA	London Metropolitan Archives
MCA	Manchester City Archives
NA	Nottinghamshire Archives
ORO	Oxfordshire Record Office
SA	Shropshire Archives
SLHL	Southwark Local History Library
SRO	Staffordshire Record Office
ULBLSC	University of Leeds, Brotherton Library, Special Collections
WCRO	Warwickshire County Record Office
WAC	Westminster Archives Centre
WYASB	West Yorkshire Archive Service, Bradford
WYASC	West Yorkshire Archive Service, Calderdale (at Halifax)
WYASK	West Yorkshire Archive Service, Kirklees (at Huddersfield)
WYASL	West Yorkshire Archive Service, Leeds
WYASW	West Yorkshire Archive Service, Wakefield
WRO	Worcestershire Record Office

Chapter 1

Industrial Change in England 1780–1820

Until late in the eighteenth century, most of England's output of woollens, worsteds, linens, fustians and cottons was produced by families in their own homes or in communal workshops. Children were fully involved in family units of production, learning to assist in a variety of ways from an early age.[1] Work was flexible and was distributed among family members less by gender or even age than by availability and competing demands of the household.[2]

As the limitations of long-term expansion through domestic or proto-industrial production became apparent, merchant manufacturers, the organisers of the system, sought alternatives.[3] Centralised production came to replace the diffuse networks of workers that had evolved since the later seventeenth century. By concentrating workers within a single unit, problems associated with embezzlement,[4] quality control and discipline were overcome, and with the additional input of new technology, productivity gains were made.[5] Many of the early 'factories' were little more than large workshops within which local labour congregated. Although initially there was no technical imperative for units to be large, increased scale of production was a feature of the first purpose-built factories, and eventually mass production became the norm.

Changes to manufacturing processes began in the textile sector in the last quarter of the eighteenth century. The cotton industry was the most significant in terms of rate of expansion, productivity gains, and innovatory working practices, but

---

1   Hans Medick, 'The proto-industrial family economy: the structural function of household and family during the transition from peasant society to industrial capitalism', in Pat Thane and Anthony Sutcliffe (eds), *Essays in Social History* (Oxford, 1986), vol. 2, pp. 32–4; Maxine Berg, *The Age of Manufactures: industry, innovation and work in Britain 1700–1820* (London, 1994), pp. 157–8; Wanda Minge-Kalman, 'The industrial revolution and the European family. The institutionalisation of "childhood" as a market for family labor', *Comparative Studies in Society and History*, 20 (1978): 455.

2   Medick, 'Proto-industrial family economy', pp. 37–9. It has been argued that the labour of children and women proliferated in proto-industry because it was cheap. Pat Hudson and W.R. Lee (eds), *Women's Work and the Family Economy in Historical Perspective* (Manchester, 1990), pp. 15–16.

3   John Hicks, *A Theory of Economic History* (Oxford, 1969), pp. 137–59; Peter Kriedte, Hans Medick, and Jurgen Schlumbohm, *Industrialization before Industrialization* (Cambridge, 1981), especially pp. 101–111 and 136–45.

4   This was seen as a customary right by many rural industrial or proto-industrial workers. Penelope Lane, 'Work on the margins: poor women and the informal economy of eighteenth and nineteenth century Leicestershire', *Midland History*, 22 (1997): 86–9.

5   Kriedte et al, *Industrialization*, pp. 136–43; Berg, *Age of Manufactures*, pp. 70–74.

most textile trades participated in the expansion of this period.[6] The organisational differences between domestic and factory production were economically significant, but location-wise there was much overlap.[7] Manufacturing in the countryside, a feature of proto-industry, was also characteristic of early factories. The search for suitable factory sites was initially driven by the requirements of water power, which dominated textile production until the early years of nineteenth century.[8] Year round availability of water, and not simply its fast-flowing nature was essential. As a result factories were often placed where few competing demands on water supply existed. However, there were early urban water mills, as those in Manchester and Sheffield illustrate;[9] and in any case, the water power imperative was only temporary. By 1810, the mule and the steam power associated with it[10] became the technology of choice over the water frame, although the two systems co-existed for some years to come.[11] As mule spinning gained in popularity,[12] it became economically expedient to locate a plant closer to existing sources of labour, and where markets and raw materials could be accessed more conveniently. Inevitably, therefore, while those rural mills with nearby towns, such as Styal, Cromford, and Burley-in-Wharfedale, remained viable well into the nineteenth century, those factories that were genuinely isolated, of which Backbarrow to the north of Lancashire is an example, mostly succumbed to the competition of urban mills.

The early textile mill owners revealed a marked preference for the labour of women and particularly children.[13] Because of technological developments, the

---

6   Textile manufacturing dominated all manufacturing at this time. Peter Lindert estimates that employment in textiles more than tripled between 1750 and 1800. Cited in Maxine Berg, 'Women's work, mechanisation and the early phases of industrialisation in England', in Patrick Joyce (ed.), *The Historical Meanings of Work* (Cambridge, 1987), p. 69.

7   Maxine Berg, 'Factories, workshops and industrial organisation', in Roderick Floud and Donald McCloskey (eds), *The Economic History of Britain since 1700*, vol. 1, 1700–1860 (Cambridge, 1994), pp. 123–36, discusses the complexity of early industrial organisation.

8   Peter Gaskell, *Artisans and Machinery* (London, 1836), p. 136; W. Ashworth, 'British industrial villages in the nineteenth century', *Economic History Review*, 3/3 (1951): 378.

9   The cotton mill of Wells, Middleton was unusually located in Sheffield. Among Manchester water cotton mills, were those of David Holt, William Douglas, and Akers and Beever.

10   Although mules could be run by water power, and water frames sometimes used the assistance of steam power, especially where supplies of water were erratic.

11   Water spinning continued in the Midlands counties until the mid-nineteenth century.

12   There were also labour implications. Mule spinning factories tended to use more men and fewer children than water mills. See Frances Collier, *The Family Economy of the Working Classes in the Cotton Industry 1784–1833* (Manchester, 1964), p. 3. Collier also states that use of apprentices was confined to water spinning. In fact, they were commonly used in mule spinning too.

13   However, as Maxine Berg points out, 'reliance on women's labour and more significantly children's labour is little remarked upon ... even in reference to early factory industry', Berg, 'Women's work', p. 68. See also Osamu Saito, 'Labour supply behaviour of the poor in the English industrial revolution', *Journal of European Economic History*, 10/3 (1981): 636–47, who, by focusing on the supply of such labour, neglects employer preference for it.

nature of work was unfamiliar. Male labour was expected to resist the discipline, monotony and unrelenting pace of work implied by the new machines, while women and children were assumed to be amenable to novel and experimental forms of labour. The need for greater managerial supervision within centralised production was also new; and different methods could be tried out on children.[14] The untested nature of production processes and the potential for costly mistakes, indicated the use of the cheapest available labour. At this stage, therefore, children were to be employed wherever possible. And because many elements of production had been taken over by machine, even very young children could perform essential tasks.[15]

For demographic reasons too, children's role in early manufacturing was inevitable. Population changes during the second half of the eighteenth century created a high dependency ratio, and thus a situation in which the labour of young people was necessary.[16] In the later eighteenth century, children aged between 5 and 14 comprised at least 20 per cent of the population.[17] The eighteenth-century demographic system, for long dominated by the Malthusian Trap, was fragile, and only consistent gains in both production and productivity would permit continued population increases. Neither population growth nor economic growth could be sustained on the productive capacity of adults alone. That children should work was hardly in question. The nature of the work conducted by children, however, was hotly contested.

During the eighteenth century, conceptions of children and childhood changed, and historians broadly agree that a benevolent child-centred ideology replaced

---

14 Large groups of children of course posed particular supervisory problems. Mary Rose, 'Social policy and business: parish apprenticeship and the early factory system 1750–1834', *Business History*, 21 (1989): 12.

15 Many of the early textile machines were specially adapted to children's physiques. Wally Seccombe, *Weathering the Storm: Working Class Families from the Industrial Revolution to the Fertility Decline* (London, 1993), p. 36.

16 According to Marjetta Rahikainen, a period of population growth is followed by an age transition that first leads to a high child dependency rate, in which child labour is widespread. Britain was among the first economies to enter this phase. *Centuries of Child Labour: European experience from the seventeenth to the twentieth century* (Aldershot, 2004), p. 9. In the seventeenth century when a substantial proportion of the poor were young, 'child labour [was] surely normal'. D.C. Coleman, 'Labour in the English economy of the seventeenth century', *Economic History Review*, 8/3 (1956): 286.

17 Berg, 'Women's work', p. 69 suggests the figure to be between one sixth and one quarter of the total population. Other sources indicate that in 1821 those under 9 years old comprised 29 per cent of the population; and those between 10 and 19 years another 22 per cent. B.R. Mitchell, *British Historical Statistics* (Cambridge, 1988), p. 15. See also E.A. Wrigley and R.S. Schofield, *The Population History of England, 1541–1871* (Cambridge, 1981), pp. 528–9; Michael Anderson, 'Population change in north-western Europe, 1750–1850', in Michael Anderson (ed.), *British Population History from the Black Death to the Present Day* (Cambridge, 1996), p. 269; John R. Gillis, *Youth and History: Tradition and Change in European Age Relations 1770 to the present* (New York, 1974), pp. 11 and 39; and Peter Kirby, *Child Labour in Britain, 1750–1870* (Basingstoke, 2003), pp. 26–30 for more discussion.

a genealogical one.[18] At the same time attitudes to child labour showed signs of shifting from one of complete acceptance to one where it was no longer taken for granted.[19] The transformation of work associated with industrialisation consolidated the critical strand of thought.[20]

Until the later eighteenth century, however, the consensus was that children should be productive for both economic and moral reasons.[21] Defoe's delight in encountering busy Yorkshire children during his Tour is well known.[22] Locke's argument that idle children was labour lost to society[23] underpinned early eighteenth century attempts to provide work for children within workhouses.[24] The productive value of children was emphasised by William Pitt in 1796, when he wrote that

> experience has already shown how much could be done by the industry of children, and the advantage of early employing them in such branches of manufacture as they were capable to execute ... If anyone would take the trouble to compute the amount of all the earnings of the children who are educated in this manner, he would be surprised, when he came to consider the weight which their support by their own labours took off the country, and the addition which, by the fruits of their toil, and the habits to which they were formed, was made to its internal opulence.[25]

---

18   Such ideas underpinned Shaftesbury's vision of aristocratic consensualism. Also relevant was a body of historical ideas in which childhood and adulthood were constructed as distinct spheres. The ideas of Locke and Rousseau, which locate the child at the centre of the educational process, are discussed in Sesbastian Mitchell, 'But cast their eyes on these little wretched beings: the innocence and experience of children in the late eighteenth century', *New Formations*, 41 (2001): 119.

19   Ludmilla Jordanova, 'Children in history: concepts of nature and society', in G. Scarre (ed.), *Children, Parents and Politics* (Cambridge, 1989), pp. 19–20. See also the discussion in Pamela Horn, *Children's Work and Welfare, 1780–1890* (Cambridge, 1995), pp. 1–4.

20   Rahikainen argues that child labour came to be seen as a social evil as it did not conform to the new sensitivity towards children or to the new ideal of 'proper' or 'normal' childhood. *Centuries of Child Labour*, p. 8.

21   John Rule, *The Labouring classes in Early Industrial England 1750–1850* (London, 1986), p. 15.

22   'Hardly anything above four years old, but its hands are sufficient to itself.' Daniel Defoe, *A Tour through the Whole Island of Great Britain* (London, 1974), introduction by G.D.H. Cole and D.C. Browning, vol. 2, p. 195. See also Coleman, 'Labour in the English economy', 286–7.

23   John Locke Report for the reform of the Poor Law, 1697; cited in Hugh Cunningham, *The Children of the Poor: Representations of Childhood since the Seventeenth Century* (Oxford, 1991), p. 22. Locke believed that children could make a productive contribution from the age of three. Peter Laslett, *The World We Have Lost* (London, 1965), p. 3.

24   Cunningham, *Children of the Poor*, pp. 18–32; J.L. Hammond and Barbara Hammond, *The Town Labourer 1760–1832: The New Civilisation* (London, 1917), p. 100.

25   Speech by William Pitt, 12 February 1796, citing Frenchman Michelet and quoted in 'Alfred' [Samuel Kydd], *The History of the Factory Movement from the Year 1802, to the Enactment of the 10 Hours Bill in 1847* (London, 1857), p. 3. See also the writings of Jeremy Bentham, who believed that children, especially teenagers, to be highly productive: UC [Manuscript collection at the Bentham Project, University College, London] cli 334; Michael Quinn, 'Jeremy Bentham and physical disability: a problem for whom?', forthcoming, ts

The Schools of Industry introduced later in the eighteenth century embodied contemporary search for social order, and received support from the Society for Bettering the Condition of the Poor, under the general principle that 'whatever encourages and promotes habits of industry, prudence, foresight, virtue, and cleanliness among the poor, is beneficial to them and to the country'.[26] Habits of work, it was believed, should be learned at an early age;[27] and children should contribute to their own subsistence.[28] The Philanthropic Society, established in 1788 to rescue abandoned and criminal children, saw 'indolence' as the root of all evil.[29] Colquhoun, at the end of the century, described idleness as 'a never-failing inroad to criminality'.[30] However, Eden stated that although 'habits of industry and perseverance are undoubtedly of so much importance, that they cannot be too early or too strongly inculcated', he preferred that these be learned at home rather 'than in working schools, or in manufactories'.[31] He was concerned that removal from parents, which such institutions entailed, damaged 'domestic connections ... and that reared in crowds, the rising generation lose the spring of health in contagion and restraint'.[32]

Child labour at an early age was customary in the domestic system and was only seriously challenged with the coming of the factory, when: 'for the first time toiling children were regarded as an outrage, not something to be admired ... something monstrous in the factory system which directed attention to the yet more monstrous exploitation of the labour of young children'.[33] From concern about the moral and physical effects of early factory work, emerged the utilitarian argument that the successful reproduction of society was endangered by such activity. It was believed that the outcome would be weak and stunted men incapable of engaging in men's work; and women unversed in household skills with bodies unable to bear healthy children. Initial criticism focused on the physical evils.[34] Like other contemporaries,

---

p. 16. I am grateful to Dr Michael Quinn for these and other communications on the subject of Jeremy Bentham's ideas about children.

26 Cunningham, *Children of the Poor*, pp. 27–8.

27 Ivy Pinchbeck and Margaret Hewitt, *Children in English Society* (2 vols, London, 1969–73), vol. 2, p. 413.

28 Sara Horrell and Jane Humphries, 'Child labour and British industrialisation', in Michael Lavalette (ed.), *A Thing of the Past? Child Labour in Britain in the Nineteenth and Twentieth Centuries* (Liverpool, 1999), p. 77.

29 Child labour fitted well with the belief in individual industry and thrift and the mischief wrought by idle hands. Anna Davin, 'Child labour, the working class family and domestic ideology in 19th century Britain', *Development and Change*, 13 (1982): 637.

30 Patrick Colquhoun, *Treatise on the Police of the Metropolis* (London, 1796), p. 95, cited in Cunningham, *Children of the Poor*, p. 24.

31 F.M. Eden, *The State of the Poor*, (London, 1797), pp. 420–21.

32 Ibid.

33 M. Dorothy George, cited in Berg, 'Women's work', p. 68; see also Cunningham, *Children of the Poor*, pp. 50–51.

34 John Aiken, *Description of the Country 30–40 miles around Manchester* (London, 1795), p. 219; Thomas Gisborne, *An Enquiry into the Duties of Men in the Higher and Middle Classes of Society in Great Britain* (2 vols, London, 1795), vol. 2, p. 363–4; Eden, *State of the poor*, pp. 421–2.

both Eden and Gisborne recognised the moral as well as the physical dangers of youthful factory employment: 'the morals of manufacturers assembled together in numerous bodies are at least as much endangered as their health';[35] and that 'numbers of both sexes, of different ages and dispositions, should be collected together in such a manner, that the contagion of example cannot but lead to profligacy and debauchery'.[36] The debate about factory employment for children initiated in the 1780s was subdued in the early years of the nineteenth century but gathered pace through the 1830s and 1840s.[37]

It is often assumed that expansion of textile production depended on labour, especially child labour, which exceeded local supplies.[38] However for many, especially the smaller scale manufacturers, sufficient labour was found nearby. Advertisements of the speculative period from the late 1780s to the early 1790s were reassuring on this point. Placing his mill buildings on the market, Dr Fearn of Pontefract, for example, indicated that 'extensive cotton works may be made, and the labour of children obtained at an easy rate'.[39] A 'cotton or worsted mill'[40] was offered for sale near Skipton in Craven, 'where labour is cheap and where the children and upgrown persons are mostly in want of employment'.[41] Where the search went beyond the neighbourhood, advertisements for large families indicated that housing would be provided for incomers. Clayton and Walshman, Keighley cotton spinners, notified the press in the spring of 1787, that 'in order to accommodate workpeople [we] are now erecting a number of convenient cottages ... any people with large families, that are desirous to have them employed ... may be assured of meeting every reasonable encouragement'.[42]

As the employers' search widened, requests for labour appeared in the newspapers of most populous towns.[43] Advertisements indicated the preferred type of worker. Employers such as Samuel Oldknow at Mellor, and Richard Arkwright at Cromford,

---

35 Gisborne, *An Enquiry*, vol. 2, p. 368.

36 Eden, *State of the Poor*, p. 422.

37 Kydd, *History of the Factory Movement*, p. 16, criticises the employment of 'stranger-children gathered together from the workhouses ... to be used up as the cheapest raw material in the market' in the early textile mills.

38 It is commonly argued that early factory employers had difficulty in recruiting a steady and productive workforce. Michael Huberman, 'How did labour markets work in Lancashire? More evidence on prices and quantities in cotton spinning, 1822–1852', *Explorations in Economic History*, 28 (1991): 90. Arthur Redford, *Labour Migration in England 1800–1850* (Manchester, 1964), pp. 19–21; S.D. Chapman, *The Early Factory Masters: The Transition to the Factory System in the Midlands Textile Industry* (Newton Abbot, 1967), p. 156; O.J. Dunlop, *English Apprenticeship and Child Labour: A history* (London, 1912), pp. 257–8.

39 *Leeds Mercury*, 24 April and 1 May 1787. A similar advert: 'extensive cotton works may be formed and the labour of children obtained at an easy rate', appeared in the same paper four years later, *Leeds Mercury*, 1 March 1791.

40 Which was, in fact, 'a parcel of land ... with a powerful fall of water'.

41 *Leeds Mercury*, 29 March 1791.

42 *Leeds Mercury*, 10, 17, 24 April and 1, 8 May 1787. This indicates that the firm expected to use labour from the wider region.

43 Most notably *Leeds Mercury* and *Manchester Mercury*. In the same papers, parishes advertised their own children who were available for factory apprenticeships.

desired young female workers and created non-factory employment for the adult males taken as a necessary price for their wives and numerous offspring required for the factory.[44] The appeal of regular work for the whole family was sufficient to encourage a substantial movement of urban underemployed to the rural mills of Cheshire, Derbyshire, Yorkshire and Lancashire. Thus a youthful labour force was accumulated, and Arkwright and many other early factory masters, never looked beyond the supply of 'free' labour for their requirements. But for increasing numbers of manufacturers, such labour on its own was inadequate. Either insufficient numbers were accessible, or problems of control and discipline were experienced. Evidence from business records and from Poor Law settlement examinations indicates how free children were neither steady not constant workers, moving from factory to factory in search of better pay and conditions. Labour turnover was costly both in search time and in wasted training.[45]

Fortuitously, during the last two decades of the eighteenth century, as the search for new industrial labour gathered pace, an alternative source of young workers, revealed itself. The rising dependency rate created high levels of poverty, especially among the young; and the Poor Law encouraged poor children into employment through apprenticeships.[46] From the employer's point of view, parish apprentices, on whom this book focuses, seemed to carry all of the advantages of free child labour with fewer of the disadvantages. In the first place, they came without parental baggage.[47] Employers were thus freed from the burden of finding work for those parents for whom there was no role in the factory, and liberated from restrictions on discipline and control.[48] The second key advantage of parish apprentice labour was its capacity for renewal. The apprentice taken on at the age of eight or nine, and surviving to the end of his or her term, provided a dozen or more years of unpaid labour. Upon release, he or she would be replaced by a 'new' apprentice.

---

44   George Unwin, *Samuel Oldknow and the Arkwrights: The Industrial Revolution at Stockport and Marple* (London, 1924), p. 167.

45   That this remained the case for many years is demonstrated in submissions to the *Royal Commission on Children's Employment* vol. 5, 1834. A letter from James Holroyd, Halifax surgeon, to Scriven includes the observation: 'I have known children to be in the habit of leaving one employer for another two or three times during the month, by this practice acquiring wandering and unsettled habits not only to the prejudice of themselves, but also to the great inconvenience and loss to their employers. Instances have occurred of twenty or thirty children having at one time left their employment, without giving the least notice ... machinery has unexpectedly been left standing, to the great loss of the factory master'. Evidence exists that parents were often responsible for this movement to avoid paying loans to factory owners or to pocket advances given.

46   Jane Humphries, 'Female headed households in early industrial Britain: the vanguard of the proletariat?', *Labour History Review*, 63/1 (1998): 50; Linda A Pollock, *Forgotten Children: Parent-child relations from 1500–1900* (Cambridge, 1993), pp. 62–3.

47   This is not to imply that no such apprentices had parents. The research on which this study is based indicates that a number were orphans, but the majority had at least one parent living, and these remained in the parish of origin.

48   This facet will be explored in Chapters 9 and 12. Several of the employers in this study explicitly noted the latter advantage.

Such replenishment would take place gradually because of the staggered timing of apprentices reaching the end of their terms.[49] 'Free' children were less expendable, as the local labour market would not provide replacement children with the same facility as the parish.[50] Thirdly, parish apprentices provided a stable workforce. Although absconding was not uncommon, apprentices were not easily able to move between factories during their term. The level of employment mobility permitted to free children caused costly inconvenience to employers. Finally, it was assumed that parish children were cheap, which for many employers was the main benefit.[51]

The transfer of children between parishes and textile manufacturers was facilitated by the consonant requirements of both parties. In the later eighteenth century parishes became burdened with growing numbers of poor children and the existing apprenticeship system came under strain. As the supply of pauper children came to exceed the number of willing local masters, parishes began to discuss the policy and practice of factory apprenticeship.[52] At much the same time, textile manufacturers struggled to find and retain labour, and instigated a search for young workers through various forms of publicity, assisted by agents with good connections within Poor Law circles.

The association of industrialisation, factory production, and the labour of young children is commonly noted in British economic histories of the late eighteenth and the early nineteenth century.[53] By concentrating on the emotive aspects of child

---

49   Employers varied in the extent to which they retained apprentice labour. Some, such as Greg, Merryweather, clearly made an effort to do so; while others, of which Backbarrow is an excellent example, made little secret of the fact that their factory ran almost entirely on successive batches of parish apprentices. See *State of Children Employed in the Manufactories of the UK: Report of the minutes of evidence taken before the Select Committee*, 1816, Sessional Paper 397 [hereafter SC1816].

50   Especially once a relationship had been developed between employer and parish officials.

51   According to Morris David Morris, early factory masters sought the cheapest labour possible. 'The recruitment of an industrial labor force in India, with British and American comparisons', *Comparative Studies in Society and History*, 2/3 (1960): 313. How cheap parish apprentices were in practice is explored in Chapter 6.

52   See meetings of 6 September 1787; 6 October 1791; 20 October 1791; 3 November 1791. Trustees of the Poor Minutes, parish of St Mary, Islington, 1786–1798, Islington Local History Centre [ILHC]; and meetings of 11, 22 and 26 December 1789, Minutes of Governors and Directors of the Poor, parish of St James, Piccadilly, D1872, Westminster Archives Centre [WAC].

53   This was actually more common in the early texts than those of more recent years. See, for example, Hammond and Hammond, *The Town Labourer*; J.L. Hammond and Barbara Hammond, *The Skilled Labourer 1760–1832* (London, 1919); J.L. Hammond and Barbara Hammond, *The Rise of Modern Industry* (London, 1925); John H. Clapham, *An Economic History of Modern Britain: The Early Railway Age 1820–1850* (Cambridge, 1930); Paul Mantoux, *The Industrial Revolution in the Eighteenth* Century (London, 1928), especially pp. 408–416. Examples of recent work which takes this approach include James Walvin, *A Child's World: A Social History of English Childhood, 1800–1914* (Harmondsworth, 1982), pp. 61–7; Brian Inglis, *Poverty and the Industrial Revolution* (London, 1971), p. 30. However, as Sara Horrell and Jane Humphries note, 'children who worked in the earliest manufactories

labour, however, such literature marginalises the real contribution that children made to early industry. Young people, especially parish apprentices, were victims of a harsh Poor Law regime and a brutal new industrial system. Their often short, always exhausting lives form the subject of voyeuristic pity, but the nature of their experience and the influence of parish apprentices on the course of Britain's industry has been neither fully investigated nor acknowledged.

Quantitative analyses of early manufacturing expansion have recently revised the revolutionary notions of change. But such work has paid scant attention to the workers who made growth possible. Historical research of a more qualitative kind has demonstrated the complex composition of the workforce and specifically the gender divisions of labour in early manufacturing industry.[54] It is well known that children as well as men and women were affected by changes in the work process. Yet the specific part played by children in the construction of the new industrial labour force is not fully recognised.[55] In discussions of their position as workers, children are often linked with women. In early nineteenth century economic thought, only men were unequivocally constructed as 'free' while women and children, occasionally to differing degrees, were seen as in need of some form of protection.[56]

The specific nature of children's work in the early industrial labour force requires further investigation. A start can be made by exploring the role of the parish apprentice as an independent worker. Parish apprentices were numerically significant and integral to the production process. It was they who facilitated the operation of new technology.[57] During the early years of industrialisation children ceased to be simply adjuncts to production, but worked as discrete units of labour for the first time. It is a contention of this work that those children who worked independently of mother, or indeed of either parent, played a particularly important role in early industrial development. This study focuses on the contribution of the parish apprentice, as a specific form of child labour. Prior to factory production, the urban parish apprentice, bound to the master or mistress of a skilled or an unskilled trade, typically engaged in menial tasks. In neither case was the parish apprentice central to the production process. Through the eighteenth century, it became increasingly common for parish children in the larger urban areas to be engaged in productive

---

are scarcely visible in mainstream economic histories of industrialisation'. 'Child labour and British industrialization', p. 76.

54 Most important in this category are Maxine Berg and Pat Hudson, 'Rehabilitating the industrial revolution', *Economic History Review*, 45/1 (1992): 24–50; Berg, *Age of Manufactures*, Chapter 6; Katrina Honeyman, *Women, Gender and Industrialization in England, 1700–1870* (Basingstoke, 2000), Chapters 1 and 3.

55 In recent years the place of women in industrial change has been increasingly recognised, but children remain neglected. Robert McIntosh, *Boys in the Pits: Child Labor in Coal Mines* (Montreal and Kingston, 2000), p. 9.

56 Such views were debated during the 1830s, but had begun to emerge during discussion over parish apprentice legislation between 1811 and 1816. *The Journal of the House of Commons*, 1811–16; and *The Parliamentary Debates* (London: Longman), vols 19–20.

57 Engels asserted that the employment of children in the mills was 'at first almost exclusively by reason of the smallness of the machine'. Frederik Engels, *The Condition of the Working Class in England* (1969 edn), p. 177.

work in local workshops, or in the parish's workhouse or school of industry.[58] To some extent such activity resembled the parish apprentice in the early textile mills, the subject of this study.

Interest in children and in child labour has grown significantly in recent years, and scholarship on the subject has entered new areas of investigation. Some research has adopted a quantitative approach, or at least has attempted to measure components of children's employment or unemployment.[59] Other work has begun to explore notions of exploitation;[60] and children's position in the family economy.[61] Comparative work has enhanced the subject.[62] The primary purpose of this book is to revisit prevailing assumptions about the nature and value of children's work within the industrial revolution. It will look beneath the tropes of dark, satanic mills and abused children workers, by taking a group of parish apprentices who comprised the first generation of factory workers, and assess both their experience of work and the role they played in the making of the industrial labour force. It will explore the connections between the Poor Law and the operation of early capitalism. It will attempt to identify ways in which children acquired a gendered work identity and how – as male and female – they came to fit into the new industrial gender division of labour.

Any attempt to explore the history of children faces the challenge of data paucity.[63] One advantage of investigating the parish apprentice, rather than any

---

58 M. Dorothy George, *London Life in the Eighteenth Century* (London, 1925), pp. 224–7.

59 Clark Nardinelli, *Child Labour and the Industrial Revolution* (Bloomington, Indiana, 1990); Hugh Cunningham, 'The employment and unemployment of children in England c.1680–1851', *Past and Present*, 126 (1990): 115–50; Kirby, *Child Labour*, pp. 79–81; Peter Kirby, 'How many children were "unemployed" in eighteenth- and nineteenth-century England?', *Past and Present*, 187 (2005): 187–202; and Hugh Cunningham, 'Reply', ibid., 203–215.

60 Nardinelli, *Child Labour*; Carolyn Tuttle, *Hard at Work in Factories and Mines: The Economics of Child Labour during the Industrial Revolution* (Boulder, Colorado, 1999); Michael Lavalette, 'Theorizing children at work. Family, state and relations of production in historical context', in Lavalette (ed.), *A Thing of the Past?*, pp. 44–68; Sara Horrell and Jane Humphries, ' "The exploitation of little children": child labour and the family economy in the industrial revolution', *Explorations in Economic History*, 32 (1995): 485–516.

61 Jane Humphries, *Through the Mill*, forthcoming.

62 Rahikainen, has offered useful European comparisons. She shows that traffic in children was managed by Foundling Homes, orphanages or poor relief authorities; in the German and Scandinavian countryside, poor children were also put up for public auction. *Centuries of Child Labour*, p. 94. See also Colin Heywood, 'Age and gender at the workplace: the historical experiences of young people in Western Europe and North America', in Margaret Walsh (ed.), *Working Out Gender: Perspectives From Labour History* (Aldershot, 1999), pp. 48–65; Colin Heywood, 'The market for child labour in nineteenth-century France', *History*, 66 (1981); and Katherine A. Lynch, *Family, Class and Ideology in Early Industrial France: Social Policy and the Working Class Family, 1825–1848* (Madison, 1988).

63 In this book the words of children are recorded by parish officials during examinations, for example.

other type of child, however, is the availability and richness of relevant sources.[64] Most parishes kept detailed records of their children put out as apprentices. A law of 1802 required a formal registering of apprentices,[65] in the belief that 'it would tend to the benefit of the children so bound as apprentices'.[66] Unlike some other contemporary regulations, this seems to have been well observed. By no means all parish apprenticeship registers survive, but it has been possible to examine a substantial selection of these.[67] Parishes also kept other kinds of records, including minutes of Vestry meetings, reports of visits to factory apprentices, and examinations of returned apprentices. Such documents inevitably varied in terms of quality and detail, but together they demonstrate how far parish children were protected by their parish after their binding had been formalised. Less substantial sources include records of manufacturing concerns to which children were apprenticed. The business records generally focus upon costs, outputs and profits, and rarely provide qualitative evidence of the lives of parish children in their care. But correspondence between firms, agents and parishes has survived in small quantities, and provides insight into the nature of the relationship that developed between parish and business.[68]

Evidence generated by governmental action has also proved to be of value. In addition to the voluminous reports, parliamentary discussions, enquiries, Select Committees and Acts of Parliament, the historical record contains written responses by Poor Law authorities and factory manufacturers to government edict. The extent to which published government record represents opinion or action is rightly questioned. Commentators have often dismissed reports of factory visitors under the 1802 Act, for example, because of alleged collusion between inspectors and factory owners. Further evidence that corroborates or contradicts such reports is vital in such cases.[69] Despite the range of information that exists, its availability is patchy. Even if the data were reasonably complete, however, it would be impossible to consult and

---

64 Kathryn M. Thompson (ed.), *Apprenticeship and Bastardy Records*, Short Guides to Records (London: Historical Association, 1997), no. 29, p. 31, suggests that the quantity of documents emanating from the parish apprenticeship system, especially that relating to the factories, exaggerated its significance.

65 42 Geo III c 46 (1802). This was distinct from the Health and Morals of Apprentices Act introduced in the same year. The Appendix to the Act contains a register pro forma, which the majority of parishes adopted. Failure to comply with the regulation a fine of £5, which the Webbs describe as a heavy penalty, was indicated but rarely applied. Sidney and Beatrice Webb, *English Local Government*, vol. 7, *English Poor Law History*, part 1, *The Old Poor Law* (London, 1927) p. 205.

66 'A Bill to require the overseers of the poor to keep a register of the several children, who shall be bound by them as apprentices', *House of Commons Parliamentary Papers*, 1801–1802, vol. 1, p. 55.

67 Rose, 'Social policy and business', pp. 18 and 28 n. 70, suggests that very few apprenticeship registers survive. In fact, although there are frustrating gaps, many hundreds exist. Only a selection of these has been examined for this study.

68 The very existence of such correspondence indicates a level of concern denied in earlier accounts.

69 In this study, it has been possible to compare reports of the same enterprise by different authors.

analyse it all.[70] Some form of selection has been necessary. It would be disingenuous to suggest that the arguments to be presented in this study are based on a 'sample' of children, or parishes or enterprises, from which confident generalisations can be drawn. Nevertheless the subjects are far from randomly collected. A degree of 'representativeness' has been achieved.

During the period selected, namely the years between 1780 and 1820, the nature of textile manufacture was transformed both by technology and perhaps more so by the centralisation of production, which permitted control of the workforce. The research presented here is based on a total of seventy textile enterprises, which include worsted, linen and silk as well as cotton manufactures, in approximately the same proportions as existed at the time. These enterprises were identified partly though the parish apprenticeship records, but also by a search of business archives, and references from secondary sources.[71] The apprenticeship registers of 164 parishes were consulted. These parishes include the main London suppliers of parish apprentices, a selection of those in the textile producing counties of Yorkshire, Lancashire, Derbyshire, Nottinghamshire, Warwickshire and Staffordshire, and a group of parishes in counties not involved in new forms of textile manufacture, namely Herefordshire, Worcestershire, Essex, Kent, Lincolnshire and Suffolk. Slightly less than 40 per cent of the 164 parishes included children bound to textile factory manufacturers.

The book is structured thematically, shaped by both the concerns of existing literature, and the issues highlighted by the exploration of the sources. The book is divided into two parts. The first part explores the process of parish factory apprenticeship; the second examines the parish apprentice experience. The early chapters establish the context within which the parish apprentice is to be examined. Thus Chapter 2 explores the nature of late eighteenth-century poverty, the operation of the Poor Law and the emergence of parish factory apprenticeship as a key feature of both the new industrial system and parish strategy towards the poor. It suggests that the construction of the parish factory apprentice should be understood in terms of changing attitudes to both children and poverty. Chapter 3 outlines the key features of the structure and process of the early parish factory apprenticeship system and its regulatory framework. It argues, contrary to the traditional notion of random disposal, that the process of parish factory apprenticeship was rigorous, well coordinated and formally recorded. The fourth chapter investigates the supply of parish apprentices, and attempts to gauge its extent and distribution. In Chapter 5, the demand for parish apprentices from a selection of textile producers during the period of peak movement in apprentices is explored. The firms were located throughout the major textile producing counties of the early industrialising period. The chapter establishes the distribution of parish apprentices, and then discusses the extent to which such labour made a difference to early industrial textile production. The final chapter in the first section attempts to specify the range and distribution of

---

70   It is hoped that a further period of sustained research will attempt to itemise all existing material.

71   The comprehensive work of Chris Aspin, *The Water Spinners* (Helmshore, 2003), was particularly valuable in identifying relevant Arkwright type mills.

the costs and benefits associated with the practice of parish factory apprenticeship, and challenges the notion that the system of parish factory apprenticeship was economically viable only in the early stages of textile factory production, if at all.

The second part of the book explores several aspects of the parish apprentice experience. Chapter 7 tests the view that parish factory apprenticeship in textile production failed to provide training in the key skills required for long-term employment in the industry. It identifies the tasks performed by children, and considers how far apprentices both received industry-specific training and acquired transferable skills. It argues that although the 'training' varied considerably among firms, parish factory apprentices learned above all how to be factory workers. Chapter 8 investigates the way in which the gender division of labour – a key feature of industrialisation – was constructed. It uses the period in which parish factory apprentices were most prominent in textile production to explore the processes – both explicit and subtle – by which work and workers were gendered within new organisational forms. Chapter 9 considers the notion of exploitation through evidence of experimentation, of compulsion, of corporal punishment and sexual abuse, of intensification of labour, and of damage to health through a combination of long hours of work and inadequate diet.

The objective of Chapter 10 is to gauge the extent to which parish apprentices both as children and as independent workers were given the opportunity to speak; and how far their voices were heard. It will offer a glimpse of how parish apprentices saw themselves: as workers; as vulnerable children separate from their families, or as semi-independent young adults. Chapter 11 revisits the assumption that during the height of the parish apprenticeship system, participating parishes were driven primarily by the desire to reduce short- and long-term responsibility for their poor children. By investigating a range of different sources, and by examining the language used, it is possible to determine the general level of care and protection provided by individual parishes. The chapter argues that many parish apprentices suffered during their term through a combination of careless placement and ineffective protective measures; but others were more effectively protected by parish and other interested parties. The final substantive chapter explores the experience of parish apprenticeship in the early textile firms, demonstrating the range of neglectful practices. It is argued that responsibility for the 'protection' of children was held jointly by parish Poor Law officials, including magistrates, the factory proprietors and the mills' managements. The concluding chapter lays out the key strands of the argument that the parish apprenticeship system was integral in the construction of the new industrial labour force. It is suggested that all children's labour was important to early manufacturing industry, but that in the initial stages of development the parish apprentice was a flexible element in an otherwise inflexible labour market. It was the parish apprentice who assisted in preparing the late eighteenth-century labour market for a period of persistent industrial growth.

Chapter 2

The Poor Law and the Parish Apprentice

In the later eighteenth century, much employment for children was situated at the interface of the Poor Law and the industrial labour market. The parish apprentice became an integral part of the early industrial labour force; he or she was also a vital component of the 'old' Poor Law. The way in which the poor child moved from the 'care' of Poor Law officialdom to the 'care' of early industrial textile entrepreneurs became a distinctive feature of late eighteenth-century England. The movement from one system, which was overburdened with needy children, to another, which required large numbers of young people, eased pressures on both.[1] Parish apprenticeship was consistent with the prevailing opinion that work both provided a route out of poverty for the individual and reduced local and national levels of pauperism.[2] The propriety of children's work was especially well established.[3] This chapter will explore the nature of late eighteenth century poverty, the operation of the Poor Law and the role of the apprentice in parish strategy towards the poor.

In the later eighteenth century the English were preoccupied with poverty. The growth in numbers seeking poor relief not only burdened ratepayers but also exposed the administrative limitations of the system.[4] Parish records indicate the scale of the financial pressure placed upon the parishioners. The cost of poor relief is estimated to have increased five-fold between 1750 and 1803, with the peak increase occurring

---

1   Approximately one-third of paupers through the nineteenth century were under the age of sixteen. At the same time, there was a strong desire to remove children from the depressing atmosphere of the workhouse. Michael E. Rose, *The English Poor Law 1780–1930* (Newton Abbot, 1971), p. 178.

2   Steve Hindle, '"Waste" children? Pauper apprenticeship under the Elizabethan Poor Laws, c.1598–1697', in Penelope Lane, Neil Raven and K.D.M. Snell (eds), *Women, Work and Wages in England, 1600–1850* (Woodbridge, 2004), p. 19.

3   This was based on the belief that children should acquire habits of work from an early age but also that they should become self-supporting in later life. See, for example, Geoffrey W. Oxley, *Poor Relief in England and Wales* (Newton Abbot, 1974), p. 73. It was also linked to the view that poor relief for families was conditional on the employment of children where appropriate. Sara Horrell and Jane Humphries, 'Child labour and British industrialisation', in Michael Lavalette (ed.), *A Thing of the Past? Child Labour in Britain in the Nineteenth and Twentieth Centuries* (Liverpool, 1999), pp. 77 and 96.

4   According to Dunlop, the industrial revolution took place at a time when the Poor Law was most inefficiently administered. O.J. Dunlop, *English Apprenticeship and Child Labour: A History* (London, 1912), p. 242. Dunkley argues that 'over the centuries the old Poor Law had grown out of an ever-increasing collection of expedients'. Peter Dunkley, *The Crisis of the Old Poor Law in England, 1795–1834: An Interpretive Essay* (New York, 1982), p. 178.

between 1785 and 1795.⁵ A 'colossal rise' in the poor rates led to parliamentary investigations into the Poor Laws.⁶ For ratepayers, the system, which had operated under consensus, lost support during the later eighteenth century,⁷ as writers such as Malthus claimed that the 'generosity' of the Poor Laws was itself responsible for the growing levels of pauperism.⁸ Those liable for paying rates, which reached 60 per cent in some places,⁹ began to question the principles upon which the Poor Law system was based.¹⁰ It was suggested with increasing frequency that the reforming and disciplining function of the Poor Law should be at least as important as the material relief of the poor.¹¹ As Lynn Hollen Lees suggests,

> even though a widespread discourse of humanitarianism continued to privilege private and public charity towards the poor, much in public culture suggested profound distrust of the impoverished ... the practice of poor relief during the eighteenth century rested on ... generosity laced with suspicion, aid tied to dependence and restriction.¹²

---

5   Lynn Hollen Lees, *The Solidarities of Strangers: The English Poor Laws and the People, 1700–1948* (Cambridge, 1998), p. 84; George R. Boyer, *An Economic History of the English Poor Law, 1750–1850* (Cambridge, 1990), pp. 26–7. Joanna Innes had argued that, because the value of land was also rising, the real increase in rates was less pronounced than the raw figures indicate. Joanna Innes, 'The distinctiveness of the English Poor Laws, 1750–1850', in Donald Winch and Patrick K. O'Brien (eds), *The Political Economy of British Historical Experience, 1688–1914*, (Oxford, 2002), p. 389.

6   £2 million in 1785 to £5.3 million in 1802. W.E. Tate, *The Parish Chest: A Study of Parochial Administration in England* (3rd edition, Cambridge, 1969), p. 21; Dunkley, *The Crisis*, p. 144. This was despite the frequency with which paupers sought alternative means of support. Paul A. Fideler, *Social Welfare in Pre-Industrial England: The Old Poor Law Tradition* (Basingstoke, 2006), p. 148.

7   Hollen Lees, *Solidarities*, pp. 19–20; Innes, 'The distinctiveness', pp. 384, and 392–3.

8   See, for example, the debate between Blaug and McCloskey. Mark Blaug, 'The Myth of the Old Poor Law and the Making of the New', *Journal of Economic History*, 23/2 (1963): 151–84; D.N. McCloskey, 'New Perspectives on the Old Poor Law', *Explorations in Economic History* (Summer 1973): 419–36. Innes argues that 'the 1790s saw the introduction of unprecedentedly generous rate-financed relief schemes', 'The distinctiveness', pp. 390. For discussion of the thought of Malthus and Bentham on poverty, see U.R.Q. Henriques, *Before the Welfare State: Social Administration in Early Industrial Britain* (London, 1979), pp. 22–4.

9   For example, the rate in Bingley, Yorkshire, in 1800 was 12s to the pound. E.E. Dodd, *Bingley: A Yorkshire Town Through Nine Centuries* (Bingley, 1958), p. 95. Such was the pressure on rates in the 1790s that central government provided financial support to parts of the West Riding. Innes, 'The distinctiveness', p. 392. Malthus identified a number of parishes in which rates had risen to similar levels. Raymond G. Cowherd, 'The humanitarian reform of the English Poor Laws from 1782–1815', *Proceedings of the American Philosophical Society*, 104/3 (1960): 339–40.

10   However, Steve King, 'Poor relief and English economic development reappraised', *Economic History Review*, 50/2 (1997): 364, questions the idea that poor rates focused elite attention on the question of poverty and how to keep down relief bills.

11   George R. Boyer, review of Hollen Lees, *Solidarities*, in 'H-Net Reviews in the Humanities and Social Sciences', May 2000.

12   Hollen Lees, *Solidarities*, p. 42; and according to Dunkley 'humanitarianism and evangelical piety ... were giving way to a more cynical and calculating approach to charity,

Responsibility for poverty and the poor became a contested subject.[13]

The 'old' Poor Law is at turns praised and derided by historians for its flexibility, its lack of uniformity and its random but sometimes generous delivery at the point of local need.[14] According to J.R. Poynter, the 'three injunctions of the Elizabethan Poor Law, which bade each parish to relieve the impotent, employ the able-bodied, and "correct" the wilfully idle, were interpreted, obeyed or neglected in a bewildering variety of local circumstances'.[15] Assessment of the system as 'relief of the poor within the framework of repression',[16] is consistent with some contemporary opinion,[17] but blanket condemnation seems misplaced.[18] The practice varied between liberality and harshness;[19] and as Steve King argues, the type and extent of relief differed substantially not just by parish but also over time.[20] Relief might be adequate or not depending on a range of factors, including competing demands on parish resources, regional economic conditions, the availability of individual opportunities to avoid dependence on the parish, as well as parish officers' attitude towards the poor.

The effectiveness of poor relief depended on 'practical men reacting to local problems with varying degrees of intelligence, integrity and zeal'.[21] The organisation

---

animated by fear of the poor'. Dunkley, *The Crisis*, p. 45.

13 Hollen Lees, *Solidarities*, p. 84.

14 Periodic debates among historians have failed to generate conclusions, though they have raised interesting themes for investigation. Since the 1960s, analyses of the Poor Laws have shifted from political and moral to economic. See Blaug, 'The myth of the Old Poor Law', and McCloskey, 'New Perspectives'; More recently issues surrounding gender have been discussed. See, for example, K.D.M. Snell, *Annals of theLabouring Poor: Social Change and Agrarian England, 1660–1900* (Cambridge, 1985), pp. 279–82; Hollen Lees, *Solidarities*, pp. 55–6; Colin Heywood, 'On learning gender roles during childhood in nineteenth century France', *French History*, 5/4 (1991): 451–66.

15 J.R. Poynter, *Society and Pauperism: English Ideas on Poor Relief 1795–1834* (London, 1969), p. xx.

16 The Webbs also suggested 'Charity in the grip of serfdom'. Sidney and Beatrice Webb, *English Local Government*, vol. 7, *English Poor Law History*, part 1, *The Old Poor Law* (London, 1927), p. 396.

17 For example, Sir Thomas Barnard and the Bettering Society, which opposed the deterrent workhouse. Poynter, *Society and Pauperism*, p. 96.

18 Steve King's critique of Solar places it in the context of that expanding view. 'Poor relief', p. 360.

19 Henriques, *Before the Welfare State*, p. 24. Henriques suggests that 'harsh attitudes were commonest among the lesser ratepayers'.

20 King, 'Poor relief', p. 365. Here he is criticising Solar's inadequate appreciation of the diversity and complexity of the Old Poor Law; and the gulf in generosity between northern and southern areas. It is true that the bulk of existing commentary on the old Poor Law is based on the relatively generous southern counties. King is one of the few to consider its operation in the northern counties. Solar points out that lower levels of relief expenditure in the northern counties might be the result of authorities' meanness, but could be because the northern populations had greater opportunities for bi-employment. Peter Solar, 'Poor relief and English economic development. A renewed plea for comparative history', *Economic History Review*, 50/2 (1997): 371.

21 Poynter, *Society and Pauperism*, p. 21; see also Hollen Lees, *Solidarities*, pp. 19–20.

of the parish, as the purveyors of the old Poor Law, varied. The poor rate was set by the parish, overseen by a core of officers, which included the incumbent Vicar or Rector, usually supported by two churchwardens, who managed the church and its fabric, but were also responsible for the administration of the Poor Law. Churchwardens were ex-officio overseers of the poor. Additional parochial officers included the overseers who assumed responsibility for the daily management of the Poor Law until the 1830s, and usually reported to the Vestry, becoming its 'principal executive servants'.[22] Late in the eighteenth century many parishes incorporated a body of Guardians of the Poor, consisting of magistrates, often seen as protectors of the poor against cruel overseers;[23] and responsible for the proper implementation of administrative procedures. 'It was in keeping with the local status of the magistracy that the collective decisions of the Quarter Sessions in relief matters were promulgated in the form of orders to the overseers of the poor'.[24] This body appointed a permanent committee of Directors, who met regularly, made policy decisions and selected a group of acting Guardians who supervised the relief distributed by the overseers.[25] Later eighteenth century practice, therefore, operated within a statutory framework, which itself provided 'an ever-increasing number of alternative procedures which could be adopted'.[26]

During the later eighteenth century, a large and growing proportion of paupers was young. Earlier marriage, and a birth rate that rose faster than the death rate,[27] altered the population's age distribution;[28] and 'each successive generation was larger than its predecessor'.[29] This generated a relatively high dependency rate, which by its nature increased the likelihood of family poverty. Other contemporary forces augmented the numbers of poor. The Napoleonic Wars, for example, 'raised the

---

22 Tate, *The Parish Chest*, p. 30; see also pp. 10–23; Dunkely, *The Crisis*, p. 51. Dunkley adds that even under a system of Select Vestries, justices often remained unhampered in their activities, and did not always observe the formalities that would ensure that the views of ratepayers and officers were heard at the level of policy making. In the 1820s, complaints were received by the House of Commons that Justices dictated relief policies in a number of parishes. *The Crisis*, p. 52.

23 While Parliamentary investigations and official surveys suggested that local justices typically intervened in favour of the poor, falling levels of relief after 1815 appears to contradict such a view. Dunkley, *The Crisis*, p. 69.

24 Dunkley, *The Crisis*, pp. 49–50.

25 Poynter, *Society and Pauperism*, p. 12.

26 Poynter, *Society and Pauperism*, pp. 8 and 13. According to Cowherd, most of the humanitarian reforms introduced between 1782 and 1815 were designed to increase the authority of the magistrates over the parish officers; and to reduce the harsh conditions of the Poor Laws. 'Humanitarian reform', p. 342.

27 See E.A. Wrigley and R.S. Schofield, *The Population History of England, 1541–1871* (Cambridge, 1981).

28 David Levine, *Family Formation in an Age of Nascent Capitalism* (New York, 1977), p. 12.

29 John Gillis, *Youth and History: Tradition and Change in European Age Relations 1770 to the Present* (New York, 1974), p. 39.

proportion of families deserted by their male head',[30] and records reveal the growing numbers of fatherless families approaching the parish for relief at this time.[31] Poor children were particularly visible as paupers, and the work of the parish concentrated on the care not only of the children of legally settled people, but also of illegitimate children who were born within the parish. Such 'care' for 'orphans, deserted children and the illegitimate' provided directly by the parish or subcontracted, was often found to be 'not very tender'.[32] Young children put out to nurse had poor survival chances; and older children sent to the House of Industry, or bound apprentice, fared little better. Pressure from Jonas Hanway generated a legislative response.[33] The 1767 Act, for example, attempted to reduce the abuses served upon London parish apprentices, by raising the standard premium to £4 2s; and spreading the payment, so that the first half of the premium be paid after seven weeks, having ascertained reasonable compatibility, and the other half after three years to encourage better quality of master and treatment.[34] An Act of 1778 applied these terms to the rest of the country.[35]

Ambiguity and contradiction; complexity and variety; irregularity and unpredictability; all characterised the Poor Law and its subjects in general. The case of the parish apprentices, and the way they were treated by officialdom both before and after the introduction of the factory, provides an excellent example of this ambiguity, itself compounded by changing attitudes to children. Although systems were in place that implied a uniform practice as far as the treatment of parish

---

30   D. Kent, ' "Gone for a soldier": family breakdown and the demography of desertion in a London parish', *Local Population Studies*, 45 (1990); cited in Jane Humphries, 'Female headed households in early industrial Britain: the vanguard of the proletariat?', *Labour History Review*, 63/1 (1998): 34.

31   This was particularly evident in Halifax, where a number of new apprentices, whose parentage was noted, had fathers enrolled in the army. A significant proportion of these would not return either because of death or incapacity or by choice. Halifax Apprenticeship Registers, HXT 192, West Yorkshire Archive Service, Calderdale [WYASC].

32   Hollen Lees, *Solidarities*, p. 53.

33   According to Hanway, of more than 2,300 children taken into the London workhouses between 1750 and 1755, only 7 per cent survived until the end of that period. Hollen Lees, *Solidarities*, p. 54. Other contemporary evidence suggests that this was not an exaggeration. According to Roy Porter, workhouse management was often farmed out to contractors primarily interested in profit. The death rate in the workhouse of St George, Middlesex was 100 per cent. Roy Porter, *English Society in the Eighteenth Century* (Harmondsworth, 1991), pp. 131–2. The material was presented in order to facilitate Hanway's Act of 1767, 'For the better regulation of the parish poor children, of the several parishes therein mentioned, within the Bills of Mortality'. A decade later fewer deaths were recorded, and although the situation remained dire, the Select Committee of 1778 resolved 'that the said Act has produced very salutary effects in the preservation of the lives of great numbers of the infant Parish poor'. *The Journal of the House of Commons*, 1778, p. 944 .

34   7 Geo III c 39 (1767), 'An Act for the better regulation of the parish poor children of the several parishes therein mentioned within the Bills of Mortality'.

35   18 Geo III c 47 (1778), 'An Act for the relief of the poor as it related to the binding of parish apprentices'. Dorothy Marshall, *The English Poor in the Eighteenth Century: A Study in Social and Administrative History* (London, 1926), pp. 204–205.

apprentices was concerned, the outcome was far from standard. Overseers of the poor were responsible for placing parish apprentices and magistrates for ascertaining the viability of such placements, yet parishes differed from one another and over time with respect to such issues as the age at apprenticeship, its term, the range of trades considered suitable for their children, the premium involved, the method and timing by which this was paid, and even the gender distribution of destinations.[36]

The late eighteenth century consensus was that children should be taught habits important for an independent adulthood. Houses or Schools of Industry,[37] which provided the visible face of many parishes' Poor Law system, were typically commercial failures, because they focused on outmoded economic activities, because of the 'difficulty of compelling the able poor to pay proper attention to work',[38] and because the predominantly youthful labour force was insufficiently productive.[39] It has been argued that workhouses succeeded in training children in

---

36 The gender issues are discussed in Chapter 8. Both Bridget Hill, *Women, Work and Sexual Politics in Eighteenth Century England* (Oxford, 1989), pp. 101–102; and Deborah Simonton, 'Apprenticeship, training and gender in eighteenth century England', in Maxine Berg (ed.), *Markets and Manufacture in Early Industrial Europe* (London, 1991), pp. 227–58, have pointed to the larger proportion of girls among parish apprentices than among private ones. Hill also argues that it was those trades still open to female apprentices that were particularly prone to overstocking. *Women, Work, and Sexual Politics*, p. 262.

37 Some of these were backed by established manufacturers; for example, Gorton and Thompson, cotton manufacturers in Cuckney, Nottinghamshire, established a workshop in St James, Piccadilly. Meetings of 29 April 1791 and 29 May 1791, Governors and Directors of the Poor, the Parish of St James, Piccadilly, D1873, WAC. For many of those in receipt of indoor relief, this was a required activity. Sometimes those receiving outdoor relief, or relief in kind, also worked in the House of Industry. By no means every parish had a workhouse: sometimes adjoining parishes shared such facilities. This was the case with St Giles in the Fields and St George, Bloomsbury. St Martins in the Fields had a large poor population, and although it had a workhouse, not all of those in poverty were relieved therein. F.M. Eden, *The State of the Poor* (2 vols, London 1797), vol. 1, p. 440. The private contracting of workhouses was increasingly common through the eighteenth century. Fideler, *Social Welfare*, p. 154.

38 For example at St Martin in the Fields. Eden, *State of the Poor*, p. 440. This also applied to the expensive and abortive project of Gorton and Thompson.

39 Webb and Webb, *Old Poor Law*, pp. 211–33, provide detailed examples of the various activities developed by parishes and on pages 233–42, indicate the extent of failure. Jeremy Bentham who believed that poverty was a spur to labour, believed that 'Industry Houses' could be profitable, specifically by exploiting the labour of children. Michael Quinn, 'Jeremy Bentham on physical disability: a problem for whom?' forthcoming; ts p. 16. Examples of profitable manufactories associated with workhouses exist, especially in the early nineteenth century. For example, the Birmingham Guardians found that 'the new method of preparing hemp and flax ... has been advantageously introduced into several houses of industry ... and particularly into some in the neighbourhood of the metropolis', 2 June 1818, Minutes of Guardians of the Poor, Birmingham Parish, GP/B/2/1/2 1806–24 BCA; and Hackney flax factory, emulated by St Pancras, 21 November 1815, Minutes of Directors of the Poor, Parish of St Pancras, P/PN/PO/1/11 (microfilm reference UTAH 652) Camden Local Studies and Archives Centre [CLSAC].

occupations at precisely the time when their skills were becoming redundant in the labour market'.⁴⁰

The picking of cotton, hair and oakum was typical of the activity of the poor in both workhouses and Schools of Industry, but some children were taught locally specific skills of value to later employment. For example, when the Shrewsbury workhouse opened in 1784, 'boys are instructed in the different workshops ... girls are employed in spinning, in making gloves ... and other labour that is suited to their sex, their ages and abilities'.⁴¹ In St Martin in the Fields, the 100 children employed in the workhouse – before they were put-out apprentices – engaged in spinning flax, picking hair and carding wool.⁴² In Ealing, in-house training was provided to enhance the children's marketability: and they were sent to 'manufactories' when sufficiently skilful.⁴³ In 1802, the Hampstead Board of Guardians expressed the opinion 'that spinning was a proper employment for women and girls' and resolved that 'the women and girls in the workhouse be employed in spinning and that the proper apparatus, machines and materials be procured for employing them in such work'.⁴⁴

Links with local industry created employment for children in emerging manufacturing areas,⁴⁵ where they were sent on a daily basis to local manufacturers, in a quasi-apprentice form. In Liverpool, for example,

> about 50 girls are bound apprentices to a person who attends in the house, and employs them in sprigging muslin ...the house receives a small weekly sum for this work during their apprenticeship. The sum is from 1s to 2s 6d a week according to their proficiency in tambour work. They are bound for three years, and provided with victuals by the parish.⁴⁶

---

40 Poynter, *Society and Pauperism*, p. 15.

41 Eden, *State of the Poor*, p. 633. In the Shrewsbury House of Industry, children were set to work in the spinning room soon after they had reached the age of 5. Jennifer Tann, *Children at Work* (London, 1981), p. 7.

42 Eden, *State of the Poor*, p. 440. After an infancy spent in the country, parish children from St Martin were taken into the workhouse at seven or eight years old for a while before being put-out apprentices.

43 Eden, *State of the Poor*, p. 424. The cotton factory on Hampstead Road, connected to the workhouse, provided employment for the children of St Pancras Parish, many of whom were subsequently apprenticed to cotton mills out of town. 31 March 1807, Minutes of Directors of the Poor, Parish of St Pancras, P/PN/PO/1/3 (microfilm reference UTAH 651) CLSAC.

44 Meeting of 5 April 1802, Hampstead Board of Guardians Minutes 1800–1816, PHA/PO/1/1, CLSAC.

45 Eden, *State of the Poor*, pp. 130, 329.

46 Eden, *State of the Poor*, p. 329.

In Derby, children from the five parishes of the town might earn from 1s to 2s 6d a week in the local silk and cotton mills.[47] In Nottingham, workhouse children were employed in a cotton mill; and earned for the workhouse around £60 per year.[48]

Other schemes to create employment for surplus children included the 1780 proposal by Mr Vaux, a lace manufacturer, to construct a number of factories around London for 'the employment of infant females, in order to prevent the habitual idleness and degeneracy so common and so destructive to that most exposed and neglected part of the community'. Potential patrons were invited to visit his existing lace factory in Marylebone, with the hope that they would assist in setting up further establishments, and recommend

> proper children viz from the age of five years and upwards ...whose situation in life are the most dangerous and who often habituated to an early idleness ... the children will be heard spell, read and say their catechise ... and every other regard will be paid to their health and morals.[49]

Diverse proposals to provide poor children with productive employment notwithstanding, the cheapest and easiest solution to the problem of child poverty was for the parish to bind children to apprenticeships as they were empowered to do under the Elizabethan Poor Law.[50] Parishes advertised for apprenticeships and were happy to pay several pounds, approaching the cost of supporting a child in the workhouse for one year, to those willing to assume the burden.[51] For a number of reasons an apprenticeship was deemed preferable to relieving a child in the workhouse. The inconvenience of inspection was the first of these.[52] The second was that the workhouse was unlikely to teach skills, or even the habit of work. Thus the

---

47   Eden, *State of the Poor*, p. 128. This money would be paid to the parish, not to the children themselves.

48   Eden, *State of the Poor*, vol. 2, p. 576.

49   This was a targeted campaign. The publicity documents were circulated nationwide among the gentry. The example I read was addressed to the Earl of Dartmouth and survives in the Staffordshire Record Office, D(W) 1778 V702.

50   Dunlop, *English Apprenticeship*, p. 242.

51   Joan Lane estimated that the cost of a child to the parish was around £4 annually. In fact this is likely to be an underestimate. Birmingham Parish estimated the weekly cost of keeping a child in the workhouse, except clothing, to be 2s 6d in 1818 (£6 10s per annum), 2 June 1818, Minutes of Guardians of the poor, Birmingham Parish, GP/B/2/1/2 1806–24 BCA; and St Mary Newington estimated the average cost per inmate to be 3s 10d, 31 March 1806, St Mary Newington Workhouse Committee Minutes 1806–1813 Ref 930 Southwark Local History Library [SLHL]. An apprenticeship premium even of £5, which was higher than average, would represent a substantial saving, given that the apprenticeship would run for seven years or more. Joan Lane, *Apprenticeship in England 1600–1914* (London, 1996), p. 84. See also Anthony Brundage, *The English Poor Laws 1700–1930* (Basingstoke, 2002), p. 16. According to Dorothy Marshall, 'there was no regular machinery to see that pauper apprenticeship was carried out to its intended conclusion'. Marshall, *English Poor*, p. 193.

52   1790 regulation giving power to justices to inspect and report on workhouses, and an act of 1792–93, which authorised punishment of overseers and constables for neglect of duty. Tate, *Parish Chest*, p. 194.

training component of apprenticeship offered long term economic advantage to both individual and parish. Short-term cost-effectiveness comprised the third relative attraction. Even accounting for the value of in-house production, the master's premium and the cost of clothing would be outweighed several times by the cost of supporting a child either in the workhouse or through outdoor relief.

Apprenticeship out of the parish carried even greater benefits. In this case, the final and perhaps most important attraction for the parish was the settlement consideration. A settlement was of particular importance under the Poor Law system as it conferred a right to poor relief.[53] Although K.D.M. Snell suggests that the complexity of the relationship between apprenticeship and settlement law has been inadequately explored,[54] for many observers the link was straightforward. According to Dorothy George, 'the law of settlement, the practice of apprenticeship and theories on social status were inextricably interwoven, though all of them underwent modifications in the eighteenth century ... [under] the act of 1691, settlement could be got by serving an apprentice'.[55] However, contemporaries and historians disagree about the point at which a settlement was gained. Snell, for example, insists that 'a full seven-year apprenticeship was one of the legal 'heads' that conferred a settlement';[56] while many contemporaries understood the situation rather differently. It was widely held that 40 days service under an apprenticeship was sufficient to gain a settlement.[57] Whatever

---

53 Paul Slack, *The English Poor Law, 1531–1782* (Cambridge, 1995), pp. 28–30; Kathryn M. Thompson (ed.), *Settlement Papers*, Short Guides to Records, no. 28 (London: Historical Association, 1997), pp. 25–8; Henriques, *Before the Welfare State*, pp. 13–14.

54 K.D.M. Snell, 'The apprenticeship system in British history: the fragmentation of a cultural institution', *History of Education*, 25/ 4 (1996): 303–304. See also, Simon Deakin and Frank Wilkinson, *The Law of the Labour Market: Industrialisation, Employment and Legal Evolution* (Oxford, 2005), pp. 115–20; Hindle, 'Pauper apprenticeship', p. 23.

55 M. Dorothy George, *London Life in the Eighteenth Century* (London, 1925), pp. 223–4. Not only did indentured apprentices acquire a settlement in the parish in which they served, but also, under the terms of the 1691 Act, servants hired for a complete year were granted settlement provided that they were unmarried. Steven King, *Poverty and Welfare in England, 1700–1850: A Regional Perspective* (Manchester, 2000), p. 273.

56 Snell, *Annals*, p. 228.

57 Tate, *Parish Chest*, p. 225. The 40-day rule is confirmed in Kathryn M. Thompson (ed.), *Apprenticeship and Bastardy Records*, Short Guides to Records, no. 29 (London: Historical Association, 1997), p. 29. In September 1808, for example, St Pancras Parish officials resisted an appeal against the removal of a former parishioner who had gained settlement in St Marylebone on the grounds of a partially served, but not cancelled, apprenticeship. 13 September 1808, Meeting of Directors of the Poor, Parish of St Pancras, P/PN/PO/1/4 (microfilm reference UTAH 650), CLSAC. Discussions on 19 December 1809 (P/PN/PO/1/5 UTAH 650) and 17 May 1814 (P/PN/PO/1/9 UTAH 651) were also relevant. According to Snell, under the Act of 1758, an apprentice would be irremovable after 40 days; but Snell's impression is that the Act was frequently ignored. Snell, *Annals*, p. 258. See Fideler, *Social Welfare*, pp. 143–6 for a historiographical comment of the settlement issue. Despite confusion and complexity, the system survived into the new Poor Law era. Michael E. Rose, 'Settlement, removal and the new Poor Law' in Derek Fraser (ed.), *The New Poor Law in the Nineteenth Century* (Basingstoke, 1976), pp. 25–44.

the contemporary understanding, once parishes had discovered the settlement opportunity, 'it became the chief use of the apprenticeship clause'.[58]

Evidence that gaining a settlement elsewhere for its young poor was a parish priority emanates from the common practice of withholding part if not all of the apprentice premium until a settlement was ascertained. In 1787, for example, the officers of Gnosall parish, agreed to 'pay him ... when ... [name] shall have gained a settlement under her indentures of Apprenticeship the sum of fifty shillings and sixpence';[59] and in the case of the binding of Mary Smith of Elmton parish in Derbyshire to Edward Marshall of Sutton in Ashfield, Notts, 'in consideration of which, the parish of Elmton had paid the said Edward Marshall the sum of £2'. Marshall 'promises to pay the overseers of the poor of Elmton the said £2 if the said Mary Smith should become chargeable to the parish of Elmton during the term of the said apprenticeship'.[60]

Dr Burn stated that not only would the parish 'take special care that the master live in another parish', but it would also 'move heaven and earth if any dispute happens about a settlement'.[61] Just as it was important for parishes to assist their poor in gaining a settlement elsewhere, it was equally a priority 'to keep an extraordinary look out to prevent persons coming to inhabit without certificates ...'.[62] It was relatively straightforward for taxpayers to stop migrants from acquiring local settlement, by identifying a loophole in the apprenticeship indenture or agreement, or by hiring servants for less than a year; and 'by the early nineteenth century, an unprecedently high proportion of apprenticeships was being deemed illegal for the purposes of settlement, with "lost" contracts or indentures, or little more than verbal agreements often being entered into'.[63]

Historians have commonly taken the view that during their apprenticeships children were 'put out of the sight and mind of the parish that had legal responsibility

---

58 Marshall, *English Poor Law*, pp. 181–3; Ivy Pinchbeck and Margaret Hewitt, *Children in English Society* (2 vols, London, 1969–73), vol. 1, pp. 434–5. The rate at which parishes appreciated this possibility varied, and continued to generate uncertainty into the factory age. See discussion 4 October 1791, Meetings of Churchwardens, Overseers and Assistants, Parish of St Clement Danes, B1147, and 6 October 1791, meeting of Vestry, Parish of St Clement Danes, B1073, WAC. James Stephen Taylor, 'A different kind of Speenhamland: nonresident relief in the industrial revolution', *Journal of British Studies*, 30 (1991): 185–8 and 207, refers to both the practice of settlement through apprenticeship, and the flexible use of the system to permit labour mobility.

59 Cited in Tate, *Parish Chest*, p. 225.

60 14 October 1797, Elmton parish apprenticeship indenture, D1462 A/PO 289, Derbyshire Record Office (DRO).

61 Dr Burn's 'animated though somewhat too highly coloured picture of a parish overseer' is quoted in Eden, *State of the Poor*, vol. 1, p. 347. In 1768 Sir John Fielding stated that the 'chief view of the overseer is to get rid of the object and fix his settlement in another parish'. Quoted in Hollen Lees, *Solidarities*, p. 55; and the Webbs cited contemporary opinion that 'the worst possible master in another parish was preferred to the best residing in the parish'. Webb and Webb, *Old Poor Law*, p. 199.

62 Cited in Tate, *Parish Chest*, p. 195.

63 Snell, 'The apprenticeship system', p. 315; see also Snell, *Annals*, pp. 252–4.

for them'.[64] As the Webbs noted in their examination of the old Poor Law, 'throughout the whole of the eighteenth century we find constant complaints of the indifference of Churchwardens and overseers to anything beyond saving the parish the keep of the boys or girls'.[65] In 1732, for example, the 'very bad practice in parish officers who, to save expense, are apt to ruin children, by putting them out as early as they can, to any sorry masters that will take them, without any concern for their education or welfare', was denounced.[66] Sir John Fielding, in 1786, spoke directly on the subject. 'The chief view of the overseer is to get rid of the object and fix his settlement in another parish'.[67] Richard Burn expressed a similar view: 'contemporaries freely admitted that they bound pauper children to virtually anyone as long as a master lived outside the parish; they also promptly forgot any need to oversee the arrangement'.[68] The potential for abuse through parish determination to apprentice out of the parish was thus substantial, and was well recognised at the time. An enquiry of 1738 observed that

> a most unhappy practice prevails in most places to apprentice poor children, no matter to what master, provided he lives out of the parish, if the child serves the first 40 days we are rid of him for ever. The master may be a tiger in cruelty, he may beat, abuse, strip naked, starve or do what he will to the poor innocent lad, few people take much notice, and the officers who put him out the least of anybody.[69]

However, a further ambiguity of the old Poor Law was the extent to which the parish retained responsibility for children once they had been handed over to the master or employer. If the Settlement rules, as well as those underpinning the apprenticeship indentures operated consistently, then in principle, the parish would cease to be in a position of care once premiums were paid. Yet, marginal notes in parish apprentice registers, and records of overseers meetings which indicate the serious pursuit of

---

64 For example, Hollen Lees, *Solidarities*, pp. 102–103; Webb and Webb, *Old Poor Law*, p. 197: 'What the Poor Law administrators were thinking about was merely how to get the boy off their hands'. It is difficult to find a historian, or even a contemporary commentator, who does not express this opinion. What is missing is conclusive, supporting evidence.

65 Webb and Webb, *Old Poor Law*, pp. 197–8. But the Webbs provide at least one example of due care, that of the parishes of St Giles and St George, Bloomsbury, where in 1781 officers were expected to 'cause strict enquiry to be made respecting the characters of the persons who from time to time apply to have them as apprentices', p. 198n. My research indicates that this case was far from unusual both before and after factory apprenticeship. See also Hill, *Women, Work and Sexual Politics*, p. 87; Charlotte Neff, 'Pauper apprenticeship in early nineteenth century Ontario', *Journal of Family History*, 21/2 (1996): 147.

66 Author of 'An account of the workhouses in Great Britain in the year 1732', cited in Webb and Webb, *Old Poor Law*, p. 198.

67 Quoted in Webb and Webb, *Old Poor Law*, p. 198.

68 Cited in Hollen Lees, *Solidarities*, p. 55. The situation had altered little by the 1830s. When the Poor Law enquiry asked how apprentices had turned out, a parish officer replied that 'we have nothing to do with them afterwards'. Quoted in Webb and Webb, *Old Poor Law*, p. 199.

69 Enquiry into the causes of the increase of the poor, 1738, cited in George, *London Life*, p. 227.

apprentices' complaints, suggest that officers of the Poor Law assumed long-term responsibility for their young poor.[70] That this continued to be the case within the context of factory apprenticeship will be demonstrated in later chapters.

A process that amounted to bulk apprenticeship, in which parishes throughout the land were involved, predated the factory. William Felkin, authority on the midlands hosiery and lace industry, for example, noted that in 1730 parishes offered £5 for each boy or girl taken off their hands, and that one manufacturer at Nottingham ran all the frames in his workshop using parish apprentices, usually 25 in number.[71] In the 1740s, the Foundling Hospital proposed sending girls to textile centres where they might be taken on as apprentices.[72] In 1774, officials of the parish of St George, Hanover Square, which subsequently engaged in the factory apprenticeship system, supplied 'young children to a London silk manufacturer, apparently without any formal apprenticeship'.[73] The death of one of these children and the ensuing enquiry, found systematic cruelty and the children were brought back to the parish.[74] During the later eighteenth century, small masters in the iron trades in Birmingham, south Staffordshire, and Worcestershire, took large numbers of apprentices into their workshops.[75]

The well-established practice of binding out of the parish permitted continuity into the factory age. The movement of parish apprentices into early textile mills gathered pace from 1780 as the number of pauper children increased,[76] but only perpetuated an existing trend. Parish factory apprenticeships may have differed from traditional forms in terms of the nature of work and possibly the distance of placements, but the principle and implications of out-of-parish bindings were unaltered. The criticisms of 'disposal' were also unchanged. The emergence of factory apprenticeship reawakened concerns about settlement. But evidence that settlement benefits motivated parish factory apprentices is unconvincing. Although the factory

---

70 Thompson, *Apprenticeship and Bastardy*, p. 30, specified the Acts of 1746–47, which permitted an apprentice to complain about ill-treatment or failure to teach a trade, and a measure of 1792–93, which included a system for checking on children sent to distant factories.

71 Felkin, quoted in Webb and Webb, *Old Poor Law*, p. 200.

72 A.P. Wadsworth and Julia de Lacy Mann, *The Cotton Trade and Industrial Lancashire, 1600–1780* (Manchester, 1931), p. 407, quoting William Maitland, *A History of London*, (1756 edn), pp. 1299–1300.

73 Quoted in Webb and Webb, *Old Poor Law*, p. 201. Ivy Pinchbeck, *Women Workers and the Industrial Revolution 1750–1850* (London, 1930), pp. 272–3.

74 This example demonstrates a level of care by St George's parish officers even if they had been less than cautious in the initial placement of the children. Such attention by this particular parish also featured during the active period of factory apprenticeship, and surpassed the level demonstrated by some other parishes both in London and elsewhere in the country. This is discussed in Chapter 11.

75 Hollen Lees, *Solidarities*, p. 101.

76 Parliamentary returns of 1803 suggest that there were 195,000 children of paupers aged between 5 and 14 who were permanently relieved by the parishes in England and Wales. Cited in Hugh Cunningham, 'The employment and unemployment of children in England c.1680–1851', *Past and Present*, 126 (1990):133.

system expanded the opportunities for resettlement, the practice of binding 'out' even to a distance was well established.

Formally equivalent to earlier forms, factory apprenticeship was nevertheless perceived by contemporaries and by historians as inherently more open to abuse, both in terms of settlement law and in how they affected the children involved. The nature of the agreements drawn up between parish and employer rendered the settlement situation even more ambiguous than previously and easier to evade; and often, but by no means always they accorded little protection to the children themselves. According to Arthur Redford,

> there were ... many ways of taking the apprentices without incurring liability. The indentures were sometimes not properly completed, and might be disowned; a still less scrupulous method was to goad the apprentice into running away before their contract was completed ... some mills owners managed to build their apprentice house in a different parish from that in which their mill stood

thus creating at best an ambiguous situation regarding both rate payments and settlement.[77]

Parishes may have varied in the extent to which they understood settlement to be an integral part of the package of the apprenticeship agreement, but they were all sensitive to the issue. The Chelmsford overseers, for example, in

> fixing up this bargain with the cotton manufacturer [Douglas, Pendleton] ... effectually discharged Chelmsford of future as well as present liability for relief of these ten young paupers, for the parishioners of Eccles would be responsible for their relief, if in need, after the completion of their apprenticeship.[78]

Discussion among the parish officers of St Clement Danes indicates the preoccupation of both parish and master with settlement. In 1791, for example, 'a letter was read from Mr Birch of Blackbarrow [sic] which stated that all children sent there gained a settlement in the parish of Cartmell [sic] that the notion that had gone forth in St

---

77 Arthur Redford, *Labour Migration in England 1800–1850* (Manchester, 1964), p. 30. Bott's factory in Tutbury is one such example; and so, as is revealed in the 1816 Select Committee, is the Backbarrow factory. Ellis Needham intentionally built the house for his apprentices within a different parish to his factory, partly it seems to pacify local residents. M.H. Mackenzie, 'Cressbrook and Litton Mills 1779–1835 Part 1', *Derbyshire Archaeological Journal*, 88 (1968): 18. Debate between Landau and Snell illustrates the absence of uniform practice. Landau argues that until 1795 in Kent, local officials routinely examined all newcomers about their settlement; while Snell believes that in the southern areas that he studied, the poor could move in search of work and remain in a parish unless they became chargeable. Norma Landau, 'The laws of settlement and the surveillance of immigration in eighteenth-century Kent', *Continuity and Change*, 3/3 (1988): 391–420; K.D.M. Snell, 'Pauper settlement and the right to poor relief in England and Wales', *Continuity and Change*, 6/3 (1991): 384–99; see also Lees, *Solidarities*, pp. 28–9; Fideler, *Social Welfare*, pp. 143–6.

78 Ten indenture papers, ERO D/P 94/14; F.G. Emmison, 'Essex children deported to a Lancashire cotton mill, 1799', *The Essex Review*, 53 (1944): 79.

Clements parish that they did not gain a settlement was erroneous'.[79] Some years later, the case of Elizabeth Anne Galloway, who had been apprenticed to Monteith and Bogle, but who was to be brought back to town, adds to the complexity of the contemporary status of settlement. The officers of St Clement Danes 'agreed that on the child being received from Glasgow, a bond should be given to indemnify the parish from any charge which might accrue therefrom, she not having gained any parochial settlement in Glasgow'.[80] Cases in Warwickshire and Oxfordshire illustrate similar concerns. Apprenticeship indentures for children bound from Coleshill parish in Warwickshire to 'William Willcock of Fazeley in the county of Stafford, cotton spinner' for example, stated that William Willcock 'will provide for the said apprentice that she be not any way a charge to the said parish or parishioners of the same; but of and from all charge shall and will save the said parish and parishioners harmless and indemnified during the term'.[81] St Clements Parish, Oxford, used very similar wording when binding its children to Benjamin Smart's Emscote mill. The proprietors 'will so provide for the said apprentice that she be not any way a charge to the said parish but of and from all charges shall and will save the said parish of St Clements harmless and indemnified during the said term'.[82]

The discovery that pauper children were bound into one poor parish from another generated an immediate response. Children were apprenticed to masters in St Mary Newington, Southwark, from other local parishes, for example; and in 1824–25, as bindings for St Mary children were sought out of the area, 21 children from St Giles, Middlesex, were apprenticed in St Mary. When requested by St Mary parish officers to remove the children, St Giles overseers replied that they would seek alternative placements and that if any of the children became chargeable in the meantime, they would be collected.[83] The apprenticeship indenture forms of a small number of parishes, especially those in the Corporation of London, required the written permission of both the sending and the recipient parish before execution, and it was not unknown for arrangements to fall because of the latter's refusal. In 1818, for example, John White from St Dunstan in the West, was to be apprenticed to John Jackson, watch finisher, Curtain Road, Shoreditch, but was not bound because 'we could not obtain the consent of the overseers of St Leonard's, Shoreditch'.[84] The

---

79 4 October 1791, Meetings of Churchwardens, Overseers and Assistants, Parish of St Clement Danes, B1147, and 6 October 1791, Meeting of Vestry, Parish of St Clement Danes, B1073, WAC.

80 28 January 1809, Meetings of Churchwardens, Overseers and Assistants, Parish of St Clement Danes, B1149, WAC.

81 For example, Hannah Jackson, 4 April 1814, Coleshill Apprenticeship indentures, Warwickshire County Record Office (WCRO).

82 Indenture dated 24 June 1811, contained in correspondence between Benjamin Smart and St Clements Parish, Oxford, Z351/2/1, WCRO.

83 St Mary Newington workhouse committee minutes, January 1826; Typescript of essay: Dorothy Hester Helena Newbold 'The Poor Law. St Mary Newington, 1790–1834' undated, p. 26, SLHL.

84 Poor apprentices register, 1803–1887, Parish of St Dunstan in the West, MS 3003, Guildhall Library (GL). It is rare to find examples of such forms, and in the course of the research for this study, only those within the Corporation of London were identified.

implication is that concerns about the cost of future settlement proved a stumbling block. Apart from a handful of such examples, little is known about the response of the recipient parish.[85] Very few indentures took the form described above, where the permission of the parish in which the master resided, in the case of an incoming apprentice, was required.

By the end of the eighteenth century, occupiers were increasingly compelled to maintain a child or pay a fine. Practice varied but usually the burden of maintaining the children, especially the older ones, was shared among the eligible ratepayers,[86] either by rotation or by casting lots. In Hope-under-Dinmore, Herefordshire, for example, 'twelve children were balloted to the respective persons named at the last meeting as liable to take parish apprentices, and the overseer is directed to call upon the persons to whom the children are respectively balloted'.[87] On occasions, the local justices chose such parishioners as they saw fit.[88] The most common means of avoiding this responsibility was the payment of a fine, but alternative measures taken by the parish in the event of refusal included the direction that the overseer 'take out summons against the person so objecting to show cause why the children shall not be bound to them'.[89] Where a fine were imposed, £10 was common, but varied according to parish need.[90] In 1819, for example, the Leeds Poor Law officials agreed 'that the fine for refusing a parish apprentice be increased to such a sum as may remove the difficulty that is now encountered in obtaining situations for the children of paupers'.[91]

The rising level of fine income at the turn of the nineteenth century indicates the growing reluctance on the part of masters, especially those in trades or professions, to take on apprentices, and the increasing use of the fine system to raise much needed

---

85 In his analysis of Suffolk apprentices, Hugh Fearn appears to associate 'outside' apprenticeship with inferior masters and substandard training, and eventually with an increase in poverty and crime within the recipient parish. Hugh Fearn, 'The apprenticing of pauper children in the incorporated hundreds of Suffolk', *Proceedings of the Suffolk Institute of Archaeology*, 26 (1955): 90.

86 Normally all occupiers rated at £10 per year or more would be liable. Webb and Webb, *Old Poor Law*, p. 208.

87 22 May 1811, Minutes of Vestry meetings, Parish of Hope under Dinmore N31/33, Herefordshire Record Office (HRO).

88 Webb and Webb, *Old Poor Law*, p. 209.

89 22 May 1811, Minutes of Vestry meetings, Parish of Hope under Dinmore N31/33, HRO.

90 Webb and Webb, *Old Poor Law*, p. 209. There were exceptions to this: in Ledbury parish, for example, a substantial number of masters opted to pay the £10 fine. These were mainly the wealthier parishioners, 'gentlemen' and 'reverends' for whom a parish child was likely to be more of hindrance than a help. Apprenticeship Register, Ledbury Parish, BO92/62, HRO.

91 12 April 1819, Leeds Workhouse Committee minute and order book 1818–, LO M/6. West Yorkshire Archive Service, Leeds (WYASL). There were cases of employers being paid back exemption fines if they subsequently took on an apprentice. Philip W. Anderson, 'The Leeds workhouse under the Old Poor Law, 1726–1844', University of Leeds, MPhil thesis, 1977, p. 88. In 1829, the Poor Law committee attempted to resolve its difficulties by ruling that all householders should take at least one apprentice. Anderson, 'Leeds workhouse', p. 89.

revenue at a time of financial pressure.[92] Fines in Calverley-cum-Farsley, for example reached a peak in 1800–1801; and the list includes many who elected to pay the fine by instalments.[93]

Many examples exist of undesirable youngsters offered to successive masters in the certain knowledge that an avoiding fine would be forthcoming.[94] Indeed there existed children whose key function appears to have been fine income-generation. The case of George Orange in Leeds seems to support this. He was offered and rejected on almost a weekly basis.[95] Such a practice was widely condemned by the Royal Commission on Poor Laws in 1834, which rightly suggested that putting children onto unwilling employers was a very bad practice.[96]

It was not uncommon for those ratepayers who neither desired an apprentice nor could afford the fine to reassign the child to another employer. Formally this required permission from Poor Law officials but only rarely was this sought. Another avoidance tactic was to complain of the unsuitability of the chosen apprentice. In a number of instances this was attempted on the grounds of gender, girls more frequently than boys being deemed unsuitable. Parishes revealed little sympathy to the master in such cases, resulting in some interesting legal rulings.[97] Ill health and disability were also contested. Ailing children were either offered with a bonus premium[98] or if not recognised as such at the outset were soon returned to the parish.

This is the moment at which the early textile factories came to play a role. The problem of finding sufficient and suitable masters was eased towards the end of the eighteenth century by mill owners who were 'willing to take' substantial numbers of pauper apprentices to attend their machinery.[99] This came to be an important strand

---

92   The reluctance of ratepayers to take pauper apprentices had been a feature of the system from the outset, and a major problem though the seventeenth century. Hindle, 'Pauper apprentices', pp. 22–6.

93   Apprentice Book, Parish of Calverley cum Farsley, BDP 17/89, WYASL.

94   The parish records of Leeds and Halifax provide many such examples. Often a girl was offered when clearly a boy was required; or a disabled child was offered when a healthy one was desired. Either way, they managed to more than pay for their own keep through the fines paid to avoid taking them.

95   Leeds Workhouse Committee minute and order book 1818–, LO M/6.WYASL. According to Anderson, George Orange had 23 employers in a two-year period. 'Leeds workhouse', p. 117. Similar examples were identified in Suffolk by Fearn, 'The apprenticing'.

96   Tweedy comment in *Report of the Royal Commission on the Poor Laws*: PP 1834, XXVII, Appndx 4, part 1, no. 20, cited in Webb and Webb, *Old Poor Law*, p. 209.

97   See, for example, the ruling provided about the term of apprenticeship and the age at termination, Wakefield Quarter Sessions QD1/555, West Yorkshire Archive Service Wakefield (WYASW).

98   For example, an agreement was reached between the officers of Stanford Bishop parish and a master in 1817, 'to take apprentices that are unhealthy, that is the one with the bad eyes and the other with something like the Kings Evil – the officers do hereby agree to defray any expense that may be brought on by either of the above complaints'. 20 February 1817, Stanford Bishop Parish Book, N5/1 HRO.

99   Oxley, *Poor Relief*, p. 76. This is somewhat of an understatement: in fact employers were in need of such child labour. Nevertheless their willingness distinguished them from many other masters.

of Poor Law administration, because it resolved, at least temporarily, a crisis of poor relief in many parishes. That it was seen as significant by contemporaries was reflected in the documentation that stemmed from it.[100] The element of compulsion on which the parish apprenticeship system depended, hardly served the interest of the child, and although the practice of factory apprenticeship has been rightly attacked for its openness to abuse, it was not unique in this respect. The key advantage of factory over other contemporary forms of apprenticeship, was that in every case the master willingly took the child; and so long as the business survived was unlikely to pass children onto another master.[101]

The construction of the parish apprentice should be understood in terms of changing attitudes to both children and poverty. As children they were seen increasingly benignly; but as 'poor' they were also seen as fearsome objects. This tension is revealed in the treatment of the parish apprentices and will be explored in later chapters.

---

100 Oxley, *Poor Relief*, p. 76. The bindings to distant parishes/mills that were to be scrutinised and approved by magistrates, augmented the range of parish documentation.

101 Business failure, however, was quite common in early textile factories.

Chapter 3

Factory Apprenticeship: Structure, Process and Legislation

In the last years of the eighteenth century, the growing number of poor children increased financial pressure on the old Poor Law. Consequently, the scale of parish apprenticeship increased as traditional forms of binding – to domestic service and farm work as well as local trades – were augmented by factory apprenticeship.[1] The requirements of the first textile factories for poor children appeared to match the requirements of the parishes for apprentice placements. The process of parish factory apprenticeship met the needs of both parish and enterprise. This chapter outlines the key features of the structure and process of the early factory apprenticeship system and the legislation implemented to regulate it. I shall argue, contrary to the traditional notion of random disposal, that the process of parish factory apprenticeship was rigorous, well coordinated and formally recorded.[2]

A bleak picture of the trade in parish children was drawn by contemporaries and subsequently replicated by scholars. Sir Samuel Romilly spoke and wrote frequently on the subject with reference to his other preoccupation, slavery:

> It is a very common practice with the great populous parishes in London to bind children in large numbers to the proprietors of cotton mills in Lancashire and Yorkshire … The children who are sent off by wagon loads at a time, are as much lost for ever to their parents as if they were shipped off to the West Indies.[3]

---

1 In many of the parishes examined for this study, binding to factory apprenticeships took place in addition to the other forms during the peak years between 1790 and 1810. See for example, the apprenticeship registers of St Clement Danes, St Martin in the Fields, St Margaret and St John. There is a substantial literature referring to this subject, for example, Charlotte Neff, 'Pauper apprenticeship in early nineteenth century Ontario', *Journal of Family History*, 21/2 (1996): 146–7.

2 This does not mean that the experience of children was as positive as the documentary legacy suggests.

3 *Memoirs of the Life of Sir Samuel Romilly, with a Selection of his Correspondence, Edited by his Sons* (1840, vol. II, Irish University Press, 1971), pp. 378–9. He expressed his strong objection to the practice in the commons' discussion of the 1811 Bill; emphasising the 'abuses which prevailed from the maladministration of the existing laws'. He regaled the House with stories of murders by masters, 'which would fill the House with horror'. *The Parliamentary Debates* (London, 1811), vol. 20, p. 517. In his diary, he understands the murders to have been prompted by the master's desire to obtain fresh premiums for a replacement batch of children. Cited in B.L. Hutchins and A. Harrison, *A History of Factory Legislation* (Westminster, 1903), p. 14.

The description provided by the Webbs is typical of traditional historical discourse:

> The progress of the industrial revolution led to a demand for child labour in one manufacture after another ... The necessary operatives had to be brought from somewhere and the cheapest source was the workhouse of the south of England. Parish officers accordingly found themselves importuned by the agents sent by manufacturers to recruit their staffs, who, without asking any premium, carried off the children literally by cartloads, taking even infants of three or four years old.[4]

Although historians have subsequently revised the analysis, the typical interpretation remains pessimistic.[5] The following discussion attempts to illuminate the operation of the parish factory apprenticeship system, which will be explored further in Chapter 4.

That early textile factories, especially in isolated rural locations, operated under labour supply constraints, is well recorded.[6] Widely advertised incentives to attract labour proved inadequate to most needs.[7] Even the powerful Richard Arkwright was compelled to obtain workers – especially juveniles – from outside the area of his factories. While in the wide search for labour he was unexceptional, he made

---

4 Sidney and Beatrice Webb, *English Local Government*, vol. 7, *English Poor Law History*, Part 1, *The Old Poor Law* (London, 1927), p. 201. They also cite Romilly describing the children taken 'in carts like so many negro slaves'. *Hansard*, 1807, p. 800. J.L. Hammond and Barbara Hammond, *The Town Labourer 1760–1832: The New Civilisation* (London, 1917), p. 101, also refer to pauper children being taken off in cartloads. Some contemporaries, including Jeremy Bentham, believed that children as young as four years old could be productive. Whether this was appropriate was more debatable. Medical evidence to the 1816 Select Committee indicated that seven years was the age at which factory employment became suitable but only for 4–5 hours per day (Matthew Baillie, MD, SC1816, p. 29). In contrast to the tendency of early writers to exaggerate the extreme youth of factory parish apprentices, the more recent trend is to underestimate the youthfulness of such workers. See, for example, Peter Kirby, *Child Labour in Britain, 1750–1870* (Basingstoke, 2003), p. 4, who asserts that it was rare for children to be employed under the age of 10; and Peter Laslett, *Family Life and Illicit Love in Earlier Generations: Essays in Historical Sociology* (Cambridge, 1977), p. 214.

5 See, for example, Pamela Horn, *Children's Work and Welfare, 1780–1890* (Cambridge, 1995), p. 19, who cites the view that children were dispatched like 'cartloads of live lumber'; Marjorie Cruickshank, *Children and Industry: Child Health and Welfare in North-west Textile Towns During the Nineteenth Century* (Manchester, 1981).

6 See for example, S.D. Chapman, *The Early Factory Masters: The Transition to the Factory System in the Midlands Textile Industry* (Newton Abbot, 1967), pp. 156–8; Mary B. Rose, 'Social policy and business: parish apprenticeship and the early factory system, 1750–1834', *Business History*, 31/4 (1989): 5–9, 13–20.

7 Incentives included generous payment systems, security of employment and low-rent housing. For example, at Cromford men comprised 13 per cent of the total. Chapman, *Early Factory Masters*, p. 165–6; details of Samuel Oldknow's productive use of this strategy is detailed in George Unwin, *Samuel Oldknow and the Arkwrights: The Industrial Revolution at Stockport and Marple* (London, 1924), pp. 159–75.

unusually little use of parish apprentices.⁸ For many other early factory employers, however, the poor parish child proved to be an ideal component of the workforce.

The first stage in establishing the system of parish factory apprenticeship was the identification of the supply of poor children and demand for their labour. Parishes were initially more proactive than employers in this regard. The practice of advertising available children was well established by parishes prior to the factory age; and continued thereafter in the search for suitable placements either in mills or in local trades. Newspapers through the second half of the eighteenth century and into the early part of the nineteenth century were replete with advertisements offering or requiring apprentices.⁹ A small number of examples are offered here to illustrate this point. In 1783, Poor Law officers of St James, Piccadilly, one of the wealthier London parishes, agreed the wording of an advertisement: '100 boys and 100 girls orderly in behaviour ... any manufacturer or tradesman willing to employ such children ... may come and look [on a date to be specified]'.¹⁰ Four years later, the parish advertised the availability of children between 7 and 14: 'the governors would be glad to treat for the employment of 70 healthy boys at any business they may be thought capable of ... [any] respectable inhabitant of this OR ANY OTHER parish' may apply.¹¹ St James continued to advertise alongside its engagement with large-scale factory apprenticing. In 1801, the following was inserted in the daily newspapers: 'A number of well educated useful and healthy children of both sexes are now in the workhouse and School of Industry of this parish qualified to be bound apprentices'.¹²

In 1784, the Birmingham Guardians, observing that there were forty surplus girls in the workhouse for whom suitable local placements had not been found, agreed that 'measures be immediately adopted for putting them out apprentices'. They advertised in the local press 'that there are many healthy girls in the Birmingham workhouse between nine and fourteen years of age which the overseers of the poor are desirous to put out apprentice and would give a proper premium with them according to the circumstances of the case not exceeding £5'. It was added that

---

8 R.S. Fitton and A.P. Wadsworth, *The Strutts and the Arkwrights, 1758–1830: A Study of the Early Factory System* (Manchester, 1958), p. 105, assert that although parish apprentices were not employed, they did use 'ordinary' apprentices and long-term hiring. They also brought juvenile labour from the textile districts of Manchester and Nottingham. Chapman, *Early Factory Masters*, p. 156–7.

9 Grantham parish advertised several stout healthy boys and girls in the Leeds Intelligencer (and no doubt elsewhere) on 19 November 1804. George Ingle, *Yorkshire Cotton: The Yorkshire Cotton Industry, 1780–1835* (Preston, 1997), p. 70.

10 21 October 1783, Minutes of Governors and Directors of the Poor, Parish of St James, Piccadilly, D1870, WAC. However the meeting of 7 November 1783 intimated that the spinning of wool would not be 'the best employment that can be procured for the children'.

11 19 October 1787, Minutes of Governors and Directors of the Poor, Parish of St James, Piccadilly, D1872 WAC.

12 Mainly skilled trades are given as examples. 5 May 1801, Minutes of Governors and Directors of the Poor, Parish of St James, Piccadilly, D1877, WAC.

children could be 'seen' at the workhouse the following week.[13] In the same year, the Oswestry Guardians announced that 'manufacturers and mechanics may be supplied with either girls or boys as parish apprentices from 8–16'.[14]

St Clement Danes engaged in pre-factory advertising but was also one of the first parishes to seek specifically factory placements. In February 1785, a meeting of Poor Law assistants 'ordered that an advertisement be inserted in the *Daily Advertiser* that there are several children, boys and girls, in the workhouse of a fit age to be placed out apprenticed';[15] and two years later its advertising of 'several stout boys' in the *Manchester Mercury* met with immediate response from John Birch cotton manufacturer of Backbarrow. Within days, twenty boys had started work there.[16] The co-dependent relationship between parish and firm that was established at that moment persisted for over fifteen years, during which time 200 children were bound, accounting for the majority of apprentices of both parties. Discovering that conditions at Backbarrow had deteriorated in the early years of the nineteenth century, St Clement Danes officials resumed the search for suitable placements for its children. On 28 January 1809: 'the clerk stated a number of children to be in the house of an age at which they might be apprenticed out and proposed advertisements for masters and mistresses'.[17]

Firms, too, placed newspaper advertisements both in the initial stages of their establishment and during periods of particular expansion.[18] The connection between parish and firm, once established, often continued for a number of years. The example of Benjamin Smart indicates the careful attention paid to the relationship with the supplying parish. Although Smart advertised widely in newspapers local to his Warwickshire cotton mill, a number of his apprentices were drawn from St Clement parish, Oxford with whom close links were nurtured. In 1812, having concluded an apprenticeship arrangement, Smart requested 'the insertion of my late advertisement for apprentices in your next week's journal'.[19] Other strong relationships included that between the parish of St Luke, Chelsea and the firm of Douglas, to whom all its apprentices were bound between 1795 and 1802;[20] and the firm of Davison and

---

13 15 June 1784, Minutes of Birmingham Board of Guardians, 1783–1806, GP/B/2/1/1, Birmingham City Archives (BCA).

14 Chris Aspin, *The Water Spinners* (Helmshore, 2003), pp. 46–7.

15 1 February 1785, Minutes of Churchwardens, Overseers and Assistants, Parish of St Clement Danes B1147, WAC.

16 Aspin, *Water Spinners*, pp. 46–7.

17 Minutes of Churchwardens, Overseers and Assistants, Parish of St Clement Danes B1148, WAC. Other examples of early nineteenth-century advertising included St Pancras parish, which advertised children in June 1805 and had apprenticed 40 of them within a week to two Lancashire cotton manufacturers. Directors of the Poor, St Pancras parish, 22 June 1805.

18 Aspin, *Water Spinners* pp. 46–7.

19 Letter from Smart to St Clement, Oxford 3 Mo6 1812; Z351(sm) WCRO.

20 Workhouse Apprenticeship Register, 1791–1802, St Luke, Chelsea, P74/LUK/116. London Metropolitan Archives [LMA].

Hawksley, Nottingham, which absorbed all the available St Luke children between 1802 and 1805.[21]

Both parishes and firms also employed a direct approach. George Merryweather, a Yorkshire millowner, for example, wrote to a number of parishes in the south of England in his search for young workers.[22] There is little doubt that a number of firms very soon became known to parishes across the nation; Samuel Greg, William Toplis, William Douglas and Robert Peel among them. Parishes sometimes made the first move, and in view of the difficulty that existed in some areas of finding local bindings, this is hardly surprising. Furthermore, a factory master found to be sound in his treatment and training of children, might be offered children by parishes as they became available. For example, in 1811 the vestry clerk of St Clement Danes parish 'reported receipt of letter ... from Messrs Henry Monteith, Bogle and Co. of Glasgow, in answer to a letter ... offering children as apprentices, consenting to take them in the spring if not previously disposed of'.[23] In 1817, the Vicar of Biddulph wrote to Samuel Greg:

> the thought has occurred to me that some of the younger branches of the poor of this parish might be useful to you as apprentices in your factory at Quarry Bank. If you are in want of any of the above, we could readily furnish you with 10 or more at from 9 to 12 years of both sexes. My wife desires to join in best wishes for Mrs Greg and family.

The reply, sent by return, included the following: 'I am much obliged by your attention and find we have room at present for about 12 young girls of from 10–12 years. For boys we have not any room at present ... we keep them one month upon trial before bound to ascertain their probable healthiness'.[24]

To supplement advertising activity and the direct approach, a range of personnel and processes were employed to expedite the matching of supply and demand. A number of mill owners, especially the larger ones, who took children from geographically dispersed parishes, engaged the services of one or more agents.[25] Several such individuals became specialists in negotiating agreements between parish and factory owner, and worked for several firms. Others appear to have been well-connected amateurs, typically local merchants with links to Boards of Guardians, who simply oiled the wheels of the process when required.

---

21 Apprenticeship Register, 1802–1813, Parish of St Luke, Chelsea, P74/ LUK/117, LMA.

22 See, for instance, its approach to Islington and to Epsom parishes. Both considered but declined the request. 22 June 1801, Trustees of the Poor Minutes, Parish of St Mary, Islington, Islington Local History Centre (ILHC); Aspin, *Water Spinners*, p. 438.

23 3 September 1811, Minutes of Vestry, Parish of St Clement Danes, B1075, WAC.

24 Greg Papers, C5/8/9/1 and C5/8/9/2, Manchester City Archives [MCA].

25 Women agents were allegedly used to attract 'free' children from their families. Arthur Redford, *Labour Migration in England, 1800–1850* (Manchester, 1964), p. 25. No instances of female agents have been identified brokering deals with Poor Law officials in the course of this study. Redford argues that 'the practice of scouring the countryside for workhouse labour seems to have been a general method of recruiting workers for the country mills until the 1830s', ibid.

Examples of professional agents were John Plant and Philip French, both of whom worked for John Douglas at his mills in Pendleton and Holywell; but for other factory masters too. John Plant negotiated with Essex parishes, and reached the agreement that led to the deportation of ten children from Chelmsford to Pendleton in 1799.[26] He is also mentioned in the Poor Law records of a number of London parishes. A meeting of St James's parish, Westminster in 1797, for example, read a 'letter from Mr French, agent to Messrs Douglas and Co. of Pendleton'.[27] Mr French as well as a Mr Burn negotiated between John Whitaker of Burley-in-Wharfedale and the parish of St Mary Newington.[28] Other specialist negotiators were Mr Robinson, agent for Backbarrow, whose letter 'requesting to have 20 or 24 children of each sex, above 10 and from that to 15 …' was considered by the officers of St Clement Danes parish;[29] and Mr Rainey, agent to Haywood and Palfreyman among others. When considering the suitability of the Wildboar Clough factory as a destination for its poor children, the St James parish officers were referred by Rainey 'to Messrs Battier Zombin and Co. of 11 Devonshire Square for enquiry as to the character and respectability of Haywood and Palfreyman'.[30] Rainey also persuaded the proprietors to include a clause in the apprenticeship indentures making provision for the children in the event of their deaths, as requested by St James parish officers.[31] Thomas Gorton, of Aldermanbury in the city of London, brokered deals between St Pancras parish and mills in the Midlands and the north of England, especially after 1814, when he operated in conjunction with a Manchester-based agent, named Joshua Barnsley.[32]

The services of agents, or equivalent were often engaged to expedite the physical transfer of children from parish to factory. Jeremiah Bury and Co, who sought children from Southwark, reassured the parish that 'our friends, Messrs Rowlandson Brown and Co., no 17 Watling Street will engage a coach to take them down to our place'.[33] In the case of Susannah Lallement, 'a girl being chosen to go on liking to Mr Merryweather at Otley', it was ordered by the Governors of the Poor of St

---

26 F.G. Emmison, 'Essex children deported to a Lancashire cotton mill, 1799', *The Essex Review*, 53 (1944): 77–87; and though the agent is referred to as Mr John Plum, this is almost certainly a transcribing error.

27 10 February 1797, Minutes of Governors and Director of the Poor, Parish of St James, Piccadilly D1878, WAC. John Plant also appears to be operating as a firm manager.

28 10 December 1813, 9 April 1814, 13 April 1914, Minutes of St Mary Newington Workhouse Committee, 930, SLHL.

29 Letter of 29 September 1789, Minutes of Churchwardens, Overseers and Assistants, Parish of St Clement Danes, B1147, WAC.

30 9 February 1796, Minutes of Governors and Directors of the Poor, Parish of St James, Piccadilly, D1875, WAC.

31 As indicated by the discussion at meetings on 23 and 26 February 1796, the proprietors initially resisted that request. Minutes of Governors and Directors of the Poor, Parish of St James, Piccadilly, D1875,WAC.

32 10 May 1814, Minutes of Directors of the Poor, Parish of St Pancras P/PN/PO/1/9 (microfilm reference UTAH 651) CLSAC; 18 June 1816, Minutes of Directors of the Poor, Parish of St Pancras P/PN/PO/1/12 (microfilm reference UTAH 652) CLSAC.

33 'Proposal from Bury and Co.', Parish records of St George the Martyr, Southwark, SLHL.

George, Hanover Square, that 'when Mr Merryweather's agent appoints the time for her being sent by the wagon she be again seen by the Board'.[34] Acting for Messrs Garnett and Horsfall, Thomas Gorton assured St Pancras Directors of the Poor that 'the children were to be conveyed to the manufactory by the coaches without any expense to the Board'.[35]

Agents not only brokered initial deals but also acted as conduits of information between employer and parish throughout the apprenticeship term. They were sometimes required by parishes to account for the practices of the factories, especially in cases of complaint. For example, early in 1792,

> Mr Johnson [another] agent to the Holywell cotton mills attended and informed the board [of St Clement Danes parish] that of the children bound to that company, seven out of nine had run away. He admitted that they were worked from 7 in the evening to 6 in the morning that they were not relieved during the night.[36]

Agents were also used as a point of contact in cases of absconding children. When John Harris ran away from Holywell in 1797, his parish (St Anne, Soho in Westminster), was informed that 'should he make his appearance to you will be obliged to you to inform Mr Philip French Wills Coffee House … who is authorised to receive him for the Holywell Twist Company'.[37] Other agents expanded their role, and their income, by offering services to the parish. For example, in April 1815, John Gorton intimated 'his intent of going shortly into Lancashire to inspect all the children sent from this parish and others into Lancashire'.[38] Although agents were less usually employed by parishes to identify outlets for parish apprentices, individuals local to the factory were often selected to act on behalf of the parish or on behalf of the children, or both, once the apprentices were in place. Frequently these were local churchmen, some of whom, given the paucity of responsible adults with time on their hands in many neighbourhoods, were employed also by the factory to provide rudimentary education for the children.[39]

---

34   14 April 1807, Minutes of meetings of Governors and Directors of the Poor, Parish of St George, Hanover Square, C925, WAC.

35   24 May 1814, Minutes of Directors of the Poor, parish of St Pancras. P/PN/PO1/9 (microfilm reference 651) CLSAC. Gorton also paid the expenses for a magistrate to accompany eight children bound to Litton mills and inspect the conditions there. 18 June 1816, Minutes of Directors of the Poor, Parish of St Pancras, P/PN/PO/1/12 (microfilm reference UTAH 652) CLSAC.

36   12 March 1792, Minutes of Churchwardens, Overseers, and Assistants, Parish of St Clement Danes, B1147, WAC. After discussion, the parish official agreed that the two remaining boys be discharged.

37   Letter dated 18 November 1797 from John Roberts, Holywell to St Anne's parish. Apprenticeship, 1702–1834, Parish of St Anne, Westminster, A2262, WAC.

38   18 April 1815, Minutes of Directors of the Poor, Parish of St Pancras P/PN/PO/10 (microfilm reference UTAH 652), CLSAC.

39   For example, local clergymen were employed by the parish of St James at Haywood and Palfreyman at Wildboar Clough, at Holt Mills, Manchester, and by the Foundling Hospital at Cuckney. This feature is considered in more detail in Chapter 11.

However, although agents smoothed communications between interested parties, their actions were by no means always benign. As businessmen, they were driven by profit, which apprentice children facilitated. Only unusually did parishes uncover misdeeds, but this probably because they chose not to look. When investigating the improperly executed indentures of children recently bound to various masters through the auspices of Thomas Gorton, who was charged to 'dispose of the children as he sees fit',[40] a committee of parish Directors suspected that this agent was paid by manufacturers before the execution of indentures,[41] and by subsequently reassigning children he stood to gain a second time. Interviewed on this subject, Gorton 'refused angrily to give any answer whatever and immediately went away'; and when pressed on a later occasion 'he refused to answer in a manner certainly offensive and insulting'.[42] Having been unfavourably impressed with Gorton, the Directors proposed to 'discountenance and do away ... all further intercourse and communication' with him; and suggested that 'a totally different arrangement should ... be resorted for the future ... and that a direct communication should be had by this Board with the masters to whom the children are to be bound'.[43]

The financial and administrative arrangements associated with factory apprentice binding were usually exactly the same as for traditional, trade apprenticeships. The form of indenture was identical; names were recorded in the same registers in the same format; and the level and payment of the premium were usually equivalent. Although the size of the premium was not universally recorded,[44] there is no suggestion that fees were not paid, nor evidence for the Webbs' assertion that factory masters did not expect a premium.[45] The payment of a fee was crucial to the deal, and a number of manufacturers depended on an up-front payment.[46] Each of the 73 children bound in the 1790s by St Clement Danes parish to John Birch of Backbarrow, for example, were sent with a premium of 3–4 guineas, providing Birch with a useful capital sum of £250–300 – enough to build an apprentice house, say, or to tide the

---

40   8 November 1814, Minutes of Directors of the Poor, Parish of St Pancras P/PN/PO/10 (microfilm reference UTAH 652) CLSAC. As such, he was given too much freedom by the parish, an action that officials came to regret.

41   He also appeared to pocket the premiums, though he may have passed some of this on to the manufacturers at a later date. 18 June 1816, Minutes of Directors of the Poor, Parish of St Pancras P/PN/PO/1/12 (microfilm reference UTAH 652) CLSAC.

42   Ibid.

43   Report of 18 June 1816. Ibid. In effect the committee felt the Board to be responsible for failing to check the circumstances of the children.

44   Of the group that went to the Fewston factory from Sculwater in Hull, for example, no fee was specified. It is most likely, however, that one was paid. Register of Apprentices, 1801–1844, Sculwater Parish, PUS 411, Hull City Archives (HCA).

45   According to Alysa Levene, the Foundling Hospital initially did not pay a fee believing that this would discourage those masters only seeking financial gain. Alysa Levene, 'Pauper apprenticeship and the Old Poor Law in London: feeding the industrial economy', forthcoming.

46   Even if a proportion was siphoned off by an agent.

business over difficult times.⁴⁷ When children at Backbarrow reached the end of their apprenticeship term, they were usually replaced by a new set of apprentices accompanied by equivalent quantities of cash.⁴⁸

A premium of £4, 2s, 0d. was commonly paid by London parishes.⁴⁹ Indeed this was the figure stipulated as a minimum under the terms of Hanway's 1767 Act.⁵⁰ Only rarely did parishes pay more. St Luke Chelsea raised its standard premium from £4 to £5 after 1813 irrespective of trade.⁵¹ The Foundling Hospital consistently paid five guineas with each poor child bound apprentice.⁵² Five guineas was also the sum paid by Arnold parish, Nottinghamshire for the binding of a girl to the local mill of Davison and Hawksley.⁵³ Many parishes paid less than the statutory minimum, but there is no evidence that fees were avoided altogether. St Pancras usually paid £3 in two installments; but varied this on request. After some negotiation, the Directors of the Poor agreed to an increase to £4, 2s, 0d with each child bound to Samuel Oldknow in 1814,⁵⁴ and to Thomas Garnett of Clitheroe later the same year.⁵⁵ The money was to be paid 'one moiety on the children being sent down to Clitheroe and the remainder in three months after and on the said indentures being duly allowed

---

47 Apprenticeship records 1784–92, Parish of St Clement Danes, B1266; and Apprenticeship records 1784–1801, Parish of St Clement Danes, B1267, WAC.

48 According to William Travers, giving evidence to the 1816 Select Committee, there were continually 120–130 apprentices at Backbarrow, suggesting a regular throughput. SC1816, p. 288. In following this practice of disposal, however, Birch was by no means typical.

49 This premium was paid by St Leonard Shoreditch, for example, as well as St Mary Newington, and St Martin in the Fields, after 1802. St Clement Danes sometimes paid £4, 2s, 0d, otherwise 3 guineas.

50 7 Geo III c 39 (1767). Clause XV read 'no … parish child shall be bound out as apprentices with a sum less than £4 2/- [sic] as an apprentice fee; forty shillings whereof to be paid to the master or mistress within seven weeks after executing the indentures, and the remaining forty two shillings after such apprentice shall have served three years of his or her apprenticeship'. Although this applied initially to London, the Act of 1778 applied the regulations everywhere else.

51 Apprenticeship Register, 1802–1813, Parish of St Luke Chelsea, P74/ LUK/117, LMA.

52 Alysa Levene asserts that the Foundling Hospital did not pay premiums, believing that such payments might attract inappropriately greedy rather than altruistic masters. This may have applied to local or non-factory bindings, or those earlier in the eighteenth century, but there is no doubt that girls sent to Samuel Oldknow's factory were accompanied by £5 apiece. See below.

53 Apprenticeship Register, Arnold Parish, PR 14062/1, Nottinghamshire Archives (NA).

54 Meetings of 8 March 1814, 29 March 1814 (when, suspecting that Oldknow might insist upon £4, 2s, 0d or even the £5 that it had received from the Foundling Hospital, the view was taken that 'no more than the usual fee of 30/- should be given with each child'), 5 April 1814 (when, discovering that Oldknow did expect at least £4, 2s, 0d, it was agreed that such an allowance be paid). Minutes of Directors of Poor, Parish of St Pancras, P/PN/PO/1/9, (microfilm reference UTAH 650), CLSAC.

55 Ibid., 10, 17 and 24 May 1814.

by the magistrates'.[56] The standard apprenticeship fee was £1, 10s, 0d in the parish of Ombersley, Worcestershire, but 2 guineas were paid for apprenticeship to linen manufacture and £4 for cotton spinning.[57] In addition to the premium, all indentures stipulated the parish's commitment to fulfilling apprentices' wardrobe requirements at the beginning and end of the term. Parishes sometimes negotiated a financial alternative. St Pancras parish, for example, gave 30 shillings (£1.50) or £2 in place of the initial clothing allowance, on condition that 'the Directors should be fully satisfied that the apprentices are properly cloathed'.[58] Some employers preferred this cash equivalent, as the case of Benjamin Smart indicates. After the arrival, an apprentice from St Clement parish Oxford, Smart wrote,

> I should prefer returning the cloaths she has brought when she is bound if you will allow me the £5 for that purpose – it might save you a few shillings but as they are not quite suitable or like the other girls' dresses should wish to provide her cloaths myself.[59]

Despite variations in premium between parishes and sometimes between trades, the amount paid with a parish factory apprentice was not out of line with that paid to masters of 'trade' apprentices. In view of the novelty of some elements of the practice it is, perhaps, surprising that premiums were not more frequently negotiated. Evidence from St Clement Danes parish indicates that officials were quick to spot an opportunity to cut costs:

> Mr Anderson stated to the Board that he had been informed that the Parish of St Anne, Soho received premiums from the proprietors for the children apprenticed to the cotton manufactures, he therefore conceived this parish might in future refuse any fee with children so apprenticed which would be a considerable saving. It being the sense of the Board, Mr Barker promised to enquire of the Churchwardens of St Anne and report the result to the next vestry.[60]

Otherwise there is no evidence that parishes attempted to reduce the premium and this indicates that their need for the apprentice arrangement matched that of employers. However the practice of paying the premium in two parts, where the second instalment was paid after the satisfaction of all parties had been established. St Martin in the Fields parish, for example, paid half of the premium up front and the remainder after three years;[61] and St James, Piccadilly ascertained that the apprentices

---

56 Ibid., 24 May 1814.

57 Register of Apprentices, Parish of Ombersley, 850 Ombersley 3572 8ii; Worcestershire Record Office (WRO).

58 24 July 1804, Minutes of Directors of Poor, Parish of St Pancras, P/PN/PO/1/1 (microfilm reference UTAH 649), CLSAC. £2 was not an unusual amount.

59 One of a series of letters between Benjamin Smart and St Clement Parish, Oxford. Z351/4 1 Mo 23 1812, Oxfordshire Record Office (ORO). Most of these letters are duplicated in the Warwickshire County Record Office.

60 9 February 1792, Minutes of Vestry, Parish of St Clement Danes, B1073, WAC. As nothing more was heard about this, it was probably a false rumour.

61 Until 1802, the premium was £4. Thereafter £4, 2s, 0d. Apprenticeship Registers, Parish of St Martin in the Fields, F4511, F4309, F4310, F4311, WAC.

'have faithfully served their masters, and have not any cause of complaint' then 'ordered that the additional apprentice fee be forthwith paid'.[62] The survival of a receipt from John Haigh to the parish of St Margaret and St John for £52, 10s, 0d in January 1797 'being the remainder of the apprentice fee', shows that in this case the second instalment was paid only after several years. The records indicate that 10 girls and 14 boys were bound to Haigh from the London parish in 1792, and the level of the second payment suggests a gratifying survival rate, if indeed the parish had ascertained the continued presence of the children.[63]

The standard indenture form applied to factory apprentices in the same way as to any other trade. In the space for the trade to be learned, an expression equivalent to 'the art and mystery of cotton spinning' was inserted. In 1795, Mary Ann Finch, for example, was indentured by the parish of St Anne, Westminster, to William Douglas of Pendleton, to learn 'the art and mystery of a cotton spinner'. Several years later, Elizabeth Davis was bound from the same parish to John Douglas of Holywell to learn the 'art and mystery of cotton manufacture'.[64] Indentures of the children bound from St Leonard, Shoreditch, to Colbeck, Ellis and Wilks were to learn 'weaving and flax dressing'; while those to Whitaker in Burley were 'to learn cotton spinning and weaving'.[65] Several parishes insisted that their children become accomplished in both spinning and weaving in order that their employment opportunities be enhanced. Birmingham parish specifically sought firms able and willing to teach both skills.[66] When considering the binding of 14 children to Messrs John Gorton,[67] St Pancras parish, concerned that learning the 'trade of a cotton spinner' on its own was insufficient, 'suggested that it would be well if Mr Gorton would undertake to instruct the children in weaving cotton also'.[68] Gorton duly agreed and it was 'ordered that the said indentures of apprentices as applying both to spinning cotton and to weaving also be ready for execution at the next General Board'.[69] Fresh indentures

---

62   4 May 1797, Minutes of Governors and Directors of the Poor, Parish of St James, Piccadilly, D1876, WAC.

63   The receipt is reproduced in Philip Charlesworth, 'Foundlers at Marsden', *Old West Riding*, vol. 10, 1990, p. 21. The figures suggest a second payment of £2, 4s, 0d per head. Or, more likely, the total premium was £5; the second installment would therefore be £2, 10s, 0d per head, indicating a total of 21 children, and thus a 'waste' of 3 children. The receipt was dated shortly before the parish visitors arrived at Marsden to investigate claims of ill treatment.

64   Apprenticeship 1702–1834, Parish of St Anne, Westminster, A2262, WAC.

65   Apprenticeship Register, 1802–, Parish of St Leonard, Shoreditch, P91/LEN/1332, LMA.

66   16 September 1795, Minutes of the Birmingham Board of Guardians, 1783–1806, GP/B/2/1/1.

67   As far as I know, he was unrelated to the Thomas Gorton, agent, linked to St Pancras.

68   9 December 1806, Minutes of the Directors of the Poor, Parish of St Pancras, P/PN/PO/1/3 (microfilm reference UTAH 649) CLSAC.

69   Ibid., 16 December 1806.

of apprenticeship in which both businesses were introduced were prepared and executed.[70]

The formal process of executing apprenticeship indentures that existed prior to the factory system continued as before. No distinction of place or trade was made in the procedure by which indentures were signed. The children selected for binding to Whitaker's Burley mill from St Mary Newington, 'to learn the art of spinning and manufacture of cotton', 'were called in and examined by the magistrates and officers. The magistrates signified their approbation that the said children should be placed under the care of Mr Whitaker as apprentices'.[71] Whitaker's agent was then told that 'the magistrates having given their consent, the children are ready whenever he shall appoint the time for their being sent'.[72] The example of St Pancras parish also indicates the formality of the procedure. The minutes of Vestry meetings indicate that those present at the formal signing of indentures included nine Directors of the Poor, the master, the child and the parent(s).[73] In July 1804, it was

> ordered that the Clerk be directed to write to Mr Sewell of the Flax Mills, Hounslow, Mddx, informing him that the Board is ready to agree to his proposal to apprentice 12 boys and 12 girls from the workhouse to be employed in his flax mills and therefore requesting Mr Sewell's attendance at the workhouse on Friday next in order to make all due arrangements on the business.[74]

In October of 1806,

> on the recommendation of the committee for General Purposes ... the Board executed indentures of apprenticeship for the binding of Sarah Barrell and Charlotte Lindsay each aged 15 years to Mr Geo Merryweather of the Liberty of Cawood, Wislow and Otley ... and agreed to give a premium of £3 with each apprentice to be paid as follows: £2 ... to be paid in the course of 3 months from the execution and completion of the said indentures and the remaining £1 at the end of three years ... the Board having just had the said [girls] called in as in attendance with the Master and the said [girls] expressing their utmost willingness and desire to be bound as aforesaid.[75]

Before indentures were formally signed an apprentice was expected to work for a few probationary weeks to ensure suitability on both parts, but particularly from the

---

70 Ibid., 23 December 1806. When Isaac Hodgson of Caton mills requested a change to the wording of the indentures, this was referred to a committee of the Directors of the Poor, who deliberated for more than seven months before agreeing. Ibid. 6 February 1816; 17 September 1816.

71 23 March 1814, St Mary Newington Workhouse Committee Minutes, 931, SLHL.

72 April 3 1815, St Mary Newington Workhouse Committee Minutes, 931, SLHL.

73 22 Jan 1805, Minutes of Directors of Poor, Parish of St Pancras, P/PN/PO/1/2 (microfilm reference UTAH 649) CLSAC. On 22 June 1805, 38 indentures of apprentices were executed by 9 of the Directors present, the 'Reverend Bromley having made due enquiry into the character and responsibility of the masters'. Ibid.

74 24 July 1804, Minutes of Directors of Poor, Parish of St Pancras, P/PN/PO/1/1 (microfilm reference UTAH 649) CLSAC.

75 Ibid., 7 October 1806. On 10 September 1808, a mother was brought in with her children to consent to the binding.

employers' perspective. Although such a 'liking' was not universal among factory proprietors, most millowners employed medical officers to check the youngsters' health before they were taken on. Those found unfit, or unable to withstand the rigours of factory work during the probationary period, were returned to their place of origin.[76]

In most respects, therefore, the administration of the factory apprenticeship system was equivalent to all other types. The area of difference was in age and therefore term. Almost all indentures stipulated the end of the term to be 21 for both sexes.[77] The age of parish factory apprentices appears to have been slightly younger than those bound to other trades,[78] and thus the term of apprenticeship longer, but there is no evidence to suggest that very young children were bound. In the course of this study, out of the several thousand children, for whom ages are available, children below the age of seven constituted a handful. The register of apprentices bound to Toplis and Co., worsted manufacturers of Cuckney in Nottinghamshire, is suggestive of the age distribution of parish factory apprentices more widely. As indicated in Table 3.1, the modal and median age was ten, and 48 per cent of children were aged under ten.[79] Other examples show a similar pattern. Of the groups of children bound from St Clement Danes to Monteith and Bogle, Glasgow between 1805 and 1809, the mean age was just under 10. Eight of the 49 children were aged seven.[80] Fifty per cent of the apprentices to Davison and Hawksley from St Luke, Chelsea were aged eight or nine.[81] Of the 200 children bound to the early textile mills from St Martin in the Fields parish after 1802, the average age was just under 11, and none was under the age of 8. The average age of apprentices to individual firms, however, varied; and the St Martin children bound to Samuel Ashton were mostly ten and under.[82]

---

76 Mary B. Rose, *The Gregs of Quarry Bank Mill: The Rise and Decline of a Family Firm, 1750–1914* (Cambridge, 1986), p. 30; Pamela Horn, 'The traffic in children and the textiles mills, 1780–1816', *Genealogists Magazine*, 24/ 5 (1993): 358.

77 Occasionally, the age of 18 was stipulated to be the end of the term. For example, some of the later bindings from St Pancras parish stipulated 18 as the terminal age. 24 May 1814, Minutes of Directors of Poor, Parish of St Pancras, P/PN/PO/1/9 (microfilm reference UTAH 651) CLSAC. The traditional regime of 24 for boys and 21 for girls was never implemented in the case of factory apprenticeships, and in any case ceased to be generally used for any apprenticeship after the 1770s.

78 Alysa Levene shows that while the age of parish apprentices was lower than that of private apprentices; children bound to factories tended to be slightly younger than those bound to other trades. Levene, 'Pauper apprenticeship', forthcoming.

79 'List of children put apprentice to William Toplis', DD 895/1, NA.

80 Apprenticeship records 1784–1792, Parish of St Clement Danes, B1266; and Apprenticeship records 1784–1801, Parish of St Clement Danes, B1267, WAC.

81 Apprenticeship Register, 1802–1813, Parish of St Luke, Chelsea, P74/ LUK/117, LMA.

82 28 of the 44 were between 8 and 10, Parish of St Martin in the Fields, Apprenticeship Registers, 1795–1803 F4313, and 1802–1824 F4311,WAC.

Table 3.1 Age of Child Apprentices to William Toplis, Cuckney, 1786–1805

Age	Number of children
5	3
6	8
7	54
8	91
9	94
10	124
11	69
12	49
13	19
14	11
15	1
16	1
17	0
18	1

Source: 'List of children put out apprentice to William Toplis', DD895/1, Nottinghamshire Archives.

The age of St Pancras children varied according to destination. Most of those bound to Lambert's Lowdham mill and to Gorton's Bury, Lancashire enterprise, for example, were under 10, while those apprenticed to Samuel Ashton and Thomas Haslam were mostly aged 11 or more.[83] Children bound from St James's Piccadilly and from St Leonard's Shoreditch, were, on average, older. The 20 boys bound to Haywood and Palfreyman in 1796 from St James, for example, were all between 11 and 15 on binding.[84] It was rare for a St Leonard's child to be bound under the age of 10, and the mean age was well above 11. Of the 35 children bound to Merryweather and Whitaker, for example, 26 were 12 and older; and nearly half of the total were 14 and above.[85] The majority of parish factory apprentices, therefore, were at least 10 years of age, with a sizeable minority who were younger. However inappropriately

---

83   19 of the 32 to Haslam; and 12 of the 23 to Ashton were 11 and over. 19 of the 40 to Lambert and 20 of the 39 to Gorton were 10 and under. Apprenticeship Register, 1802–1867, Parish of St Pancras, P90/PANI/362, LMA.

84   Their birth dates were all between 1781 and 1784. 26 February 1796, Minutes of the Governors and Directors of the Poor, Parish of St James, Piccadilly, D1875, WAC. The statement of Margaret Chamberlain to the meeting of 29 February [*sic*] 1797 confirmed that she had been bound to Douglas, Pendleton at the age of 12 or 13. As her term had ended after eight years and five months, this indicates that she was 12 years and 7 months at binding.

85   Apprenticeship Register, 1802–, Parish of St Leonard, Shoreditch, P91/LEN/1332, LMA.

youthful these children were, they were clearly older than that suggested by the early writers on the subject.[86]

The format of apprenticing to factory masters was the same as for other types with the same scrutiny by magistrates.[87] This may indicate that those in authority to agree apprenticeships made no distinction between the two types. Discussions in Vestry meetings, visits to masters, enquiries before apprenticing, and subsequent inspections occurred equally irrespective of 'type' of apprenticeship or distance from the parish. However, complaints about laxity in the system increased at the end of the eighteenth century which may suggest awareness of problems in all apprenticeships or may indicate a concern specific to factory apprenticeships.[88]

The system of parish factory apprenticeship was subject to traditional laws and regulations which, by the end of the eighteenth century, became perceived as inadequate to the task. The remainder of this chapter considers the evolution of the legislative framework within which the parish factory apprenticeship system operated from the early nineteenth century. Pressure for regulation generated by the perceived trade in pauper children to mills around the country resulted in the 1802 Act.[89] The background debate to the 1802 Act has been carefully analysed by historians.[90] According to Joanna Innes, growth of judicial concern about factory apprentices paralleled broader developments in thinking about children. From the 1780s, growing numbers of child-centred charities, and other philanthropic groups, focused their activities on conditions of children's work. The Society for Bettering the Condition of the Poor, established by Thomas Bernard, which was particularly interested in the fate of apprentice children, helped to shape the 1802 Act.[91] Such was the momentum generated by the various forces supporting the protection of

---

86 For example, Webb and Webb, *Old Poor Law*, p. 201. Although some historians accepted the Webb's position, more recently it has been suggested that only rarely were children bound to factories under the age of 10. Kirby, *Child Labour*, p. 4.

87 This itself was variable, however. Steve King, for example, disputes the extent to which magistrates were an active force in Poor Law administration, enforcing minimum standards. King, 'Poor relief and English economic development reappraised', *Economic History Review*, 50/2 (1997): 363.

88 In 1800, for example, the Middlesex Quarter Sessions attempted to tighten up the system whereby the magistrates appeared to be giving consent as a matter of course, by requiring that the magistrates carefully investigate the circumstances of the proposed master. See Webb and Webb, *Old Poor Law*, pp. 4–5. Evidence of magistrates refusing to approve an apprenticeship arrangement is sparse; though Theodore Price, speaking to the 1816 Select Committee, referred to his vehement opposition to factory apprentices and his refusal to sign such indentures. 'I will never sign an indenture as long as I live, that is, under the present existing laws'. SC1816, p. 122.

89 *An Act for the Preservation of the Health and Morals of Apprentices and Others, Employed in Cotton and Other Mills, and Cotton and other Factories*, 42 Geo III c 73, (hereafter referred to as HMA Act) passed on 22 June 1802. The passage of this first piece of protective legislation encountered some resistance.

90 Among the most thorough is Joanna Innes. See 'Origins of the Factory Acts: the Health and Morals of Apprentices Act, 1802' in Norma Landau (ed) *Law, Crime and English Society, 1660–1830* (Cambridge, 2002), pp. 30–55.

91 Innes, 'Origins', pp. 243–7.

parish apprentices that those who might object, the factory owners for example, had little time to organise their opposition. Despite the individual efforts of key manufacturers, the Act proceeded into the statute books.[92]

Because the Act was concerned only with the employment of parish apprentices in cotton mills, it has been criticised as narrowly conceived. However, it targeted the key component of the early factory labour force as well as its most vulnerable. The 1802 Act also marked the point at which legislation protecting apprentices evolved into factory legislation;[93] even though many contemporaries typically perceived it as an extension of the Poor Laws.[94] The act was intended to 'preserve the health and morals of such apprentices and other persons'.[95] It aimed to protect the health by maintaining certain standards of cleanliness and ventilation in the factories; restricting total hours worked and outlawing night work; providing sufficient change of clothing; and ensuring that the services of a physician were available to treat illness or injury. The morals were protected in a number of ways: by the physical segregation of boy and girl apprentices in their sleeping accommodation; by religious instruction; and by a thorough programme of basic education. The sixth clause of the Act decreed that every apprentice

> shall be instructed in some part of every working day, for the first four years at least of his or her apprenticeship ... in reading, writing and arithmetick ... according to the age and abilities of such apprentice, by some discreet and proper person, to be provided and paid by the master of mistress ... in some room ... set aside for that purpose.[96]

---

92 John Douglas of Holywell, for example, tried to persuade Peel to delay; and William Hey, surgeon friend of Wilberforce, submitted a glowing report on working conditions at Burley-in-Wharfedale. Innes, 'Origins', p. 251.

93 It is difficult to interpret the Act solely as a piece of factory legislation though some have tried. For example, T.K. Djang, *Factory Inspection in Great Britain* (London, 1942), pp. 26–30; M.W. Thomas, *The Early Factory Legislation: A Study in Legislative and Administrative Evolution* (Leigh-on-Sea, Essex, 1948), pp. 9–13.

94 It was viewed by contemporaries as an extension of the Poor Law. Sonya Rose, 'Protective labor legislation in nineteenth-century Britain: gender, class and the liberal state' in Laura L. Frader and Sonya O. Rose (eds), *Class and Gender in Modern Europe* (Ithaca, NY, 1996), p. 194. Hutchins and Harrison, *History of Factory Legislation*, p. 2 assert that the Act may be regarded more as an extension of the old Poor Law than as a conscious assumption of control over industry; and (on p. 16) they state that 'It was in reality not a Factory Act properly speaking, but merely an extension of the Elizabethan Poor Laws relating to parish apprentices'. Equally, the 1784 resolution of the Manchester magistrates 'was only an administrative regulation under the Poor Law and had no bearing on the question of the restriction of child labour generally'. Hutchins and Harrison, *History of Factory Legislation*, p. 9. See also Mark Blaug, 'The classical economists and the factory acts – a re-examination', *Quarterly Journal of Economics*, 72 (1958): 212. The 1833 Act has also been seen as a social policy measure as much as a piece of factory legislation. Howard P. Marvel, 'Factory legislation: a reinterpretation of early English experience', *Journal of Law and Economics*, 20 (1977): 379; Simon Deakin and Frank Wilkinson, *The Law of the Labour Market: Industrialization, Employment and Legal Evolution* (Oxford, 2005), p. 227.

95 HMA Act, p. 418.

96 HMA Act, p. 418.

To encourage the observation of the terms of the act, magistrates from every area in which liable mills were located were to 'appoint two persons, not interested in, or in any way connected with any such mills or factories, to be visitors ...; one of who shall be a Justice of the Peace ... and the other shall be a clergyman', to inspect the liable factories and 'report from time to time in writing, to the Quarter Sessions of the Peace'.[97] The reporting was to encompass the extent to which the act was observed, with particular reference to the cleanliness (whitewashing), ventilation of the mill; and whether or not the proprietor had hung 'printed written copies' of the act in 'two or more conspicuous places' in the mill. Fines of between £5 and £10 were to be imposed on proprietors who prevented the visitors from fulfilling their duty; and a penalty of £2 to £5 for failure to observe any of the Act's terms. The owner of each factory employing 3 or more apprentices, and/or 20 or more 'other persons', was required annually to so inform the Clerk of the Peace.[98]

A separate Act of 1802 required the overseers and Guardians of the poor to keep a register of all children bound by them as apprentices.[99] Failure to comply incurred a fine of up to £5.[100] Most parishes had kept apprenticeship registers for many years before this legislation and continued to do so subsequently. The few recorded instances of non-compliance noted do not appear to have been harshly disciplined. For example, a letter dated 17 March 1812 from the *House of Commons Committee on Parish Apprentices* and addressed to the parish of St Swithin London Stone, 'ordered that the churchwardens ... do make returns of apprentices ... as directed by the Act ... returns to be made ... to 1811 inclusive'.[101]

---

97 Significantly, there is no evidence that such visiting and reporting was compulsory. The wording is vague, i.e. the visitors shall report from time to time. There is no evidence from any of the Quarter Sessions records that I examined, that reports were written either fully or for more than a year or so. See also the *Account of the Cotton and Woolen Mills and Factories in the UK, Great Britain, and Ireland 1803–18*. House of Lords, The Sessional Papers, 1819, vol. 108 (Hereafter HL1819 vol 108); and Thomas, *Early Factory Legislation*, pp. 12–13.

98 The Clerk of the Peace then kept a record of this information for which he was paid 'the sum of two shillings and no more'. Innes, 'Origins', p. 420.

99 42 Geo III c 46 (1802). This requirement was typically reproduced at the front of the registers. Most parishes appear to have adopted the standard style as suggested in the appendix to the act.

100 Discussion of the Bill 'to require the overseers of the poor to keep a register of the several children who shall be bound by them as apprentices' published in *The House of Commons Parliamentary Papers*, 1801–1802, vol. 1, pp. 55–61. The frequency with which such registers appear in the parish records, and the apparent completeness of them, suggests that this act was taken seriously. There seems little doubt that parishes had previously maintained a record of their children bound apprentice, even if these can only be found buried in the minutes of Vestry meetings.

101 This letter was contained in the Apprenticeship Register, 1809–1815, for St Swithin London Stone, MS565,GL. It implied that no such register had been kept since the Act of 1802. The omission had presumably only recently come to light. No reference was made to the £5 penalty specified in the terms of the Act.

Resistance from employers to the HMA Act was evident.[102] Many factory owners responded formally and immediately to its passage.[103] During February of 1803, a number of petitions objecting to the Act were presented to the House of Commons from employers in all textile factory districts.[104] They argued that the act would be prejudicial to the trade;[105] that it would be 'injurious and oppressive not only to the cotton, woollen and flaxen spinners, but to manufacturers at large';[106] and that existing laws were sufficient to 'protect Apprentices and Servants against every species of abuse or improper treatment of masters'[107] All the petitions were read and 'laid on the table', and there is little sign that much notice was taken of them. Other manufacturers enlisted eminent support. George Merryweather of Burley, for example, whose cotton spinning enterprise apparently depended on 24-hour working, asked his friend the eminent surgeon William Hey of Leeds to provide medical evidence of the healthful effects of night work.[108] The same manufacturer contended that through his factory and others like it, a 'great number of children' had been rescued from vice and misery and trained to be upright workers.[109] It was also argued that the system of inspection by visitors would undermine their authority in the eyes of apprentices who, because they allegedly came from 'low and vicious surroundings' required plenty of discipline to keep them in order.[110] A group of Yorkshire spinners believed that 'the price of labour is excessive and the consequent insubordination amongst the labourers very great. The operation of the apprentice Act will greatly tend to increase this evil'.[111]

---

102 Also, it was more concerted than had been their response to the bill. According to Inglis, 'there had been no concerted campaign by the mill owners against the bill. They were not established men like the master clothiers. And Peel being a millowner himself made it difficult to protest'. Brian Inglis, *Poverty and the Industrial Rrevolution*, (London, 1971), p. 111.

103 The Webbs remark that 'even this very little amount of protection of children against ill-usage was opposed by mill owners', *Old Poor Law*, p. 202.

104 The similar wording of the petitions indicates a concerted campaign, as indeed there was. Innes, 'Origins', pp 252–3.

105 Cotton spinners from Manchester, Stockport, Bolton, Glasgow and Preston, read 11 February 1803, published in *The Journal of the House of Commons*, 1803, p. 149.

106 Manufacturers from Leeds and Keighley, read 14 February 1803, *The Journal of the House of Commons*, 1803, p. 160. Exactly the same wording came from proprietors of cotton mills at Holywell, Flint, read 25 February 1803, *The Journal of the House of Commons*, 1803, p. 206.

107 Manufacturers from Tutbury, Alrewas, Namptwich [sic], Ashbourn and Newcastle-under-Lyme, read 22 February 1803, *The Journal of the House of Commons*, 1803, p. 191.

108 William Hey 'Visit to the cotton mills at Burley', *The Reports of the Society for Bettering the Condition and Increasing the Comforts of the Poor*, vol. 4, 1805, appendix 1, supplement II, pp. 16–19; 'Report of a Select Committee of the Society upon some observations on the late act respecting cotton mills, and on the account of Mr Hey's visit to a cotton mill at Burley', ibid., pp. 1–16; Innes, 'Origins', p. 252.

109 Inglis, *Poverty and the Industrial Revolution*, p. 112.

110 J.L. Hammond and Barbara Hammond, *The Town Labourer 1760–1832* (London, 1917), p. 106.

111 Aspin, *Water Spinners*, p. 53.

While a number of factory owners, especially those dependent on apprentices, noisily objected to several terms of the Act, others seemed unaware of its implications. Despite a newspaper advertising campaign by magistrates drawing proprietors' attention to the need to register, as well as the requirement that copies of the Act be placed prominently in all liable factories, it appears that a number of firms remained ignorant. Registration was desultory; and of those who did initially comply, the majority did so for only a year or two.[112] Others registered late, pleading ignorance of the requirement to register.[113] As far as inspection was concerned, magistrates in the majority of counties duly appointed visitors, but in the absence of a specific procedure for inspection, the level of reporting in most parts of the country was desultory.[114] Although the Act was enforced only limply, it was later claimed by Peel to have removed the worst abuses of the system.[115] Any improvement in conditions, however, were only partly attributable to the legislation. The intervention of local magistrates appears to have reduced the amount of night working; and limited the practice of distant bindings.[116]

The HMA Act did not alter the structure of the parish factory apprenticeship system. It was designed to protect parish apprentices already bound to textile factories, and those yet to be bound, rather than to amend the process of apprenticing, hence its link between Poor Law and factory legislation. The 1816 Act, however, aimed to protect poor children by curtailing distant placements, and can therefore be interpreted as a piece of Poor Law legislation. Initially introduced as a seemingly unexceptionable bill in 1811,[117] it became weakened by several years of committee

---

112 In West Yorkshire, only Wells, Middleton of Sheffield responded zealously; in Warwickshire only Bott. The return in Derbyshire was rather better. HL1819, vol. 108, pp. 77–136. Records collected by the Home Office in 1810 demonstrate a suspiciously low rate of return. A request had been made to all counties for return on records kept between 1802 and 1809. Many counties, some plausibly, stated that there were no eligible mills in their county. Others reported that they had no information. Officials at Worcestershire, for example, were 'not aware of their being any cotton and woolen factories within the county of Worcester. No one has ever been entered with the Clerk of the Peace'; and from Wiltshire: 'no entry has been made in this office of any mill or factory since the passage of that act and consequently no visitor has been appointed nor any report made of the state of any such mills and factories'. As far as Ireland was concerned, 'it appears that in no county or city whatever have any steps been taken in consequence of the act ... and that in very few counties are there any establishments of the descriptions pointed out in the act'. Returns of factories, 8 March 1810, HO42/104, National Archives.

113 Returns of Cotton and other mills, 1803–1806, QE 33/1 WYASW.

114 It seems that after a while, magistrates forgot to visit the mills. This is what some magistrates told Parliament. Innes, 'Origins', p. 252.

115 *The Parliamentary Debates,* 1811; SC1816. Although this is debatable, the significance of the Act was greater than suggested by Kathryn Thompson, who argues that it 'was already redundant by the time it was enacted', because of new technology's reduced demand for apprentices. *Apprenticeship and Bastardy,* p. 30.

116 Innes, 'Origins', p. 253.

117 *House of Commons Parliamentary Papers,* 10 April 1811. The terms of the Bill ran to 11 pages. A number of its clauses did not appear in the 1816 Act because of the opposition

work and vigorous debate.[118] The Act to regulate the binding of parish apprentices was passed, after several amendments on 2 July 1816.[119] Its core element was the 40-mile limit, which applied specifically, but not exclusively, to London children:

> no child shall be bound apprentice ... at a greater distance than 40 miles from the parish ... unless such a child shall belong to some parish or place which shall be more than 40 miles from the city of *London*, in which case it shall be lawful for the justices ... to make a special order for that purpose.

This was based on the belief, reinforced by the assumption on which the 1815 report had been prepared, that the worst abuses emanated from the trade between the London parishes and factories in the Midlands and the north of England.[120] Such a limit was designed to prevent estrangement between parent and child; and to allow both parents and parish officers to know 'the manner in which such children are treated'.[121] A fine of £10 was to be imposed on both parties to the transaction in case of evasion. Other clauses rendered unlawful the apprenticing of a child under the age of nine, and the need for overseers' approval for removal or reassignment.[122] A clause to restrict numbers of apprentices in a single enterprise, included in the 1811 Bill, had been quietly dropped.

Described as a 'dead letter'[123] even before its final assent, the direct impact of the 1816 Act was limited. Parishes had already begun to restrict the practice of long-distance factory apprenticeship, and after 30 years in which parish apprentices had dominated the labour force of many textile factories, 'free' children became employed in larger numbers. Legislative attention, therefore, having fulfilled its

---

of Peel and others. These included the proposed restriction – to nine – on the total number of apprentices a master might take.

118 In 1815, reference was made to the objection of some London parishes, who had 'menaced an opposition to the Bill', *House of Commons Parliamentary Papers*, session 1814–15, *Report from the Committee on Parish Apprentices*, 19 May 1815, p. 5. Early factory legislation should also be seen in terms of the structural and technical changes within the industry. See John Foster, 'The making of the first six Factory Acts', conference report in *Bulletin of the Society for the Study of Labour History*, 18 (1969): 4–5.

119 56 Geo III c 139 (1816) 'Act for the better regulating the binding out parish apprentices'.

120 Scotland was rarely mentioned.

121 No reference to grandparents in the Act, though they had been identified in the bill. There had also been reference in the bill of 30 May 1816 to the imposition of a fine. Any overseer who 'shall bind an apprentice to any master or mistress whose residence or ... business shall not be in the same county or within the distance of 40 miles ... and said master or mistress shall each respectively forfeit the sum of £10 for each apprentice so bound'. The same sum was to be the penalty for transferring a parish apprentice from one master to another without consent. 56 Geo III c 139 (1816).

122 A fine also imposed on any contravention; and a further clause made provision for collecting the debt if it were not forthcoming, p. 1070.

123 Redford, *Labour Migration*, p. 29; SC1816, pp. 316–17, 319–22.

obligation to parish apprentices, moved to focus on other children.[124] Commons discussion of the 1818 Bill centred on the concept of 'free labour' and whether any children fitted this category. That parish apprentices were not 'free labour' was more readily accepted than that of other children. Advocates of free labour felt that it was wrong to 'interfere between the parent and the child, the master and the juvenile work-person',[125] and that the proposed Act 'would destroy the cotton trade and, by compelling the masters to dismiss from their employment those who were subject to its restrictions, it would involve the children in hardship and their parents in ruin'.[126] The House of Lords raised many objections, and while the bill passed through the Commons after a battle, it fell in the Lords. A further enquiry was ordered before the Bill[127] was reintroduced and the Factories Regulation Act was passed in 1819.[128]

This chapter has argued that from the outset parish factory apprenticeship was formally and consistently ordered. Prior to early nineteenth century legislation specific to its operation, the system functioned efficiently under the existing rules for 'traditional' apprenticeships. Many of these persisted after the 1802 HMA Act, which was more concerned to add a layer of protection for parish apprentices than to instigate structural change. The surviving record confirms the regular use of standard

---

124 This had already been set in motion by 1816. The attempt to include free children in the 1802 HMA was derailed by Peel and by others, believing it wrong to interfere with the labour of children who lived at home. The Select Committee that took evidence from 25 April to 18 June 1816 (SC1816), was chaired by Robert Peel except when his own mills were under the spotlight. Hammond and Hammond, *Town Labourer*, pp. 110–11.

125 *The Parliamentary Debates*, (London, 1818). During its first reading, pp. 559–66, there was extensive debate about free labour and whether or not parish apprentices should be included in this category, during which Peel made the following statement: 'Those who were employers of children, seeing them from day to day, were not so sensible of the injury that they sustained from this practice as strangers who were strongly impressed by it'. During its second reading, evidence was presented that suggested that parish apprentices were anyway a declining proportion of total textile factory labour, p. 584.

126 If parents could 'not draw a profit from children in their very early years, they might not waste so much of their own time, they would work harder and probably obtain better wages for better work'. Quoted in Hutchins and Harrison, *History of Factory Legislation*, p. 26. Sir Francis Burdett, for example, felt that 'it could not upon any grounds be contended that these helpless children should be sacrificed to the avarice and cupidity of their unfeeling parents'. Discussion surrounding Hobhouse Bill, 1825, quoted in Thomas, *Early Factory Legislation*, p. 27.

127 A watered-down version according to Aspin, *Water Spinners*, p. 370.

128 *The Parliamentary Debates* (London, 1818), pp. 559–66 and pp. 581–4; Hammond and Hammond, *Town Labourer*, pp. 113–15. The 1819 Act established that only if subjects could be considered unfree would the state protect them in economic transactions. Rose, 'Protective labor legislation', p. 197. Support for the 1819 Act in the form of the 1818 Manchester 'gentry' petition which was signed largely by the calico printing and merchanting community. Foster, 'The making of the first six Factory Acts', p. 4. The Act was the result of some compromise, and made inadequate provision of inspection. This was rectified by the 1825 (Hobhouse) Act, in preparation for which a survey of factories was made, which revealed widespread evasion of the lower age limit of nine years. Sometimes employers pleaded ignorance; and children were told to lie about their ages. Factory Reports, HO44/14, National Archives.

procedures for binding parish children to factories and elsewhere. Continuity in the interaction of parish, magistrates and employer, and the documentation generated, was evident everywhere. The impact of measures introduced to protect parish apprentices will be considered in the later chapters of the book. The following chapter explores the way in which the system operated to distribute parish children to the early textile factories.

Chapter 4

The Supply and Distribution of Parish Apprentices

For several decades, historians have emphasised the need to identify those parishes that bound children to textile mills, in order to estimate the extent of factory apprenticeship; to assess the outcome of the policies that moved children from parish to mill; and to challenge conventional wisdom that the trade in poor children was simply a northward movement from London.[1] It is unlikely that the true extent of parish factory apprenticeship during early industrialisation will ever be known, but as evidence so far presented is very limited, any progress must be welcome. Until recently it was assumed that during the early years of factory production, the country was awash with swarms of 'savage, uncontrolled children',[2] plucked from the workhouses of the metropolis[3] and put to work in newly established textile mills. Implicit in this view was the notion that such children played an important, if exploited, role in the labour force of the early textile industry. In contrast, research of the last few years has tended to underplay the significance of these young workers in the overall process, suggesting that parish apprentices comprised a small proportion of the total labour force. Joanna Innes, for example, has argued that the majority of apprenticeships were organised by parents or by charities, and that parish officials apprenticed only about 5 per cent of the relevant age group. This estimate, however, appears to be based on just two local studies, and it seems likely that the situation

---

1   Geoffrey W. Oxley, for example, states that more needs to be known about the general context of policies, the number of parishes participating in apprenticing to mills, and the achievement of the strategy. See his *Poor Relief in England and Wales 1601–1834* (Newton Abbot, 1974), pp. 77–8. Eden's incomplete survey of 1797 has not been superseded. Yet many more indentures and Apprenticeship Registes survive than is assumed, by, for example, Mary B. Rose, 'Social policy and business: parish apprentices and the early factory system 1750–1834', *Business History*, 31/4 (1989): 18 and 27 n. 56; and Lynn Hollen Lees, *The Solidarities of Strangers: The English Poor Laws and the People, 1700–1948* (Cambridge, 1998), pp. 101–102. Kathryn Thompson asserts that Apprenticeship Registers 'do not survive as often as historians would like', *Apprenticeship and Bastardy Records*, Short Guides to Records, no. 30 (London: Historical Association, 1997), p. 30.
2   This was the way in which parish children were 'imagined'. Hollen Lees, *The Solidarities of Strangers*, p. 127. Maurice W. Thomas, *The Early Factory Legislation: A Study in Legislative and Administrative Evolution* (Leigh-on-Sea, Essex, 1948), pp. 5–7.
3   Some accounts include other, usually unspecified, large cities.

varied regionally and locally according to such factors as economic structure, employment opportunity, and the extent and condition of the poor.[4]

The previous chapter demonstrated that the process of parish factory apprenticeship was formal and well-regulated. This chapter confirms that in practice the system of factory apprenticeship consisted of a much more controlled distribution than is often recognised. It argues that the system permitted a substantial redistribution of labour even though the movement of parish apprentices often took place over short distances. While this chapter considers the supply of parish apprentices, the next chapter will assess the significance of such apprentices for a sample of contemporary textile enterprises. It is impossible to identify all parishes involved in the process of factory apprenticeship because the necessary documentation has not survived or is not traceable, or because parishes failed to keep proper records.[5] However, by investigating a sample of regions, a much fuller picture can be obtained of the geography of participation than currently exists. The purpose of this chapter is to present the results of this research.

Information about parish apprentices emanates from many sources. The parish records, where they have survived, provide the most systematic data. These consist of apprenticeship indentures; Apprenticeship Registers, which were required by law from 1802,[6] but in many cases existed prior to that; and minutes of meetings of the churchwardens and overseers, the 'Directors of the Poor' or Vestry, all of which provide discursive information or indirect reference to apprentices and their location. Records of firms also generate data but these are disappointingly sparse. More random still is information from parliamentary enquiries. The Select Committee of 1816, for example, presents the evidence of Joseph Meyer, cotton manufacturer of Stockport, that 'at one time [he had] nearly 200 apprentices', who came from 'London and elsewhere'.[7] Intriguing but even less specific is the reference in the 1815

---

4 Joanna Innes, 'Origins of the Factory Acts: the Health and Morals of Apprentices Act 1802', in Norma Landau (ed.), *Law, Crime and English Society, 1660–1830* (Cambridge, 2002), p. 235. Hugh Cunningham has also suggested figures, 'The employment and unemployment of children in England c.1680–1851', *Past and Present*, 126 (1990): 146. See also his 'Reply' to Kirby in *Past and Present*, 187 (2005): 203–215. Also relevant is Joan Lane, *Apprenticeship in England 1600–1914* (London, 1996), pp. 5–6. Although parish factory apprentices may have accounted for only a small proportion of total apprentices, or total children within the age group, they formed an important proportion of the factory labour force.

5 Both before and after the 1802 Act, lists of apprentices were kept, if at all, more or less haphazardly by parishes, sometimes kept in separate registers, sometimes in random places in Vestry Minute Books. The 1802 Act required that a proper register be kept, and although Tate suggests that such registers were 'rarely met with'. W.E. Tate, *The Parish Chest: A Study of Parochial Administration in England* (3rd edn, Cambridge, 1969), p. 226. My research for this study suggests that these can often be found though not always fully completed or up to date.

6 The relevant act was separate from the HMA Act.

7 *Report of the Minutes of Evidence taken before the Select Committee on the State of the Children Employed in the Manufacturers of the United Kingdom*, 1816, (SC1816) p. 55. Meyer's evidence also stated that there are 'a hundred remaining in our works having served their apprenticeship with us'; of those who did not stay, 'some of them have returned home after their apprenticeship'.

Report from the Committee on Parish Apprentices to the 25 children apprenticed to a manufacturer from the parish of Bermondsey.[8]

Other indirect evidence indicates wider practice of parish apprenticeship than can be substantiated from complete sources. No apprentice registers survive for the parishes of Tottenham and Hornsey, but the archives contain a document 'relating to the journey of Tottenham and Hornsey parish apprentices to the North'.[9] Some, but probably not all of those children, terminated their journey at Toplis's Cuckney mill.[10] The complete register of parish apprentices at Cuckney shows the arrival of 8 Tottenham children in 1790, 11 in 1792, and 4 in 1795. None from Hornsey is mentioned in the Cuckney register, so those apprentices together with a portion of the Tottenham children were destined to a different mill on their northwards journey. Large numbers of children from Edmonton and St Marylebone parishes were registered at Cuckney, and undoubtedly were widely distributed. Yet, the absence of parish records precludes the specification of numbers and locations.

A total of 164 parishes were selected for examination. While these do not comprise a proper sample, they include parishes from a variety of regions, some of which were expected to have participated in factory apprenticing, such as several London parishes, and some where this seemed less likely, such as in the rural West Country. As it turned out, all the counties, if not all the parishes explored, made a contribution to the process of creating the early industrial labour force.[11] This suggests that a nationwide study would reveal a much greater participation in the parish factory apprenticeship system than has hitherto been supposed. The most serious bias in the selection here is the weight of London parishes. Although an inevitable outcome of source availability, it could be argued that such bias will serve to confirm the partiality of conventional wisdom. However, known data could not be ignored, and by also investigating under-researched collections such bias would be at least partly rectified. The justification of such an approach will be indicated through the following discussion.

The key findings are presented in the tables below, and further discussion of selected examples draws conclusions about the nature and prevalence of factory apprentices, and the impact of the system on the local labour market. Only impressionistic evidence exists about the number of children who worked in the early factories.[12] At this stage of research, it is not possible to estimate aggregate

---

8   Select Committee on Parish Apprentices, PP1814–5, V, p. 5. The report gives no date and no indication of name or location of manufacturer; states that 16 did not go, but no was reason given.

9   Overseers records, Parish of Tottenham, ldbcm:a/1/PT/5C/10, Haringey Archives Service (HAS).

10 Located in Nottinghamshire, this mill was not strictly in the north; but sufficiently distant from London to be considered so by contemporary southerners.

11 Sixty-four of the parish Apprenticeship Registers and indentures included children bound to textile factories. This is slightly less than 40 per cent of the total.

12 Patrick Colquhoun, *Survey of Arkwright Textile Mills* (1787) Baker Library, Harvard University. Colquhoun says nothing about ages of children, for example, not least because this was not his purpose, and it is possible that he concentrated on the very young. Also, no distinction was made between parish apprentices and other children.

numbers of parish apprentices. The more modest aim of this study is to indicate broad patterns of apprenticeship, from which an overall level of significance may be inferred. The distribution of factory apprenticeship is undoubtedly more complex than hitherto imagined. Not only was the geographical range of both parishes and firms more extensive than typically assumed, but the interaction of 'factory' and other manufacturing apprenticeships blurs the distinction between them. It was noted in the previous chapter that, administratively and financially, factory apprenticeships were barely distinguished from other forms. The discussion of the local labour markets that follows partly explains why this was the case.

As predicted, a small number of London parishes contributed disproportionately to the transfer of factory apprentices from south to north. The geography and demography of poverty, in addition to source bias, rendered this inevitable. For 30 or more years, large numbers of children supported by the poorer districts of the capital were made available to the areas of industrial expansion. Yet although these young people formed a significant proportion of total known apprentices, the parishes from which they originated comprised only a small proportion of total known contributing parishes. Similarly, although a substantial proportion of total known apprentices were bound to textile mills distant from their birth parish, a significant number of journeys were less than fifty miles. Placements within the locality or the region were much more common than previously understood. This is partly because early textile factories were distributed beyond pockets of the North and Midlands. It is also because mills in well-populated areas, which tended not to seek labour from a distance, nevertheless employed local parish children. Further, not only was cotton produced outside of these areas, but textiles other than cotton moved into factory manufacture towards the end of the eighteenth century and made full use of parish apprentice labour. Silk and flax, in addition to cotton, wool and worsted were factory-produced in the south of England, drawing upon the region's poor children. Finally, many of those London parishes binding children northwards sought to restrict the mileage as far as possible.[13] In other words, long-distance apprenticeship was neither a consistent goal nor a typical outcome.

The distribution of parish apprentices suggested by this research adjusts the assumptions that parish apprentices were drawn mainly from towns, and sent mainly to isolated country mills.[14] Late eighteenth-century poverty was as much a rural as an urban phenomenon; and, although total numbers varied greatly, the ratio of poor children to apprenticeship opportunities was likely to be similar in countryside and town. Many, but by no means all, of the early textile factories were country-based yet not necessarily isolated. Apprentice labour was drawn from local villages and towns

---

13 The parish of St Margaret and St John, for example, saw the advantage, however slight, of binding children to Toplis, 120 miles from London rather than Haigh, at 200 miles distant. 'Report of a visit to the different manufactories when children are apprenticed from the parishes of St Margaret and St John the Evangelist, Westminster', September 1802, E3371/95, WAC (Hereafter 1802 Report, St Margaret and St John).

14 J.L Hammond and Barbara Hammond, *The Town Labourer 1760–1832* (London, 1917), p. xxv.

in the region and further afield. Urban factories existed from the outset, employing local free children and apprentices as well as those from elsewhere.

The complex transfers of parish children during the period of early industrialisation were not confined to factory employment. Parish apprentices were vital to a range of textile trades and other trades that contributed to industrial expansion. Such labour also supported sectors of manufacturing separate from but closely connected to factory production. For example, large numbers of apprentices were employed in non-factory handweaving, particularly in textile districts where free children comprised a growing proportion of the factory labour force. In testimony to the 1816 Select Committee, surgeon Kinder Wood stated that 'it is common to take apprentices in that business [hand weaving] which is not in the mills … there are many come from London. There are hundreds out of St Giles workhouse.'[15] The following analysis indicates the wider contribution of parish apprentices to the process of early industrialisation. The discussion is organised around groups of parishes, beginning with London.

Table 4.1 St Clement Danes Parish Factory Apprentices

Firm	Location	Nature of business	Date	Girl apprentices	Boy apprentices
Douglas	Pendleton	Cotton spinning	1786	1	8
Atherton	Holywell	Cotton spinning	1787	3	1
John Birch	Cartmel/Backbarrow	Cotton manufacturer	1787	6	29
John Birch	Cartmel/Backbarrow	Cotton manufacturer	1789	10	14
John Birch	Cartmel/Backbarrow	Cotton manufacturer	1790	3	9
Wells	Sheffield	Cotton manufacturer	1790	3	0
John Birch	Cartmel/Backbarrow	Cotton manufacturer	1791	5	12
John Watson	Salmesbury, near Preston	Cotton manufacturer	1791	5	8
John Birch	Cartmel/Backbarrow	Cotton manufacturer	1792	7	13
John Birch	Cartmel/Backbarrow	Cotton manufacturer	1793	2	5
John Birch	Cartmel/Backbarrow	Cotton manufacturer	1795	8	10
John Birch	Cartmel/Backbarrow	Cotton manufacturer	1798	8	7
John Birch	Cartmel/Backbarrow	Cotton manufacturer	1799	3	9

---

15 SC 1816, pp. 203–205. Also Wood makes reference to the long hours and poor conditions of work of such outworkers.

John Birch	Cartmel/Backbarrow	Cotton manufacturer	1800	8	7
John Birch	Cartmel/Backbarrow	Cotton manufacturer	1801	1	6
Monteith and Bogle	Blantyre, Glasgow	Cotton manufacturer	1805	9	17
Monteith and Bogle	Blantyre, Glasgow	Cotton manufacturer	1806	2	3
Monteith and Bogle	Blantyre, Glasgow	Cotton manufacture	1807	2	2
Monteith and Bogle	Blantyre, Glasgow	Cotton manufacturer	1809	11	8
David Ainsworth	Cartmell	Cotton manufacturer	1811	0	1
David Ainsworth	Cartmell	Cotton manufacturer	1813	0	3
David Ainsworth	Cartmell	Cotton manufacturer	1814	0	3
James Newton	Cressbrook	Cotton manufacturer	?	?	?
William Garth	Colne, Lancs	Cotton manufacturer	1813	2	0
William Garth	Colne, Lancs	Cotton manufacturer	1814	2	1
William Garth	Colne, Lancs	Cotton manufacturer	1815	3	4

Sources: St Clement Danes Apprenticeship Records 1784–1792, B1266; St Clement Danes Apprenticeship Records 1784–1801, B1267; St Clement Danes Apprenticeship Register 1803–1822, B1268. Westminster Archives Centre.

The London parishes of St Clement Danes, Lambeth, St Giles in the Field, St Luke Chelsea, St Pancras, and St Martin in the Fields were among those most heavily engaged in the transfer of apprentices to the early factories. Each of them sent groups of children, at peak times accounting for 90 per cent of their bindings, to the new textile factories. In the 1790s, for example, almost all the poor children from St Clement Danes were bound apprentice to Mr John Birch at Cartmel (Backbarrow).[16] (See Table 4.1). Between 1787 and 1801, almost 200 children were bound there and only a handful locally. The transmission of such large numbers to a single location in so short a space of time was unusual but not unique.[17] In 1805, 26 children were sent to Glasgow, most of them having entered the St Clement Danes workhouse only

---

16 Apprenticeship Records 1784–1792, Parish of St Clement Danes, B1266; and Apprenticeship Records 1784–1801, Parish of St Clement Danes, B1267, WAC.

17 According to William Travers, giving evidence to the 1816 Select Committee, there were continually 120–30 apprentices at Backbarrow, suggesting a regular throughput. SC1816, p. 288.

shortly before they were bound out;[18] and only 6 within London.[19] Long distance apprenticing from St Clement Danes continued until 1815, when the main clients included David Ainsworth, successor to John Birch at Backbarrow,[20] and Monteith and Bogle of Blantyre, near Glasgow.[21] Factory apprentices comprised a significant proportion of those originating in St Giles in the Fields parish (see Table 4.2). They were dispersed throughout the early textile manufacturing region, both to key players, such as William Douglas and Robert Peel, whose dependence on parish apprentices is renown, and to smaller enterprises in the Lancashire weaving trade.[22]

Table 4.2 St Giles in the Fields Parish Factory Apprentices

Firm	Location	Nature of business	Date	Girl apprentices	Boy apprentices
William Douglas	Pendleton	Cotton manufacturer	1786	5	3
William Douglas	Pendleton	Cotton manufacturer	1787	0	3
William Douglas	Pendleton	Cotton manufacturer	1789	?	?
William Douglas	Pendleton	Cotton manufacturer	1790	1	0
Ellis, Needham, Frith	Tideswell	Cotton manufacturer	1789	2	10
Ellis, Needham, Frith	Tideswell	Cotton manufacturer	1790	9	2
Ellis, Needham, Frith	Tideswell	Cotton manufacturer	1793	3	5
Ellis, Needham, Frith	Tideswell	Cotton manufacturer	1794	0	4
Ellis, Needham, Frith	Tideswell	Cotton manufacturer	1795	2	3
Ellis, Needham, Frith	Tideswell	Cotton manufacturer	1796	2	0
Peter Atherton	Holywell	Cotton spinner	1790	5	0
Needham, Smithand Heywood	Tideswell	Cotton spinner	1791	0	5
John Cowpe	Pleasley	Cotton manufacturer	1791	10	0

---

18   Pamela Horn, 'The traffic in children and the textile mills, 1780–1816', *Genealogists' Magazine*, 24/5 (1993): 354–6.
19   Horn, 'The traffic', p. 354–6.
20   Apprenticeship Register 1803–22, Parish of St Clement Danes, B1268, WAC.
21   This was one of the very few Scottish mills which absorbed English parish children.
22   Register of Apprentices 1780–1802, Parish of St Giles in the Fields P/GF/PO/4, CLSAC; Chris Aspin, *The Water Spinners* (Helmshore, 2003), p. 208.

John Charles Bott, William Lucas and Francis Greasely	Tutbury, Staffs	Cotton manufacturer	1791	0	24
John Charles Bott, William Lucas and Francis Greasely	Tutbury, Staffs	Cotton manufacturer	1793	2	1
John Charles Bott, William Lucas and Francis Greasely	Tutbury, Staffs	Cotton manufacturer	1794	1	1
John Charles Bott, William Lucas and Francis Greasely	Tutbury, Staffs	Cotton manufacturer	1795	0	6
John Charles Bott, William Lucas and Francis Greasely	Tutbury, Staffs	Cotton manufacturer	1796	0	3
John Charles Bott, William Lucas and Francis Greasely	Tutbury, Staffs	Cotton manufacturer	1800	0	9
William Harrison and Peter Atherton	Kirk mill, Chipping, Preston	Cotton manufacturer	1795	9	0
Hollins and Co.	Pleasley, Derbyshire	Cotton manufacturer	1797	1	0
Chavat and Co.	Southwell	Cotton manufacturer	1797	0	5
Joseph Wells	Sheffield	Cotton manufacturer	1797	4	0
Joseph Wells	Sheffield	Cotton manufacturer	1799	7	0
Joseph Wells	Sheffield	Cotton manufacturer	1800	8	0
Joseph Wells	Sheffield	Cotton manufacturer	1801	3	0
Joseph Wells	Sheffield	Cotton manufacturer	1802	2	2
John Douglas	Pendleton	Cotton manufacturer	1799	2	4
Nathaniel Pattison	Congleton	Silk manufacturer	1799	20? children	0
Nathaniel Pattison	Congleton	Silk manufacturer	1801	20 children	0
Peel	Bury	Cotton manufacturer	1803	65 children	0
Peel	Bury	Cotton manufacturer	1807	18 children	0
John Edward Hudson	Gauxholme, Todmorden	Cotton manufacturer	1807	29 children	0

Sources: St Giles in the Fields parish, Register of Parish apprentices 1780–1802. P/GF/PO/4, Camden Local Studies and Archives Centre; Chris Aspin, *The Water Spinners*, p. 254.

Table 4.3 St Luke, Chelsea Parish Factory Apprentices

Firm	Location	Nature of business	Date	Girl apprentices	Boy apprentices
William Douglas	Pendleton	Cotton spinning	1795	15	12
William Douglas	Pendleton	Cotton spinning	1797	2	3
William Douglas	Holywell	Cotton spinning	1797	3	8
Davison and Hawksley	Arnold, Notts	Worsted and cotton manufacturer	1802	10	11
Davison and Hawksley	Arnold, Notts	Worsted and cotton manufacturer	1803	4	11
Davison and Hawksley	Arnold, Notts	Worsted and cotton manufacturer	1804	3	0
Davison and Hawksley	Arnold, Notts	Worsted and cotton manufacturer	1805	3	3
Benjamin Smart	Milverton, Warwickshire	Cotton manufacturer	1814	6	0
Benjamin Smart	Milverton, Warwickshire	Cotton manufacturer	1815	3	0

Sources: St Luke Chelsea Workhouse Apprenticeship Register 1791–1802 P74/LUK/116; St Luke Chelsea Apprenticeship Register 1802–1813 P74/LUK/117. London Metropolitan Archives.

Only a small proportion of poor children in the care of St Luke Chelsea (see Table 4.3) were retained in the parish during the early industrial period. During the early 1790s, the majority of boys were apprenticed to coal-carrying ships in the north-east of England; and from 1795 to 1800, most of the parish's girls and boys were bound to the Douglas cotton-spinning enterprises.[23] Between 1802 and 1805, all but five apprentices were sent to Davidson and Hawksley, worsted and cotton manufacturers of Arnold, Nottingham. Only six names appear in the register for the years from 1805 to 1813 and all were apprenticed locally. Between 1813 and 1815, the long-distance trade resumed with all the boys, 24 in number, being sent to mines in Bilston, Staffordshire and all the girls, of whom there were 9, to Benjamin Smart's cotton-spinning mill in nearby Milverton, Warwickshire.[24] St Pancras parish (see Table 4.4) revealed a similar pattern. During the late 1780s and early 1790s, a

---

23 Workhouse Apprenticeship Register, 1791–1802, Parish of St Luke Chelsea, P74/LUK/116, LMA.

24 Apprenticeship Register, 1802–13, Parish of St Luke Chelsea., P74/LUK/117, LMA.

handful of apprentices to Marsland and Kelsall and Douglas were interspersed with groups of poor boys bound to mariners in Hull and Whitby. From 1796 onwards, a clear majority of parish apprentices were bound to textile factories, both local (Hounslow) and further afield. The proportion sent to the more distant factories, mainly in Lancashire, rose over time.[25] During the years 1802–1806, 92 from a total of 132 apprentices were bound to three cotton manufacturers around Bury in Lancashire; and a further two girls were apprenticed to Merryweather's Burley-in-Wharfedale mill. No further apprentices were bound until 1814, when 72 from a total of 92 children apprenticed from St Pancras were sent to Lancashire firms.[26] During the final two years in which the parish openly engaged in the practice, a total of 16 children were bound to several Lancashire firms.[27]

Table 4.4 St Pancras Parish Factory Apprentices

Firm	Location	Nature of business	Date	Girl apprentices	Boy apprentices
Marsland and Kelsall	Glossop	Cotton manufacturer	1788	0	6
Marsland and Kelsall	Glossop	Cotton manufacturer	1796	4	4
William Douglas	Pendleton	Cotton manufacturer	1790	0	3
Messrs Lambert	Nottingham	Cotton spinning, etc.	1799	15	14 (including Robert Blincoe)
Messrs Lambert	Nottingham	Cotton spinning, etc.	1800	0	11
Samuel Ashton	Middleton, Lancs	Cotton manufacturer	1802	18	7
Thomas Haslam	Bury	Cotton spinner	1803	18	6
Sewell and McMurdo	Hounslow	Flax spinner	1804	17	17
Sewell and McMurdo	Hounslow	Flax spinner	1805	5	8
John Gorton	Bury	Cotton spinner	1805	13	12
John Gorton	Bury	Cotton spinner	1806	6 (who did not go nor cause any indentures executed)	8
Merryweather	Burley	Cotton manufacturer	1806	2	0

---

25 Register of Apprentices 1778–1801, Parish of St Pancras, P90/PANI/361, LMA.

26 Most of the remainder were apprenticed to trades within the London area but usually outside the parish. Apprenticeship Register, 1802–67, Parish of St Pancras, P90/PANI/362 LMA; Directors of the Poor minutes, Parish of St Pancras, P/PN/PO/1/9–10, CLSAC.

27 Apprenticeship Register, 1802–67, Parish of St Pancras, P90/PANI/362, LMA.

Firm	Location	Nature of business	Date	Girl apprentices	Boy apprentices
Jeremiah Garnett	Clitheroe	Cotton manufacturer	1814	12	10
Samuel Oldknow	Mellor, Lancs	Cotton manufacturer	1814	18	1
Isaac Hodgson	Caton Mills, Lancs	Cotton manufacturer	1814	5	13
Isaac Hodgson	Caton Mills, Lancs	Cotton manufacturer	1816	4	8
Joseph Wolfenden	Heyride [sic], Oldham	Fustian manufacturer	1814	0	1
Ottiwell Kershaw	Heyride [sic], Oldham	Fustian manufacturer	1814	0	2
James Buckley	Heyride [sic], Oldham	Fustian manufacturer	1814	0	4
James Buckley	Heyride [sic], Oldham	Fustian manufacturer	1815	0	1
John Clegg	Heyride [sic], Oldham	Fustian manufacturer	1814	0	1
James Collier	Heyride [sic], Oldham	Fustian manufacturer	1814	0	1
William Marlow	Prestwich	Cotton weaver	1814	1	1
John McGarrick	Manchester	Cotton manufacturer	1814	0	1
John McGarrick	Manchester	Fustian manufacturer	1815	0	1
John Wild	Heyside, Oldham	Cotton manufacturer	1815	0	1

Sources: St Pancras Register of Apprentices, 1778–1801, P90/PANI/361; St Pancras Apprenticeship Register, 1802–1867, P90/PANI/362, London Metropolitan Archives; St Pancras Minutes of meetings of Directors of the Poor, 1804–1820, P/PN/PO/1/1–17 (microfilm references UTAH 649–654), Camden Local Studies and Archives Centre.

Table 4.5 St Martin in the Fields Parish Factory Apprentices

Firm	Location	Nature of business	Date	Girl apprentices	Boy apprentices
William Douglas	Pendleton	Cotton spinner	1785	0	15
William Douglas	Holywell	Cotton spinner	1786	5	16

Peter Atherton	Holywell	Cotton spinner	1787	10	15
William Douglas	Pendleton	Cotton spinner	1787	0	8
Wells Middleton	Sheffield	Cotton spinner	1789	4	0
William Douglas	Pendleton	Cotton spinner	1798	3	7
George Rickards	Bakewell	Cotton spinner	1791	0	10
Richard Gorton	Cuckney	Weaver	1791	0	12
John/Isaac Hodgson	Caton Mills, Lancaster	Cotton manufacturer	1791	0	14
William Douglas	Eccles/ Pendleton	Cotton manufacturer	1794	2	4
William/John Douglas	Pendleton	Cotton manufacturer	1795	0	3
Thomas Watson	Watford	Silk throwster	1796	14	8
William/John Douglas	Pendleton	Cotton manufacturer	1797 ('agreed that as many children in the school as may be eligible')	3	10
Palfreyman	Cragg works, Prestbury	Cotton manufacturer and printer	1796	0	7
John Douglas	Holywell	Cotton manufacturer	1800	1	6
Wells, Middleton	Sheffield	Cotton spinner	1789 (Aspin, but no numbers)	?	?
Wells, Middleton	Sheffield	Cotton spinner	1798	4	0
Wells, Middleton	Sheffield	Cotton spinner	1799	2	6
Wells, Middleton	Sheffield	Cotton spinner	1800	4	8
Wells, Middleton	Sheffield	Cotton spinner	1801	1	0
Wells, Middleton	Sheffield	Cotton spinner	1802	4	3
Wells, Middleton	Sheffield	Cotton spinner	1808	2	2
Mitchell and Co.	Holt Town, Manchester	Cotton spinner	1801	8	4

John and William Singleton	Wigan	Cotton spinner	1802	0	6
John Middleton	Sheffield	Cotton spinner	1802	0	3
John Middleton	Sheffield	Cotton spinner	1808 'all failed'	2	2
Samuel Ashton	Middleton, Lancs	Cotton manufacturer	1802 'as many boys and girls as apprentices as may suit him'	9	35
Thomas Haslam	Bury, Lancs	Cotton spinner	1803	0	4
Thomas Dixon	Ormskirk, Lancs	Cotton spinner	1803	0	5
John Head	Masham, Yorks	Worsted manufacturer	1803	8	0
John Head	Masham, Yorks	Worsted manufacturer	1804	8	0
John Head	Masham, Yorks	Worsted manufacturer	1809	0	3
John/Jeremiah Bury and Co.	Stockport	Cotton spinners and weavers	1805	5	11
John/Jeremiah Bury and Co.	Stockport	Cotton spinners and weavers	1806	3	0
John/Jeremiah Bury and Co.	Stockport	Cotton spinners and weavers	1807	1	4
John/Jeremiah Bury and Co.	Stockport	Cotton spinners and weavers	1810	2	0
Merryweather	Otley	Cotton weaver	1806	0	2
Merryweather	Otley		1807	1	4
Charles Harding	Tamworth	Cotton weavers and spinners	1807	4	14
James Lees	Roberttown, Birstall, West Yorkshire	Cotton spinners	1807	0	3

Peel	Bury	Cotton manufacturer	1807 agreed 'that the children made choice of for Sir Robert Peel and Co. be bound apprentice'	'a group'	?
Peel	Bury	Cotton manufacturer	1808		3	5
Peel	Tamworth	Cotton manufacturer	1810 agree 'that as many boys as are eligible be bound to Sir Robert Peel at Tamworth'	?	?
Thomas Yates	Tamworth	Cotton spinner and weaver	1809		3	5
Thomas Yates and Co.	Bury, Lancs	Cotton spinners and weavers	1810		1	8
Thomas Yates and Co.	Bury, Lancs	Cotton spinners and weavers	1811		1	3
Edward Collyer	Ingersley Mills, Rainow, Macclesfield	Cotton weaver	1811		0	2
James Whitelegg	Nr Manchester	Cotton weaver	1814		0	6
Thomas Andrew	Harpurhey, nr Manchester	Calico printer	1815		0	5
William Calrow	Bury	Cotton manufacturer	1815		4	2
David Ainsworth	Backbarrow, Cartmel	Cotton spinner	1815		2	4
Joseph Broster	Rainow, Macclesfield	Cotton spinner	1816		0	2

Sources: St Martin in the Fields Apprenticeship Register, 1784–1794, F4309; St Martin in the Fields Apprenticeship Register, 1795–1803, F4310; St Martin in the Fields Apprenticeship Register, 1802–1824, F4311, Westminster Archives Centre.

St Martin in the Fields parish maintained detailed records of apprenticeships from 1761. During the 1760s, many of the local poor boys were apprenticed to the Essex fishing trade, and to mariners in Whitby, Newcastle, and South Shields, a trend that continued through the 1770s.[28] From 1785, the transfer of children to cotton

---

28   Apprenticeship records 1761–1784, Parish of St Martin in the Fields, F4511, WAC.

mills began.[29] (See Table 4.5.) For several years from the late eighteenth century to the early nineteenth century, these parish factory apprentices formed well over 70 per cent of the total. Throughout the period from 1802–1816, 200 of the 347 St Martins children registered as apprentices were sent to textile mills.[30] A number of firms, such as Douglas, Wells and Middleton, and Peel were regular and substantial customers, who, judging from parish discussions were accorded priority treatment.[31] Others received just single batches, either from choice, or because they were not among the parish's preferred masters.[32]

Table 4.6   St Mary at Lambeth Parish Factory Apprentices

Firm	Location	Nature of business	Date	Girl apprentices	Boy apprentices
Douglas	Pendleton	Cotton manufacturer	1786	1	8
Douglas	Pendleton	Cotton manufacturer	1787	2	0
Douglas	Pendleton	Cotton manufacturer	1796	2	2
William Harrison	Holliwell	Cotton spinner	1790	9	8
Joseph Wells	Sheffield	Cotton manufacturer	1790	14	4
Joseph Wells	Sheffield	Cotton manufacturer	1798	3	0
Haigh	Almondbury, Marsden	Cotton manufacturer	1792	0	12
Haigh	Almondbury, Marsden	Cotton manufacturer	1793	0	16
Haigh	Almondbury, Marsden	Cotton manufacturer	1795	0	1
Haigh	Almondbury, Marsden	Cotton manufacturer	1796	0	9
Haigh	Almondbury, Marsden	Cotton manufacturer	1803	15	8
Nathaniel Mason	Iver, Bucks	Cotton spinner	1793	0	15

---

29   Apprenticeship Register, 1784–1794, Parish of St Martin in the Fields, F4309, WAC.

30   These numbers were distributed unevenly over the years, as follows: in 1802, 53 of 72; in 1803, 18 of 28; almost all in 1805 and 1807; and the majority between 1810 and 1814, when, as was often the case, rather smaller groups were sent to rather smaller enterprises.

31   For example, on 6 September 1797, it was agreed 'that as many children in the Schools as may be eligible be bound to Mr John Douglas'; and on 28 November 1810, it was agreed 'that as many boys as are eligible be bound to Sir Robert Peel and Co. at Tamworth, Staffs', Minutes of meetings of officers of the parish, St Martin in the Fields, F2075, WAC.

32   Apprenticeship Register, 1795–1803, Parish of St Martin in the Fields, F4310; and Apprenticeship Register, 1802–1824, Parish of St Martin in the Fields, F4311, WAC.

Workman, Brummell and Hall	Dartford, Kent	Cotton spinners	1793	0	15
Workman, Brummell and Hall	Dartford, Kent	Cotton spinners	1795	0	3
Charles Jackson	Cuckney, Notts	Worsted manufacturer	1794	14	12
Charles Jackson	Cuckney, Notts	Worsted manufacturer	1795	6	9
Davison and Hawksley	Arnold, Notts	Worsted manufacturer	1795	5? Or 10	6
Davison and Hawksley	Arnold, Notts	Worsted manufacturer	1796	6	17
Davison and Hawksley	Arnold, Notts	Worsted manufacturer	1797	1	1
Davison and Hawksley	Arnold, Notts	Worsted manufacturer	1798	4	4
Nicholas Cresswell	Castleton	Cotton spinner	1796	15	1
Nicholas Cresswell	Castleton	Cotton spinner	1797	4	0
Nicholas Cresswell	Castleton	Cotton spinner	1798	5	0
Nicholas Cresswell	Castleton	Cotton spinner	1799	4	0
Nicholas Cresswell	Castleton	Cotton spinner	1800	3	0
Nicholas Cresswell	Castleton	Cotton spinner	1801	6	0
Royds, Toplis and Toplis	Cuckney	Worsted manufacturer	1800	0	6
Royds, Toplis and Toplis	Cuckney	Worsted manufacturer	1805	9	10
John Watson	Preston	Cotton spinner	1803	5	12
Colbeck	West House, Fewston	Flax manufacturer	1803	4	0
Merryweather	Burley-in-Wharfedale	Cotton manufacturer	1806	0	3
Merryweather	Burley-in-Wharfedale	Cotton manufacturer	1807	6	1
Merryweather	Burley-in-Wharfedale	Cotton manufacturer	1809	0	3
Whitaker	Otley	Cotton manufacturer	1806	12	0
Whitaker	Otley	Cotton manufacturer	1807	2	0
Whitaker	Burley	Cotton manufacturer	1810	3	0

Whitaker	Burley	Cotton manufacturer	1811	4	0	
Whitaker	Burley	Cotton manufacturer	1813–14	22	0	
R&G Hodgkinson	Worksop	Cotton weaver	1807	0	9	
William Pearce	Pleasley, Derbyshire	Cotton spinner	1809	5	0	
Robert Blackwall	Edale, Castelton	Cotton spinner	1810	6	0	
Merryweather	Manchester	Calico weaver	1810	0	3	
George Andrew	Stockport	Calico printer	1816	0	9	

Sources: St Mary at Lambeth, Apprenticeship Register, 1782–1833, P85/MRY1/270; St Mary at Lambeth Apprenticeship Register, 1802–1826 P85/MRY1/271;St Mary at Lambeth, Apprenticeship Register, 1827–56, P85/MRY1/272, London Metropolitan Archives.

Between 1786 and 1816, Lambeth parish bound 374, more than 80 per cent, of its poor children as apprentices to distant mills, and several groups to cotton mills in the south (see Table 4.6). During the 1790s, the majority of Lambeth parish apprentices were bound to factories in Marsden and Burley-in-Wharfedale in Yorkshire, in Nottingham, and in Castleton in Derbyshire.[33] St George the Martyr parish in Southwark engaged enthusiastically in factory apprenticeship (see Table 4.7). Throughout a 30-year period from 1786, 90 per cent of its apprentices were bound northwards to textile mills. During the period from which evidence for St Leonard's apprenticeships survives, 1802–1816, a large proportion (80 per cent) were bound to the Midlands and North, always to the eastern side of the country. Yorkshire features unusually prominently in the arrangements (see Table 4.8).

Table 4.7   St George the Martyr Southwark Parish Factory Apprentices

Firm	Location	Nature of business	Date	Girl apprentices	Boy apprentices
Cooke and Kilner	Taplow, Bucks	Cotton manufacturer	1787	1	0
Ellis Needham	Tideswell, Derbyshire	Cotton manufacturer	c. 1790	n/a	n/a**
Hugh Lecky	St George in the East	Flax manufacturer	1799	6	0
Jeremiah Bury	Heaton Norris, Stockport	Muslin manufacturer	1800?	n/a	n/a*
Davison and Hawksley	Arnold, Notts	Worsted spinner	1800	1	6

---

33   Apprenticeship Registers, 1782–1833, Parish of St Mary at Lambeth, P85/MRY1/270, LMA.

John Watson	Preston, Lancs	Cotton manufacturer	1800	5	8
John Watson	Preston, Lancs	Cotton manufacturer	1802	12	10
Edmund and Thomas Yates	Bury, Lancs	Cotton manufacturer	1802	5	4
Colbeck and Co.	West House, Otley, Yorks	Flax manufacturer	1803	11	0
John Rushworth	Clough Head, Marsden and Colne, Lancs	Wool comber and worsted spinner	1803	0	1
Colbeck and Co.	Otley	Flax manufacturer	1804	14	6
John Watson	Preston, Lancs	Cotton manufacturer	1805	2	16
John Watson	Preston, Lancs	Cotton manufacturer	1806	10	16
Peel, Yates and Co.	Bury, Lancs	Cotton spinner	1806	5	7
John Watson	Preston, Lancs	Cotton manufacturer	1807	3	5
Jonas Whitaker	Otley, Yorks	Calico weaver	1809	6	0
George Merryweather	Otley, Yorks	Cotton manufacturer	1809	6	2
Jonas Whitaker	Otley, Yorks	Calico weaver	1810	10	0
George Merryweather	Otley, Yorks	Cotton manufacturer	1810	1	1
Jonas Whitaker	Otley, Yorks	Calico weaver	1811	5	0
Geary and Ranyard	Leicester	Framework knitter	1811	0	3
Jonas Whitaker	Otley, Yorks	Calico weaver	1812	7	0
Colbeck and Co. (Colbeck, Wilks and Ellis)	Otley, Yorks	Flax manufacturer	1814	7	10
Robert Needham	Tideswell, Derbyshire	Cotton manufacturer	1816	2	0

* Bury applied for 200. It is not clear how many, if indeed any, went. ** Referred to in Report from St James Piccadilly 1803.

Sources: St George the Martyr Vestry Minutes 1785–1809, 555–9; St George the Martyr, Apprenticeship indentures 1799–1836, 1/boxes 51–2; St George the Martyr Annual register of the parish poor children until they are apprenticed out 1789–1807, 764; St George the Martyr 'Plan of disposing of 200 parish children wanted by J. Bury and Co., Muslin Manufacturers of Hope Hill, near Stockport, Cheshire', Southwark Local History Library.

Table 4.8 St Leonard, Shoreditch Parish Factory Apprentices

Firm	Location	Nature of business	Date	Girl apprentices	Boy apprentices
Davison and Hawksley	Arnold, Nottingham	Worsted spinner	1803	4	6
Middleton	Sheffield	Cotton spinner	1805	2	13
Merryweather	Otley, Yorks	Cotton spinner	1808	3	6
Merryweather	Otley, Yorks	Cotton spinner	1809	1	5
Whitaker	Burley	Cotton spinner	1809	8	0
Merryweather	Otley, Yorks	Cotton spinner	1810	0	4
Colbeck, Ellis, Wilks	West House, Fewston	Flax spinners and manufacturers	1811	3	14
Whitaker	Burley	Cotton spinner	1811	4	0
Whitaker	Burley	Cotton spinner	1812	2	0
Needham	Litton	Cotton spinners	1814	7	13
Whitaker	Burley	Cotton spinner	1816	3	0

Sources: St Leonard Shoreditch, Apprenticeship Register 1802–, P91/LEN/1332, microfilm reference 020/172, London Metropolitan Archives.

It is hard to avoid the conclusion that the binding of apprentices to distant textile factories was associated with London parishes overwhelmed with poor children. For parishes with less child poverty and access to more local placements, not only were the numbers and proportion of factory apprentices smaller, but the enterprises selected by such parishes were more likely to include some closer to home. London parishes that participated sporadically in factory apprenticeship include St George, Hanover Square (Table 4.9), St James, Piccadilly (Table 4.10), St Paul, Covent Garden (Table 4.11), St Mary Newington (Table 4.12), St Anne, Soho (Table 4.13) and St Botolph (Tables 4.14 and 4.15), where factory bindings of small groups of children constituted a minority of total placements.[34] For other London parishes, the factory system appeared to be used intermittently either to clear a backlog or to deal speedily with a sudden influx of poor children.[35] It is even possible that some parishes operated as a labour exchange and organised the transfer of children from other parts of the capital. During the whole of 1780, the parish of St Margaret and St John apprenticed a total of 23 children to various trades' people in the London area; in one week in October 1794, 50 children were bound to Toplis's Cuckney worsted mill (see Table 4.16). This supports Horn's suggestion that factory apprenticeship was not always a 'natural' process.[36]

---

34 These also tended to be among the least distant.

35 This appears to have been the case with the Foundling Hospital in the second half of the eighteenth century. See Levene, 'Parish apprenticeship', forthcoming. In addition, there are those parishes that engaged in the process of factory apprenticeship but, because of data deficiency, the extent of the activity remains unknown.

36 Horn, 'The traffic', pp. 354–6.

Table 4.9 St George, Hanover Square Parish Factory Apprentices

Firm	Location	Nature of business	Date	Girl apprentices	Boy apprentices
David Holt	Holt Town, Manchester	Cotton spinner	1790–1808	n/a but several groups	n/a but several groups
Haywood and Palfreyman	Wildboar Clough, near Macclesfield, Cheshire	Calico printer	1796	15 children*	0
Merryweather	Burley, Yorkshire	Cotton spinner and weaver	1790–1808	n/a but several groups, including but not exclusively below	0
Merryweather	Burley, Yorkshire	Cotton spinner and weaver	1802	6	6
Ellis Needham	Tideswell, Derbyshire	Cotton spinner	1803	5 approx*	5 approx*
Merryweather	Burley, Yorkshire	Cotton spinner and weaver	1805	5	2
Merryweather	Burley, Yorkshire	Cotton spinner and weaver	1807	1	0
Davison and Hawksley	Nottingham	Worsted spinner and weaver	1790–1807	n/a but several groups	n/a but several groups
John Bott	Tutbury	Cotton spinner	1790–1807	n/a but several groups	n/a but several groups
Cooper and Matchett	Woodeaves, Derbyshire	Cotton spinner	1790–1808	n/a but several groups	n/a but several groups
Churchill	Sheepshead, Leicester	Cotton spinner	1790–1808	n/a but several groups	n/a but several groups
Sewell and McMurdo	Hounslow	Flax spinner	1790–1808	n/a but several groups	n/a but several groups

*The children sent to Litton were brought back to the parish because of poor treatment and conditions. *Sources*: St George, Hanover Square, Meetings of the Governors and Directors of the Poor, C925, Westminster Archives Centre. No apprenticeship registers or indentures survive, and most of the above is derived from the minutes of meetings of the Governors and Directors of the Poor, which describe visits to the factories. In most cases, more than one and possibly several groups were sent, the size of each averaging 12–15. In 1808, there were still children at several of the factories, indicating that more had been sent from mid-1790s and probably later.* Information from St James parish.

Table 4.10 St James, Piccadilly Parish Factory Apprentices

Firm	Location	Nature of business	Date	Girl apprentices	Boy apprentices
Messrs Strutt	Rickmansworth	Cotton spinner	1786	6	6
Messrs Strutt	Rickmansworth	Cotton spinner	1787	4	6
Gorton and Thompson	Cuckney, Nottinghamshire	Woolen and cotton manufacture	1787		c. 35
Douglas	Pendleton	Cotton spinner	1787	8	0
Messrs Strutt	Rickmansworth	Cotton spinner	1788	7 children	0
Haywood and Palfreyman	Wildboar Clough, near Macclesfield, Cheshire	Cotton winder and calico printer and bleacher	1790 (I think this was 1796)	1	32
Ellis Needham	Tideswell, Derbyshire	Cotton spinner	c. 1790	11	0
Douglas	Pendleton	Cotton spinner	1797	11	11
Ellis Needham	Tideswell, Derbyshire	Cotton spinner	1797	11	0
David Holt	Holt Town, Manchester	Cotton spinner	1801	14 children	0
Douglas	Holywell	Cotton spinner	1801	20 children?	0
Sewell and Jones	Hounslow	Flax spinner	1818	7	7

Sources: St James Piccadilly Minutes of Governors and Directors of the Poor 1782–1805, D1870–D1878, Westminster Archives Centre; Transfer of Apprentices to Sewell and Jones 1 March 1821, Turner Collection ACC/0526/36, London Metropolitan Archives.

Table 4.11 St Pauls, Covent Garden Parish Factory Apprentices

Firm	Location	Nature of business	Date	Girl apprentices	Boy apprentices
Ellis Needham	Litton	Cotton spinner	1796	4	0
Haywood and Palfreyman	Cragg works, Wildboar Clough	Calico printer	1796	0	8
Haywood and Palfreyman	Cragg works, Wildboar Clough	Calico printer	1797	0	4

Source: St Paul Covent Garden, Minutes of Churchwardens and Overseers H879, Westminster Archives Centre.

Table 4.12 St Mary Newington (Southwark) Parish Factory Apprentices

Firm	Location	Nature of business	Date	Girl apprentices	Boy apprentices
Jonas Whitaker	Otley	Calico weaver	1813	12	0
Jonas Whitaker	Otley	Calico weaver	1814	5	0
Jonas Whitaker	Otley	Calico weaver	1815	6	0

Sources: St Mary Newington, Apprenticeship Register, 1802–1831. 891; St Mary Newington, Workhouse Committee Minutes, 1806–1820. 930–3; St Mary Newington, Minutes of the Governors and Guardians, 1814–23. 892. Southwark Local History Library.

Table 4.13 St Anne, Soho Parish Factory Apprentices

Firm	Location	Nature of business	Date	Girl apprentices	Boy apprentices
Douglas	Pendleton	Cotton spinner	1794	n/a (1 named but almost certainly one of a group)	?
Douglas	Pendleton	Cotton spinner	1795	n/a (but indenture of 1 girl survives, likely to be one of a group)	?
Douglas	Holywell	Cotton spinner	1796		n/a (1 runaway; again, almost certainly one of a group)
Douglas	Holywell	Cotton spinner	1799	n/a (but indenture of 1 girl survives, likely to be one of a group)	?

Source: St Anne parish, Apprenticeship 1702–1834 A2262, Westminster Archives Centre. A handful of indentures survive. It is almost certain that more than this number was sent.

Table 4.14 St Botolph Aldergate Parish Factory Apprentices

Firm	Location	Nature of business	Date	Girl apprentices	Boy apprentices
Haywood and Palfreyman	Wildboar Clough	Linen factory	1796	0	2
William Mitchell and David Holt	Holt Town, Manchester	Cotton manufacturer	1802	5	6

Source: St Botolph Aldergate parish, Apprenticeship Register, 1769–1805, MS 2658, Guildhall Library.

Table 4.15 St Botolph Without Aldergate Parish Factory Apprentices

Firm	Location	Nature of business	Date	Girl apprentices	Boy apprentices
Joseph Brosser	Rainow, Macclesfield	Cotton manufacturer	1805	0	3
Joseph Brosser	Rainow, Macclesfield	Cotton manufacturer	1806	0	3

Source: St Botolph without Aldersgate parish, Apprenticeship Register, 1802–, MS 1471, Guildhall Library.

Table 4.16 St Margaret and St John the Evangelist, Westminster Parish Factory Apprentices

Firm	Location	Nature of business	Date	Girl apprentices	Boy apprentices
Haigh	Marsden	Cotton spinner	1792	8	16
Royds, Toplis and Co.	Cuckney	Worsted manufacturer	1794	13	37
Royds, Toplis and Co.	Cuckney	Worsted manufacturer	1795	0	4
Merryweather	Burley	Cotton spinner	1797	36	32
Merryweather	Burley	Cotton spinner	1798	12	10
Watson	Walton, Lancaster	Cotton manufacture	1798	8	8
Royds, Toplis and Co.	Cuckney	Worsted manufacturer	1799	0	10
Merryweather	Burley	Cotton spinner	1799	2	5
Merryweather	Burley	Cotton spinner	1800	2	7
Royds, Toplis and Co.	Cuckney	Worsted manufacturer	1800	2	5
Merryweather	Burley	Cotton spinner	1801	16	8
Royds, Toplis and Co.	Cuckney	Worsted manufacturer	1801	8	8
John Morley	Chingford, Essex	Silk manufacturer	1801	5	4

Sources: St Margaret Apprenticeship Indentures 1680–1802 E3384; St Margaret and St John, 'Report of a visit to the different manufactories where children are apprenticed from the parishes of St Margaret and St John the Evangelist, Westminster', September 1802 E3371/95, Westminster Archives Centre.

For the parishes concerned and for the firms to which they provided children, the transfer of factory apprentices was especially marked in the years between 1790 and 1810. But the majority of London parishes played little or no part in the provision of new industrial labour.[37] They were either cautious about factory apprenticeships and stipulated relatively nearby destinations in Hounslow, Rickmansworth, Kent and Essex, for example, or did not participate at all. For Islington, this was a policy decision;[38] for others, such as Clapham, the supply of apprenticeship opportunities in the locality was sufficient to cope with the needs of the parish and its poor children.[39]

The importance of the transfer of child labour from the South to the Midlands and North of England cannot be denied, yet as the following section illustrates, the majority of apprentice agreements involved short-to-medium distances and included traditional trades as well as the emergent textile manufactures of the time. Proximity of apprentice bindings varied regionally according to economic structure and availability of occupational opportunities. In economically buoyant areas, apprenticeship opportunities roughly matched the quantity of poor children. Conversely, where industrial progress was sluggish and poverty high, apprenticeship prospects were limited. In the context of late eighteenth century economic change, experience varied within as well as between regions.

Among parishes in the emergent textile regions, the industrially dynamic town of Leeds was able to apprentice many of its poor children to 'respectable' trades.[40] Small numbers only were sent to the Thompsons' cotton spinning mills at Thorner, five miles from the centre of Leeds; and to Merryweather at Otley. Exceptionally, children were apprenticed out of the area.[41] In the township of Halifax, the majority of apprenticeships before 1790 were 'proper' apprenticeships. The majority were local, and there was a clear gendering of trades. Boys were sent to learn trades, especially cordwaining, or cardmaking; while girls were taught the 'honest and lawful calling' of housewifery. During the 1790s and 1800s, girls become more visible in the parish apprenticeship register and many were apprenticed to cotton spinning, mostly within the parish – John Horsfall being the main recipient – but also to such Oldham manufacturers as Benjamin Clegg. This latter destination increased so that

---

37 In addition to those identified above, a number of parishes engaged in the process of factory apprenticeship but because of data deficiency, the extent of the activity remains unknown.

38 For example, Islington Trustees of the poor made a policy decision on 6 October 1791 to reject applications from distant factory masters, though its children went to silk mills in east London and Essex, including that of George Courtauld in Barking. See meeting of Trustees 2 December 1813, Trustees of the Poor Minute Book, ILHL.

39 The local silk industry was important here. Register of Apprentices 1804–1822, Parish of Holy Trinity, Clapham, P95/TRI/ 1/27, LMA.

40 Philip W. Anderson, 'The Leeds workhouse under the Old Poor Law, 1726–1844', University of Leeds, MPhil thesis, 1977, p. 83. The diverse and dynamic structure of the Leeds economy permitted this.

41 Leeds Parish Apprenticeship Register, LO/AR1, WYASL. Towards 1820, the parish encountered more resistance on the part of masters to take on apprentices and although the fine income for refusal formed a welcome addition to the parish pot, this only partly compensated for the inconvenience caused, Leeds Workhouse Committee Minute and Order Book 1818– LO M/6, WYASL. In the adjoining parish of Calverley cum Farsley exists a very large list of fines paid in lieu of taking an apprentice, Apprentice Book, Parish of Calverley cum Farsley BDP 17/89, WYASL.

by 1810 around 40 per cent of parish apprentices were sent to Oldham, which, while in a different county, was not far away.[42] In cases where children were apprenticed outside of the parish, provisions were made to protect the parish financially in case of failure. 'If the apprentice shall return in to Halifax to be chargeable before the time ... the money ... is to be returned at the same time by the masters'.[43] The Warley registers reveal the same tendency for boys to be apprenticed to local trades while girls were more likely to be apprenticed out of the area, at a younger age and to textile factory manufacture.[44] In Heptonstall, almost all of the poor girls were apprenticed to weaving or cotton spinning, only a few cases outside of the area, and the boys mostly to local trades.[45]

In Keighley the situation was rather different, partly because of the bounty of the Bowcock Charity, which supported the apprenticeship of boys to local trades, and partly because of the strength of early cotton spinning in and about the town. The strength of the local economy ensured plentiful openings for parish apprentices. Parish apprentices of both sexes were mostly bound within the Keighley area, girls mainly to be instructed in the 'mistery of housewifery', and boys to destinations that included serge weaver, cordwainer and, especially after 1802, spindle making, shuttle making, brass and iron founding, all of which were integral to new forms of manufacturing.[46] The cotton spinning enterprises absorbed a handful of parish apprentices, but their requirement of children was typically met through local families.[47] A number of Keighley settlement examinations provide insight into the informal nature of some apprenticeships, as well as experience of master bankruptcy, which may have wider relevance.[48] In the rural parishes around Bradford, such as Calverley cum Farsley, Carleton and Wilsden, parish children were bound mainly to farmers and weavers within the parish. Cotton and worsted spinners accounted for a small number.[49] Worsted spinning was a relatively common destination of the small number of parish apprentices in Sutton.

Few parish children from Manchester and surrounding areas were apprenticed extra-parochially. Because of the region's full participation in new forms of textile manufacturing, the supply of children, whether parish or 'free', rarely exceeded demand

---

42   Indentures of apprentices, Halifax parish OR:328; Register of pauper apprentices 1802–1832, Halifax parish, OR:88, WYASC.
43   Apprenticeship books, 1729–1839, Halifax township, HXT: 192 WYASC.
44   Register of Pauper Apprentices 1802–1843, Parish of Warley, OR: 143, WYASC.
45   Apprenticeship Register, 1802–1841, Parish of Heptonstall HPC/A:20/226; Apprenticeship indentures, 1703–1847, Parish of Heptonstall HPC/A: 20/1–225 WYASC.
46   Parish of Keighley, Apprenticeship Papers, 1664–1832, BK1/2; Apprenticeship Indentures, 1664–1812, BK 1/2/1; Assignment of apprentices to new masters and Register of Apprentices,1802–1832, BK 1/2/2, Keighley Library (KL).
47   George Ingle, *Yorkshire Cotton. The Yorkshire Cotton Industry, 1780–1835* (Preston, 1997), pp. 64–75; Returns of Cotton and other mills. 1803–1806, QE 33/1, WYASW.
48   Keighley settlement examinations, 1745–1840 BK1/17/1, KL.
49   Apprenticeship indentures, Parish of Calverley cum Farsley, MM86/3/1; Apprenticeship Register, Parish of Carleton, BDP 18/138; Apprenticeship indentures, Parish of Allerton cum Wilsden, 69D82/9/4; Apprenticeship Register, Parish of Sutton, 69D82/9/3, West Yorkshire Archive Service, Bradford, WYASB.

at the parish level even in the unmodernised sectors. The apprenticeship registers of both Oldham St Mary, and Prestwich, where children were bound to local weaving trades, bear this out.[50] As pressure on hand weaving increased through the growth of mechanised spinning, apprentices were additionally sought from outside the region.[51] Other parishes in Lancashire, notably Liverpool, participated in the expansion of its region's textile factory production through the provision of parish apprentices.[52]

In the East Midlands textile region, while parish apprentices may have quite often crossed parish boundaries, they rarely travelled long distances. The majority of Alfreton apprentices, for example, remained within the Derbyshire parish, several being sent to Hulse's cotton mill.[53] The handful sent away remained close to the border with Nottinghamshire. Several textile factories, including Thomas Jewsbury's calico weaving plant at Measham, and Thomas Hawksworth's linen manufacture in Tamworth, provided the destination for a handful of apprentices from Denby, Repton and Foremark.[54] Nine of the 20 Church Broughton parish apprentices left the parish mainly to destinations in nearby Staffordshire.[55] Most of the Dale Abbey parish apprentices were sent to framework knitters in nearby Nottinghamshire;[56] while 40 per cent of the Melborne parish apprentices were bound to framework knitters in the surrounding counties of Nottinghamshire, Leicestershire and Staffordshire.[57] Nottinghamshire parish boys were typically bound to framework knitters,[58] and although girls were not excluded from such activity, they were more likely to be sent to spinning factories or to employers out of the parish.[59] The county's largest textile factories, Toplis at Cuckney and Davison and Hawksely in Arnold, near Nottingham, initially drew on local children especially from Mansfield before casting their net more widely to permit rapid expansion. Arnold parish, in which Davison and

50   Apprenticeship indentures, Parish of Oldham St Mary, 1999/81 DRO 24; Apprenticeship Register, Parish of Prestwich, L 160/10/5, MCA.

51   Including St Giles in the Fields. SC 1816, p. 233. According to Kinder Wood, an Oldham surgeon, 'it is common to take apprentices in [hand weaving], which is not in the mills', p. 203; 'there are many come from London. There are hundreds out of St Giles workhouse', SC1816, p. 205.

52   Liverpool was an important supplier of children to Backbarrow, to Gregs and to Derbyshire mills after the 1820s.

53   Apprenticeship indentures 1805–1824, Alfreton parish, D654 A/PO 244–77, DRO.

54   Apprenticeship indentures, Parish of Denby, D1428 A/PO/72–142; Apprenticeship indentures, Parish of Repton, D638 A/PO 510 and 512, DRO.

55   Apprenticeship Register, Church Broughton, D854 A/PO 120–129, DRO.

56   Apprenticeship indentures, Parish of Dale Abbey. D1061 A/PO/12/1–11, DRO.

57   Melborne parish register, D655 A/PI 1/3, DRO.

58   The case of Mansfield Woodhouse is a good example; Apprenticeship Register, Mansfield Woodhouse, NA.

59   Apprenticeship Register, 1803–1815, Parish of Carlton-in-Lindrick shows both girls and boys leaving the parish; none is bound parochially. Although one boy is bound to a nailmaker in Tickhill, Yorkshire, this parish is closer to his place of origin, located in the northern reaches of Nottinghamshire, than many Nottinghamshire parishes. In fact, another boy, apprenticed to a framework knitter in Arnold is sent much further away. Those bound at the greatest distance are two girls sent in 1811 to a candlewick and sack manufacture in Harlsthorpe to the north of Goole, PR 1394, NA.

Hawksley's factory was situated, recorded only one child being bound there. It has not been possible to refute such a statistic yet it seems unlikely that the parish would have ignored the potential of such a major local employer.[60]

Evidence from the Essex parishes indicates a similar pattern of intra-regional but often extra-parochial apprenticeship. The majority of Chelmsford apprentices were bound outside of the parish, as were those of Coggeshall, Thaxted and Whitham among others. Many Essex girls and boys were bound to one of the county's numerous silk factories; and only a small proportion were dispatched the longer distance to textile factories in the Midlands and North. Apart from the ten children bound to Douglas's Pendleton cotton mill from Chelmsford, the fifteen to Haigh's Marsden factory from Halstead parish, and batches to Toplis's mill at Cuckney from a handful of parishes, there is little indication of a 'trade' in parish apprentices. In Middlesex, the Hanwell parish plan to send pauper children as apprentices to a mill at Cuckney 'seems to have been rarely applied'; not least because of parental opposition to the practice.[61] The pattern of parish apprenticeship within the emerging textile regions demonstrates the intraregional flow of children to diverse trades, which included the new textile industries. It was relatively unusual for children to be bound to factories outside the region.

The discussion now turns to regions where textile manufacturing was less pronounced. Because of the manufacturing dynamism of the western half of the Midlands, parish apprentices were unlikely to be sent long distances even if they were not bound parochially. The Shrewsbury linen factories of Marshall Hutton and Hives, and Benyon and Benyon, comprised the major textile activity in Shropshire. Production began in the early 1800s, and altered the distribution of the town's apprentices. Before 1802, a significant proportion of Shrewsbury's young were apprenticed to Staffordshire mining and glass making, and to the Wolverhampton metal trades. Thereafter, except for a small group sent to Greg's Styal mill in 1804, the majority of parish children were found parochial placements, usually to one of the linen factories.[62] These two firms absorbed small numbers of children from surrounding rural parishes, which also sent apprentices to the Kidderminster carpet weaving trade.[63]

---

60 Apprenticeship indenture (no name), Parish of Arnold, for a 'girl to go to Davison and Hawksley in consideration of the sum of five pounds and five shillings ... The trade or business of worsted spinning ... and will teach and instruct', PR 14062/1, NA; Eden shows that children from the Nottingham workhouse worked in a local cotton mill, which is most likely to have been Davison and Hawksley, on a daily basis, and would not therefore have been recorded as apprentices. F.M. Eden, *The State of the Poor* (London, 1797), p. 329.

61 Hanwell Vestry Minutes 21 March 1792, 11 June 1792 and 1 April 1793, cited in Susan Reynolds, (ed.), *A History of the County of Middlesex*, vol. 3, p. 229. The threat of distant apprenticeship, however, was used by the parish to extract compliant behaviour from its families Canewdon parish. E.J. Erith, *Essex Parish Records, 1240–1894* (Chelmsford, 1950), p. 72. As long as they 'behave orderly', the children would not be compelled to go.

62 Register of apprentices 1802–1818, Shrewsbury Incorporation of the Poor, PL 2/7/1/1, Shropshire Archives (SA).

63 Local farmers were the most common destination of most rural children, however. Bridgnorth contained ten distinct parishes, including Astley Abbotts and Clesbury Mortimer.

The incompleteness of Staffordshire apprentice records precludes robust conclusions. It is highly likely that some of the county's children were apprenticed to the local cotton mills at Tutbury (Botts) and Tamworth (Peels), yet little written evidence of this survives. Children from Gnosall have elsewhere been identified as providing labour for distant mills but this is not confirmed by the parish records;[64] and Madeley parish sent a handful of children to Greg's Styal factory.[65] Several parishes bound children to Kidderminster carpet weavers, which drew children from throughout the Midlands,[66] and to small metal masters in the Black Country. Otherwise apprentices were retained within the region, whose dynamic metal industries provided many options. Many of Pattingham's poor children, for example, were bound to screwmakers, blacksmiths, or nailors;[67] and those from the parish of Blymhill and Tettenhall were mostly bound to local trades.[68]

Because of the strength of the county's industrial activity, the Poor Law officers of most of Warwickshire's parishes were able to find apprenticeships for its children within the region if not within the immediate locality. Expansion in the many traditional trades, especially in metal making, but also in ribbon and carpet weaving, and framework knitting, took place alongside the growth of factory textile production. Parish children were bound to one of the region's textile – mostly cotton – factories in small groups or even singly; and were treated identically to those apprenticed to 'real' trades.[69] This was the case in Coleshill parish, for example, when in 1814 the indenture for Hannah Jackson, 13, to be bound to William Willcock of Fazeley in the county of Stafford, cotton spinner, read that she was 'to be taught the art, trade or business of cotton, spinning and weaving'.[70]

Bulkington parish children were mainly bound either to nearby ribbon weavers, or to framework knitters in the region.[71] A similar distribution of Bedworth apprentice

---

Apprentice registers, Parish of Bridgnorth, BB/G/1/10/1–10; Apprentice register, Parish Westbury, P297/L/9/1; Apprenticeship Register, Parish of Stanton-upon-Hine, P167/L/4/1/2/; Apprenticeship Register, Parish of Rodington P230/L/7; Vestry meetings, Parish of Edgemond, P102/L/5/1, SA.

64 The formal record shows that more than 90 per cent of the parish's poor children were apprenticed to local farmers, and a handful to the Wolverhampton metal trades. Gnosall Apprenticeship indentures D951/5/95; Apprenticeship Register, 1802–, Parish of Gnosall, D95/5/93 Staffordshire Record Office (SRO).

65 Apprenticeship Register, 1802–, Parish of Madeley, D3412/5688; and correspondence with Gregs, Madeley parish, D3412/5/703, SRO.

66 Webb and Webb, *Old Poor Law*, p. 203, suggest an example of Gloucester, and also cite an eye witness account of 1833 that parish apprentices were brought into the industry by the cartload, but my research shows that from many Warwickshire, Worcestershire and other counties, apprentice boys (no girls?) were sent to Kidderminster. The distance from home parish was rarely extensive but it did mean that a substantial proportion of the population of Kidderminster did emanate from outside the town/parish.

67 Apprenticeship Register, Parish of Pattingham, D3451/5/380, SRO.

68 'A list of the children put out prentice by the parish of Blymhill, 1769–1791', D1044/4/1, SRO; Apprenticeship Register, Parish of Tettenhall, D571/1/PO/145, SRO.

69 See Chapter 5 on detail of where they all went.

70 Apprenticeship Indenture, 4 April 1814, Parish of Colleshill, WRCO.

71 Apprenticeship Register, 1802–1834, Parish of Bulkington, DR198/120 WCRO.

children is indicated by the parish records. In addition, individual children were apprenticed to two Derbyshire calico weaving enterprises, one of which was owned by Thomas Jewsbury,[72] and a Kidderminster carpet weaver. In 1809, a group of 20 girls was sent to Charles Harding cotton spinners and weavers at Tamworth.[73] The apprenticeship records of Coleshill parish also reveal a combination of ribbon weaving, framework knitting, supplemented by the metalware trades of Coventry, Birmingham and Wednesbury. Others were bound to the Peels' and William Willcock's cotton factories at Fazeley,[74] and a single child to Robert Waterfield, calico printer of Oakthorpe.[75] A good range of regional trades, and some larger textile enterprises was represented in the 53 entries for Kingsbury parish. Coventry silk manufacturers took a number of the children, as did the Fowler brothers, cotton spinners of Alder Mills, and Thomas Jewsbury, calico weaver at Measham, Derbyshire.[76]

A total of 339 children were apprenticed by Nuneaton parish in the years between 1802 and 1834, especially in the earlier part of the period. In view of its diverse urban economy, it is surprising that a large proportion of the parish's poor children were apprenticed outside of the locality. During 1802 and 1803, several groups of children were sent to Joseph Peel's Fazeley cotton spinning enterprise, and to Thomas Jewsbury of Measham, Derbyshire. Otherwise, most of the children were bound to framework knitting or ribbon weaving; or to the occasional locksmith at Willenhall.[77] A significant proportion of the 23 children apprenticed by Shustoke parish,[78] were bound to Wilks and Jewsbury at Measham and William Willcock, cotton manufacturer of Fazeley. Most of the rest were apprenticed out of town, some to Bilston miners and others to Birmingham metal trades.[79] Jewsbury also received six children from the small parish of Attleborough, near Nuneaton.[80]

---

72 A firm that engaged in spinning as well as weaving, a characteristic that found the approval of the Birmingham Guardians of the Poor, which believed that experience of spinning only was too narrow a training for its children.
73 Register of apprentices 1802–, Parish of Bedworth, DR 225/34, WCRO.
74 Formerly this firm had been styled Harding and Peel.
75 Apprenticeship Indentures, Parish of Colleshill, WCRO. The small rural parish of Monks Kirby apprenticed 23 of its poor children between 1802 and 1815. Most were sent, with a substantial premium of 5 or 6 guineas to learn framework knitting in Nottingham (over 40 miles distant), or in Hinckley or Burbage, both in Leicestershire and about 20–25 miles away; others were bound to ribbon weaving in nearby Coventry. Register of Apprentices 1802–1815, Parish of Monks Kirby, DR 155/62, WCRO.
76 Register of Apprentices, 1802–1819, Kingsbury Parish, DR(B) 3/126, WCRO. Children from Alcester and Tanworth parishes near Redditch were apprenticed mainly to the local trade of needlemaking. Apprenticeship Register, 1802–1823, Parish of Alcester, DR 360/78, WCRO; Register of apprentices 1802–1838, Parish of Tanworth, DRB 19/90, WCRO.
77 Register of apprentices 1802–1834, Parish of Nuneaton, DR137/20, WCRO.
78 This is 13 miles from Birmingham.
79 Register of Apprentices 1802–1830, Parish of Shustoke, DRB 39/65, WCRO.
80 Apprenticeship Register, 1802, Parish of Attleborough, DR 137/20, WCRO. Among the apprentices from St Nicholas parish, Warwick, were a number to Coventry ribbon weaving and Northampton woolcombing. Apprentice Certificate Book, Parish of St Nicholas Warwick, DR115/210, WCRO.

Table 4.17 Birmingham Factory Apprentices

Firm	Location	Nature of business	Date	Girl apprentices	Boy apprentices
Dicken and Finlow	Burton	Cotton spinner	1795	16 children	?
John Peel	Burton	Cotton spinner	1795	'a number of children'	?
Joseph Peel	Fazeley	Cotton spinner	1795–	Some plus 1 girl and 1 boy reassigned from Summerseat	?
Peel, Yates and Co.	Ratcliffe Bridge	Cotton spinner	1796		16 [though 5 absconded]
Peel	Hind mill	Cotton spinner	1796	28	4
Peel	Summerseat	Cotton spinner	1796	37	9
Dicken and Finlow	Burton	Cotton spinner	1798	34	6
Bott, Bower, Birch and Co.	Nantwich	Cotton spinner	1798	'a number of children'	?
Toplis	Cuckney	Worsted spinner	1802	11	12
Bott and Co.	Tutbury	Cotton spinner	1808	21 children (all girls?) (Also 1 girl from Edgbaston parish)	?
Dicken	Alrewas	Cotton spinner and weaver	1808	34 (all girls?)	?
Jewsbury	Appleby	Cotton weaver	1808	38 children (mostly girls)	?
Jewsbury	Measham	Cotton spinner and weaver	1808	c. 30?	?
Jewsbury	Ashby	Cotton spinner and weaver	1808	large number, unstated	?
James Robinson	Papplewick	Cotton spinner	1808	23 children	?
Hancox and Wakefield	Mansfield	Cotton spinner	1808	1, reassigned from Cuckney	?
Davison and Hawksley	Arnold	Worsted spinner and weaver?	1808	2 reassigned from Cuckney	1
Jewsbury	Appleby	Cotton weaver	1813	47 [all girls?]	?
Jewsbury	Measham	Cotton spinner and weaver	1813	20 children, mostly girls	?
Jewsbury	Ashby	Cotton weaver	1813	66	3

Note: in all cases except Toplis, the numbers apply to those children who were there at that time; not the date at which sent. In some cases, for example, Jewsbury, there may be overlap and /or double counting, that is some, but probably not all those in 1813 were the same as in 1808, but cannot be sure as we do not know when the 1808 children, mostly girls, were bound.

Sources: Minute Book of the Birmingham Board of Guardians, 1783–1806. GP/B/2/1/1; Minute Book of the Birmingham Board of Guardians, 1806–24, GP/B/2/1/2. Birmingham City Archives.

Before the spread of factory production, Birmingham's large but fluctuating numbers of poor children were apprenticed mainly to the small metal trades within the parish.[81] The majority of placements were for boys, however, and from the early 1780s many of the surplus girls were taken by textile factory proprietors, initially in Lancashire but thereafter mostly within the region (see Table 4.17).[82] Factory bindings from parishes on the outskirts of Birmingham, however, were unusual. The apprenticeship indentures for St George's parish, Edgbaston, for example, indicate diverse placements. A large proportion of boys and some girls were bound to local metal trades, and during the period 1780–1820, only one girl was apprenticed to a mill outside the area: to Bott and Co., Tutbury to 'learn the art of a cotton spinner and weaver'.[83]

The Worcestershire records[84] indicate that children were apprenticed to a combination of local farmers and tradesmen within the wider region, including some textile manufacturers. Many of the 120 registered children in Ombersley, for example, were apprenticed to local farmers; but a substantial minority were bound to Kidderminster carpet weavers, and to Marshall's Shrewsbury linen factory. One child was apprenticed to a cotton spinner in Lancashire.[85] Benyon's linen factory and Kidderminster carpet weavers received a large share of the apprentices from Worcester St John parish.[86] The strength of the West Midlands trades notwithstanding, the textile factories within and outside of the region shared in the distribution of the area's parish apprentices.

The records of several parishes in the south west of England including Bristol and those in Herefordshire were examined. In Bristol 'the demand for child labour consequent upon the industrial revolution apparently made it possible for the Corporation to insist upon apprenticeship for all children above a certain age for whom relief was asked'.[87] By the end of the eighteenth century, the supply of poor children rose in line with demand for them from factory employers. Bristol

81 A premium of £5 was given to encourage good masters.
82 Minutes of the Birmingham Board of Guardians, GP/B/2/1/1, BCA. The Apprenticeship Register has not survived, so proportions cannot be ascertained.
83 Apprenticeship indentures, Parish of St George, Edgbaston, MS515/59, BCA.
84 In some registers, sadly, no trade or location is noted. This is relatively unusual but disappointing when it does occur. This was the case in Winchenford, where apprentices were listed in the Parish Book 1769–1829, 850/2253/1, Worcestershire Record Office.
85 The £4 premium for this placement was significantly greater than the £1 10s standard fee, and the 2 guineas usually paid for an apprenticeship to Marshalls. Register of Parish Apprentices, Parish of Ombersley, 850 Ombersley 3572 8ii; 3572/17/I, WRO.
86 Worcester St John Parish Register. A large proportion of Feckenham's poor children were apprenticed to the local specialism of needlemaking. Feckenham Register of Parish Apprentices. Worcestershire Record Office, 705:89 3586/12/1. From Droitwich, six children were bound to the Kidderminster carpet trade, and the rest to metal trades in and out of the area. Droitwich register of Parish Apprentices, B850 BA 839/14, WRO.
87 E.E. Butcher, *Bristol Corporation of the Poor: Selected Records, 1696–1834* (Bristol, 1932), p. 23.

children were sent, with some circumspection, to mills in Holyhead, Preston, and midlands counties during a twenty year period from 1790 (see Table 4.18).[88] In rural Herefordshire, the majority of children were put out to farmers in the same parish,[89] or to short-term local placements.[90] The only parish found to have been involved in the practice of factory apprenticing was Hereford, possibly because of the declining fortunes of glove making, formerly a major local employer. It began in 1789, relatively early, by sending 20 children to Toplis's Cuckney mill. It is unlikely that further children were not bound to textile factories but records do not exist to indicate how many more groups were sent and to where.

Table 4.18 Bristol Factory Apprentices

Firm	Location	Nature of business	Date	Girl apprentices	Boy apprentices
John Watson	Near Preston	Cotton manufacturer	c. 1795	n/a	n/a
Smalley	Holywell	Cotton spinner	1795	n/a	n/a*
Benjamin Churchill	Sheepshead, near Loughborough	Silk and cotton manufacturer	1796	10?	10?
Davison and Hawlesley	Arnold, Nottingham	Worsted and cotton manufacturer	1797 (more than one batch)	n/a	n/a
Newton	Cressbrook	Cotton manufacturer	1800?	n/a	n/a
Needham	Tideswell, Derbyshire	Cotton manufacturer	1800?	n/a	n/a

* Several groups were apparently sent to Holywell.

---

88 Butcher, *Bristol Corporation*, p. 22.

89 For example, Apprenticeship Register, Parish of Ledbury, BO 92/62 Herefordshire Record Office (HRO); Register of apprentices 1722–1822, Parish of Yarpole, S14/10–11HRO; Register of apprentices 1803–1834, Parish of Eardisland, AJ32/90, HRO; Register of Apprentices 1801–1830, Parish of Felton, G45/52, HRO. The Cuckney register identifies a number of children from Hereford, but none of the extant registers in either the township of Hereford or other parishes in the county provide confirmation of this. Although the bulk of parishes in Hereford sent their children to local masters/mistresses, this was by no means always straightforward. In Ledbury parish, for example, a significant number of masters chose to pay a fine rather than take an apprentice; and in Hope-under Dinmore, liable persons were balloted. Register of apprentices 1802–1810 (contained within the Minutes of Vestry meetings), Parish of Hope-under-Dinmore, N31/33, HRO.

90 Apprenticeship Register, Parish of Ledbury, BO 92/62; Register of Apprentices 1722–1822, Parish of Yarpole, S14/10–11; Parish Book, Parish of Stanford Bishop N5/1; Apprenticeship Records, Parish of Tarrington, K14/72; Register of Apprentices 1802–1810, Parish of Hope under Dinmore, N31/33; Parish Vestry Minute Book, Parish of Almeley, G73/3; Register of Parish Apprentices 1801–1830, Parish of Felton, G45/52; Parish Register of Apprentices 1790–1831, Parish of Burrington, G61/1; Register of Apprentices, 1803–1834, Parish of Eardisland, AJ32 /90, HRO.

Sources: The information in this table is derived with assistance from archives staff at Bristol Record Office; from E.E. Butcher, *Bristol Corporation of the Poor: Selected Records, 1696–1834* (Bristol, 1932), which constitutes the only surviving information on Bristol apprenticeships. In 1816 the Deputy Governor visited the 'several manufactories' to which the parish sent apprentices 'for some years past', which suggests that the practice continued at least until 1810 and that there may well have been other factories involved.

Because of evidence that poor girls from the area were bound to Benjamin Smart's Warwickshire cotton mill, the Oxfordshire parish records were consulted. However, the Smart connection turned out to be exceptional. According to the parish records of Witney, Oxfordshire for the period 1780 to 1812, a number of boys were apprenticed out of the parish but mainly to trades, and the majority of indentures were to local blanket weavers. Other than in 1805, when an abortive attempt was made to bind a group of Witney girls to Benjamin Smart's cotton mill in Warwickshire, no children were bound to factories.[91] The St Clement parish apprenticeship records show that the majority of the poor children[92] were apprenticed within the parish. The handful of girls sent to Smart were the result of a personal approach by the proprietor.[93]

Both direct and indirect evidence suggests that parishes on the eastern side of England participated in the parish factory apprenticeship system. Parishes in the Hull area formally apprenticed their poor children to local trades. Most boys from Sculwater parish, for example, were bound to shipbuilding and associated trades; the girls – fewer in number – mostly to domestic service. In 1814, a group of children was apprenticed to the flax spinning mill at Fewston in the Yorkshire Dales.[94] In 1836, according to Derbyshire records, nine girls were bound from Hull parish to Lorenzo Christie's Edale cotton mill. Because these children were bound outside of the stipulated 40-mile radius, it is possible that Hull parish did not formally record the arrangement. It may also have neglected to register other factory bindings, irregular or otherwise.[95] In the rural north-east, overseers bound pauper children as apprentices to craft occupations or sent them into Lancashire cotton mills.[96] In Lincoln, although the full range of bindings cannot be ascertained, children were

---

91 Apprenticeship Indentures pre-1803, Parish of Witney. Most of the 47 indentures related to the 1790s when the majority of bindings were to blanket weavers or fullers. A small number went to Rotherhithe and Southwark. Apprenticeship Indentures, 1807–1812, mostly applied to Witney blanket weavers, and a few fullers. A small number were bound out of town, for example, to Cheltenham, plaisterer; Gloucester; Clerkenwell Green, paper hanger. MS DD Par Oxford Witney, ORO.

92 Only 24 indentures were completed through the eighteenth and early nineteenth century.

93 MS DD Par. Oxford St Clements, ORO.

94 Register of Parish apprentices, 1802–1844, Parish of Sculwater, PUS411, HCA.

95 Edale mill, Castleton, prop, Lorenzo Christie. Three of the Hull children bound at that time were dead by 1840, Q/AG 20, DRO.

96 R.P. Hastings, 'Poverty and the Poor Law in the north Riding of Yorkshire, c. 1780–1837', *Borthwick Papers*, 61 (1982): 20–21; R.P. Hastings, *Essays in North Riding History 1780–1850* (Northallerton, 1981), p. 89.

apprenticed in groups from the House of Industry[97] to textile mills in the Midlands and North. In 1797, for example, 22 pauper girls and boys, with an average age of 10, were apprenticed to the 'Lancashire cotton mill at Bolton' and the employers were given £5 towards the expense of removing them.[98] Apprentice activity in Suffolk was 'determined by the vicissitudes of an agrarian county and by limited scope of occupational opportunity'.[99] Although there is evidence that parish children from Bury St Edmunds were apprenticed to Bank mill, Salford in the 1790s,[100] and it is likely that there were other groups, the records which might confirm this no longer survive.[101]

Other parishes for which indirect or partial information exists include Doncaster where the surviving evidence consists of an Overseers Memorandum book of 1794–5. This document reveals a strong desire among parish officers to apprentice a large proportion of its poor children to Davison and Hawksley cotton and worsted producers of Arnold, Nottingham, the resistance of family members notwithstanding.[102] Chatham in Kent, was not an unusually large provider of poor children for textile factories; but despite the proximity of at least one cotton factory in nearby Dartford, and other local opportunities, the parish bound groups of its children to Douglas's Pendleton factory.[103]

A traffic in children is only partly indicated by the findings of this chapter. Despite a small number of cases where it appears that factory apprentices were recorded separately, parishes did not typically distinguish between factory apprenticeship and traditional apprenticeship; or between long distance and short distance. Each indenture was executed with equivalent care. Apprenticeships in factories became more numerous as the allocation of poor children to local trades people became difficult for parish officials. Outside of London, most parishes that bound children

---

97 Which, as in other towns and cities of the time, served several parishes within the area.

98 Within a few months of their departure, an anonymous complaint about their welfare was received by the Board of Directors; but although an enquiry was ordered, no record has been preserved of any action taken on their behalf.

99 Hugh Fearn, 'The apprenticing of pauper children in the incorporated hundreds of Suffolk', *Proceedings of the Suffolk Institute of Archaeology*, 26 (1955): 92.

100 Aspin, *Water Spinners*, p. 159; Advertisement in *Manchester Chronicle*, 24 December 1796 for runaways including two who had originated from Bury St Edmunds. Information leading to their return was to be 'handsomely rewarded'.

101 Fearn, 'The apprenticing', pp. 88–92, suggests that fine income was so substantial within Suffolk parishes that there was a reluctance to apprentice children extra-parochially.

102 Overseers of the poor records, Memorandum Book of the Overseers 1794–95, Doncaster township, PL/D/1, Doncaster Archives, (DA), pp. 69–70. It seemed that the parish attempted to remove children both those in the workhouse and those on the weekly list to Davison and Hawksley. No other mill was mentioned.

103 Elizabeth Melling (ed.), *The Poor: A Collection of Examples from Original Sources in the Kent Archives Office from the Sixteenth to the Nineteenth Century* (Maidstone, 1964). Chatham parish, Kent, P85/8/3, p. 135. The Vestry meeting that agreed the visit was held on 11 April 1792.

to factory apprenticeships usually did so locally or regionally. Typically, a factory destination was viewed as just one of a number of options.[104]

On the basis of the parishes investigated for this study, the pattern of supply of parish factory apprentices described in existing texts on the subject is broadly confirmed. In terms of the numbers of children involved, a large proportion originated in the poor London parishes and was bound northwards. Some revision to the traditional version is, however, possible. Firstly the widespread distribution of parishes contributing to the movement of factory apprentices should be emphasised. Other large cities, such as Bristol, Birmingham and Liverpool were important providers of factory apprentices; but so too were smaller towns and even rural parishes. A significant proportion of the parishes examined here, even quite unexpected ones, bound some of their children to factories. In terms of the total numbers involved, the significance is less, but in terms of actual participation, hardly a county was excluded. Thus, although the total numbers of parish children involved will probably remain forever elusive, the indication that more parishes participated in the practice than previously recognised also suggests higher overall figures.

The second, connected revision relates to distance. The trade was not overwhelmingly dominated by distances of 200 miles or more. A number of groups of children, such as those bound from London to Yorkshire and the north of Lancashire, travelled those distances; but many others, even those of London origin were sent rather closer to home. The silk mills of Essex and Hertfordshire; the Middlesex flax mills; and even the lesser known cotton trade of Kent and Rickmansworth, joined the many Midlands mills in absorbing the capital's children. More importantly, despite frustrating gaps in evidence, it is possible to conclude that local parish children supplied at least some of the requirements of the majority of early textile mills. As indicated above, the nature of the local labour market influenced the numbers involved, but even where non-textile trades were buoyant, the factories recruited some of their labour through the parishes.[105] An important component of the parish factory apprentice labour, therefore, was recruited in the region if not the locality.

Thirdly, the process of factory parish apprenticeship was much more controlled than conventionally believed. The distribution of children sometimes involved large groups generating a sense of random disposal. Yet small groups and individuals, often contained within their region of birth, contributed to the overall pattern. The surviving record, disappointingly erratic as it is, nevertheless indicates the careful registering of all movements.[106] Finally, the trade in parish factory apprentices continued well after the first decade of the nineteenth century. Parishes, or other institutions caring for poor children, may have disguised the extent of this activity,

---

104 From time to time, the reluctance of local masters to accept parish children became a real problem, such periods often coinciding with a relaxing of attitudes towards cotton spinners. Problems persisted as demonstrated in the discussion of the Leeds Workhouse Committee on 12 April 1819 when it was agreed 'that the fine for refusing a parish apprentice be increased to such a sum as may remove the difficulty that is now encountered in obtaining situations for the children of paupers,' Leeds Workhouse Query Book 1803–1810, LO/Q 2. WYASL.

105 The gender distribution of this labour is discussed in Chapter 8.

106 The implications of such record keeping will be explored in Chapter 11.

but traces of its persistence can be identified. The extent to which parish apprentices contributed to individual textile enterprises and thus to the expansion of the textile industries nationwide will be considered in the next chapter.

Chapter 5

Textile Enterprise and the Parish Apprentice

Although the importance of parish apprenticeship to early textile manufacture is the subject of some debate,[1] several strands of conventional wisdom remain. For example, it is still believed that the use of parish apprentices in early textile production was confined to isolated areas; that such children were drawn from long distances; that they were directed mainly to large enterprises; that they were used only for a short period; and that they were most commonly associated with failed enterprises. Together such assumptions question the overall value of parish apprentices to individual enterprises and to the industrial economy as a whole.[2]

The previous chapters focused on the role played by the parishes in distributing apprentices to early textile factories. Yet the process of recruitment was not determined solely by parishes.[3] Interaction between firms and parishes gained momentum from the later 1780s, which enhanced the efficient distribution of parish apprentices. This chapter gauges the extent to which parish apprentices made a difference to early textile factory production. The discussion is based on the demand for parish apprentices from a selection of textile producers during the period of peak movement in apprentices. The firms, which represent the key groups of textiles, were located throughout the major textile producing counties of the early industrialising period. The discussion turns firstly to the distribution of parish apprentices to firms

---

1 Early writers on the industrial revolution assumed this importance. For example, Paul Mantoux, *The Industrial Revolution in the Eighteenth Century* (London, 1928); J.L. Hammond and Barbara Hammond, *The Town Labourer 1760–1832: The New Civilisation* (London, 1917); J.L. Hammond and Barbara Hammond, *The Skilled Labourer, 1760–1832* (London, 1919).

2 S.D. Chapman, *The Early Factory Masters: The Transition to the Factory System in the Midlands Textile Industry* (Newton Abbot, 1967), pp. 156–73; Sidney Pollard, *The Genesis of Modern Management: A Study of the Industrial Revolution in Britain* (London, 1965), pp. 191–6; James Walvin, *A Child's World: A Social History of English Childhood, 1800–1914* (Harmondsworth, 1982), pp. 61–7. See also Peter Kirby, *Child Labour in Britain, 1750–1870* (Basingstoke, 2003), pp. 71–7, although most of his discussion focuses on the 1830s and 1840s. Mary Rose believes in the importance of such labour at least in the early stages of industrialisation, and has begun to explore some of the early assumptions. Mary B. Rose, *The Gregs of Quarry Bank Mill: The Rise and Decline of a Family Firm, 1750–1914* (Cambridge, 1986), pp. 28–33 and 54–7; Mary Rose, 'Social policy and business: parish apprenticeship and the early factory system, 1750–1834', *Business History*, 21/4 (1989): 13–17.

3 Rose, 'Social policy and business', pp. 13–20.

by region and product, considering the chronology and geography of the practice. Having established the shape and extent of the employment of parish apprentices, the second part of the discussion will consider how far such labour made a difference to early industrial textile production. It will investigate the use made by individual enterprises of parish apprentices; and it will explore the traditional assumptions that larger enterprises and those most likely to fail made particular use of parish apprentices.

Table 5.1 indicates the known number of parish apprentices bound to each of the firms selected for this study, during the period *c.* 1785 and 1815. Further detail about the origin of apprentices is provided in the Appendix. In almost all cases, because of data limitations, the figures presented understate the true extent of parish apprentices. No attempt has been made to estimate or to rectify the shortfall; but it is hoped that further research will fill some of the remaining gaps.

Table 5.1 The Distribution of Parish Apprentices in Early Textile Production

Firm	Location	Nature of business	No. of parish apprentices (known or best estimate)
Akers and Beever	Salford, Lancashire	Cotton spinner	*c.* 200
George Andrew	Stockport, Cheshire	Calico printer	9
Thomas Andrew	Harpurhey, Lancashire	Calico printer	5
Samuel Ashton	Middleton, Lancashire	Cotton manufacturer	78
Atherton and Harrison	Chipping, Lancashire	Cotton manufacturer	9
John Birch	Backbarrow, Lancashire	Cotton spinner	256
Benyon and Co.	Shrewsbury, Salop	Linen manufacturer	15
Bott, Bower and Co.	Nantwich, Cheshire	Cotton spinner	41
John Bott	Tutbury, Staffordshire	Cotton spinner	108
Brosser	Macclesfield, Cheshire	Cotton manufacturer	8
Jeremiah Bury	Stockport, Cheshire	Cotton manufacturer	64
Calrow	Bury, Lancashire	Cotton manufacturer	6
Benjamin Churchill	Loughborough, Leicestershire	Silk and cotton manufacturer	40
Benjamin Clegg	Oldham, Lancashire	Cotton spinner	*c.* 50
Cooper and Matchett	Tissington, Derbyshire	Cotton spinner	*c.* 12
Cowpe, Hollins, Oldknow	Mansfield, Nottinghamshire	Cotton spinner	17
Cresswell	Edale, Derbyshire	Cotton manufacturer	44
Davison and Hawksley	Arnold, Nottinghamshire	Worsted manufacturer	262
Dicken and Finlow	Burton, Staffordshire	Cotton manufacturer	66

Douglas	Holywell, Flintshire	Cotton spinner	98+
Douglas	Pendleton, Lancashire	Cotton spinner	151+
Fowler	Tamworth, Staffordshire	Cotton manufacturer	5
Jeremiah Garnett	Clitheroe, Lancashire	Cotton manufacturer	22
William Garth	Colne, Lancashire	Cotton manufacturer	12
John Gorton	Bury, Lancashire	Cotton spinner	38
Gorton and Thompson	Cuckney, Nottinghamshire	Cotton spinner	32
Samuel Greg	Styal, Cheshire	Cotton spinner	150
John Haigh	Marsden, Yorks	Cotton manufacturer	101
Charles Harding	Tamworth, Staffordshire	Cotton spinner	39
Hardnumm, Norris and Co.	Bury, Lancashire	Cotton spinner	23
Harrison and Leyland	Euxton, Lancashire	Cotton twist manufacturer	40
Thomas Haslam	Bury, Lancashire	Cotton spinner	40
Haywood and Palfreyman	Macclesfield, Cheshire	Linen manufacturer	73
John Head	Masham, Yorks	Worsted manufacturer	16
R & G Hodgkinson	Worksop, Nottinghamshire	Cotton weaver	29
Isaac Hodgson	Lancaster, Lancashire	Cotton spinner	105
David Holt	Manchester, Lancashire	Cotton spinner	67+
John Edward Hudson	Gauxholme, Lancashire	Cotton spinner	29
Joseph Hulse	Shirland, Derbyshire	Cotton weaver	4
Thomas Jewsbury	Measham, Derbyshire	Cotton/calico spinner and weaver	230
Lambert	Lowdham, Nottinghamshire	Cotton/hosiery	41
Marshall, Hutton and Hives	Shrewsbury, Salop	Linen manufacturer	82
Marsland and Kelsall	Glossop, Derbyshire	Cotton manufacturer	14
Nathaniel Mason	Iver, Bucks	Cotton spinner	15
George Merryweather	Otley, Yorks	Cotton spinner	210
George Merryweather	Manchester, Lancashire	Cotton weaver	90
Monteith, Bogle	Glasgow	Cotton manufacturer	54
John Morley	Chingford, Essex	Silk manufacturer	18
Ellis Needham	Tideswell, Derbyshire	Cotton manufacturer	95

Newton	Cressbrook, Derbyshire	Cotton manufacturer	300+ (including after 1820)
Samuel Oldknow	Mellor, Derbyshire	Cotton spinner	100+
James Pattison	Congleton, Cheshire	Silk manufacturer	93
Joseph Peel	Tamworth, Staffordshire	Cotton manufacturer	63+
Robert Peel	Summerseat, Lancashire	Cotton spinner	47+
Robert Peel	Radcliffe Bridge, Lancashire	Cotton spinner	37+
Robert Peel	Bury, Lancashire	Cotton spinner	42+
Robert Peel	Bury Lancashire	Cotton spinner	102+
Robinson	Papplewick, Nottinghamshire	Cotton manufacturer	23
Sewell and McMurdo	Hounslow Heath, Mddx	Flax spinner	31
Shute, Thomas Rock	Watford, Herts	Silk throwster	10
John and William Singleton	Wigan, Lancashire	Cotton spinner	6
Benjamin Smart	Milverton, Warwks	Cotton spinner	28
Strutt	Rickmansworth, Herts	Cotton manufacturer	23
Toplis	Cuckney, Nottinghamshire	Worsted manufacturer	762
Walton Twist	Walton-le-Dale, Lancashire	Cotton manufacturer	80
John Watson	Preston, Lancashire	Cotton manufacturer	143
Thomas Watson	Watford, Herts	Silk manufacturer	10
John Weir	Wokingham Berks	Silk manufacturer	17
Wells, Middleton	Sheffield, Yorks	Cotton spinner	100
John Whitaker	Burley, Yorks	Cotton spinner	200
James Whitelegg	Manchester, Lancashire	Cotton weaver	6
Charles Woollan	Hertford, Herts	Silk throwster	11
Woolley and McQueen	Matlock, Derbyshire	Cotton spinner	7
Workman, Brummel and Hall	Dartford, Kent	Cotton spinner	18
Thomas Yates	Tamworth, Staffordshire	Cotton spinner and weaver	17

Sources: see Appendix.

The mills selected for this study broadly reflect the overall pattern of product and place. The majority (75 per cent) of firms considered here produced cotton yarn;

some additionally wove cloth. Seven of the enterprises produced silk; five were flax spinners and three produced worsted yarn and/or cloth. Between them a range of organisational forms was represented.[4] In terms of geographical location, the 'northern' mills, consisting of those located in Lancashire, Yorkshire and Cheshire, accounted for 50 per cent (37) of the total. Those in the Midlands counties of Derbyshire, Leicestershire, Nottinghamshire, Shropshire, Staffordshire and Warwickshire comprised a further 35 per cent (26). Nine enterprises were located in the 'south' and one each in Scotland and Wales.

Each of the enterprises made use of parish apprentices. For some, such labour was partial and temporary. For others, poor children formed the bulk of the labour force for 30 years or more. The variation in dependence can be attributed to the nature of the local labour market, specifically the availability of local child labour, and competition for such labour. This supports conventional wisdom that the more isolated the factory or mill, the greater the likelihood that parish apprentices would provide at least part of the labour force. But this was not the only determinant. Others will be explored below.

The quantitative dominance of a small number of London parishes in the longer distance trade is unmistakeable. Awareness of the importance of the capital's poor children to the early industrial labour market has, however, led to the neglect of the contribution of other areas. The supply of parish apprentices was discussed in the previous chapter. The demands of the early textile mills, equally important to the geographical distribution of such labour, will be discussed here. In their search for labour, entrepreneurs considered its price and quality as well as its availability. Although a small number of parishes indicated a preference for long-distance binding, mainly for long-term financial reasons connected with settlement, the gains for employers from such a practice were less tangible. It is possible that apprentices whose birth parish was at a distance were less likely to abscond; that distant parishes were less likely to interfere with factory practice; and that employers were attracted by the larger group-size available from parishes in London and other big cities. A minority of firms among those selected here were explicitly drawn by such benefits, which in any case were offset by the cost of transportation, correspondence and agents; and the more difficult and extended negotiation between parish and firm. Evidence suggests that the majority of firms took apprentices from a long distance only when closer sources proved unreliable or insufficient, or when respondents to their advertised labour requirements were distant parishes. Because the relationship between parish and firm often continued for many years, an initial long-distance binding might generate long term practice.[5]

---

4   All were described as factories but varied in terms of scale and capital intensity. For more discussion of diversity of organisational forms within the textile industry, see Maxine Berg, 'Factories, workshops and industrial organisation', in Roderick Floud and Donald McCloskey (eds), *The Economic History of Britain since 1700*, vol. 1, 1700–1860 (2nd edn, Cambridge, 1994), pp. 123–36.

5   This was the case between the parish of St Clement Danes and John Birch, Backbarrow; and St Luke, Chelsea to Douglas and Davison and Hawksley, for example. St Luke Chelsea Workhouse Apprenticeship Register 1791–1802 P74/LUK/116; St Luke Chelsea Apprenticeship Register 1802–1813 P74/LUK/117; St Luke Chelsea Poor Relief

The mills in the north of England, and the one in north Wales, were more likely than those in the Midlands to draw upon distant sources of labour, usually as a supplement to, not instead of, local children. In parts of the northern textile region, local parish apprentices and 'free' children[6] comprised the bulk of textile workers. This was particularly the case in Halifax, Keighley, Manchester and surrounding towns and villages, where labour market conditions reduced factories' wholesale dependence on parish children. Elsewhere large groups of parish children from London and other large cities, including Liverpool, Birmingham, and Bristol, were more important to the expansion and survival of early textile businesses.[7] As suggested by conventional wisdom, these included isolated water mills, but were not confined to this type. John Birch's Backbarrow factory provides an example of a rural mill, distant from population centres, whose labour for nearly twenty years came from a single London parish – St Clement Danes – supplemented by a handful of local 'free' children. The Holywell Twist company employed 400 apprentices, mainly from Liverpool, Bristol and the South, among its employees who also included outworkers from neighbouring parishes.[8] Similarly Haigh's modest-sized mill in the Pennine village of Marsden, depended entirely on London and Essex parish children; and Colbeck's flax mill in the Yorkshire Dales village of Fewston, drew apprentice workers from Hull and London.

Not all rural mills were 'isolated'.[9] Merryweather and Whitaker's Burley-in-Wharfedale mill, for example, whose labour force from the outset consisted of parish apprentices from within the region as well as various London parishes, was located a short distance from Otley and only several miles from Leeds. Haywood and Palfreyman's Wildboar Clough enterprise was close to Macclesfield; James Pattison's silk mill in Congleton had access to local labour; and even Greg's Styal mill was situated within walking distance of a supply of parish apprentices. However, because none of these locations was supplied bountifully with parish or free children, additional, more distant, sources were sought.

Other mills selected for this study were located in or very close to substantial population centres, but where competition for young workers was fierce. Bank mill, Salford, Holt and Mitchell, Chorlton, and Douglas, Pendleton, all water spinners, were, despite their urban base, voracious users of parish apprentice labour. Akers and Beever, proprietors of Bank mill brought apprentices from Liverpool, Bury St Edmunds and Gosport; William Douglas's Pendleton factory was supplied mainly from London but also from Chelmsford and Chatham; and David Holt focused his

---

Book 1806–1810 P74/LUK/019, LMA; St Clement Danes Apprenticeship Records 1784–1792. B1266; St Clement Danes Apprenticeship Records 1784–1801. B1267; St Clement Danes Vestry Minutes: 1782–1790 B1072, 1791–1797 B1073, 1797–1805 B1074, 1805–1814 B1075, WAC.

6   Commonly more of the latter than the former.

7   It is possible that the 1784 decision by Manchester magistrates to forbid factory apprenticeships was rigorously imposed.

8   Established by John Smalley and subsequently run by his son Christopher and partners including John Douglas by whose name the firm was commonly known. A.H. Dodd, *The Industrial Revolution in North Wales* (Cardiff, 1951), pp. 284–5.

9   Many rural factories have been erroneously described as such.

search on London to supplement local supplies of 'free' labour. The Peel family's mills in Bury and surrounding districts depended almost entirely on parish labour from London, Liverpool and Birmingham.[10] Several other Bury mills including those belonging to Thomas Haslam, and John Gorton employed London apprentices, as did mills in Stockport, including Jeremiah Bury's. The early cotton mills in Preston and Lancaster supplemented London sources of parish children with those from other cities. John Watson, for example, drew additionally on Liverpool, as did Isaac Hodgson, whose apprentices also came from Bristol. Samuel Ashton's successful Middleton mill used mostly parish apprentices from London. The sole Sheffield cotton factory, run by London merchants Wells and Middleton, depended throughout its existence on the apprentice labour of London parishes, moving from one to another as its poor reputation spread and supply contracted. Most of the remaining northern mills in the study were of modest scale with comparably modest appetite for parish apprentices. These included James Whitelegg, William Garth and John and William Singleton.

The discussion above has shown that although a large proportion of the London parishes which engaged in the transfer of factory apprentices bound children to the North, factories in that region diversified their supply and supplemented the London children with parish apprentices from other large towns. With only a few exceptions, London was just one of several sources.

The majority of mills in the Midlands' counties, drew more extensively on parishes within the region than those at a distance for their supply of children workers. The only firm for which complete evidence survives is William and John Toplis and Co., worsted spinner and weaver of Cuckney, near Mansfield in Nottinghamshire. Its labour force consisted almost entirely of parish apprentices. No local 'free' children were recorded. A small number of adults were appointed as overlookers. During the early years of gentle expansion, 1786–8, the business obtained the bulk of its apprentice labour from neighbouring Mansfield, elsewhere in Nottinghamshire or occasionally from Derbyshire. The following two years witnessed both accelerating growth and a wider geographical search for child workers. Parishes in Essex, and in north and east London augmented local supplies, and from 1792 to 1794 – the years of fastest growth – the metropolis provided the bulk of new labour. The towns of Birmingham, Bristol and Hereford provided a useful supplement; and the region's poor children a consistent trickle. A total of 57 parishes provided 762 apprentices for Toplis in the space of eighteen years. The apprenticeship register of Toplis is unique, and for no other firm, except perhaps Greg, is it possible to reconstruct the apprentice body with such confidence. However, there is no compelling reason to suppose that the firm was unique in the size and diversity of its parish apprentice labour, and elements of its practice were undoubtedly replicated elsewhere.

---

10   Because, he later alleged, there was none other that he could get. SC1816. The wage book of Peel's Burrs mill in Bury covering the period 1800 to 1803 indicates only a small number of paid workers, suggesting that the majority of its workforce consisted of parish apprentices. Frances Collier, *The Family Economy of the Working Classes in the Cotton Industry 1784–1833* (Manchester, 1964), pp. 29–31.

Other firms in the region also depended heavily on apprentice labour. Typically, the greater the requirement of parish apprentices the more widespread the search. Although only partial evidence survives for the Nottingham cotton and worsted firm of Davison and Hawksley, for example, its expansion was facilitated by parish apprentices. About 50 were reassigned to the business following Toplis's failure; and substantial groups came from London parishes, from Birmingham and Bristol, and smaller numbers from nearby Doncaster and Nottinghamshire villages.[11] It is also the case that parish children from the locality were employed, but not formally as apprentices. This could well have been a widespread phenomenon that seriously understates the use of parish children in the early industrial labour force.[12] Robinson's Papplewick cotton spinning enterprise employed parish apprentices from St Marylebone in London and Birmingham as well as local free and parish children. Cowpe, Hollins and Oldknow of Pleasley mill drew on local parishes in addition to those in London.

The Derbyshire cotton spinning enterprises of Newton at Cressbrook, and Cooper and Matchett at Tissington illustrate a similar pattern of parish apprentice recruitment to that described above. The long-term success of both firms was founded on the profitable use of locally recruited parish apprentices before the partners diversified their search to London and other large cities. From 1820, the sources of institutional child labour changed. While Liverpool provided both mills with parish apprentices, Newton's Cressbrook mill drew additionally on the Royal Military Asylum (RMA), and Cooper and Matchett on Leicester. Local parishes continued to provide. Wooley and McQueen employed small numbers of apprentices from the local parish of Winster as well as 'free' local children at their cotton spinning mill. Hulse's cotton weaving enterprise also used local parish children. Thomas Jewsbury, cotton and calico spinner and weaver of Measham in Derbyshire, satisfied a significant proportion of its labour requirements from the Birmingham workhouse, and smaller groups from both urban and rural parishes in Derbyshire, Nottinghamshire and Warwickshire. It appears from the formal record that Benjamin Churchill's unusually located cotton and silk enterprise near Loughborough depended on poor children from London and Bristol, but it is likely that local child labour was used too.

---

11   The destruction of Bristol records precludes precise quantification of its apprentices to Davison and Hawksley, although we know from a study completed while the relevant sources still existed, that more than one group was sent there from the city. E.E. Butcher, *Bristol Corporation of the Poor: Select Records, 1696–1834* (Bristol, 1932), p. 22. Indirect evidence, such as 'Mental recreation' by William Stumbles, 1875, for example, suggest that the firm's young workers emanated mainly from London and Bristol. DD 568/30, NA. Although the apprenticeship register for Arnold does not indicate the binding of children to its local factory, workhouse accounts show adults and children employed by the factory. Chapman, *The Early Factory Masters*, p. 184.

12   There is evidence that most of the pauper children employed at the Evans cotton mill at Darley Abbey in Derbyshire were not formally apprenticed. There is no reason to suppose that this was an unusual occurrence. Jean Lindsay, 'An early industrial community: The Evans cotton mill at Darley Abbey, Derbyshire, 1783–1810', *Business History Review*, 34/5 (1960), pp. 295–6.

The Warwickshire cotton spinning business of Benjamin Smart depended almost entirely on female parish apprentices for its workforce. Its initial supply came from a 30-mile radius of the mill, mostly Warwickshire and Oxfordshire villages or small towns; and only much later were two groups of girls brought from London. Surprisingly, Birmingham was not one of Smart's sources, yet the town's surplus of poor girls supplied a number of other textile mills in the region. Several modest-sized cotton spinning enterprises in Tamworth, those of Joseph Peel, Charles Harding and Messrs Fowler acquired a large proportion of their apprentice labour from neighbouring parishes in Warwickshire. Birmingham provided apprentices for the Tutbury and Nantwich enterprises of John Bott and Co., the former additionally drawing poor children from Coventry and London. The smaller cotton spinning mill of Dicken and Finlow mainly used Birmingham apprentices. In so far as it has been possible to trace the origins of apprentices bound to the Shrewsbury linen factories of Marshall Hutton and Hives, and Benyon and Benyon, it appears that the majority originated from the town's workhouse, with a handful more from surrounding rural parishes, and a number from Hull.[13]

Several midlands mills demonstrated variations to the usual pattern. The notorious Litton mill run by Ellis Needham was unusual in making little recorded use of local apprentices. In addition to groups from several London parishes, Needham also 'adopted' numbers of parish apprentices from Lambert's local failed enterprise, who themselves had originated in London.[14] A preference for London children was also demonstrated at Cresswell's Castleton enterprise, which formed a long-term bond with Lambeth parish. Toplis's neighbour in Cuckney, Gorton and Thompson, formed a close relationship with St James, Piccadilly, setting up a workhouse enterprise in the Westminster parish and drawing upon the supply of poor St James children for its Nottinghamshire factory. Samuel Oldknow's pattern of recruitment was unusual, using private institutions more than parishes. A group of children was recruited from St Pancras parish;[15] but the majority of apprentices, who supplemented local 'free' children, came initially from the Foundling Hospital and, after 1820, like the other successful Derbyshire cotton mills, from the RMA at Chelsea and Southampton. The majority of midlands firms therefore avoided the London parishes at least initially, and drew upon parishes within the region as far as possible.

Textile mills in the south of England, like those elsewhere in the country, depended on parish apprentice labour, most of which was drawn from the metropolis. Unsurprisingly, there was no reverse movement of children from north to south. The

---

13 The Hull children are mentioned in Arthur Redford, *Labour Migration in England 1800–1850* (Manchester, 1964), p. 27, who refers to a Shrewsbury cotton mill. As the linen factories were the only mills in the town, one of these must have been their destination.

14 Some of these, including Robert Blincoe, had originated in St Pancras, which sent a group of eight children to Litton in December 1815, shortly before the 40-mile restriction was imposed. Report of 18 June 1816, Minutes of Directors of the Poor, Parish of St Pancras, P/PN/PO/1/12 (microfilm reference UTAH 652) CLSAC.

15 By coincidence, Robert Blincoe arrived at Mellor seeking work, just as officials from his birth parish were completing the handover of this group. John Brown, *A Memoir of Robert Blincoe* (Manchester, 1832), p. 82; John Waller, *The Real Oliver Twist: Robert Blincoe: A Life That Illuminates an Age* (Cambridge, 2005), pp. 207–208.

silk mills of Essex used the county's poor children as well as those from London, as Morley's Chingford mill illustrates.[16] Hertfordshire and Berkshire silk mills drew on London, especially such parishes as St Barts the Great and St Sepulchre, which otherwise did not participate in the factory apprenticeship system.[17] The cotton mills of Hertfordshire, Kent and Buckinghamshire used children from London and Surrey. St James Piccadilly was the main supplier of Strutt's Rickmansworth mill.[18] Both Mason's Iver mill and Workman and Co.'s Dartford factory focused on Lambeth parish for their supply of apprentices. It is likely that Chatham parish, which bound children to Lancashire cotton mills, also sent apprentices to the Dartford mill and others in the county. The large Hounslow flax mill employed apprentices from at least three London parishes, each of which were enthusiastic participants in factory apprenticeship more widely.[19]

Table 5.2 Chronology of Factory Parish Apprenticeship

Date	No. of firms taking apprentices	Total no. of apprentices
1784	1	?
1786	3	53
1787	5	97
1788	2	61
1789	6	90
1790	11	163
1791	6	107
1792	6	186
1793	7	71
1794	4	153
1795	12	302
1796	16	267
1797	9	158
1798	7	142
1799	10	143
1800	16	238

16 Courtauld's Braintree factory requested and received children from Islington, a parish that was generally averse to factory apprenticeship. Trustees of the Poor Minutes, 2 December 1813, ILHL.

17 It is assumed that such parishes found the shorter distance placements more justifiable than those to factories further afield.

18 The only Arkwright type mill in the South. Chris Aspin, *The Water Spinners* (Helmshore, 2003).

19 These included St Pancras parish, which continued to bind children there after 1816. A number were sent in the spring of 1818. 6 January 1818, 19 May 1818, 9 June 1818, 28 July 1818 Minutes of Directors of the Poor, Parish of St Pancras P/PN/PO/15 (microfilm reference UTAH 653).

1801	10	139
1802	15	230
1803	13	186
1804	5	43
1805	15	366*
1806	9	94
1807	12	131
1808	8	114
1809	7	82
1810	9	62
1811	5	31
1812	6	19
1813	4	77
1814	12	143
1815	7	54
1816	7	30
1817	1	1
1818	1	21
1819	1	40
Total		**4414**

*about 60 of these were known reassignments. Reassignment was a common enough feature but evidence is insufficiently reliable or consistent to draw confident conclusions.
Source: see Appendix.

Table 5.2 demonstrates the chronology of factory apprentice bindings taken from the selection of parishes and firms in this study. The outcome is not the normal distribution implied by traditional accounts, which suggests numbers rising to a peak in the 1790s followed by continuous decline. The pattern is a fluctuating one. Some of the vacillation can be attributed to data deficiency; the remainder to variation in supply of as well as demand for poor children. Beneath the fluctuations however, it can be seen that activity was sustained, if weakly, until 1816, and even beyond. This provides at least some challenge to accounts that emphasise the short duration of parish apprentice usage, and specifically that the practice had passed its maximum level by 1800.

A range of sources indicate that parish children provided a vital kick-start to enterprises that otherwise would either not have been established or whose subsequent growth would have been constrained.[20] It is traditionally believed that most participating firms used parish apprentices only in the initial stages of

---

20 Peel stated to the 1816 Select Committee that this was the case with his own business. It is clear from the statistics that it applied to other businesses. Backbarrow, for example, recruited the bulk of its initial labour force from St Clement Danes. See Appendix; Table 4.1; and St Clement Danes Apprenticeship Records 1784–1801, B1267, WAC.

production, relying subsequently on expanding local supplies of 'free' labour, some of which was produced by the first generation of parish apprentices. Several firms in this study clearly followed this practice;[21] while others treated parish apprentices as expendable, replacing those at the end of their term with fresh supplies.[22] A number of enterprises, of which Greg's Styal mill and Newton's Cressbrook are examples, fit somewhere in between. They gradually built up local supplies of child labour, but depended for many decades on parish apprentices for part of their requirement. Turnover of parish apprentices, together with the regular emergence of new firms and the expansion of others, ensured some continuity in demand until late in the Napoleonic Wars. It also explains why, as Table 5.2 suggests, the practice of parish factory apprenticeship was quite buoyant for about 30 years.

Apprenticeship arrangements continued beyond 1816, despite the act of that year, but were not always formally recorded.[23] Aggregate officially registered children had fallen yet the number of firms involved and even the quantity of parishes was well-sustained. Several parishes including Hull, Edinburgh, Liverpool, Leicester[24] and at least two in Southwark, for example, engaged in the factory apprenticeship system until the 1820s and beyond.[25] This casts some doubt both on the notion that firms no longer found parish children of value, and on the argument that parishes had become ideologically ill-disposed to factory apprenticing. As will be argued in a later chapter, many parishes had expressed reservations about factory bindings from an early date, but such concerns did not always prevent engagement in the factory apprenticeship system.[26] Textile factories, of all sizes and types,[27] continued to seek what appeared to them to be cost-effective labour. The demand for institutional apprentices persisted to a greater extent than was previously believed; even if the sources of supply had altered. The supply of poor parish children in any case fluctuated during most of the 30 years in question, but appeared to decline after 1820.[28]

---

21 For example, Merryweather and Whitaker.

22 The Backbarrow mill was an example of this practice.

23 For example, parish children from Hull were apprenticed to Lorenzo Christie, according to the business record. There is no evidence from this in the parish documents.

24 Greg Apprentice Indentures, 1815–37, show the participation of Liverpool, which also sent children to parts of Derbyshire. Greg records, C5/5/3/1–125, MCA.

25 And Leeds, for example, apprenticed children to Oldham which may have been outside of the 40-mile limit, through the 1820s. Leeds Workhouse Committee Minutes and order book 1818–23 LO/M/6.

26 St Clement Danes and Birmingham provide examples of such inconsistency. 12 September 1797, Minutes of Churchwardens, Overseers and Assistants, Parish of St Clement Danes, B1147, WAC; 14 September 1802, Minutes of Churchwardens, Overseers and Assistants, Parish of St Clement Danes, B1148, WAC; 2 June 1818, 29 October 1822, Minutes of Birmingham Board of Guardians, GP/B/2/1/2, BCA.

27 Mostly, but not exclusively, water powered.

28 Those parishes for which apprenticeship registers survive, indicate a decline in the total number of bindings. That is, the decline in numbers sent to factories was not being compensated for elsewhere. The decline in numbers to factories, therefore, was an indication of declining supply, or less likely, a change in record-keeping practices.

Children in the care of parishes were replaced by those supported by other institutions, in providing a youthful factory labour force. For much of the eighteenth century, the Foundling Hospital had led the way in directing large numbers of orphan children to expanding areas of manufacturing activity,[29] and organised the distribution of many groups to textile factories around the country.[30] It was also among the first to curtail the practice.[31] Other institutions, however, provided children for textile factories, among which the RMA, based in Chelsea and Southampton, was the most important. Established midway through the Napoleonic Wars, it sustained the children of dead or serving soldiers; and for those who were not reclaimed by parents, gender-specific apprenticeship was common. Boy children were typically sent to the Navy, while girls were bound to domestic service or to textile factories. The end of the war and legislative change provided ideal conditions for a trade in female apprentices between the RMA and textile factories with an established girl preference seeking a means of evading the 1816 Act. Among the main beneficiaries were Oldknow, Newton, and later Lorenzo Christie at Cressbrook, who also found children from parishes apparently impervious to the 40-mile restriction of the Act.[32] Greg continued to make use of parish apprentices until the later 1840s when rising costs of maintaining such children rendered the practice no longer viable for the firm.[33]

Parish authorities sought industrial outlets for their charges, and industrialists sought parish apprentices, through the remainder of the nineteenth century. In late 1844, for example, 'the Leicester Board of Guardians received an offer from a Mr Chambers, the owner of a cotton mill at Mayfield, just outside Ashbourne on the border between Derbyshire and Staffordshire. He was looking for 'girls to train as doublers ... and would provide them with food, lodging and clothing for three

---

29 Rose, 'Social policy and business', pp. 8–12; R.K. McClure, *Coram's Children: The London Foundling Hospital in the Eighteenth Century* (New Haven, 1981), p. 132.

30 Oldknow and Toplis were important among the recipients. The Foundling Hospital provided a model for structures of protection of apprentices, especially those bound to a distance.

31 This was partly because it was more sensitive than many parishes to the potential abuses of the factory apprenticeship system; but also because, by the early years of the nineteenth century, it had cleared its backlog of surplus children. Information from Alysa Levene.

32 The Act of 1816 applied specifically, but not exclusively to London. For parishes outside a 40-mile radius of London, the limit could be exceeded with special dispensation by the magistrates. The spirit of the law, however, was that the movement of parish children to a distance was to be strongly discouraged. Liverpool during the 1820s and beyond; Both Hull and Edinburgh sent children to Cressbrook during the 1830s; and Leicester as late as 1850.

33 Collier, *The Family Economy*, p. 46. The Greg enterprise also made use of poor families who migrated from the south of England under a Poor Law scheme of 1835. Rose, *Gregs*, pp. 76–77. Greg was one of the few northern manufacturers who made use of such labour. The number of paupers who eventually moved north was small. John Knott, *Popular Opposition to the 1834 Poor Law* (London, 1986), pp. 253–4. Just like many parish apprentices, they had been persuaded by false promises. Mills in Derby and Stockport also sought labour under the scheme. Samuel Kydd ('Alfred'), *The History of the Factory Movement from the Year 1802, to the Enactment of the 10 hours Bill in 1847* (2 vols, London, 1857), vol. 2, p. 70.

years'.³⁴ The Guardians were apparently keen to comply, but were not permitted to make a formal apprenticeship arrangement, because of the settlement implications. The local Board of Guardians went ahead notwithstanding the opposition of the Poor Law Commissioners. The arrangement appeared to work well and continued to about 1859. Girls were sent at intervals both to Mayfield and to the neighbouring Hanging Bridge mill owned by a Mr Cooper. In 1853, the Board of Guardians of Leicester informed the Ashby de la Zouch union that, 'all the girls we have sent have turned out exceedingly well, and they were treated in the kindest manner and provided for most comfortably'.³⁵ This demonstrated continuity of care by the Guardians, who remained concerned for the welfare of their children.

Two late nineteenth-century cases demonstrate the longevity of the practice. The textile firm of I & C Calvert, of Luddenden Dean in the Calder Valley, apparently facing a severe labour shortage, brought 100 children from Liverpool during the 1880s and 1890s, in what is described locally as a 'tragic tale'. The children, orphans drawn from the Industrial Schools, boarded in the equivalent of an apprentice house,³⁶ and received no wages. All the children, except one, were girls, and the majority remained at the mill as adults. Interviewed by the local press in 1966, former Director and Company Secretary, Mr William Henry Murgatroyd, who had worked in the mill 60 years earlier and knew many of the girls, stated: 'bringing them from Liverpool did good to both sides. They got a new start in life and the firm kept production going'.³⁷ In all respects, this resembled the parish factory apprenticeship system instigated over a century earlier. The second example involved groups of children brought from the Hull workhouse to work in the Halifax factory of J. Akroyd in 1884. The pauper apprenticeship nature of the arrangement was disguised by the euphemistic description of the children as 'young mill workers to be trained by the firm', but their experience, as with those at Luddenden Dean, resembled that of much earlier generations of factory apprentices. The agreement between the mill proprietor and the Hull Guardians included clauses to 'provide the said children with sufficient and proper food ... clothing, medical attendance', and to train them in 'truthfulness, obedience, personal cleanliness and industry as well as the said business of spinners'.³⁸

Having established that the practice of parish factory apprenticeship was widespread, and, for a number of decades, substantial, the discussion now turns to the significance of the practice. The existence of parish apprentices within the labour force of an enterprise does not by itself demonstrate the importance of such workers. Where it has been possible to estimate the proportion of parish apprentices in the total workforce in the firms considered for this study, this is indicated in Table 5.3.

---

34 Kathryn M Thompson, 'Apprenticeship and the New Poor Law: a Leicester example', *The Local Historian*, 19 (1989): 55.

35 Thompson, 'Apprenticeship', p. 55.

36 Apparently, they were known as hostels: rows of two or three cottages knocked together. Issy Shannon, 'The orphans of Luddenden Dean', *Milltown Memories* (Summer 2005): 11.

37 Shannon, 'The orphans of Luddenden Dean', pp. 11–12.

38 Agreement reproduced in Janet Burns, 'The West Riding half-timer', *Old West Riding*, 9 (1989): 25.

Table 5.3 The Estimated Proportion of Parish Apprentices in a Sample of Textile Factories

Firm	Date	No. of parish apprentices	No. of 'free' children	Estimated no. of employees	Percentage of parish apprentices in total
Samuel Ashton	1803	110 + 4 servants		115*	95
John Birch, Backbarrow	1797	210	50?	310?	70
Jeremiah Bury, Stockport	1790	200	50	300	67
Clayton and Walshman, Keighley		20	90	180	12
Cowpe, Hollins, Oldknow	1802	55	5?	60	90
Davidson and Hawksley	1800	60* 280 (1805: kh)	?	600?	50
Douglas, Holywell	1796	300	30	380	80
Gorton, Bury				48*	
Samuel Greg, Styal	1790	150?	?	205 (mostly apps?)*	
Haigh, Marsden	1802	90		100	90
Hodgson, Caton				137 (1818)*	
Hollins and Co., Pleasley	1802	60*		240*	25
Merryweather and Whitaker	1802	260	20	300	87
Needham, Litton	1802				
Toplis	1804	600	0	600 (plus a handful of overlookers)	99
Walton Twist Co	1819 (H of L)	80*		175*	
Wells, Middleton, Sheffield	1802	150 (mostly non local)	10	180	85

*Mary B. Rose, 'Social policy and business: parish apprenticeship and the early factory system, 1750–1834', *Business History*, 30 April 1989.

Sources: see Appendix.

It is often asserted that most parish apprentices were dispatched to the larger enterprises.[39] Because labour requirements of larger enterprises often exceeded local supply, especially in rural areas, some in-migration was inevitable. In the early stages of textile factory production, parish apprentices formed the most flexible component of the labour market and facilitated such inward movement of people. Small as well as large firms made variable use of parish apprentices. The input of such children permitted the rapid initial expansion of many of the largest textile enterprises of the early industrialising period. The limited appetite of smaller enterprises for parish apprentices meant that they were less likely to require 'batches' of poor children. Nevertheless they did contribute to the overall demand. Although small numbers were more feasibly obtained locally, they were sometimes transported from further afield. Small groups of children would be lodged with local families or landladies obviating the need for additional apprentice housing.[40]

Table 5.3 indicates the varied scale of factories making use of parish apprentices. The data is disappointingly sparse, and generalisation impossible. Yet it appears that parish apprentices were used, to different degrees, in a range of factory types. Among those using the most, where the proportion of total labour was also high, were Toplis and Co, John Birch, Davison and Hawksley, Merryweather and Whitaker, Wells and Middleton, Douglas, Samuel Greg and Samuel Oldknow. Of more moderate size but still using a large proportion of parish apprentices were Messrs Haigh, Samuel Ashton, Isaac Hodgson and Cowpe, Hollins and Oldknow. The smaller firms included William Calrow, Joseph Hulse, John and William Singleton and James Whitelegg. Among firms where the estimated total of parish apprentices was 50 per cent or less was Hollins and Co., at Pleasley mill. The smaller proportion does not mean that parish apprentices were necessarily of marginal importance; indeed they may have played a crucial role in the expansion or survival of the firm.

The association of zealous employment of parish apprentices and enterprise failure has often been assumed. This section will assess the evidence for this alleged relationship, and argues that the prevalence of bankruptcy during the period in which parish apprentices were used does not confirm a causal relationship. Business failure was a feature of competitive capitalism; and was also more likely during the early, experimental, period of technical and organisational change, when risks were greatest. Textile businesses suffered vagaries of trade in the middle years of the Napoleonic Wars. The firms in this study operated in a climate of economic uncertainty and, therefore, were particularly vulnerable to contraction or collapse. Evidence has not survived for all firms in this study, but that which exists indicates that while some, as predicted, succumbed in the years between 1805 and 1808, the majority enjoyed

---

39   For example, Joanna Innes, 'Origins of the factory acts: the Health and Morals of Apprenticeship Act, 1802', in Norma Landau (ed.), *Law, Crime and English Society, 1660–1830* (Cambridge, 2002), p. 233.

40   Boys and girls were boarded by contract at 2s 6d per week at Bott, Birch, Bowyer and Randall at Nantwich, recorded in the report of the firm to the Birmingham Guardians of the Poor, 21 August 1798, GP/B/2/1/1, 1783–1806, BCA. It also seems that the Board of some of the children apprenticed at Oldknow's Mellor factory was contracted out. 12 September 1815, Minutes of Directors of the Poor, St Pancras parish, refers to a bill for Messrs Pickford's 'charge of keep of 20 children', P/PN/PO/1/11 (microfilm reference UTAH 652) CLSAC.

at least moderate success. A number experienced long-term prosperity. Most of the latter based their success on continued use of parish apprentices. Although it is not possible to generalise from the cases in this study, it appears that parish apprentices were associated with a cross-section of outcomes, including a solid proportion of successes.

The sample contains at least as many known successes as known failures. Descriptions of failure have been more extensively publicised than accounts of success. Contemporary criticism of the use and abuse of parish apprentices drew heavily on their experiences in the circumstances of factory closure. This approach, while rightly emphasising the greater potential suffering of parish children than 'free' ones, may have exaggerated the frequency of such occurrence. The enterprise of Haywood and Palfreyman was exceptional in its brevity. Established in 1796 and employing many apprentices from several London parishes, it disappeared without warning in 1799.[41] Several other major users of parish apprentices ceased trading in the first decade of the nineteenth century having survived for between ten and twenty years. The Marsden enterprise of John, Thomas and Samuel Haigh, merchants and manufacturers, began business upon the arrival of its first group of London parish apprentices in 1792. The enterprise was not properly overseen by owners more interested in their London and Manchester interests, and it failed in the difficult trading conditions of 1805.[42]

Among the largest users of parish apprentices, the Toplis's business, ceased trading in 1805 following several challenging years during which costs, especially those associated with the children, were cut to a minimum.[43] By contrast, production at Lambert's much smaller Lowdham mill ended less than a year after implementing costly improvements to the upkeep of its parish apprentices.[44] The Preston firm of Watson failed in 1807; and the Backbarrow mill run by John Birch a year later. Both had depended heavily on parish apprentice labour. Backbarrow continued to operate under new ownership for at least another decade. The firm of Ellis Needham, notorious for its abuse of parish apprentices, survived with increasing difficulty, for almost 30 years. Although Robert Blincoe remained at the mill at the expiry of his apprenticeship term, the majority its apprentices did not do so. Because of ratepayer complaints about the financial burden of former apprentices, Needham was forced to quit the mill in 1814. His brother Robert took over for a short time, bringing more

---

41 Only months before, the business appeared to have been thriving. Report, dated 6 September 1799, of Messrs Johnson, Freeman and Ideson relative to poor children belonging to those Parish apprenticed to Messrs Hayward and Palfreyman in Cheshire. Minutes of meeting of Governors and Directors of the Poor, St James Piccadilly 7 September 1799, D1877, WAC.

42 Philip Charlesworth, 'Foundlers at Marsden', *Old West Riding*, 10 (1990): 25, states that 'John Haigh was gazetted bankrupt on 28 December 1805' but that 'in June 1805 crofts, cottages and closes, a mill and mill dam were put up for sale'. The main buildings were offered in March 1806. See also Aspin, *Water Spinners*, pp. 248–9.

43 Following Toplis's failure, his youthful workforce was distributed to other mills in the area. Toplis Apprentice Register, 'List of children put out apprentice to William Toplis', DD895/1.

44 Described in Brown, *Memoir*, p. 27; and Waller, *The Real Oliver Twist*, pp. 127–8.

poor children from London.[45] The factory of Davison and Hawksley, used firstly for worsted and then for cotton production, was built in 1788, and grew very rapidly between 1793 and 1800 when it employed 600 apprentices. The partners, while committed to technological improvement,[46] neglected their parish apprentices, and, unable to make a long-term success of the business, were taken over in 1810.[47]

Such examples suggest a link between heavy use of parish apprentice and unsuccessful enterprise. Some failures were the result of opportunism on the part of entrepreneurs either already overcommitted to other activities or insufficiently experienced in textile manufacture. Ill-prepared manufacturers were a common feature of the early industrial landscape, and although the cheapness of parish apprentices may have induced the entry of inadequate masters unlikely to succeed,[48] in the group of firms studied here, the failures were a minority. And among those that ceased production before 1820 or even 1810, the majority had contributed to textile manufacturing activity for ten or more years. Most businesses in this study were at least moderately successful, trading for at least 20 years. Among these, Benjamin Smart's Warwickshire enterprise, survived trading difficulties during the later years of the Napoleonic Wars. Smart raised income wherever possible. Negotiating an apprentice deal from the Oxford parish of St Clements in 1812, Smart stipulated an increase in premium: 'As the times are much worse I now expect to have two new dresses and a premium of £5 with each girl'.[49] After a further decade of moderate profitability, the business ceased production during 1822.[50] Thomas Jewsbury's Derbyshire cotton spinning and weaving enterprise, established during the 1790s, enjoyed at least 20 years of successful trading before its sale in 1818.[51] The Sheffield cotton mill, established in 1788, and supplied with apprentices by St Martin in the Fields parish for at least 20 years, ran an eventful course. In 1792, fire destroyed the mill buildings, which were rebuilt in 1796; an apprentice house was added in 1804. The enterprise expanded in 1812, and in 1813 diversified into worsted handcombing and spinning as well as silk before its failure in 1815.[52] Isaac Hodgson, proprietor of

---

45 Chapman, *The Early Factory Masters*, p. 203.

46 As demonstrated in correspondence with Boulton and Watt DD 452/6/1–13, NA.

47 Details of the 'Sale of Arnold Mills' 14 May 1810, DD568/5, NA.

48 This appears to lie behind the conventional wisdom associating the use of parish apprentices with early failure.

49 1 mo 1 1812. Letter from Benjamin Smart to overseers at St Clements Parish, Oxford. Z531, Oxfordshire Record Office (ORO).

50 Joan Lane, 'Apprenticeship in Warwickshire cotton mills, 1790–1830', *Textile History*, 10 (1979): 171.

51 Thomas Jewsbury, an associate of Robert Peel before establishing himself as manufacturer, moved to Manchester to become a cotton merchant, which he combined with duties of agent to the West of England Insurance Company. Website about author Maria Jane Jewsbury, his daughter, produced by the Convey Project on women writers at Sheffield Hallam University. <http://www.shu.ac.uk/schools/cs/corvey/corinne/CorinneAuthors/Jewsbury/biog.html>

52 George Ingle, *Yorkshire Cotton: The Yorkshire Cotton Industry, 1780–1835* (Preston, 1997); David T. Jenkins, 'The cotton industry in Yorkshire, 1780–1900', *Textile History*, 10 (1979): 75–95.

the small but reasonably successful Caton mill, and business partner in the mercantile branch of Samuel Greg and company, which incurred heavy losses while trading in Spain, passed the small mill on to Greg in 1817 in partial payment of his debts.[53]

The failures and moderate successes were distributed throughout the early textile manufacturing regions. So too were the highly successful and enduring enterprises. Particularly notable for their longevity among the northern factories were Samuel Ashton's well-regarded business in Middleton;[54] Samuel Greg's Styal concern, whose long-term success on the basis of parish apprentices has been thoroughly recorded;[55] and Whitaker's Greenholme mill in Burley-in-Wharfedale. Founded on the labour of parish apprentices, the enterprise eventually became self-sustaining in labour as the apprentices became adult workers and produced the next generation of young workers. The factory remained productive until well into the twentieth century. Consolidation enabled the Peel empire to continue, and its initial dependence on parish apprentice labour was gradually reduced.[56] The firm of Mitchell and Holt, established in 1789 by David Holt, had by 1815 become an exhibition factory shown to foreign dignitaries.[57] The Pendleton and Holywell enterprises of William Douglas similarly flourished for some years, and the evidence of parliamentary committees suggests that a large proportion of parish apprentices were retained by the firm in the long term.[58] James Pattision's silk mill in Congleton was established in 1753, and according to his evidence to the 1816 Select Committee, parish apprentices supplemented local free labour only intermittently, and had by then discontinued the practice.[59]

Many textile enterprises of well-recorded longevity were located in the Midlands.[60] These included Newton's Cressbrook mill; Cooper and Matchett's enterprise at Tissington; Robinson's Papplewick concern and Wooley and McQueen, cotton spinners of Matlock. Established in the late eighteenth century as a small concern,

---

53   Rose, *The Gregs*, pp. 34–8. The enterprise was found to be in need of renovation, and machines in need of updating. Greg Papers C5/1/2/5, MCA. Hodgson's Spanish adventure was noted in St Pancras parish records in the context of his failure to sign his apprentices' indentures. Report presented to the Poor Law officers, 18 June 1816; Minutes of Directors of the Poor, Parish of St Pancras, P/PN/PO/1/12 (microfilm reference UTAH 652) CLSAC.

54   The business was showered with praise by Edward Baines in his *History of the Cotton Manufacture in Great Britain* (London, 1835), pp. 444–51.

55   Rose, *The Gregs*, especially pp. 54–7.

56   SC1816; HL 1819.

57   Aspin, *Water Spinners*, pp. 161–4.

58   Testimony of Samuel Jones and Samuel Gardner, HL1819 vol. 110, pp. 180–81; Robert Plant, 36, spinner, Appleton and Plant. Also testimony from John Houldsworth, an Oldham weaver, HL1819 vol. 110, pp. 133–6, 241. According to Dodd, *Industrial Revolution in North Wales*, p. 287, the Holywell enterprise flourished until the late 1830s, but then declined rapidly and was liquidated in the early 1840s.

59   SC1816, p. 76.

60   The records of Derbyshire mills are particularly useful, especially from an 1841 investigation. It may be that this has tended to exaggerate the relative weight of the county's mills in the total of successes.

the Newton family's Cressbrook mill employed at most 60 apprentices before 1810.[61] Like many other enterprises, it struggled between 1805 and 1809, but then expanded before 1815 on the labour of parish apprentices from Liverpool, Chester, Bristol and London.[62] Growth continued, and in 1823, a third mill and an apprentice house were built. Over 300 apprentices were brought from RMA Chelsea and Southampton. In 1835, the mill was taken over by Henry McConnell and continued to operate at least until the 1840s.[63] Evidence for the longevity of the Cooper and Matchett business is drawn from the 1841 survey of the Derbyshire mill when it was still using parish apprentices. Children from the Liverpool workhouse had been transferred to the mill during the 1820s and 1830s,[64] and further apprentices were sent by the Leicester Poor Law authorities during the 1850s.[65] Finally, in the South, the Hounslow Heath flax spinning enterprise founded by Sewell and McMurdo survived well beyond 1820, with some change in ownership, and continued to employ parish apprentice labour.[66] Parish apprentices, therefore, were used in all types of firms, large and small, successful and unsuccessful. For a time, these constituted the most appropriate labour. They cannot be blamed for firm failure, nor can success be attributed solely to them. Efficient firms succeeded with parish labour; inefficient firms failed with them.

The data so far produced are limited, and more local and national research is required before confident conclusions can be drawn. Nevertheless, it has been shown here that the distribution of factory-based parish apprentices was more complicated than the simple story of traffic from London to the North of conventional wisdom. Although surviving evidence demonstrates that children from a relatively small number of London parishes formed an important source of factory apprentice labour, its dominance in such a market has been overstated. Most counties were involved in the distribution of children from areas of population pressure to those where supplies of labour were, at least in the short run, inadequate to the needs of expanding industries. No area outside London contained the level of surplus characteristic of the poorer parishes of the capital, but even the smallest contributor played a part. This chapter has shown that the majority of firms, especially in the Midlands, drew initially at least upon parishes in the region for their supplies of parish apprentices.

---

61 In 1807, Cressbrook apparently employed 30 apprentices, though numbers rose thereafter. 1807 report of Derbyshire mills, HL 1819 vol. 108.

62 *Ashton Chronicle,* 23 June 1849, quoted in full, Aspin, *Water Spinners,* p. 477.

63 For detail on the development of Cressbrook mill, see M.H. MacKenzie 'Cressbrook and Litton Mills, 1779–1835. Part 1', *Derbyshire Archaeological Journal,* 88 (1968): 8–14; M.H. MacKenzie, 'Cressbrook Mill, 1810–1835', *Derbyshire Archaeological Journal,* 90 (1970): 62–3; Factories Inquiry, Royal Commission, 1st report, 1833 (450) XX 24.

64 2 April 1841, from J. Cooper, Woodeaves mill to Mr George Hodgkinson, Clerk to magistrates, Wirksworth DRO Q/AG/16/11, DRO.

65 Thompson, 'Apprenticeship', p. 55.

66 Transfer of apprentices to Sewell and Jones, 1 March 1821. Although not selected for this study, the silk business of Samuel Courtauld, a long-term success, drew upon the labour of London parish apprentices. Turner Collection: ACC/0526/36, LMA.

The practice of factory parish apprenticeship, was large in scale,[67] extended over a wide geographical area, and liberated the industrial labour market. The increasingly flexible, unconstrained labour market that emerged later in the eighteenth century, facilitated the establishment and growth of nascent textile manufacturing enterprises, a number of which would not have existed without parish apprentices. Those that were founded almost entirely on the labour of poor children from local and more distant parishes included some that were very short lived, but others that were successful into the medium-term and long-term.

The employment of parish apprentices made a difference to the early factory manufacture of textiles. Because of such labour, early industrial expansion took place at a rate not otherwise likely. The availability of unpaid labour may have permitted the emergence of inefficient firms that added little to the manufacturing sector, except in the short run; but among users of parish apprentices were many long-term successes too. Such positive outcomes made a difference not only to the longer-term employment of poor children, but also to the profitability of the enterprise and the economy as a whole. Several components of conventional wisdom have been revisited and adjusted in this chapter. The value of the system has been demonstrated. Textile firms, varying in scale, product and location depended on parish apprentices throughout the period from 1785 to 1815 and often for much longer. Many enterprises apprenticed poor children from the local region either as well as, or in preference to, those of more distant origin. The association of the practice of parish apprenticeship with successful enterprise more than with failure will be explored in the next chapter, which considers the costs and benefits of the system to both parish and factory.

---

67 Much larger than has yet been possible to quantify.

Chapter 6

The Costs and Benefits of Parish Apprenticeship

It is often argued that the system of parish factory apprenticeship was economically viable only in the early stages of textile factory production, if at all; and that it was already in decline before the introduction of the legislation that rendered the use of parish apprentices unviable.[1] The reason for the decline, it is suggested, was that the 'economics' of the system – that is not only costs and benefits, but also the operation of the labour market – ceased to favour the employer. Chapter 5 demonstrated that many employers continued to use parish apprentices up to the implementation of the 1816 legislation, and some for a long time after. For businesses which depended on parish apprentices for as much as forty or fifty years, the benefits appeared to have outweighed the costs. Other textile manufacturers dispensed with the system or used it less enthusiastically, as indigenous labour replaced the parish apprentice. Yet other users of parish apprentices failed but not necessarily because the system was economically inefficient.[2] Whatever the explanation for failure, the persistent use of parish or other institutional apprentices well into the 1840s suggests that there were some benefits. The purpose of this chapter is to attempt to specify the range and distribution of the costs and benefits associated with the practice of parish factory apprenticeship. There can be no formal measurement of such factors – in particular no value can be attributed to the possession of a controlled, disciplined and docile labour force at a time when free children were aware of their marketability and hence mobile – but an attempt will be made to indicate where gains and losses were most likely to fall.

The following discussion focuses on the economic implications for textile manufacturers of parish factory apprenticeship. Some attempt will also be made to gauge its impact on the donating parish. By investigating the 'economics' of the parish apprenticeship system, this chapter will explore the traditional wisdom that the system ultimately furthered the interest of the donating parish more than the recipient firm. The system of parish factory apprentices entailed a greater range of costs than is often assumed or that many employers expected. Although the children

---

1   For example, Neil J. Smelser, *Social Change in the Industrial Revolution: An Application of Theory to the Lancashire Cotton Industry 1770–1840* (London, 1959), pp. 103–105; Mary B. Rose, 'Social policy and business: parish apprenticeship and the early factory system, 1750–1834', *Business History*, 31/4 (1989): 24.

2   Such firms, however, may have been inappropriately lured into the industry by the expectation of cheap labour.

were exploited in the economic sense that they were not rewarded through pay for their product, they were by no means a free resource.

In view of the variation in usage of parish apprentices and of children more generally among early textile factory owners, it is impossible to estimate the overall balance of costs and benefits. A number of factors influenced the value of parish apprentice labour including the extent to which such labour was seen as expendable, short- term labour or part of a longer-term strategy of labour recruitment; the nature of technology and power and the size and organisation of the enterprise. During the early, experimental stage of textile factory production, the age and gender composition of the labour force varied between firms. Some employers made full use of children workers, which may have included parish apprentice labour, while others preferred to use a larger proportion of adult labour. The precise measurement of the value of parish apprentice labour is impossible, not just because of the variety of outcomes but also because not all costs and benefits were of a quantifiable kind. This chapter will identify the wide range of issues that need to be taken into account when exploring the economics of the parish apprenticeship system. It will begin with an assessment of the costs and benefits that accrued to the parish from the system before engaging with the more complex implications for employers. It will conclude by suggesting that the decline of the system, which took place much more gradually than is usually believed, was only partly the result of a shifting balance of costs and benefits, and was also related to social and cultural changes.

The parish factory apprenticeship system drew upon the mutual interest of Poor Law authorities and employer. The benefits to the parish of apprenticeship were clear. Whether the child was apprenticed locally or outside the parish, the authorities were relieved of financial and other responsibilities for the child at least during the period of the apprenticeship; and if the apprenticeship served its longer-term purpose, the child would be better placed to find work as an adult and remain financially independent. In the case of extra-parochial apprenticeship, long-term liability shifted to the new parish.

In the early years of the parish factory apprenticeship system, most of the parish costs were transparent and uncontroversial. The apprentice indenture formalised components of the financial arrangement, which typically consisted of the payment by the parish of a premium in one or two parts to the employer. The parish also committed to providing several sets of clothing for the apprentice at the beginning and the end of the term. However, the distribution of additional expenses for which neither parish nor employer had an obvious commitment was negotiated on an *ad hoc* basis.[3] Such extras included transport expenses and the costs of education. In view of the distances covered under the new system, the costs of transporting children from parish to factory could be considerable. The travel was commonly arranged by the agent but paid for by the parish. For example, the cost of sending the ten children from Chelmsford parish to Douglas's Pendleton factory, organised by John Plant, agent, was £3, 6s, 0d.[4] The employer sometimes bore the cost; and

---

3   Often an agent played a negotiating role here.
4   Chris Aspin, *The Water Spinners* (Helmshore, 2003), p. 172.

this was certainly the case where absconders were to be returned.⁵ In the case of a single child sent from St George Hanover Square parish to Merryweather, the Board 'order that when Mr Merryweather's agent appoints the time for her being sent by the waggon she be again seen by the Board'.⁶ The 22 children bound from St Pancras parish to Jeremiah/Thomas Garnett's mill in Clitheroe 'were to be conveyed to the manufactory by the coaches without any expense to the Board'.⁷

Expenses associated with instruction in basic literacy, numeracy and religious knowledge could be substantial and continuous. The more observant firms established educational provision from the outset; but where this was not already in place, 'protective' parishes both organised and paid for the services of a local instructor. However, where a negligent parish converged with a negligent employer, the provision of education was likely to be overlooked. The 1802 Act established employer responsibility for organising and meeting the costs of education and religious training. Not all employers met this obligation, and the Act lacked the powers to force them to comply; yet a surprising number, including those under economic pressure, provided at least a modicum of general education.⁸

Most of the employers to whom the parish of St James, Piccadilly bound its children provided for the instruction and care of the apprentices, and the parish itself intervened only if arrangements proved inadequate. In their initial approach to St James, the proprietors of Holt and Mitchell declared their intention to

> pay due attention to the morals of the children we may take, having established a Sunday School upon the premises for which suitable masters having been long engaged and every requisite provided for the improvement of the children. Its our intention to go beyond this and allow them an opportunity of learning to read etc in some part of the working hours.⁹

---

5   For example, 5 August 1806, Directors of the Poor, Parish of St Pancras, P/PN/PO/1/3 (microfilm reference UTAH 649), CLSAC.

6   14 April 1807, Minutes of Governors and Directors of the Poor, Parish of St George, Hanover Square, C925, WAC. It seems that Merryweather organised the wagon and collected the London children. During a short period in 1807, Merryweather took children from several parishes including St Martin in the Fields (5), Lambeth (9) as well as the St George's girl who could easily be accommodated with the others.

7   24 May 1814, Directors of the Poor, Parish of St Pancras, P/PN/PO/1/9 (microfilm ref UTAH 652), CLSAC. This applied to all dealings with agent Thomas Gorton, who also met parish officers expenses when children were bound. Report 18 June 1816, Directors of the Poor, Parish of St Pancras P/PN/PO/1/12 (microfilm reference UTAH 652) CLSAC.

8   The situation was rather different from that asserted by Hollen Lees that 'unsupervised by either government or parish authorities, their levels of training, education and treatment were the choice of the entrepreneur', Lynn Hollen Lees, *The Solidarities of Strangers: The English Poor Laws and the People, 1700 –1948* (Cambridge, 1998), p. 102. Both employer and parish hoped that education would instil moral discipline. Joanna Innes, 'Origins of the factory acts: the Health and Morals of Apprenticeship Act, 1802' in Norma Landau (ed.), *Law, Crime and English Society, 1660 –1830* (Cambridge, 2002), p. 248.

9   17? September 1801, Minutes of Governors and Directors of the Poor, Parish of St James, Piccadilly, D1878, WAC.

To supplement these apparently rigorous arrangements, St James engaged the services of a local clergyman with whom close links were retained. Similarly, although Messrs Haywood and Palfreyman allowed 'the boys time to write and have provided a person to instruct them',[10] the parish deemed it necessary to negotiate a more thorough job from a local clergyman. In each case, the parish paid amounts totalling £5 or £10 per annum for the clergyman to instruct children and generally keep an eye on their welfare.[11] William Douglas at Pendleton 'employed and paid a clergyman of the Church of England to instruct them in their Bible catechism and other religious duties on Sunday'.[12] Whether the parish or the employer paid, the per capita cost of between 1d and 2d per week constituted an unanticipated and unwanted supplement, at a time when cost containment was the driving force. Clearly not all – neither employers not parishes – fulfilled their responsibility in this respect; and when business was poor, it might be assumed that education costs would be one of the first to be cut; followed by clothing and food for the children.

The support system for parish apprentices, to be discussed in Chapter 11, added, sometimes considerably, to the costs entailed in the process of factory bindings. Parishes did not engage equally in establishing protective measures for their children, and for the poorer or more reluctant parishes expenses might be minimal. But for those that visited distant factories both before and during the period of their children's apprenticeship, and who paid for local clergymen to ensure good treatment for their apprentices, as well as incidental postal and local travelling and subsistence expenses, the costs were substantial.[13] For example, when the children from Chelmsford parish were visited at Douglas's Pendleton factory in response to complaints of improper treatment, Mr Culling was thanked for his (satisfactory) report and 'paid the expenses of his journey by the overseers amounting to the sum of £10.7.6 ... and three guineas be paid to Mr John Culling as a gratuity and compensation for the loss of time in attending to the Manchester business'.[14] William Pepall, a St Pancras Beadle, a man not averse to fiddling expenses, charged his parish £8 for 'the expenses of his journey into Lancashire', and also claimed £4, 15s, 0d for 'coachhire and expenses' from Thomas Gorton, agent.[15] In the case where

---

10   23 February 1796, Minutes of Governors and Directors of the Poor, Parish of St James, Piccadilly, D1876, WAC.

11   A fee was established but additional, *ad hoc* payments were made in the light of the level of service provided. See Minutes of meetings of the Directors and Governors of the Poor, Parish of St James, Piccadilly, 6 May 1796, 4 May 1797, 17 September 1802, 12 May 1803, D1876, 1877, 1878, WAC.

12   Statement of Margaret Chamberlain, former apprentice 29 February 1797, Minutes of Governors and Directors of the Poor, Parish of St James, Piccadilly, D1876, WAC.

13   It was not always the parish which bore the cost of local support. David Holt was among the entrepreneurs who financed some educational and welfare provision.

14   4 May 1802, vestry meeting, Chelmsford parish, D/P 94/12/12, Essex Record Office (ERO).

15   This had taken place in May and July 1814, but was only brought to the parish's attention in a report of 18 June 1816. Minutes of Directors of the Poor, Parish of St Pancras, P/PN/PO/1/12 (microfilm reference UTAH 652) CLSAC. Despite being 'strongly reprimanded' by the Board for such a misdemeanour, he was sent again into Lancashire – probably because

a group of visitors was involved in visited multiple placements, the costs would rise to several times these amounts. If visiting were taken seriously and conducted annually, the expenditure might easily approach that of keeping several children in the workhouse. This became increasingly well recognized, and the withdrawal of parishes from binding to the most distant factories was often explained in terms of the difficulty and expense of regular and effective visiting.[16]

Parishes hoping for a cheap disposal of their children might have been disappointed. Some employers were exacting in their expectations of the parish and added to their financial burden. Samuel Greg, for example, stipulated his requirements to Biddulph parish:

> I am much obliged by your attention and find we have room at present for about 12 young girls of from 10–12 years. Terms: 2 guineas with each child and clothing: 2 shifts; 2 pairs of stockings; 2 frocks or bedgowns; 2 brats or aprons. And 2 guineas to provide them other necessaries.[17]

Benjamin Smart could also be quite demanding. In correspondence with the overseers of St Clement parish, Oxford, Smart stated, 'I want active, healthy girls ... I now expect to have 2 new dresses and a premium of £5 with each girl'.[18] Having taken one such apprentice, he complained about the quality of the clothing which had been sent with her. This may reflect high standards but it might also suggest that Smart was seeking additional cash.

> The girl is come and I feel no objection to her being bound immediately. I should prefer returning the cloaths she has brought when she is bound if you will allow me the £5 for that purpose – and when speaking of two dresses, I expect three articles of each kind which require weekly washing it being more convenient to wash once a fortnight only ... I will send you a bill for the latter which you may enter in the Parish accounts as having expended on her for cloaths.[19]

---

he was familiar with the geography – to bring home a group of children whose indentures were cancelled.

16 For example, in the conclusion to their 1802 report, the visitors from the parish of St Margaret and St John to factories in Nottinghamshire, Lancashire and Yorkshire expressed concern about the distance between parish and factory and asked, 'could the children be kept nearer home by apprenticing them to manufactories in London or the neighbourhood or what would be still more desirable, the establishment of manufactories in the workhouse, it would be much more satisfactory to all parties', 1802 Report of St Margaret and St John; St Luke Chelsea, in the conclusion to their report of the visit to Davison and Hawksley on 20 June 1807, state that the parish would not send any more children to Arnold not least because its distance from London precluded 'those frequent visits which are essential to the good of the children', P74/LUK/019 (microfilm reference X D26/008), LMA.

17 Letter to James Sewell, Vicar of Biddulph, February 27 1817, Greg business records, C5/8/9/2, MCA.

18 Letter dated 1 mo 1 (January) 1812, Rock mills, from Benjamin Smart to St Clement parish, Oxford (William Parsons, overseer) Z351/3, WCRO.

19 One of a series of letters between Benjamin Smart and St Clement parish, Oxford, Z351/5/1, WCRO.

Parishes as well as employers practised cost containment. The premium was assumed to be an obligatory cost. Nevertheless, attempts were made to reduce its burden on the parish.[20] Although there is no evidence that employers ever paid for the children;[21] the premium could be lowered or paid in instalments. This not only deferred payment but in the case of 'wastage' – children who died or absconded – the second instalment was avoided altogether. Together, the cost of an average premium and the clothing allowance, amounted to between £5 and £6 per child. Such a sum rarely exceeded the cost of the annual upkeep of a parish workhouse child. After 12 months, therefore, as long as the child had not returned 'home', the parish had made a net gain on the deal.

The benefits to the parish of factory apprenticeship seem to be unambiguous; and most took the form of saving, or reducing long-term expenditure. Even before the era of factory expansion, parishes were intent on identifying ways of cutting costs to the parish entailed in maintaining poor children.[22] There is some evidence that parishes, including St Leonards, Hackney, St Olave, Southwark, and St Giles in the Fields resented paying the Foundling Hospital the cost of supporting 'their' children, and from the 1770s began to withdraw them.[23] St Clement Danes began to seek alternatives from the early 1780s if not before. In June 1782, for example, the Vestry discussed whether children under six should be sent to the Foundling Hospital, and it was agreed unanimously that 'all those above the age of six years to be sent to the silk mills at Watford *or elsewhere* [my italics] as great savings might be made to the parish'.[24] As a result of apprenticing out of the parish, which was typically the case with factory apprentices, the parish: 'disposed' of the short-term and long-term costs of maintaining a poor, and sometimes sickly child;[25] was able to reduce overcrowding in the workhouse, provide better services for the remaining paupers; and, where groups of children were sent at one time, reduce administrative costs. The factory employer was, by definition, a willing master so apprenticeship in this case was more likely to secure a long-term placement and even a positive

---

20 A rumour that some factory employers were paying parishes for the privilege of sending their children was discussed by the officers of St Clement Danes, but later discovered to be without foundation, 9 February 1792, Minutes of Vestry, Parish of St Clement Danes, B1073, WAC.

21 The fact that this was discussed, however, suggests that although the allocation of a premium with the parish apprentice indicated that factory apprentices were viewed in much the same way as other apprenticeships, the fact that this alternative option was even mentioned indicates that the distribution of the benefits of the arrangements had not been explicitly agreed.

22 Young people and old people naturally constituting the expensive groups.

23 R.K. McClure, *Coram's Children: The London Foundling Hospital in the Eighteenth Century* (New Haven, 1981), p. 146.

24 12 June 1782, Minutes of Vestry, Parish of St Clement Danes, B1072, WAC.

25 Joan Lane, *Apprenticeship in England 1600–1914* (London, 1996), pp. 83–4. Many employers, however, stipulated healthy children in advertisements and correspondence and some would return substandard children.

experience for the child. However, for some parishes, this resulted in the loss of 'fine income'.[26]

Factory apprenticeship generated costs to the parish, but these were usually far outweighed by the benefits or savings that accrued. For the employers, the costs and benefits were more complicated and less predictable. The initial premium and clothing provision offset apprenticeship costs for at least a year, if the fee were not used for capital projects, but in the longer term, expenditure mounted up. It was the potential excess of apprentices' costs over their product that led Smelser to describe the system as 'economically irrational'. Although wages were low, or zero, Smelser argued that this advantage was diminished by the cost of maintenance, and responsibility for apprentices' welfare, which 'must have been a source of continuous distraction from the economic management of the mill'.[27] In the following sections, the costs associated with parish apprentices will be identified; and an attempt made to assess the benefits. It will be suggested that each cost either had an offsetting benefit, or would have been matched or exceeded by the price of the 'free' labour equivalent. Those who have argued that the economics of parish apprentices did not operate in employers' favour except for a short period have typically emphasised absolute costs, and disadvantages, with little consideration of the costs of providing the same service through an alternative means.[28]

Board and lodging comprised the minimum continuous costs of maintaining an apprentice. In practice, the quality of provision and thus the cost of apprentice upkeep varied. In at least 50 per cent of the businesses examined in this study, apprentice accommodation was allocated in a separate, often purpose-built house. A number of factory owners were already in possession of suitable premises; others chose to construct afresh. Although adding to the fixed costs of the enterprise, such building could be financed by the apprentice premium, and in turn comprised an asset of some value. Research on the costs of apprentice houses suggests an average of £300 to accommodate 100 apprentices.[29] The initial fee paid by the parish would cover this outlay in the case of a large group of apprentices.

Evidence from Greg's Quarry Bank mill, where a substantial apprentice house was built, suggests that the weekly cost per head of keeping an apprentice was 3s, 6d in 1790; and between 4s and 5s in 1822–40.[30] It is argued that the steep rise in costs

---

26 A number of parishes in Suffolk, as well as Leeds and Halifax parishes, appeared to depend on fines, which could total substantial amounts, in order to finance indenture premiums.

27 Smelser, *Social Change*, p. 104, asserts that 'clearly this method of employment was economically irrational from certain standpoints', p. 104.

28 Neil Smelser emphasised the costs and disadvantages of the parish factory apprenticeship system with little regard for the costs of the alternatives. *Social Change*, pp. 104–105.

29 Pamela Horn, *Children's Work and Welfare, 1780–1890* (Cambridge, 1995), p. 20.

30 Pamela Horn, 'The traffic in children and the textile mills, 1780–1816', *Genealogists' Magazine*, 24/5 (1993): 365; Carol O'Mahoney (ed.), *Quarry Bank Mill Memoranda*, vol. 1 (Styal, 1989), p. 56; Frances Collier, *The Family Economy of the Working Classes in the Cotton Industry, 1784–1833* (Manchester, 1964), p. 46. The Gregs also spent substantial sums on medical treatment. See Chapter 12, note 10.

and a slower growth in wages during the 1840s resulted in the firm's abandonment of the parish apprentice system in 1847.[31] Mr Morley of the silk mills at Sewardstone requested, apparently in lieu of a premium, 2s a week per child 'for which they are to be properly taken care of'.[32] Among those factories choosing to subcontract responsibility for apprentice board and lodging[33] was the Nantwich cotton spinning enterprise of Bott, Birch, Bower and Randall, where 'boys and girls boarded by contract at 2/6 per week each'.[34] Such a sum, while less than the costs incurred by the generous Greg, was equivalent to the price of contemporary workhouse upkeep. For example, it was reported by the Birmingham Guardians that, in 1818, 399 children were maintained in the Asylum at an average cost of 2s, 6d per week for everything except clothing.[35] In Bristol, the equivalent was 2s per head per week.[36] William Newton of Cressbrook mill, calculated the net costs of his 30 apprentices brought from London in 1816 to be minimal, 'the expenses upon them will be about £66, but in three years there will be about £63.0.0 to receive from the parish the children came from, so it will bring the expenses to about £3.0.0'.[37]

In the early stages of factory production, therefore, the weekly cost of maintaining a parish apprentice lay between 2s, 6d and 3s, 6d. Such figures need to be considered against estimates of the value of their output and the cost of the alternative 'free' labour. Nardinelli has calculated the annual value of the marginal product of a child under 13 in cotton factories to be £7, 7s in 1833 at a time when the yearly wage costs of such labour was £7, 9s.[38] Even if accurate for the 1830s, such figures cannot be easily extrapolated backwards to the beginning of the nineteenth century. Nevertheless, evidence of high profits in the early decades of factory production suggests that children's marginal product would not be less at this time than in the 1830s, and in

---

31 Collier, *Family Economy*, p. 46. As wages for 'free' children rose less than costs, so apprentice children who had been relatively cheap up to c. 1820, probably became slightly more expensive in 1830. By 1822, when there were 90–95 apprentices, the unit cost had risen to 4s, 11d per week plus 1¼d a head for clothing. Thereafter, the trend continued upwards until by 1846, when the number of apprentices had dwindled to 15, they were costing 9s, 2d each. During this decade, 'free' children were paid about 5s a week. Horn, 'The traffic', p. 365; O'Mahoney (ed.), *Quarry Bank Mill*, p. 56.

32 3 August 1807, Vestry minutes, Woodford parish, D/P 167/8/3 ERO.

33 Sometimes, but not always, such enterprises had relatively small parish apprentice numbers.

34 This amounts to £6 a year; the estimated cost of keeping children in the workhouse. Rose, 'Social policy', p. 7, 27 August 1798, Minutes of the Birmingham Board of Guardians, GP/B/2/1/1, BCA.

35 Report of the Asylum Committee of the Birmingham Guardians, 2 June 1818, Minutes of Birmingham Board of Guardians, GP/B/2/1/2. At St Mary Newington, Southwark, the average weekly expenditure per head was 3s, 10d per week for adults and children, 31 March 1806, St Mary Newington Workhouse Committee Minutes 1806–1813, 930, SLHL.

36 E.E. Butcher, *Bristol Corporation of the Poor: Selected Records 1696–1834* (Bristol, 1932), p. 15.

37 M.H. MacKenzie, 'Cressbrook Mill 1810–1835', *Derbyshire Archaeological Journal*, 90 (1970): 63.

38 Clark Nardinelli, 'Were children exploited during the industrial revolution?', *Research in Economic History*, 11 (1988): 251.

the successful firms may easily have been higher. Evidence that the average weekly wage of a 'free' child in 1800 was 4s,[39] suggests that marginal productivity was likely to have been at least the 3s, 6d per week indicated by Nardinelli's study.

Historians have suggested that expense of parish apprentice upkeep alone exceeded the wage that would have been paid to a 'free' child living at home with parents.[40] However, while the cost of maintaining a child in the factory, as in the workhouse, changed little as he or she got older, the value of apprentice labour almost certainly increased with age. Not only was efficiency and productivity likely to rise over time, but the difference between the wage of the 'free' child and the cost of the apprentice also increased. The relative cost of parish apprentice labour and that of 'free' children was not constant. It varied not only between factories and locations, but also over the term of the apprenticeship and the age of the child. In principle, the factory apprentice would become more beneficial to the employer over time, not only as he or she became a more efficient and more productive worker, but also, in relation to the increasingly expensive paid alternative.[41]

Wally Seccombe estimates that by the ages of 8–10, children could offset the costs of their own upkeep.[42] Marshall preferred 'children of 11 or 12' for his Holbeck concern. 'They do more work and require less superintendence than younger children provided they have been previously brought up in habits of order and obedience; otherwise they made worse servants than those who begin to work at 9 or 10 years of age'.[43] The marginal cost of the parish apprentice varied according to age. At the beginning of the apprenticeship when extreme youth combined with inexperience suggested that cost of feeding, clothing and accommodating the parish child was probably only just offset by its productive capacity. The poor value of parish apprentices in their early days was remarked upon by Mr Jones of Sewell and Jones, flax spinner of Rickmansworth, referring to the £5 premium, stated that it was 'more than sunk in the time consumed in teaching them and the waste of materials'.[44] Yet the length of the term, which in the case of parish factory apprenticeships could be 12 years or more, constituted not only a long period in which employers enjoyed non-waged labour, but also one during which gains would increase. The value of the

---

39 Aspin, *Water Spinners*, p. 38. Other evidence such as workhouse employment suggests weekly payments of 2s, 6d per unit of labour. For example, Gorton and Thompson's proposal, discussed by the Directors and Governors of the Poor of the parish of St James Picccadilly on 29 April 1791 and 29 May 1791, D1873, WAC.

40 Jennifer Tann, *Children at Work* (London, 1981), p. 34, using the example of Greg.

41 Contemporary Jeremy Bentham recognised that after the age of seven or eight 'value will for 6 or 7 years to come be every year on the increase'. Also that a 'boy' of 20 could produce 16–20 times that of a 4-year-old, while consuming only twice as much. 'Situation and relief of the poor', *Annals of Agriculture*, xxix (1797), pp. 400–405.

42 In the case of 'free' labour 'and thereafter became indispensable contributors'. Wally Seccombe, *Weathering the Storm: Working Class Families from the Industrial Revolution to the Fertility Decline* (London, 1993), p. 31.

43 Marshalls Mss, MS200/14/2, Special Collections, Brotherton Library, University of Leeds. (SCBLUL)

44 6 January 1818, Directors of the Poor, St Pancras parish, P/PN/PO/1/15 (microfilm reference UTAH 653), CLSAC. Such wastage would also apply to 'free' children workers.

apprentice would rise over time in line with the growing strength and experience, and associated productivity that came with age.[45] Although an increasing appetite for food and replacement clothes would raise subsistence costs, such was the parsimony of most diets, and most garb, that such increases were minimal.

As most indentures specified the end of term to be the age of 21, the saving made by using both experienced and non-waged parish apprentices could be substantial. The wage rates of several firms illustrate the potential significance of this. The example of William Douglas's cotton mills in Pendleton as described by his manager to the parish of St James, indicated that free hands were paid much more as they got older. Children under 10 were typically paid between 2 and 4 shillings per week, equivalent to the subsistence costs of the apprentice, but by 14 and certainly by 16 their earnings lay between 6 and 7 shillings a week.[46] While the source of this information lacks objectivity, as the motivation was to persuade the parish officers of the buoyancy of long-term earnings potential for the apprentices, these sums amounted to considerably more than the cost of maintaining a parish apprentice of the same age who technically was paid nothing at all.[47]

Parish apprentices reaching their mid to late teens working alongside 'free' teenage labour could not avoid becoming aware of their value. Research on apprenticeship in North America highlights the high rate of absconding in the later years of apprenticeship, as boys especially sought paid work that valued their training and experience.[48] Parish children in England seemed to run away at all stages of their apprenticeship for a host of reasons, but those absconding in the later years of their term were more likely than others to be driven by the desire to earn a wage that matched their level of competency. This is also the point at which employers, recognising such young men and women's value, exerted much time and energy in retrieving such runaways. Wages paid at Holt and Mitchell's Manchester factory also rose substantially with age and experience: 'our drawers and rovers girls get from 5s, 8d to 8s per week – boys in the other departments of the card room from 4s, 6d to 11s – when employed as mule spinners their earnings are much more – we have now both boys and girls about 20 who have been with us some years and whose

---

45 The growing productivity of teenagers especially from the ages of 16 to 21 is asserted in Peter Scholliers, *Wages, Manufacturers and Workers in the Nineteenth-Century Factory: The Voortman Cotton Mill in Ghent* (Oxford, 1996), pp. 92–8. Jeremy Bentham noted, and attempted to quantify, the incremental growth in the value of young people to their peak at 20, when their productive capacity was as substantial as an adult. In his proposed system, he reckoned that a male aged 20 could make a gross profit on his labour of £20. Net profit, subtracting maintenance at £5, was predicted to be £15. UC cli 334. Bentham project Mss, University College London. I am grateful to Dr Michael Quinn for this reference.

46 Letter dated 21 January 1797 from John Plant to the Governors and Directors of the Poor, Parish of St James, Piccadilly, D1876, WAC.

47 Parish children were paid pocket money for overtime work, but nothing for the usual 12–14 hour day.

48 Gillian Hamilton, 'Enforcement in apprenticeship contracts: were runaways a serious problem? Evidence from Montreal', *Journal of Economic History*, 55/3 (1995): 553–4. See also John E. Murray and Ruth Wallis Herndon, 'Markets for children in early America: a political economy of pauper apprenticeship', *Journal of Economic History*, 62/2 (2002): 356–82.

weekly earnings are from 23s, 6d to 31s, 6d per week'.⁴⁹ In 1802 officials from the parish of St James visited the factory of Mitchell and Holt and reported that '2 girls about 18 years old [earned] £1.10.0 and 150 girls [not apprentices] from 10 to 15 years old 6/6 each'.⁵⁰ At the end of the term, the employer was in possession of a fully trained factory worker familiar with the particular ways of the enterprise; and if the mill owner had incurred costs in providing education for the parish apprentices,⁵¹ the higher quality labour thus produced would more than repay the expense.

From the early years of parish factory apprenticeship, wastage though death and disappearance cost employers dearly. Evidence is impressionistic, yet at some factories the wastage rate was high. Of the seven apprentices recruited by Toplis from Hackney parish in June 1794, for example, 'three ran away, two had to be returned, one died and the other left … a year after arriving at Cuckney'.⁵² Such a record was certainly not typical but neither was it unique. In March 1792, 'Mr Johnson agent to the Holywell cotton mills attended and informed the board that of the children bound to that company, seven out of nine had run away'.⁵³ High mortality at Wells and Middleton's Sheffield mill was recorded from the examination of former apprentice Harriet Russell who recalled that 'about 20 children buried while she was there some with the waste – ie decline'.⁵⁴ Investigating allegations of a high death rate at Davison and Hawksley, Stanley Chapman found that the burial register of Arnold parish contained a large number of entries for the firm's parish apprentices just after the turn of the century. These, he suggests, may have been the result of 'famine and fever' rather than overwork.⁵⁵ Apprentice debilitation through intensification of labour and inadequate diet certainly raised the probability of turnover through death. Although all labour turnover had a cost in terms of wasted training and experience, this could be offset by healthy and vigorous replacement apprentices.

Judging from the efforts made by employers to retrieve absconders, apprentices sufficiently healthy to run away were less cheaply replaced. Before the factory, a disappearing apprentice may have been an intended outcome for some masters, whose need for the premium exceeded that for the child; yet, although much

---

49 A letter, dated 14 September 1801, from Messrs Mitchell and Holt of Holt Town to the Parish of St James, Piccadilly, was considered on 19 September 1801, Minutes of Governors and Director of the Poor, Parish of St James, Piccadilly, D1878, WAC.

50 Report of officers visit to Holt and Mitchell 19 February 1802, Minutes of Governors and Directors of the Poor, Parish of St James, Piccadilly, D1878, WAC.

51 As was noted above, parishes often bore this cost, even though under the terms of the 1802 HMA, it became the employers' responsibility.

52 S.D. Chapman, *The Early Factory Masters: The Transition to the Factory System in the Midlands Textile Industry* (Newton Abbot: David and Charles, 1967), p. 171. Chapman attributes the high death rate among parish apprentices there not necessarily to harsh treatment, but at least partly because 'they were collected from the unhealthy dregs of society'. This raises the important issue of the quality of apprentice labour which was undoubtedly variable.

53 12 March 1792, Minutes of Churchwardens, Overseers and Assistants, Parish of St Clement Danes, B1147, WAC.

54 Probably tuberculosis. 12 September 1797, Minutes of Churchwardens, Overseers and Assistants, Parish of St Clement Danes, B1147, WAC.

55 Chapman, *Early Factory Masters*, p. 179.

less likely within the factory system, trade fluctuations and water power failures created erratic labour demand conditions. Nevertheless, for factory employers, apprentice absconding was a nuisance at best, and a serious cost at worst. Newspaper advertisements indicate the expenses that employers were willing to incur in order to retrieve absconders. The cost of the missing labour was compounded by the cost of advertising and rewards. For example, Bott and Co. of Nantwich distributed a notice that read: 'whoever will restore to the proprietors any of the runaway apprentices shall be allowed one guinea ... and sixpence per mile as expenses for every mile exceeding eight necessarily traveled by them for that purpose'.[56] Some employers cooperated to expedite apprentice retrieval. Robert Blincoe, himself thwarted in attempts to escape from at least two Midlands mills, described how a local inn was used as a collection point for runaway apprentices; and a reward of five shillings paid for each child returned.[57] Other employers attempted to prevent the absconding. At Robert Peel's factories, for example, children were deprived of shoes.[58]

Apprentice children were clearly more valuable and less expendable than might be assumed. Employer frustration over absconding children was driven by cost as well as inconvenience. The parish officers of St James, Piccadilly, for example, received the following itemisation from Gorton and Thompson:

> the gentlemen will consider also that whenever those boys have run away they have always taken their new cloaths and all their cloaths with them that we have been at much expense in sending after them, and therefore that the second fee [i.e. the one paid half way through the apprenticeship] is nothing equal to our loss exclusive of our loss by their labour for the last years of their apprenticeship ... .[59]

As parish apprentices gained in value through their term, so the cost of runaways increased over time.[60] As apprentices became aware of their increased value, and by their late teens might well be working alongside well paid 'free' labour of the same age, the temptation to seek paid employment in a different factory must have been irresistible. Early factories depended upon a settled and reliable workforce. Despite the financial and organisational costs of absconding, the disciplinary controls imposed upon parish apprentices rendered them more stable than their free equivalents. Non-parish children were typically employed on weekly contracts, and in factory districts, movement between mills, as children sought out higher pay and more congenial surroundings, resulted in substantial, costly, but unpredictable turnover. Despite the extent of absconding, therefore, parish apprentices were more captive, and thus provided more workplace stability than free children.

Although it is sometimes suggested that children, and especially parish apprentices, were docile and biddable, evidence that they were troublesome and

---

56 Aspin, *Water Spinners*, p. 49.
57 John Brown, *A Memoir of Robert Blincoe* (Manchester, 1832), p. 24.
58 28 June 1796, Minutes of the Birmingham Board of Guardians, GP/B/2/1/1, BCA.
59 Meeting of 17 November 1795, reading a letter from Gorton and Thompson, dated 15 October 1795, Minutes of the Governors and Directors of the Poor, Parish of St James, Piccadilly, D1876, WAC.
60 Murray and Herndon, 'Markets for children', p. 363.

lacked concentration is more convincing. This was rectified by experimental forms of control. The supervisory costs of the disciplinary regime under which parish apprentices laboured were offset not only by a more compliant and stable workforce than would otherwise have existed, but also by gains derived through intensification of labour and other exploitative forms of work such as night working. Experimentation in ways of working as well as in methods of disciplining was important to the development of factory practice. The objective of rigid workplace discipline at the parish apprentice stage was to instigate a tight regulatory system for the long-term control of workers. Apprentices were contained not only to enhance productivity in the short term but also so that they would become accustomed to regulation, and accept it when adult. The benefits of parish apprentices over other types of labour at this experimental stage were substantial.[61]

Despite maintenance costs, parish apprentices were cheaper than the alternatives. Without them, millowners using water power would have had to pay higher wages and invest more on cottages, to attract families'.[62] Because children workers were preferred and work for adult labour was difficult to find, parish apprentices arriving without parents carried more benefits than 'free' children.[63] As was demonstrated in Chapter 5, several employers replied almost exclusively on parish children.[64] Whether or nor parish apprentice labour was cost effective, for some employers it was the only labour available. The parish apprentice was thus most beneficial to employers because of the essential labour it provided; and because it assisted in the process of enhancing the flexibility of the labour market. Children became an increasingly important component of the new industrial labour market and parish apprentices led the way. The widespread use of parish apprentices indicated in the previous two chapters, demonstrates their value in redistributing industrial labour from areas of surplus to areas where child labour was scarce.[65] It is impossible to estimate how many children were apprenticed by their parishes into the cotton and other factory textile industries, but this study supports Mary Rose's assertion that 'since a high proportion of urban parishes and indeed rural mill owners were involved in the transfer, the numbers must have been considerable'.[66] Although labour was often imported, typically this was quite nearby and anyway was easily come by.[67]

Parish apprenticeship also carried wider, and longer-term implications, both economic and social in nature. For example, there were longer-term benefits to the employers, in the form of either disposable, or quiescent labour; and to the economy as the basis for a new industrial labour force was formed. 'For the first time in history,

---

61 Peter Scholliers, 'Grown-ups, boys and girls in the Ghent cotton industry: the Voortman mills, 1835–1914', *Social History*, 20 (1995): 217, shows that this was the case in his examination of the cotton industry in the Low Countries.

62 Mary B. Rose, *The Gregs of Quarry Bank Mill: The Rise and Decline of a Family Firm 1750–1914* (Cambridge, 1986), p. 30.

63 Rose, 'Social policy', p. 19.

64 Rose, *The Gregs*, p. 31. Rose identifies the Peel, David Dale at New Lanark, and Douglas at Holywell. There were of course others.

65 Rose, *The Gregs*, pp. 26–8.

66 Rose, *The Gregs*, p. 30.

67 Rose, *The Gregs*, p. 33.

children became important factors in the economic system',[68] a labour force that was inured to control and discipline; to long hours of monotonous work, and impersonal, crowded conditions. The system of parish factory apprenticeship also benefitted the economy in terms of declining costs of poor relief. Children apprenticed to factories were more likely to acquire long-term employment than those who remained in the workhouse. The longer the children stayed, the more beneficial would be the practice for the employer, and possibly even for the child.

Many historians have emphasised the short-lived nature of parish apprentice labour. As some employers had used such labour because none other was available, it is implied that once other types were available then the practice would cease. It is argued that the 1802 legislation had aggravated the inconvenience of employing parish children. Conforming to the requirements of the Act imposed costs, which were not trivial. Augmenting the expense of providing education and gender-segregated sleeping arrangements, was the cost of annual whitewashing. It has been demonstrated that the job could be time-consuming and expensive. The 1824 Factory Visitors reports indicate that cleaning and whitewashing were performed to a variable standard; and generally seen to be a nuisance. One firm employed a man solely for that purpose.[69] Whitewashing also incurred loss of time: 'We are informed that the process of whitewashing properly is tedious and troublesome, that is occasions a delay of nearly a week and is very destructive to the machinery if not carefully preserved'.[70]

It has been argued that employers found parish apprentice labour to be a 'headache'.[71] To some they were found to be 'troublesome, inconvenient and objectionable in almost every point of view…'.[72] At Pleasley mill they were 'so much trouble to have in the House', and proprietors replaced them with young people on a seven-year indenture, and adults on long-term contracts, thus 'obtaining the advantages of a stable labour force without the cares and responsibilities of maintaining a large number of young children …'.[73] Although the practice of parish factory apprenticeship waned in some regions prior to 1820, it persisted elsewhere until mid-century, despite alleged inconvenience. In 1835, for example,

> James McConnell, a large Manchester spinner, purchased a Derbyshire factory with apprentices and decided to continue with them. In 1843 he complained that they had given him little else than headaches. He had foreseen a cost advantage because of their low wages, but the expenses for housing, the waste of food, the care of clothing, the

---

68   Edgar Royston Pike, *Human Documents of the Industrial Revolution in Britain* (London, 1966), p. 75.

69   1824 Factory Reports, HO44/14, National Archives.

70   Detailed report, dated 2 March 1824, from John Hargreaves and Laurence Halstead of the higher division of the Hundred of Blackburn. 'careful inspection of 35 of the most considerable cotton mills and factories', 1824 Factory Reports, HO44/14, National Archives.

71   Smelser, *Social Change*, p. 187.

72   *Children's Employment Commission*, PP, 1843 (210), XIV, pp. 211–12. Rose, *Gregs*, p. 78.

73   Chapman, *Early Factory Masters*, p. 173, quoting Alderman Howitt, partner in the Pleasley enterprise.

apprentices complaints that they were working for nothing, and their ineffective labour led McConnell to believe that 'in reality [apprentice labour] is more expensive than paid labour ... and ... troublesome, inconvenient ... and objectionable in almost every point of view'. He believed that there were almost no apprentices in the early 1840s, general experience having 'decided against the system'.[74]

Such a detailed critique is rare and although some elements of it are convincing, none was new, and free children were not devoid of inconvenient qualities. Also while McConnell's statement usefully itemises the costs of parish apprentices, it fails to indicate the benefits that had permitted his Cressbrook mill and others in the area to remain profitable for several decades. Although Samuel Greg found apprentices increasingly expensive, he also retained the system for over 60 years.[75]

Those who have argued that the economics of parish apprentices did not operate in the employers' favour except for a short period in the early stages of factory production have typically overlooked the expense of parish apprentices as a proportion of the total costs of establishing and running the factory. In most cases, the costs unrelated to parish apprentices, namely fixed capital expenditure in the form of factory premises, machines, power, as well as such working capital costs as raw materials and stocks, were huge compared with the total spent on the parish children, even where this might be inflated by a purpose-built apprentice house.[76]

In the early textile mills, new technology rather than labour was responsible for production and productivity increases. Factories needed cheap labour to ensure that machines kept running. Evidence from the records of a number of businesses suggests that those which invested substantially in initial fixed capital were more likely than others to focus their attention and their capital on overcoming technological problems, developing machinery and improving their power sources. Davison and Hawksley, for example, which depended on parish apprentice labour, demonstrated greater interest in technical innovation that in the welfare of their young workers. Machinery drained their time and their money; and the resulting containment of labour costs minimised the quality of apprentices' food and clothing.[77] Also in Nottinghamshire, the Robinsons of the extensive Papplewick enterprise appeared to act in a similar fashion. The family was wealthy, having built up a cotton empire during the 1740s through cotton bleaching, before constructing several mills and converting corn mills along the river Leen. While the partners depended substantially on parish apprentices for their labour,[78] thousands of pounds were spent in machine development, in creating dams and water channels to harness water power in the

---

74 Smelser, *Social Change*, p. 187, quoting McConnell from Parliamentary papers 1843 XIV, CEC, pp. 211–12.

75 Rose, *Gregs*, p. 78; Collier, *Family Economy*, p. 46.

76 The cost of apprentice labour rather than the cost of millowners' rates bill. Benjamin Smart, for example, was the the third largest ratepayer in the parish. Joan Lane, 'Apprenticeship in Warwickshire cotton mills, 1790–1830', *Textile History*, 10 (1979): 171.

77 Their communications with Boulton and Watt demonstrate technical competence, DD 452/6/1–13, NA.

78 Many were drawn from the Parish of St Marylebone.

unpromising environment of Papplewick; and in litigation with adjacent landowners.[79] In neither case was capital short; yet the labour costs were minimised.

During the early period of industrialisation, children were the most suitable form of labour in the new factories. Technological innovation permitted production with the minimum of direct intervention. It was rational to use the youngest and cheapest labour possible. Parish apprentices were ideal; not only were they cheap, but, because they were effectively captive labour, they were the least likely to object to the new, experimental conditions of work. While children were a minor element in overall costs, parish apprentices were not a free resource. Like all labour, they had a cost. The expenses associated with parish apprentices were board and lodging rather than wages. The cost of workplace supervision was the same for 'free' children as for parish apprentices, and although the latter also incurred non-work supervision costs, such was the length of the working day that these were minimal. The benefits of parish apprentices, like their costs, included measurable and less tangible components. These included their output in the short term, but also a quiescent labour force in the longer term.

The first part of this book has explored the process of the parish factory apprenticeship system. It has demonstrated the existence of a formally regulated and well documented transfer of poor children from parishes with insufficient placements to meet all requirements to textile mills seeking to enhance labour supply. It has revealed a complex pattern of distribution as apprentices from parishes throughout the land travelled varying distances to textile factory placements. While not always the very cheap option anticipated by some mill owners, such apprentices provided cost effective labour for much of the early textile industry. The value of parish apprentices will continue to be explored in the second part of the book, which considers their experience as factory workers.

---

79   Website: <www.papplewick.org/local/millinfo.htm> (last accessed 19 June 2007); Also Robinsons of Papplewick Account book, DDBM 197/1–2, NA.

Chapter 7

Parish Factory Apprenticeship and the Nature of Work

The assumption that apprenticeships should provide a formal training in skilled work has led some historians to describe apprenticeships to factory or manufacturing shop as 'fictive'.[1] Yet the juxtaposition of pre-industrial 'trade' apprenticeship and early industrial factory apprenticeship has generated misleading comparisons. The two types were more alike than commonly believed. 'Real' apprenticeships involved training in the skills necessary for a particular trade but also included 'apprehension' and 'inculcating of skilled instinct', as well as instruction in literacy, numeracy, and housewifery.[2] This was also the case in the more carefully regulated factory apprenticeships where a range of 'transferable' skills, as well as those specific to textile production, were learned. Some historians have suggested that even 'real' apprenticeship was never primarily 'economic' in the 'strict sense of being rationally functional to the purpose of skilled training'; and K.D.M. Snell has argued that the system was a form of moral and social control as well as a means of market and labour force supervision.[3] Again there are parallels with factory apprenticeships which will be explored below. As far as parish apprentices were concerned, few were taught a profitable trade, and through the later eighteenth century, a large proportion of boys were placed in overcrowded and vulnerable trades, while girls were commonly bound to domestic service. Despite the allegedly unskilled nature of much factory work, textile factory apprenticeship had at least two advantages over dead-end non-factory placements: firstly, it provided experience in a new, if experimental, form of work; and secondly it provided experience in an expanding area of activity in which employment prospects appeared buoyant.

---

1   Lynn Hollen Lees, *The Solidarities of Strangers: The English Poor Laws and the People, 1700–1948* (Cambridge, 1998), p. 56. Dunlop also argued that although capitalism was inimical to apprenticeship, much work in skilled trades was of low-grade, assistant type; and apprentices were taught a small component of the trade so that they were unable to work on their own account after apprentice. O.J. Dunlop, *English Apprenticeship and Child Labour: A History* (London, 1912), p. 231. She also states, on page 227, that apprenticeship was more congenial to the domestic than to the factory system. According to Pamela Horn, 'the training was minimal ... and of little value in providing the child with the experience needed for a secure job in later life'. *Children's Work and Welfare, 1780–1890* (Cambridge, 1995), p. 10.

2   K.D.M. Snell, 'The apprenticeship system in British history: the fragmentation of a cultural institution', *History of Education*, 25/ 4 (1996): 3.

3   Snell, 'Apprenticeship system', p. 4.

The sources reveal little about the nature of the training that factory apprentices received or even on the nature of work that they undertook.[4] Nevertheless, by combining several forms of evidence it is possible to derive a sense of the apprentices' working experience and hence what was learned during their term. This chapter will test the view that parish factory apprenticeship in textile production did not provide training in the key skills required for long-term employment in the industry. It identifies the tasks performed by children and young adults, and assesses evidence about the long-term value of their apprenticeships. It considers evidence about the extent to which apprentices acquired specialist and transferable skills. It argues that what parish factory apprentices learned above all was how to be factory workers, and that this was important.

From an early stage of their apprenticeship, even very young children were 'independent' workers.[5] They were not simply assistants. New technology, which raised labour productivity to previously unknown levels, increased the demand for child labour not just as helpers but also as substitutes for adult workers in the main process.[6] The operation of the factory was dependent on the labour of such children. As machine minders, parish apprentices were accountable for the output of their machines, and therefore had more responsibility than had hitherto been the case.[7] The work performed by children was essential to the production process.[8] According to Samuel Fox who, together with his son, worked at Hancox and Wakefield at Mansfield, 'We [the factory] cannot work without the children ... children can do the work better than grown persons'.[9] The Backbarrow concern clearly 'could not have succeeded without the pauper apprentices who tended many of the machines'.[10] Subject to adequate age or size on entry, parish factory apprentices quickly reached the position of independent workers, without whom many early textile mills would not have continued profitably. Unlike other apprenticeships, where parish children spent much of their term 'helping' in the productive process by conducting ancillary tasks, those in factories soon became independent machine minders, performing intermittent remedial tasks. They were supervised by overlookers, the only adults in the workforce of many mills. The very youngest children, those apprenticed at seven

---

4   This is suggested in Dorothy Marshall, *The English Poor Law in the Eighteenth Century: A Study in Social and Administrative History* (London, 1926), p. 193, who adds that 'it was no one's business to find out'.

5   They were independent not in a financial sense but with respect to separation from family or Poor Law dependence. Also they had responsibility in the workplace and were not simply helpers.

6   Marjetta Rahikainen, *Centuries of Child Labour: European Experience from the Seventeenth to the Twentieth Century* (Aldershot, 2004), p. 10. All stages of production relied to varying degrees on child labour. Michael Winstanley, 'The factory workforce', in Mary B. Rose (ed.), *The Lancashire Cotton Industry: A History since 1700* (Preston, 1996), p. 131.

7   Dunlop, *English Apprenticeship*, p. 266.

8   Peter Gaskell, *Artisan and Machinery* (London, 1836), pp. 168–70.

9   HL 1818, vol. 96, p. 183. He referred to throstle spinning. This is the corollary of the view expressed by Dr Pennington, surgeon at Papplewick, 'that it is out of the question that we should put men to do it'. SC1816, p. 225.

10 Chris Aspin, *The Water Spinners* (Helmshore, 2003), p. 346.

or eight years old, began their factory working life as scavengers, cleaners, sweepers and bobbin doffers,[11] before progressing to machine minders and piecers.

Many early accounts emphasise the responsibility placed on children for factory profitability, and children's own recognition of their value. Children had a sense of importance at being in charge of a machine. The Marquis de Bombelles described his visit to the Bromsgrove factory of Watson and Co. in 1784. The parish apprentices 'work with a charming assiduity; nothing seems to distract them, and everything shows that they take pride in feeling useful ... the busy child is rarely tempted to do wrong'.[12] Robert Dale Owen, in his autobiography, emphasised the value of young workers at New Lanark, 'a tiny superintendent, boy or girls, took the place of a multitude of adult workpeople ... I had a thousand opportunities to witness the skill and vitality with which these child-rulers acquitted themselves'.[13] And John Aikin observed: 'the children are soon very dextrous ... it is wonderful to see with what dispatch they can raise a system, connect threads, and drop it again into work almost instantaneously'.[14]

Some writers ascribe the independence of children workers to the 'automatic' nature of the technology. In the early factories, it has been suggested, were machines that under one roof were able to convert bales of cotton into bundles of thread, almost automatically. They needed only the 'nimble fingers of children' to keep them in motion. A visitor to Cromford in 1785 said, 'I can only say that the whole process of cleaning, carding, combing, twisting and compleating the yarn for the loom seems to be done almost without human aid'.[15] Certainly the new machines replicated many of the movements of hand spinning. Chris Aspin describes how the rollers replaced finger and thumb to draw out fibres, 'before a revolving flyer imparted the required twist'. By this means a stronger and uniform quality yarn was produced.[16] But the machines were by no means automatic; and were imperfect in many ways.[17]

In the water-spinning mills to which the majority of early parish apprentices were bound, the tasks performed by children were not easy. Evidence to the House of Lords committee illustrates the complex manoeuvres involved. Hodgson stated that water spinning 'required quickness of the hands' and it could take two or three years for a child to acquire the required skill. Also joining broken threads was more complicated an operation for a water spinner than a piecer in a mule mill. And while a child could learn to piece one thread, he or she might not be able to attend too many spindles at one time. Laurence Gardner, a former Douglas apprentice, agreed

---

11 This consisted of removing and replacing bobbins. Pamela Horn, 'The traffic in children and the textile mills, 1780–1816', *Genealogists' Magazine*, 24/5 (1993), describes the main tasks performed by the youngest parish apprentices. See also Horn, *Children's Work and Welfare*, p. 21; and Rahikainen, *Centuries of Child Labour*, p. 130.

12 Aspin, *Water Spinners*, p. 52.

13 Aspin, *Water Spinners*, p. 13.

14 John Aikin, *A Description of the Country from Thirty to Forty Miles round Manchester* (London, 1795), p. 173. He is here describing work on a cotton twist machine.

15 Cited in Aspin, *Water Spinners*, p. 13.

16 Aspin, *Water Spinners*, pp. 14–17.

17 Katrina Honeyman, *Origins of Enterprise: Business Leadership in the Industrial Revolution* (Manchester, 1982), p. 77.

that 'in the water spinning the spinner is a piecer as well as a spinner', whereas 'in the mule spinning the frame comes forward, but in the other it is on one frame, and if the thread breaks you piece it up. In water spinning the spinner has to piece the threads? Yes'.[18] When younger, John Houldsworth, a 47-year-old Oldham weaver, had worked at Douglas, 'attending the water frames and piecing the ends'.[19]

Very young children began with picking cotton.[20] The first task allocated to seven-year-old Robert Blincoe, for example, 'was to pick up the loose cotton, that fell upon the floor. Apparently nothing could be easier, and he set to with diligence'.[21] Otherwise, young apprentices were given as range of scavenging jobs to do. At Douglas's mill, '... we have two little wenches continually cleaning [the machinery]; and we stop three or four frames at once, and wipe them down, and then stop some more'.[22] At Pendleton, 'We take ... scavengers to wipe down for the mule spinners';[23] at David Holt, 'each scavenger has to go under to clean the wheels'.[24]

Two runaway apprentices from Samuel Greg's Styal mill described the tasks they performed. Thomas Priestly's job was 'to attend two machines for spinning cotton, each of which spun about 50 threads, my business was to supply these machines, to guide the threads occasionally and to twist them when they snapt'. He also oiled the machinery 'a matter that required some care'.[25] His younger co-absconder, Joseph Sefton, 'was first employed to doff bobbins ... I then secured straps and put lists round the binders ... I used to oil the machinery every morning in fact I was employed in the mill work I did not spin'.[26]

The factory visits of neither parish officials nor magistrates provide much insight into the nature of parish apprentices' work. It appears not to have been of interest. It is extraordinary that parish officers travelled hundreds of miles apparently to ascertain the well being of their children without observing them at work. But in the majority of cases, even when the 'inspection' of the mill was apparently thorough in terms of duration of visit and interviews with individual children, there is no evidence that the nature and intensity of work and the tasks performed was studied. Apprentices were seldom asked about their work. If the children were witnessed

---

18   Laurence Gardner, employed at Douglas, HL 1819, vol. 110, p. 181.

19   Evidence to HL 1819, vol. 110.

20   Aspin, *Water Spinners*, p. 333. Tasks were allocated on the basis of age more than sex.

21   John Brown, *A Memoir of Robert Blincoe* (Manchester, 1832), p. 20.

22   Laurence Gardner, HL, 1819, vol. 110, p. 181.

23   Hugh Batho, 42, cotton factory manager, Douglas, Pendleton, HL 1819, vol. 110, p. 421.

24   James Kerby, spinner, had worked some time at David Holt, HL 1819, vol. 110, pp. 202–203.

25   'Examination of Thomas Priestly who did on Sunday the 22nd day of June last elope from and desert the employment of his master' by Middlesex magistrates, 2 August 1806. Greg papers C5/8/9/5, MCA.

26   'Examination of Joseph Sefton brought under a warrant of the Rev. Croxton Johnston Clerk one of his Majesty's Justices of the Peace for the County of Chester for his having eloped and deserted the service of Samuel Greg ... to whom he was apprentice', 2 August 1806. Greg papers C5/8/9/4, MCA.

at their labour, a cursory impressionistic statement was given, typically remarking upon the ease of the work. For example, at Haighs mill in Marsden in 1797, parish officers noted that

> we went to the mills, where we were shewn by the said Mr J H —, their different operations, and the children assiduously employed. There is no part of the business that appeared to us to be laborious; it is divided into the different branches of picking and preparing cotton for the machines, spinning and weaving; all of which except the two first, are by the effect of mechanism rendered much easier than the ordinary methods of performing them.[27]

The Birmingham Poor Law officials conducted an inspection of Jewsbury's Measham factory in the autumn of 1813 and found that the work was 'by no means very labourious';[28] and at Cuckney, 'the employment of the children seemed light and easy', according to visitors from London.[29] Visitors never stayed long enough to witness the true arduousness and monotony of the apprentices' labour.

Employers themselves emphasised the ease of work in pre-binding correspondence with parishes. William Douglas asserted that at Pendleton, 'the work in the factory is all light';[30] and at David Holt's Manchester mill

> the children we are desirous of obtaining are intended to be employed in the several branches of the cotton business, such as carding, roving, drawing and spinning none of which require much bodily exertion as the application of power by steam or water supersedes that necessity, the hours of labour seldom exceed 12 in the day – in the night we never work.[31]

In later testimony, Isaac Hodgson, proprietor of Caton mill, insisted that 'there is no other employment where large numbers of children are employed where the work is so easy';[32] while the owner of Pleasley mill near Mansfield stated that 'I think we cannot call it labour, but it is merely attention; they do it with great ease to themselves'.[33]

---

27   Jospeh Moser, 'Report of the Situation of the children apprenticed by the churchwardens, overseers, and governors of the poor, of the united parishes of St Margaret and St John in the city of Westminster to the cotton manufactory of Messrs H ... at M ... and Messrs J and T at Cuckney mills ... Addressed to the workhouse board of the said parishes, 10 April 1797', Published in the *European Magazine*, vol. 34 1798 (Hereafter 1797 Report, St Margaret and St John).
28   The inspections were made on 14 and 15 September 1813, and discussed by the Birmingham Guardians on 12 October 1813, when the visitors were thanked for 'their great attention to the welfare of the children'.
29   1797 Report, St Margaret and St John.
30   Meeting 10 February 1797 the Governors and Directors of the Poor, St James Piccadilly, to discuss letter 21 January 1797 from John Plant, on behalf of Douglas, Pendleton, D1876, WAC.
31   Letter dated 14 September 1801 from Messrs Mitchell and Holt to the Governors and Directors of the Poor, St James Piccadilly, D1878, WAC.
32   HL 1818, p. 206.
33   HL 1818, p. 200.

Although Andrew Ure's suggestions that child labour in factories, 'seemed to resemble a sport', and that most of the time was spent in 'idle contemplation',[34] are derided by historians and were criticised by contemporaries,[35] the 'lightness' of children's work is a recurring theme in early nineteenth century documentation.[36] It is possible that this was a sincere interpretation of the children's effort following a brief workplace visit.[37] Inspectors may have anticipated more intensely arduous work, or children may have been allocated light work or machines slowed for the duration of the inspection. Compared to the labour in the workhouse, with which many visitors were familiar, factory work may have seemed automatic, as machines bore the bulk of physical strain. More likely, however, such remarks were propagandist in intent. Emphasis on the lightness of work comprised an element in the attempt to legitimise children's factory labour, which by the second decade of the nineteenth century was beginning to be challenged. Readiness to emphasise the ease of work indicates a defensive response to the prevailing belief that children were 'naturally ill-suited to heavy labour'.[38]

Medical opinion presented to the parliamentary committees of 1816, 1818 and 1819 reiterated the relative ease of factory employment. In evidence later discredited because it was not based on direct observation,[39] Edward Holme asserted that 'children that are unfit for other employment, may find employment in cotton factories without detriment to their health'.[40] Dr Whatton, after visiting 40 factories, asserted that minding a shop was worse;[41] and another 'I know of no employment whatever less laborious than that in the cotton factories'.[42] William Paulson, a

---

34 Mark Blaug, 'The Classical Economists and the Factory Acts – a re-examination', *Quarterly Journal of Economics*, 72 (1958): 216.

35 In 1835, McCulloch devoted a major article to Ure's philosophy of manufactures.

36 Employers themselves were at pains to emphasise this point. Engels himself was prepared to accept this but argued that precisely because of its lightness it was 'more enervating than any other' employment. Frederik Engels, *The Condition of the Working Class in England* (London, 1969), p. 183. Samuel Kydd too thought the lightness of the work to be a red herring: 'it is the wearisome uniformity of the employment ... which are ... fatiguing to mind and body'. *The Factory Movement*, vol. 1, p. 172. Evidence to the Factory Commission of 1833 alleged the long periods of idleness. Tufnell, for example, 'if a child remains during twelve hours per day for nine hours he performs no actual labour'. Quoted by Edward Baines, *History of the Cotton Manufacture in Great Britain* (London, 1835), p. 459.

37 In his critique of Ure, Charles Wing suggested that 'if he had prolonged his visit to an undue length, he would have found langour ... as to his never having seen an instance of corporal punishment, nor having found the children in ill-humour, perhaps he did not enter the spinning rooms quite so unexpectedly as he imagined'. Charles Wing, *The Evils of the Factory System Demonstrated by Parliamentary Evidence* (London, 1837), p. liii. Such observations may also be relevant to the parish factory visits used in this study.

38 Ludmilla Jordanova, 'Children in history: concepts of nature and society', in G. Scarre (ed.), *Children, Parents and Politics* (Cambridge, 1989), pp. 19–20.

39 HL 1818, p. 10. Other medical evidence was undermined by lack of direct observation.

40 HL 1818, p. 45.

41 HL 1818, p. 35.

42 HL 1818, p. 165.

Mansfield surgeon, believed that factory work 'cannot be called labour'.[43] So easy was the work that at the end of a 12- or 14-hour shift, children had energy to spare. The superintendent of mills at Holywell described the children playing outside after work for hours, even in winter;[44] and Samuel Fox's son was 'ready for play at night when he comes home'.[45]

That children's factory labour included long periods of play was frequently asserted, in response to leading questions. Thomas Turner, house surgeon and apothecary of Manchester Poor House, for example, 'saw various persons at play during the time we were at Mc and K; they were at play whenever we entered the room, but they resumed their work as soon as their employers entered the room'.[46] When Samuel Fox was asked if his son's labour at a Mansfield factory was 'not more play than work?' replied, 'Yes, it is'; and 'More an amusement than a labour?', 'Yes it is'.[47] Major General Doveton, MP for Lancaster found the children at Horrocks factory Preston 'running about and to be playful: it appeared to me to be absolutely an amusement'.[48]

Not all contemporaries approached the subject so benignly, but that children were excessively overworked, however, was a minority opinion in early nineteenth century public documents. References to the intensity of children's work were typically linked to health matters. Testimony to the House of Lords Committee of 1819 indicated the long hours and laboriousness of children's employment, and the damage inflicted on their health by such work. The medical evidence in this enquiry, which emphasised the hazards of intensive early work, contrasted with that presented to the 1816 Select Committee. 'The children's work was very laborious' stated several respondents simply.[49] William Royle commented that the 'children worked so hard, they perspired'.[50] The arduousness of work was commonly associated with the excessive length of the working day. The damage to children's bodies during the period of major growth resulted in permanent 'deformity', and was connected to long hours attending machines without respite, often standing in awkward positions.[51] In evidence to the 1816 Select Committee, William Tomlinson, surgeon

---

43 HL 1818, p. 137.
44 Edward Kenworthy, 45, superintendent of mills at Holywell, evidence to HL1819 vol. 110, p. 390.
45 HL 1818, pp. 178–83.
46 HL 1818, p. 155.
47 HL 1818, pp. 178–83.
48 HL 1818, p. 196.
49 Roger Haslam, 34, spinner, at Thomas Ainsworth; and Joseph Mercer, 37, employed at Lightollers, Chorley, HL 1819, vol. 110, pp. 73 and 84.
50 William Royle, 30, spinner, at Thomas Ainsworth, HL 1819, vol. 110, p. 75.
51 Peter Kirby points out that frequency of such observation notwithstanding, little statistical evidence is available before the later nineteenth century that compares groups of employed and non-employed children. *Child Labour in Britain, 1750–1870* (Basingstoke, 2003), p. 15. John Rule, too, believes that it is not always easy to 'attribute specifically to working conditions poor health which was in part a product of the total living environment'. *The Labouring Classes in Early Industrial England 1750–1850* (London, 1986), p. 144. W.H. Hutt, a robust apologist for the factory system and criticiser of the Hammonds, suggests both

in Preston 'says that he attended the Penwortham factory 4 or 5 times a week, when in possession of Mr Watson; that the children were in a wretched condition from being overworked; a great number of them had crooked legs'.[52] Jeremiah Wood, master cotton spinner, Bolton, when asked if the children employed in factories at an early age frequently become deformed, replied: 'Not so much in mule spinning as in the old water spinning in my opinion'.[53]

In the early years of textile factory production, experimentation with technology, organisation of processes and the nature of work, meant that apprentice training was not yet standard. Not only did practice vary between factories but changes also took place over time in the same factory. From the descriptions of the nature of work and the tasks involved in early textile factory production, it can be argued that in the absence of standard practice, some components of factory work required training while others required experience. Overall, training and experience merged.

Evidence of the apprentices' indentures and the apprenticeship registers indicate that children were to learn a specific trade or skill, such as the 'art of cotton spinning', or 'the art and mystery of flax dressing'. The training programme was rarely specified, though hints are sometimes provided in correspondence between employer and parish. Only occasionally did parishes insist upon receiving a training schedule, to ascertain that their children would be employable as adults. The Guardians of Birmingham, by placing their children only to those factories that provided experience in both spinning and weaving, demonstrated an awareness of the long-term value of 'breadth' of training: 'In consequence of a resolution appearing in our parish books that no children should be put to places where spinning only could be learnt, and finding that some of the best situations (for girls in particular) being of that description'.[54] Such stipulation was founded on the belief that spinning was mostly performed by children, and therefore, with respect to future prospects, this component of the training was of limited value. The Directors of the Poor of St Pancras also ascertained that their children bound to factories be taught a range of relevant skills in order to enhance their chances of employability; and insisted that Messrs Gorton, Chorley and Co., for example, added weaving to the spinning already described on the indentures;[55] and when Isaac Hodgson requested an alteration of the original agreement to teach spinning and weaving, to the vaguer 'cotton manufacturing', the Directors referred

---

that deformities were prevalent at the time irrespective of occupation; and that if there were a larger proportion of deformities among factory children, this might be because weaker children were sent to factories because of the ease of work there. W.H. Hutt, 'The factory system of the early nineteenth century', in F.A.Hayek (ed.), *Capitalism and the Historians* (London, 1954), pp. 177–8.

52 SC1816, p. 295.

53 HL 1819 vol. 110, p. 331.

54 Visit of the factory of Dicken and Co. on Friday 1 July 1808, reported to the Birmingham Guardians at their meeting of 12 July 1808. Minutes of the Birmingham Board of Guardians, GP/B/2/1/2, BCA.

55 9, 16 and 23 December 1806 Minutes of Directors of the Poor, Parish of St Pancras P/PN/PO/1/3 (Microfilm reference UTAH 649) CLSAC.

the matter for consideration by a special committee before fresh indentures were prepared.[56]

Children bound from the parish of St James Piccadilly to Haywood and Palfreyman were to be taught 'spinning, weaving, bleaching, printing and dyeing cotton and other goods ... and there is not the least doubt but that when the children are out of their apprenticeship they will be able to get a very comfortable livelihood at any of the before mentioned trades, except spinning which will always be done principally by children'.[57] A progressive 'training programme' for parish apprentices was outlined by William Douglas for his Pendleton cotton factory. 'In the first stages of their apprenticeships the smallest children are set to wind rovings, to spread cotton upon carding cloths, and to look at the spinners and learn to piece up the ends'. Then children move onto the 'business of the carding rooms'.[58] The apprentices to Marshall, Hutton and Hives, Shrewsbury were to be taught how to manufacture linen yarn and were initially employed in processes that involved separating and cleaning flax fibres prior to spinning;[59] while those to Colbeck, Ellis and Wilks, flax spinners, West House mills, Fewston were to learn 'weaving or flax dressing'.[60] Whatever arrangements were made, children's own awareness of their formal 'apprentice' status, and thus their training schedule, was by no means universal.[61]

Formal training, or more commonly informal on-the-job training, was at least as important for where it would lead as for what was learned. Visitors from St James Piccadilly, for example, having observed the existing conditions at Mitchell and Holt, and 'consulted on their probable prospects', expressed doubts about the value of factory apprenticeships, 'for so simple and unvaried is the labour to which they have been accustomed and so limited is the knowledge to be required in the contracted routine of their occupation that they are by no means qualified to avail themselves of other pursuits ... with very few exceptions by no means warrant the

---

56 6 and 13 February 1816, Minutes of Directors of the Poor Parish of St Pancras. P/PN/PO/1/11 (microfilm reference UTAH 652) CLSAC. In fact, it was not until September, following further enquiries into Hodgson's 'respectability and character' that the change was accepted. The newly amended indentures were executed by 'nine Directors present', and then sent for 'allowing' by two magistrates. 17 September 1816, Minutes of Directors of the Poor, Parish of St Pancras P/PN/PO/1/12 (microfilm reference UTAH 653) CLSAC.

57 6 May 1796 'Report of Messrs Johnson, Charlton and Ideson relative to poor children belonging to this parish upon liking in Cheshire and Derbyshire and apprenticed out in Nottinghamshire', Minutes of Governors and Directors of the Poor, Parish of St James Piccadilly, D1876, WAC.

58 10 February 1797, Minutes of Governors and Directors of the Poor, Parish of St James Piccadilly, to discuss letter 21 January 1797 from John Plant on behalf of Douglas, Pendleton, D1876, WAC.

59 For example, Mary Parsons was apprenticed from the parish of Prees, Shropshire, PL2/7/1/1, SA.

60 8 October 1811. Apprenticeship Register 1802– Parish of St Leonard, Shoreditch, P91/LEN/1332, LMA.

61 The example of an apprentice to Toplis's factory, presented in Chapter 10, provides an illustration of this. Voluntary examination of Jane Bounds of Norton in the parish of Cuckney 'singlewoman', 11 September 1809, DD4P67/71, NA.

prospect of obtaining that comfortable livelihood which your committee are well aware it is the anxious wish of the board should prove the result of their care and management ... to pass several years in the acquisition of a business [i.e. trade or skill] which requires no exercise of intellect, calls forth no ingenuity and excites no emulation'.[62] Doubts were also expressed by the Vestry of St Luke Finsbury: 'Application having been made for a number of children to be apprenticed to the proprietors of the cotton mills at Pendelton ... but several of the governors of the poor [have] doubts whether such children can obtain employ at the expiration of their indenture sufficient to maintain them'.[63] The Foundling Hospital investigated the children's prospects prior to binding at Toplis's Cuckney factory. The response they received did not bode well:

> Considering how their apprentices were to procure their living when out of their times, he said that as the worsted spinning by mills was a recent invention and everybody were getting into it more and more every year several mills have been lately erected in this and the neighbouring counties he could not but foresee however good the intentions of Messrs Toplis were with regard to employing their apprentices in future when out of their time it must be frustrated by the numbers that would want employ from all the various mills who would certainly like them employ all the children ... he should not for all these reasons advise the apprenticed the children as proposed except there was a great difficulty of providing otherwise for them so as render it more eligible to attempt any risk of their future well being.[64]

Testimony to the 1816 Select Committee generated some discussion of the learning experience of parish apprenticeships. The evidence of John Moss, late Governor of the apprentice house at Backbarrow, which referred to his recent encounter with three of the apprentices who were out of their time, but had not yet found employment, suggested that they were trained for very little. 'They spun so coarse; they knew very little about [cotton spinning] ... They might have obtained a living if they were bound to a proper trade'.[65] Such a position was confirmed by Robert Plant, 36, spinner, Appleton and Plant, who, when asked by the House of Lords committee in 1819, whether 'employment in the cotton factories qualify them for any other employment?', replied: 'It does not; a man who has worked in a mill cannot work at anything else'.[66] Theodore Price deplored factory apprenticeships because they had no prospects for the adult female whose 'fingers were too large to go between the

---

62 'Report of Messrs Johnson and Halfhide accompanied by the clerk to the governors of the poor relative to their children apprenticed from the Parish of St James, Westminster, at Manufactures in Lancashire, Cheshire, and Derbyshire', Considered on 3 November 1803, at the meeting of Governors and Directors of the Poor, Parish of St James, Piccadilly. A few months later, however, the parish noted the value of factory apprenticeship for providing good discipline for unruly parish children. 13 March 1804, Meeting of the Governors and Directors of the Poor, Parish of St James, Piccadilly, D1878, WAC.

63 5 October 1797,Vestry Minutes, Parish of St Luke Finsbury, ILHL.

64 Letter from Secretary of Foundling Hospital to Treasurer, June 1792, DD 212/1/5–6, NA.

65 SC1816, p. 182.

66 House of Lords, vol. 110, 1819.

threads to twist cotton'. He was vehemently opposed to factory apprenticeships and refused to sign such indentures.[67]

A key objective of parish apprenticeship was to provide poor children with the means for future support. The more solicitous parishes selected bindings most likely to fulfil this aim. Many of those parishes engaging with the factory apprenticeship system for the first time made careful enquiry into the long-term potential of such placements. Indeed it became common practice for parish officers to ascertain that work was likely to be forthcoming at the end of the apprentice term.[68] Directors of the Poor of St Pancras were cautious about placements, and when investigating the propriety of masters also 'took especial care from the enquiries which they may cause to be made that there is every prospect of full employment for the children when they shall be out of their time'.[69] Prior to binding, employers were usually reassuring on this point. Evidence suggests, however, that while a large proportion of employers would retain the better quality apprentices on expiry of their term, many parish children bound to textile factories were destined to seek employment either at other textile mills, or in altogether different trades. In order that parish factory apprentices be employable beyond the factory, the acquisition of a range of general or 'transferable' skills was essential.[70]

The parishes' interest in training reflected the priority placed on long-term employability.[71] Both parishes and other officials doubted that much of value was acquired during a factory apprenticeship and feared that employment prospects were consequently poor. Hence the emphasis placed on transferable skills.[72] From the

---

67 SC1816.

68 The Foundling Hospital was among the first to do this; and had some misgivings about the post-apprenticeship employment opportunities, for example at Toplis. Letter from Secretary of Foundling Hospital to Treasurer, June 1792, DD 212/1/5–6, NA.

69 In the context of Isaac Hodgson of Caton Mills near Lancaster. 16 August 1814, Minutes of Directors of the Poor, St Pancras Parish, P/PN/PO/1/10(microfilm reference UTAH 652), CLSAC. Before agreeing to the binding of their children to Jeremiah Garnett of Clitheroe, the officials of St Pancras parish were 'requested to take especial care from the enquiries which they may cause to be made, that there is every prospect of full employment for the children when they should be out of their time'. 10 May 1814, Minutes of Directors of the Poor, St Pancras Parish, P/PN/PO/1/9 (microfilm reference UTAH 652), CLSAC.

70 As Snell has shown, this had traditionally been the case.

71 The emphasis placed by the Poor Law on the training of pauper children was enduring and formed the subject of a Poor Law commissioners' report in 1841. Finding that almost 65,000 children under the age of 16 were workhouse residents, it deemed it necessary to ascertain the quality of education and training 'of this class of children' and if necessary to improve it for the purpose of ensuring long-term employability and independence. Report to the Secretary of State for the Home Department from the Poor Law Commissioners on the Training of Pauper children, 1841, pp. iii–vi. A substantial section, pp. 127–200, focused on pauper children and apprenticeship. According to Dorothy Marshall, it was taken for granted in the late eighteenth century that apprenticeship was the only way to train children to play a useful part in the world. Dorothy Marshall, *The English Poor in the Eighteenth Century: A Study in Social and Administrative History* (London, 1926), p. 202.

72 It was feared that factory employment 'consumed the energies of the child by excessive toil in an unhealthy environment, casting the young adrift at the close of their apprenticeship

earliest days of factory apprenticeship, parishes expected that during their term, the children would acquire basic literacy skills and sometimes facility in numeracy too, in much the same way as they would have done had they remained under the direct control of the parish in the workhouse.[73] Such expectation was later enshrined in legislation.[74] It appears that greater care was taken by parishes to ensure that such transferable skills were taught than in confirming the content of industrial training. In post-binding enquiries, and during factory visits, parishes ascertained the quality and quantity of educational provision much more rigorously than the teaching of workplace skills. It may be that the officers of the parish believed that the ability to read and write provided for a more secure future and increased the employability of their children more than competence in industrial work. It is possible that the children thought so too. Several accounts exist that indicate the determination of many children to acquire literacy skills, or to sustain the level reached prior to their factory placement.[75]

The 1802 Act stipulated that parish apprentices should, at least for the first four years of their indentures, be taught the three Rs for some time each day in a dedicated room, by some 'discreet and proper person'.[76] Prior to the clarification provided by the Act, and even for some time afterwards, practice varied, but most commonly children were taught literacy, often in conjunction with religious instruction, by a local clergyman. In some cases, the arrangement was explicitly negotiated between parish and employer. In others, a system of education already existed at the factory prior to placement.[77] In yet others, parish officers made local arrangements without apparent reference to the employers. This was the case of St James parish children at Wildboar Clough, the parish officers arranged for 'their' children to be educated by a local clergyman. The Reverend Bromley appears to have taught the St James children to read and to write, but children from the other parishes, it appears, received no such benefits.[78] David Holt, Quaker educationalist and cotton spinner provided for the instruction of his parish apprentices. He announced to the parish officers of

---

with faculties impaired and without the training requisite to a future career'. A.E. Dobbs, *Education and Social Movements 1700–1850* (London, 1919), p. 132.

73 Not all children acquired literacy skills in the workhouse but instruction was usually provided.

74 The 1802 HMA Act stipulated that time and space be put aside each day for the purpose of educating the apprentices.

75 Examples of this are explored in Chapter 10.

76 42 Geo III c 73 (1802) p. 418.

77 Many employers recognised the value of an educated workforce. Wanda Minge-Kalman, 'The industrial revolution and the European family. The institutionalization of 'childhood' as a market for family labour', *Comparative Studies in Society and History*, 20 (1978): 457. It has been suggested that the 'socialising' outcome of a programme of education was more important than the acquisition of literacy or numeracy skills. David F. Mitch, 'The role of human capital in the first industrial revolution', in Joel Mokyr (ed.), *The British Industrial Revolution: an Economic Perspective* (Boulder, Oxford, 1993), p. 295.

78 Extensive correspondence between Rev. William Bromley and the officers of St James parish took place between May 1796 and January 1797, Minutes of Governors and Directors of the Poor, Parish of St James, Piccadilly, D1876, WAC.

St James Piccadilly that in addition to religious and moral teaching he intended 'to go beyond this and allow them an opportunity of learning to read etc in some part of the working hours'.[79] A dedicated schoolmaster was duly appointed.[80]

Education at Backbarrow, according to evidence of a long-serving overlooker to Peel's Committee, had for some time been satisfactorily provided by a clergyman during his Sunday visits; 'but latterly there have been two men appointed to attend every Sunday in the house, to read prayers and address the children' for which the proprietors pay.[81] In this case and probably many others, Sunday was specified for the apprentices' general education, it being too much of an intrusion into the working days. At Backbarrow, even Sunday was, for those selected to clean machinery, a working day. At the better-run enterprises, parish apprentices received an education at least on a par with that provided in the workhouse. Some children ended their term both literate and numerate; with the potential to transfer these skills to non-factory employments if they so wished. Less solicitous employers failed to provide fully for their apprentices' educational needs. So in a number of cases the children's education was at best sporadic, at worst entirely neglected.[82] Where these appear to have been neglected, complaints were made, most vociferously by the children as demonstrated in Chapter 10.

Religious education was often linked with more general education, when instruction in literacy was provided by local clergymen, using bibles and prayer books as reading matter. Both parish and state insisted upon moral and religious teaching, to which much of Sunday was typically dedicated. The required church attendance filled the local pews with parish apprentices.[83] The growth of Sunday Schools, mainly in the urban areas, was associated with the infant population – more often 'free' children than parish apprentices – of textile factories. For many children, such institutions provided the major component of their educational experience.[84] Child labour in the cotton-manufacturing town of Stockport produced the largest Sunday school in the world.[85] In some areas, children employed in factories were given preference to Sunday school admission.[86] The research of K.D.M Snell demonstrates a strong correlation between Sunday school pupils and employment in manufacturing; also connected with high levels of religious attendance, relatively

---

79 17 September 1801, Minutes of the Governors and Directors of the Poor, Parish of St James, Piccadilly, D1878, WAC.

80 17 September 1802, Minutes of the Governors and Directors of the Poor, Parish of St James Piccadilly, D1878, WAC.

81 Testimony of William Travers, SC1816, p. 288.

82 Even after the 1833 Factory Act, which introduced compulsory schooling, the education component was often neglected. Janet Burns, 'The west riding half timer' in *Old West Riding*, 9 (1989): 21.

83 For example, in Cark-in-Cartmel. Aspin, *Water Spinners*, pp. 352–60.

84 W.B. Stephens, *Education, Literacy and Society, 1830–1870: The Geography of Diversity in Provincial England* (Manchester, 1987), p. 93; Mitch, 'The role of human capital', p. 281.

85 K.D.M. Snell, 'The Sunday school movement in England and Wales: child labour, denominational control and working class culture', *Past and Present*, 164 (1999), p. 142.

86 Snell, 'Sunday school', p. 142.

high wages and low per capita relief costs in the Midlands and northern counties.[87] He concludes that

> those areas most exploiting child labour were the ones that leaned most heavily on primary religious education for their youth ... It was in many ways a facilitating response to the problems created by those patterns of child labour, and to what was probably an intensified work-discipline affecting children and teenagers during the working week.[88]

Other 'transferable' skills were gender specific.[89] The domestication of the female apprentices was commonly referred to in the parish and business records, despite its evident incompatibility with the productive activities of the factory. Employers appeared to be conscious of their responsibility in this respect, yet perceived it as less pressing than did the parish officers. Although female apprentices were often retained in the factory as young adults, it was expected that on marriage or childbirth, they would either take a 'career break' or quit the factory altogether and later pursue other occupations.[90] Both sexes, however, appear to have had access to employment beyond the factory. A range of evidence, including parish examinations and parliamentary investigations, indicates that child workers were able to later enter many other occupations.[91] Not only were many parish apprentices literate but they had also acquired the ability to work hard and retain a focus on even the most monotonous of tasks.

If much of the work performed in factories was repetitive and easy to learn, to what extent did apprenticeship have value? And what skills did children acquire? The most important element of 'training' was the adaptation to factory discipline acquired by having grown up in that context.[92] Although parish officers were concerned about the limitations of factory apprenticeship, it was nevertheless the case that such an apprenticeship was a prerequisite for adult factory employment, without which the chances of obtaining such work were slim.[93] If the 'skills' acquired were negligible, factory apprentices nevertheless learned to be factory workers, though on-the-job training and socialisation.[94] This section of the chapter argues not only

---

87 Snell, 'Sunday school', pp. 145–6.
88 Snell, 'Sunday school', pp. 167–8.
89 Programmes of education often coupled the learning of the three Rs with 'sewing for the girls'. John Marshall did this in his factory school in Holbeck, for example. Burns, 'The West Riding half-timer', p. 23.
90 Aspin, *Water Spinners*, p. 259; R.S. Fitton and A.P. Wadsworth, *The Strutts and the Arkwrights, 1758–1830: A Study of the Early Factory System* (Manchester, 1958), pp. 230–32.
91 Aspin, *Water Spinners*, p. 260; the 1819 report contains several tables of information about employment of former factory workers.
92 Douglas A Galbi, 'Child labor and the division of labor in the early English cotton mills', *Journal of Population Economics*, 10/4 (1997): 357–75. The firm of Samuel Greg recognised this in retaining apprentices as adult labour: 'the best families for good conduct have sprung from this source'. Mary B. Rose, *The Gregs of Quarry Bank Mill: The Rise and Decline of a Family Firm, 1750–1914* (Cambridge,1986), p. 57.
93 John Lyons, 'Family response to economic decline: Handloom weavers in early nineteenth-century Lancashire', *Research in Economic History*, 12 (1989): 71.
94 Mitch, 'The role of human capital', pp. 295–307.

that in enduring a factory apprenticeship parish children learned what it meant to be a factory worker, but also that such training was recognised by employers to equip young people for factory employment without which their prospects were reduced. Finally, it provides evidence that parish factory apprentices who so desired secured long-term employment in textile mills.

Prior to entry into the factory setting, parish apprentices were already familiar with the discipline of routine and regular working which was alien to 'free' children and adults.[95] E.P. Thompson's contrast between flexible pre-industrial notions of time and the regular time divisions of industrial society, has been challenged by Tadmor's argument that there were regular notions of time and work even before the shift to the factory.[96] In any case, the workhouse regime was likely to have provided a valuable introduction to factory work. For employers, 'the formation of a disciplined factory labour force was an awkward hurdle',[97] if not 'one of the most difficult transformations required'[98] during industrialisation, and one that children, and especially parish apprentices were most likely to help them overcome.[99] The work of Douglas Galbi has provided a framework within which to understand the 'training' element of children's factory labour.[100] Learning to be a factory worker included becoming accustomed to working in a managed and supervised way[101] – itself necessitated by the machine – and acquiring the ability to work in disagreeable

---

95 For example, the Bristol workhouse, see E.E. Butcher, *Bristol Corporation of the Poor: Selected Records, 1696–1834* (Bristol, 1932); and the Manchester workhouse, which, like others also prepared children for harshness and deprivation. G.B. Hindle, *Provision for the Relief of the Poor in Manchester 1754–1826* (Manchester, 1975), pp. 40–48.

96 Naomi Tadmor, *Family and Friends in Eighteenth Century England: Household, Kinship and Patronage* (Cambridge, 2001), pp. 66–7. Equally, familial cooperation did not necessarily negate individual economic action or a desire for economic gain. Tadmor, *Family and Friends*, p. 178.

97 Colin Heywood, 'The market for child labour in nineteenth-century France', *History*, 66 (1981): 46; though Heywood also believed that *les enfants assistes* were only a *pis aller* for employers.

98 Sidney Pollard, 'Factory discipline in the industrial revolution', *Economic History Review*, 16/2 (1963): 254.

99 Not least because parish apprentices were not in a position to resist, as could adults and 'free' children, entry into the new factories. Pollard, 'Factory discipline', p. 254.

100 Galbi's focus is on 'free' children, though his findings are relevant to parish apprentices too. There may not have been a great difference between the early workplace training of parish apprentices and free children.

101 Kristine Bruland, 'The transformation of work in European industrialisation', in Peter Mathias and John A. Davis (eds), *The First Industrial Revolutions* (Oxford, 1989), pp. 158–62; Stephen A. Marglin, 'What do bosses do? The origins and functions of hierarchy in capitalist production', *The Review of Radical Political Economics*, 6/2 (1974): 94–100; Maxine Berg, 'Factories, workshops and industrial organisation', in Roderick Floud and Donald McCloskey (eds), *The Economic History of Britain since 1700*, vol. 1, 1700–1860, (2nd edn, Cambridge, 1994), pp. 146–7. The tendency of workers to shirk generated a range of disciplinary and monitoring devices. Michael Huberman, 'How did labour markets work in Lancashire? More evidence on prices and quantities in cotton spinning, 1822–1852', *Explorations in Economic History*, 28 (1991): 88.

conditions for the very long hours demanded by the factory regime. Early inuring to (or socialisation into) the new environment of the factory was essential, and early manufacturers found difficulty in 'training human beings to renounce their desultory habits of work, and identify themselves with the unvarying regularity of the complex automaton'.[102]

The new environment was unpleasant and unhealthy.[103] In the descriptions of the health hazards of early factory work, medical men among others noted the intense heat in which many children laboured.[104] Extremely hot conditions were more likely in the mule spinning factories powered by steam, than in the water frame mills to which most parish apprentices were indentured, but the latter were by no means exempt.[105] Mill visitors who reported to the parliamentary committees of 1816–19[106] may have been struck by the uncomfortable temperatures endured by workers and believed them to be unhealthy, yet evidence indicates that they did not experience the full impact of the factory heat. Other testimony suggests that special measures were taken on the day of the visit to reduce temperatures.[107] The factory atmosphere was also polluted by cotton particles that, ingested by young apprentices, required resolution by emetics.[108] Cotton dust was combined with that from the chalk rubbed on the rollers of the water frames to prevent the fibres sticking, and worsened the environment still further. Robert Blincoe described being 'not a little affected by the dust and flue with which he was half suffocated',[109] and apprentices learned to withstand the discomfort of spending hours in unventilated sheds full of flying cotton fibres that inflamed the eyes and damaged the lungs.[110]

---

102 Pollard, 'Factory discipline', p. 258; see also Mitch, 'The role of human capital', pp. 295–6.

103 Michael Watkins submitted written reports of his factory visits to the House of Lords 1819 Committee, which indicated that conditions were worse where steam engines are used. Water wheels generated a more wholesome atmosphere and the appearance of children better, HL 1819, vol. 110, p. 279.

104 Even though some had no first-hand experience of this.

105 Very few of the parish visitors' reports, for example, criticised the temperature; though some referred to the level of ventilation, a feature stipulated in the 1802 HMA Act.

106 In HL 1818, the medical witnesses were specifically asked about the heat in which the children worked.

107 This indicated that most proprietors received some warning of an impending visit. John Broadbent evidence to HL 1819, vol. 110, p. 144; Evidence from George Chapel, Joseph Tavner, George Brennan, Matthew Carter, who also noted that very young children were sent away on the day and others were spruced up; and John Haigh, HL 1819, vol. 110. M.H. MacKenzie, 'Cressbrook and Litton mills: a reply', *Derbyshire Archaeological Journal*, 90 (1970): 58.

108 Aspin, *Water Spinners*, p. 26.

109 John Brown, *A Memoir of Robert Blincoe* (Manchester, 1832).

110 Such conditions persisted throughout the nineteenth century. Engels described the ailments resulting from working in rooms full of fibrous dust. Engels, *Condition*, pp. 91–100. Flax spinning was particularly damaging to health. Workers were not only affected by dust but also by the damp atmosphere created by 'wet spinning'. Ivy Pinchbeck, *Women Workers and the Industrial Revolution 1750–1850* (London, 1930), p. 187. See Samuel Kydd (Alfred), *The History of the Factory Movement from the Year 1802, to the Enactment of the Ten Hours'*

The use of fish oil for lighting generated a number of disorders; and the oil required for machine lubrication had a particularly unpleasant smell.[111] The smell of the factory was one of the many disagreeable features to which apprentice children had to become accustomed. Blincoe first noticed the smell even before he entered the factory, caused by the oil 'with which the axles of twenty thousand wheels and spindles were bathed. The moment he entered the doors, the noise appalled him and the stench seemed intolerable'.[112] Other unhealthy practices were referred to in the second volume of Ferriar's *Medical Histories* published in 1795. He particularly identified the habit of night children getting into beds 'which have just been quitted by other children who labour during the day. This is, alone a very noxious practice. But such is the natural appetite for fresh air, that many of these little creatures prefer rambling in the fields during part of the time allotted to then for sleep'.[113]

Parish apprentices also became accustomed, often the hard way, to the dangers of factory machinery.[114] For very young children, scavenging and collecting cotton involved moving under machinery and even between motive parts. Lapse of concentration could lead to a serious injury. Crushed hands and fingers were common, and so were head injuries. Unguarded machinery in textile factories rendered mutilations commonplace.[115] Parish apprentices and other children were also 'trained' or gained experience in working in crowded, noisy conditions. Blincoe was 'terrified by the whirring motion and noise of the machinery' but all apprentices became inured or deafened by the clatter of spinning machines.[116] They also came to terms with close supervision. Resistance to disciplined working conditions was more likely when entry took place after childhood. Galbi suggests that 'work in mechanised factories required regular attendance and consistent effort, respect for tools ... used but not owned ... and the ability to work in close quarters with a large number of persons. In late eighteenth century England, these were largely new kinds of skills'.[117]

Bill in 1847 (London, 1857), pp. 166–9, for more detail on conditions in flax spinning and in silk and worsted mills. Few contemporary occupations were without dangers and discomfort, some of them, such as the mercury poisoning suffered by hatters and the muscular conditions of miners, were considerably worse than those endured by factory workers. John Rule, *The Labouring Classes in Early Industrial England 1750–1850* (London, 1986), pp. 139–44.

111 1802 Report, St Margaret and St John.
112 Brown, *Memoir*, p. 20.
113 Cited in Aspin, *Water Spinners*, p. 28.
114 The dangers associated with factory work were very real, but worse existed in coal mines. See Ray Devlin, *Children of the Pits: Child Labour and Child Fatality in the Coal Mines of Whitehaven and District* (Whitehaven, 1988), p. 38; Peter Kirby, 'The viability of child labour and the Mines Act of 1842' (University of Sunderland occasional paper, 1996); P.E.H. Hair, 'Mortality from violence in British coal mines, 1800–1850', *Economic History Review*, 21/3 (1968): 549–59.
115 Roy Porter, *English Society in the Eighteenth Century* (Harmondsworth, 1991), p. 335. He also connected the damp atmosphere of factories to the rise in tuberculosis.
116 Brown, *Memoir*, p. 20.
117 Galbi, 'Child labor', p. 358.

Galbi uses evidence from the early nineteenth century to argue that factory managers considered child labour in the factory to be important, if not essential training for future factory work; and that most adult factory labour had worked in factories as children. Because the requirements of factory work were so different from any other form of employment, employers strongly preferred those who had worked in factories at a young age. His argument is that child labour, including parish apprentices, was important in shaping the size and characteristics of the pool of future adult factory workers.[118] This must have specifically applied to parish apprenticeship, which was therefore more than disposable labour. It was, rather, an entry point into the labour market for the early English cotton mills. The learned experience as children, not only sustained factory production, but also ensured continuity into adult labour.[119] The best adult labour was that which had learned the ways of the factory from childhood. Galbi and others argue that apprenticeship from a young age in factories was the best way to learn to become an adult factory worker. This is confirmed by Colin Heywood in the context of France. In the factories there, a training element was implicit in much child labour, which often constituted a first rung on a ladder that might lead to a skilled position as an adult.[120] Evidence that employers preferred apprentices when selecting adult workers was collected by parishes. St James Piccadilly sponsored an enquiry in the Manchester area by a representative of Holts who found that 'a very great preference is given to those hands who have been employed in the business several years and consequently to those who have served apprenticeships to it'.[121]

Indeed, unless factory experience had been gained as a child, the chance of becoming a competent adult worker was slim. In the opinion of Andrew Ure: 'it is found nearly impossible to convert persons past the age of puberty ... into useful factory hands'.[122] Factory employees preferred workers who had begun to work in the factory at a young age because the requirements of the factory were so different from the requirements of other jobs at that time. Above all, the children learned to be factory workers. Adult workers who had not worked in the factories as children generally could not find jobs in the factories even if they were willing to work at low wages.

The discussion finally turns to the extent to which parish apprentices used their experience to gain adult employment.[123] Systematic data on what became of

---

118 Galbi, 'Child labor', pp. 357–75. See also Douglas A. Galbi, 'Economic change and sex discrimination in the early English cotton factories', Discussion Paper, Centre for History and Economics, King's College Cambridge. Social Science Research Network Electronic Paper Collection.

119 This is consistent with traditional apprenticeship where it was important that in order to acquire a competency, it was necessary to begin work at an early age.

120 Heywood, 'The market for child labour', p. 44.

121 Letter dated 3 May 1803, from Rev. Johnson and read to the meeting of the Governors and Directors of the Poor, Parish of St James Piccadilly, 12 May 1803, D1878, WAC.

122 Andrew Ure, *Philosophy of Manufactures* (London, 1835), p. 16.

123 This is considered further in the following chapter, which considers the gender division of labour.

apprentices at the end of their term do not exist,[124] but there is sufficient evidence to suggest that employment opportunities existed either in the mill in which the apprenticeship had been served, or in equivalent factories. The following illustrations from individual businesses and parishes demonstrate that even firms reputed to dispose of their apprentices retained a significant proportion. Birch's Backbarrow mill is an example. In testimony to the 1816 Select Committee, it was claimed that apprentices were released on completion of their apprenticeship, yet an investigation by the parish of St Clement Danes indicates a satisfactory retention rate at least among the girls.[125] At Litton mill, where conditions were allegedly poor and expendability might be expected, retention was substantial. In 1803, parish officers from St James Piccadilly reported seeing boys from St George the Martyr working at Litton after the end of their terms.[126] Even Robert Blincoe, whose criticisms of the factory's organisation are well known, remained at the end of his apprenticeship though he left of his own accord some months later.[127]

Other cases indicate the intention for apprentices to stay on at the end of their term; even if this did not always work out in practice. Pre-binding correspondence in which proprietors assured parishes of the long-term opportunities at their mills may be interpreted as a cynical means of extracting suitable children. The Holywell Twist Company, for example, in setting out its terms for the apprenticeship arrangement to the Hertfordshire parish of Royston, stated that 'when out of their time – girls may then earn from 5 to 7s per week, boys from 10 to 15s or more according to their ability'.[128] Evidence from settlement examinations, letters from former apprentices and later parliamentary enquiries confirms that Douglas's factories at Holywell and Pendleton had good retention rates, which would have been even better had all those given the opportunity to remain done so. Of those choosing to leave, a large proportion sought employment in neighbouring mills. The statement of Margaret Chamberlain, formerly an apprentice at Douglas's Pendleton factory, reveals that 'it was universally the custom in that country to employ those who had served their apprenticeship in the neighbourhood in preference to any others'. She also stated that she had known some girls who had initially left at the end of their apprenticeship to go into domestic service but that they had subsequently returned.[129] Two other former apprentices at Pendleton provided written evidence. Letters from Elizabeth Cuthbert

---

124 This requires detailed research on local-level record linkage. See Pat Hudson, 'A new history from below: computers and the maturing of local and regional history', *The Local Historian* (1995): 217–18; and Steve King, 'Reconstructing Lives: The Poor, the Poor Law and Welfare in Calverley, 1650–1820', *Social History*, 22/ 3 (1997): 318–38.

125 Of the 11 girls who had completed their term, 7 remained; but only 6 of the 38 boys, 5 November 1801, Minutes of Vestry, Parish of St Clement Dane, B1074, WAC.

126 4 November 1803, Minutes of the Governors and Directors of the Poor, Parish of St James, Piccadilly, D1878, WAC.

127 John Waller, *The Real Oliver Twist: Robert Blincoe – A Life That Illuminates An Age* (Cambridge, 2005), pp. 194–5; Brown, *Memoir*, p. 79.

128 Undated Letter to Royston parish from Holywell Twist Company, Royston parish records, D/P87/14/1/6, Hertfordshire Archives and Local Studies (HALS).

129 29 [*sic*] February 1797, special meeting of the Governors and Directors of the Poor, Parish of St James, Piccadilly, D1876, WAC.

and Mary Bennett stated that they both still worked in the area but not at Douglas's factory. Mary Bennett says that 'I now work at a factory in the neighbourhood of Pendleton ... I had no reason for leaving Mr Douglas's employ only that a very intimate acquaintance of mine who is married and lives near the place where I now work and with whom I now live'.[130]

Several testimonies to the parliamentary committees of 1816–19 came from former apprentices at Douglas's Holywell and Pendleton factories, who themselves had remained at their original factory and claimed that this was the norm. Samuel Jones, for example, had been apprenticed to Douglas at the age of eight, and remained there as a spinner. Laurence Gardner, 33, originally a parish apprentice, had left the firm at the end of his term but subsequently returned to Douglas because that was what he knew and 'better than a strange place'. Both men confirmed that twenty or thirty of their cohort of parish apprentices still worked at the mill and that it was standard practice to be retained.[131] Other former apprentices at Douglas had moved on but remained in the trade, including Robert Plant who established his own small cotton spinning enterprise.[132]

Later evidence from Derbyshire suggests that former apprentices comprised an important component of the local factory labour supply. In 1841, for example, John Smedley of Lea mill, Ashover testified that he 'employed hands who have completed their apprenticeship at other mills and have found them honest, industrious and respectable in their conduct and valuable hands. I now employ some who were formerly apprentices to Mr Newton at Cressbrook mill and are now settled here; and some have families now in my employ'.[133] The relatively high retention of female apprentices, which partly reflects preferential sorting by early textile manufacturers, is explored in the following chapter. The experience of parish apprentices at Greg's Styal mill illustrates this tendency. Seventy per cent of apprentices were female and many of these became adult workers.[134] Few rose to positions of authority, though two, after years of service, become overlookers.[135] At least 70 women became spinners.[136] Others became weavers, and several former apprentices became employed in the Greg household. Few of the male apprentices became spinners; mostly they were carders, scutchers and a small number of weavers. Others joined the army.[137]

---

130 10 March 1797, Minutes of the Governors and Directors of the Poor, Parish of St James, Piccadilly, D1876. WAC.

131 Testimony of Samuel Jones and Samuel Gardner, HL1819, vol. 110, pp. 180–81.

132 Robert Plant, 36, spinner, Appleton and Plant. Also testimony from John Houldsworth, an Oldham weaver, HL1819, vol. 110, pp. 133–6, 241.

133 Q/AG/18, DRO.

134 It was increasingly the practice at Gregs for apprentices to be retained. Writing in 1833, W.R. Greg asserted that ex-apprentices 'almost always marry, very often amongst themselves and remain with us as workmen'. Rose, *The Gregs*, p. 57. See also Frances Collier, *The Family Economy of the Working Classes in the Cotton Industry 1784–1833* (Manchester, 1964), p. 44.

135 Keith Robinson, *What Became of the Quarry Bank Mill Apprentices? The Origins, Childhood and Adult Lives of 200 Cotton Workers* (Styal, 1996), p. 18.

136 Robinson, *What Became...?*, p. 23.

137 Robinson, *What Became...?*, p. 35.

Female apprentices who formed the majority at Merryweather and Whitaker also expected to be retained. A parish officer from St Mary Newington

> attended and reported that he had been to Mr Whitakers at Burley near Ottley in the county of York and had seen and examined the children apprenticed there ... that on the day he was there 8 young women came out of their time all of whom wishing to remain in Jn Whitaker, he had retained them all in the work of the factory.[138]

William Wood, one of the first apprentices to reach Burley worked at the factory for almost 50 years.[139] Birmingham girls at Bott's Tutbury factory, at Dicken and Finlow's cotton factory in Burton, Staffordshire, and at Thomas Jewsbury's Derbyshire enterprises were expected to remain at the termination of their apprenticeship. It was neither intended nor expected that parish apprenticeship should provide opportunities for upward social mobility. Yet several cases exist. At Gregs, a handful of male apprentices attained management positions. Robert Blincoe started his own, intermittently successful, business.[140] Clement Dodenhoff, originally bound from St Martin in the Fields parish to Isaac Hodgson's Preston mill, was at the time of the Lord, committee manager at Thomas Darwell's Wigan factory.[141]

By the end of their term, parish factory apprentices had as much as ten or twelve years experience of factory work. While undoubtedly not 'skilled' in the traditional sense, such children were better placed to gain factory employment, including the relatively well-paid sort, than those adults who had not worked in mills as children. It may have been less a 'training' than an 'experience of work', and specifically unvarying work, but in most cases the acquisition of transferable skills together with the learned capacity to labour for long hours permitted access to jobs outside as well as inside the world of the factory. The explicit intention of all parish apprenticeships was to enhance the employment chances of poor children. Research is at too early a stage to judge the success of factory apprenticeships in this respect, yet the evidence of this chapter is that it was not unusual for parish children to remain in factory employment at the end of their term of apprenticeship, and that the apprenticeship experience allowed them to do so. Apprentices became preferred labour. Most factory employment consisted of rudimentary manual labour and availability of work was unpredictable. Nevertheless, the expansion of textile factory manufacturing in the first half of the nineteenth century provided plentiful opportunities for former apprentices.

---

138 Meeting of 24 July 1817, St Mary Newington Workhouse Committee Minutes 1815–20, 932, SLHL.
139 Aspin, *Water Spinners*, p. 436.
140 Brown, *Memoirs*, pp. 60–63.
141 HL 1819, vol. 110, pp. 97–105.

Chapter 8

The Making of a Gendered Labour Force?

Gender differences between children in the early industrial workforce have been inadequately explored by historians. Colin Heywood argues that 'specialists in child labour have often focused on the age dimension and neglected gender; and scholars interested in the gender division of labour have emphasized adults'.[1] Jane Humphries and Sara Horrell suggest that contemporaries generally did not distinguish prepubescent boys and girls. Sex only became significant at puberty whereupon it led to the condemnation of the employment of adolescent girls outside the confines of the family.[2] This chapter is concerned with how the gender division of labour – a key feature of industrialisation – was constructed.[3] It will use the period in which parish factory apprentices were most prominent in textile production to explore the processes by which work and workers were gendered within new organizational forms.

Gender divisions at work in pre-industrial England were constructed and perpetuated through the institutions of apprenticeship and guild. The latter became less important from the seventeenth century but the former remained a key driver of gender distinctions until the nineteenth century. Recent research has demonstrated how the apprenticeship system offered quite different opportunities to girls and boys. A study of private apprenticeships has indicated a growing gender inequality in scale and scope of binding from the seventeenth through to the nineteenth century. Boys comprised the majority of apprentices, and were more likely to be bound to skilled trades than girls who were destined to 'domestic' trades.[4] Boys' apprenticeships concentrated on the acquisition of a trade, emphasizing skill and self-reliance. What

---

1   Colin Heywood, 'Age and gender at the workplace: the historical experiences of young people in Western Europe and North America', in Margaret Walsh (ed.), *Working Out Gender: Perspectives from Labour History* (Aldershot, 1999), p. 48.

2   Sara Horrell and Jane Humphries, '"The exploitation of little children": child labour and the family economy in the industrial revolution', *Explorations in Economic History*, 32 (1995): 487; Jane Humphries, '"The most free from objection"': The sexual division of labour and women's work in nineteenth century England', *Journal of Economic History*, 67/4 (1987).

3   Horrell and Humphries, '"The exploitation"', pp. 488–510. In the article, the authors discuss the 'gendered aspects of children's work', but do so in the context of family participation in factory work, and is therefore driven by different perspectives than this study which is concerned with the independent parish apprentice.

4   K.D.M. Snell, *Annals of the Labouring Poor: Social Change and Agrarian England, 1660–1900* (Cambridge, 1985).

girls were expected to learn through apprenticeship or in other ways, was to be adaptable and flexible.[5]

Although it is an exaggeration to suggest, as Lynn Hollen Lees has done, that the Poor Law did not make gender distinctions,[6] the parish apprenticeship system offered more opportunities to girls than did the private equivalent. The priority of the Poor Law officials was to rid the parish of the burden of poor children, irrespective of gender, and to provide all children with the means to become self supporting in later life. Nevertheless boys appeared more frequently in parish registers,[7] and they were more likely than girls to be placed in skilled trades.[8] Thus girls were more likely to receive an apprenticeship if they were poor, but because the bindings were 'gendered', parish apprenticeships generated unequal outcomes for girls and boys. Parish boys were given a wider range of opportunities than were girls who were largely confined to textiles and 'service' trades, and were generally subject to an inferior occupational training.[9] However well girls performed during their apprenticeship, their futures lay in low-status occupations with indifferent prospects. In principle, therefore, the system of factory parish apprenticeship offered a different outlook for girls, and one with greater equality with boys. There is no evidence that parishes were more 'protective' of girls; there are no examples that they were prevented from being sent to factories on account of distance, or for any other reason. After hearing the testimony of Margaret Chamberlain, a former apprentice, the officers of St James, Piccadilly, 'Resolved unanimously that the whole of the foregoing statement is very satisfactory to the committee and that the situation of Messrs Douglas and Co. appears very proper for apprentices of either sex'.[10]

The extent to which children were divided by gender depended on their age and availability.[11] In much contemporary discussion of children workers, certainly before the 1830s, their sex was rarely specified; and 'as long as they were regarded

---

5   Deborah Simonton, 'Apprenticeship: training and gender in eighteenth-century England', Maxine Berg, *Markets and Manufacture in Early Industrial Europe* (London, 1991), p. 255; O.J. Dunlop, *English Apprenticeship and Child Labour* (London, 1912), p. 149; Katrina Honeyman, *Women, Gender and Industrialisation in England, 1700–1870* (Basingstoke, 2000), pp. 25–7.

6   Lynn Hollen Lees, *Solidarities of Strangers: The English Poor Laws and the People, 1700–1948* (Cambridge, 1998), p. 56.

7   Snell, *Annals*, pp. 279–82.

8   Girls were most likely to be bound to domestic or farm service. Simonton, 'Apprenticeship', pp. 243–7.

9   Simonton, 'Apprenticeship', p. 252; and in Suffolk, for example, because of such unwillingness, a practice of short-term apprenticeship often for one year only, was commonly used to persuade masters to take girls. Hugh Fearn, 'The apprenticing of pauper children in the incorporated hundreds of Suffolk', *Proceedings of the Suffolk Institute of Archaeology*, 26 (1955): 92.

10   29 February 1797 Special meeting of the Governors and Directors of the Poor, Parish of St James, Piccadilly, convened to hear the testimony of Margaret Chamberlain. D1876, WAC.

11   Anna Davin 'Child labour, the working class family, and domestic ideology in 19th century Britain', *Development and Change*, 13 (1982): 634–5.

as children, the division of labour between boys and girls appears to have been more flexible than in the case of adolescents or the adult labour force'.[12] The textile factories established in the 1780s and 1790s were based upon new ways of working, with no precedent in terms of the gender division of labour. The children workers in the first textile mills were described in non-gendered terms.[13] At first sight, it appears that parish children were bound to factory apprenticeships as undifferentiated labour; yet emerged at the end of their term as gendered workers and paid differentially. This chapter will consider if and why this was the case. Firstly it will explore the view that employers were unconcerned about the sex of their parish apprentices. The evidence presented in Table 8.1 suggests that while many employers appeared indifferent to sex and received boys and girls in roughly equal numbers, others appeared to have very clear preferences. However, the gender structure of the intake may have reflected a gendered supply of children as much as a gendered demand. In areas where local trades provided placements mainly for boys, the majority of those available for factory apprenticeships were girls. This was evidently the case in the Midlands, for example. Parishes with a surfeit of boys available for factory apprenticeships existed but were less common.

Because many parish apprentices were undifferentiated by sex at the point of binding,[14] the second strand of the chapter explores how parish boys and girls 'learned' to be gendered workers, so that by the end of their terms, tasks and wage differentials were justified. The extent to which gendered practices were introduced through the package of training offered to parish apprentices, will be considered. A range of evidence will be used to demonstrate how parishes and other institutions shared with employers in developing strategies to socialise children into gender roles appropriate to work and life. It is quite likely that puberty was the point at which the pursuit of gender socialisation began,[15] but preoccupation with puberty, was less apparent between 1780 and 1820[16] than in the 1830s and 1840s.[17]

---

12 Marjetta Rahikainen, *Centuries of Child Labour: European Experience from the Seventeenth to the Twentieth Century* (Aldershot, 2004), p. 13.

13 Colquhoun provides no indication of ages and it seems likely that those identified would be the younger age groups, say, under 13. It is assumed that his assessment was done by eye rather than on the basis of written confirmation of age. Colquhoun's survey of 143 Arkright type mills, 1788, Baker Library, Harvard.

14 The physical differences between male and female and the expectation that at puberty boys would be stronger than girls, will not be discussed here, not least because physical strength was not a key requisite of factory work. In any case, this issue has been discussed elsewhere, for example, by Joyce Burnette, 'An investigation of male-female wage gap during the industrial revolution in Britain', *Economic History Review*, 50/2 (1997): 257–81.

15 This focused mostly on girls; boys appeared to have less to learn.

16 The 1802 Act, concerned as it was with morality, required the segregation of male and female sleeping accommodation, but otherwise made little explicit reference to the particular issues surrounding adolescent girls and boys.

17 Especially the testimony of 'medical men' in the Royal Commissions. This preoccupation has been reflected in the work of historians. See, for example, Robert Gray, 'Medical men, industrial labour and the state in Britain, 1830–50', *Social History*, 16/1 (1991): 19–43; Sophie Hamilton, 'Images of femininity in the 1830s and 1840s', in Eileen Janes Yeo

This section considers the way in which gender preferences were developed during the apprenticeship period, but also the possibility that some 'sorting' occurred during the initial selection stage. Douglas Galbi has argued that the gendering of factory work partly stemmed from the preferential sorting of labour.[18] The extent to which employers revealed a gendered preference for parish apprentices in the early period of textile factory production in indicated in Table 8.1. Because factory production had no precedent with respect to the gender division of labour, it is likely that employers in the flexible early stage of factory manufacturing selected whichever gendering of tasks – if any – suited the organisation of their enterprise. It was not until the 1820s and 1830s that the gender division of labour became generally implemented. Even then, perceptible differences existed between regions, such as Manchester and Glasgow, which may have originated in the differential use of parish apprentices.[19]

Table 8.1 Parish Factory Apprenticeship by Gender

Firm	Girl apprentices	Boy apprentices
George Andrew	0	9
Thomas Andrew	0	5
Samuel Ashton	36	42
Atherton and Harrison	9	0
John Birch	93	163
Benyon	15	0
Bott, Nantwich	21	20
Bott, Tutbury	42	66
Brosser	0	8
Jeremiah Bury	26	38
William Calrow	4	2
Benjamin Churchill	20	20
Benjamin Clegg	?	?
Colbeck, Ellis and Wilks	49	30

(ed.), *Radical Femininity: Women's Self-Representation in the Public Sphere* (Manchester, 1998), pp. 79–105; Marjorie Levine-Clark, *Beyond the Reproductive Body: The Politics of Women's Health and Work in Early Victorian England* (Columbus, Ohio, 2004), especially pp. 17–56.

18   Galbi uses this notion in his analysis of the gendering of work in the cotton mills of the 1830s and 1840s; and shows that youth was much less segregated by sex than the adult labour force. Douglas Galbi, 'Child labour and the division of labour in the early English cotton mills', *Journal of Population Economics*, 10/4 (1997): 357–75; and Douglas Galbi, 'Economic change and sex discrimination in the early English cotton factories', Discussion Paper, Centre for History and Economics, Kings College, Cambridge (1994), pp. 15–18.

19   The more robust gendering of work that emerged was mostly likely the outcome of forces additional to employer preferences, including trade union action as well as developments in technology and power.

Cooper and Matchett	5	7
Cowpe, Hollins, Oldknow	17	0
Cresswell	43	1
Davison and Hawksley	121	141
Dicken and Finlow	49	17
Douglas, Holywell	63+	35+
Douglas, Pendleton	61+	90+
Fowler	5	0
Jeremiah Garnett	12	10
William Garth	7	5
John Gorton	19	19
Gorton and Thompson	0	32
Greg	?	?
Haigh	32	69
Charles Harding	24	15
Hardnumm	11	12
Harrison and Leyland	20	20
Thomas Haslam	24	16
Haywood and Palfreyman	11? At most, possibly all boys	62/73
John Head	13	3
R&G Hodgkinson	10	19
Isaac Hodgson	42	63
David Holt	35+	32+
John Edward Hudson	15	14
Joseph Hulse	4	0
Thomas Jewsbury	176	54
Lambert	15	26
Marshall, Hutton and Hives	55	27
Marsland and Kelsall	1	13
Nathaniel Mason	0	15
Merryweather	160	134
Monteith, Bogle	24	30
John Morley	9	9
Ellis Needham	53	42
Newton	? too many unknowns but definite girl preference	
Samuel Oldknow	100+ Many unknowns but explicit girl preference	
James Pattison	46	47

Peel, various	179	100
Robinson	18	5
Sewell and McMurdo	12	19
Shute, Thomas Rock	5	5
John and William Singleton	0	6
Benjamin Smart	28	0
Strutt	10	13
Toplis	304	458
Walton Twist	31	49
John Watson	55	88
Thomas Watson	5	5
John Weir	8	9
Wells, Middleton	56	44
James Whitelegg	0	6
Charles Woollan	7	4
Woolley and McQueen	7	0
Workman, Brummell and Hall	0	18
Thomas Yates	4	13
Total	**2816**	**2380**

+ Certainly more than this, but a number of unknown quantities prevents definite totals to be produced. *Sources*: see Appendix.

Among the firms studied, 55 per cent of parish factory apprentices were girls; 18 of the 57 firms preferred girls, 16 preferred boys, and the remaining 23 were apparently indifferent.[20] In a number of cases the evidence is not transparent about gender. Apprenticeship registers always specified the sex of the child; but in other parish and business documentation this was not so consistent and reference is made to 'children'; or groups of 'either sex'. Several dominant early textile manufacturers appeared to have a preference for girls as workers.[21] Richard Arkwright advertised for cheerful girls[22] and his associate, Samuel Oldknow confined his search to female apprentices: 'I will thank you to inform me … whether it would be compatible with your engagement there to procure for me 40 or 50 females from 8–12 years old at

---

20 The preference for girls suggested here is less marked than that proposed by Joan Lane, *Apprenticeship in England 1600–1914* (London, 1996), pp. 177–8.

21 There appears to be a connection between firms that preferred girls, good treatment during the apprenticeship, retention at the end of the term and longevity and prosperity of business.

22 Newspaper advertisements from manufacturers commonly requested 'healthy strong girls'. Louise A. Tilly and Joan W. Scott, *Women, Work and Family* (New York, 1978), p. 112.

the different workhouses in London'.[23] Benjamin Smart of Emscote mill[24] always specified girls in newspaper advertisements[25] and in letters to parish officials. 'I want active, healthy girls about 14 years of age and not under 4ft 6" in height', he wrote to St Clement parish, Oxford.[26] Peter Noaille, silk manufacturer and thrower at Greatness, near Sevenoaks only employed girls who 'seldom leave me unless they are bribed to leave me to go to any other manufactories or to go to service'.[27] Benyon and Co., Shrewsbury flax spinners took only girls, as did Newton at Cressbrook mill, Whitaker at Burley, Woolley and McQueen, Atherton and Harrison, and Cresswell at Edale. It appears that Jewsbury, and Dicken and Finlow would have taken only girls from Birmingham had the parish been prepared to provide these. Mitchell and Holt also preferred girls but were willing to take some boys. In negotiation with the parish of St James, Piccadilly, Holt stated that 'we should prefer the majority of them girls and could now take 40 girls and 20 boys'.[28]

Almost as many firms appeared to prefer boys. Notable among these were Gorton and Thompson of Cuckney; and Turner of Godley who both specifically requested boys. Brosser, Haywood and Palfreyman, Nathaniel Mason, Workman, Brummell and Hall took only boys; while Haigh at Marsden, and Marsland and Kelsall of Glossop used mostly male apprentices.

Some, such as Birch specifically requested both sexes: the parish of St Clement Danes received a 'letter from Mr Robinson the agent for the Blackbarrow [sic] cotton mills requesting to have 20 or 24 children of each sex'.[29] Other firms expressed no preference. J. Bury of Stockport appeared to offer equal opportunities: 'We take them at 9 or 10 years old both sexes to be employed during their younger years in various departments ... but it is ultimately intended to make them into weavers, as they grow up they will be taught to weave different kinds of goods'.[30] The proposal of James Noble a Leicester Hosier to employ children in the St James workhouse

---

23 Correspondence with London Foundling Hospital about apprentices. Letter, 13 November 1813, from Samuel Oldknow to Mr Livesey of the Foundling Hospital. MF 1020, MCA.

24 According to Price, 'the children at Emscot Mill are 34 in number; are apprentices and all females' SC1816, p. 171.

25 'Healthy, active girls of 14 years of age ... A premium of five pounds with each will be expected'. Joan Lane, 'Apprenticeship in Warwickshire cotton mills, 1790–1830', *Textile History*, 10 (1979): 164.

26 Letter dated 1 mo 1 (January) 1812, Rock mills, from Benjamin Smart to St Clement parish Oxford. (William Parsons, overseer) Z351/3, ORO; Letter from Benjamin Smart to St Clement parish Oxford, dated 1 Mo 23 1812, Z351/4, ORO.

27 SC1816, p. 76.

28 A letter, dated 14 September 1801, from Messrs Mitchell and Holt of Holt Town was delivered to the Board and read 17 September 1801. Minutes of Governors and Directors of the Poor, D1878, WAC.

29 29 September 1789, Minutes of Vestry, Parish of St Clement Danes, B1072, WAC.

30 Proposal from Bury and Co. 'The following is a short sketch of a plan of disposing of 200 parish children wanted by J. Bury and Co, muslin manufacturers of Hope hill, near Stockport, Cheshire, particularly the weaving branch'. Records of the Parish of St George the Martyr, Southwark, SLHL.

indicates that young children were not differentiated by sex. 'The employment is light and easy, such as small boys or girls ... may do without fatigue'.[31]

Although some firms expressed a clear gendered preference, supply conditions influenced the sex ratio. In many Midlands parishes, for example, more apprenticeships were available to boys among the local skilled trades, leaving 'spare' girls to be bound to factories.[32] In the poorer London parishes, such as St Martin in the Fields and St Giles in the Fields, placements for boys were scarcer, providing a healthy supply for the factory employers. Dicken and Finlow were obliged to take a few boys along with a more substantial quantity of his preferred girls. Charles Harding seemed to have a girl preference, and Bedworth parish provided him with 19 girls and 1 boy. This may have been supply driven because from St Martin in the Fields, he received 4 girls and 14 boys. Similarly John Bott received only girls from Birmingham for his Tutbury mill; while St Giles in the Fields provided only boys.

The following section aims to explain gender preference where it existed. Preference was determined either by short-term interests or by long-term labour requirements or both. Conventional wisdom on the subject of parish apprentices suggests that such children were used as expendable labour; employed intensively before release at the end of their term. Although evidence collected for this study suggests that such practice was not the norm, many employers included short-term expedience in their selection procedure. The preference for a single sex may have stemmed from the desire to avoid the costly inconvenience of segregated accommodation;[33] and the expensive superintendence of moral standards; or from the perceived differential qualities of boys and girls.[34] In so far as employers anticipated long-term labour requirements, these were often, but not always, associated with a preference for girls.[35] This may have a technical explanation: users of the water frame were more likely to select girls if they intended to retain their apprentices into

---

31 28 October 1800, Minutes of Governors and Directors of the Poor, Parish of St James, Piccadilly, D1877, WAC.

32 Birmingham was a good example of this, and consistently dealt with a surfeit of girls. For example, 8 December 1783, Minutes of Birmingham Board of Guardians, GP/B/2/1/1. On 15 June 1784, 'that there are many healthy girls in the Birmingham workhouse between nine and fourteen years of age which the overseers of the poor are desirous to put out apprentice and would give a proper premium with them according to the circumstances of the case not exceeding £5'. Minutes of Birmingham Board of Guardians GP/B/2/1/1, BCA.

33 Required by the 1802 HMA.

34 These included female conformism and patience; and male strength and courage.

35 The firms of Dicken and Finlow, Burton, and Samuel Oldknow, Mellor are examples of such practice. In any event, it may be surmised that where the employer specified the desired gender(s) of the apprentices, the particular choice may have been reflected in the long-term plans of the millowner; he may have had a specific gender division of labour in mind. Such a finding challenges the view, expressed by Farey among others, that girls were more likely to be turned away at the end of their term. Ivy Pinchbeck, *Women Workers and the Industrial Revolution 1750–1850* (London, 1930), p. 183; but supports the more recent work of Galbi who finds, for a slightly later period, that more girls than boys stayed on in factories. 'Child labour', pp. 364–5.

adulthood.[36] Several proprietors of rural Midlands mills selected girls for longer-term employment. Thomas Jewsbury did so. At John Bott's Nantwich mill, girls were likely to be retained when out of their time, but 'boys are not their peculiar choice'.[37] The future prospects of the Birmingham children, all girls, at his Tutbury factory looked good. They were to be retained and paid quite well: 'we had the pleasure of seeing many who had been employed in the spinning mills for several years beyond the term of their apprenticeship'.[38] Dicken and Finlow's preference for girls indicated long-term plans, which pleased the Birmingham Guardians. 'We conceive that there needs no stronger proof of this place being a very comfortable one than this viz that several young women who have served out the time of their apprenticeship still remain at these works earning from 6s to 8s per week'.[39]

It was not just for technical reasons that girls were sometimes preferred. The robust female constitution was recognised by contemporary factory owners.[40] Examples of differential health can be found both in parish visitors' reports and in medical evidence to parliamentary committees. At Backbarrow the children 'appear in a good state of health....the Girls better than the Boys'.[41] The visitors to Merryweather found that 'the Boys looked healthy and happy and were well grown; the Girls particularly so ...;[42] and a separate visitation remarked that 'The girls seemed uniformly healthy and happy'.[43] When asked by the House of Lords committee of 1818, if he had noticed any material difference between the boys and the girls, Thomas Turner, surgeon and apothecary replied 'the boys certainly did not look so healthy as the girls'.[44] In evidence to the Lords 1819 Committee, Edmund Lyon, a Manchester doctor, referred to his inspection of Sunday School children, which found 30 of the

---

36   This is consistent with Maxine Berg's argument that water frame production relied especially on the labour of girls and young women, 'Women's work, mechanisation, and the early phases of industrialisation in England', in Patrick Joyce (ed.), *The Historical Meanings of Work* (Cambridge, 1987), p. 79. In Scotland, girls were more likely to be retained as spinners and in weaving operations, as boys went to other trades when they were grown up, Archibald Buchanan, SC1816, p. 9. According to the same source, girls were able to earn more than boys, both as teenagers and subsequently.

37   Report received by the Birmingham Guardians 27 August 1798. Minutes of Birmingham Board of Guardians, GP/B/2/1/1, BCA. Many others married and settled in the area. 30 June 1808, Minutes of Birmingham Board of Guardians GP/B/2/1/2, BCA.

38   30 June 1808. Minutes of Birmingham Board of Guardians, GP/B/2/1/2, BCA.

39   1 July 1808. Minutes of Birmingham Board of Guardians, GP/B/2/1/2, BCA.

40   Advertisements from such factory owners as Richard Arkwright, for example, expressed preference for active healthy girls. Lane, *Apprenticeship*, pp. 177–8. Some boys, after puberty, may have been physically stronger than girls but this was not an advantage in textile factory employment.

41   Report of the Brighton Directors and Guardians of the Poor 'to visit the children lately sent to the cotton manufactory at Backbarrow' June 1805. Quoted in Chris Aspin, *The Water Spinners* (Helmshore, 2003), p. 349.

42   1802 Report, St Margaret and St John.

43   William Hey, 'Account of a visit to the cotton mills at Burley', published, with a critique in *The Reports of the Society for Bettering the Condition and Increasing the Comforts of the Poor*, vol. IV, 1805, Appendix, supplement II, pp. 16–19.

44   HL 1818, p. 157.

121 boys, but only 3 of the 129 girls to be of 'sickly appearance'. Other testimony observed that 'we cannot here avoid noticing the striking superiority, in point of appearance, which the girls possessed over the boys';[45] and 'the appearance in the cotton factories of the girls was much better than of the boys'.[46]

Girls were more likely than boys to be described as cheerful and amenable, which may have been related to their superior health. At Toplis's mill in Cuckney, 'the girls are all in the new mill and being by nature more suited to bear confinement – are better grown – look more healthy'.[47] There may well have been a widespread expectation among employers that girls would be more patient, more reliable and less likely to abscond.[48] Evidence on runaways is by no means conclusive, but indicates that while girls were not averse to running away, boys had a higher absconding rate. Samuel Greg's growing preference for girls after 1800 was related to boys' ill-discipline.[49] In view of all this, it is surprising that boys were tolerated at all.

Research on the gendering of the early factory labour force has hitherto concentrated on the 1830s and has typically argued that before puberty, gender differences in employment and pay were imperceptible, but thereafter differentials emerged and gradually widened.[50] This section considers the extent to which an initial preference led to a longer term gender division of labour and longer term employment. There is little indication that girls and boys performed different tasks before their mid teens at the earliest. In terms of work performed, girls and boys were interchangeable.[51] Girls may have been preferred as longer-term factory workers because of their anticipated cheapness.[52] Evidence that pay differentials set in as

---

45   HL 1819, vol. 110, p. 354.
46   Thomas Jarrold, MD, Manchester, HL 1819 vol. 110, p. 311.
47   1802 Report, St Margaret and St John.
48   Joan Lane suggests that there is evidence for this. *Apprenticeship*, p. 180.
49   Lane, *Apprenticeship*, p. 15. Lane also suggests, on pages 202 and 227, that absconding increased during years of warfare, which may have reflected the increase in soldiering opportunities for boys.
50   Wally Seccombe, *Weathering the Storm: Working Class Families from the Industrial Revolution to the Fertility Decline* (London, 1993), pp. 36–9; Humphries, 'The most free …', pp. 946–7, links the segregation of the sexes in the workplace with the control of sexuality; Clare Evans, 'The separation of work and home?', University of Manchester PhD thesis, 1990; Pat Hudson and W.R. Lee (eds), *Women's Work and the Family Economy in Historical Perspective* (Manchester, 1990), p. 249.
51   Evidence from textile factories elsewhere in Europe suggests a similar pattern of interchangeability at least among younger children. Colin Heywood, 'On learning gender roles during childhood in nineteenth century France', *French History*, 5/4 (1991): 455; Katherine A. Lynch, *Family, Class and Ideology in Early Industrial France: Social Policy and the Working Class Family 1825–1848* (Madison, 1988), pp. 176–7.
52   Ivy Pinchbeck and Margaret Hewitt, *Children in English Society* (2 vols, London, 1969–1973) vol. 2, p. 413. In her discussion of gender pay differentials, Burnette considers the extent to which wage discrimination existed during the early industrial period. She concludes that 'women seem to have been paid market wages, and the assertion that women were paid customary wages needs to be revised'. Burnette, 'An investigation', p. 278. However, Burnette argues, on p. 272, that girls received less training than boys, thus creating an imbalance in human capital. This argument is not convincing in the case of factory parish apprentices.

apprenticeship ended is found in business correspondence. At the Holywell Twist Company, for example, 'when out of their time ... girls may then earn from 5 to 7s per week, boys from 10 to 15s or more according to their ability'.[53] Confirmation that this was within the usual range of pay for girls is provided in the case of the Nantwich firm of John Bott where 'girls when grown up may earn from 4/6 to 6/- per week if attentive to business'.[54] At Bott's Tutbury factory, the average for girls was a little higher at 6s to 8s a week;[55] and at Jewsbury's Measham enterprise it was claimed that 'at the expiry of their term a girl was 'able to get 7/6 to 10/- a week'.[56] At Backbarrow, once apprenticeship was completed, 'the girls get from 6s to 7s per week. The men from 12s to 14s and upwards they can board in the neighbourhood men for 6s women 5s per week'.[57] Four years later, wages had stayed much the same although the cost of board and lodging had risen: 'those ... who are out of their time and stay at Backbarrow can board not according to what they eat but what they earn. A woman who can earn 8/- a week can board for 6/-, a man who earns 12/- must pay 8 or 9/-'. This was verified by the examination of Mary Cramp who said 'she could have earned 7 or 8 shillings per week but declined staying 'as her friends in London had sent for her'.[58]

Officials from the parish of St Clement Danes received information about wages from another source. '[On] Sunday morning in our way from Cartmell to Backbarrow we conversed with a woman who belonged to Messrs Birch and Robinson's Mills, she informed [them] that she and her children had worked there many years and that she earned eight shillings per week'.[59] A comparison of two different firms to which St James, Piccadilly bound children also illustrates the gender pay gap.

> Mr Strutt of Rickmansworth cotton manufacturer ... stated that being informed Mary Robinson his late apprentice from this parish has made a complaint to a former committee that the utmost wages she could earn would not exceed 3/- per week if she continued in

---

53 Letter to parish from Holywell Twist Company stating 'Terms for taken apprentices by the Holywell Twist Company', Royston parish. D/P87/14/1/6, HALS.

54 Visit of 21 August 1798 reported to Birmingham Guardians on 27 August 1798. Minutes of the Birmingham Board of Guardians, GP/B/2/1/1, BCA.

55 Thursday 30 June 1808, Minutes of the Birmingham Board of Guardians, GP/B/2/1/1, BCA.

56 The inspections were made on 14 and 15 September 1813, and discussed by the Birmingham Guardians on 12 October 1813, when the visitors were thanked for 'their great attention to the welfare of the children'. Minutes of the Birmingham Board of Guardians, GP/B/2/1/2, BCA.

57 2 November 1797 'Read a report of Messrs Ritchie and Buck of the children at the cotton mills at Backbarrow,' .Minutes of Vestry, Parish of St Clement Danes, B1147, WAC.

58 St Clement Danes, 5 November 1801, Report of Messrs Pouden and Davidson respecting the children at Cartmell. Discussed at the meeting of 14 January 1802, convened to discuss the compared reports Minutes of Vestry, Parish of St Clement Danes, B1148, WAC.

59 5 November 1801 Report by Messrs Pouden and Davidson respecting the children at Cartmell. This was discussed with the report from 1797 at a meeting of the Vestry of St Clement Danes 14 January 1802. Minutes of Vestry, Parish of St Clement Danes, B1148, WAC.

his service ... in answer stated that he intended to have allowed his said late apprentice five shillings per week ....[60]

By contrast, Gorton and Thompson alleged that at Cuckney, 'according to the prices now given for weaving I think a boy would earn from 1 guinea to 1 ½ guineas per week certain'.[61] In a reply to a query from their neighbour, Toplis, Messrs Gorton and Thompson, 'tell us that the worst hands they have can earn 16 and 18s per week, but the general sum per week is from 24 to 25s'.[62] At Litton mills near Tideswell, visitors from the parish of St James found that although girls and boys were both retained by the firm at the end of their term, the latter were able to earn twice as much as the former. In 1803

> Catherine Burrows, Louisa Bontfante, Elizabeth Hastings and Sophia Smith [had] severally served the full term of their apprenticeship and were employed at the factory at the accustomed wages of 2/6 and 2/8 per week with board and lodging ... In the further progress of enquiry it appeared that Thos Lockhart apprenticed by the parish of St George the Martyr, Middlesex, continued with Mr Needham three years after the expiration of his apprenticeship having saved from his weekly wages of 5/6 exclusive of board and lodging.[63]

Evidence from Douglas's Pendleton factory suggests that during their apprenticeship, girls and boys were prepared for later pay differentials. Apprentices were given 'pocket money' for working 'over hours', to which boys had greater access. 'Henry Churchill ... has 2/- a week allowed him for pocket money and is nearly out of his time ... Martha Kelly almost out of her time has long had 1/- a week for pocket money'.[64] Although it was claimed, by Douglas and other proprietors in the area, that

---

60 6 December 1791, Minutes of Governors and Directors of the Poor, Parish of St James, Piccadilly, D1872, WAC.

61 Letter from Gorton and Thompson, Cuckney, read at meeting of Governors and Directors of the Poor, 12 October 1792. Minutes of Governors and Directors of the Poor, Parish of St James, Piccadilly, D1872, WAC.

62 Reply from Toplis to 1802 Report, St Margaret and St John, 11 September 1802, E3371/1, WAC.

63 Report of Messrs Johnson and Halfhide accompanied by the clerk to the Governors of the Poor relative to their children apprenticed from the Parish of St James, Westminster to Litton Mills. Meeting, 4 November 1803, Minutes of Governors and Directors of the Poor, Parish of St James, Piccadilly, D1878, WAC.

Some years after this information was collected, Robert Blincoe, a St Pancras parish apprentice, who remained at Litton mill on expiry of his term, found a discrepancy between the promised rate of pay, 4s, 6d a week, and the actual payment he received which was very little. His wages were to have been paid monthly; but 'month after month elapsed, and instead of an honest settlement, there was nothing but shuffling! He then worked and lived like others, till his master owed him nearly half a years labour'. John Brown, *Memoir of Robert Blincoe* (Manchester, 1832), p. 55. Blincoe departed soon after this to earn real money.

64 Letter 21 January 1797 from John Plant, Pendleton, read at meeting 10 February 1797, Minutes of Governors and Directors of the Poor, Parish of St James, Piccadilly, D1876, WAC. Margaret Chamberlain suggested that there was an element of choice in the amount of pocket money earned: that she 'could earn sufficient pocket money when she pleased'. Examination

it was possible for young people to earn £1, 5s, 0d to £2, 2s, 0d a week on completion of their apprenticeship,

> this uniform and it should seem, preconcerted reply of proprietors in general, was however completely controverted by several persons actively employed at different factories, who on being interrogated, all agreed in stating that the women so employed, seldom received more than 8s nor the men more that 10s per week except the master or principal of each room whose weekly allowance amounted to 14s.[65]

These examples indicate that higher male wages were the norm. However, equal pay, and even higher wages for women did exist. In Scotland young women commonly commanded higher rates of pay than young men who anyway were more likely to seek non-factory employment.[66] Although this was unusual south of the border, in Manchester, for example, it was possible for girls to earn as much as boys or even more, at the end of their apprenticeships. Prior to binding children to Holt's mill, the officials of St James, Piccadilly, 'reported that they had made particular enquiry ... of Mr Mitchell and Holt, from whom it appeared that the children already apprenticed from other parishes ... that several boys and girls have been employed by them for several years are enabled to earn from 23/- to 31/- per week'.[67] An earlier letter from Holt himself, however, indicates a more complex story:

> our drawers and rovers girls get from 5/6 to 8s per week – boys in the other departments of the card room from 4/6 to 11/- when employed as mule spinners their earnings are much more – we have now both boys and girls about 20 who have been with us some years and whose weekly earnings are from 23/6 to 31/6 per week.[68]

A few months later, the officers of St James parish visited Mitchell and Holt to check for themselves. They

> were permitted to examine the books of the Manufactory with a view of ascertaining the emoluments of the children when their term of apprenticeship should expire, from whence it appeared that 30 men had earned 2 guineas per week each, 150 women 9/6 each, 2 girls about 18 years old, £1.10.0 and 150 girls [not apprentices] from 10 to 15 years old, 6/6

---

of Margaret Chamberlain at specially convened meeting of governors and directors of the poor of St James Piccadilly, 29 February [sic] 1797. Minutes of Governors and Directors of the Poor, Parish of St James, Piccadilly, D1876, WAC.

65 Report of Messrs Johnson and Halfhide accompanied by the clerk to the governors of the poor relative to their children apprenticed from the Parish of St James, Westminster, at Manufactures in Lancashire, Cheshire ... considered by the meeting of the Governors and Directors of the Poor, St James, Piccadilly, 4 November 1803. Minutes of Governors and Directors of the Poor, Parish of St James, Piccadilly, D1878, WAC.

66 Evidence of Archibald Buchanan to SC1816, p. 9.

67 2 October 1801 Minutes of Governors and Directors of the Poor, Parish of St James, Piccadilly, D1878, WAC.

68 Letter, dated 14 September 1801, from Messrs Mitchell and Holt of Holt Town was delivered to the Board and read; meeting of Governors and Directors of the Poor, St James Piccadilly, 17 September 1801. Minutes of Governors and Directors of the Poor, Parish of St James, Piccadilly, D1878, WAC.

each. That there was one department in the business in which the women can earn £1.11.6 per week each and that it was the manufacturers' intention to place all the children from this parish who served their apprenticeship with them to that employment ... by which the girls will be placed in that employ and thereby ... be enabled to earn from 9/6 to £1.11.6 weekly according to their respective abilities.[69]

Other evidence collected for the parish by a representative of Holts suggested that 'good hands whether male or female will get from 25s to 35s per week'.[70]

Thus it appears that although 'free' girls and young women apprentices out of their time, were in some circumstances able to earn as much as male equivalents, the norm was a female wage around 50 per cent of the male. The following section examines how experience of work and life at the mill influenced the parish apprentices' longer term expectations as workers and specifically their earnings potential. Evidence on 'training', discussed in Chapter 7 indicates that the extent to which parish apprentices learned to perform particular tasks, was not specifically gendered. At least until puberty, and probably for some time thereafter, children were typically employed on tasks irrespective of sex.

In addition to the long and grueling working day, parish apprentices were expected to receive 'instruction' in basic literacy and religious knowledge. In most factories, both sexes were educated to the same level; any gendering of the educational provision was confined to separate classes for boys and girls.[71] At Backbarrow, all the apprentices were 'taught to read and wrote [sic] by a gentleman intended for the church who is instructing Mr Barkers one of the partners children. Many of them write extremely well and some are accomptants as far as the rule of three whose books we examined'.[72] Yet in some cases boys were given priority, and were expected to progress further than girls.[73] Although both girls and boys were sent from St James parish to Mitchell and Holt, a letter from the local clergyman emphasised the educational progress of the boys. 'Last Thursday all St James boys were ordered to meet me in the large school room erected for that sole purpose', he wrote.

> [8 boys names] read two chapters in the old testament [3 boys names] one chapter in the new testament and the rest of the boys are coming forward pretty well ... Mrs Johnson

---

69   19 February 1802 Report of the committee appointed to visit the poor children placed out upon liking to the manufactory of Messrs Mitchell and Holt. Minutes of Governors and Directors of the Poor, Parish of St James, Piccadilly, D1878, WAC.

70   Letter dated 3 May 1803, from Rev. Johnson and read to the meeting of the Governors and Directors of the Poor, St James Piccadilly, 12 May 1803. Minutes of Governors and Directors of the Poor, Parish of St James, Piccadilly, D1878, WAC.

71   At several enterprises, including Gregs, the girls were additionally taught to sew and trained in housework. Frances Collier, *The Family Economy of the Working Classes in the Cotton Industry 1784–1833* (Manchester, 1964), p. 45. This was also the case at Marshall's Holbeck factory. Janet Burns, 'The west riding half timer' in *Old West Riding*, 9 (1989): 23.

72   2 November 1797, Minutes of Vestry, Parish of St Clement Danes, B1074, WAC.

73   In the Bristol workhouse, for example, both boys and girls were taught to read but only boys to write. E.E. Butcher, *Bristol Corporation of the Poor: Selected Records 1696–1834* (Bristol, 1932), p. 17.

undertakes to inspect the circumstances and welfare of the girls and a more particular account respecting their improvement will be given in my next.[74]

This report, however, failed to materialise. At Bury's factory in Stockport, the plan was that 'the boys and girls will be taught reading, writing and the common rules of arithmetic and those boys who evince a genius and disposition for it, will have an opportunity if they behave well to learn some of the higher branches of science'.[75]

It is such differential expectations, which are subtle rather than dramatically divergent, which leads into the analysis of 'socialisation'. This refers to the way in which gender identities were constructed during the period of apprenticeship; and specifically the way in which female children were constructed as lesser workers. During the period of factory parish apprenticeship, a tension existed between the identity of girls as workers and as domestic beings.[76] Such a tension, which existed in pre-factory apprenticeships and remained in the factory context, was connected to two assumptions. Firstly that girls needed to be 'trained' in domesticity for their future as wives and mothers, and secondly that they were most likely to find employment in domestic service.[77] Apprenticeships for boys, therefore, both in factories and other trades, were more likely to focus on 'work' and on their identity as workers, than apprenticeships for girls, which even in factories were bound up in a larger package

---

74   17 September 1802, Letter from Rev Johnson, dated 14 September 1802, delivered to the Board and read. Minutes of Governors and Directors of the Poor, Parish of St James, Piccadilly, D1878, WAC.

75   'Plan of disposing of 200 parish children wanted by J. Bury and Co., Muslin Manufacturers of Hope Hill, near Stockport, Cheshire', undated document, estimated by archivist to be *c*. 1780, SLHL.

76   Some early nineteenth century observers pointed out that factory work was no worse than most occupations, including agricultural labour and domestic industry in 'unfitting girls to look after a house or for domestic life'. Harold Perkin, *The Origins of Modern English Society 1780–1880* (London, 1985), p. 151. By the 1830s, such concerns had become much more pronounced. Kydd, for example, stated that 'the females are wholly uninterested in sewing, knitting and other domestic affairs', Samuel Kydd (Alfred), *The History of the Factory Movement from the Year 1802, to the Enactment of the Ten Hours' Bill in 1847*, vol. 1 (1857), p. 12, and pp. 338–40. According to Kay, 'the early age at which girls are admitted into the factories, prevents their acquiring much knowledge of domestic economy'. James Phillips Kay, *The Moral and Physical Condition of the Working Classes Employed in the Cotton Manufacture in Manchester* (London, 1832), p. 69. Robert Owen desired legislation which included a clause precluding girls' entry into any manufactory until they were 'competent to sew their common garments of clothing'. Robert Owen, *Observations on the Effect of the Manufacturing System* (London, 1817), p. 11. See also Catherine Robson, 'The ideal girl in industrial England', *Journal of Victorian Culture*, 3/2 (1998): 204.

77   Though the irony of this was that it encouraged girls into domestic service, which was one of the lowest status, lowest paid occupations with modest future prospects. Prior to the practice of factory bindings, parish girls were frequently apprenticed to domestic service in the expectation that their future would lie in this area. Bridget Hill, *Women, Work and Sexual Politics in Eighteenth Century England* (Oxford, 1989), p. 88; K.D.M. Snell, *Annals of the Labouring Poor: Social Change and Agrarian England, 1660–1900* (Cambridge, 1985), p. 281; Deborah Valenze, *The First Industrial Woman* (Oxford, 1995), pp. 159–62.

of socialization. For girls, work was only one component of the making of their more complicated identity. Socialisation for girls was not simply about acquiring cooking and cleaning skills, but also about learning to be flexible, polite, to deport themselves appropriately and to acquire a cheerful demeanour.[78] The expectation that girls were to be accomplished in domestic tasks, which were symbolically, if not practically, at variance with the tasks of the factory, and which generated a primary identity distinct from work, provided the justification for their lower wages. The irony of the socialisation of girl apprentices was that they were expected to acquire the modesty and domesticity, nurturing and obedience that would distinguish them from boys while working alongside their male counterparts for fourteen hours a day.[79]

The emphasis placed upon a gendered socialisation even for the poorest children in society can be seen in the correspondence between employer and parish officials in the context of factory parish apprenticeship. The proposal of Bury and Co., muslin manufacturers of Hope Hill, near Stockport, Cheshire, to take children from St George the Martyr parish, Southwark, for example, included the promise that the boys only were to have the chance to 'be promoted to superior places as overlookers etc. ... the girls as they grow up, will be taken by turns into the kitchen in order to make them acquainted with household matters'.[80] At Merryweather, 'there were several Boys employed in the various trades required to keep in Repair the complicated Machinery of this Mill, such as Carpenters, Mill Wrights and Turners, both in brass and wood, all of which we saw the Boys performing with much dexterity ... One girl is nursery maid'.[81] At Toplis,

> the girls by turns, were taught to do household work, so that many of them become good servants; and that there was besides employment in the manufactory for a number of women in framing the webb, by a machine which we saw, and some engaged in that avocation. The boys, he informed us, were, when they grew too large for the employment of the mils, turned over chiefly to woolcombers and machine-smiths, [or] into the counting-house.[82]

At the end of a visit to Toplis, the overseers observed to the proprietors that 'the boys should be encouraged to bathe in fine weather', and that 'the provision of the boys should be increased particularly on dumplin days', whereas, 'the girls should be taught to sew and their hair cut shorter'; and 'the older girls should be taught household work, previous to the expiration of their apprenticeship'.[83]

The Vestry of St Clement Danes parish in discussing the condition of girls at Backbarrow mill, could not 'avoid remarking that some few alterations might be

---

78 In the harsh conditions of factory work, such skill was hard won. The belief persisted, however, that this was naturally occurring.

79 Heywood, 'Age and gender', pp. 56 and 60.

80 'Plan of disposing of 200 parish children wanted by J. Bury and Co., Muslin Manufacturers of Hope Hill, near Stockport, Cheshire', undated document, estimated by archivist to be c. 1780, SLHL.

81 1802 Report, St Margaret and St John.

82 1802 Report, St Margaret and St John.

83 1802 Report, St Margaret and St John.

adopted respecting the females in future ... to make them more useful on their entrance into the world, particularly their being put alternately to Household work'.[84] Later it was reported that at the mill 'the servant maids are selected from the girls who attended to washing ironing cooking mending and making of cloaths, etc.'[85] When the parish officers from St Clement Danes arrived at Backbarrow for an inspection, 'the house was delicately clean; three of our girls were busily employed two of them rubbing the furniture and one scrubbing the floor'.[86]

As girls were directed into domestic activity particularly during the latter period of their apprenticeship, their consciousness as factory workers was inevitably weakened. A less pronounced work identity may have justified lower pay. Ellis Needham, proprietor of Litton mills, reassured St James parish, which was concerned that girls there received insufficient training in domestic skills, suggesting that girls' competence in domestic tasks was as important as the ability to earn a living wage. 'I think it exceeding proper that every woman should know something of household business', said Needham who also emphasised that the girls could make a good living: 'they will be able to get considerably more than 6s per week when they are loose, we have now a number of girls of 12 and 14 years of age that gets that money, and we have several of 17 and 18 years that gets 8, 9 and 10 s per week'.[87] Later Needham wrote that 'I assure you that many thousand women get a very good living by the same business in this country as well as in Lancashire and Cheshire ... I however think it exceeding proper that every women should understand the management of a family.[88]

Thus girls were expected to become both competent workers and properly domesticated women. The juxtaposition of the two objectives indicates a tension in the socialisation of girls.[89] The female identity was undoubtedly bound up with domesticity, as well as other 'female' attributes such as demeanour, deportment, modesty. Work identity was only a part and possibly the smaller part of this identity. The expectation that girls would be accomplished in domestic tasks and that their primary identity was not with work, may have been a justification for lower wages.

---

84   14 January 1802, meeting to compare the two reports on Backbarrow, Minutes of Vestry, Parish of St Clement Danes, B1074, WAC.

85   2 November 1797, Minutes of Vestry, Parish of St Clement Danes, B1074, WAC.

86   5 November 1801, Report by Messrs Pouden and Davidson respecting the children at Cartmell. Minutes of Vestry, Parish of St Clement Danes, B1074, WAC.

87   31 May 1796, Minutes of Governors and Directors of the Poor, Parish of St James, Piccadilly, D1876, WAC.

88   8 September 1796, letter from Ellis Needham, recorded in Minutes of Governors and Directors of the Poor, Parish of St James, Piccadilly, D1876, WAC.

89   The tension between factory work and domesticity that was recognised by parish officers, employers and sometimes by older boy apprentices, was not articulated by the girls themselves during this period. Recent research indicates that this was more prevalent by the 1830s. Testimony to the 1833 Factory Commission suggests that the female experience of child labour, though not necessarily as parish apprentice, may have shaped their response to the ideal of woman. Douglas A. Galbi, 'Through eyes in the storm: aspects of the personal history of women workers in the industrial revolution', *Social History*, 21, (1996): 143 and 158–9.

Even at this early stage, therefore, the pay differential may have had little to do with differences between girls and boys with respect to productivity, or output or ability to do the job, but more the result of a differently constructed work identity.

It seems that at the end of their apprenticeship girls recognised that their future employment would consist of either factory work or domestic service. Evidence of settlement examinations and interviews with former apprentices indicate the frequency with which young women obtained domestic service employment at the end of their term of factory apprenticeship which in some cases had lasted for twelve or more years. Margaret Chamberlain, for example, 'one of the girls who served her apprenticeship with Messrs Douglas and Co. at Pendleton ... is now a servant to an apothecary in Bridge Street Westminster'.[90] Then, at a meeting specially convened to examine Ms Chamberlain, it was revealed

> that several young women when out of their time had gone to service but generally returned back to follow their trade preferring it to service – that she should have continued either with her master or gone to Manchester but had relations in London who persuaded her to come to Town.[91]

In Scotland it was the case too, as Buchanan pointed out to the 1816 committee: 'when the girls grow up, we do not object to their going into service; we rather recommend it; they go away for six months and twelve months; and if they let us know when they wish to return to the works again, we endeavour to employ them'.[92]

Despite the emphasis by parish and proprietor on female domesticity, priority on providing female apprentices with a long-term livelihood remained. Although it was clearly believed that girls should have the opportunity to gain employment in domestic service, their right to a factory career was never questioned.[93] There were, however, other concerns about the employment of young women. In the 1830s, factory girls were seen as objects of pity; and anxiety focused on female puberty,[94] and the 'peculiar' physical susceptibilities of young girls, their morals and their fitness to

---

90   24 February 1797, Minutes of Governors and Directors of the Poor, Parish of St James, Piccadilly, D1876, WAC.

91   Testimony of Margaret Chamberlain presented to meeting of 29 February [sic] 1797, Minutes of Governors and Directors of the Poor, Parish of St James Piccadilly, D1876, WAC.

92   Evidence of Archie Buchanan, SC1816, p. 51.

93   The tension between the domestic and the working female explored fully during the 1830s and 1840s, was then used as an argument against women's factory labour. Meg Gomersall, *Working Class Girls in Nineteenth-Century England: Life, Work and Schooling* (London, 1997), p. 9. This was not the case in the earlier period.

94   Robert Gray, 'Factory legislation and the gendering of jobs in the north of England, 1830–1860', *Gender and History*, 5/1 (1993): 69. Female puberty was discussed more than the male because maturing women's bodies were understood to be more prone to damage by factory work, with implications for safe/successful reproduction. Gray also argues that 'the rhetorical figure of the helpless and vulnerable child was often associated with femininity'. Robert Gray, *The Factory Question and Industrial England 1830–1860* (Cambridge, 1996), p. 34; Robson, 'The ideal girl', p. 206. According to medical opinion, puberty was both retarded and hastened by factory employment. Engels, *Condition*, pp. 190 and 228.

be wives and mothers'.[95] Such discussion was barely evident in the early nineteenth century. By the time of the 1816 Select Committee, reference to puberty can be found but much less frequently than in the commissions of the 1830s. A medical man's observation was that children in cotton mills, 'grow quicker: I am inclined to think there is a more early arrival to puberty'.[96] More typical was concern about the challenge posed by factory work to the specific health of girls. Mr Simmons, surgeon, for example, observed: 'in passing into the state of womanhood, the health is often peculiarly delicate; and should they survive that critical period, distortion of the spine may be seriously apprehended. This deformity is not uncommon, and when situated low down the spine, will aggravate the period of child-birth'.[97] In evidence to the 1819 Lords committee, William Dean, a Slaithwaite surgeon, agreed that employment in cotton factories was more damaging to girls than to boys: 'it has a great tendency to stint their growth, and make them puny, and it subjected them to great difficulty in gestation, and in labour ... distortion of the pelvis takes place and makes the labour protracted and difficult and in some instances fatal';[98] and Llewellyn Jones MD, Chester noted that, 'during the short period of my practice at Holywell [8–10 years] I met with more cases requiring the aid of instruments ... than a gentleman of great practice in Birmingham [had met with] the whole of his life'. He also suggested that their progeny was more delicate, and the girls' 'general appearance bespeaks the absence of average health'.[99]

However, medical opinion before 1820 was more equivocal than in the early 1830s. Edward Holme, MD, for example, had no particular concerns about girls engaged in factory work: When asked, 'Have you any reason to suppose that the employment in the manufactures affected the females in any way prejudicial?', he replied, 'None whatsoever'.[100] Gavin Hamilton, a Manchester surgeon when asked by the House of Lords Committee of 1818: 'is not the age of fourteen what you would call a delicate time of life, both for male and female children, when the constitution undergoes considerable change?', replied, 'It certainly is in the female sex, a delicate period; but I did not find it had that effect upon them which I expected'. He added, 'a boy of fourteen ... is in as healthy a state as at any age', and 'I can hardly say that they did suffer from it at all'.[101]

---

95 Sonya O. Rose, 'Protective labor legislation in nineteenth-century Britain: gender, class and the liberal state', in Laura L. Frader and Sonya O. Rose (eds), *Class and Gender in Modern Europe* (Ithaca, NY, 1996), p. 200. Marjorie Levine-Clark argues that puberty was seen to be hastened or retarded, but never 'normal'. *Beyond the Reproductive Body*, pp. 27–33. Frederick Engels argued that the factory employment of young girls 'produces all sorts of irregularities during the period of development', *Condition*, pp. 190, 228. Only rarely was male puberty mentioned.

96 28 May 1816, Kinder Wood, surgeon, Oldham, examined. SC1816, p. 199.

97 SC1816, p. 287.

98 HL 1819, vol. 110, p. 290.

99 HL 1819, vol. 110, pp. 315–20. Evidence of headaches among girls at puberty was provided by Dr Carbutt, HL 1818, p. 121. He later acknowledged that all girls of that age are prone to headaches not just those in factories.

100 HL 1818, p. 11.

101 HL 1818, p. 102.

During the period of this study, observation on sexuality was hardly explicit. Anxiety about pregnancy and illegitimacy undoubtedly existed but was discussed less openly at the end of the eighteenth century than in the 1830s.[102] Nevertheless concern with morality and sexual propriety was obvious in the public record, if not in factory documentation.[103] Objections to the mingling of the sexes could be heard,[104] and the 1802 Act specifically required that boys and girls had separate sleeping apartments.[105] The evidence presented below suggests the development of a general practice of gender segregation, possibly prompted by the terms of the 1802 Act, and a growing tendency to discuss the differential implications of sex and gender at adolescence.

Gender-segregated sleeping accommodation was commonly referred to in the reports of parish and magisterial visits, as well as in the testimony of children themselves. The separation of sexes at sleep – perhaps more than the quality of diet and overall child welfare – indicated a soundly organised enterprise. Consistency of observation was marked. At Douglas's Pendleton factory, for example, 'the Boys and Girls during their apprenticeship ... lodge in different Houses at a considerable distance from one another';[106] or, as a spokesman for the firm said, 'the lodgings of our apprentices the boys and girls are separate from each other, by a greater distance than most of the streets in London are broad'.[107] The situation at Douglas's Holywell factory was described in the writings of Thomas Pennant who observed that the

---

102 Lane, *Apprenticeship*, p. 194; Humphries, '"The most free from objection ..."', especially pp. 942–48; Horrell and Humphries, 'The exploitation of little children', p. 487. By the 1830s, dangers to the moral welfare of girls were believed to undermine their fitness for domestic duties and for future marriage and motherhood. Robert Gray, 'Languages of factory reform in Britain, c. 1830–1860' in Patrick Joyce (ed) *The Historical Meanings of Work* (Cambridge, 1987), pp. 150–52. Hamilton, 'Images of femininity', p. 92, also emphasises contemporary anxiety about the potential for 'rampant sexual intercourse'. Edward Baines, *History of the Cotton Manufacture in Great Britain* (London, 1835), p. 481. Not all contemporaries were concerned about sexual congress within the factory. In ninety per cent of cases, according to William Cooke–Taylor, 'the seducers do not belong to the same mill as the seduced'. Quoted in Harold Perkin, *The Origins of Modern English Society 1780–1880* (London, 1969), p. 152.

103 As Sidney Pollard remarked, 'sexual morals rarely became an important issue to the factory disciplinarians (as distinct from outside moralists)'. The raising of levels of respectability and morality among the working class was, however, seen generally as 'an aspect of building up a new factory discipline'. 'Factory discipline in the industrial revolution', *Economic History Review*, 16/2 (1963): 270.

104 Rose, 'Protective labor legislation', p. 199, though it was not yet the metaphor for social disorder that it was to become.

105 The sources indicate the existence of a distinction between the employment of young children and adolescents.

106 Testimony of Margaret Chamberlain presented to meeting of 29 February [sic] 1797 Minutes of Governors and Directors of the Poor, Parish of St James Piccadilly, D1876, WAC.

107 Letter 21 January 1797 from John Plant, Pendleton to St James Parish read to meeting of Governors and Directors of the Poor, Parish of St James, Piccadilly, 10 February 1797, D1876, WAC.

apprentices were fed and clothed 'in commodious houses built for that purpose, the boys and girls in separate houses ...'.[108] An unnamed [and unreferenced] visitor to Cuckney about 1794 wrote that the children 'employed at the respective mills ... Are kept in excellent order. They live in cottages built for the purpose, under the care of superintendents; boys under one roof and girls under another'.[109] In a report of 1803, the visitors to John Watson's Preston mill found that the terms of the 1802 Act had been complied with and the apartments of boys and girls were separate; and 'no more than two sleep in one bed'.[110] At several factories boys and girls lodged in a single house, but most likely in separate 'apartments'. At Cressbrook, for example, 'there are about 30 apprentices, male and female ... separate apartments in a lodging house a short distance from the mill ... small ... clean, not crowded and apparently well-conducted';[111] and at Styal, the single apprentice house apparently managed to accommodate large numbers of boys and girls quite separately. The examination of two runaway apprentices from Samuel Greg's mill emphasised the propriety of conditions at the house. 'The boys slept at one side of the house and the girls on the other. The girls all slept in one room, the boys in three. There was a door betwixt their apartments which was locked of a night'.[112] The parish apprentices at Haigh's Marsden factory were housed in a building known as 'Throstles Nest'. Although boys and girls slept and ate in the same house, there was segregation within the building.[113] The Walton Twist company at Walton-le-Dale conformed to the minimal requirements of the 1802 Act as reported by the visitors; specifically the 'apartments were agreeable to the Act'.[114] The regulation was adhered to well beyond the early years of enactment. When, in 1818, parish officers from St Pancras investigated conditions at Jones and Sewell, the Hounslow flax mills, 'they found that every care is taken to separate and keep apart the two sexes by appropriating them detached apartments for living and sleeping'.[115] At Backbarrow, at the time of the 1824

---

108 Thomas Pennant, *The History of the Parishes of Whiteford and Holywell* (London, 1796), p. 215.

109 S.D. Chapman, *The Early Factory Masters: The Transition to the Factory System in the Midlands Textile Industry* (Newton Abbot, 1967), p. 171. Also an Anglican clergyman was advertised for, to take a full-time appointment at the Cuckney mills. *Nottingham Journal*, 31 August 1793. Separate accommodations for girls and boys were confirmed in the 1797 Report, St Margaret and St John; and reiterated in the 1802 Report, St Margaret and St John.

110 Lancashire W: 1803 Samlesbury: only one cotton mill, HL 1819, vol. 108.

111 Derbyshire, G 1807, Cressbrook, HL 1819, vol. 108.

112 'Examination of Joseph Sefton brought under a warrant of the Rev. Croxton Johnston Clerk one of his Majesty's Justices of the Peace for the County of Chester for his having eloped and deserted the service of Samuel Greg ... to whom he was apprentice', 2 August 1806. Greg papers C5/8/9/4, MCA. His co-absconder concurred.

113 1802 Report, St Margaret and St John.

114 Report of 1803, HL 1819, vol. 108.

115 6 January 1818, Minutes of Directors of the Poor, Parish of St Pancras, P/PN/PO/1/15 (microfilm reference UTAH 653) CLSAC.

Factory inspections, boys and girls slept in separate rooms and 'not more than two apprentices sleep in the same bed.'[116]

In other instances, recognition of the purpose of gender segregation was observed. At Merryweather's factory, to obviate undesirable intermingling, 'the apartments of the Girls are perfectly distinct from those of the Boys and they are even separated at dinner'. In Jewsbury's Measham mill, visitors found

> nothing that could attach blame to ... we questioned the children apart from their employers and found them satisfied with every part of the treatment ... except the restraints they are subject to after the hours of business, which restraints are thought necessary for the preservation of their morals there being great numbers of both sexes employed in the same factory.[117]

In 1813, it was again noted 'that no improper intercourse should take place'.[118] At Backbarrow, 'the girls when advanced in years worked separately from the young men';[119] and it was noted with satisfaction that 'not one act of Bastardy has happened among their apprentices during their conducting the business, a period of twenty years'.[120] Toplis was proud of his record in this respect: because the 'habitations of the boys and girls totally distinct and separate as it renders them much more liable to observation than they would otherwise be, and prevents those early connections which would perhaps, in their maturer years, expand into vicious habits and lead to serious consequences ...'; and from the '*four hundred* young persons under their care, yet but one irregular connexion had taken place; and that the further spreading of such an example had probably been stopped, by their obliging the youth to marry the girl whom he had seduced'.[121]

Only rarely did firms fail to provide appropriate accommodation. One example, ironically, was the enterprise of Robert Peel, author of the 1802 Act. Inspections of his Lancashire factories identified numerous deficiencies. At Radcliffe Bridge the apprentices' lodging was 'very indifferent'; and at Hind mill there were 'no sheets' on the bed. In neither place was reference made to separation of the sexes; but at the third mill, Summerseat, 'the sheets and linen [were] decent' but 'the rooms where they lodge and eat are very small and close. Boys and Girls in same rooms'. Although

---

116 1824 Factory Reports, Mills in the Hundred of Lonsdale in the county of Lancaster, inspected by James Crosfield, J.P. and J. Sunderland, Minister of Ulverton. Report dated 1 March 1824, HO44/14, National Archives.

117 Reports from Birmingham Guardians discussed at meeting of 12 July 1808, Minutes of Birmingham Board of Guardians, GP/B/2/1/2, BCA.

118 The inspections were made on 14 and 15 September 1813, and discussed by the Birmingham Guardians on 12 October 1813, when the visitors were thanked for 'their great attention to the welfare of the children'. Minutes of Birmingham Board of Guardians, GP/B/2/1/2, BCA.

119 Discussion of the two reports of Backbarrow mill, 14 January 1802, Minutes of Vestry meetings, Parish of St Clement Danes, B1074, WAC. A later report from Brighton Directors and Guardians of the Poor. June 1805. Cited in Aspin, *Water Spinners*, pp. 245–51.

120 A report from Brighton Directors and Guardians of the Poor, June 1805. Cited in Aspin, *Water Spinners*, pp. 245–51.

121 1797 Report, St Margaret and St John.

the inspection was conducted prior to the 1802 Act, such disregard for the propriety of the time reflected a more widespread neglect of the apprentices' welfare.[122] At Needham's place in Litton, 'The house we have hitherto had them in being much too small for the number we now have we are erecting a new one on a more convenient plan, and which will be more healthy for the children'.[123] Although at Holt's mill, the sleeping accommodation was not specifically described, the Officers of St James parish were disconcerted to witness a

> scene of confusion which was exhibited in the hours of relaxation by the promiscuous assemblage of the sexes and the improper language which too frequently assailed the ear, from the want of that due control and restraint which it seems almost impracticable to impose upon such large numbers collected together at the periods of recreation.[124]

Before the emergence of factory apprenticeships, parish bindings were mostly gendered.[125] This chapter tested the proposition that employment in the early factories might allow greater equality in gendered practices; and has demonstrated that the organisation of work, including the gender division of labour within the 'new' sectors of manufacturing was subject to variation and experimentation. After thirty years of factory production, the distribution of tasks by gender remained flexible, and differed by region. No obvious preference emerged. Variations in gendered practices existed not only between industries within textile manufacturing, but also within a single industry. As far as any pattern emerged, those firms with a preference – whether for girls or boys – appeared to have longer-term objectives in mind; while those 'indifferent' to sex were more likely to be indifferent to outcomes and a longer-term use for its parish apprentices. Whether or not girls and boys were taught different tasks during the course of their apprenticeship, they nevertheless learned to be different. Gendered socialisation meant that girls, who were instructed in the ways of domesticity alongside their factory labour, emerged with a less pronounced work identity than boys. The physical separation of boys and girls for sleeping and often for eating and instruction as well, was explicitly driven by moral concerns, yet facilitated the gendering of the factory, even if the work itself was not so clearly segregated.

---

122 28 June 1796, Report of Birmingham Guardians visit to Peels' Lancashire mills, Minutes of the Birmingham Board of Guardians, GP/B/2/1/1, BCA.

123 8 September 1796, letter from Ellis Needham to officers of St James Piccadilly. Minutes of the Governors and Directors of the Poor, Parish of St James, Piccadilly, D1876, WAC.

124 'Report of Messrs Johnson and Halfhide accompanied by the clerk to the governors of the poor relative to their children apprenticed from the Parish of St James, Westminster to Mitchell and Holt', considered by the meeting of the Governors and Directors of the Poor, Parish of St James, Piccadilly, 4 November 1803, D1878, WAC

125 Except in some agricultural activities.

Chapter 9

The Exploitation of Little Children

According to E.P. Thompson, 'the exploitation of little children' was one of the most shameful aspects of British industrialisation.[1] As the first children to experience the experimental nature of factory life separate from direct protection, parish apprentices were potentially subject to rigid discipline and other forms of exploitation.[2] Yet whether parish factory apprentices encountered more abuse than pre-factory apprentices is hotly contested by historians. The Romantic view, which juxtaposes the harshness of factory life with a pre-industrial golden age, is a minority position.[3] Most historians, while highly critical of the abusive conditions endured by children in textile factories, recognise the grim reality of earlier apprenticeships.[4] Nevertheless the peculiar features of industrial capitalism originating in the late eighteenth century have not been disregarded. Michael Lavalette, for example, argues that 'the transition to a capitalist market system and the commodification of labour power that came with it marked a significant intensification in child labour exploitation';[5] and Wally Seccombe warns of minimising the difference in exploitation potential between factory manufacturing and pre-industrial work. Industrial capitalism, Seccombe

---

1   E.P. Thompson, *The Making of the English Working* Class (London, 1963), p. 331; alluded to in Sara Horrell and Jane Humphries, '"The exploitation of little children": child labour and the family economy in the industrial revolution', *Explorations in Economic History*, 32 (1995): 485.

2   In the early factories there was considerable scope for cruelty and overwork on a mass scale. Anna Davin 'Child labour, the working class family, and domestic ideology in 19th century Britain', *Development and Change*, 13 (1982): 636.

3   Paul Mantoux, *The Industrial Revolution in the Eighteenth Century* (London, 1928), pp. 399–439; J.H. Clapham, *An Economic History of Modern Britain: the Early Railway Age, 1820–1850* (Cambridge, 1930), pp. 3–52; Clark Nardinelli, *Child Labour and the Industrial Revolution* (Bloomington, Indiana, 1990), pp. 17–21; James Walvin, *A Child's World: A Social History of English Childhood, 1800–1914* (Harmondsworth, 1982), pp. 61–3. As Peter Kirby observes, Walvin's position is based on several brief extracts from E. Royston Pike, *Human Documents of the Industrial Revolution* (London, 1966). Peter Kirby, *Child Labour in Britain, 1750–1870* (Basingstoke, 2003), p. 5 n. 3.

4   Among the many authorities who have contributed to this approach are M. Dorothy George, *London Life in the Eighteenth Century* (London, 1925), especially pp. 224–50; O.J. Dunlop, *English Apprenticeship and Child Labour: A History* (London, 1912), pp. 188–94; Anthony Brundage, *The English Poor Laws 1700–1930* (Basingstoke, 2002), p. 16; Roy Porter, *English Society in the Eighteenth Century* (Harmondsworth, 1991), pp. 85–6; John Rule, *The Labouring Classes in Early Industrial England 1750–1850* (London, 1986), p. 142; and Horrell and Humphries, 'The exploitation', p. 512.

5   Quoted in Marjetta Rahikainen, *Centuries of Child Labour: European Experience from the Seventeenth to the Twentieth Century* (Aldershot, 2004), p. 211.

argues, did not inaugurate the use of child labour, but transformed the context. The result of industrial change was 'a greater intensity of work ... a more voracious consumption of youthful labour power, sapping people's energy and debilitating their health'.[6]

This chapter is not concerned with quantifying exploitation,[7] nor with comparing the early factory age with other periods in terms of the experience of parish apprentices or other children workers.[8] Rather, it aims to assess the experience of parish apprentices, the first generation of textile factory workers, by adapting Clark Nardinelli's concept of indirect exploitation. It considers evidence of compulsion, experimentation, corporal punishment and sexual abuse, intensification of labour, and damage to health through a combination of long hours of work and inadequate diet. It takes for granted that parish apprentices were directly exploited by their employers.[9] Textile enterprises remained profitable as a result of their labour, for which they received only shelter and food.[10] Equally, parish apprentices were used, in ways that free children could not have been, to experiment in factory practices, and to prolong abusive and inefficient firms through cost containment. No attempt is made to challenge exploitation, or to 'correct its emphasis', but rather to explore its nature and outcomes.[11]

Previous chapters have shown that the process of parish factory apprenticeship gained momentum and shape through negotiation between parish and factory, and that the relationship between child, parish and factory owner, did not cease upon the signing of indentures. This chapter will introduce the argument that employers and parishes colluded in the exploitation of the apprentices.

That the parish was complicit in the exploitation of their children was most obvious in the involuntary nature of the apprentice binding. Parochially enforced

---

6   Wally Seccombe, *Weathering the Storm: Working Class Families from the Industrial Revolution to the Fertility Decline* (London, 1993), pp. 35–6.

7   Clark Nardinelli is one of the few to have tried to do this. See 'Were children exploited during the industrial revolution?', *Research in Economic History*, 11 (1988): 243–76; and *Child Labor and the Industrial Revolution*, especially pp. 76–94. Most work on children's factory labour has tended to focus on the period after 1830 because of the paucity of data prior to this.

8   The 'evils' of the parish apprenticeship system were still apparent in the mid nineteenth century. George Nicholls, *A History of the English Poor Law* (2 vols, London, 1898), vol. 2, pp. 317–18. Examples of the abuse of very young children in the workplace in the second half of the nineteenth century can be found in the Royal Commission of 1863; cited in Lionel Rose, *The Erosion of Childhood: Child Oppression in Britain 1860–1918* (London, 1991).

9   It therefore conflicts with Nardinelli's controversial conclusion is that exploitation fell during industrialisation because of increased labour market competitiveness. 'Were children exploited?' p. 268.

10   The costs of 'extras' like decent clothing and schooling were often met by their birth parish.

11   Rule, *The Labouring Classes*, p. 145. Among those intent on 'reassessing' exploitation are defenders of the market economy who suggest that child labour was a necessary but passing stage in the birth of the industrial economy.

labour grew in the later eighteenth century as numbers of poor increased.[12] Apprenticeship to manufactories from workhouses was seen as the best remedy for the idleness of children.[13] Demand for children 'stemmed from the recruitment and discipline problems faced by early industrial entrepreneurs', but because its supply was contained by initial reluctance,[14] a degree of compulsion seemed inevitable. The strategy of many parishes, however, was to replace direct force with robust persuasion. The signed consent of children to the apprentice placement was obligatory; and parental approval was also frequently sought. Yet the acquiescence of the child in the face of domineering parish officials, or false promises, meant nothing; and parental resistance carried little weight. Only rarely, as in the case of St Mary Newington for example, did the parish accept a parent's refusal without reprisal.[15] More commonly, the opposition of parents was countered by the threat to withhold benefits, or was simply overruled.[16] After discussing the case of a mother who requested the return of her daughter, a St Pancras child recently sent 'on a liking', the parish officers concluded that because the woman could not

> indemnify the Parish against such children again becoming chargeable, and their appearing from the account of the care, every probability that further trouble and expense would ensue by consenting to the measure ... that such application ... be refused and the clerk was directed to write to Mr Gorton the master in Lancashire to desire him that if any application should be made for the girl by any person to resist the same.[17]

When Martha Etheridge's father refused to allow her to go to Toplis's factory and took her home, Woodford parish asserted that 'she is in future to be at his charge and no further burthensome to this parish'.[18] The tension between consent and compulsion was palpable. Parish apprentices did not enter the labour market as free agents. Decisions were made for them by others, and although by signing their apprenticeship indentures they formally agreed to the deal, in effect, as Sara

---

12 Rahikainen, *Centuries of Child Labour*, p. 33. Compulsion also applied to masters, though rarely were factory employers unwilling. Bridget Hill, *Women, Work and Sexual Politics in Eighteenth Century England* (Oxford, 1989), p. 88.

13 Rahikainen, *Centuries of Child Labour*, p. 37.

14 Rahikainen, *Centuries of Child Labour*, p. 124. This observation applies to 'free' children.

15 On 13 April 1814, 'Charlotte Smith's mother applied to take her from the house, she having been selected by Mr Burne for Mr Whitaker – but the mother insisted on taking her from the house', Minutes of St Mary Newington Workhouse Committee, 931, SLHL.

16 Steve Hindle demonstrates how the withholding of poor relief as a means of securing compliance, or punishing non-compliance was implemented from the early years of 'compulsory' pauper apprenticeship. "'Waste' children? Pauper apprenticeship under the Elizabethan Poor Laws, c. 1598–1697', in Penelope Lane, Neil Raven and K.D.M. Snell (eds), *Women, Work and Wages in England, 1600–1850* (Woodbridge 2004), p. 21.

17 22 June 1805, Minutes of Directors of the Poor, Parish of St Pancras, P/PN/PO/1/1 (microfilm reference UTAH 649), CLSAC.

18 4 February 1788, Minutes of Woodford Vestry, D/P 167/8/3 ERO.

Horrell and Jane Humphries have argued, they were 'commandeered by Poor Law officials'.[19]

Compulsion continued into the workplace. The new textile technology replaced heavy labour but required consistent minding to run effectively. Because of their nimble fingers and slight physique, children constituted ideal labour. But they were manifestly ill-equipped to sustain the necessary attention. Experimental methods to assist the development of children's powers of concentration and stamina were introduced in the early textile factories.[20] The role of corporal punishment in enhancing levels of production was assumed from the early days of textile factory production, and can be seen as part of the factory 'experiment'.[21] Beating existed, even in 'humanitarian' enterprises where practices may have been more subtle,[22] and was apparently accepted by children and parish officers. Despite variations in the manifestation of discipline, some form of 'control' became embedded in factory organisation.[23]

The disciplinary options available to early factory manufacturers were discussed over 40 years ago by Sidney Pollard.[24] The use of 'stick' on children workers exceeded many times the offering of 'carrots', and only gradually did a new ethos of work discipline evolve.[25] Most of the existing 'stick' options, namely fines, dismissals, complaints to parents, were not relevant to parish apprentices, to whom only beating applied. With respect to the positive inducements, these were uncommonly employed, but two examples from firms in the present study indicate the nature of the carrots that parish apprentices might expect. Financial inducements were used at Birch's Backbarrow mill. For good work and behaviour, apprentices received a 'bounty'

---

19 Horrell and Humphries, 'Exploitation', p. 89; Sara Horrell and Jane Humphries, 'Child labour and British industrialisation', in Michael Lavalette (ed.), *A Thing of the Past? Child Labour in Britain in the Nineteenth and Twentieth Centuries* (Liverpool, 1999), p. 76. Rahikainen, *Centuries of Child Labour*, p. 32 shows that this compulsion existed in many economies. To send young children away from their 'home' or 'birth parish' to an unknown, and often distant, destination was an act of cruelty.

20 Diane Elson refers to submissiveness through sanctions. 'The differentiation of children's labour in the capitalist labour market', *Development and Change*, 13 (1982): 492.

21 Nardinelli suggests that a good thrashing would raise children's output/wages by 16–18 per cent. *Child Labor*, p. 92. Gregory Clark emphasises the importance of a coordinated and hardworking labour force, which required discipline to achieve. 'Factory discipline' *Journal of Economic History*, 54/1 (1994): 129–30.

22 Neil J. Smelser, *Social Change in the Industrial Revolution: An Application of Theory to the Lancashire Cotton Industry 1770–1840* (London, 1959), p. 105–107.

23 Commissions of the 1830s and 1840s were replete with descriptions of the abuse of 'free' children. Clark's coercion theory suggests that by the mid-nineteenth century, 'discipline was profitable primarily because it forced workers to increase their efforts not because it reduced costs by coordinating their labour.' Clark, 'Factory discipline', pp. 136 and 148.

24 Sidney Pollard, 'Factory discipline in the industrial revolution', *Economic History Review*, 16/2 (1963), pp. 254–71.

25 According to Michael Huberman, methods of supervision remained unsophisticated through much of the nineteenth century. 'How did labour markets work in Lancashire? More evidence on prices and quantities in cotton spinning, 1822–1852', *Explorations in Economic History*, 28 (1991), pp. 88–90.

of 6d or 1s, which were taken away if offences were committed.²⁶ The intention at Jeremiah Bury's Stockport factory was to adapt Robert Owen's approach:

> Their punishments for faults will be chiefly badges of disgrace and for good conduct they will receive rewards and marks of favour and distinction. We have cards of honour and a large folio book with a page or two allotted to each name, in which is registered their merit or demerit every Christmas they will have a feast, when the contents of this book will be published to them, and rewards distributed to the deserving ... (one mode of distinction to the deserving will be to teach them to sing scientifically if they evince a taste for it).²⁷

Mostly, however, apprentices were encouraged through physical means to work hard and obediently.

Experiments in corporal punishment involved testing the effectiveness of disciplinary methods. Chastisement was employed in several situations: where children's concentration slipped; where children made mistakes; where children fell asleep; and where they engaged in playful activities.²⁸ The type and level of physical force deemed necessary in each case, varied between firms and individuals. Gratuitous beating on the part of sadistic or frustrated overlookers was also common.²⁹ Parish apprentices played an important role in the corporal punishment 'experiment', which because of its persistence can be judged a success. Joan Lane has used the evidence of legal proceedings to argue that apprentices in early textile factories were more likely than other contemporary workers to experience abuse. Parish factory apprentices, generally unable to protect themselves except by absconding, suffered most acutely from trade variations and harsh masters.³⁰

The following section explores the experience of and attitudes towards the different levels of corporal punishment, and argues that while brutal beating was condemned, milder forms of 'correction' were condoned by most 'protective' parishes. Many of the tales of factory life portrayed in parliamentary reports, involve the role of the overlooker in keeping children awake during the long hours of labour by constant prodding and poking with a stick.³¹ 'Gentler' methods were also used. At Marshall's Shrewsbury factory, 'if a child became sleepy, the overlooker touches the child on the shoulder and says "come here". In the corner of the room there is an

---

26 Pollard, 'Factory discipline', p. 266.

27 'A plan of disposing of 200 parish children wanted by J Bury and Co., muslin manufacturers of Hope hill, near Stockport, Cheshire', addressed to St George the Martyr parish, c. 1790, SLHL.

28 Samuel Jones, a spinner and former apprentice at Douglas's Pendleton enterprise stated to the 1819 Lords Committee that children beaten by masters 'because they cannot follow close enough to their work; they cannot do work enough for them; they get fatigued and tired', HL 1819 vol. 110, p. 174.

29 European scholars argue that English disciplinary methods were peculiarly harsh. Marjetta Rahikainen, oral presentation to the ESRC First Labour market seminar, University of Birmingham, 28 April 2006.

30 Joan Lane, *Apprenticeship in England 1600–1914* (London, 1996), p. 186. Lane cites the example of Ann Hinds who became the subject of a contemporary pamphlet, p. 222.

31 In one action, this demonstrated the twin evils of overwork and physical abuse.

iron cistern filled with water. He takes the boy by the legs and dips him in the cistern, and then sends him back to work'.[32]

The familiarity of parish apprentices with routines of workhouse discipline may have prepared them for the factory experience.[33] If not, it seems that they quickly adapted to a regime in which minor misdemeanours were punished. When describing episodes of punishment to visiting parish officials, apprentices indicated, almost apologetically, that it happened 'only when I deserved it'.[34] This suggests that apprentices came to recognise the collusive relationship between employers and parish officials who were unlikely to 'protect' them from abuse. It also indicates that the experiment in discipline and control was successful. Powerless children were cowed into submission.

A certain amount of 'disciplining' appears to have been the norm and some degree of brutality came to be expected; recipients as well as perpetrators came to be inured to the practice.[35] Beating was rarely mentioned in factory visitors' reports; either because it was not witnessed during inspections – and it almost certainly would not have been – or because it was implicitly condoned. Parish collusion in the physical abuse of early factory apprentices should be recognised. The parish either ignored the existence of beating or, where this was impossible, condoned the employers actions. Only very rarely did the parish position itself with the child. Typically, the officers described punishment without comment, or implicitly held the child responsible.

Although 'numerous complaints respecting the treatment of the children' at Merryweather and Whitaker's Burley mill had reached the ears of parish officials, they were pleasantly surprised by the circumstances in which they found the apprentices. The officers assumed that apprentices required discipline, and descriptions were presented matter-of-factly. 'When [not if] the boys are beat it is with a leather strap'.[36] The Leeds officials visiting several years later, observed that 'the boys said when they were corrected it was with a small stick on the palm of the hand'.[37] At Peel's Hind mill, the Birmingham visitors noted that, by way of punishment, the children were 'beat with sticks'.[38] Although their visit to Lancashire was prompted by a runaway apprentice who 'gave a miserable account of her usage', the Birmingham officials

---

32 Jonathan Downe, who was seven years old when sent to Marshalls, interviewed in June 1832.

33 The abusive conditions in many workhouses are well recorded. See, for example, G.B. Hindle, *Provision for the Relief of the Poor in Manchester 1754–1826* (Manchester, 1975), pp. 40–48. Despite its prohibition, discipline was also usual in schools. Jane Humphries' forthcoming work indicates that children's experience of beating in schools was worse than that in factories. It has been argued that beating was a common experience for all young people during this period. Porter, *English Society*, p. 17.

34 The example of William Green at Merryweather's mill exemplifies this. 1802 Report, St Margaret and St John.

35 Evidence to the SC1816; HL 1818; HL 1819 vol. 110, suggests that many factory workers barely noticed its existence.

36 1802 Report, St Margaret and St John.

37 The visit took place on 28 August 1805; the group reported to the workhouse committee on 4 September 1805, Leeds Workhouse Query Book, 1803–1810, LO/Q 2, WYASL.

38 28 June 1796, Minutes of Birmingham Board of Guardians GP/B/2/1/1, BCA.

did not comment on the punishment regime at Peel's other mills in the area.[39] Nor did they mention in their report the beating that was described by a former apprentice at John Bott's Nantwich mill and may have accounted for its high rate of absconding.[40] Parishes' reluctance to acknowledge abuse even where it may have been excessive is illustrated by visitors to John Watson's Preston factory who were disconcerted to notice 'a large pair of stocks at end [of the eating room] for refractory children to be fastened to and whipped at'. They were persuaded that 'no child had been whipped in the recollection of the overlooker'.[41] This appeared to appease the visitors, and the subject was not referred to again.

Parishes commonly underplayed children's complaints of abuse. In October 1796, for example,

> Mr Churchwarden Butler reports that in consequence of a complaint made of the children with Mr Watson at Watford being ill-treated, he, with Mr Taylor and Mr Lemage went on Wednesday last very unexpectedly to visit them, when it appeared to them that the children were all perfectly satisfied, very well treated and comfortably accommodated and upon the whole the situation appears eligible and the complaint malicious and unfounded.[42]

And at Douglas's Pendleton plant, visitors reports were silent on the subject of abuse, which is suspicious given the complaint received by Chelmsford parish that children at Pendleton were being 'improperly treated'.[43] Upon investigation, the treatment of the children was found to be 'highly satisfactory' and the 'representations made to the parish groundless'.[44] Greenwood's damning critique of the Pendleton factory was partly corroborated by evidence of former apprentices to the House of Lords Committees of 1818 and 1819, who complained of long hours and damage to health and physique, though none actually referred to brutal beating.[45]

---

39 14 May 1796, Minutes of Birmingham Board of Guardians GP/B/2/1/1, BCA.

40 Report received by Birmingham Guardians, 27 August 1798 Minutes of Birmingham Board of Guardians GP/B/2/1/1, BCA; Testimony of Samuel Jones to HL 1819, vol. 110, p. 173.

41 1802 Report, St Margaret and St John.

42 19 October 1796, Minutes of meetings of Officers of the Parish, Parish of St Martin in the Fields F2075, WAC.

43 The euphemistic terminology that permeates contemporary discussions on corporal punishment indicates reluctance to confront the issue directly.

44 Chelmsford Parish, D/P94, p. 75, Vestry Minutes 1794–1823 regarding apprenticing of pauper children to Lancashire cotton manufacturer. Evidence from the Vestry minutes indicates that it was Douglas who took the initiative, with subsequent complaints of ill treatment found to be unjustified 1799–1802, D/P 94/14, ERO; see also F.G. Emmison 'Essex children deported to a Lancashire cotton mill, 1899' *The Essex Review*, 53 (1944): 77–87; and detailed criticism by Walter Greenwood, writer, who wrote that Douglas was notable … for never having once in his lifetime performed a single generous action'. Chris Aspin, *The Water Spinners* (Helmshore, 2003), p. 165.

45 By the time of the House of Lords Committees, a former apprentice, still employed by the mill, asserted that 'we never allow them [children] to be beaten'. Hugh Batho, HL 1819, vol. 110, pp. 421–5.

The extent to which parish children were chastised for their inadequacies at Douglas's Holywell factory, not mentioned in earlier parish reports or apprentices' testimony,[46] was the subject of some discussion in the House of Lords Committee.[47] The mill superintendent for example, denied allowing the children to be 'beaten for neglect or carelessness' or knowing of any complaints 'either by the children or by the parents'. Yet, when pressed it transpired that he had been convicted of cruelty.[48] James Knott, a manager at the mill argued that children were not punished, merely reprimanded; yet John Broadbent, a spinner at the works, said that he had seen children beaten 'for different purposes; neglect of their work, and carelessness, and doing mischief and such like'.[49] Colbeck, Ellis and Wilks was renown for the brutal treatment of its parish apprentices[50] though this was not noted by the visitors under the 1802 Act, who believed that 'the mills seem under very proper care'.[51]

Parishes were also complicit in workplace compulsion by encouraging children to tolerate discipline. Although children from St James parish bound to Strutt's Rickmansworth mill in 1788, for example, encountered abuse almost immediately,[52] and were later found by parish officers to have been 'very severely chastised for trifling offences'.[53] However, the children were exhorted to be courageous and obedient: 'they talked with every child in rotation and recommend them to behave dutifully to their masters and teachers and to be diligent and faithful in the performance of their duty'.[54] Even at Haigh's Marsden enterprise, which parish officers visited in response to complaints from local residents of over-zealous beating there, the children were encouraged to be stoical. Acknowledging that 'boys and girls who have generally more vivacity than prudence, will frequently deserve and must receive correction', the parish officers continued that while 'it is not perhaps very easy theoretically to describe with precision the quantum of chastisement necessary. In the case of our children, it is by all parties allowed that correction was formerly carried to excess'. Nevertheless, it was the visitors' shared opinion 'that it was better to let

---

46 The high rate of absconding, however, indicates a far from benign establishment.

47 The beating of children was openly discussed for the first time during the Factory Commissions of the 1830s, when it became one of the main complaints against factory owners. Pollard, 'Factory discipline', p. 260.

48 Testimony of Edward Kenworthy, HL 1819 vol. 110, p. 392. In his eyes however, although he was found guilty, because he paid the fine imposed, he believed he was 'liberated'.

49 Testimony to the HL 1819, vol. 110, p. 144.

50 I.D.B. Ferguson, 'Fewston mill', BA Dissertation, University of Leeds, Folk Life Studies, 1967.

51 Returns of Cotton and other mills 1803–1806, QE 33/1, WYASW.

52 29 April 1788, Minutes of Governors and Directors of the Poor, Parish of St James, Piccadilly, D1873, WAC.

53 28 October 1792, Minutes of Governors and Directors of the Poor, Parish of St James, Piccadilly, D1874, WAC.

54 17 September 1790, Minutes of Governors and Directors of the Poor, Parish of St James, Piccadilly, D1873, WAC.

pass unnoticed a complaint, the ground of which seems entirely to be removed, and even the remembrance of which has long lain dormant'.⁵⁵

Evidence that absconders were returned to abusive employers confirms parish complicity. In August 1806, the Directors of the Poor of St Pancras parish, which had earlier failed to protect Robert Blincoe and his young associates, considered evidence that four boys had been beaten at Haslam's Bury mill, and specifically that one of the said boys 'had received a very severe blow in the side'. A letter of explanation from the employer, and a visit to the factory by the Beadle were reassuring, and 'the said four boys be taken back to Mr Haslam at his expense'. The Beadle was 'authorised to take such steps as may be necessary to prevent any ill-treatment to them in future', though it is difficult to see how practically he could have done so.⁵⁶

As children were reluctant to complain to parish factory visitors about chastisement,⁵⁷ most descriptions of abuse, particularly the excessive type, came from the safety of geographical or chronological distance. Evidence suggests that children resisted excessively violent discipline by running away.⁵⁸ In evidence to parish officers of St Clement Danes, Harriet Russell, a former apprentice at Wells, Middleton, emphasised the harsh discipline: 'they are strapped for not working and allowances taken away and [though] some were beat much not disabled'.⁵⁹ Three of the boys bound to Mitchell and Holt from St James parish eloped and returned 'home'. On being questioned by officers they complained of being 'improperly corrected in a continuance for 4 or 5 days'.⁶⁰

Autobiographical accounts provide vivid descriptions of abuse. From Robert Blincoe's well-known memoirs, we have learned that St Pancras parish apprentices

---

55 1797 Report, St Margaret and St John. Joseph Moser, 'Report of the situation of the children apprenticed by the churchwardens, overseers and governors of the poor of the United parishes of St Margaret and St John in the City of Westminster to the cotton manufactory of Messrs H— at M— and Messrs J and T at Cuckney Mills, addressed to the workhouse Board of the said parishes, April 10 1797', *European Magazine and London Review*, 34 (September 1798): 201.

56 5 August 1806, Directors of Poor minutes, Parish of St Pancras, P/PN/PO/1/2 (microfilm reference UTAH 649) CLSAC. The boy most affected, Lary Madden, had been apprenticed in April 1803, aged 13, together with his sister Ann, aged 10. Apprenticeship Register 1802–1867, Parish of St Pancras, P90/ PANI/ 362. LMA.

57 At Cuckney, for example, 'There was but one complaint against the masters, 'but many against the overlookers'. In this case, the officials were aware that the children needed their protection but took little action. 1802 Report, St Margaret and St John.

58 John Brown, *Memoir of Robert Blincoe* (Manchester, 1832); parish examinations of runaways, such as, 5 August 1806, Minutes of Directors of the Poor, Parish of St Pancras, P/PN/PO/1/2 (microfilm reference UTAH 649), CLSAC. On the spot complaints were relatively unusual.

59 12 September 1797 Special meeting called to consider the examination of Harriet Russell. Minutes of Vestry, Parish of St Clement Danes, B1074, WAC.

60 These were unlikely to have the children's exact words, but the sentiment may have been accurately expressed. 20 July 1802, Minutes of Governors and Directors of the Poor, Parish of St James, Piccadilly, D1878, WAC. Other complaints included the requirement to work from five in the morning to ten at night with insufficient provisions.

were beaten or threatened from the moment they arrived at Lowdham;[61] and again at Litton, where overlookers, driven by the need to meet production targets, compounded regular cruelty with intermittent sadistic acts. Several pages of the *Memoir* are dedicated to descriptions of savage practices. Those more mentionable include the hanging of heavy weights onto the tiny Blincoe as entertainment: 'under this cruel torture he soon sank; when to make the sport last longer ... [more weights added so that] Blincoe could not lift his arm to the roller'.[62] Such extreme usage may have been exceptional but was not unique.[63] A former apprentice recalled:

> There were no inspectors, no public opinion to put down flagrant cases of oppression, or of cruel usage. Some of the overlookers were brutal beyond what would now be believed, while the master was feared and almost worshipped by turns ... the mortality among millhands was very great ... had a fair record been kept of the doings of some overlookers it would read more like the doings of a West Indian slave driver than a sober record of English life.[64]

A former apprentice at Newton's Cressbrook plant, writing years after the event, described the nature of abuse there. 'An overlooker called William Hughes ... starting beating me with a stick, and when he had done I told him I would let my mother know. He then went out and fetched the master in to me. The master started beating me with a stick over the head till it was full of lumps and bled'.[65]

Even if parish officers were reluctant to take action against cruel masters, not all punishment was condoned. Uncontrolled beating and other cruel practices, a feature of firms and personnel under pressure, were subject to legal action.[66] Andrew Hides, overseer at the Sheffield mill, spent six months in York Castle in 1799 'for beating an apprentice Edward Garrett so violently with a leather strap that the child's life was greatly despaired of'.[67] At Merryweather's Manchester plant, physical abuse was not mentioned in the critical report of 1810, but later evidence demonstrates its

---

61 Though this did abate following parish protests. See debate about accuracy of Blincoe: described by Rule, *The Labouring Classes*, pp. 147–9.

62 Brown, *Memoir*, pp. 39–44.

63 For example, 'in a mill at Wigan the children, for any slight neglect, are loaded with weights of twenty pounds, placed over their shoulders, and hanging behind their backs'. Oastler, quoted by Kydd, *The Factory Movement*, vol. 2, p. 10. According to Sidney Pollard, 'Robert Blincoe's sadistic master was untypical', and 'serious beatings were neither very widespread, nor very effective'. 'Factory discipline', p. 260.

64 Autobiography of Thomas Wood, engineer, from John Burnett (ed.), *Useful Toil: Autobiographies of Working People from the 1820s to the 1920s* (London, 1994), p. 306.

65 Sarah Carpenter, *Ashton Chronicle*, 23 June 1849. This paper which advocated radical social reform published a number of testimonies of parish apprentices.

66 According to Lane, the masters of textile apprentices figured prominently in legal proceedings. *Apprenticeship*, p. 186.

67 But was fined only 6d for hitting a girl apprentice at the mill. In 1803, St George's Westminster resolved that no more children be apprenticed there. 24 February, Minutes of Governors and Directors of the Poor, Parish of St George, Hanover Square, C925, WAC; Aspin, *Water Spinners*, p. 241.

existence. Testimony to the 1816 Select Committee refers to a case of abuse some years earlier

> in a factory where a great number of apprentices had been taken from the metropolis ... a complaint of ill-usage of the apprentices employed there was taken up by the then magistrates and parochial officers of the place and a prosecution instituted at the expense of the churchwardens ... what finally became of it I do not know; I think it was removed by certiorari into the Court of Kings Bench ... the man's name was Merryweather.[68]

In spite of Jeremiah Bury's good intentions and allegedly Owenite disciplinary strategy,[69] cruelty at his Stockport mill was reported in the local press. An overlooker had been taken into custody 'for a most violent assault' with a hand whip on two boys and for 'fastening a chain to the leg of one of them'.[70] Even Richard Arkwright, who did not take parish apprentices, was found to have abuse taking place in his enterprises. In 1786, an overlooker at his Bakewell mill was imprisoned for six months and fined £20 for having 'kicked and otherwise abused' a child worker 'in a very unmerciful Manner, and afterwards drew it up by the neck with a cord. The child was brought into court and appeared a shocking spectacle'.[71]

However violent and unjustified the act, employers lacked remorse and were quick to defend themselves. At Davison and Hawksley, several cases of assault against the children were brought by local residents, though none was proven. A statement issued by Davison following a protest meeting of inhabitants denied general abuse but admitted that some level of necessary 'correction' had occurred. 'In so great a number of apprentices, there will be some base and refractory ones, you who are framework knitters and keep but few; know this by experience – and you also know that correction may be occasionally necessary'. The particular child whose case had given rise to some unrest, 'had destroyed and wasted work to a most shameful degree; and to a very large amount – she had been in the county Bridewell for her vices, and instead of being reformed, came out more wicked and base than ever'.[72]

In an environment in which physical abuse was endemic, and applied equally to girls and boys,[73] sexual exploitation was likely to occur. Robert Gray's research suggests the prevalence of the sexual abuse of young girls by overlookers and

---

68 Testimony of David Evans, Barrister and Magistrate in Manchester to the SC1816, p. 321.

69 Rewards and punishments took the form of badges.

70 *Manchester Chronicle*, 21 August 1808, cited in Aspin, *Water Spinners*, p. 189.

71 Quoted in Frances Collier, *The Family Economy of the Working Classes in the Cotton Industry 1784–1833* (Manchester, 1964), p. 70.

72 Statement by Robert Davison, Arnold, 18 July 1798, DD 568/34, NA.

73 The Sadler Committee of 1832 found that bosses made 'no distinction of sex in administering punishment ... yes, the females of this country, no matter whether children or grown up'. Quoted in Inglis, *Poverty and the Industrial Revolution*, p. 331. Marshall, however, argues that young girls were particularly defenceless and were the victims in some of the worst cases. Dorothy Marshall, *The English Poor in the Eighteenth century: A Study in Social and Administrative History* (London, 1926), pp. 199–200.

managers in the textile factories of the 1830s and 1840s;[74] and Lane argues that 'parliamentary commissions were to reveal widespread sexual abuse of child labour by both masters and overlookers'.[75] However, the subject was not discussed openly in the age of factory reform and even less in the period of this study. The 1802 Act emphasised moral issues and by stipulating sex-segregated sleeping quarters, focused on potential impropriety between apprentices of the same age, rather than sexual exploitation by elders. Common sense tells us that this must have happened but only snippets of evidence are available. Sexual abuse was a hidden form of exploitation. It was not even hinted at in parish reports; yet the small number of examples that exist suggests at least the blurring of the line between physical and sexual abuse.

The apprentices at Litton mill were subject to many forms of abuse including that of a sexual nature. According to Robert Blincoe, 'to boys, he [John Needham] was a tyrant and an oppressor! To the girls, the same, with the additional odium of treating them with an indecency as disgusting as his cruelty was terrific. Those unhappy creatures were at once the victims of his ferocity and his lust'.[76] Blincoe also made specific reference to girls having petticoats lifted up by the Needham boys for fun;[77] and further that 'the girls were frequently prostituted to the carnal lusts of the young masters, who did not (as occasion required) scruple to make use of the most base means of screening their own infamy'.[78] Sexual abuse at Newton's Cressbrook plant was described by a former female apprentice.

> The master carder's name was Thomas Birks; but he never went by any other name than Tom the Devil. He was a very bad man – he was encouraged by the master in ill-treating all the hands, but particularly the children. I have often seen him pull up the clothes of big girls, seventeen or eighteen years of age, and throw them across his knee, and then flog them with his hand in the sight of both men and boys.[79]

Evidence to the 1816 Select Committee criticised Mr Moss, governor of the apprentice house at Backbarrow for 'making too free' with the children. He allegedly 'took a stick and put it to a girl's petticoats, and heave them up a little, and say, let us see what sort of legs you have got: and I thought he was rather too lose there'.[80] Mrs

---

74 Robert Gray, 'Medical men, industrial labour and the state in Britain, 1830–50, *Social History*, 16/1 (1991): 19–43.

75 Joan Lane, 'Apprenticeship in Warwickshire cotton mills 1790–1830', *Textile History*, 10 (1979), p. 168.

76 Brown, *Memoir*, p. 43.

77 John Waller suggests that Blincoe through Brown refrained from exposing further detail to avoid charges of lewdness. If this were a genuine concern, it may explain why not more contemporary accounts survive. John Waller, *The Real Oliver Twist: Robert Blincoe – A Life that Illuminates an Age* (Cambridge, 2005), p. 155.

78 Waller, *The Real Oliver Twist*, p. 282. At a Scottish mill, a young girl was severely beaten because she had rejected the advances of her boss who had 'wanted familiarities with her'. Waller, *The Real Oliver Twist*, p. 300, citing the 1832 Select Committee.

79 Sarah Carpenter, *Ashton Chronicle*, 23 June 1849. This paper, which advocated radical social reform, published a number of testimonies of parish apprentices.

80 Evidence of Travers, SC1816, p. 289.

Moss who shared the care of the apprentices failed to prevent this abuse; and the children believed that 'he was too familiar with some of them'.[81]

Intensification of labour, reflected in long hours of unremitting labour, was characteristic of early factory practice,[82] and constituted the most consistent component of abuse during the apprentices' tenure. While it was generally agreed that habits of industry were to be encouraged as early as possible, contemporary opinion on the prolonged labour of young children was clearly divided. Some commentators welcomed the practice of extended working days. A document of 1770 argued that 'being constantly employed at least twelve hours in a day ... we hope the rising generation will be so habituated to constant employment, that it would at length prove agreeable and entertaining to them'.[83] It was also argued that children were not overworked and in any case long hours brought moral benefits.[84] Growing evidence that prolonged labour damaged young bodies, however, shaped a more critical strand of thought, illustrated by the work of Marx, Marshall and Mill.[85]

The working day of early parish apprentices was at least twelve hours but usually more.[86] The norm appeared to lengthen and, by 1816, daily labour of fourteen and fifteen hours appeared to be commonplace.[87] Night working was not unusual, even after the 1802 Act. Visitors' reports made surprisingly little reference to hours of work; assessments were founded on apprentices' appearance: 'the children appeared

---

81 Evidence of Travers, SC1816, p. 292. Hopkins, however, questions the motives of Moss's accusers and thus the accuracy of their statements. Eric Hopkins, *Childhood Transformed: Working-class Children in Nineteenth-Century England* (Manchester, 1994), p. 84.

82 Expansion of industrial output during the early period of industrialisation was at least partly the result of increased hours of physical work, achieved by increasing the number of days of labour per year rather than growing number of hours per day. It has been argued that hours worked increased by 20 per cent between 1760 and 1830; the peak occurring in 1800. Hans-Joachim Voth, *Time and Work in England 1750–1830* (Oxford, 2000), pp. 242 and 268–70.

83 Quoted in B.L. Hutchins and A. Harrison, *A History of Factory Legislation* (Westminster, 1903), p. 5. A working day of at least 12 hours was typical in workhouses or parishes' Houses of Industry. See, for example, E.E. Butcher, *Bristol Corporation of the Poor: Selected Records, 1696–1834* (Bristol, 1932); and the Manchester workhouse, which, like others, also prepared children for harshness and deprivation. G.B. Hindle, *Provision for the Relief of the Poor in Manchester 1754–1826* (Manchester, 1975), p. 40.

84 Most evidence to the 1816 Select Committee, with the exception of Robert Peel and Robert Owen, dismissed the idea that factory children were overworked, and argued that they were healthier, more intelligent and more moral than others. J.L. Hammond and Barbara Hammond, *The Town Labourer 1760–1832: The new civilisation* (London, 1917), pp. 111–12.

85 Basu Kaushik, 'Child labour: cause, consequence and cure, with remarks on international labour standards', *Journal of Economic Literature*, 37 (1999): 1094–1095.

86 A number of firms made overtime payments when hours exceeded twelve in one day. The list of such payments at Gregs, typically viewed as a benevolent employer, indicates the frequency of 'overtime', and thus very long working days. Collier, *The Family Economy*, p. 42.

87 Testimony presented to 1816 Select Committee indicates a standard working day 6 am to 7 or 8 pm; particularly vicious employers might work the children from 5 am to 9 pm.

overworked', for example, or even 'the children did not appear overworked'. The impact of such incessant labour on fragile young bodies and spirits can be measured in terms of disability and deformity.[88] One boy, who worked at Haighs in Marsden, was carried to the mill when he was too ill to walk and made to work the usual shift.[89] Even at the exemplary Styal mill of Samuel Greg, medical records include many cases of apprentices being treated for injuries to legs and eyes.

Excessive hours of work were compounded by the erosion of dinner breaks. The luxury of an hour's leisure at midday was unusual. At Toplis, for example, half an hour was allowed for dinner but this included walking to and from the eating room which was half a mile away.[90] Many parish apprentices were retained during dinner breaks, or at weekends to clean and lubricate the machinery. Small payments were made, or promised on these occasions.[91] Through the practice of machinery cleaning during the dinner hour, children were deprived of much-needed breaks and essential nourishment. When forced to work through meal times, the child's food was brought into the factory for him or her to eat, but was more often left to congeal under a covering of fibre dust, thus rendering it at best unpalatable; at worst a danger to health.[92] At Litton, for example, 'the dinner was brought up in tin cans, and often has Blincoe's allowance stood till night, whilst he was almost famished with hunger, and he has often carried it back, or rather eaten it on the road, cold, nauseous, and covered with flue'.[93] Children were also kept back after work to clean and maintain the machines;[94] and weekends were often set aside for that purpose. At Backbarrow, for example, a large part of Sunday was dedicated to machinery maintenance and repair. John Moss, once superintendent of the apprentice house, claimed that every Sunday morning some children worked from 6 till 12 in cleaning the machinery;[95] and at Lowdham 'once in ten days or a fortnight, the whole of the finer machinery used to be taken to pieces and cleaned and then they had to remain at the mill from morning to night'.[96]

---

88   This is discussed at length in the 1830s commissions but features less prominently in earlier investigations. Medical priorities changed over the first three decades of the nineteenth century.

89   Pamela Horn, 'The traffic in children and the textile mills, 1780–1816', *Genealogists' Magazine*, 24/5 (1993): 361.

90   1802 Report, St Margaret and St John.

91   Brown, *Memoir*, p. 33.

92   Douglas Hay uses case law to show how agricultural labourers resisted encroachment onto their meal breaks during harvest time. Paper delivered to the ESRC First Labour Market seminar, Oxford, January 2006.

93   Brown, *Memoir*, p. 22.

94   Joseph Sefton, for example, a runaway from Greg's Styal mill, complained that he missed his education because of being kept after work to clean the machines. 2 August 1806, Greg papers C5/8/9/4, MCA.

95   SC1816, p. 177. The criticism that some of the children had to work on Sunday rather than attend church was played down by William Travers, overlooker at the plant. It is possible that only a proportion of the apprentices were 'chosen' to do this work; but for those involved their working week would thus approach 90 hours. SC1816, p. 288.

96   Brown, *Memoir*, p. 22.

Production at water spinning mills was subject to greater irregularity than in mule spinning, and periodic overtime working resulted. Summer drought was particularly problematic and upon restoration of power, extra hours were worked to clear the backlog of orders.[97] Apprentices, who received no wage, were paid the odd penny to work overtime, which was described, erroneously, as 'voluntary'. In response to parish complaints that children were overworked at Cuckney, Toplis defended himself at great length. He stated that long hours were worked only when necessary to make up time lost through lack of water; and that the parish apprentices chose to work 'overtime' as they were paid for this; and were disappointed when they could not.

> To vindicate our characters from the charge you have made ... we shall here observe that since last Tuesday we have strictly confined ourselves to 12 hours in the day, and if we give over at our usual time this evening, we shall only have 11 hours for this day – it is necessary to state what effect this alteration has made. The children being deprived of their little emoluments which they have obtained for their extra time have been nearly in a state of rebellion, and we are afraid they will be sometime before their minds are settled so as to work with that cheerfulness and alacrity they have been used to.[98]

A letter from Douglas at Pendleton to St James parish makes reference to overtime working: 'and our own apprentices that chuse to work (for it is at their option) are paid 1d per hour for all the surplus hours that they work and this is paid to them weekly'.[99] Laurence Gardner, in evidence to the House of Lords in 1819 recalls learning his trade as a water spinner from the age of nine [which would have been in 1794] when 'most of the labour consisted of parish apprentices'. He disputes the voluntary nature of overtime: 'we were obliged to work overtime and greatly against my will'.[100] At Peel's Lancashire factories, the standard 15 hours of labour was supplemented by some paid overtime.[101]

Although the assumption that parish apprentices were subject to greater exploitation than 'free' children has not been proven, the potential for abuse through overtime and night working was clear. A number of employers, including Merryweather, insisted that night working was necessary to the firm's profitability. Such enterprises also defended strongly the rectitude of such a practice. William Toplis, for example, when asked 'if he did not think that working *by night* was injurious to the health of the children?', replied,

---

97 Water mills continued to be prone to irregular working through the 1830s and later because of the vagaries of flood and drought. A.E. Peacock, 'Factory Act prosecutions: a hidden consensus?', *Economic History Review*, 38/3 (1985): 432.

98 Cuckney, 11 September 1802 reply by Toplis to the 1802 Report, St Margaret and St John, E3371/17, WAC.

99 Meeting 10 February 1797 called to discuss letter 21 January 1797 from John Plant, on behalf of Douglas, Pendleton. Minutes of Governors and Directors of the Poor, Parish of St James, Piccadilly, D1876, WAC.

100 Testimony of Laurence Gardner, HL1819, vol. 110, p. 181.

101 28 June 1796, Birmingham Guardians report. Minutes of Birmingham Board of Guardians, GP/B/2/1/1, BCA. Blincoe records that promised payments were not always delivered. Brown, *Memoir*, p. 33.

so far from it that those thus employed were as healthy as any in the factory; that men, who have practised it all their lives, have lived to a very great age; that the children who were fond of it, because they worked two hours less than the others; so that, when the place of a nightworker fell, they had many candidates for it, and bestowed it as a kind of reward for *day diligence*.[102]

Visitors to Merryweather's Burley-in-Wharfedale mill expressed positive sentiments about night work, with supporting testimony.[103]

> With respect to those boys who work all night, we found them looking better in general, and better educated than the day boys, they have some advantages over the day workers – their employment being two hours in the 24 less, and having 4 hours from six to 10 in the morning – that time is devoted to Air, exercise and improvement, A circumstance particularly noticeable is – that no death has yet occurred among the Night Workers.

In spite of such advantages, most night boys 'would rather work during the day'. While acknowledging this, the visitors apparently found that 'many of the day boys on the other hand, expressed a wish to work at Night – this we attributed to that love of variety so natural at their age'.[104] Apprentices at Douglas's Holywell enterprise disliked night working. Seven out of nine children bound there from St Clement Danes had run away. 'Mr Johnson agent to the Holywell cotton mills' attended the parish meeting to discuss the issue, 'admitted that they were worked from 7 in the evening to 6 in the morning that they were not relieved during the night'.[105]

The health of parish apprentices, undermined by intense labour, was further impaired by inadequate attention to daily sustenance. The accommodation and food of the factory apprentices may have paralleled those of workhouse children,[106] but dietary requirements of the former greatly exceeded those of the latter. Parish visitors to Strutt's Rickmansworth factory, for example, alleged 'that the food allowed them was inadequate to the many hours they were kept to work'.[107] Dietary deprivation was tantamount to abuse in at least two ways. In the first place, apprentices' health was damaged. The importance of food was recognised by contemporary doctors.[108]

---

102 1797 Report, St Margaret and St John.

103 William Hey, 'Account of a visit to the cotton mills at Burley', *The Reports of the Society for Bettering the Condition and Increasing the Comforts of the Poor*, vol. IV (1805), Appendix, supplement II, pp. 16–19. The tenor of his report was repeated by more than one parish report. 1802 Report, St Margaret and St John; Leeds report discussed 4 September 1805, Leeds Workhouse Query Book 1803–1810, LO/Q 2 WYASL.

104 1802 Report, St Margaret and St John.

105 The parish was not pleased and the boys were brought home again. 12 March 1792, Minutes of the Churchwardens, Overseers and Assistants, Parish of St Clement Danes, B1147, WAC.

106 According to Allen, forthcoming, children in both institutions were served a diet, 95 per cent of which was cereal. Descriptions of the grim workhouse diets under the new Poor Law proliferate in G.R. Wythen Baxter, *The Book of the Bastilles* (London, 1841).

107 28 October 1792, Minutes of the Governors and Directors of the Poor, Parish of St James, Piccadilly, D1874, WAC.

108 Edmund Lyon, a Manchester MD, in evidence to the House of Lords Committee 1819, said 'I attributed the unhealthy appearance of some to the deficiency of good food'. HL 1819,

Secondly, where apprentices subsisted on low-calorie diets they had less energy to work, and became less efficient workers, which in turn attracted a higher level of abuse.[109]

The food provided by employers of parish apprentices varied both in quality and quantity.[110] The superior enterprises provided ample nourishment, but the majority concentrated on subsistence fare. The cheapest nutritionally adequate diet consisted of the least expensive grain cooked as porridge. Bread was more expensive, and a number of parish apprentices complained of its absence in their diet.[111] The inadequate fare of many parish factory apprentices was compounded by its repetitive, unpalatable nature.[112] The way in which diets were described also varied; the variation being attributable to the source of information. Evidence emanated from mill owners or agents; from visitors to the mill; and from apprentices or other factory workers. The blandest and meanest of regimes could be talked up – usually by employers – by describing food as 'locally produced'; 'grown on neighbouring farms', or 'wholesome'. Toplis for example, responding to parish criticism, stated that 'the provisions we may speak in the strongest terms it is of the best quality. Our beef we have from an opulent butcher who supplies Lord Newark and several other families of consequence in the neighbourhood. The corn we grind ourselves. The soup and bread you tasted and were allow'd by the party to be good'.[113] The agent of Douglas's Pendleton factory, John Plant, described the diet:

> the breakfast of our children is five or six days in the week bread and broth made with 140lbs [?] of beef; the dinners are beef potatoes and bread 2 or 3 days in the week, beef potatoes and onions seasoned with pepper and baked in pies make their dinners twice a week; and puddings made from flour ... this they have the other two days each week, our suppers are rice milk, milk pottage, bread and butter, cheese and bread etc.[114]

A visitor emphasised the appetising fare at Holywell:

---

vol. 110, p. 359.

109 Robert C. Allen, forthcoming. Cheap food comprised a key component in employers' cost containment strategy, and a deteriorating diet was an indication that the business was under pressure, but because it reduced worker efficiency, it proved a false economy. For further discussion on the relationship between supply of nutrients and work effort, see Herman Freudenberger and Gaylord Cummins, 'Health, work and leisure before the industrial revolution', *Explorations in Economic History*, 13 (1976): 1–12; Voth, *Time and Work*, pp. 161–84.

110 As was also the case in workhouses. The stark contrast between the Manchester workhouse and that at Shrewsbury during the 1790s in this regard, was recognised by contemporaries. Hindle, *Provision of Poor Relief*, p. 48.

111 This was particularly noticeable at Merryweather's Burley-in-Wharfedale factory.

112 Palsaert, cited in Allen, forthcoming.

113 Toplis reply to 1802 Report, St Margaret and St John, 11 September 1802, E3371/17, WAC.

114 Meeting date 10 February 1797; Letter 21 January 1797 from John Plant, manager/agent of Douglas, Pendleton. Minutes of Governors and Directors of the Poor, Parish of St James, Piccadilly, D1876, WAC.

> Their food for dinner is beef or pork and potatoes three or four times a week, the other days herrings and potatoes, or soup and bread and cheese, as much as they please to eat. Their breakfasts and suppers in summer is milk and bread; in the winter, when milk cannot be had, they drink porridge or broth, with bread and cheese.[115]

The quantities of food provided were occasionally specified in terms of weight, or capacity; but amounts were more commonly implied by phrases such as 'sufficiency'; 'eat until they had their fill'; 'if still hungry could have leftovers'; or insufficiency, which was a frequent complaint of children, whose awareness of hunger was highly tuned.

Parish visitors and children were most likely to criticise factory diets and used such terms as 'coarse' or 'watery'. The Blincoe memoir indicates the poverty of the diet at Lowdham mill, especially in contrast to the roast meat and plum puddings promised by Lambert's agent prior to binding. The source highlights the importance not only of the composition of the diet and its quality and quantity; but also the circumstances within which food was eaten – whether at the machine or in the dining room – and the timing and regularity of its serving. At Lowdham mill, for example, apprentices breakfasted on rising at 5 am, then ate nothing till lunch at 12. No further food was served until supper at the end of the working day.[116] At Litton mill 'the breakfast hour was eight o'clock; but the machinery did not stop, and so irregular were their meals, it sometimes did not arrive till ten or eleven o'clock. At other times the overlookers would not allow the apprentices to eat it, and it stood till it grew cold and covered with flue!'. Much of the food was close to inedible. 'The supper ... consisted of milk-porridge, of a very blue complexion! The bread was partly made of rye – very black, and so soft, they could scarcely swallow it, as it stuck like bird lime to their teeth'. After a few minutes, one of the girls 'flung a dab of bread against the wall, where it stuck fast, as if it had been plaister'.[117] The diet at Litton was even worse;

> their first meal was water-porridge and oaten cakes – the former thin and ill-made – the latter, baked in flat cakes, on iron griddles, about an inch thick – and being piled up in heaps, was liable to heat, ferment and grow mouldy. This was a new and not a very palatable diet.[118]

This was no Blincoesque exaggeration: the diet was described identically by the visitors to the mill in 1811.[119]

The method of serving such unappetising fare only compounded its inadequacy. At Lowdham, the absence of crockery and cutlery meant that at meal times, 'the

---

115 Thomas Pennant, *The History of the Parishes of Whiteford, and Holywell* (London, 1796), p. 215.
116 Brown, *Memoir*, pp. 20–22.
117 Brown, *Memoir*, p. 17.
118 Brown, *Memoir*, p. 32.
119 Records of Quarter Sessions. Documents relating to Cotton Mill apprentices Q/AG/1–36; Reports of cotton mills and factories inspected from the last midsummer sessions to the present. Brief notes on the conditions of the mills by Marmaduke Middleton Middleton, 18 April 1811 Q/AG/7, DRO.

boys pull out the fore-part of their shirts, and holding it up with both hands, received the hot boiled potatoes ... the girls ... held up their dirty greasy ... aprons that were saturated with grease and dirt, and having received their allowance, scampered off as hard as they could ... each apprentice devoured her allowance, and seemed anxiously to look about for more'.[120] 'Overtime' money tended to be spent on food; often so rich compared with the usual fare that it made the children ill.[121] Reports of diet at Merryweather's Manchester concern soon after his arrival in the town in 1810 make grim reading: 'the potatoes for dinner were boiling with their skins on in a state of great dirtiness, and eight cow heads boiling in another pot for dinner; a great portion of the food we were told was of a liquid nature'.[122]

That insufficient food compounded other damage done by the nature of work can be seen in contemporary observations on height. The impact of a poor diet on growth was noted. Because 'height is a function of net nutritional status, the balance between calorie intake and energy expenditure, during childhood and adolescence', food consumption at such key moments needed to exceed calories burned in a routine working day.[123] The apprentices at Davison and Hawksley, for example, were fed a bland and monotonous diet which, finding unpalatable, ate only sparingly. After visiting the factory, the officers from St Luke, Chelsea, observed 'to Mr H that some of the children were in appearance less in size now than at the time of their being sent to him several years ago ... a strong proof that a more nutritious diet is absolutely necessary'.[124] In 1802, visitors to Toplis observed the children and remarked

> that their growth should be checked and their bodies emaciated – it did not occur at the moment to measure their height but we are confident of not exceeding the truth, when we declare that, none of the boys who are 17 and 18 years (except 4 or 5) stand 5 feet in height – but most of those of that age, have the appearance and are the size of children from 13 to 15 years old.[125]

---

120 Brown, *Memoir*, p. 18.
121 Brown, *Memoir*, p. 48.
122 HL 1819, vol. 108.
123 Especially as calories for work took precedence over calories for growth. Voth, *Time and Work*, pp. 162 and 171–2. See also Sara Horrell, Jane Humphries and Hans-Joachim Voth, 'Stature and relative deprivation: fatherless children in early industrial Britain', *Continuity and Change*, 13 (1998): 73–115.
124 Report by Messrs Rolls and Whitfield at Arnold mill, recorded with minutes of the meeting of 23 June 1807, Poor Relief Book 1806–1810, parish of St Luke, Chelsea, P74/LUK/019 (microfilm reference X 026/008), LMA.
125 1802 Report, St Margaret and St John. Recent scholarship that has explored the heights of adolescents in a historical context demonstrates that the most rapid growth in young persons took place between the ages of 15 and 16. Presumably this was the time at which plentiful and nourishing food was essential. Roderick Floud, Kenneth Wachter and Annabel Gregory, *Height, Health and History: Nutritional Status in the United Kingdom, 1750–1980* (Cambridge, 1990), p. 173. See also their discussion on pp. 163–75. The unequal gender distribution of food which applied to households during this period and which generated a relative fall in heights for English females was not apparent among parish apprentices. Stephen Nicholas and Deborah Oxley, 'The living standards of women during the industrial revolution, 1795–1820', *Economic History Review*, 46/4 (1993): 739–46. Peter Kirby challenges the assumption that

Five years earlier, the children's plump bodies had been admired.[126]

Many of the factors discussed above, especially the long hours of labour and zealous disciplining, applied to 'free' children as well as parish apprentices. The absence of parental protection and the isolated location of many early mills, however, provided opportunities for excessive treatment of the latter. The potential for exploitation by distant employers was explicitly recognised by the parish visitors to Marsden in 1797:

> that the parochial children who are sent to such remote distances as those, for instance, at the manufactory at M— are, from this circumstance alone, placed too far beyond the limits of general observation; nor can they be properly attended to without considerable inconvenience and *expense*; they are consequently left much more in the power of their masters than those of whom we may figuratively say, 'their cries may be heard' and who are, in reality, nearer home.[127]

Such concern was well-founded. The parish officials had been surprised at the prevalence of local children who 'might have been made useful, at play or totally unemployed' and asked the factory manager to explain:

> if we were to employ the children of persons on the neighbourhood, we should have their parents continually complaining of their being kept too many hours at work of their food their clothing and many other matters of much less importance: indeed nothing, however frivolous, would be suffered to pass without an appeal to us. They would always have a train of relations after them; they would by them be led to wish for indulgencies incompatible with our system, and the refusing of which would be a source of discontent and a continual reasons for murmuring and inveighing against us. All these disagreeable consequences are prevented or obviated by having apprentices from a remote distance, and by taking them from persons who consign them entirely to our management and direction.[128]

That the officials did not immediately remove their children from the situation indicates collusion. George Merryweather also recognised the difference. Night working, so important to his business, depended on parish apprentices because 'free

---

heights provide an index of general welfare. In the case of short coal-mining children, he argues that it was occupational environment rather than poor nutrition that accounted for their shirt stature. 'Causes of short stature among coal mining children, 1823–1850', *Economic History Review*, 48/4 (1995): 688. This argument was robustly criticised by Jane Humphries, 'Short stature among coal-mining children: a comment', *Economic History Review*, 50/3 (1997): 351–7.

126 1797 Report, St Margaret and St John.
127 1797 Report, St Margaret and St John.
128 1797 Report, St Margaret and St John; Moser Joseph 'Report of the situation of the children apprenticed by the churchwardens, overseers and governors of the poor of the United parishes of St Margaret and St John in the City of Westminster to the cotton manufactory of Messrs H— at M— and Messrs J and T at Cuckney Mills, addressed to the workhouse Board of the said parishes, April 10 1797', *European Magazine and London Review*, 34 (September 1798): 200.

labourers cannot be obtained to perform night work except on very disadvantageous terms ...'.[129]

The treatment of parish children at the time of factory failures, further indicates their relative disadvantage. The impact on parish apprentices of the bankruptcy of their master was unsettling at best and traumatic at worst.[130] Business failure was a feature of competitive capitalism, but was not a novel occurrence. Parishes had long contended with bankrupt masters and mistresses failing to provide for the children or inform the parish.[131] It was not unusual for apprentices to be cast adrift. In the pre-factory era, however, distances between master and parish were quite short, communication easier, and apprentices better placed to find their way home. The implications of factory failure were potentially more serious: the number of children at any one business was greater; and so, often, was the distance from home. The outcome was not necessarily grim; and the learned stoicism of parish apprentices sustained them as they sought other placements or attempted to find their way back 'home'. Floating apprentices were 'adopted' by local enterprises; or continuity was provided by the early appearance of new owners. But typically the already uncertain future of parish apprentices was compounded by bankruptcy and the failure of proprietor or parish to make proper provision for them. It is perhaps not surprising that amidst the severe anxiety that inevitably accompanied the circumstances of insolvency, the welfare of apprentices was neglected. Management at Toplis's Cuckney factory was unusual by not only organising alternative placements for their apprentices but also in carefully recording them. Some of the children had already been dispersed, many to mills in the region, as the business declined.[132] In the case of the children rendered unemployed by the failure of Lambert's Lowdham mill, unsuccessful attempts were made to return them to the parish, before the bulk were reassigned to a dismal future with Ellis Needham at Litton mill.[133]

Otherwise the picture was more predictable. News of the collapse of Haywood and Palfreyman, for example, only reached the parish of St James several weeks after the event, by which time several children had made their way home and others taken in by local proprietors. Five were reassigned to 'Mr Collier a cotton manufacturer at Wildboar Clough', and the parish also discovered that 'Mr Frost a grocer in Macclesfield had been pleased from motives of humanity to take John Grant one other of the children into his employ'.[134] Some were subsequently discovered at the factory of Davison and Hawksley, having been reassigned. After the failure of the

---

129 Hammond and Hammond, *The Town Labourer*, p. 152; Sidney Webb and Beatrice Webb, *English Poor Law History: Part 1 The Old Poor Law* (London, 1927), p. 202; Aspin, *Water Spinners*, p. 436.

130 The eventual outcome might work in the apprentices' favour, but they still suffered in the short term.

131 Nicholls, *English Poor Law*, pp. 104–105, which also refers to the death of master or mistress.

132 List of children put apprentice to William Toplis, DD 895/1, NA.

133 The Lamberts contacted the apprentices' parishes of origin but apparently received no reply. Waller, *The Real Oliver Twist*, p. 128.

134 Meeting 7 September 1799 to discuss report, dated 6 September 1799, of 'Messrs Johnson, Freeman and Ideson relative to poor children belonging to those Parish apprenticed

Haigh's enterprise in Marsden, its remaining parish apprentices were distributed to other mills in the area. Merryweather and Whitaker took in a group; and several became reassigned to Thomas and Joseph Turner, cotton manufacturers at Godley in Cheshire.[135] Following Needham's bankruptcy in 1816, Litton mill was vacated and the 'apprentices were left destitute of support other than from the township of Taddington to the number of eighty and upwards', most of whom, with the help of local magistrates, were transferred to other masters. The 'rest being too debilitated for work, were obliged to be supported by the Township'.[136]

Birch and Robinson apparently walked away from their Backbarrow enterprise leaving the children to fend for themselves.[137] For some of these apprentices the experience was familiar, having only recently arrived at Backbarrow following the failure of Watson,[138] when they had been similarly cast adrift.[139] 'A great many [of the Backbarrow children] went towards Kennell [sic], others to Lancaster'. Most 'ended up at Lancaster workhouse' before being returned to Messrs Ainsworth, the next owners.[140] William Travers, the former Backbarrow overlooker, however, denied that the children were all 'desired to leave the mill', and asserts that there was plenty of food in the house. 'Do you mean then to say that the children's going away was a voluntary act of their own?'; 'they had liberty to go or to stay', he replied.[141] These and other examples indicate that while parish apprentices were often 'rescued', their welfare was typically disregarded. Significantly, the home parish rarely intervened in the aftermath of firm failure and rarely retrieved the children, a minority of whom nevertheless made their way back to their 'birth' parish.

Only rarely was it suggested that parish apprentices in the early textile mills received favourable treatment over free children. When asked by the House of Lords committee if he believed that 'if the master spinners employed apprentices they would make them work as long as they make their people work now that they can get fresh hands when they choose?', Clement Dodenhoff replied, 'No there is an act I believe against it, which prevents them; they would work them as long as they were able'; and when 'If they employed apprentices instead of other children, do you think they would make them work such long hours?' he answered simply 'No'.[142]

---

to Messrs Hayward and Palfreyman in Cheshire'. Minutes of Governors and Directors of the Poor, Parish of St James, Piccadilly, D1877, WAC.

135 This was the evidence of Robert Miller to Battersea parish in 1817. Quoted in Aspin, *Water Spinners*, p. 249.

136 Tideswell burial register, M.H. MacKenzie, 'Cressbrook and Litton mills, 1779–1835, Part 1', *Derbyshire Archaeological Journal*, 88 (1968), p. 21.

137 SC1816.

138 For example, the sixty children from St George the Martyr, Southwark, Aspin, *Water Spinners*, p. 273. Apprenticeship Register, Parish of St George, Southwark, SLHL.

139 Mr William Tomlinson, surgeon in Preston ... recollects 'very well the circumstances of the parish apprentices from Mr Watson's factory at Penwortham, when he failed, having been turned out upon the common to find their way home as they could'. SC1816, p. 181.

140 SC1816, p. 181.

141 SC1816, p. 291.

142 Clement Dodenhoff, 39, manager at Thomas Darwell, Wigan, testimony to HL 1819, vol. 110, p. 10.

Early factory experiments in forms of discipline and supervision, and in the length and structure of the working day became embedded in factory practice. All young labour was eventually subject to conditions of work initially tested on parish apprentices. The evidence presented in this chapter suggests that parish apprentices endured a range of levels of exploitation. Factory regimes varied from the 'brutal' at one extreme to the 'humanitarian' at the other, with the majority falling somewhere in between.[143] However, factory masters were not alone in exploiting early apprentices. However bad factory conditions were for the young apprentices, they would otherwise have been bound to the worst conditions available locally.[144] Parishes were complicit. The argument introduced in this chapter, that employers, parishes and magistrates colluded in the exploitation of apprentices, will be developed in Chapters 11 and 12.

---

143 Smelser classified early capitalists into these two extreme types. In fact, the majority fell somewhere in between. *Social Change*, pp. 105–107.

144 George, *London Life*, p. 267. George also points out that because factory conditions were brought to light, some remedy was possible. John Rule also points to poor pre-existing conditions. *The Labouring Classes*, p. 142.

Chapter 10

The Voices of the Children

Parish apprentices were children in some respects but not in others.[1] They were at the same time dependent children and independent workers.[2] The objective of this chapter is to gauge the extent to which parish apprentices both as children and as independent workers were given the opportunity to speak; and the extent to which their voices were heard.[3] It will thus glimpse how this particular group of children saw themselves and their situation. Uncovering the voices of the past is always difficult but particularly so if the voices belong to the poor, the dispossessed and the young.[4] Yet the words of parish factory apprentices were reproduced in a surprisingly large number of sources. Letters, parish examinations, and interviews conducted by visiting parish officials, provide mediated voices of the parish apprentices. These children also articulated opinion through actions. The practice of absconding, for example, expressed both the simple desire to escape from unpleasant conditions and the more complex longing to return 'home'.

Despite the difficulty of hearing voices unsullied by the interference of the dominant discourse of the time, it is hoped to isolate apprentices' expressions of satisfaction and complaint. Distinguishing the words of parish apprentices from the expectations of contemporaries or historians is not straightforward. The language of early factory apprentices has been mediated by parish, by political campaigners and by historians. Parish officials wished 'their' children to be stoical and uncomplaining,

---

1   Ludmilla Jordanova discusses this idea in, 'Children in history: Concepts of nature and society', in Geoffrey Scarre (ed.), *Children, Parents and Politics* (Cambridge, 1989), pp. 3–24.

2   Clearly they were not independent in the economic sense, but they were often in sole charge of machines rather than working as helpers. Gillis refers to a period of semi-dependence for many young apprentices at the time. John R. Gillis, *Youth and History: Tradition and Change in European Age Relations 1770 to the Present* (New York, 1974), p. 2. See also Pat Thane, 'Childhood in history', in Michael King (ed.), *Childhood, Welfare and Justice: A Critical Examination of Children in the Legal and Childcare Systems* (London, 1981), pp. 16–17.

3   This dimension has been absent from previous accounts. Colin Creighton has argued that 'we should pay more attention to the views and actions of children themselves'. Comment on 'Where are we now in the analysis of child labour in the industrial revolution?', paper to the ESRC First Labour Market seminar, University of Birmingham, 28 April 2006.

4   As a historian of childhood has recently observed, 'given that the sources have been written and compiled by adults ... not only is the voice of the child more or less absent ... but the historian will be tempted to omit any representation of the child's viewpoint or ... even fail to recognize that such a perspective exists'. Harry Hendrick, *Children, Childhood and English Society, 1880–1990* (Cambridge, 1997), p. 3. See also Irina Stickland, *The Voices of Children 1700–1914* (Oxford, 1973); and Carolyn Steedman, *Strange Dislocations: Childhood and the Idea of Human Interiority, 1780–1830* (London, 1995).

partly to salve their consciences and partly because it was believed that poor children should accept hard work and discomfort into their lives. Therefore Guardians and overseers may have discouraged complaint by the tenor of questioning, or failed to hear the underlying meaning of the children's responses.[5] Political campaigners, especially those associated with factory reform, were more alert to the complaints of children workers.

Many of the children's voices will have been mediated before they reach the historians, who in turn, interpret still further through their 'implicit value systems'. Historians have understood the existence and experience of children workers in the context of a society which took children labour for granted, for example, or sought explanations such as poverty for the harsh treatment of children. Ludmilla Jordanova, who emphasises the difficulty in interpreting contemporary observations,[6] has identified an alternative approach, where historians accept that the problem exists, then seek to interpret it in 'terms of the value system of the time'.[7] For the purpose of the present study, analysis must take into account the social and cultural setting. Parish apprentices spoke in the context of the adult world of the factory. The tension between the adult nature of the work and the children who performed that work is relevant to both how the children spoke and how they were listened to.

The context of factory apprenticeship changed during the period of its operation. The system emerged at the moment when challenges to the rectitude of children's work resulted in greater protective controls. As the need to regulate children's work in general and parish apprenticeship in particular gained acceptance, the interpretation of what was seen by contemporaries changed. In this light, the frequency with which parish visitors to factories and witnesses to parliamentary enquiries emphasised the ease and lightness of the children's work in factories can be understood. Such a defensive position may well have reflected discomfort about the reality of the harshness of factory labour.

What can be achieved here is limited. This chapter does not pretend to find the 'authentic voice of childhood',[8] but rather assesses the words of parish apprentices and how far these were interpreted through the agency of the parish and other institutions. The words of children have survived in autobiography,[9] in such parish records as settlement examinations, factory visitors' reports, and interviews with former apprentices, and in parliamentary commissions.[10] In all except the former,

---

5   As late as 1853, girls sent from Ashby de la Zouche union to a Derbyshire cotton mill were discouraged by the Guardians from being 'inclined to grumble at trifles'. Kathryn M. Thompson, 'Apprenticeship and the New Poor Law: a Leicester example', *The Local Historian* (1989): 55.

6   Ludmilla Jordanova, 'Conceptualising childhood in the eighteenth century: the problem of child labour', *British Journal for Eighteenth Century Studies*, 10/2 (1987): 189.

7   Jordanova, 'Children in history', p. 9. See also Ludmilla Jordanova 'New worlds for children in the eighteenth century: problems of historical interpretation', *History of the Human Sciences*, 3/1 (1990): 70.

8   Jordanova, 'Children in history', p. 6.

9   See Jane Humphries, *Through the Mill*, forthcoming.

10   The commissions of the period 1816–19, however, hear testimony from former apprentices. The emphasis in this chapter is on existing parish children apprentices to textile mills.

the words, spoken by the apprentices in response to questions posed by adult investigators, were recorded by those same individuals with an unknown level of accuracy. This chapter will highlight the key themes of parish apprentices' articulation of satisfaction and complaint. It is certainly not a comprehensive exploration but will at least provide examples of what parish children wished to speak about, or what they were encouraged to speak about through the questions of adults; and how their words were acted upon.

The first section discusses voices of satisfaction. Parish apprentices' expressions of contentment could be interpreted cynically, with substantial reservation, or as a measure of children's tendency to make the best of their situations.[11] Parish officers wanted their children to be content, or to be stoical and to express contentment, and the apprentices knew this. Thus, voices of satisfaction, sometimes extracted by leading questioning, reflected the apprentices' consciousness of what the questioner wanted to hear and their fear of reprisals if they failed to fulfil the officials' wishes. Such anxiety was recognised by the Bettering Society for example, which in 1805 wondered 'what inducement would the children have had to make known the ill-usage they had received? What could they have expected from it, but punishment and increased severity?'[12] A former apprentice recalled his own sense of intimidation:

> When the committee began their investigation, as to the treatment and condition of the children sent from St Pancras workhouse, Blincoe was called up among others and admonished to speak the truth and nothing but the truth! So great however was the terror of the stick and strap, being applied to their persons, after these great dons should be at a great distance, it rendered him, and no doubt the great majority of his fellow sufferers extremely cautious and timid.[13]

Richard Muggeridge, migration agent for the Poor Law Commissioners in 1836, believed that pauper apprentices might be reluctant to speak their mind because they were 'universally regarded as a distinct class' and were 'lower in the scale of society than their companions in labour'... and

> being in all cases far from their friends and in many without natural protectors, and so entirely under the authority of the master and the overlookers that any appeal to the one against the other was regarded as altogether useless, as more than likely to lead to lead to increased severity and cause of complaint.[14]

---

11   Eric Hopkins, *Childhood Transformed: Working-Class Children in Nineteenth-Century England* (Manchester, 1994), p. 94.

12   *The Reports of the Society for Bettering the Condition and Increasing the Comforts of the Poor*, vol. IV, 1805, Appendix no. 1, 'Report of a Select Committee of the society upon some observations on the late Act respecting cotton mills, and on the account of Mr Hey's visit to a cotton mill at Burley', p. 7. Kathryn Thompson noted that 'evidence of ill-usage is not as common as might be expected but, considering how difficult it was for an apprentice to draw attention to ill-treatment ... it was almost certainly more prevalent than the records indicate'. Apprenticeship and Bastardy, p. 30.

13   John Brown, *A Memoir of Robert Blincoe* (Manchester, 1832), pp. 27–8.

14   Cited in Chris Aspin, *The Water Spinners* (Helmshore, 2003), p. 50. According to M. Dorothy George, *London Life in the Eighteenth Century* (London, 1925), p. 265, 'those who

Even if threats did not serve to quell the children's complaints, style of interpretation might. Quite often parish officers failed to hear the children's message. At Gorton and Thompson's Cuckney factory, the children were apparently 'content except one who wished to return to town but upon being separately examined he had no complaint nor any reason to give but that he liked to be near his friends in town'.[15] It is significant that although the child was clearly homesick, he was judged to have no reason to be unhappy. The report of Merryweather commented that most of the children 'feel better off than in London'. Such sentiment was assumed by officials rather than a spontaneous majority view.[16] Many reports refer to the appearance of well-being of the apprentices, which sometimes indicated a tacit expression of satisfaction. At Oldknow's Mellor mill, where the owner's 'very meritorious conduct towards the apprentices under his care' was underlined, the children 'were all looking very well and extremely clean'.[17] Similarly at Newton, Cressbrook mill, 'they looked well and appeared perfectly satisfied with their situation'.[18] 'To shew the satisfaction of the children' at Holywell, parish officers asserted that

> they expressed a wish that your committee would communicate to their parents their anxiety that their brothers and sisters should be sent down from their confidence that their situation promised much comfort and a decent and respectable livelihood. Some of the children wrote to their parents to this effect and others entrusted your committee with similar messages.[19]

A general level of satisfaction was inferred by parish officials from dietary sufficiency. At Haywood and Palfreyman's Wildboar Clough enterprise, for example, the children from St James parish were, apparently, 'quite satisfied with their diet';[20] and the local clergyman was 'certain they have good meal and they all look well'.[21] At Mitchell

---

appealed to a justice were often barbarously used for having dared to complain'.

15 'Report of the committee appointed to enquire into the present state of the children put apprentice to Mr Strutt ..., and also the nature of the employment, trade, and business in which the boys on liking with Messrs Gorton and Thompson ...', read at 19 September 1790, Minutes of Governors and Directors of the Poor, Parish of St James, Piccadilly, D1873, WAC.

16 1802 Report, St Margaret and St John.

17 'Reports of cotton mills and factories inspected from the last midsummer sessions to the present'. Brief notes on the conditions of the mills by Marmaduke Middleton Middleton. 18 April 1811, Q/AG/7, DRO.

18 Ibid.

19 'Report of the committee appointed to visit the poor children placed out upon liking to the manufactory of Messrs MH ... and Messrs Douglas and Co. Holywell, Flintshire', presented to meeting of 19 February 1802, Minutes of Governors and Directors of the Poor, Parish of St James, Piccadilly, D1878, WAC.

20 'Report of Messrs Johnson, Charlton and Ideson', presented to meeting of 6 May 1796, Minutes of Governors and Directors of the Poor, Parish of St James, Piccadilly, D1876, WAC.

21 Letter from Mr (Rev) Bromeley, 16 January 1797, read to meeting of 26 January 1797, Minutes of the Governors and Directors of the Poor, Parish of St James, Piccadilly, D1876, WAC; also letter of 1 May 1797.

and Holt, officers from St James parish Piccadilly, 'examined the children separately and apart and found them [14 in number] respectively satisfied with their diet ...'.[22] The 38 Birmingham apprentices at Thomas Jewsbury, Measham, 'were ... all in good health and satisfied with their situations and employment ... the provisions good and the children very well satisfied'. The children, who were 'questioned separately (and not in the presence of their employers) seemed pleased with the treatment they received'.[23] At Haigh's factory in Marsden, the children had the appearance of being satisfied: 'in short no fault was to be found, either with their portions or the quality of their provision; nor did their seem to be any want of appetite among those that partook of them, who were indeed suffered to eat until they were satisfied'.[24] The several meanings of satisfaction are evident in the above examples.

Children were also deemed to be satisfied even when unsatisfactory conditions had been revealed through *in situ* enquiry. In 1797, parish officials' report on Haigh's Marsden mill, where conditions were bleak, concluded that 'in consequence of our interrogations, would here be unnecessary, as they will be found subjoined to the lists which we carried with us. It may be sufficient to state that, that they generally declared that they were satisfied with their situation'.[25] And at Toplis five years later, 'the conduct of the boys was much to be admired – for many of those who made no complaint and declared themselves satisfied, had the effects of labour and confinement strongly marked in their persons and on their countenances'. The girls were described as 'better grown' and they 'do not complain'.[26]

Other expressions of satisfaction were obtained from children away from the mill. Two absconders from Greg's Styal mill, alleged that their reasons for running away were unrelated to conditions at the mill. 'I have no reason to complain of the usage I received during the time that I was at the factory, nor do I know that the other apprentices who were I believe about 90 had', said Thomas Priestly, who wished to see his mother. 'I am very willing to go back again', he added.[27] Similar expressions of satisfaction, or reluctance to complain, were found in letters from former apprentices. Two girls asked by their birth parish for comments on their experience at William Douglas's Pendleton factory wrote in positive terms, saying all the right things, even though neither had stayed on at the firm. Mary Bennett, for example, went to work nearby where a close friend was employed. She wrote that 'during the whole of my apprenticeship, my lodging was very clean and good, my food quite sufficient both

---

22 19 February 1802, Minutes of the Governors and Directors of the Poor, Parish of St James, Piccadilly, D1878, WAC.

23 The inspections were made on 14 and 15 September 1813, and discussed by the Birmingham Guardians on 12 October 1813, when the visitors were thanked for 'their great attention to the welfare of the children'. Minutes of Birmingham Board of Guardians, GP/B/2/1/2, BCA.

24 1797 Report, St Margaret and St John.

25 1797 Report, St Margaret and St John. The low rate of absconding may have been taken as an indication of satisfaction.

26 1802 Report, Saint Margaret and St John.

27 'Examination of Thomas Priestly who did on Sunday the 22nd day of June last elope from and desert the employment of his master' by Middlesex magistrates, 2 August 1806. Greg papers C5/8/9/5, MCA.

in respect to quantity and quality, and my master's treatment to me and every other apprentice, during my apprenticeship I have not the least fault to find ... Mr Douglas was nearly the same as I have at my present place'.[28] Elizabeth Cuthbert had 'the satisfaction to inform you I was well treated had a sufficiency of meat, drink and proper cloathing, good clean comfortable lodgings ... I never had a blow from either master or mistress during my apprenticeship. As to other apprentices, I have nothing more to say as we were all treated alike'.[29]

Historians investigating the experience of parish apprentices anticipate voices of complaint. Yet fear of censure, which may have underpinned statements of satisfaction, may equally have muted expressions of grievance. It is also possible that parish apprentices complained less than might have been expected because of the belief that nothing positive would be gained.[30] Furthermore, parish enquiries were sometimes constrained by the actions of factory owners. Although most officials strove to interview their children without proprietors present, this was not always permitted.[31] Although complaints were fewer and more moderate in tone than might have appeared justified, the sources indicate a number of recurring concerns. The following sections illustrate the dissatisfaction of parish apprentices through three key areas: diet; homesickness; and sense of exploitation.

The frequency of complaints about factory diets reflects the importance of food to both apprentices and parish officials. For the children, food marked the only potentially positive feature in otherwise monotonous or miserable lives. The satisfaction of hunger and the pleasure of eating combined with a period of relaxation and sociability created rare moments of enjoyment. Apprentices complained about dietary inadequacy not only because it was sorely felt but also because they sensed that parish officers took the matter seriously. Children also recognised that food was a less controversial issue than working conditions, for example, and a dietary complaint was less likely to incur their employers' wrath than one about hours of work. From the parish's perspective, diet was frequently examined during factory visits for several reasons.[32] The first of these was officials' genuine concern for their children's welfare; the second was that the issue was relatively uncontentious; and thirdly because food problems were relatively easily soluble. Children's concerns about food were investigated more carefully than were other complaints; and as the discussion below indicates, the parish revealed a level of sympathy in this context that was not demonstrated elsewhere. Food was an issue where, unlike any other, a meeting of minds existed between children and adults. Both saw it as fundamental to wellbeing.

---

28 Letter dated 26 February 1797, read at meeting of 10 March 1797, Minutes of Governors and Directors of the Poor, Parish of St James, Piccadilly, D1876, WAC.

29 Letter dated 5 March 1797 (from Pendleton) read at meeting of 10 March 1797. Minutes of Governors and Directors of the Poor, Parish of St James, Piccadilly, D1876, WAC.

30 For the most part, this assessment was probably right; but as Chapter 11 demonstrates, apprentices' complaints did sometimes lead to change for the better.

31 1802 Report, St Margaret and St John.

32 There is evidence that parish officials often requested a list of weekly menus in writing, which would be included in their reports.

Whatever the reason, parish apprentices often complained about the quality, quantity and variety of food. Evidence of dissatisfaction about food emanated from interviews with runaway or returned children; or via parish visitors' reports. Examples of runaway children, whose voices might be more 'open' because of distance from the factory – include two boys from Backbarrow mill, who made the extremely long and arduous journey from the north of Lancashire to St Clement Danes, their parish of origin, during the winter of 1793. When called in to speak to the parish officers, the boys 'say'd that they had meat but twice a week, that they never had butter or cheese, nor any small beer'.[33] The inadequacy of the diet appeared to be their major complaint. The examination of Harriet Russell, recently returned to her 'home' parish of St Clement Danes from Middleton, Wells and Co., Sheffield, revealed the bleakness of factory life in Sheffield. The diet, 'is a little heavy on the milk porridge ['some a pint some a pint and a half'] which is had every breakfast and some days for lunch as well; and other starchy items; every afternoon a halfpenny roll ... they never have butter or cheese ... beer only on meat days [twice a week] – then the can is held while they drink ... their food did not satisfy them they had not enough'.[34]

Apprentices spoken to *in situ* revealed their dietary preoccupations. Parish officials from St Luke parish, Chelsea, visited their children apprenticed to Davison and Hawksley, and found 'not only the children of the parish of Chelsea complained much, but the children generally from other parishes declared they could not eat the food offered them for their dinner and a considerable number (to our knowledge) went without their meal, consequently very injurious to the health'.[35] The visitors took action less because the children had complained than because they had observed for themselves the inadequacy of the diet. 'We represented to [the proprietor] with the full conviction of mind that the food was not sufficiently nutritious to nourish the bodies of the children to keep them in good health.'[36] At Merryweather's Yorkshire factory, according to the officials from St Margaret and St John parish who visited in 1802, 'the only complaint we heard, and that a general one, was want of bread', which they attributed to the children's natural longing 'to have the food of their infant days'. The proprietor promised to rectify the bread problem 'as soon as the present harvest was got in',[37] but failed to do so. In August 1805, six members of the Leeds workhouse committee inspected Merryweather's Burley concern. The first child examined, Eliz Bates, stated 'that they had milk porridge for their suppers of

---

33 Absence of beer was a common complaint. 5 February 1793, Minutes of Churchwardens, Overseers and Assistants, Parish of St Clement Danes, B1147, WAC. The boys' complaints were deemed sufficiently serious that the committee 'ordered that the boys' depositions be taken before a magistrate'.

34 12 September 1797, special meeting called to consider the examination of Harriet Russell. Minutes of Vestry, Parish of St Clement Danes, B1074, WAC.

35 Report by Messrs Rolls and Whitfield at Arnold mill, recorded with minutes of the meeting of 23 June 1807. 'Messrs Rolls and Whitfield, overseers, report of their enquiry made on 20 June 1807 at Arnold Mills in the Parish of Arnold in the county of Nottingham. Poor Relief Book 1806–10, Parish of St Luke, Chelsea, P74/LUK/019 (microfilm reference X026/008) LMA.

36 Ibid.

37 1802 Report, St Margaret and St John.

which and of other food she had as much as she could eat, but from what we could learn their having no bread at all was considered a great hardship'.[38] This particular complaint, followed up by two different sets of parish officers, was ignored by the employer. The children at John Watson's Preston factory complained of mouldy bread and of lack of meat. On the visit to the mill from officers of the parish of St Margaret and St John in 1802, 'Ann Walton said and which was corroborated by the rest of the children that they had no particular meat days, that they have had meat twice only since Christmas Day'.[39] The children insisted they had eaten meat only twice since Christmas Day; and as the visit took place in September, this was cause for concern. The visitors confirmed that the children's 'appearance indicates the want of meat', and described meals consisting largely of milk, porridge, potatoes and bread. The latter 'appeared to be made of oats baked in tins, very heavy and from its great moisture apt to be mouldy, of which the children complained'.[40] In 1802, parish visitors to Toplis's Cuckney factory noted that the majority of the boys there grumbled about insufficiency of foodstuffs.[41]

Less specific than complaints about diet were the nevertheless clear messages of homesickness. Evidence in this section and elsewhere illustrates the association of birth parish and 'home' for parish apprentices. Homesickness was expressed through a desire to see family and friends. It also indicated a general level of misery. The practice of absconding reflected deep discontent with factory life combined with a yearning to go home. The majority of runaways about whom information exists either successfully reached their birth parish or had been heading in that direction when apprehended. Parish officials appeared unsympathetic to expressions of homesickness, which were generally ignored.

The sensation of homesickness among parish apprentices was revealed in both overt and subtle ways. Examples survive of unambiguous cries for help. Among the most poignant are those of the traumatised children at Peel's Lancashire factories. Following complaints, parish officials from Birmingham parish visited the children late in June 1796. The message of the reports they returned was unequivocal. Such was the children's desperation to escape, that not only had several run away but those remaining were deprived of shoes to discourage thoughts of absconding. At Hind mill, the children were dirty, poorly clothed, without shoes and were 'beat with sticks'. They received no 'instruction' and because of the poor state of their clothing, did not attend church. Unsurprisingly 'many of the children cryed to come home'. At Radcliffe Bridge, from where several of the Birmingham boy apprentices had run away, food and lodging was poor, clothes ragged, hours of work from 5 am to 8 pm, and the only instruction they received was that which they paid for themselves, 'the boys begged they might no stay longer'. At Summerseat, conditions appeared slightly better, but still 'many of the poor children flocked round us and cryed to

---

38 The visit took place on 28 August 1805; the group reported to the workhouse committee on 4 September 1805, Leeds Workhouse Query Book 1803–1810, LO/Q 2 ,WYASL.
39 1802 Report, St Margaret and St John.
40 1802 Report, St Margaret and St John.
41 1802 Report, St Margaret and St John. None of these matched the level of complaint by Blincoe described in Chapter 9. Brown, *Memoir*, pp. 17 and 32.

come home'.⁴² The visitors' report emphasised the specific complaints about food and lack of education, yet the most profound message was one of homesickness. There is no indication that the children were returned to their Birmingham 'home'.

Visitors to Birch's Backbarrow mill from St Clement Danes parish encountered a spontaneous manifestation of homesickness from a number of their apprentices:

> Many of the senior girls burst into tears: we paused a few minutes; when the tears subsided we asked them the cause; they hesitated; but at last said they had no cause of complaint but it was a long time to be there: a few minutes now passed in reasoning and all was tranquility again. They spoke very highly of and had great confidence in Mr Birch and Robinson.⁴³

Brushed aside by parish officials who emphasised the expression of satisfaction which the girls obligingly provided, this example illustrates the profound unhappiness endured by parish apprentices.

Thus 'homesickness' reflected a generalised misery associated with harsh conditions or cruel treatment. Because it surfaced on arrival of parish officers who served as a reminder of a former, and possibly happier existence, expressions of homesickness indicate that the workhouse was seen as home. In other cases, the homesickness referred specifically to the desire to see, or to have news of, family members. Parish apprentices are frequently portrayed as orphans.⁴⁴ The apprenticeship registers indicate that only a minority had in fact lost both parents. A much larger number had at least one living parent with perhaps a second of unknown whereabouts. It was uncommon for parish factory apprentices to be in possession of two cohabiting parents, but not as rare as is often assumed. The children at Merryweather's Burley-in-Wharfedale factory illustrate this. Many children were clearly homesick, though none was recorded as crying to be taken home. The emotion was presented as a desire for more contact with family or friends. Mary Ann Lovatt, for example, 'wishes to know how her mother is'; Catharine Porter 'has not heard from her [mother] a long while, wishes to hear'; James Hickey, like William Burt 'wishes to hear from his friends'; while John Stone 'has not heard of his Father for five years'.⁴⁵ Two thirds of the children at Burley-in-Wharfedale had at least one living parent, only a minority of whom resided in the workhouse, and some mentioned siblings. The pain of such separations was seemingly underestimated by the parish officials. Requests for more companionship included a 'letter from John Ward, one of the boys apprenticed to the said Messrs Haywood and Palfreyman was read, [to the officers of St James parish]

---

42 Reports recorded in full in the minutes of meetings of the Birmingham Guardians, 28 June 1796. Minutes of Birmingham Board of Guardians, GP/B/2/1/2, BCA.

43 St Clement Danes Vestry, 5 November 1801. Report of Messrs Pouden and Davidson respecting the children at Cartmell.

44 Sara Horrell and Jane Humphries, 'Child labour and British industrialisation' in M. Lavalette (ed.), *A Thing of the Past? Child Labour in Britain in the Nineteenth and Twentieth Centuries* (Liverpool, 1999), pp. 80, 97–8.

45 This may have pre-dated his placement which had taken place only four years' previously.

whereby it appeared that all the children were in good health and very happy, and expressing his wishes some more boys would come down'.[46]

Reference to homesickness or requests for family news were particularly common among children at firms judged to have been particularly negligent or where conditions were deteriorating. Circumstances at the firm of Toplis, for example, which had been regarded as exemplary in 1797, gave cause for concern in 1802, when children expressed discontent. Parish interviews with their apprentices revealed a number who longed to hear from family:

> Ann Sophia Burgess ... wishes to know where her parents are, no complaints; Jane Ford ...wishes to know how her parents are. No complaints; Harriet Powell ...sister apprenticed at Whitechapel from the House, wishes to hear of her, satisfied; Jos Bateman ... sister went to service from workhouse two years ago wishes to know how and where she is – and that she would come to see him – no complaints; Thos Wareham ... wishes to see his parents; reads a little has no complaints; William Finch ... mother lived near St Margaret Church – wishes to see her, not enough to eat.[47]

It is significant that such unambiguous messages of homesickness are presented as consistent with having 'no complaints'.[48] While generally admiring the children's stoicism, the visitors do not appear to have actively listened to the children's pleas for contact with their families. The list of those features of the children's experience which required attention by the proprietors included that:

> the children should on no account work above twelve hours in the day and have two hours of relaxation in the course of the day; they should be washed and combed every day and a sufficiency of soap allowed; they should have some person to hear them say their prayers every evening; the boys should be encouraged to bathe in hot weather; the provisions of the boys should be increased particularly on dumpling days; the children should have more instruction than they now receive, and part of the weekdays should be appropriated to that purpose

and, as noted in Chapter 8, girls towards the end of their term were to be taught a range of domestic skills.[49] No explicit attempt to resolve the homesickness problem was identified.

The Marsden factory of the Haigh brothers, classified as negligent in this study, contained many unhappy apprentices. Parish visitors to the mill in 1797 provided the opportunity for the children to speak openly. Yet it does not appear, despite the assurances from the parish officials that 'they had listened attentively to all the objections that they made to their situation' that the children's message of homesickness was heard.

---

46   28 July 1797, Minutes of the Governors and Directors of the Poor, Parish of St James, Piccadilly, D1876, WAC.

47   Although the children were interviewed individually, there is common ground between adjacent children in terms of specified complaint.

48   1802 Report, Saint Margaret and St John.

49   1802 Report, Saint Margaret and St John.

The author of the report, concluded that 'the only causes of dissatisfaction which they [the children] had, they said, arose from the remote distance at which they were from London, from not hearing from their relations and friends, and from their not having the power, *for want of education*, to correspond with them'.[50] Although the parish officials 'heard' the children's complaint of lack of education, they failed to take seriously their underlying homesickness; and rejected several other complaints out of hand. According to their report, the majority of the children's complaints were considered 'frivolous'; and there were yet others, not recorded because they were deemed 'unecessary to state'.[51]

Absconding was a further expression of homesickness or underlying dissatisfaction rarely recognised as such by the parish. That runaways headed for their birth parish and, remarkably, often succeeded in reaching their destination, indicates that they considered this place home, or that family and friends still lived there. The level of absconding cannot be quantified, yet discursive evidence, autobiography, publicity documents, correspondence between parishes and proprietors and marginal comments in apprenticeship registers indicate its frequency. Examples from Birmingham records suggest that running away was common if typically abortive. When Poor Law officials from the town arrived at the Nantwich factory of Bott, Birch Bower and Randall to carry out an inspection, they were not able to see the Governor of the apprentice boarding house, Alexander Hewitt, because 'he was gone after 2 boys who had absconded'.[52] A decade, but only two or three inspections later, the experience was repeated when Birmingham visitors to Dicken and Finlow were 'sorry to learn that Mr D had gone towards Birmingham after two girls who had run away early the same morning'.[53] Even in the extremely unlikely event that these were coincidental, it still indicates a common occurrence. The examples also suggest that the children were making for 'home'.

Absconding was not without purpose. The aim to get home was driven by the need for protection. Robert Blincoe ran towards his birth parish from Lowdham mill in the belief that officers would be shocked by his description of conditions there, and instigate immediate improvements.[54] His apprehension, not far from the mill, was typical. In relatively rural communities in which the mills in these examples were located, factory children would stand out. A child on the run from Merryweather's Burley-in-Wharfedale mill was conveniently intercepted by the magistrate and diarist William Vavasour. On 6 May 1808, he wrote, 'this day found an apprentice boy who had run away from the service of Mr Merryweather – had

---

50   1797 Report, Parish of St Margaret and St John.

51   1797 Report, Parish of St Margaret and St John.

52   'The gentlemen appointed ... to visit the children at the cotton mill with Bott, Birch, Bower and Randall, Nantwich, all attended and brought a favourable report as follows'. This was reported to a meeting of the Birmingham poor officers on 27 August 1798. It is significant that the person in charge of apprentices, rather than a hired hand is the person searching for them Minutes of Birmingham Board of Guardians, GP/B/2/1/1, BCA.

53   1 July 1808, Minutes of Birmingham Board of Guardians, GP/B/2/1/2, BCA.

54   Blincoe was doubtless misguided in such hope, but was apprehended before he could discover this.

him returned'.[55] The case of two absconders from Greg's Styal mill, indicated that homesickness did not necessarily stem from deep-rooted dissatisfaction. Thomas Priestly, for example, implied general contentment. A factory accident precipitated his homesickness. A machine

> caught my finger and tore it off, it was the forefinger of my left hand ... during my illness I thot of my mother, and wanted to see her. She sent me a crown so I set out with Joseph Sefton, we enquired the road and walked nearly all the way to town.[56]

Sefton was also missing his mother. He asked Greg for permission 'to be absent for a month ... and he refused me, so I set off without his consent'.[57]

The final section explores the voice of children through their sense of exploitation, which was reflected in several strands of discontent. One of these stemmed from lack of access to sufficient education, which in the case of children at Haigh, described above, was connected, by the parish, to homesickness. The officers assumed that by providing literacy skills the children's homesickness would evaporate.[58] Apprentices from St James parish at Haywood and Palfreyman's Wildboar Clough factory, complained to the parish visitors about the insufficiency of their education. In their report it was noted that 'the children have not had their books about which they are very anxious'.[59] Thirty-four children from Birmingham parish apprentices to Messrs Dickens and Co., were found

> on minute examination appeared perfectly satisfied with their situation except that they were not allowed the privilege of learning to write which privilege it appears was denied them on account of some bad girls having made an improper use of it at some former period. They strongly requested us to use our influence in endeavouring to get their advantage restored to them.[60]

Even at the generally well-regarded mill of Samuel Greg, there were limitations in educational opportunities. According to the examination of Joseph Sefton,

---

55 6 May 1808. William Vavasour, private diaries 1798–1827. WYL639/398, WYASL.

56 'Examination of Thomas Priestly who did on Sunday the 22nd day of June last elope from and desert the employment of his master' by Middlesex magistrates 2 August 1806. Greg papers C5/8/9/5, MCA.

57 'Examination of Joseph Sefton brought under a warrant of the Rev Croxton Johnston Clerk one of his Majesty's Justices of the Peace for the County of Chester for his having eloped and deserted the service of Samuel Greg ... to whom he was apprentice' 2 August 1806. Greg papers C5/8/9/4, MCA.

58 1797 Report, St Margaret and St John.

59 'Report of Messrs Johnson, Charlton and Ideson relative to poor children belonging to this parish upon liking in Cheshire and Derbyshire and apprenticed out in Nottinghamshire', considered by the meeting of theGovernors and Directors of the Poor, St James parish, 6 May 1796. This event preceded the appointment of the local clergyman to oversee the children's education. Minutes of the Governors and Directors of the Poor, Parish of St James, Piccadilly, D1876, WAC.

60 Report of Birmingham parish officials of a visit to Messrs Dicken and Co., Friday 1 July 1808, Minutes of Birmingham Board of Guardians, GP/B/2/1/2, BCA.

I was obliged to make overtime every night but I did not like this as I wanted to learn my books we had a school every night but we used to attend about once a week (besides Sundays when we all attended) ... I wanted to go oftener to school than twice a week including Sundays but Richard Bamford [mill manager] would not let me go.

Despite this evident complaint he continues, 'I have no reason to complain of my master Mr Greg nor Richard Bamford who overlooks the works'.[61]

Children also complained, often in a muted way, about the level of chastisement received. The incidence of beating was explored in Chapter 9, where parish complicity in the discipline experiment was emphasised. Children's complaints of being ill-used are recorded but rarely found to be justified.[62] Complaints of severity were registered and sometimes pursued, though it appears that 'cruelty by masters had to be very severe before any complaint on the part of a child was seriously considered'.[63] This was the case at Marsden, where the problem was ostensibly resolved, or at least a considerable relaxation of discipline had taken place',[64] and the children encouraged to forgive and forget. Complaints of ill treatment at Douglas's Pendleton mill were found by Chelmsford parish officials to be unjustified.[65] Similarly at Mr Watson's Watford silk mill, children's complaints of ill treatment were found to be 'malicious and unfounded';[66] and complaints from St James's parish children at Strutts cotton spinning enterprise at Rickmansworth were considered but only upheld on one occasion.[67]

Parish apprentices rarely complained about conditions and hours of work. This indicates both children's awareness that these were contentious areas, and visitors' reluctance to entertain discussion of the subject. One example where parish apprentices did complain on this issue was reported by factory Visitors appointed under the 1802 Act, who portrayed the complainers as unusually assertive. The children at Needham's Litton mill approached one of the visitors

> with a complaint of being worked too hard, and of not having sufficient support. I thought it right to examine some of the apprentices upon both as to the facts they complained of,

---

61 Examination of Joseph Sefton brought under a warrant of the Rev. Croxton Johnston Clerk one of his Majesty's Justices of the Peace for the County of Chester for his having eloped and deserted the service of Samuel Greg ... to whom he was apprentice' 2 August 1806. Greg papers C5/8/9/4, MCA.

62 The parish officials arrived at the mill at noon on Monday 6 September and left in the evening of Tuesday 7 September 1802. Such a timetable would allow them to spend between 12 and 16 hours to interview the children if they had devoted the bulk of their time to this exercise. As there were 133 children of the parish there, this would allow 6–7 minutes per child, and therefore a cursory level of examination.

63 E.J. Erith, *Essex Parish Records, 1240–1894* (Chelmsford, 1950), p. 28.

64 1797 Report, St Margaret and St John.

65 Frith, *Essex Parish Records*, p. 75; F.G. Emmison, 'Essex children deported to a Lancashire cotton mill,1799', *The Essex Review*, 53 (1944): 77–81.

66 19 October 1796, Minutes of meeting of Officers of the Parish of St Martin in the Fields, F2075, WAC.

67 29 April 1788, 28 October 1792, Minutes of Governors and Directors of the Poor, Parish of St James, Piccadilly, D1872–4, WAC.

and the substance of their deposition is as follows viz: that they go into the mill about 10 minutes before six o-clock in the morning, and stay there till from ten to fifteen minutes after nine in the evening, excepting the time allowed for dinner, which is from half to three quarters of an hour.[68]

The visitors to Litton took up the issue with John Needham, whose explanation for the very long hours was 'that the mill was useless and the apprentices unemployed for a month in the winter in consequence of putting down a water wheel'. So the children's complaint was listened to and the visitors were sufficiently moved to follow it up, but there is no evidence that they directly intervened to reduce hours.

The nature and term of the apprenticeship arrangement often compounded the parish child's sense of exploitation. This subject permeates Blincoe's memoir and is referred to in settlement examinations. The voluntary examination of Jane Bounds of Norton in the parish of Cuckney and recorded in 1809 for example, describes how, 'born in London, and early confined to the Edmonton workhouse' at the age of seven Jane was separated from her mother and sent to Toplis 'to work ... merely for her maintenance without any wages for her service in which she continued several years, that she believes herself to have been an apprentice ... but she never saw any indenture by which she may have been bound'.[69] While Jane says nothing of her life in the mill, her sense of powerlessness is clear. She was aware of not being recompensed for her labour; and to her, her situation was ambiguous. She assumed that she was an apprentice, 'and was upon the same footing as all the other girls', but had no knowledge of the formality of the situation or of her rights.

Parish apprentices' sense of exploitation was also indicated by the long term they served as unpaid labour.[70] The traditional term of apprenticeship was seven years. Under the factory apprenticeship system, when age at binding was commonly ten or less and could be as low as six, such a term would be considered short. Because the term almost always ended at 21, many apprentices worked for 11 or 12 years – possibly half of their working lives – without recompense. In at least one case the already excessive term was lengthened by the falsification of certificates. Birmingham apprentices at Dicken and Finlow's factory, for example, expressed dissatisfaction

---

68   Records of Quarter Sessions. Documents relating to Cotton Mill apprentices Q/AG/1–36, DRO; Reports of cotton mills and factories inspected from the last midsummer sessions to the present. Brief notes on the conditions of the mills by Marmaduke Middleton Middleton, 18 April 1811 Q/AG/7, DRO. Even by the standards of the day, the 15-hour day described was unusually long. At neighbouring Cressbrook for example, the children went 'into the mill at six o'clock in the morning and come out again at eight o'clock in the evening'.

69   The name of Jane Bounds does not appear in the Cuckney register, though several batches were brought from Edmonton, including some very early in the life of the enterprise. It could be that her name changed? Or that there was a transcribing error. There was a child named Jane Beard for example. DD4P67/71, NA. It could be that she was one of the children bound 'informally', leaving no written record.

70   Such children received 'pocket money' for working overtime, but were not paid a wage until out of their time.

with the entries of their ages in the indentures and agreements by which they were bound to serve. Many declared that they were older when they were bound that what they were put down to be and several complained that they were actually serving beyond the age specified and strongly claimed our interference with their employers.

If true this carried a strong implication of exploitation. The Guardians took the complaint seriously and 'promised to enquire into this affair and we think some explanation on this subject is essentially necessary. As these errors in the ages are the cause of a considerable degree of misunderstanding between the children and the masters we recommend in future the best means be used for ascertaining the age of children before they are bound'; 'At Aldrewas [sic] several girls declared that they signed their names or made their marks to agreements binding them to serve till they were nineteen years of age and that such agreements were afterwards altered to bind them to service till they were twenty one ... we promised to enquire into this affair and we think some explanation on this subject is essentially necessary'.[71]

Parish apprentices were given more opportunity than other children workers to verbalise feelings of gratification or misery.[72] In all the reports, settlement examinations and interviews identified in the course of this study, the children's words as written by officials were most restrained in their complaints or criticism of their working and living conditions. Even though the voices of parish apprentices presented in this chapter are mostly heard through the agency of parish officials, it is possible to detect an underlying message of dissatisfaction or even distress. The extent to which the children's voices were heard depended on the subject matter. In the case of complaints about insufficient food, the parish tended to listen, and even to act. Complaints about education were taken equally seriously. However if the concern had an emotional root, as was the case with homesickness, for example, the voices were not heard. The extent to which children's concerns about corporal punishment were heard varied. Malicious brutality was acted upon, but rarely with urgency and children learned that a level of discipline was not only to be endured but was a necessary component of the apprentice experience, and learning to be a good worker. The extent to which children were protected by parish officials is explored further in the following chapter.

---

71 1 July 1808, Minutes of Birmingham Board of Guardians, GP/B/2/1/2, BCA.
72 This applied not only to the interviews with parish officers but also to parliamentary investigations, such as SC1816.

Chapter 11

The Protection of Parish Apprentices

For they [magistrates] are empowered by this Act of Parliament [Elizabethan Poor Law] to take children out of the arms of their parents, and to bind them out as apprentices till they are 21 years of age. The law has made them the guardians for those children, who have no others to take care of them. And who ought to judge of the fitness of the persons, to whom the poor children are thus to be apprenticed? Not the overseers – they are frequently obscure people, and perhaps in managing the business of the parish are not always attentive to the feelings of parent. But the legislation intended that the magistrates should have a check or control over the parish officers in this instance; and in my mind they are called upon to examine with the most minute and anxious attention to situations of the masters to whom the apprentices are to be bound, and to exercise their judgment solemnly and soberly before they allow or disallow the act of the parish officers; for which purpose it is necessary that they should confer together.[1]

This 1789 ruling by Lord Kenyon emphasises the importance of the role of the magistrates in 'protecting' parish children within the apprenticeship system.[2] The signature of two Justices[3] formed an essential component of the indenture. It was not intended as a rubber-stamping exercise even if it were sometimes seen as such.[4] The judgment of parish Poor Law officials was not to be relied upon. Financial responsibilities dominated the concerns of churchwardens and overseers of the poor, and while many such individuals expressed concern for their poor children, their expertise in caring for or protecting their children was typically limited. Parish officials were not selected for their background in this area; indeed many 'guardians' of the poor were unwilling participants in that role.

The notion that parishes wantonly disposed of their children through factory apprenticeships (and failed to offer any follow-up care) permeates the literature.[5]

---

1   'The King against the inhabitants of Hamstall Ridware'. Saturday 27 June 1789. An indenture of a parish apprentice assented to by the two justices separately is void: and no settlement is gained by serving under it. *English Reports,* vol. 100, p. 631–3. Thanks to Joanna Innes for drawing my attention to this reference.
2   This view was not uncommon in contemporary legal circles.
3   Acting together; a key ruling of the Hamstall Ridware case.
4   Articulated by the Bettering Society, for example. *The Reports of the Society for Bettering the Condition and Increasing the Comforts of the Poor*, vol. IV, 1805, Appendix no. 1 pp. 3–6; Report dated December 1802: 'It is the spirit of our poor laws, that all poor apprentices should be, peculiarly and immediately, under the view, controul and protection of the magistrate'. And not all parishes conformed to the requirement in any case. Geoffrey W. Oxley, *Poor Relief in England and Wales 1601–1834* (Newton Abbot, 1974), p. 76.
5   Roy Porter, *English Society in the Eighteenth Century* (Harmondsworth, 1991), pp. 85–6; Dorothy Marshall, *The English Poor in the Eighteenth Century: A Study in Social*

This chapter revisits two related assumptions: firstly that during the height of the factory apprenticeship system, participating parishes were motivated by the desire to reduce financial responsibility for their poor children; and secondly that parishes and other institutions failed to provide support for those children bound to factories.[6]

A range of surviving sources, including minutes of parish meetings, reports of factory visits and business correspondence, indicates that parishes rarely disregarded the welfare of their children following formal binding. Bearing in mind the potentially precarious position of children for whom the parish acted as guardian,[7] this chapter considers the systems established to protect them during their apprenticeship term. Protective measures were implemented incrementally, erratically, and through trial and error; and only rarely were they not introduced at all.[8] Formal structures were complemented by the informal and random actions of family, friends, community and well-meaning, impartial observers. The discussion that follows suggests that the majority of early factory parish apprentices were not as alone and neglected

---

and *Administrative History* (London, 1926), p. 186; Robert W. Malcolmson, *Life and Labour in England 1700–1780* (London, 1981), p. 64; Lynn Hollen Lees, *The Solidarities of Strangers: The English Poor Laws and the People, 1700–1948* (Cambridge, 1998), pp. 55 and 103; Anthony Brundage, *The English Poor Laws 1700–1930* (Basingstoke, 2002), p. 16; O.J. Dunlop, *English Apprenticeship and Child Labour: A History* (London, 1912), p. 256; M. Dorothy George, *London Life in the Eighteenth Century* (London, 1925), pp. 227 and 256; Pamela Horn, 'The traffic in children and the textile mills, 1780–1816', *Genealogists' Magazine*, 24/5 (1993): 353; B.L. Hutchins and A. Harrison, *A History of Factory Legislation* (Westminster, 1903), p. 7; Brian Inglis, *Poverty and the Industrial Revolution* (London, 1972), p. 79; Joan Lane, *Apprenticeship in England, 1600–1914* (London, 1996), pp. 1 and 81.

6   The notion of disposal and a cavalier attitude towards binding was coupled with the idea that parishes showed no sign of interest in what happened to the children subsequently. It was 'nobody's concern. The parish was unlikely to interest itself in their subsequent fate'. Inglis, *Poverty and the Industrial Revolution*, p. 108. More recently, Lynn Hollen Lees has asserted that factory apprentices were 'literally exiled from their home communities and put out of sight and mind of the parish'. Lees, *The Solidarities of Strangers*, p. 103; Ivy Pinchbeck and Margaret Hewitt, *Children in English Society* (2 vols, London 1969–1973), vol. 1, p. 245, assert that there is plenty of evidence to suggest that the apprenticing of children out of their birth parish resulted in 'the neglect of the children and the corruption of apprenticeship'. According to Kydd, the children served 'unknown, protected and forgotten'. Samuel Kydd (Alfred), *The History of the Factory Movement from the Year 1802, to the Enactment of the Ten Hours' Bill in 1847* (2 vols, London, 1857), vol. 1, p. 12.

7   Parishes did recognise their position as *in loco parentis*. Officials from the parish of St Margaret and St John, for example, concluded their report on a visit to Toplis's factory: 'This consideration … ought to make you, Gentlemen, particularly cautious with respect to the characters of those manufacturers that in future apply for the children to whom, though not naturally, you legally are the PARENTS …'. 1797 Report, St Margaret and St John. Evidence suggests that parish apprentices, the majority of whom were not orphans, also understood this to be the case. Also relevant are John Brown, *Memoir of Robert Blincoe* (Manchester, 1832), passim; 1802 Report, St Margaret and St John.

8   The Webbs stated that 'here and there, a well-managed parish would make its own inspection', but it now seems that it was the unusual parish that did not conduct some level of investigation. Sidney Webb and Beatrice Webb, *English Local Government, vol. 7, English Poor Law History, part 1 The Old Poor Law* (London, 1927), p. 202.

as conventional wisdom indicates; yet the activities of various agencies were no guarantee of 'protection'. Practice and procedure for ascertaining apprenticeship arrangements varied both between parishes and within parishes over time as a result of changes in personnel.

The performance of parishes varied greatly in terms of the care and protection they offered to their children; but few appear to have ceased all contact following the signing of factory apprenticeship indentures. Evidence from meetings of parish officers indicates sympathy towards apprenticed children. Minutes cannot fully convey the extent or depth of relevant discussions, yet sufficient clues survive to suggest that while not all Poor Law officers were well equipped for the task of child care, neither were they universally indifferent to the children's needs. Compassion undoubtedly drove many overseers, even if financial constraints often limited the manifestation of such emotion.

In Table 11.1 an attempt has been made to categorise parishes, and other institutions, such as the Foundling Hospital, in terms of the extent to which they implemented specific protective measures.

Table 11.1 Indicators of Parish Protection of Apprentices

Parish or groups of parishes	1	2	3	4	5	6	7	8	9	10	11
Birmingham	✓		✓	✓	✓	✓	✓	✓	✓	✓	
Brighton			✓	✓	✓		✓	✓			
Bristol	✓			✓		✓	✓	✓	✓	✓	
Canewdon, Essex		✓				✓					
Chatham, Kent		✓		✓				✓	✓		
Chelmsford	✓			✓		✓					
City of London	?									?	
Clapham	✓					✓		✓			✓
Coventry							✓	✓	✓		
Derbyshire											
Doncaster											
Epsom	✓							✓			✓
Halstead											
Hampstead								✓			
Hanwell	✓	✓						✓	✓		
Hereford											
Hull	✓								✓		
Islington	✓								✓		✓
Lambeth				✓			✓				
Leeds	✓		✓	✓		✓	✓	✓	✓	✓	
Manchester	✓									✓	
Nottinghamshire											
Oxford, St Clements	✓							✓	✓		

Parish	1	2	3	4	5	6	7	8	9	10	11
Oxfordshire, Witney	✓							✓	✓		
St Anne Soho								✓	✓		
St Clement Danes			✓	✓	✓	✓	✓	✓	✓		
St George Hanover Square	✓			✓				✓	✓	✓	
St George the Martyr				✓					✓		
St Giles in the Fields											
St James Piccadilly	✓	✓	✓	✓	✓	✓	✓	✓	✓	✓	✓
St Leonards, Shoreditch											
St Luke, Chelsea			✓	✓			✓		✓		
St Luke, Finsbury			✓						✓	✓	
St Margaret and St John		✓	✓	✓	✓		✓		✓		
St Martin in the Fields	✓		✓		✓			✓	✓		
St Mary Newington	✓	✓	✓	✓	✓	✓		✓	✓	✓	
St Pancras			✓					✓	✓		
St Paul Covent Garden	✓							✓	✓		
Shrewsbury	✓	✓	✓					✓		✓	
Staffordshire											
Suffolk									?		?
Warwickshire parishes	✓							✓	✓		
Worcestershire parishes											
Foundling Hospital	✓	✓	✓	✓	✓	✓	✓	✓	✓	✓	✓

Key:

1 Prior investigation of employers; and/or confirmation through 'liking'
2 Parental and/or child permission sought; no direct compulsion
3 Establish support system *in situ*
4 Visits, inspections and reports
5 Recommendation for change
6 Interview children, during or after apprenticeship; constructive response to children's complaints
7 Follow-up visit; check change; taken action (including ceasing to send children to factories)
8 Communication between parish and employer
9 Parish discussion of general or particular issues
10 Investigate/enquire into long-term career opportunities
11 No factory apprenticeships; policy decision

Level of protection	Parishes
1 most protective	Birmingham; Clapham; Epsom; Islington; Leeds; St James, Piccadilly; St Mary Newington; Foundling Hospital
2 protective	Bristol; St Clement Danes; St Margaret and St John
3 averagely protective	Brighton; Chatham; Hanwell; St George, Hanover Square; St Luke, Chelsea; St Martin in the Fields; Shrewsbury
4 not very protective	Canewdon; Chelmsford; Coventry; Lambeth; Hull; Oxford; St Anne, Soho; St George the Martyr Southwark; St Luke, Finsbury; St Pancras; St Paul, Covent Garden
5 least protective	Doncaster
6 insufficient data	Derbyshire; Halstead; Hereford; Nottinghamshire; St Giles; St Leonard; Shoreditch; Staffordshire; Suffolk; Warwickshire; Worcestershire

The findings reflect the quality of record keeping and the survival of sources as much as protective practice. For some parishes, no relevant data could be found; for many others the information is partial. It will be assumed that a parish that scored highly on 'protective indicators' adopted a responsible approach to its children; and that while those scoring poorly were probably less protective, reluctant record keeping might have disguised the level of activity.[9] Table 11.2 focuses on neglect. Relevant information is very limited but in a number of cases sufficient evidence exists to correct unduly positive interpretations. Where possible, therefore, the 'protection ratings' suggested by Table 11.1 will be checked by the 'negligence ratings' in Table 11.2.

Among the 'most protective' institutions, the Foundling Hospital established strict procedures for ascertaining the quality of factory situations. During the 1760s, several groups of children were successfully bound to manufactories with good retention intentions.[10] Two unsuccessful factory placements in the following decade – one in Leeds, the other in Stockport – encouraged the Hospital not only to exercise caution in the future but also to establish robust local support systems.[11] After appropriate checks, Samuel Oldknow of Mellor and J & W Toplis of Cuckney near Mansfield became recipients of Foundlers in the early 1790s.[12] Several months

---

9   Or that records have not survived.

10 The first of such groups – 16 girls – was sent to John Arbuthnot, a calico printer of Ravensbury, Surrey in 1760–61. Several years later, a 'batch' of 24 children were sent to Plaistow, to Felix Ehrliholtzer, embroidered and tambour worker, who expressed a willingness to provide skilled work for the girls on completion of their 'service'. R.K. McClure, *Coram's Children: The London Foundling Hospital in the Eighteenth Century* (New Haven, 1981), p. 128.

11 In both cases, the children were neglected. Mc Clure, *Coram's Children*, p. 128.

12 6 June 1792, 'Rough minutes of the General Committee of the Foundling Hospital'. DD212/1, NA. This decision was not made lightly: the report was considered at two separate meetings in conjunction with Toplis's own proposals and assurances. Toplis's register indicates the ages of the children apprenticed from the Hospital in July 1792. Ten of the 35 children [6 boys and 4 girls] were aged 7; a further 9 were aged 8. 'List of children put apprentice to William Toplis'. DD895/1, NA.

Table 11.2 Indicators of Parish Negligence of Apprentices

Parishes or groups of parishes	1	2	3	4	5	6	7	8	9	10	11	12	13	14	15	16
Birmingham	✓			✓			✓	✓	✓		✓	✓		✓		
Brighton														✓	✓	
Bristol				✓			✓	✓	✓		✓	✓		✓		
Canewdon, Essex				✓												
Chatham, Kent	?						✓	✓								
Chelmsford				✓	?		✓	✓	✓		✓	✓				
City of London					?		✓									
Coventry							✓	✓								
Derbyshire																✓
Doncaster	✓		✓				✓	✓	✓		✓	✓		✓		
Halstead	✓		✓	✓			✓	✓	✓	✓						
Hanwell				✓												
Hereford	✓						✓									
Hull							✓									✓
Islington										✓						
Lambeth		✓	✓				✓?									
Leeds							✓	✓						✓	✓	?
Manchester	?															
Notts	✓						✓									
Oxford, St Clements							✓									
Oxford, Witney				✓												
St Anne Soho	✓				?		?									
St Clement Danes		✓	✓		✓		✓			✓			✓	✓	✓	
St George, Hanover Square							✓	✓	✓		✓	✓			✓	
St George the Martyr, Southwark				✓		✓	✓	✓	✓							
St Giles in the Fields		✓	✓			?	✓?									
St James Piccadilly	?						✓				✓	✓	✓			
St Leonard Shoreditch		?	✓			?										
St Luke Chelsea							✓					✓			✓	
St Luke Finsbury					✓		✓									
St Margaret and St John							✓		✓		✓	✓		✓	✓	
St Martin in the Fields			✓				✓	✓	✓		✓?	✓	✓		✓	
St Mary Newington							✓	?								
St Pancras	?	✓	✓		✓		✓		✓		✓	✓		✓	✓	
St Paul Covent Garden					✓		✓					✓				
Shrewsbury							✓									
Suffolk					✓		✓									
Warwickshire							✓									
Worcestershire							✓									

Key:

1. Inaccurate recording; failure to record fully parish apprentices in register
2. Children apprenticed at early age [either under 8; or majority under 10]
3. More than 50 per cent of parish's children to factory during period 1785–1815
4. Force, compulsion; send children against wish of parent or child Threat; using factory apprenticeship as a means of extracting compliance behaviour
5. No prior check on employer
6. No inspection/visit/reporting
7. Very infrequent visiting [more than 4 years]
8. Inadequate inspection [less than a day spent]; treated as corporate jaunt; uncritical report – blind eye turned to abuse; expressly permitted night working
9. Inadequate check on local arrangements for protection/offloading responsibility; local arrangements unsatisfactory
10. Inconsistent policy; shift from benign to less benign
11. Failure to respond, or sluggishness in response to children's 'voice'
12. Failure to bring children home after discovery of abuse
13. Continue to send children despite poor report or discovery of abuse
14. Failure to implement change; or insist on change in face of recalcitrant employer
15. Failure to follow-up; check change
16. Persistent apprenticing after 1816 legislation

Level of negligence	Parish
High	Birmingham; Doncaster; St Clement Danes; St Martin in the Fields; St Pancras; Bristol
Moderate	Chelmsford; Halstead; St George, Hanover Square; St Margaret and St John; St George the Martyr, Southwark
Low	Leeds; St James, Piccadilly

after the departure of the children for Cuckney, the treasurer reported that 'the Rev Mr Hume, rector of Carlton in Lendrick [Notts] has obligingly undertaken to visit the children placed under the care of Messrs Toplis and Co. at Cuckney ... as occasion may require and to communicate any observations which he may think proper to this committee'.[13] As it turned out, the Reverend's assistance was needed, and upon Toplis's bankruptcy in 1805, Hume ensured the speedy transfer of the children to other employments.[14] The Oldknow papers indicate the Hospital's long-term concern for its children's welfare. A letter from Oldknow to Mr Livesey of the Foundling Hospital reported on the progress of 'Mary Smith ... out of her time ...

---

13 Foundling Hospital General Committee Minutes, DD121/1, NA.
14 McClure, *Coram's Children*, pp. 150–53.

and has fixed herself in a reputable family near to my mill where she still works ... and Sarah Cole will be out of her time next month and intends abiding here'.[15]

Islington is also rated highly because of its policy not to apprentice its children to factories despite several opportunities to do so.[16] The decision was reached after careful consideration,[17] and the policy was not reversed until 1814 when it agreed to bind children to Courtauld's silk mill in Braintree.[18] Also among the top performers, the parish of Leeds was placed in both the 'most protective' and the 'least negligent' categories. Accordingly, the records of the Leeds Poor Law officials indicate a judicious approach to the apprenticing of all its children. Potential masters, whether factory proprietors or not were carefully screened,[19] and cases of cruelty taken seriously. Because of the buoyancy of the Leeds economy, most of the town's children were placed in 'real' trades. Only two mills in the area received Leeds apprentices. One was the relatively modest enterprise of Thompson in Thorner; the other, the larger factory of Merryweather and Whitaker on the banks of the Wharfe near Otley. The Leeds' officials visited the latter enterprise soon after the arrival of the first group of children, and their glowing report recommended the immediate dispatch of more children. The gap of four years before the next recorded visit in 1809 suggested a confidence in the proprietor which, in view of appalling conditions that met visitors to Merryweather's later enterprise in Manchester, may have been misplaced.[20] Nevertheless, in other ways the parish officials demonstrated concern for its children's future.[21]

The relatively prosperous parish of St James Piccadilly also scored well on the protective indicators and was rated among the least negligent.[22] According to

---

15 Letter 13 November 1813. Correspondence with London Foundling Hospital about apprentices. MF 1020 MCA. The file also contains a letter from a former apprentice fallen on hard times and seeking the Hospital's assistance, 26 November 1843.

16 It rejected offers from Toplis and Merryweather. 6 September 1787, June 1801, Minutes of the Trustees of the Poor, Parish of St Mary, Islington, ILHL.

17 The issue was discussed at several meetings of the Trustees of the Poor, 6 September 1787, 6 October 1791, 20 October 1791, 3 November 1791, 22 June 1801, 27 May 1802, Minutes of the Trustees of the Poor, Parish of St Mary, Islington, ILHL.

18 Late in 1813, Courtauld, through his agent Mr Wilson of Highbury Hill, applied to St Mary Islington for a number of girl apprentices to his silk mill in Braintree. 2 December 1813, Minutes of the Trustees of the Poor, Parish of St Mary, Islington, ILHL. They were bound in 1814 according to the Annual Register of parish poor children, Islington. See Dorothy Hester Helena Newbold, 'The Poor Law: St Mary Newington, 1790–1834', undated typescript, P 25. SLHL. The proximity of the mill may have swayed the decision to reverse the policy.

19 In 25 May 1803, it was ordered that in future, 'no children employed in calico weaving shall be put out apprentice without ... having the sanction of the subcommittee', Leeds Workhouse Query Book 1803–1810 LO/Q 2, WYASL.

20 Because of the mill's proximity to the parish, the proprietors were connected to some or all of the Poor Law officials, which may have biased the appraisal.

21 In 1819, officers travelled to New Lanark to gather new ideas on child education and welfare. Also they pursued cases of complaint, for example, in Oldham, 1823. Leeds Workhouse Committee Minutes and order book 1818–23, LO/M/6, WYASL.

22 For example, a list of boys apprenticed to Haywood and Palfreyman, with birth dates, recording in minutes of meeting of Governors and Directors of the Poor, St James Piccadilly,

Dorothy George, it was surprising to find the parish 'which undoubtedly gave real consideration to the fate of their children, among the London parishes sending apprentices to cotton mills'.[23] Parish officers engaged with most of the stages of 'protection' identified in Table 11.1. Formal enquiries were made of all potential masters, whether 'factory' or 'trade';[24] and a number in both categories were rejected as unsuitable.[25] Parental permission was required before placement. After ascertaining the suitability of Messrs Holt and Mitchell, for example, the clerk was ordered to 'prepare a list of children from the age of 10 and upwards and affix the same on the door of the workhouse' with the following notice: 'It is intended to place the under mentioned children apprentices to Messrs M & H ... unless objected to by their parents ... The most minute and strict enquiry has been made... '.[26] Once a master was approved, and parental agreement obtained, children were sent on a 'liking', a practice by no means universal in the case of factory apprenticeships.[27] St James was one of the few parishes to withhold part of the premium until the children's satisfaction was ascertained.[28] At all the factories to which St James's children were bound, the protection of a local priest was organised.[29] At Wildboar Clough, for example, parish officers appointed Rev William Bromley to, 'visit the children and to catechise and instruct them every Sabbath day and at other times ... occasionally to enquire into their conduct and behaviour and also their treatment by

---

26 February 1796. The positive record, however, was blemished by several reversals of decisions to cease binding children to textile factories. Meeting of 23 July 1790, Minutes of the Governors and Directors of the Poor, Parish of St James, Piccadilly, D1873. Report (dated 6 September 1799) of 'Messrs Johnson, Freeman and Ideson relative to poor children belonging to those Parish apprenticed to Messrs Hayward and Palfreyman in Cheshire', discussed at meeting 7 September 1799, Minutes of the Governors and Directors of the Poor, Parish of St James, Piccadilly, D1876, WAC.

23   George, *London Life*, pp. 249–56. George also included St George, Hanover Square among the surprise participants.

24   On 7 October 1783, for example, it was 'ordered that a list of the children who have been bound apprentices for the last seven years be printed and delivered the Governors and Directors of the Poor and the churchwardens and overseers for them occasionally to enquire into the behaviour of the children and the conduct of the masters', Minutes of the Governors and Directors of the Poor, Parish of St James, Piccadilly, D1872, WAC.

25   11 July 1783, that enquiries are made of all potential masters of apprentices as to suitability. And decisions are deferred pending report. Then, 'they being found on enquiry proper places for apprentices' agreed; but this was not always the case. On 13 January 1786, for example, the committee 'found the business of Mr Patrick, engraver, 'to be a very improper place'; and on 24 July 1787 only one out of four masters who applied was found 'fit and proper to take an apprentice'. Minutes of the Governors and Directors of the Poor, Parish of St James, Piccadilly, D1872, WAC.

26   St James Piccadilly, 2 October 1801, Minutes of the Governors and Directors of the Poor, Parish of St James, Piccadilly, D1878, WAC.

27   Birmingham and St James were in a minority in this respect.

28   4 May 1797, Minutes of the Governors and Directors of the Poor, Parish of St James, Piccadilly, D1876, WAC.

29   It seems that the Foundling Hospital instigated such a practice.

their masters'.[30] Although the intention was sound, recognising that from a distance of 180 miles regular inspection was not feasible, such practice also amounted to a devolving of responsibility.

St James established good channels of communication with other parishes,[31] with current and former apprentices, with factory employers, and with the local priests. Special meetings were arranged to record the testimony of former apprentices.[32] The parish officials responded to the children's complaints, investigated them, and took action. In October 1792, for example, the overseers reported that they, with several other governors, visited the poor children bound apprentice to Strutt and found that 'seven of them had been very severely chastised for trifling offences that the food allowed them was inadequate to the many hours they were kept to work and that they were universally dissatisfied'.[33] The parish also responded quickly to requests for books and writing materials.[34] All evidence indicates the priority of the parish for the long-term interest of their children, being prepared to bring them 'home' if this were in doubt. For example, the girls at Litton mills, were thought neither to be acquainted with basic domestic skills nor likely to gain secure employment in the future: 'for all which reasons ... the said girls ought to be bound apprentices to be brought home again'.[35] Frequent reporting was a key element in the parish's strategy of protection. This was most obviously the case at the beginning of the nineteenth century when children at Holt and Mitchell and Douglas were visited every few

---

30   6 May 1796, Minutes of the Governors and Directors of the Poor, Parish of St James, Piccadilly, D1876, WAC.

31   They gleaned information about factory conditions from other parishes. For example, in the case of Haywood and Palfreyman, 'Mr Ideson ... informed the meeting that he had waited on Mr Leigh of St George's and conversed with him on the subject ... And that from every enquiry that could be made they were perfectly satisfied with the character and situation of the applicants'. 23 February 1796, Minutes of Governors and Directors of the Poor, Parish of St James, Piccadilly, D1876, WAC.

32   29 [sic] February 1797 special committee meeting to hear the testimony of Margaret Chamberlain Minutes of Governors and Directors of the Poor, Parish of St James, Piccadilly, D1876, WAC.

33   'Ordered that the Clerk do write to Mr Strutt relative thereto'. 28 October 1792, Minutes of Governors and Directors of the Poor, Parish of St James, Piccadilly, D1873, WAC.

34   9 September 1796, letter from Rev. Bromeley at Wildboar Clough, Macclesfield, 'If they learn to write they will want paper, ink and quills ... they seem very well pleased with their governors sending them books'; reply to this letter from Mr Luke Ideson. 'They have been pleased to have paper and quills to be sent for the use of the children and beg you to buy ink for them from time to time. The expense they will thankfully repay you. They have also sent half a dozen books of the great importance of a religious life'. 26 January 1797, Rev. Bromeley writes thanking for 'books, writing paper and quills for the use of the poor children'. Minutes of Governors and Directors of the Poor, Parish of St James, Piccadilly, D1876, WAC.

35   6 May 1796, Minutes of Governors and Directors of the Poor, Parish of St James, Piccadilly, D1876, WAC.

months.[36] St James parish maintained a close watch on its children before, during and after apprenticeship, recognising an enduring responsibility to them.

The parish of St Mary Newington was rated among the most protective parishes examined, and expressed consistent concern for the welfare of its young poor.[37] Because of insufficient data, no check by negligence rating has been possible. Children placed in textile factories from the parish formed a small proportion of the total except during the years 1813–15.[38] Before binding children to Whitaker's Burley mill, a report by Lambeth parish into the condition of its own apprentices there, was scrutinised by St Mary parish officials, and magistrates, and read to the children and their parents.[39] Parental permission was required before binding, and a parent's refusal in this case was not resisted.[40] Factory visiting was part of the child protection strategy, though its frequency is unclear. The Workhouse Committee recorded positive findings of a parish visit to Whitaker's mill in 1817, five years after the initial bindings.[41] Factory apprenticing from St Mary parish continued after the 1816 legislation but conformed to the stipulated 40-mile limit. In 1824, the Guardians inspected a lace factory in Bermondsey to which nine children were subsequently bound.[42] A fuller inspection took place the following year to check on the condition of the children from St Mary as well as 62 children from other parishes.[43] Concerns about a rod and cane, overwork and some dietary deficiency were raised with the proprietors, but there is no sign that the children were to be removed.[44]

Placed among the 'most protective' parishes, Birmingham was also among the 'most negligent'. Such anomalous rankings stemmed from inconsistency in strategy and action. In 1783, the Birmingham Board of Guardians was empowered to put children out as apprentices. Initially the search for suitable placements was locally

---

36   For example, 14 September 1801, 20 October 1801, 19 February 1802, 17 September 1802, Minutes of Governors and Directors of the Poor, Parish of St James, Piccadilly, D1878, WAC.

37   St Mary Newington, Governors and Guardians General minutes 1814–23, 892, SLHL. Close attention was also paid to the care of the very young children at the nursery who were visited 'regularly once every month or oftener if requisite'. This was agreed 10 November 1814, ibid.

38   In these years, factory apprenticeships comprised the majority.

39   3 December 1813, St Mary Newington Workhouse Committee Minutes, 931, SLHL. The copy of the Lambeth report does not survive, but that it existed is significant, as there is no indication in the Lambeth parish records that officials visited and reported on factories in this way.

40   St Mary Newington Workhouse Committee Minutes, vol. 11, 13 April 1814, 931, SLHL.

41   The visit also coincided with the ending of the term of some of the girls. 24 July 1817, St Mary Newington Workhouse Committee Minutes, 932, SLHL.

42   St Mary Newington Workhouse Committee Minutes, vol. III, 5 February 1824, 933, SLHL.

43   This is a rare example where inspection included children from other parishes. The case of the Lambeth report on Whitaker's mill does indicate that some sharing of information occurred.

44   Dorothy Hester Helena Newbold, 'The Poor Law: St Mary Newington, 1790–1834', pp. 20–22, unpublished typescript, held at SLHL.

confined and carefully conducted. Only later, in response to severe overcrowding, were masters outside the town considered and scrutinised: 'any person not living in Birmingham who offers to take one of the children shall bring a recommendation from the minister of the parish'.[45] Records for the years between 1785 and 1795 have not survived, yet evidently 'a great number of girls have been sent to the cotton mills', during that time.[46] The Birmingham practice was to send children initially 'on a liking' and to confirm periodically the rectitude of the placement.[47] Reporting by the Birmingham Guardians was satisfactory in extent and impressively detailed in content. Visits to Peel's Lancashire mills,[48] verified the miserable conditions described by a returned apprentice, but no recorded action was taken in the wake of the findings.[49] Nevertheless procedures were thereafter tightened up, and in 1798 the suitability of Bott, Bower's Nantwich mill, much nearer to the parish, was established by a 'deputation' delegated to 'go down and acquaint themselves with the situation of the children already engaged in such business with the general tenor of the treatment they meet with'.[50] During the same year, the firm of Dicken and Fowler was also checked; and the indentures duly sanctioned by magistrates.[51] Like the Foundling Hospital and other 'protective' parishes, local clergymen were appointed to maintain regular supervision of the apprentices.[52] The next energetic reporting session occurred in 1808 when several days were spent visiting the children, mainly girls, employed in a number of Midlands cotton mills.[53] The conditions of the girls and their future prospects – apparently all good – were investigated carefully and dutifully recorded.[54] It was then resolved that 'the overseers be requested to visit the cotton mills and make a report annually'.[55] Accordingly, in the autumn of 1810 and the spring of 1811, mill visits were recorded but no report appended.[56] The next full

---

45   19 January 1784, Minutes of Birmingham Board of Guardians, GP/B/2/1/1, BCA.

46   16 September 1795, Minutes of Birmingham Board of Guardians, GP/B/2/1/1, BCA.

47   23 September 1795, Minutes of Birmingham Board of Guardians, GP/B/2/1/1, BCA.

48   On 14 May 1796, an interview with a girl 'lately returned from Hind Mill ... who gave a miserable account of her usage' led to a resolution, reaffirming one made on 24 February 1796 to visit the children at Peels, 'that it appears necessary for one or more of the overseers to enquire personally into the truth of such assertions and also respecting the general treatment of the children and act ...'.

49   In 1816 Select Committee, Theodore Price referred to an agreement made by the Birmingham Guardians not to send any more children to Peel's factories, though acknowledged that this may have been tacit or not formally agreed in writing. But there is no mention at all of the children being brought 'home' as they so fervently requested.

50   13 August 1798 Minutes of Birmingham Board of Guardians, GP/B/2/1/1, BCA.

51   29 August 1798, 20 August 1800, Minutes of Birmingham Board of Guardians, GP/B/2/1/1, BCA.

52   Rev. Hutchinson was perceived by the Guardians to have played a valuable supportive role.

53   Though other pieces of Poor Law business are transacted.

54   The report, five pages of closely written foolscap, was impressively detailed. 12 July 1808, Minutes of Birmingham Board of Guardians, GP/B/2/1/2, BCA.

55   12 July 1808, Minutes of Birmingham Board of Guardians, GP/B/2/1/2, BCA.

56   16 October 1810: 'resolved that the thanks of this meeting be given to the Overseers for visiting the children placed out apprentices by this parish at the different cotton mills'. Also:

report was recorded in 1813. By then factory apprenticeship had declined, and future requests from manufacturers declined.[57]

Despite paucity of data, it appears that the parishes in the relatively wealthy City of London exercised care when apprenticing their poor children. The surviving parish records indicate that masters within the parish, which tended to be the best bindings, were preferred. A very small number of children were bound to textile factories in the Midlands and the North. In the cases of St Botolph Aldergate and St Botolph without Aldergate, where such examples can be found, textile factory apprenticeships accounted for less than 5 per cent of the total.[58] It can be speculated, for no evidence can be found, that personal contacts formed the basis of such apprenticeships.

The Middlesex parish of Hanwell was among the more responsible parishes.[59] In 1792, the officers informed its poor families of an offer by John Toplis, the Nottinghamshire textile entrepreneur to provide their children with an apprenticeship and that 'all persons chusing to send their children must send in their names to ye churchwarden'. The offer was generally spurned, and although the Vestry stiffened its resolve, only two pauper children were eventually sent.[60] At this stage, no compulsion was used when parents refused to comply. The issue re-emerged in 1805 as relief expenditure increased, and the 'overseer reported that he had made contact with a factory in Watford which was willing to take pauper children'. Again parental resistance rendered unsuccessful 'the strategy of removing pauper children'.[61] While this suggests that children were not forced to go against their parents' wishes, the case of Widow Stevenitts indicates that recalcitrant parents were made to suffer. In 1805, when some of her children were identified as 'proper objects' to be sent to the Watford factory, she appeared before the vestry and refused her consent. But she was punished and later found in great distress.[62]

'the thanks of this meeting be given to the reverend Mr Hutchinson of Tutbury [Minister] for his very great attention and religious instruction of the children placed from this parish at the works of Messrs Bott and Co.; and on 2 April 1811, '... thanks of this meeting be given to Messrs William Christian and Henry Evans for visiting the children at the respective cotton mills', Minutes of Birmingham Board of Guardians, GP/B/2/1/2, BCA.

57   In October 1822, for example, Mr Merry, ribbon manufacturer of Coventry and Ashby de la Zouch, requested some parish children for his factories, and although his request was treated sympathetically, it was felt 'unnecessary to resort to distant places for employment (a system which in the opinion of this meeting nothing short of the most absolute necessity can justify). This meeting deems it inexpedient to enter into any negotiation with Mr Merry on the subject'. 29 October 1822, Minutes of Birmingham Board of Guardians, GP/B/2/1/2, BCA.

58   Apprenticeship Register 1769–1805, St Botolph Aldergate, MS 2658; Apprenticeship Register 1802–, Parish of St Botolph without Aldergate, MS 1471, GL.

59   Hanwell Vestry Minutes, 21 March 1792, 11 June 1792 and 1 April 1793; cited in *Victoria County History of Middlesex*, vol. 3, p. 229.

60   Paul Carter, 'Poor relief strategies – women, children and enclosure in Hanwell, Middlesex, 1780 to 1816', *The Local Historian*, 25 (1995): 170.

61   Carter, 'Poor relief strategies', p. 170.

62   Carter, 'Poor relief strategies', p. 171.

The parish of St Clement Danes was engaged fully in the practice of factory apprenticeship; and for 30 years from 1786, more than 80 per cent of its apprentice children were bound, often in substantial groups, to textile factory employers.[63] Although such a high proportion indicates negligence, the children were not forgotten and their situation was discussed regularly at parish meetings. The parish interviewed its children both *in situ* during factory visits; and more randomly following expiration of their indentures. Parish officers communicated informally with representatives in the locality of relevant mills;[64] and inspected factories thoroughly if infrequently. The first recorded visit took place in 1791 following a recommendation that officers 'attend the several cotton manufactories where the children belonging to this parish are placed ... observe their appearance as to health and look into the employ allotted them'.[65] When, the following year, the parish enquired into the high absconding rates from Douglas's Holywell factory, and found that apprentices were being worked all night, the officers took the unusual step of recalling their remaining children.[66]

Interviews and reports of inspections were carefully discussed, yet decisions taken were not consistently implemented. The examination of Harriet Russell, for example, former apprentice at Wells Middleton's Sheffield factory, raised doubts about the rectitude of factory apprenticeship, and at a specially convened meeting, it was 'resolved that no more children be sent to the cotton mills till a Vestry give directions concerning them'.[67] No further apprentices were sent to Sheffield, but it was agreed, after reading 'letters from Backbarrow from some boys there and from Mr Birch and considering the subject ... that the children at present at Enfield fixed upon by Messrs Birch and Co. be sent on to the manufactory'.[68] For some years Birch's mill was the sole destination of St Clement Danes children, and throughout, the parish perused letters from children, and depositions from runaways, visited the factory, interviewed the children, sought information from local contacts,[69] and

---

63 This reflected the difficulty in finding sufficient local bindings. After 1816, when long-distance factory apprenticeship was curtailed, the apprenticeship register for St Clement Danes showed a contraction in the total number of bindings. In other words, the total number of children bound rose during the time in which factory bindings dominated, and shrunk thereafter. This pattern was replicated in many of the parishes for which information is available.

64 At a meeting of the Guardians of the Poor on 7 September 1797, 'Mr Burnthwaite and Mr Bury be requested to write to their friends in Lancaster to request an account of the treatment of the children at the manufactory'. Minutes of Vestry, Parish of St Clement Danes, B1074, WAC.

65 2 June 1791, Minutes of Vestry, Parish of St Clement Danes, B1073, WAC. This also demonstrates financial caution and that factory visits were not perceived as corporate jaunts.

66 12 March 1792, Minutes of Churchwardens, Overseers and Assistants, Parish of St Clement Danes, B1147, WAC. Such practice was rarely recorded elsewhere.

67 12 September 1797, Minutes of Vestry, Parish of St Clement Danes, B1073, WAC.

68 5 October 1797, Minutes of Minutes of Vestry, Parish of St Clement Danes, B1073, WAC.

69 For example, 6 October 1791, Minutes of Vestry, Parish of St Clement Danes, B1073, WAC. 'Mr Milburn the Treasurer reported that he had a friend who went their 10 or 12 times in the year and who confirmed him that they were well treated and taken great care of ... whereupon it was moved that the sanction of this vestry be given to the churchwardens and

proposed improvements to the proprietor.[70] Two reports on Backbarrow survive. The first, conducted in 1797 reassured the parish.[71] The second, produced four years later, indicated significant differences, particularly in diet, hours of work and quantity of education.[72] In view of the deteriorating conditions, it was agreed that 'Mr Jennings the vestry clerk should be directed to enter into a friendly correspondence with Birch and Co. stating the different reports of 1797 and 1801 and to submit to them that it is expected by this Vestry that the labour of their apprentices should be reduced to their original hours; that their food should be the same as when the former report was made; that the regular times for instruction might be renewed; and that all might be obliged to attend Divine worship when health and weather permitted'. The committee also suggested changes specific to the training of the girls to ensure competence in domestic work; and that the 'welfare of the children' would be enhanced if inspection were frequent and that 'an account of [the apprentices] situation should be requested of the proprietors of the mills annually'.[73] Regrettably the proprietor's persistent recalcitrance impeded the good intentions of the parish officers towards 'their' children, yet despite little alteration in conditions at Backbarrow, it was agreed that 'as it did not appear that any better mode of disposing of the children can be found or proposed that they be sent as usual to the mills at Cartmel'.[74] Such an inadequate conclusion to persistent attempts to improve apprentices' situation was not unusual. The outcome of parishes' protective measures was often disappointingly at variance with the effort expended.

The parish of Chatham in Kent was rated average on the protective criteria. Insufficient data exist to assess its negligence rating. It participated in textile factory

---

overseers of this parish for binding out such poor children as they shall in their discretion think fit to the proprietors of the manufactory at Blackbarrow ... The question put and carried unanimously in the affirmative'.

70   7 February 1793, agreed that the 'vestry clerk write Messrs. Birch that – the time from dinner to supper is too long to last without something – that cheese should be given the children once or twice a week from super – that they should have small beer – that care be taken the bread is not too stale for them and that they should have a little more relaxation'. On 4 April 1793 the committee received 'Mr Birch's reply stating that he could not alter the provision of the children, at the request of any one; and that he fancy'd the company would have no objection to give up the indenture of all the children of this parish'. Minutes of Vestry, Parish of St Clement Danes, B1073, WAC.

71   December 5 1791. 'A letter from Messrs Wilks and Co. of the Pleasley Cotton mill offering to take the children as apprentices'. Minutes of Vestry, Parish of St Clement Danes, B1073, WAC.

72   The report was received in 5 November 1801; the report on the differences between the two reports received on 14 January 1802. It was discovered that although some children had been questioned, the proprietors had provided the bulk of the evidence for the first report. By contrast, the second report was based upon the 'information of the proprietors; their servants; the examination of all the apprentices at different times and ways and also from some knowledge acquired from independent witnesses'. Minutes of Vestry, Parish of St Clement Danes, B1074, WAC.

73   14 January 1802. Minutes of Vestry, Parish of St Clement Danes, B1073, WAC.

74   14 September 1802. Minutes of Vestry, Parish of St Clement Danes, B1073, WAC. Thereafter, no more went to Backbarrow; instead to the more distant Glasgow.

apprenticeship to a limited extent only after much discussion and inspection of 'the cotton mills and enquire how the children there are treated'.[75] The report produced was considered carefully. At a special meeting, it was 'unanimously ordered and agreed that such of the poor now resident in the Poor House who shall ... be deemed proper objects be (with the consent of those persons who ought legally to be consulted) bound out apprentice to the proprietors of such manufactories'.[76] A committee was established 'to consult on and direct those measures necessary to carry the intentions of this vestry into execution'.[77] Although the number of children to be apprenticed was not recorded, the effort expended in agreeing and organising this particular group was substantial, indicating a form of protection.

The relatively sparse distribution of Essex children to textile factories out of the region was more the result of plentiful alternatives within the county than unusual care on the part of the authorities. The parish of Woodford acted according to the regulations by sending children to Toplis's Cuckney factory only after consultation with and consent of the parents 'as far as could be found'.[78] Parish children were also bound nearer to home. In 1807, for example, a group of boys was bound to Morley's silk mills at Sewardstone, Waltham Cross. Despite the apparent negligence in including a 5-year-old child within the group, together with his 8-year-old brother, the parish did conduct a pre-binding inspection from which officers were 'perfectly satisfied in the general mode of treating the children and attention to their morals'.[79]

Other Essex parishes also gained a mixed record. Insufficient data exist on the protective records of Chelmsford parish[80] which is otherwise rated moderately negligent. In response to the 'several representations that the children placed apprentice, by this parish, to John Douglas ... Pendleton ... are improperly treated', one of the officers was dispatched to the mill to inspect conditions and 'take such steps as he shall think proper to obtain redress'.[81] Culling's report of his visit indicated the 'highly satisfactory' nature of conditions at Pendleton factory, and no further action was taken at that time.[82] The parish of Halstead, similarly categorised, exercised insufficient care in dispatching some of their children to an uncertain

---

75   From Melling (ed.), *The Poor*, p. 135.

76   Chatham Parish Vestry, 2 May 1792. Melling (ed.), *The Poor*, p. 135.

77   The names of a committee consisting of the constable, the two churchwardens, the four overseers and ten other people.

78   7 January 1788 and 4 February 1788, Minutes of Woodford Vestry, D/P 167/8/3, ERO.

79   3 August 1807, Minutes of Woodford Vestry, D/P 167/8/3, ERO.

80   Although it did reject the offer from a Coggershall silk manufacturer to take pauper apprentices, which might be classed as 'protective'. Select Vestry, 1819–1832, Chelmsford parish, D/P 94, ERO.

81   April 1802, Vestry minutes, Parish of Chelmsford, D/P 94/12/12, ERO. The complainants included a Mrs Smith, probably the mother of one of the apprentices. The children had been bound in 1799 according to the indentures. See also F.G. Emmison, 'Essex children deported to a Lancashire cotton mill, 1799', *The Essex Review*, 53 (1944): 77–81.

82   4 May 1802, Vestry Minutes, Parish of Chelmsford, D/P 94/12/12, ERO. See also E.J. Erith, *Essex Parish Records, 1240–1894* (Chelmsford, 1950); Chelmsford Parish D/P 94 ERO. According to Erith, 'the proportion of apprentices discharged by justices in these grounds was so small that one imagines incidents of cruelty by masters had to be very severe

fate in the unforgiving Pennine village of Marsden; and several parishes were less than protective in sending groups of children over the course of several years to the Cuckney worsted factory of Toplis and Co. The parish of Canewdon, recognising the antipathy of parents to the practice of distant factory apprenticeship used it as a threat to keep recalcitrant parishioners in line.[83]

The negligent status of Doncaster parish rests on its practice of apprenticing a large proportion of its poor children to Davison and Hawksley of Arnold, Nottingham, the resistance of family members notwithstanding.[84] The apparently high apprentice mortality rate at the Nottingham factory did not deter the officials, but may well explain the familial reluctance. These factory bindings were forced upon the children and their families on pain of losing outdoor relief. Large numbers of adults were 'struck off the weekly list' for refusal 'to permit them' to go to Davison and Hawksley. This included a grandfather, as well as mother and fathers.[85] The punishment – loss of relief – was a cruel blow for families whose stand against a factory apprenticeship pushed them closer to destitution.

Hull enters the annals of neglectful parishes largely because of its apparently poor record keeping, and its engagement in factory apprenticeship in contravention of the 1816 Act. The existing apprenticeship records indicate the dominance of charity apprenticeship, mainly for boys to local trades. Not a rich town,[86] Hull's coastal location provided career opportunities in fishing and boatbuilding. Very few cases of factory apprenticeship were recorded – the group in 1814 to Fewston being the key exception.[87] In the 1830s, a group of children were also sent to Christie's Castleton mill in Derbyshire though this information is derived from the Derbyshire records rather than those in Hull. No discussions of factory conditions exist but this does not prove that inspection and reporting did not take place.

In common with other poor London parishes, St George the Martyr, Southwark enthusiastically grasped the opportunities offered by factory apprenticeship. Large groups of children were sent to several textile factories in the Midlands and the North, and over a 30-year period these constituted 80–90 per cent of the total. Only

---

before any complaint on the part of a child was seriously considered', *Essex Parish Records*, p. 28.

83   Vestry Minutes, 1801–1816, Canewdon parish, 2/P219, Erith *Essex Parish Records*, p. 72. The meeting included a resolution to apprentice some pauper children to a Lancashire cotton manufacturer, 1802, subsequently rescinded, provided the poor 'behave orderly' and bring their families to church.

84   Overseers of the poor records, Doncaster township: Memorandum book of the overseers, 1794–95 PL/D/1, DA, pp. 69–70.

85   For example, 26 December 1794. A similar strategy was recorded in Abedare, Glamorgan in 1819. The vestry meeting in Abedare, Glamorgan, declared that those apprentices who had been indentured, and 'whose parents have refused to let them go to their different Masters, be taken as soon as possible by the respective parish officers to such places. Resolved that on no pretence whatever, relief of any description be given to the parents so refusing'. Raymond K.J. Grant, *On the Parish* (Glamorgan, 1988), p. 19, cited in Horn, 'The traffic', p. 355.

86   In 1777, the workhouse contained 200 paupers.

87   Apprenticeship Register, Sculwater Parish, PUS 411, HCA.

one document, which records a parish officer's commendation of John Watson's Preston factory, remains. The children there were found to be 'well and hearty' and upon this judgement the parish sent several groups to Watson's mill during the period from 1800 to its failure in 1807.[88]

The positive protective ratings of a number of parishes were negated by instances of negligence. The case of St Pancras parish provides a particularly good example of the difficulty of interpreting the data provided by a range of Poor Law, autobiography and business sources. The Poor Law material alone provides conflicting evidence. Outstanding as a parish whose actions, following stringent inspection, resulted in a rare case of improved factory conditions;[89] in bringing children home when irregularities in the execution of their indentures were discovered;[90] and in investigating and sacking an agent in a case of exceeding his remit;[91] and generally responsible in choosing placements and in executing indentures, by checking out employers, turning down those deemed unsuitable;[92] was also 'negligent' both in the level of compulsion used in binding children against parental wishes,[93] in returning abused factory apprentices to the scene of their suffering,[94] in delegating too much

---

88 Chris Aspin, *The Water Spinners* (Helmshore, 2003), p. 273.

89 See discussion of Lowdham mill in Chapter 12.

90 However, more than a year elapsed between discovering that a group of children had not been bound to the masters initially agreed and named on the indentures, and ascertaining their wellbeing. In February 1815, the irregularity was uncovered and although agent Thomas Gorton assured the Directors that all was well, a committee was appointed to investigate. 21 and 28 February 1815, Minutes of Directors of the Poor, Parish of St Pancras, P/PN/PO/1/10 (microfilm reference UTAH 652) CLSAC. A very detailed report was presented on 18 June 1816 and partly acted upon in October 1816. The children were collected and finally brought 'home' in December 1816. 18 June 1816, P/PN/PO/1/12 (microfilm reference UTAH 652); 8 October 1816, 3 December 1816, P/PN/PO/1/13 (microfilm reference UTAH 653).

91 St Pancras parish was partly responsible by carelessly giving Gorton more powers than were appropriate given his deficiencies and the parish officers limited knowledge of him. 1 November 1814 Minutes of Directors of the Poor, Parish of St Pancras, P/PN/PO/1/10 (microfilm reference UTAH 652) CLSAC. However, once his limited skills had been discovered, the parish not only 'did away' with Gorton's services, but also implemented more robust procedures for the future. 18 June 1816, Minutes of Directors of the Poor, Parish of St Pancras, P/PN/PO/1/12 (microfilm reference UTAH 652) CLSAC.

92 For example, when the agent of Messrs Goodall, silk crape manufacturers of Burton Latimore [*sic*] Northamptonshire, transmitted a request for a 'number of girls', he was interviewed about the nature of the work and conditions at the factory. Feary made all the right noises about attention to morals and so forth, but the Directors nevertheless 'resolved unanimously ... to decline ... to comply with the application'. 23 November 1813, Minutes of Directors of the Poor, Parish of St Pancras, P/PN/PO/1/9 (microfilm reference UTAH 651), CLSAC.

93 22 June 1805, Minutes of Directors of the Poor, Parish of St Pancras, P/PN/PO/1/2 (microfilm reference UTAH 649) CLSAC; John Waller, *The Real Oliver Twist: Robert Blincoe – A Life that Illuminates an Age* (Cambridge, 2005), p. 81.

94 5 August 1806, Minutes of Directors of the Poor, Parish of St Pancras, P/PN/PO/1/3 (microfilm reference UTAH 649), CLSAC.

of their powers to an untested agent,[95] and sending a group of children to a mill which some years earlier had neglected a number of St Pancras children.[96] When Samuel Oldknow recruited apprentices from Clerkenwell in November 1795, his London agent reported that 'some of the Children's parents, hearing of their intended destination, and fearing that it is a kind of transportation, have come, crying to beg that they may have their children out again' but their pleas were unavailing. 35 boys and 35 girls were sent to Mellor the following January.[97] The Bristol Incorporation of the Poor,[98] was also in this category being both reasonably protective on occasions and highly negligent on others. From the limited record that survives,[99] it appears that the level of factory apprenticeships from the parish was typical of populous urban areas of the time;[100] and the 'wholesale demands for pauper apprentices in the days of the industrial revolution seem always to have been received by the Bristol Guardians with careful consideration'.[101] Sadly, this cannot be confirmed but it does appear that the Corporation 'did not wash its hands of its apprentices with the signing of the indentures', and that it took action against cruel masters. Its aftercare work, however, is represented by only one example; that of the visit by the Deputy Governor, William Stock, in 1816 to 'all the factories where the Corporation had placed out apprentices during the few years preceeding';[102] and raises questions about the prior level of protection of the children.[103] His complete findings have not survived, but although conditions were 'not in every respect agreeable to the wishes of the Guardians ... Mr Stock found no case of actual ill-treatment. He was allowed to question the children by themselves'.[104] The outcome of his visit and his luke-warm report is unknown.[105] Such evidence of care should be juxtaposed with

---

95 18 June 1816, Minutes of Directors of the Poor, Parish of St Pancras, P/PN/PO/1/12 (microfilm reference UTAH 652) CLSAC.

96 Eight children were bound to Needham's Litton mill in December 1815. This enterprise had been the scene of the abuse of Blincoe and his co-apprentices in the early 1800s, when some of the same parish officials were signatories of the indentures. The 1815 binding was reported in 18 June 1816, Minutes of Directors of the Poor, Parish of St Pancras, P/PN/PO/1/12 (microfilm reference UTAH 652) CLSAC. John Brown, *A Memoir of Robert Blincoe*, (Manchester, 1832).

97 Horn, 'The traffic', p. 356; George Unwin, *Samuel Oldknow and the Arkwrights: The Industrial Revolution at Stockport and Marple* (London, 1924), p. 171.

98 Formed though 18 city parishes and the Castle precincts district by local Act of Parliament.

99 The Bristol workhouse and all its records were destroyed by enemy action in 1940. A valuable history of the Incorporation was published in 1932, using records later destroyed. This contains examples of group factory parish apprenticeships but by no means a full indication of the extent of this

100 E.E. Butcher, *Bristol Corporation of the Poor: Selected Records, 1696–1834* (Bristol, 1932), p. 22.

101 Butcher, *Bristol Corporation*, p. 22.

102 Butcher, *Bristol Corporation*, p. 23.

103 Bristol had apprenticed children since 1795, if not earlier.

104 Butcher, *Bristol Corporation*, p. 23.

105 That substantial numbers of Bristol children were still indentured to factory masters in 1816 indicates that the practice was sustained for at least as long as the average.

Bristol's failure to inform parents of factory apprentices of their whereabouts. The testimony of Sarah Carpenter whose brother was sent from Bristol workhouse to Cressbrook mill expresses the desperation felt by families kept in ignorance: 'my mother did not know where he was for two years. He was taken off in the dead of night without her knowledge, and the parish officers would never tell her where he was. It was the mother of Joseph Russell who first found out where the children were and told my mother'.[106]

As parishes varied in the extent to which they protected factory apprentices, so did magistrates who were also responsible for these children's condition.[107] Before the end of the eighteenth century, magistrates in several textile regions adopted measures to protect factory apprentices. The 1784 actions of the Manchester magistrates in precluding the employment of parish apprentices in factories that worked at night or for more than 12 hours during the day, effectively restricted the practice locally. In 1800, Wakefield sessions agreed a strategy towards the protection of the parish children within its ambit, along the lines of the Manchester agreement and using similar terminology as that contained within Lord Kenyon's ruling. It was 'strongly recommended to all other magistrates of the West Riding to adopt the same regulations', but it appears they failed to do so.[108]

The 1802 Act enhanced the powers of Justices, who became responsible for the inspection of factories using parish children; but even before this they were expected to verify the suitability of placements. Potentially, therefore, the magistrates provided a further level of protection for parish apprentices. For a number of reasons the 'protection' provided by magistrates was little more effective than that offered by the parishes. It was not uncommon for magistrates and factory owners to move in the same social circles making impartial assessment impossible.[109] Networks undoubtedly played a part in minimising the criticism of Merryweather, Needham and Toplis among many others, but were not solely responsible for the inadequate checks. Other factors included poor communication;[110] pressure of work; lack of desire; inadequate

---

106 Interview with Sarah Carpenter, published in the *Ashton Chronicle*, 23 June 1849. Although there are few other such explicit statements of parish deceit, interviews with factory apprentices frequently called for news of their families, which at the very least indicates that communication between distant family members was discouraged.

107 Steve King disputes the view that magistrates were active in Poor Law administration or enforced minimum standards. 'Poor relief and English economic development reappraised', *Economic History Review*, 50/2 (1997): 363.

108 Wakefield adjourned sessions, 22 May 1800, QD1/219, WYASW.

109 A clear example of this is the relationship between George Merryweather and local magistrate, William Vavasour. Private diaries of William Vavasour, 1798–1827, WYL639/398, WYASL. More detail is provided in Chapter 12. See also Waller, *Oliver Twist*, pp. 162–9; McKenzie, 'Cressbrook mill', pp. 61–9. Recognising this potential problem, the authors of the act explicitly stated that mill visitors appointed under the act should not be known to factory owners. *An Act for the Preservation of the Health and Morals of Apprentices and Others, Employed in Cotton and Other Mills, and Cotton and Other Factories*, 42 Geo III c 73 (1802). HMA, 1802.

110 In the West Riding of Yorkshire, for example, several factory owners professed not to be aware of the requirement to register. Returns of Cotton and other mills 1803–1806, QE

training; and insufficient power. The Act required that the two visitors appointed in each district annually visit all mills with three or more apprentices or 20 or more employees, but made no provision for ensuring that visits be made[111] or for action to be taken – other than fining transgressors – following the submission of reports.

Evidence from Quarter Session records indicates that the appointment of visitors was reasonably complete, at least in 1803, the first year of the Act's operation. However, only a minority of these visitors fulfilled their duty to inspect the relevant mills from the outset; and after 1803, in many areas, the formal practice largely disappeared.[112] In any case, the visitors' reports were usually terse and bland.[113] The superior level of activity demonstrated by Derbyshire magistrates can be explained partly by the high proportion of its mills using parish apprentices, partly because networks of relevant parties were well integrated, and partly because of close communication among magistrates, and between these and chairs of Quarter Sessions.[114] In 1840 when the practice appears to have ceased or substantially reduced in other regions, the persistent use of parish apprentices in Derbyshire mills led the then chairman of the Quarter Sessions to request an investigation into their circumstances. Millowners were to submit returns, and visitors were to report on factory conditions.[115] The inspections, like visits under the 1802 Act, found rather little to criticise, which may reflect a genuinely satisfactory level of care on the part of the factory owners, or an uncritical approach by the visitors.[116]

The formal mechanisms of protection described above were, if well-intentioned, limited in effect. Informal attempts to protect parish apprentices are, naturally, incompletely recorded, but such evidence as exists suggests some impact. Only a minority of parish factory apprentices were orphans, and family members often provided vital support. By withholding consent to factory bindings a number of parents sought to protect their offspring. Not all parishes respected parents' wishes and either sent the children regardless, or punished the family in others ways;[117] but

---

33/1, WYASW.

111 Or even that visitors be appointed.

112 It is possible that magistrates simply forgot; or that they paid regular visits to local mills on an informal basis. The diaries of William Vavasour, Otley magistrate, suggest that this is what he did in the cases of Merryweather and later Whitaker. It is highly unlikely that he was unique. William Vavasour private diaries 1798–1827, WYL639/398, WYASL.

113 T.K. Djang, *Factory Inspection in Great Britain* (London, 1942), pp. 26–30, interprets this as humorous. However the actions were interpreted, it seems that visiting and report writing were not taken seriously.

114 In principle, children could appeal to the magistrates and Quarter Sessions if they had a serious complaint about their treatment; in practice there is very little evidence that they did this.

115 John Smedley, Lea mill Ashover, Q/AG/18, DRO.

116 Castleton, Edale mill, prop., Lorenzo Christie, Q/AG 20; Darley Abbey mill, prop. William and Samuel Evans, Q/AG 23&24; Glossop, Mellor mill, prop. John Clayton and Co., Q/AG/25 and Q/AG 26; Tideswell, Cressbrook mills, prop. McConnel Brothers, Q/AG 29, DRO.

117 As did Doncaster and Hanwell. See discussion above.

evidence of successful avoidance exists.[118] Family visits to factories occasionally resulted in improved situations. Some mills provided open days for such visits, when conditions were presented at their best.[119] On other occasions family members simply arrived.[120] The highly effective visit by the mother of two children bound by St Pancras parish to Lowdham mill was exceptional. After spending two weeks observing conditions there, she reported her findings to the parish officers, who in turn inspected the mill. Clearly dismayed by conditions there, improvements were immediately required and implemented.[121]

Other factory apprentices were protected by members of the community both within the birth parish and in the factory locale. The clearest example of the former is provided by the activists in the Oxfordshire parish of Witney who by physical force, prevented the removal of six local girls to a Warwickshire cotton mill. Such action, which incurred a stiff financial penalty for the perpetrators, not only 'rescued' these children, but clearly discouraged the parish from contemplating further factory apprenticeships.[122] Cases where residents of factory neighbourhoods intervened to prevent persistent abuse include that in Marsden, where inhabitants, shocked by the scale of physical abuse meted out by the overlooker, precipitated the visit to Haigh's mill by the parish officers of St Margaret and St John in 1797.[123] However it appears that the parish did not respond with due urgency and by the time the officials had arrived, the immediate problem had been resolved.[124] Apprentices at the Nottingham factory of Davison and Hawksley, also enjoyed the 'protection' of the surrounding community. The ill-treatment of the children was the subject of much local complaint, but although several court cases were heard, none was proved.[125] In this case, the direct action of the community may not have transformed the treatment of the children but it forced the proprietors to consider their actions more carefully. Testimony of members of the local community, as impartial and informed observers, was frequently sought by parish officials when conducting a factory inspection.[126]

---

118 Neither St James, Piccadilly nor St Mary Newington, probably the most compassionate parishes in this study, compelled parents to permit children to be bound to factory apprenticeships.

119 Both Davison and Hawksley, and Cressbrook, for example, opened their factories to visitors. Statement by Robert Davison, Arnold, 18 July 1798 'To those inhabitants of Arnold who have aided or abetted the late riotous proceedings', NRO DD 568/34, NA; MacKenzie, 'Cressbrook mill', p. 68.

120 A Bristol mother arrived unannounced at Cressbrook mill, and was persuaded that conditions were fine. Interview with Sarah Carpenter, published in the *Ashton Chronicle*, 23 June 1849.

121 Waller, *The Real Oliver Twist*, pp. 124–6.

122 Witney parish apprenticeship records show no instances of factory bindings.

123 1797 Report, St Margaret and St John.

124 Nevertheless the opportunity was taken to inspect the factory.

125 Statement by Robert Davison, Arnold, 18 July 1798, DD 568/34, NA.

126 The 1801 inspection of Backbarrow by the parish officers of St Clement Danes, included such dialogue, 5 November 1801, Minutes of Vestry meetings, Parish of St Clement Danes, B1074, WAC. The enquiry of St James parish officials into the rectitude of Haywood

The role of children in their own protection was considered in Chapter 10. Potential apprentices were required to assent to their binding.[127] In the case of factory apprenticeship, consent was rarely informed. Children apprenticed in the 1780s and early 1790s rarely understood the implications of a factory binding.[128] That children were fed misinformation is suggested by the example of Robert Blincoe. He and the other St Pancras children were strongly encouraged to believe that they were to enter a better world than the one they inhabited in the workhouse. They had no reason to doubt the stories of plentiful food and comfortable surroundings and eagerly agreed to be transported; a decision they quickly came to regret.[129]

The period of parish factory apprenticeship coincided with growth in judicial concern about conditions of apprentices.[130] This apparent irony is mirrored in the simultaneous disposal and protection practised by parishes. The outcomes of the 'protective' measures identified in this chapter were variable but generally disappointing. Despite the range of activity by both parishes and magistrates, most 'protection' was a matter of report only, and resulted in only limited changes. In very few cases, children were brought home;[131] in others, changes promised by proprietors were not confirmed by subsequent inspection.[132] More examples exist of employers resisting or refusing to make changes.[133] The most successful intervention appears to have been that by St Pancras parish at Lambert's Lowdham mill. Acknowledging their shortcomings, the proprietors implemented the required changes to the immediate benefit of its apprentice children.[134]

This chapter has revisited the conventional view that, in apprenticing their poor children to factories, parishes disposed of their responsibility towards them. The evidence is difficult to interpret, but broadly indicates a balance of 'harshness and humanity'.[135] Against the plentiful indications of time and energy spent by parish officials in providing follow-up care, must be placed their seeming cruelty in separating children and parents potentially for ever. The hope that the children would

---

and Palfreyman also included conversations with local residents. 6 May 1796, Minutes of Governors and Directors of the Poor, Parish of St James Piccadilly, D1876, WAC.

127 The child's mark, or very occasionally his or her signature, was present on all the indentures examined in the course of the research for this book.

128 Subsequently, however, communication flows from former apprentices are likely to have improved the level of awareness.

129 Brown, *Memoir*, pp. 17–23.

130 Innes, 'Origins', p. 243.

131 For example, St Clement Danes children brought back from Holywell, 12 March 1792, Minutes of Churchwardens, Overseers and Assistants, Parish of St Clement Danes, B1147, WAC.

132 Merryweather's promise to provide bread, for example, never materialised.

133 John Birch, of Backbarrow, for example, responded to the 1805 report of the Brighton Directors and Guardians of the Poor, which contained mild criticism by saying that the parish 'might take them again or they would at a moments notice transfer them over to any person they might appoint'. Cited in Aspin, *Water Spinners*, p. 349.

134 Waller, *The Real Oliver Twist*, pp. 127–8; St Pancras parish meeting. Sadly the mill closed within the year; and the parish refused to 'reclaim' their children.

135 King, 'Poor relief', p. 366.

make their own way in the world, was tempered by parish support, which often persisted beyond the term of their apprenticeship. Parish officials may have been motivated by financial rather than welfare concerns, but the majority of parishes maintained at least a modicum of contact with their children. Chapter 10 showed that parish apprentices continued to perceive their birth parish as 'home'; a view shared to some extent by the parishes. However in terms of providing real protection for their apprenticed children, the evidence is quite clear. The Poor Law authorities were able to instigate marginal changes at best. While parish officers noted that 'the children were delighted to see us and looked up to us for protection';[136] many parish apprentices 'did not find parish officers effective substitutes' for parental succour.[137] The majority of parishes developed *ad hoc* procedures intended to minimise the risk of exploitation, but ultimately made little difference. Poor Law officials had neither the competence nor the power to transform their children's situation even had they desired to do so. Deeply moved by the sight of their children, parish officers from St Margaret and St John, for example, 'consulted what further could be done for the immediate relief of these poor children – their oppressed situation had made too deep an impression to be for one moment forgotten'.[138] Their wholly inadequate response was to compose a letter to the proprietor requesting changes.

This chapter and the one that follows together indicate that all parties to the apprenticeship deal, except the apprentices themselves, shared responsibility for the outcome. An element of collusion certainly existed. The children themselves looked to the parish, whom they assumed was on their side, for protection; but while they may sometimes have received sympathy, the parish was ultimately as keen as the employer for the arrangement to work.

---

136 1802 Report, St Margaret and St John.

137 Lynn Hollen Lees, *The Solidarities of Strangers: The English Poor Laws and the People, 1700–1948* (Cambridge, 1998), p. 56.

138 1802 Report, St Margaret and St John. This report compared most unfavourably with that taken five years earlier. It is quite possible that conditions had deteriorated in the meantime; it is also possible that a change of personnel resulted in a different perception of conditions.

Chapter 12

The Neglect of Parish Apprentices

This chapter explores the experience of parish apprenticeship in the early textile firms, demonstrating the range of neglectful and caring proprietors. It identifies the relationship between conditions of the parish apprentices and performance of the enterprise; and tests the proposition that the more 'protective' parishes bound children to the more caring and successful proprietors with good future prospects, while the more neglectful, less discerning parishes disadvantaged their children in the long term. It is argued here that responsibility for the 'protection' of children was held jointly by the parish Poor Law officials, including the magistrates, the factory proprietors and the mills' managements. This is consistent with, but does not justify, the response of negligent factory masters to attacks upon their own competence. When conditions at his own mills were criticised, for example, Robert Peel acknowledged only limited responsibility, identifying also the failures of Poor Law officials: 'I found it impossible to get overseers to act in the way I thought they ought to conduct themselves'.[1] Like Peel, Adam Bogle, of Bogle and Montheith, had outside interests, and visited his plant near Glasgow only occasionally, leaving day-to-day management to another;[2] and James Pattison, a Congleton silk manufacturer confessed that because of his duties as an East Indian Company Director, he did not run his factory, but simply visited from time to time.[3]

Detailed reports on all the firms in the 'sample' of this study do not survive, but sufficient information exists to assess the circumstances of children at 50 mills. For a number of reasons, parish reports alone do not provide conclusive evidence on the nature of an enterprise. Firstly, many of the visits by parish officials were, judging by the time spent at a mill, only cursory. Secondly, proprietors were given ample warning of such visits, providing the opportunity to present their concerns in the best possible light.[4] Thirdly, as discussed in Chapter 10, even if the parish children themselves were 'interviewed' apart from their employer, they were unlikely to complain too much, for fear of reprisals.[5] Although some apprentices

---

1   21 May 1816, Viscount Lascelles in the chair, SC1816, p. 136.
2   SC1816, pp. 163–77.
3   SC1816, p. 76.
4   M.H. MacKenzie, 'Cressbrook and Litton mills: a reply', *Derbyshire Archaeological Journal*, 90 (1970): 58. Evidence suggests that mill visits conducted for the House of Lords Committee of 1819 were forewarned; and testimony describes the measures taken to reduce factory temperature, improve ventilation, enhance the appearance of the children and remove those obviously of very tender years. HL 1819, vol. 108.
5   Robert Blincoe's memoirs provide ample evidence of this. John Brown, *A Memoir of Robert Blincoe* (Manchester, 1832), passim. Evidence that reprisals occurred is offered, for example, on pp. 74–5.

looked to parish officials for 'protection', they remained in awe of such powerful individuals. Children doubted that the chance of amelioration exceeded the risk of complaining.[6] Fourthly, professional or personal connections between parish officials and proprietors, precluded consistently objective judgment. Instances of plagiarism in factory reports indicate [possible] collusion.[7]

Evidence collected for this study is summarised in Table 12.1, which indicates the protective and neglectful features of the fifty enterprises; and in Table 12.2, which presents the findings of visitors appointed under the terms of the 1802 Act.[8]

Table 12.1 Conditions in Early Textile Factories

Firm/indicator	1	2	3	4	5	6	7	8	9	10	11	12	13	14
Samuel Ashton	?	?	?	A	A	A	A	A	A	A	G	A	A	A
Birch, Backbarrow	P	P	?	P	A	A	P	P	P	P	A	A	P	P
Bott, Nantwich	A	P	P	A	A	A	?	A	A	P	A	?	P	A
Bott, Tutbury	A	?	?	G	G	G	A	G	G	G	G	G	?	G
Jeremiah Bury	A	?	P	A	A	A	A	A	?	?	?	G	?	A
Catterall and Ainsworth, Backbarrow	P	P	P	P	?	P	P	?	?	A	P	A	P	P
Cark in Cartmel	?	?	?	A	G	G	A	A	A	A	?	?	?	?
Colbeck Ellis and Wilks	P	?	P	A	A	?	?	?	?	A	A	?	A
Davison and Hawksley	P	P	P	?	?	P	P	P	A	A	P	?	P	P
Dicken and Finlow	?	?	?	G	P	A	?	G	G	G	A	?	P	A
Douglas, Holywell	P	P	P	A	A	A	?	P	P	P	?	A	P	A
Douglas, Pendleton	P	P	P	A	A	P	?	P	P	P	P	?	P	A

6 Improvements were likely to be negligible. For example, parish officials from St James, Piccadilly, visited Strutt, Rickmansworth to investigate children's grumbles, but found 'there does not appear any just cause for complaint'.17 September 1790, Minutes of Governors and Directors of the Poor, Parish of St James, Piccadilly, D1873, WAC.

7 The several surviving reports on Merryweather's Burley-in-Wharfedale concern, for example, suggest lack of independence. There is considerable overlap in content and identical wording in sections of the first of these reports by William Hey in April 1802, and that produced by the officers of St Margaret and St John in September of the same year. The Leeds officers who reported in 1805 had clearly read Hey's report using some of the same, unusual words, of which 'seminary' is an example. The tenor of all the reports is similar. *The Reports of the Society for Bettering the Condition and Increasing the Comforts of the Poor*, vol. IV, 1805, Appendix No. 1, Supplement II, pp. 16–19; 1802 Report, St Margaret and St John; Leeds report submitted 28 August 1805, and discussed 4 September 1805, Leeds Workhouse Query Book 1803–1810, LO/Q 2, WYASL.

8 Inspections under the 1802 Act were formally recorded, and found, on about 25 per cent of firms in this study, which, while a small proportion, is greater than that often suggested in historical accounts. Some magistrates told parliament that they overlooked this obligation, especially after the first year or so. See, for an informed version of this, Joanna Innes, 'Origins of the Factory Acts; the Health and Morals of Apprentices Act 1802', in Norma Landau (ed.), *Law, Crime and English Society, 1660–1830* (Cambridge, 2002), p. 252.

Evans, Darley Abbey	?	?	?	A	A	A	A	A	A	A	A	?	?	?
Gorton and Thompson	?	?	?	A	A	A	?	A	A	A	A	A	A
Samuel Greg	A	?	?	G	G	G	A	A	A	A	G	G	A	A
Haigh, Marsden	P	P	P	P	P	P	P	A	P	P	P	P	P	P
Harrison and Leyland	A	?	?	?	A	A	?	A	A	A	A	A	?	A
Haywood and Palfreyman	P	?	?	A	A	P	P	A	P	A	A	A	P	?
Isaac Hodgson, Caton mill	P	?	?	?	A	A	A	?	A	P/A	?	P	?
David Holt	P	?	?	A	A	A	A	A	A	P	A	P	A
Thomas Jewsbury	?	?	?	G	G	G	A	G	G	A	G	G	A	G
Kirk mill Chipping	?	?	?	A	A	A	?	?	?	A	A	?	A	A
Messrs Lambert, Lowdham	P	P	P	P	P	P	P	P	P	P	P	P	P	?
Marshall, Hutton and Hives	P	?	?	G	G	A	A	A	A	A	A	A	?	A
George Merryweather, Burley	P	P	P	A	?	?	A*	A	G	A	A	A	P	A
George Merryweather, Manchester	P	P	P	P	P	P	P	P	P	P	P	?	?	?
Monteith, Bogle	P	?	?	A	?	A	?	?	A	A	?	?	A	A
John Morley, Chingford	?	?	?	A	P	A	A	A	P	A	A	A	P	A
Ellis Needham, Litton 1802 (only marginally better prior to that)	P	?	P	P	P	P	P	P	P	P	P	A	P	A
Newton, Cressbrook	P	P	?	A	?	A	A	A	?	A	A	?	?	A
Samuel Oldknow, Mellor	?	?	?	A	A	A	A	G	G	G	A	A	A	A
James Pattison, Macclesfield	?	?	?	A	A	A	?	?	?	?	A	?	?	P
Peel (various)	P	P	P	A	A	P	P	P	P	P	P	P	P	P
Benjamin Smart	P	G	?	A	A	P	P	?	G	G	P	?	?	A
Strutt, Rickmansworth	P	?	P	A	A	A	A	P	A	A	P	?	P	?
Toplis, Cuckney (1797)	P	P	?	?	?	G	?	G	G	G	G	?	P	P
Toplis, Cuckney (1802)	P	P	P	P	P	P	P	P	P	P	P	?	?	P	P
Turner, Godley	P	?	?	A	A	A	?	?	?	?	?	A	?	A
Wakefield and Hancox, Mansfield	A	?	?	G	G	G	G	A	A	A	A	?	?	A
Walton Twist	?	?	?	A	A	A	A	A	A	?	A	?	A	?
John Watson, Preston (1802)	P	?	P	?	A	P	A	P	A	A	P	A	P	?
Thomas Watson, Watford	P	?	P	?	?	A	A	A	A	A	A	A	P	?

Wells, Middleton, Sheffield (1797)	P	?	P	?	?	P	P	P	P	P	P	A	P	P
John Whitaker, Burley	?	?	G	A	A	G	A	A	A	G	A	A	A	A
Woolley and McQueen	P	G	?	?	A	?	?	?	?	A	A	A	?	A

Note. The assessments given above are derived from a combination of parish reports, visitors under the 1802 Act, examination of apprentices, evidence from local residents, and autobiographies. *Although hours of work were long (13+ hours), it was explicitly stated that children were free to walk around as they wished on Sundays. Also the night workers spent from 6 to 10 in the morning at leisure.

Undoubtedly such an attempt at 'measuring' neglect is deficient in a number of ways of which two are particularly serious. Firstly, the surviving information varies greatly in objectivity and accuracy. For some firms in the sample, corroborative documentation permits quite confident conclusions; but otherwise the assessment is based upon a single source and thus potentially partial.[9] The second major deficiency is the variable quantity of data. Because of insufficient evidence, strict comparisons cannot be made. Some of the firms above appear negligent because data exist to support this; other firms appear less negligent because data do not exist to confirm their negligence. Yet they may well have been. Partial though the data contained in Table 12.1 is, it enables tentative observations to be made. On the basis of the findings in Table 12.1, firms have been ranked as follows:

Key: G = good; A = adequate; P = poor; ? = no information

1. Hours of work (G = 12 or less; A = 13–14; P = 14+)
2. Night work (G = no night work; P = night work)
3. Discipline (G = no evidence of beating; P = evidence of beating)
4. Training
5. Education
6. Welfare
7. Leisure and recreation (in some cases play areas and other entertainments were provided; but if the time allowed to enjoy such facilities was inadequate, the firm is assessed as 'poor')
8. Diet
9. Clothing
10. Accommodation
11. Health/physique
12. Medical treatment
13. Complaints/runaway
14. Retention at end of apprenticeship term

---

9   This applies particularly to the information in Table 12.2. Mill reports were sometimes produced by individuals known to, but not necessarily supporters of, the proprietors.

Group		Firms
1	most negligent	Birch; Catterall and Ainsworth; Davison and Hawksley; Haigh; Lambert; Merryweather, Manchester; Needham; Peel, Toplis; Wells, Middleton
2	below average	Bott, Nantwich; Bury; Douglas, Pendleton; Douglas Holywell; Haywood and Palfreyman; Hodgson; Strutt, Rickmansworth; John Watson
3	average	Colbeck; Evans; Gorton and Thompson; Harrison and Leyland; Holt; Kirk mill; Marshall; Merryweather, Burley; Monteith Bogle; Morley; Newton; Pattison; Smart; Turner; Walton Twist; Thomas Watson; Woollen and McQueen
4	better than average	Ashton; Cark in Cartmel; Dicken and Finlow; Greg; Oldknow; Wakefield and Hancox; Whitaker
5	least negligent	Jewsbury; Bott, Tutbury

This study does not aim to judge factories except in terms of contemporary observations. The distribution presented above indicates that parish children were, according to assessment at the time, rather more likely to have been bound to a neglectful or erratic master than to have been well supported. Nevertheless several firms appear to have fulfilled the requirements of responsible apprenticing. Most of these enjoyed long-term success. Among these are the well-rehearsed examples of Samuel Greg,[10] Samuel Ashton and Samuel Oldknow, but also the lesser known Wakefield and Hancox, Dicken and Finlow and John Whitaker. John Bott's Tutbury mill is also placed in this category. Of particular merit is the firm of Thomas Jewsbury, which was perceived by the Birmingham Guardians to provide a consistently first-rate apprenticeship experience over the period of some years. Common to them all was a healthy trading performance, attention to the training, education and welfare of their apprentices; and a striking tendency to retain their apprentices on the expiration of their term. Several – namely Oldknow, Dicken and Finlow, Whitaker, Jewsbury, and Greg – also revealed a marked or a marginal preference for girl apprentices.[11]

---

10 Because Greg's mill has been extensively researched, relatively little will be said here. It should be noted, and this is not always recognised, that the firm's medical records indicate thorough attention to the apprentices well being. Detailed doctor's notes, not all of them legible, describe treatments and follow-up inspections from which the range of ailments can be deduced. Greg papers, 'Record of medical treatment of apprentices 1802–1845', C5/4/2/1–2, MCA.

11 See Table 8.1, bearing in mind that the distribution of apprentices by gender was often a compromise so the real preference of the employer is not always fully revealed in the figures.

Table 12.2 Reports on Firms Visited Under the 1802 Act

Firm/clause	White-wash	Ventilation	No night work	Max 12-hour day	Boys and girls sleep separately	No more than two in a bed	Attend church on Sunday	Religious teaching	Three Rs every day	New clothes every year	Act displayed
Ainsworth Catterall Backbarrow	✓	✓	?	?	✓	✓	✓	?	?	✓	?
Samuel Ashton, Middleton	✓	✓	✓	?	✓	✓	✓	✓	✓	✓	✓
Colbeck, Ellis, Fewston	✓	✓	✓	?	✓	✓	✓	✓	✓	✓	✓
Evans, Darley Abbey+	✓	✓	?	?	?	?	?	?	?	?	?
Fletcher and Smethurst	✓	✓	✓	✓	✓	✓	✓	✓	✗	✓	✓
Samuel Greg, Styal	✓	✓	?	?	✓	✓	✓	✓	✓	✓	✓
Harrison and Leyland	✓	✓	✓	?	✓	✓	✓	✓	✓	✓	✗
David Holt, Manchester*	✓	✓	✓	✗	?	?	✓	✓	✓	?	?
Jewsbury	✓	✓	✓	?	?	✗	✓	✓	✓	?	?
Kirk mill, Chipping*	?	?	?	?	✓	✓	✓	✓	?	?	?
George Merryweather Manchester	✗	✗	?	✗	?	✗	?	?	?	✗	?

Firm								
Ellis Needham, Litton	?	✗	✗	✓	?	✗	✗	?
Newton Cressbrook	?	?	?	✓	✓	✓	?	?
Samuel Oldknow, Mellor	✓	✓	✓	✓	✓	✓	✓	✓
Benjamin Smart, Emscote	✗	✗	✗	Girls only	✓	✓	✓	?
Walton Twist company	✓	✓	?	✓	✓	✓	✓	✓
John Watson, Preston	✓	✓	✗	✓	✓	✓	✓	✓
Wells, Middleton, Sheffield	✓	✓	✓	✓	✓	✓	✓	✓
Woolley and McQueen	✓	✓	✓	✓	✓	✓	✓	✓

Note. ? = no evidence; * evidence from 1824 Factory inspectors report; + 1833 Commission. Where report states that the 1802 Act is 'strictly complied with', it is assumed that all categories are positive. However, it is unlikely that any mill restricted their hours of work to 12; and no visitors report referred to this specifically. It is striking how few firms failed to comply with the terms of the act. Some of these were reported poorly elsewhere. A comparison of Tables 1 and 2 suggests that even where inspection was carried out under the act, it was unlikely to identify poor performers let alone instigate improvement.

The Birmingham Guardians visited Jewsbury's enterprise several times during the 20 years of its existence, on each occasion reporting favourably on the condition of the children, and their prospects.[12] The Birmingham children were found to be 'all in good health and satisfied with their situations and employment' and 'throughout the whole of the works of Messrs Jewsbury and Co. we found nothing that could attach blame to ... The overlookers ... appeared to be men of feeling and humanity and seemed much interested in the children's welfare ...'.[13] Two subsequent visits were recorded of which no written report has survived.[14] A fourth visit by the Birmingham Poor Law officials conducted in the autumn of 1813 sustained the favourable image. The children were well, the beds and apparel clean and the food plentiful and wholesome; attention was paid to their religious upbringing and education and 'that no improper intercourse should take place'. The work apparently, was 'by no means very labourious' and 'sufficient time for recreation' was allowed. 'Mr Jewsbury ... gentleman ... [of] liberal and humane disposition ... we are of the opinion that the situation and employment of these works for poor girls (both for their health and moral as well as being able to get their living) are infinitely superior to anything of the kind we have seen and strongly recommend them'.[15]

John Bott's Tutbury mill, which depended largely on parish apprentices from the region, was also viewed favourably by at least one providing parish and a clergyman *in situ*. Birmingham had chosen Bott's enterprise, and others in the region, as suitable destinations for its poor children because it 'trained' children in both spinning and weaving operations. In 1808, Birmingham visitors found a large number of children at the mill

> 21 of which from Birmingham ... all clean and healthy, examined the provisions which we found excellent ... sleeping rooms ... clean and airy and convenient ... was more highly gratified with the account we received of the pains taken in their instruction than at any other place. The worthy clergyman of the place, Mr Hutchinson continues to pay the most zealous attention to the improvement of these poor children. They are all visited and instructed by several respectable ladies of the place ... we took great pains to learn what became of young persons after they were out of their time ... at every place they were glad to keep such in their service as were of good character ... we had the pleasure of seeing many who had been employed in the spinning mills for several years beyond the term of their apprenticeship.[16]

---

12 The positive findings were confirmed by Theodore Price, Warwickshire magistrate in his evidence to the 1816 Select Committee. He compared Jewsbury's concern very favourably with Smart's Emscote mills. SC1816, p. 121.

13 Reports from Birmingham Guardians, discussed at meeting of 12 July 1808, Minutes of Birmingham Board of Guardians, GP/B/2/1/2, BCA.

14 16 October 1810 and 2 April 1811, Minutes of Birmingham Board of Guardians, GP/B/2/1/2, BCA.

15 The inspections were made on 14 and 15 September 1813, and discussed by the Birmingham Guardians on 12 October 1813, when the visitors were thanked for 'their great attention to the welfare of the children'.

16 Birmingham Guardians, Thursday 30 June 1808, Minutes of Birmingham Board of Guardians, GP/B/2/1/2, BCA.

The mill was visited again in 1810, when the Guardians noted the Vicar's 'very great attention and religious instruction of the children';[17] and finally in 1811.[18] The Vicar of Tutbury, with local churchwardens and magistrates, signed Bott's 1816 eulogy of his own factory in which he refers to its contribution to the apprentices' well being and the character of Tutbury.[19]

An enterprise that drew upon child labour of both a parish apprentice and 'free' type, Wakefield and Hancox was quite well regarded. The Birmingham Guardians visited a parish apprentice reassigned there on the failure of Toplis. Commenting only briefly on general conditions, the Guardians noted that she was 'a very promising and intelligent girl who does great credit to those who instruct at this place'.[20] Evidence to the Select Committee portrayed the firm in glowing terms;[21] and Samuel Fox in evidence to the House of Lords, spoke positively about the experience of his nine-year-old son who worked at Wakefield's.[22] Upon Merryweather's departure in 1808, John Whitaker took charge of the Burley-in-Wharfedale mill and continued to take apprentices from a range of parishes, including St Mary Newington, which, in 1813, discussed Whitaker's suitability as an employer, using a positive report from Lambeth parish as a guide.[23] When the 22 children sent at this time were visited in 1817, they were 'found all in good health and expressing themselves fully satisfied with their treatment ... that on the day he was there 8 young women came out of their time all of whom wishing to remain in Jn Whitaker, he had retained them all in the work of the factory'.[24]

The contrast between the firms discussed above and those in the 'most negligent' category is palpable. At their worst, the enterprises of Needham, Peel, Merryweather at Manchester and Toplis created grim conditions for the parish apprentices on whom their businesses depended. While the least negligent firms were consistent in both business performance and treatment of apprentices, the enterprises of the worst offenders were unstable, providing an inconsistent apprenticeship experience. Common elements included: dependence on parish apprentices but low retention; erratic performance preceding bankruptcy; cost containment strategies based on reduced diet and education; and intensification of labour. Exploitation and abuse mounted in line with business difficulties.

---

17 Birmingham Guardians, 16 October 1810. Minutes of Birmingham Board of Guardians, GP/B/2/1/2, BCA.
18 2 April 1811 Minutes of Birmingham Board of Guardians, GP/B/2/1/2, BCA.
19 SC1816, pp. 83–5.
20 Report of visit to factories, June 1808, Minutes of Birmingham Board of Guardians, GP/B/2/1/2, BCA.
21 SC1816, p. 220.
22 HL 1818, pp, 178–80.
23 Apprenticeship Register 1802–1833, parish of St Mary Newington, 891, SLHL; 3 December 1813, Minutes of St Mary Newington Workhouse Committee, 931, SLHL. The copy of the Lambeth report does not survive, but that it existed is significant, as there is no indication in the Lambeth parish records that officials visited and reported on factories in this way.
24 24 July 1817, Minutes of St Mary Newington Workhouse Committee, 932, SLHL.

Not all of the most negligent firms had always been so. Toplis's Cuckney enterprise, for example, initially demonstrated the characteristics of an 'average' firm, receiving considerable praise from parish visitors. The proprietors maintained unusually careful records of its large parish apprentice labour force, which suggests a well-regulated enterprise.[25] A positive description of early conditions at Cuckney was published by Throsby in 1790,[26] followed two years later by a report from the Secretary of the Foundling Hospital, who inspected the factory prior to sending children there, and found that 'the young people ... seem to be very well provided for in every respect ... they work 12 hours only in the 24 hours and the rest is taken up with their meals recreation etc'.[27] A visitor in 1794 observed that the children 'are kept in excellent order. They live in cottages built for the purpose, under the care of superintendants ... an apothecary attends them at stated times to preserve health. They are trained to the duties of religion and are fed plentifully'.[28] Parish visitors in 1797 praised the circumstances effusively. 'The first appearance [of the children] gave us great pleasure.... the glow of health that seemed to animate their features, and the plumpness of their figures...They were all, notwithstanding their employment, *very clean*, the girls in particular, remarkably so, and they seemed..very orderly and well behaved'. Also 'every part was distinguished by the same attention to cleanliness'. The stairs, for example, were 'white as if just scoured'. Their food was also of excellent quality. Overall the factory was described as 'a happy asylum for those children who have either been abandoned by, or have dissolute parents ... and equal care is taken of their health, their education and their morals'.[29]

Five years later, the firm, facing trading difficulties, had become negligent. Visitors from the same parish interviewed the children individually, listened to their complaints about beating, poor diet and long hours, and noted: 'the children were delighted to see us and looked up to us for protection, from such a state of slavery and oppression as we had no expection of meeting with .... and excited our sympathy to a very high degree'.[30] Such contrasting reports may be the result of change in authorship but there is little doubt that conditions at Cuckney had deteriorated and continued to do so. Toplis, offended by the list of required changes, responded defensively and in detail. His reply began,

We have conceived it a duty we owe to ourselves to thoroughly investigate the two principal complaints you made: namely that of the children being compelled to work for

---

25 Toplis register is a unique example and demonstrates the quality of his record keeping. List of children put apprentice to William Toplis DD 895/1, NA.

26 J. Throsby (ed.), *Thoroton's History of Nottinghamshire* (London, 1797) vol. III, p. 376. S.D. Chapman, *The Early Factory Masters: The Transition to the Factory System in the Midlands Textile Industry* (Newton Abbot, 1967), p. 174. Much of the favourable comment about Toplis seems to have emanated from an uncritical reading of Throsby.

27 Letter from Secretary of Foundling Hospital to Treasurer, June 1792], DD 212/1/5–6, NA.

28 Chapman, *Early Factory Masters*, p. 171. *Nottingham Journal,* 31 August 1793.

29 1797 Report, St Margaret and St John.

30 1802 Report, St Margaret and St John.

so many hours and the short allowance of provisions. We have devoted the whole of this week to the investigation

and so it continued for several pages.[31] Toplis was unable to save his business, which failed in 1805.[32]

The businesses of George Merryweather also illustrate the impact of financial difficulties on the treatment of parish apprentices. Favourable reports on the well-visited Burley-in-Wharfedale mill,[33] partly relied on the strength of Merryweather's social network. In 1802, London parish visitors 'were perfectly satisfied with the disposition of Messrs Whitaker and Merryweather to make the Children comfortable and happy' and pleased to note that the apprentices would, 'when out of their time … obtain a sufficient for the future support'.[34] In 1805, Leeds Poor Law officers inspected 'the dining room, kitchen, workshops etc all of which we approved,' and both the Leeds and London boys and girls appeared content.[35] The parish of St George, Hanover Square, was also impressed, and in 1807, after rejecting several other requests for apprentices, concluded 'but that if Mr Merryweather of Otley near Leeds applies for more apprentices he may have them'.[36] Neither apprentices' complaints about food, which were not remedied,[37] nor the mill's practice of nightworking, outlawed by the 1802 Act, appear to have interfered with the parishes' positive perception of the enterprise. William Hey's opinion that night working did not damage the health of apprentices, accepted by at least two parishes, was

---

31 11 September 1802, Toplis reply, E3371/17, WAC.

32 To his credit, Toplis not only found all the children alternative placements, but kept a careful record of their destinations. This was by no means common practice. In Toplis's case, not all the children were well suited to their next placement, and later absconded, or, as in the case of one Birmingham girl, was moved from Toplis to Hancock and Wakefield, and then went on to Davison and Hawksley. 'List of children put apprentice to William Toplis', DD 895/1, NA.

33 Founded in 1792, when a number of children from Leeds parish were placed there, in line with a common practice of initially taking children from the locality. Seventy-two children were sent in 1797 from the parish of St Margaret and St John, the first large group to arrive there. Many of the apprentices remained at the mill at the end of their terms. In 1833, a number of workers had descended from the first generation of parish apprentices. Evidence to Royal Commission, 1833.

34 1802 Report, St Margaret and St John.

35 28 August 1805. It was 'ordered that the following persons of the committee viz Mr Wells, Mr Parkinson, Mr Cassons, Mr Hebden, Mr Peacock and Mr Pickering do go to Otley in order to inspect into the situations of the children put out apprentices to Mr Merryweather and report thereon to the Board'. Report discussed 4 September 1805, Leeds Workhouse Query Book 1803–1810, LO/Q 2, WYASL.

36 Meeting of 24 February 1807, Governors and Directors of the Poor, Parish of St George, Hanover Square, C925, WAC. St George was a parish with high standards to the extent that Dorothy George was surprised to find it among the London parishes sending apprentices to cotton mills. *London Life in the Eighteenth Century* (London, 1925), p. 249–56.

37 1802 Report, St Margaret and St John; Leeds report discussed 4 September 1805, Leeds Workhouse Query Book 1803–1810, LO/Q 2 WYASL.

condemned by the Bettering Society for endangering the health of parish children.[38] Another 'friend', local magistrate and diarist William Vavasour, provided support when Merryweather faced abuse charges, both in Burley[39] and later in connection with his Manchester enterprise.[40]

Relocation to Manchester in 1810, taking with him all his parish apprentices,[41] witnessed a shift in Merryweather's status to negligent. Visitors to Merryweather's Manchester weaving concern found grim conditions: the sleeping apartments were overcrowded and generally there was 'a great want of ventilation in this factory'. The diet was inadequate; 'the privies were too offensive to be approached by us; some of the apprentices complained of being overworked'.[42] Horrible though this description is, it does not mention physical abuse; yet soon knowledge of such activity reached the public domain.[43] Economic difficulties, which probably lay at the root of Merryweather's decision to leave the West Riding, appear to have worsened in Manchester, resulting in abuse and exploitation of the parish apprentices before inevitable bankruptcy.

Correspondence between Davison and Hawksley, partners in the Arnold mill, and Boulton and Watt, reveal the proprietors' technical competence,[44] while other evidence indicates a less careful attention to the parish apprentices on which the business depended.[45] Although the proprietors provided good apprentice accommodation and presented themselves as benevolent,[46] complaints from members of the local community about their abusive behaviour suggested otherwise. The owners offered to open their mill for the inspection of 'food, raiment, lodging, morals [and] medicines

---

38   *The Reports of the Society for Bettering the Condition and Increasing the Comforts of the Poor*, vol. IV 1805, Appendix no. 1, p. 3, 1802 Report, St Margaret and St John; Leeds report discussed 4 September 1805, Leeds Workhouse Query Book 1803–1810, LO/Q 2 WYASL.

39   27 May 1806, 'Revd Wm Bailey called to ask me to attend with him and visit the cotton mills at Otley'; 29 May 1806, 'Went to Otley and with Mr Bailey visited the cotton mills at Otley – was very much pleased with Mr Merryweather's factory; 13 October 1808, 'Went to Otley and looked over the cotton factory of Mr Merryweather with Rev. Mr Bailey'. Private diaries of William Vavasour, 1798–1827, WYL639/398, WYASL. Limited corporal punishment was referred to in parish reports, but not cited as a problem.

40   20 April 1807 and 24 April 1807; entertained Merryweather to breakfast and visited his factory. Private diaries of William Vavasour, 1798–1827. WYL639/398, WYASL.

41   Who were forced to walk the entire distance over the unforgiving Pennine terrain.

42   HL 1819, vol. 108.

43   The circumstances of Merryweather's prosecution for abuse were described in Testimony of David Evans, Barrister and Magistrate in Manchester to SC1816, p. 321.

44   DD 452/6/1–13, NA.

45   Davison and Hawksley also took children reassigned from Toplis and from Hancox and Wakefield. List of children put apprentice to William Toplis DD 895/1, NA.

46   Sale of the Arnold mills, 14 May 1810, DD 568/5, NA; Chapman, *Early Factory Masters*, pp. 180–82. Chapman, who presents the positive image of Davison and Hawksley also refers to their kindness to the local community, including the donation of a piece of land for the purpose of building a corn mill. Chapman believes that because the mill managers were Methodist preachers, it is 'unlikely that [they] would have been callous or indifferent to the welfare of the Arnold millworkers'.

for the sick', to counter local opinion that the mill's regime was cruel. A statement issued by Davison following a protest meeting of inhabitants reveals a defensive position not unusual among the 'neglectful'.[47] Parish reports indicate deficiencies in the parish apprentices' care. In 1807, the quality and quantity of food was shown to be inadequate to the children's needs; and hours of work to be excessive.[48] By 1808, when Birmingham Guardians, found 'about 300 children in a most dirty condition' the circumstances of apprentices appear to have deteriorated in line with business pressures.[49]

The impact of the declining fortunes of John Birch's Backbarrow concern on its parish apprentices was highlighted by officers of St Clement Danes parish in an attempt to secure improvements. The first visitor's report on the mill, in 1797, commented favourably on all aspects of the children's experience.[50] The second full report four years later indicated significant deterioration in the apprentices' circumstances. Education had ceased, working hours had risen[51] and the diet deficient in protein. Water porridge for breakfast, for example, replaced bread and milk. A report in 1805 from the Brighton Poor Law officials raised concerns about the quality of the bread and the level of education. Responding to these complaints, as they had to St Clement Danes some years earlier, the proprietors 'concluded that the parish might if they were not perfectly satisfied with their treatment of the children, take them again or they would at a moments notice transfer them over to any person they might appoint'.[52] When the business ceased trading in 1807, the proprietors neglected to ensure continuity of care for its parish apprentices.[53]

Conditions at Ellis Needham's Litton mills, described by Robert Blincoe, through the pen of John Brown, and fictionalised by Frances Trollope,[54] have been

---

47 Statement by Robert Davison, Arnold, 18 July 1798, DD 568/34, NA.

48 Report by Messrs Rolls and Whitfield of an enquiry at Arnold mill on 20 June 1807, recorded with minutes of the meeting of the overseers of the poor of 23 June 1807. Poor Relief Book 1806–1810, Parish of St Luke, Chelsea, P74/LUK/019 [microfiche no. X026/008], LMA.

49 Visit on 29 June 1808, recorded in the Minutes of the Birmingham Board of Guardians GP/B/2/1/2, BCA.

50 2 November 1797, report received by the Churchwardens, Overseers and Assistant, Parish of St Clement Danes, B1147, WAC.

51 5 November 1801, Minutes of Churchwardens, Overseers and Assistant, Parish of St Clement Danes, B1148, WAC.

52 Report of the Brighton Directors and Guardians of the Poor 'to visit the children lately sent to the cotton manufactory at Backbarrow' June 1805, quoted in Chris Aspin, *The Water Spinners* (Helmshore, 2003), p. 349.

53 Although most were later taken back by the new owners, it was alleged that they were abandoned by Birch. John Moss, SC1816, p. 183. This seems to be hearsay, and Moss himself appears to have an axe to grind.

54 In her 387-page novel, the appalling Deep Valley mill run by Elgood Sharpton is a thinly disguised version of Needham's enterprise, and draws closely on Robert Blincoe's account. Frances Trollope, *The Life and Adventures of Michael Armstrong: The Factory Boy* (London, 1840), pp. 118–22 and 185–7. The fever that killed numbers of children at the factory is described on pages 217–19.

vigorously debated by historians.[55] Several groups of apprentices had reached Litton mill from London parishes prior to Blincoe's arrival in 1803. When visited by parish officers in 1796, the apprentices seemed 'tolerably content' and were quite well-fed and cared for.[56] Deteriorating conditions at the mill described by Blincoe were confirmed in 1807 by visitors appointed under the 1802 Act. The 'apprentices work successively in the night, though this is expressly prohibited by the act. It is by no means certain to what hours they are confined. They are not instructed during the working hours ... though there are separate apartments for males and females in the lodging house, the rooms appear crowded'.[57] It is not clear what action, if any was taken in the light of such damning findings, there being no formal mechanism for feedback, but a further report four years later suggests that little, except the visitor's interpretation, had changed. Although 'I found the house in which the apprentices board or lodge, very clean', the children's complaints of poor diet and long hours, were upon investigation born out.[58] A modicum of teaching had been added since the 1807 report, but the food, consisting mainly of water porridge and treacle was clearly insufficient to sustain life properly, particularly in view of the extraordinary length of the working day.[59] No improvements were instigated as a result of the reports; indeed the firm's deteriorating trading conditions was matched by the apprentices'

---

55 The debate among historians about conditions at Litton is characterised by the position of M.H. McKenzie, who concludes that Needham was a poor employer, and S.D. Chapman who argues that Needham was not an unduly cruel master in the light of conditions of the day, but recognises that as a businessman he may have had limitations and operated in difficult circumstances. M.H. MacKenzie, 'Cressbrook and Litton mills, 1779–1835. Part 1', *Derbyshire Archaeological Journal*, 88 (1968): 1–25; S.D. Chapman, 'Cressbrook and Litton mills: an alternative view', *Derbyshire Archaeological Journal*, 89 (1969); MacKenzie, 'Cressbrook and Litton mills: a reply', pp. 56–9. In assessing the value of Robert Blincoe's testimony, on which much of the debate rests, Musson contributes to this debate. He is critical of Chapman's position. A.E. Musson, 'Robert Blincoe and the early factory system', in A.E. Musson, *Trade Union and Social History* (London, 1974), pp. 195–206. See also John Rule, *The Labouring Classes in Early Industrial England 1750–1850* (London, 1986), pp. 147–9 for a discussion of the debate; Trollope, *Michael Armstrong*; and W.H. Chaloner, 'Mrs Trollope and the early factory system', *Victorian Studies*, 4/2 (1960): 159–66. My own findings show that while Blincoe exaggerated the number of children apprenticed with him, his description of meeting, by chance, St Pancras parish officers at Oldknow's Mellor factory, which seemed far-fetched, was according to the evidence, entirely plausible. See, for example, 5 April 1814, Minutes of Directors of the Poor, Parish of St Pancras, P/PN/PO/9 (microfilm reference UTAH 651), CLSAC.

56 6 May 1796, Minutes of Governors and Directors of the Poor, Parish of St James, Piccadilly, D1876, WAC.

57 The report of 1807 was recorded in HL1819, vol. 108, C: County of Derby; Scarsdale G: 1807.

58 Records of Quarter Sessions, QQ/AG/1–36, DRO, focuses on Cotton Mill Apprentices. 18 April 1811 'Reports of cotton mills and factories inspected from the last midsummer sessions to the present' Marmaduke Middleton Middleton. Brief notes on condition of the mills, Q/AG/7, DRO.

59 According to Chapman, the water wheel broke in 1811, which halted production for a month. *Early Factory Masters*, p. 203.

experience. The grim conditions persisted to the end, even if the reports failed to capture fully the level of abuse and exploitation.[60]

Other firms in this category were negligent from the outset. These included several of Robert Peel's mills in the Midlands and Lancashire,[61] one of them described in a 1784 report that recommended improvements to personal cleanliness, hours of work, and ventilation.[62] Peel acknowledged some deficiencies but argued that strict attention was paid to the children's health, cleanliness and clothing in accordance with their indentures. He educated them and enabled them to make their living.[63] Significantly, he refused to end the heavily criticised night working.[64] Further evidence on Peel's Lancashire factories was provided by the Birmingham Guardians whose initial visit to its apprentices February 1796, returned a 'satisfactory account'.[65] Within two months, a damning account of 'the usage of the poor children apprenticed from this parish to Peel and Co', was heard by officials.[66] The second visit, which quickly followed, returned with detailed and unequivocally unfavourable findings.[67] Among the more serious of the discoveries were the hours of work;[68] a bland, starchy and monotonous diet, overcrowded and dirty sleeping accommodation; complaints of brutality; inadequate clothing, and overt expressions of misery and homesickness. At Radcliffe Bridge, the children were given no stockings or shoes because the Guardians were told, 'if they gave them shoes they would run away'.[69] No further Birmingham children were placed with Peel, either in Lancashire or Staffordshire.[70]

Parish apprentices at Haigh's Marsden enterprise suffered persistent neglect and abuse. Local complaints of cruelty at the mill generated the first parish inspection in 1797,[71] which revealed absentee proprietors and a poorly supervised enterprise.

---

60 See MacKenzie, 'Cressbrook and Litton mills', pp. 1–25; Chapman, 'Cressbrook and Litton mills: an alternative view'; MacKenzie, 'Cressbrook and Litton mills: a reply', pp. 56–9.

61 21 May 1816, Viscount Lascelles in the chair, SC1816, p. 132; Frances Collier, *The Family Economy of the Working Classes in the Cotton Industry 1784–1833* (Manchester, 1964), pp. 29–31.

62 The outbreak of fever at the Radcliffe mill factory in Bury led to this medical report. See Anon, 'The putrid fever at Robert Peel's Radcliff Mill', *Notes and Queries*, 203 (1958): 28. As Aspin points out, although the doctors criticised the long hours of work, they made no specific reference to night working. *Water Spinners*, p. 196. Aikin writes favourably about Radcliffe mill in its earlier, calico printing guise. J. Aiken, *A description of the country from thirty to forty miles around Manchester* (London, 1795), p. 268.

63 'The putrid fever', p. 34.

64 Aspin, *Water Spinners*, p. 27.

65 30 March 1796, Minutes of Birmingham Board of Guardians, GP/B/2/1/1, BCA.

66 May 1796, Minutes of Birmingham Board of Guardians, GP/B/2/1/1, BCA.

67 28 June 1796, Minutes of Birmingham Board of Guardians, GP/B/2/1/1, BCA.

68 Fifteen per day with some paid overtime.

69 28 June 1796, Minutes of Birmingham Board of Guardians, GP/B/2/1/1, BCA.

70 28 June 1796, Minutes of Birmingham Board of Guardians, GP/B/2/1/1, BCA.

71 1797 Report, St Margaret and St John; Moser Joseph, 'Report of the situation of the children apprenticed by the churchwardens, overseers and governors of the poor of the United parishes of St Margaret and St John in the City of Westminster to the cotton manufactory of Messrs H— at M— and Messrs J and T at Cuckney mills, addressed to the workhouse Board

Although the children were found to be fit and healthy, and the level of punishment apparently reduced, the lack of education caused concern. The local clergyman, held responsible for this deficiency, promised to rectify the situation.[72] A follow-up visit, conducted in 1802, indicated the persistence of poor conditions. After speaking to a small group of surviving children, the parish officials 'were sufficiently satisfied by the account ... received, that the children at this factory had been extremely ill treated'.[73] The enterprise folded in 1805, when a number of the remaining apprentices from all parishes were reassigned to the more salubrious environment of Merryweather's Burley factory, and Messrs Turner in Godley.

Despite the cruel regime imposed by Wells and Middleton at the only Sheffield cotton mill, their proper and punctual response to the requirements of the 1802 Act, ironically singled them out as exemplary. The bleakness of life at their factory, the starchy, monotonous and insufficient diet, inadequate clothing, sickness and frequent abuse so clearly expressed by former apprentice Harriet Russell, was entirely missing from the report of the visitors appointed under the Act. According to Russell, the children 'are strapped for not working ... Some were beat much'; and 'the flue of the cotton made them sick'.[74] The terse visitors' report of November 1803, by contrast 'found the children all well except three – the rooms airy and clean – the provisions all good ... their morals well attended to'.[75] As suggested elsewhere, compliance with the terms of the 1802 Act, as ascertained by appointed visitors, was no guarantee of child protection.

Alone among the 'most negligent' firms to effect improvement in response to parish criticism, was Lambert's Lowdham mill. After a visit that lasted several days, dissatisfied officers of St Pancras demanded changes.[76] Despite financial pressures, which had accounted for the long hours of labour and dietary restrictions, the Lamberts did attempt to redeem themselves, and in the weeks after the parish officials' visit the mill was transformed. A new apprentice house was built; more meat was added to the diet; hours of work were reduced; and the brutal governor discharged.[77] Expenditure on such alterations may have improved the experience of the apprentices but did little to help the business, which closed less than a year later.[78]

Newton's Cressbrook mill also improved, but without parish stimulus, and achieved long-term success. In the early years of the nineteenth century, when the

---

of the said parishes, April 10 1797', *European Magazine and London Review*, 34 (September 1798): 197–201.

72 Ibid p. 199.

73 1802 Report, St Margaret and St John.

74 12 September 1797, special meeting called to consider the examination of Harriet Russell. Minutes of Vestry, parish of St Clement Danes, B1073, WAC.

75 Report delivered 29 November 1803, Returns of Cotton and other mills 1803–1806, QE 33/1, WYASW.

76 They also asked local magistrates to check the implementation of these improvements. John Waller, *The Real Oliver Twist: Robert Blincoe – A Life that Illuminates an Age* (Cambridge, 2005), pp. 124–6; John Brown, *A Memoir of Robert Blincoe* (Manchester 1832), pp. 26, and 38–9.

77 Brown, *Memoir*, p. 39.

78 Waller, *The Real Oliver Twist*, p. 128.

business struggled,[79] apprentices described the poor diet and instances of physical and sexual abuse.[80] Even the reports of the magistrates, typically generous, were cool in this instance. The visitors appointed under the terms of the 1802 Act recorded, in 1807, that 'this is a small concern, the mill is not in so exact a state as might be wished particularly as to the cleanliness of the floors'.[81] The 1811 report recorded improved conditions for the apprentices and thereafter the business expanded.[82] Reports in the early 1830s from 'inspectors from the quarter sessions, from London workhouses and from factory Enquiries Commission ... all wrote warmly about some aspect of the enterprise or of Newton'.[83] The apprentices were apparently happy with their situation, their health was good, and they had plenty of leisure time. Relatives were allowed to visit the apprentices and hospitality was provided for them. But the hours of work were long and night work was practised.[84] Cressbrook, a successful firm enjoying rare longevity, appeared to have offered apprentice children both a reasonable experience during their term[85] and reasonable prospects of long-term employment with the firm.

Among the one-third of firms categorised as 'average' were those who returned a mediocre performance in most areas, as well as those who were seen to demonstrate both concern and neglect. Examples include Isaac Hodgson's Caton mill, whose long-term success was based on continued use of parish apprentices some of whom recalled their experience with pleasure[86] while others, tormented by the level of overwork, ran away.[87] Local dignitaries were satisfied with the character of Hodgson and the healthy situation in which the apprentices were kept.[88] David Holt's

---

79 MacKenzie, 'Cressbrook and Litton mills', pp. 8–14. During the middle years of the Napoleonic Wars, many textile enterprises felt under pressure.

80 See Chapter 7 for further detail on this.

81 HL 1819, vol. 108, Derbyshire, G 1807, Cressbrook. The cool report was particularly surprising in view of the Newton's strong local connections, as indicated in M.H. MacKenzie, 'Cressbrook mill, 1810–35', *Derbyshire Archaeological Journal*, 90 (1970): 61–9.

82 MacKenzie, 'Cressbrook mill', p. 63.

83 MacKenzie, 'Cressbrook mill', p. 68.

84 Again arguing that the law did not apply in this case. MacKenzie, 'Cressbrook mill', p. 69; Q/AG29 DRO. The 46 who had been bound between 1829 and 1834 with William Newton were transferred to the McConnell brothers by the commissioners for managing the affairs of the Royal Military Asylum, Southampton.

85 MacKenzie shows, on the basis of correspondence that, at least from 1814 to 1826, relationships between employers and apprentices were good. 'Cressbrook mill', p. 62.

86 One former apprentice, Kitty Seward, brought from the Liverpool workhouse in 1798, recalls the apprentice house (for 100 children) as 'a heaven on earth, where we were brought up in ignorance of evil, and where Mr Norton, the manager was a father to all'. Cited in Aspin, *Water Spinners*, p. 334; original source not given.

87 On 30 October 1792, for example, an advertisement appeared in the *Manchester Mercury* offered a reward for 10 apprentices originally from the Liverpool workhouse who had runaway. Reproduced in Aspin, *Water Spinners*, p. 333. It is assumed that this is just one of many instances of absconding children.

88 Prior to binding children to Hodgson's mill in 1814, St Pancras Poor Law officers received a testimonial from Minister of Caton and a local surgeon, asserting that the children were very healthy 'and that great attention was paid to their health, morals and instruction'. 16

Manchester cotton spinning firm received mixed reports. Prior to binding its own children, officers of the parish of St James, Piccadilly found that 'the children already apprenticed from other parishes were treated with the greatest humanity'; and the proprietors demonstrated 'earnest endeavour to enable them to earn a comfortable livelihood at the expiration of their apprenticeship in various branches of trade'.[89] A subsequent visit concluded that 'Messrs Mitchell and Holt [were] eminently qualified to take apprentices', the children were treated with care and found to be 'satisfied with their diet, lodging and employment'.[90] Although the proprietors provided well for the children's education, and religious and moral training, concerns were raised about the 'promiscuous intermingling of the sexes' during leisure time; and about the erosion of dinner hours by the practice of machinery cleaning. After a disappointing inspection, officials from St George, Hanover Square 'resolved not to send any more children to Mr Mitchell at Holt [sic]'.[91] In testimony to the House of Lords in 1818 and 1819, conditions of apprentices at Mitchell and Holt were alluded to frequently, by both medical men and former apprentices. The latter, including several young men still in Holt's employ, recalled the loss of dinner hours for machine cleaning and other detrimental working conditions.[92] Others remarked how the heating was turned down in preparation for the doctors' visits.[93] In the visitors' terse report of 1824, Holt's factory was described a 'tolerably clean'.[94]

An equivocal assessment of Smart's Emscote mill stems from the surviving evidence. The care with which he negotiated for two Oxford parish apprentices suggests a considerate employer.[95] The mill, which was dutifully registered following the 1802 Act,[96] also conformed to the regulations on night work and education. However, conditions at Emscote – especially lack of ventilation and air thick with dust – were criticised by Theodore Price in evidence to the 1816 Select Committee. Price 'thought the children short and they had a hectic appearance probably from constant work and the warmth of the room'. The apprentices, all girls,[97] enjoyed an hour's dinner break but ate breakfast at their machines. Although 'the house was

---

August 1814, Minutes of Directors of the Poor, Parish of St Pancras, P/PN/PO/1/10 (microfilm reference UTAH 652), CLSAC.

89   2 October 1801, Minutes of the Governors and Directors of the Poor, Parish of St James, Piccadilly, D1878, WAC.

90   9 February 1802, Minutes of the Governors and Directors of the Poor, Parish of St James, Piccadilly, D1878, WAC.

91   9 September 1807 and 2 February 1808, Minutes of Overseers of the Poor, Parish of St George, Hanover Square, C925, WAC.

92   HL1819, vol. 110, George Chapel, 21, piecer, Quaker Holts, pp. 167–8.

93   For example,George Paxton, HL1819, vol. 110, p. 226.

94   1824 Factory Reports, HO44/14, National Archives.

95   Lengthy correspondence between Smart and the parish of St Clement, Oxford. Z351(sm), WCRO.

96   Benjamin Smart's was the only cotton mill listed in the county each year from 1803 to 1815; but 'no written report has been made by the visitors to the Court of Quarter Sessions … at any time between the passing of [the] Act and the end of the year 1818'. HL 1819, vol. 108, County of Warwickshire.

97   According to the evidence to SC1816, p. 171, there were 34 girls.

very clean, the beds very good and comfortable, and the children's clothes very good and comfortable; all that struck me and afflicted my mind, was their want of recreation, their solitude and unvarying scenes'.[98]

Two flax spinners, Colbeck, Ellis and Wilks, of West House mills, Fewston and Sewell and McMurdo, at Hounslow Heath, were also 'average'. The former, accused by some of brutal treatment of parish apprentices,[99] was nevertheless viewed satisfactorily by Visitors appointed under the 1802 Act: 'The mill is whitewashed twice a year. The children employed appear healthy and there are casements sufficient in the window for the necessary change of air. The mills seem under very proper care'.[100] The latter was removed from the approved list of St George's, Hanover Square,[101] but other parishes, continued to send children into the long term.[102]

The silk mills of Thomas Watson of Watford and John Morley of Sewardstone near Chingford were also mid-range performers. The former was visited by officials of St Martin in the Fields,[103] because of complaints of ill treatment by the apprentices, but it 'appeared to them that the children were all perfectly satisfied, very well treated and comfortably accommodated and upon the whole the situation appears eligible and the complaint malicious and unfounded'.[104] Such was the parish's confidence in Watson as an employer of young children that a further thirteen children were sent there in the following year.[105] The latter, which took apprentices from Essex and London, was visited in 1802 by parish officials who, while able to[106] report positively about the working and living arrangements, criticised the deficient education. 'On the whole the children at this mill are extremely well treated ... the principal fault is want of instruction.' Also 'on a representation to Mr Morley that the outer garments of the girls were not in good condition, he informed us that they were about to have new cloathing as the boys had about a fortnight ago'.[107]

Among the 'quite negligent' firms, William Douglas's enterprises at both Holywell and Pendleton received mixed reviews. The factories were criticised particularly for

---

98 SC1816, pp. 121–5.
99 8 October 1811, Apprenticeship Register 1802–, Parish of St Leonard's, Shoreditch, P91/LEN/1332, LMA; I.D.B. Ferguson, 'Fewston mill', BA Dissertation, Folk Life Studies, University of Leeds, 1967.
100 Returns of Cotton and other mills 1803–1806, QE 33/1, WYASW.
101 24 February1807, Minutes of Overseers of the Poor, Parish of St George, Hanover Square, C925, WAC.
102 In 1818, children were bound from St Pancras and St James Piccadilly. Deed of covenant and indemnity in respect of apprentices belonging to the flax mills at Hounslow, 1 March 1821, Turner ACC/0526/36 LMA.
103 18 May 1796, Minutes of meetings of Officers of the Parish of St Martin in the Fields, F2075, WAC.
104 19 October 1796, Minutes of meetings of Officers of the Parish of St Martin in the Fields, F2075, WAC.
105 Apprenticeship Register, Parish of St Martin in the fields, F4311, F4511, WAC.
106 At the end of the tour the officials recommended that more children be apprenticed to manufactures in London and environs, of which this mill was, presumably, an example. 1802 Report, St Margaret and St John.
107 1802 Report, St Margaret and St John.

physical abuse and persistent night working.[108] Nevertheless, the rate of retention was good: apprentices, who comprised the bulk of the workforce, were expected to remain, and many chose to do so.[109] Parish apprentices at the very short-lived Haywood and Palfreyman, 1796–9, enjoyed mixed fortunes. Only the children from St James, for whom special provision had been made by the parish, received the full benefits of education, and the support of a local clergyman.[110] The proprietors were most neglectful in failing to provide for the children upon their bankruptcy.[111] The condition of the parish apprentices at John Watson of Preston[112] has been variously described: critically by Joseph Livesey;[113] and positively by Stephen Holloway, who found the children there 'well and hearty'.[114] Parish visitors to the mill in 1802 found some satisfactory elements, but much to be condemned. The bedrooms were 'well ordered and airy', for example, clothing good and eating rooms clean. The situation was healthy, 'a physician regularly attends the factory, four school masters are appointed to instruct the children, and prayers are read every other night – a bath is also provided for them'.[115] However, hours of work were long, the diet monotonous and inadequate in meat, and there were signs of overzealous disciplining.[116] Although the mill abided by the limited rules of the 1802 Act,[117] evidence to the 1816 Select Committee indicated that long hours remained a feature of parish apprentice life.[118]

Complaints from parish apprentices at Strutt's cotton mill at Rickmansworth began soon after their binding.[119] Conditions appeared to improve following a parish visit;[120] but by 1792 complaints resurfaced: 'the overseers reported that they [found that] seven of them had been very severely chastised for trifling offences that the food allowed them was inadequate to the many hours they were kept to work and

---

108 Night working, at Holywell, was condemned by the Poor Law officers of St Clement Danes. 12 March 1792, Minutes of Churchwardens, Overseers, and Assistants, Parish of St Clement Danes, B1147, WAC. Absconding was high.

109 For example, Testimony of Samuel Jones and Samuel Gardner, HL 1819, vol. 110, pp. 180–81; Robert Plant, 36, spinner, Appleton and Plant. Also testimony from John Houldsworth, and Oldham weaver, HL 1819, vol. 110, pp. 133–6, 241.

110 Letter from Reverend Bromley, 9 September 1796, Minutes of Governors and Directors of the Poor, Parish of St James, Piccadilly, D1876, WAC.

111 Report of 6 September to meeting of 7 September 1799, Minutes of Governors and Directors of the Poor, Parish of St James, Piccadilly, D1877, WAC.

112 Evidence of Clement Dodenhoff to House of Lords, HL1819, vol. 110, pp. 103–105. He had been apprenticed to John Watson among others.

113 Aspin, *Water Spinners*, p. 272.

114 Aspin, *Water Spinners*, p. 273. Holloway visited the mill on behalf of St George the Martyr parish, Southwark.

115 1802 Report, St Margaret and St John.

116 1802 Report, St Margaret and St John.

117 HL 1819, vol. 108. Appendix: consists of reports, including W: 1803 Samlesbury: only one cotton mill.

118 SC1816, p. 295.

119 25 August 1786, Minutes of Governors and Directors of the Poor, Parish of St James, Piccadilly, D1873, WAC.

120 29 April 1788, 17 September 1790, Minutes of Governors and Directors of the Poor, Parish of St James, Piccadilly, D1873, WAC.

that they were universally dissatisfied'. The clerk was ordered to write to Mr Strutt.[121] In their 'plan of disposal' Jeremiah Bury and Co.[122] presented themselves as superior employers who promised not only to care for the children during their term, but also to ensure a longer-term livelihood.[123] Although they promised a benign disciplinary regime, evidence of cruelty at the mill was reported in the local press.[124]

The discussion above has indicated the range of experience of early parish factory apprentices. Place of birth and other chance variables determined factory destination and thus the level of protection or neglect. There was some association between protective parishes and the least neglectful firms. Birmingham and St Mary Newington, for example, appeared to choose wisely, and together were associated with more than half of the protective firms as well as those that were economically the most successful.[125] At the lower end of the scale, some connections are observable. Among the least protective parishes, Doncaster bound children to one of the most neglectful firms, Davison and Hawksley. However, parishes such as St James implemented protective procedures but because of errors of judgment – of which Needham was a notable one – it failed to actually protect its children.

Perhaps the most important conclusion that can be drawn from the findings presented in this chapter is that well-organised firms that made proper provision for their parish apprentices were more likely to succeed in the longer term; and conversely that firms that neglected their apprentices were doomed to failure. Although the causal link is not proven, and a range of other forces were relevant to the outcome, it remains the case that the use of parish apprentices into the longer term could be associated with business success. Among the most successful business were those whose labour consisted largely of parish apprentices well beyond 1820. This success, however, was contingent on maintaining the physical and mental well being of the children and upon training them appropriately. The association of poor treatment and failure is equally clear and the causal relationship more so. It appears that trading difficulties and financial pressures resulted in the implementation of cost containment strategies, the burden of which was felt acutely by the apprentices. In the majority of the 'most negligent' firms identified above, conditions of the apprentices deteriorated from adequate to poor as diet worsened, labour became more intensive and education provision removed. Typically, such conditions marked the imminence of bankruptcy.

---

121 28 October 1792, Minutes of Governors and Directors of the Poor, Parish of St James Piccadilly, D1874, WAC.

122 The firm had been established with 200 parish apprentices, 100 of whom remained at the end of their term. This was a larger proportion than conventionally believed to have been the case at early textile factories. SC1816, p. 55.

123 The document, entitled 'The following is a short sketch of a plan of disposing of 200 parish children wanted by J Bury and Co., muslin manufacturers of Hope hill, near Stockport, Cheshire, particularly the weaving branch', is undated. It is estimated by the archivist Stephen Humphries to be around 1780. I would argue that it was more likely to be between 1790 and 1800. SLHL.

124 *Manchester Chronicle*, 21 August 1808, cited in Aspin, *Water Spinners*, p. 189.

125 On the other hand, Birmingham had also bound children to Peel's Lancashire factories, which were among the most negligent in the country.

This chapter and Chapter 11 have discussed evidence challenging the notion that parish factory apprentices were disposed of and forgotten by parishes providing employers with the freedom to ill-treat the children at will. There is no doubt that children were exploited, abused and neglected – and sometimes even well-used and protected – in the context of factory parish apprenticeship but the responsibility for this was quite clearly shared between parish and employer in ways that have not previously been fully explored.

Chapter 13

Conclusion

This study has been concerned with illuminating both the process of parish factory apprenticing, and the experience of the parish apprentices themselves. In doing so, it has supported some elements of conventional wisdom, but adjusted others. In particular, it has challenged the random nature of the distribution of parish children, and the lack of interest in their subsequent welfare exhibited by their birth parishes.

While not claiming to offer conclusive evidence either about the scale of early factory apprenticeship or its significance, this work has drawn on a 'sample' of parishes and a 'sample' of early textile factories to suggest a more complex interpretation than has been hitherto presented. The full extent of the practice will never be known, but there is more evidence to be retrieved, and a more complete picture to be presented. It has been argued here that the system of factory apprenticeship, established through the interaction of Poor Law officials and early factory proprietors, facilitated the expansion of the nascent textile industry. The cotton industry was the major beneficiary, but parish apprentices also permitted the growth of factory production in silk, linen and worsted. The woollen industry was only involved in this process to a minor extent.[1] The system of parish factory apprenticeship was important in the construction of an industrial labour force with the general and specialised skills required for textile factory employment. Parish apprentices were independent workers from an early stage. The extent to which parish children remained in the factory to which they had been apprenticed remains unknown, but the evidence presented in this study suggests that those settling in the area and producing the next generation of factory workers formed the majority. Thus the system supported the permanent movement of labour into the industrialising regions.

Without doubt, the system of factory parish apprenticeship, or the transfer of a proportion of parish children from traditional to modern forms of manufacture, facilitated the expansion of the textile trade during the early decades of industrialisation. Factory parish apprenticeship, even long-distance transfer of children, did not end in 1820. The practice declined, but continued through the 1840s and into the 1850s. As the practice of factory apprenticing ceased to be important, parishes found alternative takers for their young poor. Well into the second half of the nineteenth century, employers continued to beat on parish doors in pursuit of cheap youthful labour. For some historians, the period in which parish children were bound to factory employers was a brief, exceptional interlude. Yet the research on which this study is based suggests not only that the period within which the practice

---

1   Redford's assertion that the West Riding woollen industry drew on parish apprentices from London workhouses notwithstanding, Arthur Redford, *Labour Migration in England 1800–1850* (Manchester, 1964), p. 28.

of parish factory apprenticeship occurred was quite long – 30 years of substantial activity and a further 20 years when the practice was perceptible – but also that there was continuity between this phase and those preceding and following.

The process of parish factory apprenticeship was both more complex and more formal than traditionally conceived. The distribution of children workers from parishes throughout the land to factories in the South as well as in the Midlands and North was well regulated. As the process of the parish factory apprenticeship system was well recorded, so too was the parish apprentice experience. Traditional descriptions of the relentless labour and gruelling conditions that awaited parish factory apprentices have not been revised here. In comparison with standards established for children's working conditions in subsequent decades, the circumstances within which parish apprentices toiled were unacceptable. In comparison with the alternatives that existed for poor children at the time, however, the conditions appear less bleak. Evidence suggests that workhouse regimes and factory regimes were similar. The nature of work, the disciplinary practices, the sleeping accommodation, the diet, and access to leisure and education were equivalent. The hours of work appear to have been shorter at the workhouse, however. Early textile factories operated a fairly standard working week, and although parish-run Houses of Industry were less likely to publish the hours of work, where evidence exists, daily labour rarely exceeded 12 hours.[2] In terms of outcomes, the factory apprentice was subsequently more employable than the poor child confined to the workhouse.

Parish children were not protected from harsh factory conditions. Yet neither were they consigned by their parish to distant mills without a further thought. This study has revisited the notion of disposal and concluded that the majority of parishes appeared to sustain responsibility for their children long after they had disappeared from daily view. It can be argued that by binding children to factory masters, especially those at a distance, the parish acted irresponsibly, and that no amount of subsequent enquiry could remedy the damage. In their eagerness to take advantage of factory placements, some parish officers neglected to investigate carefully the circumstances. Nevertheless, factory placements were not universally worse than other contemporary apprenticeships either in terms of conditions, training or outcomes. Attention was paid to the longer-term prospects of the children, even if self-interest provided the motivation for such concern. Few of the parishes in this study failed to investigate the conditions in which 'their' children were to be apprenticed, to visit them at least once during their term, to consider carefully what might happen to them on completion of their apprenticeship, to take seriously any complaint on the part of the apprentice and to keep careful record of such practices and other activities relating to the binding.

Businesses too maintained records, though regrettably few have survived. The following two examples illustrate the effectiveness of record keeping by both businesses and parish, which permits historians to trace apprentices beyond the initial binding. The apprenticeship register maintained by Toplis and Co., indicates the firm's exemplary record keeping. At the time of the firm's failure in 1805, the

---

2   This was the case in Bristol, for example, E.E. Butcher, *Bristol Corporation of the Poor: Selected Records 1696–1834* (Bristol, 1932), pp. 6–9.

employers found alternative placements for the apprentices which were dutifully registered. One of these children, originally from Birmingham parish, was reassigned to Hancox and Wakefield, in nearby Mansfield, and some months later moved from there to Davison and Hawskley. On a tour of inspection of the factories to which Birmingham children had been bound, the Birmingham Guardians tracked the child to her new binding where she was promptly produced by the owners. The child had moved several times, yet sufficient records were kept to allow her to be traced. This case also demonstrates the determination of the parish officials to find her.[3] Thus the long-term responsibility of the parish for the factory apprentices, typically overlooked in historical accounts was an important influence on the experience of these children. The second example also illustrates the capacity of parishes to trace former charges despite their removal from the original place of binding but also provides a clue for the reason for this concern. When, early in 1815, parish officers from St Pancras discovered that the indentures of several apprentices had not been properly executed – indeed that they had been 'altered and erased without any communication with or knowledge on the part of the Directors' – and finding that they were not with their intended masters, set about locating their present situation. The appointed committee, while slow to report, nevertheless found the children and eventually retrieved them. The lengthy report, which demonstrated the lengths to which officials would go to track down the children who were technically no longer their responsibility, seemed very concerned to follow the proper procedures, and to maintain the propriety of the apprenticeship system. It was particularly critical of the agents involved, and censured the Directors for carelessness; yet the settlement issue was an underlying anxiety: 'the Board of Directors must unquestionably consider the indentures which have been so altered and executed by new masters as described to be completely void and therefore such as will not confer legal settlement on the children and which may be calculated as one of the objects of the apprenticeship'.[4]

It could be argued that the paper work surrounding the parish factory apprentices was more praiseworthy than actions, yet the paper trail – provided by both parish officials and businesses – suggests greater consideration for the welfare of children than has hitherto been imagined. There were no penalties for failing to visit children or listen to their complaints, yet the majority of parishes provided at least a modicum of follow-up care for years. Such findings do not condone the actions of parishes that separated children from their families and failed to provide real protection from the cruelty and neglect of factory masters. The suffering of parish children was real, and parish officers colluded with mill owners in its perpetuation. This study has not revised such a perspective. It has, rather, argued that parish apprentices were not subject to random disposal, and that parish officers appeared to care about what became of them. Grim as conditions were in early textile mills, for many parish children the alternatives were equally bleak.

---

3   29 June 1808, Minutes of the Birmingham Board of Guardians, GP/B/2/1/2, BCA.
4   18 June 1816, Minutes of Directors of the Poor, parish of St Pancras, P/PN/PO/1/12 (microfilm reference UTAH 652), CLSAC. The committee suggested approaching 'Counsel for advice'.

Less well recorded is the outcome of parish apprenticeship. A number of enterprises in this study retained a substantial proportion of their apprentices, and such children, the majority of whom were girls, settled in the area and built an adult family life. Several firms had fewer openings for adult workers and, upon the expiration of their apprenticeship the children moved on, their places taken by a fresh batch of apprentices or by free children of the locality. About the fate of children who were obliged or chose to leave, little is known. A handful of settlement examinations, evidence offered to the 1816 Select Committee and autobiographical accounts, indicate that as intended, a factory apprenticeship might well be considered sufficient training for adult employment in textile factories.

Parish apprentices were integral to the construction of the new industrial labour force. All children's labour was important to early manufacturing industry, but in the initial stages of development, the parish apprentice was a flexible element in an otherwise inflexible labour market. It was the parish apprentice who assisted in freeing the labour market in the late eighteenth century in preparation for a period of persistent industrial growth. In doing so, the poor parish child was an active force. Yet the parish factory apprentice was subject to a range of experiences based upon compulsion. He or she had little choice. Like all labour in the new industrial sphere, the parish apprentice was required to work at times and in conditions determined by others. This study has shown, however, that the early factory apprentices were not simply passive victims of callous Poor Law officials and cruel factory masters. They responded to their situation in numerous ways. Twenty years ago, it was written: 'the lives of pauper apprentices constituted a social limbo with only isolated narratives like that of Robert Blincoe to throw any light on the early lives of these children'.[5] It is hoped that this study contributes to the process of rectifying this anomaly.

---

5 E.G. Thomas, 'Pauper apprenticeship', *The Local Historian*, 14 (1981): 405.

Appendix

Origin of apprentices to Ackers and Beever, cotton spinners, Bank mill, Salford

Parish	Date	Girl apprentices	Boy apprentices
Gosport	1790	?	?
Bury St Edmunds	1790	?	?
Manchester	1796	?	?
Liverpool?		?	?

Sources: *Manchester Chronicle*, 23 December 1796; Chris Aspin, *The Water Spinners*, pp. 156–9. Insurance value of apprentice house suggests about 150–200 apprentices.

Origin of apprentices to George Andrew, calico printer, Stockport

Parish	Date	Girl apprentices	Boy apprentices
Lambeth	1816	0	9

Source: St Mary at Lambeth Apprenticeship Register, 1802–1826, P85/MRY1/271, LMA.

Thomas Andrew, calico printer, Harpurhey

Parish	Date	Girl apprentices	Boy apprentices
St Martin in the Fields	1815	0	5

Source: St Martin in the Fields Apprenticeship Register, 1802–1824. F4311, WAC.

Origin of apprentices to Samuel Ashton, cotton manufacturer, Middleton, Lancs

Parish	Date	Girl apprentices	Boy apprentices
St Martin in the Fields	1802	9	35
St Pancras	1802	18	7
St Martin in the Fields	1814	9	0

Sources: St Martin in the Fields Apprenticeship Register 1802–1824, F4311, WAC; St Pancras Apprenticeship Register, 1802–1867, P90/PANI/362, LMA. According to the House of Lords, The Sessional Papers, 1801–1833, vol. 108 (1819), in 1803–1804 Ashton employed 66 boy and 45 girl apprentices, and 4 servants; 'all in a remarkable good state of health; with regard to cleanliness, instruction of the children, attention to their morals, and other provisions of the act, they are, as far as we can perceive, strictly complied with.

Origin of apprentices to Atherton and Harrison, cotton manufacturers, Kirk mill, Chipping

Parish	Date	Girl apprentices	Boy apprentices
St Giles in the Fields	1795	9	0

Source: St Giles in the Fields parish, Register of Parish Apprentices, 1780–1802, P/GF/PO/4, CLSAC.

Origin of apprentices to John Birch [later Robinson] cotton spinners, Backbarrow mill, Cartmel

Parish	Date	Girl apprentices	Boy apprentices
St Clement Danes	1787	6	29
St Clement Danes	1789	10	14
St Clement Danes	1790	3	9
St Clement Danes	1791	5	12
St Clement Danes	1792	7	13
St Clement Danes	1793	2	5
St Clement Danes	1795	8	10
St Clement Danes	1798	8	7
St Clement Danes	1799	3	9
St Clement Danes	1800	8	7
St Clement Danes	1801	1	6
Liverpool	c. 1800	20?	20?*
Brighton	c. 1802+	10?	10?
St Clement Danes	1810	0	1
St Clement Danes	1811	0	1
St Clement Danes	1813	0	3
St Clement Danes	1814	0	3
St Martin in the Fields	1815	2	4

* guestimate: 10 ran away, so there may well have been more than 40 in total. There were additional children, originally sent from St George the Martyr, to John Watson of Preston and reassigned to Birch in 1807.

+ Brighton poor law officials visited their children at the mill in 1805, when there were 140 apprentices in total. A large proportion of these would have been the St Clement Danes children coming to the end of their time. According to John Moss, superintendent of the apprentice house in 1814–15, children also came from St James (but I found no evidence in the St James records, which appear to have been well maintained) and Whitechapel. 1816 Select Committee, p. 177.

Sources: St Clement Danes Apprenticeship Records 1784–1792, B1266; St Clement Danes Apprenticeship Records, 1784–1801, B1267; St Clement Danes Apprenticeship Register, 1803–1822, B1268; St Martin in the Fields Apprenticeship Register, 1802–1824, F4311, WAC; Aspin, *Water Spinners*, 343–51.

Origin of apprentices to Benyon and Co., linen manufacture, Shrewsbury

Parish	Date	Girl apprentices	Boy apprentices
Westbury, Shropshire	1803	4	0
Shrewsbury Incorporation	1805	6	0
Shrewsbury House of Industry	1808	1	0
Westbury Shropshire	1809	3	0
Fitz Shropshire	1809	1	0

Sources: Fitz parish apprenticeship, 1772–1925, P109/L/6; Shrewsbury Incorporation of the Poor, Register of Apprentices 1802–1818, PL2/7/1/1; Westbury Parish Apprenticeship Register 1764–1833, P297/L/9/1, Shropshire Archives.

Origin of apprentices to Bott, Bower and Co., cotton spinners, Nantwich

Parish	Date	Girl apprentices	Boy apprentices
Birmingham	1796	*c.* 20*	*c.* 20*
St George, Edgbaston	1799	1	0

* This is a guestimate, based on description of the sleeping arrangements from Birmingham visitors to the mill, as well as typical group size sent to other mills from Birmingham.
Sources: Minute Book of the Birmingham Board of Guardians, 1783–1806. GP/B/2/1/1; St George Parish Edgbaston Apprenticeship Indentures, MS515/59, BCA.

Origin of apprentices to John Bott, cotton spinner, Tutbury

Parish	Date	Girl apprentices	Boy apprentices
St Giles in the Fields	1791	0	24
St Giles in the Fields	1793	2	1
St Giles in the Fields	1794	1	1
St George, Hanover Square	*c.* 1795	*c.* 10	*c.* 10
St Giles in the Fields	1795	0	6
St Giles in the Fields	1796	0	3
Birmingham	*c.* 1800	28 children	
St Giles in the Fields	1800	0	9
Coventry	1802	15	0

Sources: Minute Book of the Birmingham Board of Guardians, 1806–. GP/B/2/1/2, BCA; St Giles in the Fields parish, Register of Parish apprentices 1780–1802, P/GF/PO/4, CLSAC; St George, Hanover Square. Meetings of the Governors and Directors of the Poor. C952, WAC; Joan Lane, 'Apprenticeship in Warwickshire cotton mills', *Textile History*, pp. 172–4.

Origin of apprentices to Brosser, cotton manufacturer, Rainow, Macclesfield

Parish	Date	Girl apprentices	Boy apprentices
St Botolph without Aldergate	1805	0	3
St Botolph without Aldergate	1806	0	3
St Martin in the Fields	1816	0	2

Sources: St Martin in the Fields Apprenticeship Register 1802–1824, F4311, WAC; St Botolph without Aldersgate parish Apprenticeship Register, 1802–, MS 1471, GL.

Origin of apprentices bound to Jeremiah Bury, cotton manufacturer, Heaton Norris, Stockport

Parish	Date	Girl apprentices	Boy apprentices
St George the Martyr, Southwark	1800	n/a	n/a*
St Martin in the Fields	1801	4?	5?
St Martin in the Fields	1805	5	11
St Martin in the Fields	1806	4	3
St Martin in the Fields	1807	1	4
St Martin in the Fields	1810	2	0

* The firm applied for 200 children. There is no indication of what happened, but it is likely that some were sent.
Sources: St George the Martyr, Apprenticeship Indentures 1799–1836. 1/boxes 51–2, SLHS; St Martin in the Fields Apprenticeship Register, 1795–1803, F4310; St Martin in the Fields Apprenticeship Register, 1802–1824, F4311, WAC.

Origin of apprentices to William Calrow, cotton manufacturer, Bury

Parish	Date	Girl apprentices	Boy apprentices
St Martin in the Fields	1815	4	2

Sources: St Martin in the Fields Apprenticeship Register, 1802–1824, F4311, WAC.

Origin of apprentices to Benjamin Churchill, silk and cotton manufacturer, Sheepshead near Loughborough

Parish	Date	Girl apprentices	Boy apprentices
Bristol*	1796	10	10
St George Hanover Square	1800	c. 10	c. 10

* No apprenticeship registers survive, but sources indicate that Bristol sent at least one and probably more groups of parish children to Churchill. Sources: E.E. Butcher, *Bristol Corporation of the Poor: Selected Records, 1696–1834*, Bristol: Bristol Record Society 1932; 23 June 1802, 5 March 1803, 24 February 1807, Minutes of meetings of Governors and Directors of the Poor, Parish of St George, Hanover Square C925, 929 and 930, WAC.

Origin of apprentices to Colbeck, Ellis and Wilks, Flax manufacturers, West House mills, Fewston

Parish	Date	Girl apprentices	Boy apprentices
St George the Martyr, Southwark	1803	11	0
Lambeth	1803	4	0
St George the Martyr, Southwark	1804	14	6
St Leonards, Shoreditch	1811	3	14
Lambeth	1811	3	0
Sculwater, Hull	1814	7	0
St George the Martyr, Southwark	1814	7	10

Sources: St George the Martyr, Apprenticeship indentures 1799–1836. 1/boxes 51–2 SLHL; St Mary at Lambeth Apprenticeship registers 1802–26 P85/MRY1/271; St Leonard Shoreditch Apprenticeship Register 1802–, P91/LEN/1332 (microfilm reference 020/172), LMA; Sculwater Register of Parish Apprentices, 1802–44, PUS/411, Hull City Archives.

Origin of apprentices to Cooper and Matchett, cotton spinners, Woodeaves, Tissington, Derbyshire

Parish	Date	Girl apprentices	Boy apprentices
?Derbyshire	1790	0	1
St George, Hanover Square	1802	n/a	n/a
Liverpool	1800–1820?	n/a	n/a
Winster	1825	0	1
Leicester	1850s	n/a	n/a

The sources of apprentices are varied even if specific information on numbers and dates are missing. *Sources*: 24 February 1807, Minutes of Governors and Directors of Poor, Parish of St George, Hanover Square; Winster Apprenticeship Register D776 A/PO 741, Derbyshire Record Office; Poor Law Leicestershire; DRO Q/AG/16/11, 2 April 1841 from J. Cooper, Woodeaves mill to Mr George Hodgkinson, Clerk to magistrates, Wirksworth: 'it is about 8 years since I had any [apprentices] at Woodeaves. They all left at that time except about half a dozen who remained as free hands, the rest I believe went into Lancashire and Cheshire, I think principally to Stockport. You will obtain the information you required from the workhouse at Liverpool from which they were all apprenticed'.

Origin of apprentices to Cowpe, Hollins, Oldknow, cotton spinners, Pleasley mill, Mansfield, Nottinghamshire

Parish	Date	Girl apprentices	Boy apprentices
St Giles in the Fields	1791	10	0
St Clement Danes	1791	?	?
St Giles in the Fields	1797	1	0
Lambeth	1809	5	0
Mansfield Woodhouse	1810	1	0

Note. In 1802, there were 60 apprentices altogether in this smallish but solid enterprise.
Sources: St Giles in the Fields parish, Register of Parish apprentices, 1780–1802, P/GF/PO/4, CLSAC; St Clement Danes Apprenticeship Records, 1784–1801, B1267, WAC; St Mary at Lambeth Apprenticeship Registers 1802–1826, P85/MRY1/271, LMA; Mansfield Woodhouse Parish Apprenticeship Register, NA.

Origin of apprentices to Edale/Castleton mill [Cresswell to 1801; Blackwall 1810–] cotton manufacturer

Parish	*Date*	*Girl apprentices*	*Boy apprentices*
Lambeth	1796	15	1
Lambeth	1797	4	0
Lambeth	1798	5	0
Lambeth	1799	4	0
Lambeth	1800	3	0
Lambeth	1801	6	0
Lambeth	1810	6	0
Hull	1836	9	0
Edinburgh	1836	9	0

Sources: St Mary at Lambeth Apprenticeship Registers, 1802–26, P85/MRY1/271; St Mary at Lambeth, Apprenticeship Registers, 1782–1833, P85/MRY1/270, LMA; Results of 1840 Enquiry; Returns of mills, Q/AG/17–33, Castleton Edale mill Q/AG/20 DRO.

Origin of apprentices to Davison and Hawksley, worsted manufacturer, Arnold, Nottinghamshire

Parish	*Date*	*Girl apprentices*	*Boy apprentices*
Doncaster township	1794	3	2
Doncaster township	1795	1	4
Arnold, Nottinghamshire	1795	1	0
Lambeth	1795	5 or 10	6
Lambeth	1796	6	17
Bristol+	1797	n/a	n/a
Lambeth	1797	1	1
Lambeth	1798	4	40
Bristol	1798	n/a	n/a
Various (including St Margaret and St John, Westminster;* reassigned from Toplis)	1798	10?	10?
St George the Martyr, Southwark	1800	1	6
St George, Hanover Square	1801 (or thereabouts)	?	?

St Luke, Chelsea	1802	10	11
St Luke, Chelsea	1803	4	11
St Leonards, Shoreditch	1803	4	6
St Luke, Chelsea	1804	3	0
St Luke, Chelsea	1805	3	3
Various [including Birmingham]; reassigned from Toplis	1805	45	45

* This information is from the 1802 Report of the visit to Toplis by parish officers of St Margaret and St John.

+ Although figures are not available, the numbers involved were probably large as other sources have suggested that most of Davidson and Hawksley's 600 apprentices came from Bristol and London.

Sources: Doncaster Township Memorandum Book of the Overseers, 1794–1795, PL/D/1, Doncaster Archives; St Mary at Lambeth, Apprenticeship Registers, 1782–1833, P85/MRY1/270, LMA; Arnold Parish Apprenticeship Indentures, PR14062/1, NA; E.E. Butcher, *Bristol Corporation of the Poor. Selected records, 1696–1834*, Bristol: Bristol Record Society 1932; St George, Hanover Square, Meetings of the Governors and Directors of the Poor, C925, 929, WAC; St George the Martyr, Apprenticeship Indentures, 1799–1836, 1/boxes 51–2, SLHL; St Leonard Shoreditch Apprenticeship Register, 1802–. P91/LEN/1332 (microfilm reference 020/172); St Luke Chelsea Apprenticeship Register, 1802–1813, P74/LUK/117, LMA; 'List of children put out apprentice to William Toplis'. DD895/1, NA.

Origin of apprentices to Dicken and Finlow, cotton manufacturers, Burton

Parish	Date	Girl apprentices	Boy apprentices
Birmingham	1795	10*	6
Birmingham	1798	34	6
Birmingham	1800	n/a	n/a

* The records indicate that Dicken and Finlow took 16 children but their marked preference for girls suggests that this figure would be distributed accordingly. In 1808, 34 Birmingham children were still serving their apprenticeship at the mill; and a number more had been retained as paid employees. *Sources*: Minute Book of the Birmingham Board of Guardians, 1783–1806. GP/B/2/1/1; Minute Book of the Birmingham Board of Guardians, 1806–?, GP/B/2/1/2, BCA.

Origin of apprentices to Douglas and Co. Holywell Twist Company

Parish	Date	Girl apprentices	Boy apprentices
St Martin in the Fields	1784	?	?
St Martin in the Fields	1785	0	15
St Martin the Fields	1786	5	16
St Martin in the Fields	1787	10	15
St Clement Danes	1787	3	1
St Clement Danes	1789	3	2

Royston parish, Hertfordshire	1790?	2	6
Lambeth	1790	9	8
St Giles in the Fields	1790	5	0
Bristol	1795–	n/a	n/a
St Giles in the Fields	1795	9	0
St Luke Chelsea	1797	3	7
St Martin in the Fields	1800	1	6
St James, Piccadilly	1801	*c.* 20 children	?
St Anne, Soho	1800		1

Sources: St Martin in the Fields Apprenticeship Register, 1784–1794 F4309; St Martin in the Fields Apprenticeship Register 1795–1803. F4310; St Clement Danes Apprenticeship Records, 1784–1792, B1266, WAC; Royston parish records, Hertfordshire Archives and Local Studies, ref D/P87/14/1/6; St Giles in the Fields parish, Register of Parish Apprentices, 1780–1802, P/GF/PO/4, CLSAC; E.E. Butcher, *Bristol Corporation of the Poor: Selected Records, 1696–1834*, Bristol: Bristol Record Society1932; St Mary at Lambeth, Apprenticeship Registers 1782–1833, P85/MRY1/270; St Luke Chelsea Workhouse Apprenticeship Register 1791–1802, P74/LUK/116, LMA; St James Parish, Minutes of Governors and Directors of the Poor, 1798–1801, D1877; St Anne Soho, Apprenticeship Records, 1702–1834, A2262.

Origin of apprentices to William Douglas, cotton spinner, Pendleton, Lancs

Parish	Date	Girl apprentices	Boy apprentices
St Martin in the Fields	1785	0	15
St Clement Danes	1786	1	8
St Giles in the Fields	1786	5	3
Lambeth	1786	1	8
St Martin in the Fields	1787	0	8
St Giles in the Fields	1787	0	3
St James Piccadilly	1787	8	0
St Martin in the Fields	1789	3	7
St Giles in the Fields	1789	?	?
St Pancras	1790	0	3
St Giles in the Fields	1790	1	0
Chatham, Kent	1792	n/a	n/a
St Martin in the Fields	1794	2	4
St Martin in the Fields	1795	0	3
St Luke Cheslsea	1795	15	11
St Luke Chelsea	1796	0	1
Lambeth	1796	2	2
St Luke Chelsea	1797	2	3

St James Piccadilly	1797	11	11
St Martin in the Fields	1797	3	10
Chelmsford	1799	0	10
St Giles in the Fields	1799	2	4
St Luke Finsbury	1799?	n/a	n/a
St James Clerkenwell	?	?	?

Sources: St Martin in the Fields Apprenticeship Register, 1784–1794, F4309; St Clement Danes Apprenticeship Records, 1784–1792, B1266, WAC; St Giles in the Fields parish, Register of Parish Apprentices, 1780–1802, P/GF/PO/4, CLSAC; St Mary at Lambeth, Apprenticeship Registers, 1782–1833, P85/MRY1/270; St Luke Chelsea Workhouse Apprenticeship Register, 1791–1802, P74/LUK/116; St Pancras Register of Apprentices, 1778–1801, P90/PANI/361, LMA; Elizabeth Melling (ed.), *The Poor: a Collection of Examples from Original Sources in the Kent Archives Office from the Sixteenth to the Nineteenth Century*, Maidstone: Kent County Council, 1964; St James Piccadilly, Minutes of Governors and Directors of the Poor, 1796–1798, D1876, WAC; Indenture Papers, Chelmsford parish, D/P 94/14; Vestry meetings, Chelmsford parish, D/P/12/12, ERO; St Luke Finsbury, Vestry Minutes, ILHC; Aspin, *Water Spinners*, p. 172.

Origin of apprentices to Fowler, cotton manufacturer, Alder mills, near Tamworth

Parish	Date	Girl apprentices	Boy apprentices
Kingsbury, Warwickshire	1807	1	0
Kingsbury, Warwickshire	1813	3	0
Kingsbury Warwickshire	1816	1	0

Source: Kingsbury Parish Register of Apprentices DR(B) 3/126, WCRO.

Origin of apprentices to Jeremiah Garnett, cotton manufacturer, Clitheroe

Parish	Date	Girl apprentices	Boy apprentices
St Pancras	1814	12	10

Source: St Pancras Apprenticeship Register, 1802–1867, P90/PANI/362, LMA.

Origin of apprentices to William Garth, cotton manufacturer, Colne, Lancs

Parish	Date	Girl apprentices	Boy apprentices
St Clement Danes	1813	2	0
St Clement Danes	1814	2	1
St Clement Danes	1815	3	4

Source: St Clement Danes Apprenticeship Register, 1803–1822, B1268, WAC.

Origin of apprentices to John Gorton, cotton spinner, Bury Lancs

Parish	Date	Girl apprentices	Boy apprentices
St Pancras	1805	13	12
St Pancras	1806	6	7

Note. St Clement Danes rejected request from Gorton in 1815.
Sources: St Pancras Apprenticeship Register, 1802–1867, P90/PANI/362, LMA; St Pancras, Minutes of meetings of Directors of the Poor, 1804–1820, P/PN/PO/1/1–17 (microfilm references UTAH 649–654).

Origin of apprentices to Gorton and Thompson, cotton spinners, Cuckney

Parish	Date	Girl apprentices	Boy apprentices
St James, Piccadilly	1789	0	6
St James, Piccadilly	1790–95	0	26
St Martin in the Fields	1791	0	12

Source: St James Parish, Minutes of Governors and Directors of the Poor, 1787–1796, D1872–D1875; St Martin in the Fields Apprenticeship Register, 1784–1794, F4309, WAC.

Origin of apprentices to Messrs Haigh, cotton manufacturers, Marsden

Parish	Date	Girl apprentices	Boy apprentices
St Margaret and St John, Westminster	1792	10	14
Lambeth	1792	–	12
Lambeth	1793	–	16
St Clement Danes	1795	–	2
Lambeth	1796	–	9
Halstead, Essex	1799	15 children	
Lambeth	1803	15	8

Sources: 1797, Report of St Margaret and St John; 1802, Report of St Margaret and St John, WAC; St Mary at Lambeth, Apprenticeship Registers, 1782–1833, P85/MRY1/270; St Mary at Lambeth Apprenticeship Registers, 1802–26, P85/MRY1/271, LMA; St Clement Danes Apprenticeship Records, 1784–1801, B1267, WAC; Halstead parish Apprenticeship Indentures, D/P/14/2, ERO.

Origin of apprentices to Charles Harding, cotton spinner, Tamworth

Parish	Date	Girl apprentices	Boy apprentices
St Martin in the Fields	1807	4	14
Bedworth, Warwickshire	1809	19	1
Coleshill, Warwickshire	1812	1	0

Sources: St Martin in the Fields Apprenticeship Register 1802–1824. F4311, WAC; Coleshill Parish Apprenticeship Indentures, DR(B) 100/108; Coleshill parish register of apprentices

1802–1835 DR(B) 100/107;Bedworth Parish Register of Apprentices 1802 DR 225/34, WCRO.

Origin of apprentices at Hardnumm, Norris and Co., Bury, Lancashire

Parish	Date	Girl apprentices	Boy apprentices
?	1819	11*	12*

* The number at the factory in 1819. Over the previous few years, there had been about 180; and there were at the time 66 workers, who had previously been apprentices at the mill. Source: House of Lords, vol. 110, 1819, pp. 466–9.

Origin of apprentices to Harrison and Leyland, cotton twist manufacturer, Euxton

Parish	Date	Girl apprentices	Boy apprentices
?	1819	40 children	

Source: The House of Lords, vol. 10, 1819, refers to the employment of 40 apprentices but does not specify whence they came.

Origins of apprentices to Thomas Haslam, cotton spinner, Bury, Lancs

Parish	Date	Girl apprentices	Boy apprentices
St Pancras	1803	18	6
St Martin in the Fields	1803	0	4
St Pancras	1805	6	6

Sources: St Martin in the Fields Apprenticeship Register 1795–1803. F4310; St Martin in the Fields Apprenticeship Register 1802–1824. F4311, WAC; St Pancras Apprenticeship Register 1802–1867, P90/PANI/362, LMA.

Origin of apprentices to Haywood and Palfreyman, linen manufacturers, Wildboar Clough, near Macclesfield, Cheshire (1799 bankrupt)

Parish	Date	Girl apprentices	Boy apprentices
St James, Piccadilly	1796	2	31
St Botolph Aldergate	1796	0	2
St George, Hanover Square	1796	15 children	
St Martin in the Fields	1796	0	7
St Sepulchres	1796	4 children	
St Paul, Covent Garden	1796	0	8
St Paul, Covent Garden	1797	0	4

Sources: St James Parish, Minutes of Governors and Directors of the Poor, 1794–1796, D1875, WAC; St Botolph Aldergate parish Apprenticeship Register, 1769–1805, MS 2658, GL; St George, Hanover Square, Meetings of the Governors and Directors of the Poor, C925; St Martin in the Fields Apprenticeship Register, 1795–1803, F4310, WAC; St Sepulchre

Holborn Apprenticeship Register, MS 3211, GL; St Paul Covent Garden, Minutes of Churchwardens and Overseers, H879, WAC.

Origin of apprentices to John Head, worsted manufacturer, Masham, Yorkshire

Parish	Date	Girl apprentices	Boy apprentices
St Martin in the Fields	1803	8	0
St Martin in the Fields	1804	5	0
St Martin in the Fields	1809	0	3

Source: St Martin in the Fields Apprenticeship Register, 1802–1824, F4311, WAC.

Origin of apprentices to R&G Hodgkinson, cotton weaver, Worksop

Parish	Date	Girl apprentices	Boy apprentices
Various (reassigned from Toplis upon bankruptcy)	1805	*c.* 10	*c.* 10
Lambeth	1807	0	9

Sources: 'List of children put out apprentice to William Toplis', DD895/1, NA; St Mary at Lambeth Apprenticeship Registers, 1802–26, P85/MRY1/271, LMA.

Origin of apprentices to Isaac Hodgson cotton spinner, Caton mill, Lancaster

Parish	Date	Girl apprentices	Boy apprentices
Liverpool	1790	*c.* 25	*c.* 25
St Martin in the Fields	1791	0	14
St George by St Paul	1803	0	3
St George the Martyr Southwark	1807	8	0
St Pancras	1814	5	13
St Pancras	1816	4	8

Sources: Aspin, *Water Spinners*, pp. 333–4; St Martin in the Fields Apprenticeship Register, 1784–1794, F4309, WAC; St George the Martyr, Apprenticeship Indentures, 1799–1836, 1/boxes 51–2, SLHL; St Pancras Apprenticeship Register, 1802–1867, P90/PANI/362, LMA.

Origin of apprentices to David Holt, cotton spinner, Manchester

Parish	Date	Girl apprentices	Boy apprentices
St Martin in the Fields	1801	8	4
St James, Piccadilly	1801	14 children*	
St James, Piccadilly	1802	?	?
St George, Hanover Square	1802	n/a	n/a
St Botolph Aldergate	1802	5	6
St George Hanover Square	1803	n/a	n/a

* Sex not specified but some of each were sent. Holt and Mitchell expressed a preference for girls. Letter, 14 September 1801 to St James Piccadilly.

Sources: St Martin in the Fields Apprenticeship Register, 1795–1803, F4310; St James Piccadilly Minutes of Governors and Directors of the Poor, 1801–1805, D1878, WAC; St Botolph Aldergate parish Apprenticeship Register, 1769–1805, MS 2658, GL; St George, Hanover Square. Meetings of the Governors and Directors of the Poor. C925, C929 and C930, WAC.

Origin of apprentices to John Edward Hudson, cotton spinner, Gauxholme mill, Todmorden, Lancs

Parish	Date	Girl apprentices	Boy apprentices
St Giles in the Fields	1807	29 children	

Source: Aspin, Water Spinners, p. 254.

Origin of apprentices to Joseph Hulse, cotton weavers, Shirland

Parish	Date	Girl apprentices	Boy apprentices
Alfreton	1811	3	0
Denby	1812	1	0

Sources: Alfreton Parish Apprenticeship Indentures, 1805–1824, D654 A/PO 244–77; Denby Parish Apprenticeship Indentures D1428 A/PO 72–142, DRO. According to the magistrates return of 1803 there were no apprentices at that date.

Origin of apprentices to Jewsbury and Co., cotton [calico?] spinners and weavers, Measham, Derbyshire

Parish	Date	Girl apprentice	Boy apprentice
Shustoke, Warwickshire	1802	1	1
Nuneaton, Warwickshire	1802	0	1
Nuneaton, Warwickshire	1803	2	6
Attleborough, Warwickshire	1803	6 children	
Shustoke, Warwickshire	1806	1	0
Birmingham	1808	38 children (mostly girls?)	
Birmingham (to Ashby)	1808	A large number of children	
Bedworth, Warwickshire	1808	1	0
Kingsbury, Warwickshire	1808	2	2
Foremark, Derbyshire	1809	0	1
Birmingham	1813	20 children	
Birmingham (to Appleby)	1813	47 children	
Birmingham (to Ashby)	1813	66	3
Kingsbury	1814	2	0

Sources: Shustoke parish Register of Apprentices 1802–1830, DRB 39/65; Nuneaton Parish Register of Apprentices, 1802–34, DR137/20; Attenborough parish Apprenticeship Register 1802–, DR 137/20 WCRO?; Minute Book of the Birmingham Board of Guardians, 1806–?, GP/B/2/1/2, BCA; Bedworth parish Register of Apprentices, 1802, DR 225/34; Kingsbury parish Register of Apprentices, DR(B) 3/126, WCRO; Foremark parish Apprenticeship Register D808 A/PO 1/1, DRO.

Origin of apprentices to Messrs Lambert, cotton spinners, Lowdham mill, Nottingham

Parish	Date	Girl apprentices	Boy apprentices
St Pancras	1799	15	15
St Pancras	1800	0	11

Source: St Pancras Register of Apprentices, 1778–1801, P90/PANI/361, LMA.

Origin of apprentices to Marshall Hutton and Hives, linen manufacturers, Shrewsbury

Parish	Date	Girl apprentices	Boy apprentices
Shrewsbury House of Industry	1805	36	21
Shrewbury House of Industry	1807	1	0
Shrewsbury House of Industry	1808	0	1
St Mary Magdalene, Bridgnorth	1808	1	0
Shrewsbury House of Industry	1809	0	1
Shrewsbury House of Industry	1812	7	4
Shrewsbury House of Industry	1814	9	0
Shrewsbury House of Industry	1817	1	0

During the period 1805–17, those bound to Marshall comprised over 50 per cent of the total from the Shrewsbury House of Industry. Source: Shrewsbury Incorporation of the Poor, Register of Apprentices, 1802–1818, PL2/7/1/1; Bridgnorth borough Apprenticeship Registers, 1802–1818, BB/G/1/10/1–10 (10 registers), SA.

Origin of apprentices to John Marsland and Henry Kelsall, cotton manufacturers, Broadbottom, Glossop

Parish	Date	Girl apprentices	Boy apprentices
St Pancras	1788	0	6
St Pancras	1796	1	7

Source: St Pancras Register of Apprentices, 1778–1801, P90/PANI/361, LMA.

Origin of apprentices to Nathaniel Mason, cotton spinner, Iver, Bucks

Parish	Date	Girl apprentices	Boy apprentices
Lambeth	1793	0	15
Epsom Surrey	1793	?	?

Sources: St Mary at Lambeth, Apprenticeship Registers, 1782–1833, P85/MRY1/270, LMA; Aspin, *Water Spinners*, p. 438.

Origin of apprentices to Merryweather and Whitaker, Burley-in-Wharfedale, Yorks

Parish	Date	Girl apprentices	Boy apprentices
Leeds	1792	2	4
St Margaret and St John, Westminster	1797	36	36
St Margaret and St John, Westminster	1798	14	7
St Margaret and St John, Westminster	1799	2	5
St Margaret and St John, Westminster	1800	2	6
St Margaret and St John, Westminster	1801	12	8
St George, Westminster	1802	6	5
St George, Westminster	1805	5	2
Leeds	1805	7	6
Lambeth via Marsden	1805	*c.* 15	*c.* 15
Leeds	1806	2	1
St Martin in the Fields	1806	–	2
St Pancras	1806	2	–
Lambeth	1806	12	3
St Martin in the Fields	1807	1	4
Lambeth	1807	8	1
St Leonards, Shoreditch	1808	3	6
St Leonards, Shoreditch	1809	9	5
Lambeth	1809	–	3
Leeds	1809	6	6
St Leonards, Shoreditch	1810	–	4
Lambeth	1810	3	5
Lambeth	1811	4	–
St Leonards, Shoreditch	1811	4	
St Leonards, Shoreditch	1812	2	
St Leonards, Shoreditch	1816	3	

Sources: Leeds Apprenticeship Register *c*. 1720–*c*. 1808 LO/AR 1, WYASL; 1797 Report of St Margaret and St John; 1802 Report of St Margaret and St John; St George, Hanover Square Meetings of the Governors and Directors of the Poor. C925, C929 and C930, WAC; St Mary at Lambeth Apprenticeship Registers, 1802–1826, P85/MRY1/271, LMA; St Martin in the Fields Apprenticeship Register, 1802–1824, F4311, WAC; St Pancras Apprenticeship Register, 1802–1867, P90/PANI/362; St Leonard Shoreditch Apprenticeship Register, 1802–, P91/LEN/1332 (microfilm reference 020/172), LMA.

Origin of apprentices to Henry Monteith, Bogle and Co., cotton manufacturer, Blantyre near Glasgow

Parish	Date	Girl apprentice	Boy apprentice
St Clement Danes	1805	9	17
St Clement Danes	1806	2	3
St Clement Danes	1807	2	2
St Clement Danes	1809	11	8

Source: St Clement Danes Apprenticeship Register, 1803–1822, B1268, WAC.

Origin of apprentices to John Morley, silk manufacturers, Seward Stone near Chingford

Parish	Date	Girl apprentices	Boy apprentices
St Margaret and St John, Westminster	*c*. 1800	4	4
Woodford, Essex	*c*. 1800	n/a	n/a
Woodford, Essex	1807	0	6

Sources: 1802 Report of St Margaret and St John; Vestry meetings, Woodford parish, D/P 167/8/3, ERO; Erith, Essex parish registers, p. 28. It is very likely that apprentices from other Essex parishes were bound here, as the silk mills of the region formed a primary destination of the county's poor children.

Origin of apprentices to Ellis Needham, cotton manufacturer, Litton mills, Tideswell

Parish	Date	Girl apprentices	Boy apprentices
St Giles in the Fields	1789	2	10
St George the Martyr Southwark	*c*. 1790	n/a	n/a*
St Giles in the Fields	1790	9	2
St Giles in the Fields	1791	0	5
St Giles in the Fields	1793	3	5
St Giles in the Fields	1794	0	4
St Giles in the Fields	1795	2	3
St James, Piccadilly	1796	11	0
St Paul, Covent Garden	1796	4	0
St Giles in the Fields	1796	2	0

St James, Piccadilly	1797	11	0
Foundling Hospital	c. 1797	c. 10	c. 10
St George, Hanover Square	1803	c. 5	c. 5
St Leonards Shoreditch	1814	7	13
St Pancras	1815	4	4
St George the Martyr, Southwark	1816	2	0

* A report from St James Piccadilly in 1803 found boys there from St George the Martyr employed after the expiration of their apprenticeship.

Sources: St Giles in the Fields parish, Register of Parish apprentices 1780–1802. P/GF/PO/4, CLSAC; St James Piccadilly Minutes of Governors and Directors of the Poor, 1794–1796, D1875; St George, Hanover Square. Meetings of the Governors and Directors of the Poor C925, C929 and C930; St Paul Covent Garden, Minutes of Churchwardens and Overseers, H879, WAC; St Leonard Shoreditch Apprenticeship Register, 1802–, P91/LEN/1332 (microfilm reference 020/172); St Pancras Apprenticeship Register, 1802–1867, P90/PANI/362, LMA; St Pancras Minutes of meetings of Directors of the Poor, 1804–1820, P/PN/PO/1/12 (microfilm reference UTAH 652), CLSAC; St George the Martyr, Apprenticeship Indentures 1799–1836, 1/boxes 51–2, SLHL.

Origin of apprentices to Messrs Newton, cotton manufacturer, Cressbrook mill

Parish	Date	Girl apprentices	Boy apprentices
Ashover, Derbyshire	1796–8	6	0
Bristol	c. 1800	n/a	n/a
St Clement Danes	1815?		
St James Piccadilly?	1810?		
Bristol			
Liverpool			
Chester			
Royal Military Asylum, Chelsea and Southampton	1823–	300	

Sources: Ashover parish register, DRO; E.E. Butcher, *Bristol Corporation of the Poor: Selected Records, 1696–1834*, 1932; St Clement Danes, Papers relating to Parish Apprentices 1802–35, B1353; St Clement Danes, Minutes of Churchwardens, Overseers and Assistants, 1809–?, B1149, WAC; Correspondence concerning enquiry into apprentices bound from a distance, made on the order of the QS at the request of Edward Sacheverell Chandos Pole, then Chairman of Quarter Sessions, who wished to forward details from the enquiry to Chelsea Orphan Asylum, Dec 1840– April 1841, Q/AG/16/1–11; Results of 1840 Enquiry; returns of mills, Q/AG/17–33, Cressbrook mills, Q/AG/29; Abstract of returns of the apprentices in the cotton mills in the county of Derby, 1840, Q/AG/36; Cressbrook mill accounts, D507; William Newton's Account Book, 1814–16, D507 B/B1, DRO.

Origin of apprentices to Samuel Oldknow, cotton spinner, Mellor

Parish	Date	Girl apprentices	Boy apprentices
Foundling Hospital	1790–	n/a but numerous	0?
St Pancras	1814	18	1
RMA Chelsea	1823	4	0
RMA Southampton	1825–8	23	0

Sources: Correspondence with London Foundling Hospital, MF1020, MCA, indicates a long-term connection between the two parties; St Pancras Apprenticeship Register, 1802–1867, P90/PANI/362, LMA; St Pancras Minutes of meetings of Directors of the Poor, 1804–1820, P/PN/PO/1/9 (microfilm references UTAH 651), CLSAC; Correspondence concerning enquiry into apprentices bound from a distance, made on the order of the QS at the request of Edward Sacheverell Chandos Pole, then Chairman of Quarter Sessions, who wished to forward details from the enquiry to Chelsea Orphan Asylum, Dec 1840– April 1841, Q/AG/16/1–11; Results of 1840 Enquiry; Returns of mills, Q/AG/17–33, including Mellor mill, Glossop Q/AG/26; Abstract of returns of the apprentices in the cotton mills in the county of Derby, 1840. Q/AG/36, DRO.

Origins of apprentices to James Pattison, silk manufacturer, Congleton

Parish	Date	Girl apprentices	Boy apprentices
St Giles in the Fields	1799	*c.* 20 children	
St Giles in the Fields	1800	*c.* 20 children	
St Andrew Holborn	1800	19 children	
St Andrew Holborn	1801	19 children	
St Andrew Holborn	1805	15 children	

Sources: St Giles in the Fields parish, Register of Parish Apprentices 1780–1802, P/GF/PO/4, CLSAC; SC1816, p. 76.

Origin of apprentices to Robert Peel, cotton spinner, Summerseat

Parish	Date	Girl apprentices	Boy apprentices
Birmingham	1796	38	9

Source: Minute Book of the Birmingham Board of Guardians, 1783–1806, GP/B/2/1/1, BCA.

Origin of apprentices to Peel, Yates and Co., cotton spinners, Radcliffe Bridge

Parish	Date	Girl apprentices	Boy apprentices
Birmingham	1796	0	16
St George the Martyr, Southwark	1802	5	4
St George the Martyr, Southwark	1806	5	7

Sources: Minute Book of the Birmingham Board of Guardians, 1783–1806, GP/B/2/1/1, BCA; St George the Martyr, Apprenticeship Indentures, 1799–1836, 1/boxes 51–2, SLHL.

Origin of apprentices to Robert Peel, cotton spinner, Hind mill, Bury

Parish	Date	Girl apprentices	Boy apprentices
Birmingham	1796	28	4
Hertfordshire	?	n/a	n/a

Sources: Minute Book of the Birmingham Board of Guardians, 1783–1806, GP/B/2/1/1, BCA; Aspin, *Water Spinners*, 197–8.

Origin of apprentices to Robert Peel, cotton spinner, Burrs mill, Bury

Parish	Date	Girl apprentices	Boy apprentices
St Giles in the Fields	1803	64 children	
St Giles in the Fields	1807	18 children	
St Martin in the Fields	1807	n/a	n/a
Hertfordshire	?	n/a	0

Sources: Aspin, *Water Spinners*; St Martin in the Fields Apprenticeship Register, 1802–1824, F4311, WAC.

Origin of apprentices to Joseph Peel, cotton manufacturer, Fazeley, Tamworth

Parish	Date	Girl apprentices	Boy apprentices
Birmingham	1796	n/a*	n/a*
Birmingham, reassigned from Peel's mill at Summerseat	1796	1	1
Nuneaton	1802	8	1
Colleshill	1803	7	1
Colleshill	1806	5	0
St Martin in the Fields	1808	3	5
St Martin in the Fields	1810	'as many as are eligible'	
Colleshill	1812	1	0

* Several groups of several children were probably sent here. Not all were formally recorded by the Birmingham Guardians.

Sources: Minute Book of the Birmingham Board of Guardians, 1783–1806, GP/B/2/1/1, BCA; Nuneaton parish Register of Apprentices, 1802–1834, DR137/20; Colleshill parish Apprenticeship Indentures; Colleshill parish Register of Apprentices, 1802–1835, DR(B) 100/107, WCRO; St Martin in the Fields Apprenticeship Register 1802–1824, F4311, WAC.

Origin of apprentices to Robinson, cotton manufacturers, Papplewick, Nottinghamshire

Parish	Date	Girl apprentices	Boy apprentices
St Marylebone	?	0	n/a
Birmingham	1808	23 children	

Sources: St Marylebone information from <www.papplewick.org/local/millinfo.htm>, Reports of Birmingham Guardians who visited this mill imply that the majority, if not all, of this number were girls. Minute Book of the Birmingham Board of Guardians, 1806–?, GP/B/2/1/2, BCA; SC1816.

Origin of apprentices to Sewell and McMurdo, flax spinners, Hounslow Heath

Parish	Date	Girl apprentices	Boy apprentices
St George, Hanover Square	1802	n/a	n/a
St Pancras	1804	17	17
St James, Piccadilly	1818	7	7
St Pancras	1818	0	7

Sources: St George, Hanover Square, Meetings of the Governors and Directors of the Poor, C925, C929 and C930, WAC; St Pancras Apprenticeship Register, 1802–1867, P90/PANI/362, LMA; St Pancras Minutes of meetings of Directors of the Poor, 1804–1820, P/PN/PO/1/15 and 16 (microfilm references UTAH 653, 654), CLSAC; Deed of covenant and indemnity in respect of apprentices belonging to the flax mills at Hounslow, 1 March 1821, LMA Turner ACC/0526/36.

Origin of apprentices to Shute, Thomas Rock, silk throwster, Watford

Parish	Date	Girl apprentices	Boy apprentices
St Barts the Great		10–15? children	

Source: St Barts the Great parish register, MS 4010A, GL.

Origin of apprentices to John and William Singleton, cotton spinner, Wigan

Parish	Date	Girl apprentices	Boy apprentices
St Martin in the Fields	1802	0	6

Source: St Martin in the Fields Apprenticeship Register, 1802–1824, F4311, WAC.

Origin of apprentices to Benjamin Smart, cotton spinner, Milverton, Warwickshire

Parish	Date	Girl apprentices	Boy apprentices
Tredington, Warwickshire	1804	1	0
Bloxham, Oxon	1804	2	0

Parish	Date	Girls	Boys
Bloxham, Oxon	1805	1	0
Stratford-upon-Avon	1805	1	0
Stratford-upon-Avon	1807	3	0
Southam, Warwickshire	1808	2	0
Weston-under-Wetherley, Warwickshire	1808	1	0
Bloxham, Oxon	1808	2	0
Butlers Marston, Warwickshire	1810	1	0
St Clements, Oxford	1811	1	0
Southam, Warwickshire	1811	1	0
Stratford-upon-Avon	1812	1	0
St Clements, Oxford	1812	1	0
St Luke, Chelsea	1814	6	0
St Luke, Chelsea	1815	3	0
Tysoe, Warwickshire	1816	1	0

Sources: Correspondence between Benjamin Smart and St Clement parish, Oxford, Z351 (sm); Correspondence between St Clement parish, Oxford, and Benjamin Smart, Z351/1-5, WCRO; Oxford St Clements parish Apprenticeship Indentures, MS DD Par, Oxford St Clements, ORO; St Luke Chelsea Apprenticeship Register, 1802–1813, P74/LUK/117, LMA; Joan Lane, 'Apprenticeship in Warwickshire cotton mills, 1790–1830', *Textile History*, 10, 1979, p. 173.

Origin of apprentices to Strutt, cotton manufacturer, Rickmansworth

Parish	Date	Girl apprentices	Boy apprentices
St James, Piccadilly	1786	6	6
St James, Piccadilly	1787	4	6
St James, Piccadilly	1790	0	1

Source: St James Piccadilly, Minutes of Governors and Directors of the Poor, 1784–1787, D1871; 1787–1790, D1872; 1790–1792, D1873, WAC.

Origin of Apprentices to Toplis, Cuckney 1786–1805

Parish	Date	Girl apprentices	Boy apprentices
Mansfield	1786	1	6
Mansfield	1788	1	0
Mansfield	1792	1	1
Mansfield	1793	0	1
Mansfield	1795	1	1
Mansfield	1796	2	2
Mansfield	1800	0	2
Mansfield	1803	1	0

Mansfield	1804	0	2
Mansfield Woodhouse	1786	2	2
Mansfield Woodhouse	1787	0	1
Worksop	1787	2	0
Worksop	1788	1	1
Worksop	1789	7	3
Carlton, Nottinghamshire	1786	0	1
Carlton, Nottinghamshire	1793	1	1
Eastwood, Nottinghamshire	1786	1	1
Barlborough, Derbyshire	1786	1	0
Barlborough, Derbyshire	1788	1	0
Torworth, Nottinghamshire	1787	0	1
Sutton, Nottinghamshire	1787	0	2
Sutton, Nottinghamshire	1792	0	1
Sutton, Nottinghamshire	1801	0	1
Walesby, Nottinghamshire	1787	1	1
Scartcliff, Nottinghamshire	1787	1	1
Scartcliff, Nottinghamshire	1791	0	1
Staveley, Nottinghamshire	1787	1	0
Staveley, Nottinghamshire	1788	1	0
Farnsfield, Nottinghamshire	1787	0	2
Elmton, Derbys	1787	2	0
Collingham, Nottinghamshire	1787	0	2
Clarborough, nr Retford Nottinghamshire	1787	2	1
Gresley	1788	0	2
Hayton, Nottinghamshire	1788	2	1
London	1788	0	1
London	1792	0	1
London	1801	3	0
Edmonton, Middlesex	1787	5	5
Edmonton, Middlesex	1788	4	6
Edmonton, Middlesex	1789	0	5
Edmonton, Middlesex	1791	0	4
Edmonton, Middlesex	1791	3	1
Edmonton, Middlesex	1794	0	1
Hackney	1787	4	3
Edmonton, Middlesex	1788	5	7

Edmonton, Middlesex	1790	0	10
Edmonton, Middlesex	1791	9	2
Edmonton, Middlesex	1792	3	7
Edmonton, Middlesex	1793	1	2
Edmonton, Middlesex	1794	0	7
Edmonton, Middlesex	1795	6	3
Woodford, Essex	1788	3	5
Woodford, Essex	1790	5	0
Woodford, Essex	1791	2	4
Low Layton, Essex	1788	0	1
Wanstead, Essex	1788	0	5
Wanstead, Essex	1790	0	2
Wanstead, Essex	1795	0	1
Braintree, Essex	1791	0	3
Barking, Essex	1792	10	9 (including a 5yr old)
Doncaster	1788	4	3
Ollerton, Nottinghamshire	1788	1	1
Ollerton, Nottinghamshire	1789	0	1
Hereford	1789	3	14
Buckminster, Leics	1790	0	1
Elksley	1790	0	1
Tottenham	1790	1	7
Tottenham	1792	2	9
Tottenham	1795	2	2
Lambeth	1790	0	1
Lambeth	1791	0	1
Lambeth	1794	14	12
Lambeth	1795	6	9
Lambeth	1800	0	6
Lambeth	1805	9	7
Spalding, Lincolnshire	1791	0	1
Warmsworth, nr Doncaster	1791	1	0
St Michael Bassishaw, city of London	1791	0	2
Abchurch, City of London	1791	1	2
Abchurch, City of London	1792	1	0
Foundling Hospital	1792	10	26
Woodborough, Nottinghamshire	1792	2	0

Cuckney, Nottinghamshire	1792	0	1
Chesterfield, Derbyshire	1792	0	1
Chesterfield, Derbyshire	1796	2	0
Luggershall, Wiltshire	1792	0	2
Collarbourn	1792	0	1
St Marylebone	1794	9	13
St Marylebone	1795	10	7
St Marylebone	1800	10	0
St Marylebone	1802	13	3
St Marylebone	1803	10	9
St Marylebone	1804	3	5
St Marylebone	1805	10	9
St Andrews, Holborn	1792	0	2
Boston, Lincolnshire	1794	0	1
Langwith, Nottinghamshire	1794	0	1
Leicester	1794	0	1
St Martin's, Leicester	1794	4	0
St Margarets, Westminster	1794	13	37
St Margarets, Westminster	1795	0	10
St Margarets, Westminster	1799	0	11
'Westminster'	1800	3	7
St Margaret and St John	1801	8	7
Birmingham	1802	0	7
Birminham	1802	11	5
St Saviours, Southwark	1795	24	25
Hanwell, Middlesex	1792	0	2
Misc. London parishes	1792	4	16
Misc. London parishes	1793	0	1
Misc. London parishes	1794	1	5
Misc. London parishes	1795	0	2
Bradford	1794	0	5
Bradford	1796	0	1
Halifax	1794	7	11
Halifax	1795	4	6
Wakefield	1795	2	0
Highworth, Wiltshire	1795	1	0
Worksworth	1799	0	2
Worksworth	1800	0	1

Ordsall, Salford	1803	0	1
Harrington, nr Spilsby	1803	1	0
Whitwell, Derbyshire	1804	2	0

Source: 'List of children put out apprentice to William Toplis', DD895/1, NA.

Origin of apprentices to Walton Twist Co., cotton manufacturer, Walton-le-dale

Parish	Date	Girl apprentices	Boy apprentices
?	c. 1800	31	49

Source: The 1803 factory returns specifies number of apprentices but not their origin. Evidence from HL1819 suggests that Liverpool is a strong possibility.

Origin of apprentices to John Watson, cotton manufacturer, Salmesbury, near Preston

Parish	Date	Girl apprentices	Boy apprentices
Liverpool	1790	n/a	n/a+
Bristol	1795	?	?*
St Margaret and St John, Westminster	1798	8	8
St George the Martyr, Southwark	1800	5	8
St George the Martyr, Southwark	1802	12	10
Lambeth	1803	5	12
St George the Martyr, Southwark	1805	2	16
St George the Martyr, Southwark	1806	10	16
St George the Martyr, Southwark	1807	3	8

* The records were destroyed in 1940 along with the workhouse; but published work from 1932 refers to request for poor children from a cotton manufacturer near Preston. Almost certainly this was John Watson. Evidence is also provided by adverts for runaways from the mill of children apprenticed from Liverpool, Aspin, *Water Spinners*, p. 51.

Sources: Lambeth parish registers; St George the Martyr, Southwark Apprenticeship Register; Report of conditions at the factory from St Margaret and St John, Westminster, 1802.

Origin of apprentices to Thomas Watson, silk manufacturer, Watford

Parish	Date	Girl apprentices	Boy apprentices
St Martin in the Fields	1796	14	8

Source: St Martin in the Fields Apprenticeship Register, 1795–1803, F4310; St Martin in the Fields Minutes of Meetings of Officers of the Parish, 1795–1806, F2075, WAC.

Origin of apprentices to John Weir, silk manufacturer, Wokingham, Berks

Parish	Date	Girl apprentices	Boy apprentices
St Giles Camberwell	1815	17 children	

Source: St Giles Camberwell Apprenticeship Register, 1803–1817, X097/239, LMA.

Origin of apprentices to Wells and Middleton, cotton spinners, Sheffield

Parish	Date	Girl apprentices	Boy apprentices
St Martin in the Fields	1789	4	0
St Clement Danes	1790	3	–
Lambeth	1790	14	4
St Giles in the Fields	1797	4	–
St Martin in the Fields	1798	4	–
Lambeth	1798	3	–
St Giles in the Fields	1799	7	–
St Martin in the Fields	1799	2	6
St Martin in the Fields	1800	3	3 [5?]
St Giles in the Fields	1800	6	2
St Giles in the Fields	1801	2	–
St Martin in the Fields	1801	1	–
St Martin in the Fields	1802	–	7
St George, Westminster	1802	3	3
St Giles in the Fields	1802	2	2
St Leonards. Shoreditch	1805	2	13
St Martin in the Fields	1808	–	4
Total		**56**	**44**

Sources: St Martin in the Fields Apprenticeship Register, 1784–1794, F4309,1795–1803, F4310, 1802–1824, F4311; St Clement Danes Apprenticeship Records, 1784–1792, B1266, 1784–1801, B1267, WAC; St Mary at Lambeth, Apprenticeship Registers 1782–1833, P85/MRY1/270, LMA; St Giles in the Fields parish, Register of Parish Apprentices, 1780–1802, P/GF/PO/4, CLSAC; St George, Hanover Square Meetings of the Governors and Directors of the Poor, C925, C929 and C930, WAC; St Leonard Shoreditch Apprenticeship Register, 1802–, P91/LEN/1332 (microfilm reference 020/172), LMA.

Origin of apprentices bound to James Whitelegg, cotton weaver, Manchester

Parish	Date	Girl apprentices	Boy apprentices
St Martin in the Fields	1814	0	6

Source: St Martin in the Fields Apprenticeship Register, 1802–1824, F4311, WAC.

Origin of apprentices of Charles Woollan, silk throwster, St Michael, Hertford

Parish	Date	Girl apprentices	Boy apprentices
St Martin in the Fields	1803	3	0
St Sepulchre, Holborn	1803	6–8?	

Source: St Martin in the Fields Apprenticeship Register, 1802–1824, F4311, WAC; St Sepulchre Holborn Apprenticeship Register, MS 3211, GL.

Origin of apprentices to Wooley and MacQueen, cotton spinners, Matlock

Parish	Date	Girl apprentices	Boy apprentices
Winster, Derbyshire	1802	7	0

Source: Winster parish Apprenticeship Indentures, D 776 A/PO 716, DRO.

Origin of apprentices to Workman, Brummell and Hall, cotton spinners, Dartford, Kent

Parish	Date	Girl apprentices	Boy apprentices
Lambeth	1793	0	15
Lambeth	1795	0	3

Source: St Mary at Lambeth Apprenticeship Registers, 1782–1833, P85/MRY1/270, LMA.

Origin of apprentices to Thomas Yates, Cotton spinner and weaver, Tamworth

Parish	Date	Girl apprentices	Boy apprentices
St Martin in the Fields	1809	3	5
St Martin in the Fields	1810	1	8

Source: St Martin in the Fields Apprenticeship Register, 1802–1824, F4311, WAC.

Bibliography

Manuscript sources

Birmingham City Archives

Minute Book of the Birmingham Board of Guardians, 1783–1806, GP/B/2/1/1.
Minute Book of the Birmingham Board of Guardians, 1806–?, GP/B/2/1/2.
St George Parish, Edgbaston Apprenticeship Indentures, MS515/59.

Bristol Record Office

Wick and Abson Parish, Gloucestershire Register of apprentices 1806–1829, P/Abs.

Camden Local Studies and Archives Centre

St Giles in the Fields Parish Register of Parish apprentices, 1780–1802, P/GF/PO/4.
Hampstead Parish Board of Guardians Minutes, 1800–1816, PHA/PO/1/1.
Hampstead Parish Vestry minutes, 1780–1805, P/HA1/M/1/2.
St Pancras Minutes of meetings of Directors of the Poor, 1804–20, P/PN/PO/1/1–17 (microfilm references UTAH 649–654).
St Pancras Minutes of Vestry, 1780–1805, P/PN/M/1/2.

Croydon Local Studies Library and Archives Service

Register of Apprentices, bound out by the Parish of Croydon, 1802–1843, PR1/1/5/1.

Derbyshire Record Office

Parish Records
Alfreton Parish Apprenticeship Indentures, 1805–24, D654 A/PO 244–77.
Church Broughton Parish Apprenticeship Indentures, 1715–1820, D854 A/PO 120–129.
Dale Abbey Parish Apprenticeship Indentures, D1061 A/PO/12/1–11.
Denby Parish Apprenticeship Indentures, D1428 A/PO 72–142.
Elmton Parish Apprenticeship Indentures, D1462 A/PO 289.
Foremark Parish Apprenticeship Register, 1809–1833, D808 A/PO 1/1.
Melbourne Parish Register, 1740–1812, D655 A/PI 1/3.
Repton Parish Apprenticeship Indentures, D638 A/PO 510, 512.

Winster Parish Apprenticeship Indentures, D 776 A/PO 716.

Records of Quarter Sessions
Documents relating to Cotton Mill apprentices Q/AG/1–36.
Reports of cotton mills and factories inspected from the last midsummer sessions to the present. Brief notes on the conditions of the mills by Marmaduke Middleton Middleton, 18 April 1811, Q/AG/7.
Note to register the mill for spinning cotton occupied by Messrs Walter Evans, William Evans, Samuel Evans, and Moses Harvey, situate at Darley in the Parish of St Alkmunds and in the County of Derby, Q/AG/12.
Registration of cotton mills and weaving shops belonging to Messrs Thomas Jewsbury and Co. at Measham, Derbyshire; plus 2 weaving sheds at Appleby, Derbyshire September 1812, Q/AG/13.
Correspondence concerning enquiry into apprentices bound from a distance, made on the order of the QS at the request of Edward Sacheverell Chandos Pole, then Chairman of Quarter Sessions, who wished to forward details from the enquiry to Chelsea Orphan Asylum, Dec 1840–April 1841, Q/AG/16/1–11.
Results of 1840 Enquiry; returns of Mills Q/AG/17–33; including: Lea mill Ashover mill, Q/AG/18; Castleton Edale mill, Q/AG/20; Darley Abbey mill, Q/AG/23–24; Mellor mill, Glossop Q/AG/26; Tideswell, Cressbrook Mills, Q/AG/29,
Mr Pole's queries and answers to them. Q/AG/34–5.
Abstract of returns of the apprentices in the cotton mills in the county of Derby, 1840, Q/AG/36.

Business Records
Cressbrook mill accounts, D507.
William Newton's Account Book, 1814–16, D507 B/B1.
Darley Abbey Cotton mill, D5231.
Litton Mills, John Baker cotton manufacturer, bankruptcy papers, 1811, D394.

Doncaster Archives

Doncaster Township Memorandum Book of the Overseers, 1794–1795, PL/D/1.

Essex Record Office, Chelmsford

Canewdon Parish Vestry minutes, 1801–1816, D/P/219.
Chelmsford Parish Indenture Papers, D/P 94/14.
Chelmsford Parish Vestry meetings, D/P/12/12.
Halstead Parish Apprenticeship indentures, D/P/14/2.
Woodford Parish Vestry meetings, D/P 167/8/3.

Goodchild

Ossett 1794–1836

Guildhall Library, Manuscripts Collection

St Andrew Holborn Parish Apprenticeship Register, 1802–1832, MS 9601.
St Barts Parish Apprenticeship Register, 1802–, MS4010.
St Barts the Great Parish register, MS 4010A.
St Botolph without Aldersgate Parish Apprenticeship Register, 1802–, MS 1471.
St Botolph Aldergate Parish Apprenticeship Register, 1769–1805, MS 2658.
St Dunstan in the west Register of Poor Apprentices, 1803–1887, MS 3003.
St Katherine by the Tower Parish Apprenticeship Register, MS 2660.
St Mary Woolchurch Haw Register of Apprentices, 1811–1830, MS 8116.
St Michael Bassishaw Poor Apprenticeship Register book, 1802– ,MS 2493.
St Michael Crooked Lane Parish Apprenticeship Register, 1807–1839, MS 2766.
St Michael le Querne Parish Apprenticeship Register, MS 7688.
St Sepulchre Holborn Apprenticeship Register, MS 3211.
St Swithin London Stone, Apprenticeship Register, 1809–1815, MS565.

Haringey Archives Service

Tottenham Parish Overseers Records, Papers relating to the journey of Tottenham and Hornsey Parish apprentices to the north (n.d.), Ldbcm:a/1/PT/5C/10.
Hornsey Parish. Re opinion of Counsel on legality of paying premiums for parish apprentices out of private charity funds, 17 July 1832, Ldbcm:a/1/PH/2B/17.
Hornsey Apprenticeship Records,1821–1866, Ldbcm:a/1/PH/3E/3.

Herefordshire Record Office

Almley Parish Vestry Minute Book, 1793–1860, G73/3.
Burrington Parish Register of Apprentices, 1790–1831, G61/1.
Eardisland Parish Register of Apprentices, 1803–1834, AJ32/90.
Felton Parish Register of Apprentices, 1801–1830, G45/52.
Hope–under–Dinmore Parish Minutes of Vestry Meetings: Register of Apprentices, 1802–10, N31/33.
Ledbury Parish Apprenticeship Register, 1805–1825, BO92/62.
Stanford Bishop Parish Book, 1797–1910, N5/1.
Tarrington Parish Apprenticeship Records, 1801–1835, K14/72.
Yarpole Parish Register of Apprentices, 1722–1822, S14/10–11.

Hertfordshire Archives and Local Studies

Royston Parish Records Letter to Royston Parish from Holywell Twist Company, DP87/14/1/6.

Hull City Archives

Parish Records
Kingston-upon-Hull Incorporation for the poor workhouse admissions and discharges, PUH/215.
Kingston-upon-Hull Incorporation for the poor Register of Parish Apprentices, 1802–1844, PUH/1.
Sculwater Register of Parish Apprentices, 1802–44, PUS/411.

Islington Local History Centre

St Mary, Islington, Trustees of the Poor Minutes, 1786–1798.
St Luke Finsbury Vestry Minutes.

Keighley Library

Huddersfield Register of poor children bound apprentice, KC311/18/7.
Thurstonland Apprenticeship Register, 1803–1843, KC271.
Keighley Township Apprenticeship papers, 1664–1832, BK1/2.
Keighley Township apprenticeship indentures, 1664–1812, BK1/2/1.
Assignment of apprentices to new masters and register of apprentices, 1802–1832, BK1/2/2.
Keighley Overseers' correspondence, BK1/11.
Keighley Overseers' miscellaneous, BK1/12.
Keighley Settlement examinations, 1745–1840, BK1/17/1.

Bowcock Charity:
particulars of money and land left by Isaac Bowcock, BK10/538.
Change in conditions of the trust, BK5/1.
Book of proforma apprenticeship indentures, BK5/26.

Lancashire Record Office

Quarter Session Orders, 1784, QSO 2/153.

London Metropolitan Archives

Holy Trinity, Clapham Register of Apprentices, 1804–22, P95/TRI/1/27.
St Andrew Holborn Register of apprentices, 1804–1844, X065/001.
St Giles Camberwell Apprenticeship Register, 1803–1817, X097/239.
St Mary Acton Register of Apprentices, 1760–1815, DRO/052/294.
St Mary at Lambeth, Apprenticeship Registers, 1782–1833, P85/MRY1/270.
St Mary at Lambeth Apprenticeship Registers, 1802–1826, P85/MRY1/271.
St Mary at Lambeth, Apprenticeship Registers, 1827–1856, P85/MRY1/272.
St John at Hampstead Parish: Church Row Camden, Register of Parish Apprentices, 1803–1836, P81/JN1/49.

St John at Hampstead Parish: Church Row Camden, Register of Parish Apprentices, 1825–37, P81/JN1/50.
St Leonard Shoreditch Apprenticeship Register, 1802–, P91/LEN/1332 (microfilm reference 020/172).
St Luke Chelsea Workhouse Apprenticeship Register, 1791–1802, P74/LUK/116.
St Luke Chelsea Apprenticeship Register, 1802–13, P74/LUK/117.
St Luke Chelsea Poor Relief Book, 1806–1810, P74/LUK/019.
St Olave Bermondsey Register of Apprentices, 1767–1782, X020/002.
St Pancras Register of Apprentices, 1778–1801, P90/PANI/361.
St Pancras Apprenticeship Register, 1802–1867, P90/PANI/362.
Transfer of Apprentices to Sewell and Jones, 1 March 1821, Turner Collection ACC/0526/36.

Manchester City Archives

Samuel Oldknow correspondence with the London Foundling Hospital about apprentices MF 1020.
Manchester Overseers of the Poor – Apprenticeship Indentures, 1700–1913, M3/9/1–163.
Parish of Oldham St Mary Apprenticeship Indentures, 1999/81 DRO 24.
Middleton Parish Apprenticeship Records, 1677–1793, M39/3/6/1–14.
Re boy from London to Richard Cobden, M87/2/2/21, 22.
Prestwich Parish Apprenticeship Indentures,1803–28, L160/10/5.
Stretford Parish Apprenticeship Indentures, 1717–1812, L89/9/16/1–97.
Tottington Parish Apprenticeship Records, 1709–1815, L21/3/32.

Greg papers
Samuel Greg Quarry Bank Apprenticeship Indentures, C5/5/2/1–98.
Samuel Greg Quarry Bank Apprenticeship Indentures, 1815–37, C5/5/3/1–125.
Correspondence between Samuel Greg and the Vicar of Biddulph, 1817, C5/8/9/1–2.
examination of Joseph Sefton, who absconded from Styal (2 August 1806), C5/8/9/4.
examination of Thomas Hardisty who absconded from Styal, C5/8/9/5.
QB, Styal, C5/8/27.
Bollin Fee, 1712–1815, C3/2/10/1–46.

National Archives

Factory returns relating to children, 8 March 1810, HO42/104.
Reports from visitors examining conditions for factory children, 1824, HO44/14.
Letters re anxiety about social unrest, 1812, (HO42.122.
Arson attacks on textile factories, HO40.1.
House of Lords Sessional Papers 1819 (PP1819CVIII p. 57, 'An account of the cotton and woollen mills and factories in the UK of GB and Ireland, 1803–18'.

Nottinghamshire Archives

Arnold Parish Apprenticeship Indentures, PR14062/1.
Carlton-in-Lindrick Parish Apprenticeship Register, 1803–15, PR1394.
Mansfield Woodhouse Parish Apprenticeship Register, PR2092.
'List of children put out apprentice to William Toplis', DD895/1.
Voluntary Examination of Jane Bounds of Norton in the parish of Cuckney 'singlewoman', 11 September 1809, DD4P67/71.
Rough Minutes of the General Committee of the Foundling Hospital, DD212/1.
Copy of letter from Secretary of Foundling Hospital to Treasurer, re Toplis, June 1792, DD212/1/5–6.
Extracts from 'Mental recreation' by William Stumbles, 1875 DD 568/30.

Business Records:
Davison and Hawsley, Arnold Mills. Correspondence with Boulton and Watt DD, 452/6/1–13.
Statement by Robert Davison, Arnold, 18 July 1798, DD 568/34.
Pleasley Works business records. Account Books, DDBM 197/1–2.

Oxfordshire Record Office

Correspondence between St Clement parish, Oxford, and Benjamin Smart, Z351/1–5.
Oxford St Clements Parish Apprenticeship Indentures, MS DD Par.
Oxford St Clements Witney Parish Register of Apprentices pre 1803, MS DD Par Oxford Witney.
Witney Parish Register of Apprentices, 1807–1812, MS DD Par Oxford Witney.

Shropshire Archives

Bridgnorth Borough Apprenticeship Registers, 1802–1818, BB/G/1/10/1–10 (10 registers).
Cardington Apprenticeship Indentures, 1665–1834, P54/L/6.
Edgemond Parish Vestry Meetings, P102/L/5/1.
Fitz Parish apprenticeship, 1772–1925, P109/L/6.
Great Ness Register of Parish Apprentices, 1812–1834, P114/L/16/1.
Milson Parish Apprenticeship Register, P189/L/3.
Pontesby list of Parish Apprentices, P220/L/12/263.
Prees Parish Apprenticeship Register, PL2/7/1/1.
Rodington Parish Apprenticeship Register, 1817–1819, P230/L/7.
Shrewsbury Incorporation of the Poor, Register of Apprentices, 1802–1818, PL2/7/1/1.
Stanton-upon-Hine Parish Apprenticeship Register, P167/4/1/2.
Stapleton Overseers accounts, containing list of 'prentices taken', 1744–1802, P268/L/4/2.
Westbury Parish Apprenticeship Register, 1764–1833, P297/L/9/1.

Southwark Local History Library

St Mary Newington, Apprenticeship Register, 1802–31. 891
St Mary Newington, Workhouse Committee Minutes, 1806–20. 930–3
St Mary Newington, Minutes of the Governors and Guardians, 1814–23, 892.
St Saviour, Workhouse Committee Minutes, 1807–30, 96.
St George the Martyr Vestry Minutes, 1785–1809, 555–9.
St George the Martyr Apprenticeship Indentures, 1799–1836. 1/boxes 51–2.
St George the Martyr Annual Register of the parish poor children until they are apprenticed out, 1789–1807, 764.
St George the Martyr 'Plan of disposing of 200 parish children wanted by J. Bury and Co., Muslin Manufacturers of Hope Hill, near Stockport, Cheshire'.
St Olave, Bermondsey Annual Register of parish poor children until they are apprenticed out, 1785–1813, 1619.
St Mary Magdalen, Bermondsesy Minutes of the Governors and Directors of the Poor, 1190–1200.

Staffordshire Record Office

'A list of the children put out prentice by the parish of Blymhill, 1769–1791', D1044/4/1.
Clifton Campville Apprenticeship Register, 1802–1815, D1059/3/10.
Gnosall Parish Apprenticeship Indentures, D951/5/95.
Gnosall Parish Apprenticeship Register, 1802–, D95/5/93.
Madeley Parish Apprenticeship Register 1802– D3412/5688.
Madeley Parish, correspondence with Samuel Greg, Quarry Bank mill, D3412/5/703.
Pattingham Parish Apprenticeship Register, D3451/5/380.
Proposal from Mr Vaux to establish lace factories in London addressed to the Earl of Dartmouth, D (W), 1778, V702.
Seighford Overseers of the Poor Accounts, 1779–1828, (at the front of which is a list of 'all of every of the parish apprentices bound', 1731–1795, D731/12.
Seighford Parish Apprentices Indentures, 1731–1808, D731/13.
Tettenhall Parish Apprenticeship Register, 1802–1829, D571/A/PO/145.

University of Leeds, Brotherton Library, Special Collections

Jonathan Akroyd (Lane Head, Ovenden, Halifax) Account Books, 1772–1802.
William Lupton and Company Ltd, Whitehall Mills, 1694–1958.
R V Marriner Ltd, Greengate Mills, Keighley, 1630–1950.
Marshall and Co., Leeds, 1788–1886.

Warwickshire County Record Office

Alcester Parish Apprenticeship Register, DR360/78
Attleborough Parish Apprenticeship Register, 1802, DR137/20.

Bedworth Parish Register of Apprentices, 1802, DR225/34.
Bulkington Parish Apprenticeship Register, 1802–34, DR198/120.
Coleshill Parish Apprenticeship Indentures, 1694–1836 DR (B) 100/108/1–245.
Coleshill Parish Register of Apprentices, 1802–1835, DR(B) 100/107.
Correspondance between Benjamin Smart and St Clement Parish, Oxford, Z351 (sm).
Kingsbury Parish Register of Apprentices, DR(B) 3/126.
Monks Kirby Parish Register of Apprentices, 1802–15, DR155/62.
Nuneaton Parish Register of Apprentices, 1802–34, DR137/20.
Shustoke Parish Register of Apprentices, 1802–30, DRB 39/65.
Tanworth Parish Register of Apprentices, 1802–38, DRB 19/90.
Temple Grafton Apprenticeship Indentures, 1712–1810, DR201/51.
Warwick St Nicholas Parish Apprentice Certificate Book, DR115/210.
Warwick St Mary Apprenticeship Indentures, DR126/7961.

Westminster Archives Centre

St Anne Soho Apprenticeship Records, 1702–1834, A2262.
St Clement Danes Apprenticeship Records, 1784–1792, B1266.
St Clement Danes Apprenticeship Records, 1784–1801, B1267.
St Clement Dane Apprenticeship Register, 1803–22, B1268.
St Clement Danes Vestry Minutes, 1782–1790, B1072.
St Clement Danes Vestry Minutes, 1791–1797, B1073.
St Clement Danes Vestry Minutes, 1797–1805, B1074.
St Clement Danes Vestry Minutes, 1805–1814, B1075.
St Clement Danes Vestry Minutes, 1814–1822, B1076.
St Clement Danes Minutes of Churchwardens, Overseers and Assistants, 1779–1798, B1147.
St Clement Danes Minutes of Churchwardens, Overseers and Assistants, 1798–1809, B1148.
St Clement Danes Minutes of Churchwardens, Overseers and Assistants, 1809–, B1149.
St Clement Danes Papers relating to Parish Apprentices, 1802–1835, B1353.
St George, Hanover Square Meetings of the Governors and Directors of the Poor, C925, C929 and C930.
St James Piccadilly Minutes of Governors and Directors of the Poor, 1782–1784, D1870.
St James Piccadilly Minutes of Governors and Directors of the Poor, 1784–1787, D1871.
St James Piccadilly Minutes of Governors and Directors of the Poor, 1787–1790, D1872.
St James Piccadilly Minutes of Governors and Directors of the Poor, 1790–1792, D1873.
St James Piccadilly Minutes of Governors and Directors of the Poor, 1792–1794, D1874.

St James Piccadilly Minutes of Governors and Directors of the Poor, 1794–1796, D1875.
St James Piccadilly Minutes of Governors and Directors of the Poor, 1796–1798, D1876.
St James Piccadilly Minutes of Governors and Directors of the Poor, 1798–1801, D1877.
St James Piccadilly Minutes of Governors and Directors of the Poor, 1801–1805, D1878.
St Margaret Apprenticeship Indentures, 1680–1802, E3384.
St Margaret and St John, 'Report of a visit to the different manufactories where children are apprenticed from the parishes of St Margaret and St John the Evangelist, Westminster', September 1802, E3371/95.
Reply from John Toplis to the 1802 Report of St Margaret and St John, 11 September 1802, E3371/17.
St Martin in the Fields Apprenticeship Register, 1761–1784, F4511.
St Martin in the Fields Apprenticeship Register, 1784–1794, F4309.
St Martin in the Fields Apprenticeship Register, 1795–1803, F4310.
St Martin in the Fields Apprenticeship Register, 1802–1824, F4311.
St Martin in the Fields Minutes of Meetings of Officers of the Parish, 1795–1806, F2075.
St Martin in the Fields Minutes of Meetings of Officers of the Parish, 1806–1818, F2076.
St Mary Le Strand Apprenticeship Register, 1767–1788, G1038.
St Paul Covent Garden Minutes of Churchwardens and Overseers, H879.

West Yorkshire Archives Service Bradford (WYASB)

Allerton parish Apprenticeship Register, ISD74/10/2/16.
Allerton-cum-Wilsden apprentices Cliffe Castle, 69D82/9/4/1–170
Barwick in Elmet Parish Book (includes 'Town prentices put out'), RDP 7 46/2.
Barwick in Elmet Parish Account Book, 1776–1813 (includes 'Town prentices put out'), RDP 7 46/3.
Bingley Parish Apprenticeship Register, 33D80.
Burley-in-Wharfedale Parish Apprenticeship Indentures, BDP 33.
Calverley cum Farsley Parish Apprentice Book, BDP 17/89.
Calverley cum Farsley Apprenticeship Indentures, 1764–99, M/86/3/1.
Carleton Parish Apprentice Indentures, BDP 18/126; 131;132; 133;138.
Guiseley Township Apprentices, 1741–1838, BDP 29/113.
Sutton-in Craven Apprentices Cliffe Castle, 69D82/9/3/1–42.
Idle Parish Apprenticeship Indentures,15D74/1/3/1a–e.
Indenture of property William Fison and Co., worsted spinners, Greenholme mill, Burley-in-Wharfedale,10D76/3/177/1.
Robert Heaton of Ponden mill Account Books, B150–155; Day Book, 1794–1807, B156; 'A brief history of the Heaton family', B164.
William Day, worsted manufacturers, Albert Mills, Bradford Account Book, 1812–1816, 10D76/3/187.

West Yorkshire Archive Service: Calderdale (WYASC), Halifax

Halifax Parish Register of Pauper Apprentices, 1802–1832, OR:88.
Halifax Parish Settlement Certificates, 1741–1815, OR:97.
Halifax Parish Settlement Certificates, 1815–43, OR:98.
Halifax Township Indentures of Apprentices, 1716–1833, OR:328.
Halifax Township Apprenticeship Books, 1729–1839, HXT: 192.
Halifax Parish Poor Law Settlements and Removals, c. 1672–1843, MISC93.
Heptonstall Township Apprenticeship Indentures, 1703–1847, HPC/A: 20/1–225.
Heptonstall Township Apprenticeship Register, 1802–1841, (also referred to as the indenture book for the Township of Heptonstall), HPC/A:20/226.
Heptonstall Affiliation Book Bastardy Records, 1807–38, HPC/A:17.
Heptonstall Langfield Parish Removal Orders, 1822–27, TT121.
Langfield Parish Removal Orders, 1844–96, TT122.
Langfield Parish Register of Apprentices, 1810–28, TT99.
Ovenden Parish Register of apprentices, 1802–1844.
Southowram Township Apprenticeship Book, 1763–1835, MISC:164/3.
Southowram Township Apprenticeship Indentures, 1763–1835, HAS/B: 22/4.
Township Settlements and Removals, 1829–48, HPC/A:13/14.
Sowerby Parish Apprenticeship Indentures, c.1783–c. 1838, SPL108.
Sowerby Parish Apprenticeship Register, 1802–, SPL 109.
Sowerby Parish Settlement Certificates, 1687–1820s, SPL 92/1–174.
Sowerby Parish removals and examinations, 1688–1843, SPL 93.
Sowerby Parish Settlement Examinations, 1712–1842, SPL 94/1–84.
Warley Parish Register of Pauper Apprentices, 1802–1843, OR: 143.

West Yorkshire Archive Service, Kirklees [WYASK], Huddersfield

A register of poor children of the township of Huddersfield bound apprentices, 1798–1844, KC 311/18/7.
Batley Township Apprenticeship Indentures, 1780–1825, KC72.
Dewsbury Register of Apprentices, 1737–1838, KC1042.
Thornhill Apprenticeship Indentures, 1729–1844, KC1044/6.
Thurstonland Township records, Apprenticeship Register, 1803–1843, KC271/46–8, 50.

West Yorkshire Archive Service, Leeds (WYASL)

Bramley Parish Apprenticeship Register, 1802–1832, LO/B11.
Bramley Parish Apprenticeship Register, 1833–1843, LO/B10.
Leeds Apprenticeship Register c. 1720–c. 1808, LO/AR 1.
Leeds Workhouse Committee Minutes and Order Book, 1762–1770, LO/M/5.
Leeds Workhouse Committee Minutes and Order Book, 1818–23?, LO/M/6.
Leeds Workhouse Query Book, 1803–1810, LO/Q 2.
Leeds Workhouse Account Book, 1801–5, LO A/1.
Hunslet Parish Apprenticeship Register, LO/HU/3.

Barwick in Elmet parish records; list of apprentices, 1709–1810.
Calverley [St Winifreds] register of poor apprentices, 1793–1810.
West End mill, Fewston: R.V. Marriner, VI, Box 12; Box 32, 46.
Fewston Deeds: 245/1/3 Box 13; 245/2/2, 245/2/3 Box 12; 286 Box 9; 407 Box 15.
William Vavasour Private Diaries, 1798–1827, WYL639/398.

West Yorkshire Archive Service Wakefield (WYASW)

Appeals against the imposition of a girl apprentice from another township, QS 10/33 1794–97.
Wakefield Adjourned Sessions, 22 May 1800, QD1/219.
Halifax 1707–54, list of apprentices, including some sent out of the parish, D53/10/1.
Returns of Cotton and other mills, 1803–1806, QE 33/1.
Sandall Parish Apprenticeship Register, D 20/9/11/3.
Sandall Parish Dame Lady Bowles bequest for binding poor children, 1720–1808, D 20/9/11/5.

William Salt Library, Stafford

Record Book of the Sedgeley Workhouse Apprentices, 1802–1823.

Worcestershire Record Office

Droitwich Register of Parish Apprentices, 1806–1826, b850 BA 839/14.
Feckenham Register of Parish Apprentices, 1805–1834, 705:89 3586/12/v.
Hallow Parish Register of Apprentices, 1802–1822, 850/4832/2/i.
Ombersley Register of Apprentices, 1803–1821, 850 Ombersley 3572 8ii; 3572/17/i.
Tenbury Wells Parish Apprenticeship Register, 1773–1826, B711.85 7406/12.
Wichenford Parish Book, 1769–1829, 850/2253/1.
Worcester St John Parish Register, 1803–1825, 850 1671/3.

Yorkshire Archaeological Society Archives

Pearson, John, 'The life of William Hey FRS', (1822).
Anning, S.T., 'William Hey FRS; the father of Leeds surgery', Leeds Philosophical and Literary Society, 17, 5 (1980), pp. 101–111.

Printed Primary Sources

7 Geo III c 39 (1767) 'An Act for the better regulation of the parish poor children of the several parishes therein mentioned within the Bills of Mortality.'
18 Geo III c 47 (1778) 'An Act for the relief of the poor as it related to the binding of parish apprentices.'
42 Geo III c 46 (1802) 'An Act to require the overseers of the poor to keep a register of the several children who shall be bound by them as apprentices.'
42 Geo III c 73 (1802) 'An Act for the preservation of the health and morals of apprentices and others, employed in cotton and other mills, and cotton and other factories.'
56 Geo III c 139 (1816) 'Act for the better regulating the binding out parish apprentices.'
House of Lords, 'Account of the cotton and woolen mills and factories in the UK, Great Britain, and Ireland 1803–18', *The Sessional Papers,* vol. 108 (1819).
House of Commons, 'Report from the Select Committee appointed to examine into the number and state of Parish apprentices bound into the country from the bills of mortality', *Parliamentary Papers* 1814–15 (304) V 1567 (printed 19 May 1815).
House of Commons, 'Report of the Minutes of Evidence taken before the Select Committee of the state of children employed in the manufactories of the UK', *Parliamentary Papers* 1816 (397) III 235.
House of Commons Parliamentary Papers, 1801–1818.
The Parliamentary Debates (London: Longman), 1803–1820.
Royal Commission on Children's Employment, vol. 5, 1834.

Newspapers and Journals

The Journal of the House of Commons, 1778–1816.
Leeds Intelligencer
Leeds Mercury

Secondary Sources: Contemporary Works

Aikin, J.A., *Description of the Country from Thirty to Forty Miles around Manchester* (London: John Stockdale, 1795).
Baines, Edward, *History of the Cotton Manufacture in Great Britain* (London: Fisher, Son and Co., 1835).
Bray, William, *Sketch of a Tour into Derbyshire and Yorkshire* (London: B.White, 1783).
Brown, John, *A Memoir of Robert Blincoe, an Orphan Boy...* (Manchester: John Doherty, 1832). (Reprinted in *British Labour Struggles: Contemporary Pamphlets 1727–1850,* New York: Arno, 1972).
Burn, Richard, *The Justice of the Peace, and the Parish Officer* (London: T. Cadell, 1793).

Cooke Taylor, W., *Notes of a Tour in the Manufacturing Districts of Lancashire* (London: Duncan and Malcolm, 1842).
Defoe, Daniel, *A Tour through the Whole Island of Great Britain* (1724) (Reprinted London: Dent 1974 with an introduction by G.D.H. Cole and D.C. Browning).
Eden, Frederick. M., *The State of the Poor* (London: B. and J. White, 1797).
Farey, John, *General View of the Agriculture and Minerals of Derbyshire* (London: M McMillan, 1811).
Fielden, John, *The Curse of the Factory System* (London: A. Cobbett, 1836; 2nd edition London: Cass, 1969).
Gaskell, Peter, *Artisans and Machinery* (London: John W. Peter, 1836; Fascimile reprint of the 1st edn, London: Cass, 1968).
Gisborne, Thomas, *An Enquiry into the Duties of Men in the Higher and Middle Classes of Society in Great Britain* (London: B and J White, 1795), 2 vols.
Greg, W.R., *An enquiry into the State of the Manufacturing Population and Causes and Curses Therein Existing* (Manchester, 1831).
Kay-Shuttleworth, James, *Moral and Physical Condition of the Working Classes Employed in the Cotton Manufacture*, 2nd edn (London: Ridgeway, 1832).
Kydd, Samuel, (Alfred), *The History of the Factory Movement from the Year 1802, to the Enactment of the Ten Hours' Bill in 1847* (London: Simpkin, Marshall,1857), 2 vols.
Langdale, Thomas, *A Topographical Dictionary of Yorkshire* (Northallerton: J. Langdale, 1822).
Moser, Joseph, 'Report of the situation of the children apprenticed by the churchwardens, overseers and governors of the poor of the United parishes of St Margaret and St John in the City of Westminster to the cotton manufactory of Messrs H— at M— and Messrs J and T at Cuckney Mills, addressed to the workhouse Board of the said parishes, April 10 1797', *European Magazine and London Review*, 34 (September 1798): 197–201; and (October 1798): 265–8.
Nicholls, George, *A History of the English Poor Law: In Connection with the State of the Country and the Condition of the People* (London: P.S. King and Son, 1898).
Owen, Robert, *An Address Delivered to the Inhabitants of New Lanark on the First of January 1816 at the Opening of the Institution Established for the Formation of Character* (London: Longman, Hurst and Co., 1817).
——, *A New View of Society: Observations on the Effect of the Manufacturing System* (London: Cadell and Davies, 1813).
Pennant, Thomas, *The History of the Parishes of Whiteford and Holywell* (London: B. and J. White, 1796).
Romilly, Sir Samuel, *Memoirs of the Life of Sir Samuel Romilly, with a Selection of his Correspondence, Edited by his Sons* (1840, vol. II, Irish University Press, 1971).
Throsby, J. (ed.), *Thoroton's History of Nottinghamshire* (vol. III, London: B. and I. White, 1797).
Trollope, Frances, *The Life and Adventures of Michael Armstrong, the Factory Boy* (London: Henry Colburn, 1840).

Ure, Andrew, *The Philosophy of Manufactures: or, an Exposition of the Scientific, Moral and Commercial Economy of the Factory System of Great Britain* (London: Charles Knight, 1835).
Wing, Charles, *Evils of the Factory System: Demonstrated by Parliamentary Evidence* (London: Saunders and Otley, 1837).
Young, Arthur, *A Six Months Tour through the North of England* (London: W. Strahan, 1770).

Secondary Sources: Modern Works

Anderson, Michael, *Family Structure in Nineteenth Century Lancashire* (Cambridge: Cambridge University Press, 1971).
Aspin, Chris, *The Water Spinners* (Helmshore: Helmshore Local History Society, 2003).
Berg, Maxine, *The Age of Manufactures 1700–1820: industry, innovation and work in Britain* (London: Routledge, 1994).
Bolin-Hort, Per, *Work, Family and the State: Child Labour and the Organisation of Production in the British Cotton Industry, 1780–1920* (Lund: Lund University Press, 1989).
Boyer, George R., *An Economic History of the English Poor Law, 1750–1850* (Cambridge: Cambridge University Press, 1990).
Brundage, Anthony, *The English Poor Laws 1700–1930* (Basingstoke: Palgrave, 2002).
Burnett, John, *Destiny Obscure: Autobiographies of Childhood, Education and Family from the 1820s to the 1920s* (London: Allen Lane, 1982).
——, *Idle Hands: the experience of unemployment, 1790–1990* (London: Routledge, 1994).
——, (ed.), *Useful Toil: Autobiographies of Working People from the 1820s to the 1920s* (London: Routledge, 1994).
——, David Vincent and David Mayall (eds), *The Autobiography of the Working Class: An Annotated, Critical Bibliography* (Brighton: Harvester Press, 1984–9).
Butcher, E.E., *Bristol Corporation of the Poor: Selected Records, 1696–1834* (Bristol: Bristol Record Society, 1932).
Chapman, S.D., *The Early Factory Masters: The Transition to the Factory System in the Midlands Textile Industry* (Newton Abbot: David and Charles, 1967).
Clapham, John H., *An Economic History of Modern Britain: the Early Railway Age 1820–1850* (Cambridge: Cambridge University Press, 1930).
Clarkson, L.A., *Proto-industrialisation: The First Phase of Industrialisation?* (Basingstoke: Macmillan, 1985).
Collier, Frances, *The Family Economy of the Working Classes in the Cotton Industry 1784–1833* (Manchester: Manchester University Press, 1964).
Crafts, N.F.R., *British Economic Growth during the Industrial Revolution* (Oxford: Clarendon, 1985).
Crompton, Frank, *Workhouse Children: Infant and Child Paupers under the Worcestershire Poor Law, 1780–1871* (Stroud: Sutton Publishing, 1997).

Crowther, M.A., *The Workhouse System, 1834–1929: The History of an English Social Institution* (London: Methuen, 1981).

Cruickshank, Marjorie, *Children and Industry: Child Health and Welfare in North-West Textile Towns During the Nineteenth Century* (Manchester: Manchester University Press, 1981).

Cunningham, Hugh, *The Children of the Poor: Representations of Childhood since the Seventeenth Century* (Oxford: Blackwell, 1991).

——, *Children and Childhood in Western Society since 1500* (Harlow: Longman, 1995).

Cunningham, Hugh, and Pier Paolos Viazzo (eds), *Child Labour in Historical Perspective 1800–1985* (Florence: UNICEF, 1996).

Cunningham, Hugh and Joanna Innes (eds), *Charity, Philanthropy and Reform: From the 1690s to 1850* (Basingstoke: Macmillan, 1998).

Cunningham, W., *The Growth of English Industry and Commerce in Modern Times* (Cambridge: Cambridge University Press, 1903).

Deakin, Simon and Frank Wilkinson, *The Law of the Labour Market: Industrialisation, Employment and Legal Evolution* (Oxford: Oxford University Press, 2005).

Devlin, Ray, *Children of the Pits: Child Labour and Child Fatality in the Coalmines of Whitehaven and District* (Whitehaven: Friends of Whitehaven Museum, 1988).

Digby, Anne, *Pauper Palaces* (London: Routledge and Kegan Paul, 1978).

Djang, T.K., *Factory Inspection in Great Britain* (London: G Allen and Unwin, 1942).

Dobbs, A.E., *Education and Social Movements 1700–1850* (London: Longmans Green and Co., 1919).

Dodd, A.H., *The Industrial Revolution in North Wales* (Cardiff: University of Wales Press, 1951).

Dodd, E.E., *Bingley: A Yorkshire Town through Nine Centuries* (Bingley: Harrison, 1958).

Dunkley, Peter, *The Crisis of the Old Poor Law in England, 1795–1834: An Interpretive Essay* (New York: Garland Publishers, 1982).

Dunlop, O.J., *English Apprenticeship and Child Labour: A History*. With a supplementary section on the modern problem of juvenile labour by O.J. Dunlop and R.D. Denman (London: T Fisher Unwin, 1912).

Edsall, Nicholas C., *The Anti-Poor Law Movement 1834–44* (Manchester: Manchester University Press, 1971).

Erith, E.J., *Essex Parish Records, 1240–1894* (Chelmsford: Essex County Council, 1950).

Fideler, Paul A., *Social Welfare in Pre-industrial England: The Old Poor Law Tradition* (Basingstoke: Palgrave Macmillan, 2006).

Fitton, R.S. and A.P. Wadsworth, *The Strutts and the Arkwrights, 1758–1830: A Study of the Early Factory System* (Manchester: Manchester University Press, 1958).

Floud, Roderick, Kenneth Wachter and Annabel Gregory, *Height, Health and History: Nutritional Status in the United Kingdom, 1750–1980* (Cambridge: Cambridge University Press, 1990).

Frow, Edmund, and Ruth Frow (eds), *The Dark Satanic Mills: Child Apprentices in Derbyshire Spinning Factories* (Salford: Working Class Library, 1987).

George, M. Dorothy, *London Life in the Eighteenth Century* (London: Kegan Paul, Trench, Trubner, 1925).

Giles, Colum and Ian H. Goodall, *Yorkshire Textile Mills: The Buildings of the Yorkshire Textile Industry, 1770–1930* (London: HMSO, 1992).

Gillis, John R., *Youth and History: Tradition and Change in European Age Relations 1770 to the Present* (New York: Academic Press, 1974).

Gomersall, Meg, *Working-Class Girls in Nineteenth-Century England: Life, Work and Schooling* (London: Macmillan, 1997).

Gordon, Linda (ed.), *Women, the State and Welfare* (Madison: University of Wisconsin Press, 1990).

Gray, Robert, *The Factory Question and Industrial England, 1830–60* (Cambridge: Cambridge University Press, 1996).

Hammond, J.L. and Barbara Hammond, *The Town Labourer 1760–1832: The New Civilisation* (London: Longmans, Green and Co., 1917).

——, *The Rise of Modern Industry* (London: Methuen, 1925).

——, *The Skilled Labourer 1760–1832* (London: Longmans, Green and Co., 1919).

Hareven, Tamara, *Family Time and Industrial Time: The Relationship Between Family and Work in a New England Industrial Community* (Cambridge: Cambridge University Press, 1982).

Hastings, R.P., *Essays in North Riding History 1780–1850* (Northallerton: North Yorkshire County Council, 1981).

——., *Poverty and the Poor Law in the North Riding of Yorkshire, c1780–1837* (York: Borthwick Institute, 1982).

Hayek, F.A. (ed.), *Capitalism and the Historians* (London: Routledge and Kegan Paul, 1954).

Heaton, Herbert, *The Yorkshire Woollen and Worsted Industries: From the Earliest Times to the Industrial Revolution* (Oxford: Clarendon Press, 1920).

Hendrick, Harry, *Child Welfare: historical dimensions, contemporary debates* (Bristol: Policy Press, 2003).

——, *Children, Childhood and English Society, 1880–1990* (Cambridge: Cambridge University Press, 1997).

—— (ed.), *Child Welfare and Social Policy: An Essential Reader* (Bristol: Policy Press, 2005).

Henriques, U.R.Q., *Before the Welfare State: Social Administration in Early Industrial Britain* (London: Longman, 1979).

——, *The Early Factory Acts and their Enforcement* (London: Historical Association, 1971).

Heywood, Colin, *A History of Childhood: Children and Childhood in the West from Medieval to Modern Times* (Oxford: Polity, 2001).

Hicks, John, *A Theory of Economic History* (Oxford: Clarendon Press, 1969).

Hill, Bridget, *Women, Work and Sexual Politics in Eighteenth Century England* (Oxford: Basil Blackwell, 1989).

Hindle, G.B., *Provision for the Relief of the Poor in Manchester 1754–1826* (Manchester: Manchester University Press for the Chetham Society, 1975).
Honeyman, Katrina, *Origins of Enterprise: Business Leadership in the Industrial Revolution* (Manchester: Manchester University Press, 1982).
——, *Women, Gender and Industrialisation in England 1700–1870* (Basingstoke: Macmillan, 2000).
Hopkins, Eric, *Childhood Transformed: Working-Class Children in Nineteenth-Century England* (Manchester: Manchester University Press, 1994).
Horn, Pamela, *Children's Work and Welfare 1780–1890* (Cambridge: Cambridge University Press, 1995).
Howe, Anthony, *The Cotton Masters, 1830–60* (Oxford: Clarendon Press, 1984).
Huberman, Michael, *Escape from the Market: Negotiating Work in Lancashire* (Cambridge: Cambridge University Press, 1996).
Hudson, Pat, *The Genesis of Industrial Capital: A Study of the West Riding Wool Textile Industry, c. 1750–1850* (Cambridge: Cambridge University Press, 1986).
——, *The Industrial Revolution* (London: Edward Arnold,1992).
Hudson, Pat and W.R. Lee (eds), *Women's Work and the Family Economy in Historical Perspective* (Manchester: Manchester University Press, 1990).
Hutchins, B.L. and A. Harrison, *A History of Factory Legislation* (Westminster: P.S. King, 1903).
Ingle, George, *Yorkshire Cotton: The Yorkshire Cotton Industry, 1780–1835* (Preston: Carnegie Publishing, 1997).
Inglis, Brian, *Poverty and the Industrial Revolution* (London: Hodder and Stoughton, 1971).
Ittmann, Karl, *Work, Gender and Family in Victorian England* (Basingstoke: Macmillan 1995).
Jennings, Bernard, *A History of Harrogate and Knaresborough* (Huddersfield: The Advertiser Press, 1970).
Joyce, Patrick (ed.), *The Historical Meanings of Work* (Cambridge: Cambridge University Press, 1987).
Keeling, Frederick, *Child Labour in the United Kingdom: A Study of the Development and Administration of the Law Relating to the Employment of Children* (London: P.S. King and Sons, 1914).
——, *The Labour Exchange in Relation to Boy and Girl Labour* (London: P.S. King and Son, 1910).
Kidd, Alan, *State, Society and the Poor in Nineteenth Century England* (Basingstoke: Macmillan, 1999).
King, Peter, *Crime, Justice and Discretion in England, 1740–1820* (Oxford: Oxford University Press, 2000).
King, Steven, *Poverty and Welfare in England 1700–1850: A Regional Perspective* (Manchester: Manchester University Press, 2000).
—— and Alannah Tomkins (eds), *The Poor in England 1700–1850: An Economy of Makeshifts* (Manchester: Manchester University Press, 2003).
Kirby, Peter, *Child Labour in Britain, 1750–1870* (Basingstoke: Palgrave, 2003).
Knott, John, *Popular Opposition to the 1834 Poor Law* (London: Croom Helm, 1986).

Lane, Joan, *Apprenticeship in England 1600–1914* (London: UCL Press, 1996).
—— (ed.), *Coventry Apprentices and their Masters 1781–1806* (Stratford-upon-Avon: Dugdale Society, 1983).
Laslett, Peter, *Family Life and Illicit Love in Earlier Generations: Essays in Historical Sociology* (Cambridge: Cambridge University Press, 1977).
——, *The World We Have Lost* (London: Methuen, 1965).
Lavalette, Michael, *Child Employment in the Capitalist Labour Market* (Aldershot: Avebury, 1994).
—— (ed.), *A Thing of the Past? Child Labour in Britain in the Nineteenth and Twentieth Centuries* (Liverpool: Liverpool University Press, 1999).
Lees, Lynn Hollen, *The Solidarities of Strangers: The English Poor Laws and the People, 1700–1948* (Cambridge: Cambridge University Press, 1998).
Levine, David, *Family Formation in an Age of Nascent Capitalism* (New York: Academic Press, 1977).
Levine-Clark, Marjorie, *Beyond the Reproductive Body: The Politics of Women's Health and Work in Early Victorian England* (Columbus, The Ohio State University Press, 2004).
Lynch, Katherine A., *Family, Class and Ideology in Early Industrial France: Social Policy and the Working Class Family, 1825–1848* (Madison: University of Wisconsin Press, 1988).
McClure, R.K., *Coram's Children: The London Foundling Hospital in the Eighteenth Century* (New Haven: Yale University Press, 1981).
McIntosh, Robert, *Boys in the Pits: Child Labor in Coal Mines* (Montreal and Kingston: McGill-Queen's University Press, 2000).
McKendrick Neil, John Brewer and J.H. Plumb, *The Birth of a Consumer Revolution: The Commercialisation of Eighteenth-Century England* (London: Europa, 1982).
McMillan, Margaret, *Child Labour and the Half Time System* (London: 'Clarion' Newspaper Company, 1896).
Malcolmson, Robert W., *Life and Labour in England 1700–1780* (London: Hutchinson, 1981).
Mandler, Peter (ed.), *The Uses of Charity: The Poor on Relief in the Nineteenth Century Metropolis* (Philadelphia: University of Pennsylvania Press, 1990).
Mantoux, Paul, *The Industrial Revolution in the Eighteenth Century: An Outline of the Beginnings of the Modern Factory System in England* (London: Jonathan Cape, 1928).
Marshall, Dorothy, *The English Poor in the Eighteenth Century: A Study in Social and Administrative History* (London: George Routledge, 1926).
Marshall, J.D., *The Old Poor Law 1795–1834* (London: Macmillan, 1968).
Melling, Elizabeth (ed.), *The Poor: A Collection of Examples from Original Sources in the Kent Archives Office from the Sixteenth to the Nineteenth Century* (Maidstone: Kent County Council, 1964).
Mitchell, B.R. *British Historical Statistics* (Cambridge: Cambridge University Press).
Nardinelli, Clark, *Child Labour and the Industrial Revolution* (Bloomington: Indiana University Press, 1990).

Neale, A.R., *The St Marylebone Workhouse and Institution 1730–1965* (London: St Marylebone Society, 1967).
O'Mahoney, Carol (ed.), *Quarry Bank Mill Memoranda*, vol. 1 (Styal: Quarry Bank Mill Trust, 1989).
Oxley, Geoffrey W., *Poor Relief in England and Wales 1601–1834* (Newton Abbot: David and Charles, 1974).
Parr, Joy, *Labouring Children: British immigrant apprentices to Canada 1869–1924* (London: Croom Helm, 1980).
Perkin, Harold, *The Origins of Modern English Society, 1780–1880* (London: Routledge and Kegan Paul, 1969).
Phillips, G.L., *England's Climbing-Boys: A History of the Long Struggle to Abolish Child Labor in Chimney-Sweeping* (Boston, Mass: Baker Library, 1949).
Pike, Edgar Royston, *Human Documents of the Industrial Revolution in Britain* (London: George Allen and Unwin, 1966).
Pinchbeck, Ivy, *Women Workers and the Industrial Revolution 1750–1850* (London: Routledge, 1930).
—— and Margaret Hewitt, *Children in English Society* (London: Routledge and Kegan Paul, 1969–1973), 2 vols.
Pollard, Sidney, *The Genesis of modern management: A Study of the Industrial Revolution in Britain* (London: Edward Arnold, 1965).
Pollock, Linda A., *Forgotten Children: Parent-child Relations from 1500–1900* (Cambridge: Cambridge University Press, 1983).
Pooley, Colin G. and Jean Turnbull, *Migration and Mobility in Britain since the Eighteenth Century* (London: UCL Press, 1998).
Porter, Roy, *English Society in the Eighteenth Century* (Harmondsworth: Penguin, 1991).
Poynter, J.R., *Society and Pauperism: English Ideas on Poor Relief 1795–1834* (London: Routledge and Kegan Paul, 1969).
Rahikainen, Marjetta, *Centuries of Child Labour: European Experience from the Seventeenth to the Twentieth Century* (Aldershot: Ashgate, 2004).
Randall, Adrian, *Before the Luddites: Custom, Community, and Machinery in the English Woollen Industry, 1776–1809* (Cambridge: Cambridge University Press, 1991).
—— and Andrew Charlesworth (eds), *Markets, Market Culture and Popular Protest in Eighteenth Century Britain and Ireland* (Liverpool: Liverpool University Press, 1996).
Redford, Arthur, *Labour Migration in England 1800–1850* (Manchester: Manchester University Press, 1964).
Reynolds, J., *The Great Paternalist: Titus Salt and the Growth of Nineteenth-Century Bradford* (London: Temple Smith, 1983).
Robinson, Keith, *What Became of the Quarry Bank Mill Apprentices? The Origins, Childhood and Adult Lives of 200 Cotton Workers* (Styal: Quarry Bank Mill Trust (Enterprises) Ltd., 1996).
Rose, Lionel, *The Erosion of Childhood: Child Oppression in Britain 1860–1918* (London: Routledge, 1991).

Rose, Mary B., *The Gregs of Quarry Bank Mill: the Rise and Decline of a Family Firm, 1750–1914* (Cambridge: Cambridge University Press, 1986).
Rose, Michael E., *The English Poor Law 1780–1930* (Newton Abbot: David and Charles 1971).
Rule, John, *The Experience of Labour in Eighteenth-Century Industry* (London: Croom Helm, 1981).
——, *The Labouring Classes in Early Industrial England, 1750–1850* (London: Longman, 1986).
Samuel, Raphael (ed.), *Village Life and Labour* (London: Routledge and Kegan Paul, 1975).
Scarre, Geoffrey (ed.), *Children, Parents and Politics* (Cambridge: Cambridge University Press, 1989).
Scholliers, Peter, *Wages, Manufacturers and Workers in the Nineteenth-Century Factory: The Voortman Cotton Mill in Ghent* (Oxford: Berg, 1996).
Seccombe, Wally, *Weathering the Storm: Working Class Families from the Industrial Revolution to the Fertility Decline* (London: Verso, 1993).
Sharpe, Pamela, *Adapting to Capitalism: Working Women in the English Economy, 1700–1850* (Basingstoke: Macmillan, 1996).
Slack, Paul, *The English Poor Law, 1531–1782* (Cambridge: Cambridge University Press, 1995).
Smelser, Neil J., *Social Change in the Industrial Revolution: An Application of Theory to the Lancashire Cotton Industry 1770–1840* (London: Routledge and Kegan Paul, 1959).
Snell, K.D.M., *Annals of the Labouring Poor: Social Change and Agrarian England, 1660–1900* (Cambridge: Cambridge University Press, 1985).
Steedman, Carolyn, *Strange Dislocations: Childhood and the Idea of Human Interiority, 1780–1830* (London: Virago, 1995).
Stephens, W.B., *Education, Literacy and Society, 1830–1870: The Geography of Diversity in Provincial England* (Manchester: Manchester University Press, 1987).
Stickland, Irina, *The Voices of Children 1700–1914* (Oxford: Basil Blackwell, 1973).
Tadmor, Naomi, *Family and Friends in Eighteenth Century England: Household, Kinship and Patronage* (Cambridge: Cambridge University Press, 2001).
Tann, Jennifer, *Children at Work* (London: Batsford, 1981).
Tate, W.E., *The Parish Chest: A Study of the Records of Parochial Administration in England*, 3rd edn (Cambridge: Cambridge University Press, 1969).
Taylor, James S., *Poverty, Migration and Settlement in the Industrial Revolution: Sojourners' Narratives* (California: The Society for the Promotion of Science and Scholarship, 1989).
Thomas, Maurice W., *The Early Factory Legislation: A Study in Legislative and Administrative Evolution* (Leigh-on-sea, Essex: Thames Bank Publishing Co., 1948).
——, *Young People in Industry 1750–1945* (London: T. Nelson, 1945).
Thompson, E.P., *The Making of the English Working Class* (London: Gollanz, 1963).

Thompson, Kathryn M. (ed.), *Settlement Papers*, Short Guides to Records, no. 28 (London: Historical Association, 1997).
——, *Apprenticeship and Bastardy Records*, Short Guides to Records, no. 30 (London: Historical Association, 1997).
Tilly, Louise A. and Joan W. Scott, *Women, Work and Family* (New York: Holt, Rinehart and Winston, 1978).
Tuttle, Carolyn, *Hard at Work in Factories and Mines: The Economics of Child Labour During the Industrial Revolution* (Boulder, Colorado: Westview Press, 1999).
Unwin, George, *Samuel Oldknow and the Arkwrights: The Industrial Revolution at Stockport and Marple* (London: Longmans, Green and Co., 1924).
Valenze, Deborah, *The First Industrial Woman* (Oxford: Oxford University Press, 1995).
Vincent, David, *Bread, Knowledge and Freedom: a study of nineteenth century working class autobiography* (London: Methuen, 1981).
Voth, Hans-Joachim, *Time and Work in England 1750–1830* (Oxford: Clarendon Press, 2000).
Wadsworth, A.P. and Julia de Lacy Mann, *The Cotton Trade and Industrial Lancashire, 1600–1780* (Manchester: Manchester University Press,1931).
Waller, John, *The Real Oliver Twist: Robert Blincoe – A Life that Illuminates an Age* (Cambridge: Icon Books, 2005).
Walvin, James, *A Child's World: A Social History of English Childhood 1800–1914* (Harmondsworth: Penguin, 1982).
Webb, Sidney and Beatrice Webb, *English Local Government, vol. 7, English Poor law History part 1. The Old Poor Law* (London: Longmans, Green and Co., 1927).
Williams, Gertrude, *Apprenticeship in Europe: The Lesson for Britain* (London: Chapman and Hall, 1963).
Winch, Donald, and Patrick K. O'Brien (eds), *The Political Economy of British Historical Experience, 1688–1914* (Oxford: Oxford University Press, 2002).
Winstanley, Michael, *Working Children in Nineteenth Century Lancashire* (Preston: Lancashire County Books, 1995).
Wrigley, E.A., *Continuity, Chance and Change: The Character of the Industrial Revolution in England* (Cambridge: Cambridge University Press, 1988).
—— and R.S. Schofield, *The Population History of England, 1541–1871: A Reconstruction* (Cambridge: Cambridge University Press, 1981).

Articles and chapters in books

Anderson, Michael, 'Population change in north-western Europe, 1750–1850', in Michael Anderson (ed.), *British Population History from the Black Death to the Present Day* (Cambridge: Cambridge University Press, 1996), pp. 191–279.
——, 'The social implications of demographic change 1750–1950', in F.M.L. Thompson (ed.), *The Cambridge Social History of Britain, 1750–1950* (Cambridge: Cambridge University Press, 1990), vol. 2, pp. 1–71.

——, 'Sociological history and the working class family: Smelser revisited', *Social History*, 1 (1976): 317–34.
Anon, 'The putrid fever at Robert Peel's Radcliffe Mill', *Notes and Queries*, 203 (January 1958): 26–35.
Arnot, Margaret L., 'Infant death, child care and the state: the baby-farming scandal and the First Infant Life Protection Legislation of 1872', *Continuity and Change* 9 (1994): 271–311.
Ashworth, William, 'British industrial villages in the nineteenth century', *Economic History Review*, 3/3 (1951): 378–87.
Basu, Kaushik, 'Child labour: cause, consequence and cure, with remarks on international labour standards', *Journal of Economic Literature* 37/3 (1999): 1083–1119.
Berg, Maxine, 'Factories, workshops and industrial organisation', in Roderick Floud and Donald McCloskey (eds), *The Economic History of Britain since 1700*, vol. 1 1700–1860, (Cambridge: Cambridge University Press, 2nd edn, 1994), pp. 123–50.
——, 'What difference did women's work make to the industrial revolution?' *History Workshop Journal*, 35/1 (1993): 22–44.
—— 'Women's work, mechanisation and the early phases of industrialisation in England' in Patrick Joyce (ed.), *The Historical Meanings of Work* (Cambridge: Cambridge University Press, 1987): 64–98.
—— and Pat Hudson, 'Rehabilitating the industrial revolution', *Economic History Review*, 45/1 (1992): 24–50.
Billingham, Bruce, 'Institution and family: an alternative view of nineteenth century child saving?', *Social Problems*, 33/6 (1986): 33–57.
Blaug, Mark, 'The myth of the old Poor Law and the making of the new', *Journal of Economic History*, 23/2 (1963): 151–84.
—— 'The Poor Law Report re-examined', *Journal of Economic History*, 24/2 (1964): 229–45.
——, 'The Classical Economists and the Factory Acts– a re-examination', *Quarterly Journal of Economics*, 72/2 (1958): 211–26.
Bray, R.A., 'The apprenticeship question', *Economic Journal*, 19/75 (1909): 404–415.
Brebner, J.B., 'Laissez-faire and state intervention in nineteenth century Britain', *Journal of Economic History,* Supplement 8 (1948): 59–73.
Brown, John C., 'The condition of England and the standard of living: the case of cotton textiles, 1806–1850', *Journal of Economic History*, 50/3 (1990): 591–614.
Bruland, Kristine, 'The transformation of work in European industrialisation', in Peter Mathias and John Davis (eds), *The First Industrial Revolutions* (Oxford: Basil Blackwell, 1989), pp. 154–69.
Burnette, Joyce, 'An investigation of female–male wage gap during the industrial revolution in Britain', *Economic History Review*, 50/2 (1997): 257–81.
——, 'Testing for occupational crowding in eighteenth-century British agriculture', *Explorations in Economic History*, 33/3 (1996): 319–45.
Burns, Janet, 'The west riding half timer', *Old West Riding*, 9 (1989): 21–25.

Camps-Cura, Enriqueta, 'Transitions in women's and children's work patterns and implications for the study of family income and household structure: a case study from the Catalan textile sector (1850–1925)', *The History of the Family*, 3/2 (1998): 137–53.

Carter, Paul, 'Poor relief strategies: women, children and enclosure in Hanwell, Middlesex, 1780 to 1816', *Local Historian*, 25 (1995): 164–77.

Caunce, S.A., 'Complexity, community structure and competitive advantage within the Yorkshire woollen industry, c. 1700–1850', *Business History*, 39/4 (1997): 26–43.

——. 'Not sprung from princes: middling society in eighteenth century West Yorkshire', in A. Kidd and D. Nicholls (eds), *The Making of the British Middle Class? Studies in Regional and Cultural Diversity since the Eighteenth Century* (Stroud: Sutton 1998): 19–41.

Chaloner, W.H., 'Mrs Trollope and the early factory system', *Victorian Studies*, 4/2 (1960): 159–66.

Chapman, S.D., 'Cressbrook and Litton Mills: an alternative view' *Derbyshire Archaeological Journal*, 89 (1969): 86–90.

Charlesworth, Philip, 'Foundlers at Marsden', *Old West Riding* 10 (1990): 20–26.

Clark, Gregory, 'Factory discipline', *Journal of Economic History*, 54/1 (1994): 128–63.

Coats, A.W., 'Changing attitudes to labour in the mid eighteenth century', *Economic History Review*, 11/1 (1958): 35–51.

Cody, Lisa Forman, 'The politics of illegitimacy in an age of reform: women, reproduction, and political economy in England's New Poor Law of 1834', *Journal of Women's History*, 11/4 (2000): 131–56.

Coleman, D.C., 'Labour in the English economy of the seventeenth century', *Economic History Review*, 8/3 (1956): 280–95.

Collier, Frances, 'An early factory community', *Economic History*, 2/1 (1930): 117–24.

Cowherd, Raymond G., 'The Humanitarian reform of the English poor laws from 1782–1815', *Proceedings of the American Philosophical Society*, 104/3 (1960): 328–42.

Cunningham, Hugh, 'Child labour in the industrial revolution', *The Historian*, 14 (Spring 1987): 3–8.

——, 'The employment and unemployment of children in England c. 1680–1851', *Past and Present*, 126 (1990): 115–50.

——, 'The decline of child labour: labour markets and family economies in Europe and North America since 1830', *Economic History Review* 53/3 (2000): 409–428.

Dale, Christabel (ed.), 'Apprentices and their masters 1710–1760', *Wiltshire Society* (1961): 1–178.

Davin, Anna, 'Child labour, the working class family and domestic ideology in 19th century Britain', *Development and Change*, 13/4 (1982): 633–52.

D'Cruz, Shani, 'Care, diligence and 'usfull pride' [*sic*]: gender, industrialisation and the domestic economy, c. 1770–.1840', *Women's History Review*, 3/3 (1994): 315–45.

Derry, T.K., 'The repeal of the apprenticeship clauses in the Statute of Apprentices', *Economic History Review*, 3/1 (1931): 67–87.

De Vries, J., 'The industrial revolution and the industrious revolution', *Journal of Economic History*, 54/2 (1994): 249–70.

Edwards, M.M. and R. Lloyd Jones, 'N.J. Smelser and the cotton factory family: a reassessment' in N.B. Harte and K.G. Ponting, *Textile History and Economic History: Essays in Honour of Miss Julia de Lacy Mann* (Manchester: Manchester University Press, 1973): 304–319.

Elbaum, Bernard, 'Why apprenticeship persisted in Britain but not in the United States', *Journal of Economic History*, 49/2 (1989): 337–49.

Elson, Diane, 'The differentiation of children's labour in the capitalist labour market', *Development and Change*, 13/4 (1982): 479–97.

Emmison, F.G., 'Essex children deported to a Lancashire cotton mill, 1799', *The Essex Review*, 53 (1944): 77–81.

Fearn, Hugh, 'The apprenticing of pauper children in the incorporated hundreds of Suffolk', *Proceedings of the Suffolk Institute of Archaeology*, 27/2 (1953): 85–97.

Freudenberger, Herman and Gaylord Cummins, 'Health, work and leisure before the industrial revolution', *Explorations in Economic History*, 13/1 (1976): 1–12.

Freudenberger, Herman, Frances J. Mather and Clark Nardinelli, 'A new look at the early factory labour force', *Journal of Economic History*, 44/4 (1984): 1085–1090.

Foster, John, 'The making of the first six Factory Acts', *Bulletin of the Society for the Study of Labour History*, 18 (1969): 4–5.

Galbi, Douglas A., 'Child labour and the division of labour in the early English cotton mills', *Journal of Population Economics*, 10/4 (1997): 357–75.

——, 'Economic change and sex discrimination in the early English cotton factories', Discussion Paper, Centre for History and Economics, King's College Cambridge. Social Science Research Network Electronic Paper Collection.

——, 'Through eyes in the storm: aspects of the personal history of women workers in the industrial revolution', *Social History*, 21 (1996): 142–59.

Gatley, D.A., 'Child workers in Victorian Warrington: the Report of the Children's Employment Commission into Child Labour', Staffordshire University, KOS Occasional Paper, 1996.

Goddard, V. and B. White, 'Child workers and capitalist development', *Development and Change*, 13/4 (1982): 465–78.

Gray, Robert, 'Factory legislation and the gendering of jobs in the north of England, 1830–1860', *Gender and History*, 5 (1993): 56–80.

——, 'The languages of factory reform in Britain, c. 1830–1860' in P. Joyce (ed.), *The Historical Meanings of Work* (Cambridge: Cambridge University Press, 1987), pp. 143–79.

——, 'Medical men, industrial labour and the state in Britain, 1830–50', *Social History*, 16 (1991): 19–43.

Gritt, A. J., 'The Census and the servant: a reassessment of the decline and distribution of farm service in early nineteenth-century England', *Economic History Review*, 53/1 (2000): 84–106.

Hair, P.E.H., 'The Lancashire collier girl, 1795', *Transactions of the Historic Society of Lancashire and Cheshire*, 120 (1968): 63–86.

——, 'Mortality from violence in British coal mines, 1800–1850', *Economic History Review*, 21/3 (1968): 545–61.

Hall, Catherine, 'The home turned upside down? The working class family in cotton textiles 1780–1950', in Elizabeth Whitelegg (ed.), *The Changing Experience of Women* (Oxford: Martin Robertson in association with the Open University, 1982): pp. 17–29.

Hamilton, Gillian, 'Enforcement in apprenticeship contracts: were runaways a serious problem? Evidence from Montreal', *Journal of Economic History*, 55/3 (1995): 551–74.

Hamilton, Sophie, 'Images of femininity in the 1830s and 1840s', in Eileen Janes Yeo (ed.), *Radical Femininity: Women's Self-representation in the Public Sphere* (Manchester: Manchester University Press, 1998): 79–105.

Hastings, R.P., 'Poverty and the Poor Law in the north Riding of Yorkshire, c1780–1837', *Borthwick Papers*, 61 (1982): 1–41.

Hendrick, Harry, 'Constructions and reconstructions of British childhood: an interpretative essay, 1800 to the present', in Allison James and Alan Prout (eds), *Constructing and Reconstructing Childhood: Contemporary Issues in the Sociological Study of Childhood* (London: Falmer, 1990), pp. 35–59.

Heywood, Colin, 'Age and gender at the workplace: the historical experiences of young people in Western Europe and North America', in Margaret Walsh (ed.), *Working Out Gender: Perspectives from Labour History* (Aldershot: Ashgate, 1999), pp. 48–65.

——, 'The market for child labour in nineteenth-century France', *History*, 66/1 (1981): 34–49.

——, 'On learning gender roles during childhood in nineteenth century France', *French History*, 5/4 (1991): 451–66.

Hindle, Steve, '"Waste"' children? Pauper apprenticeship under the Elizabethan poor laws, c. 1598–1697', in Penelope Lane, Neil Raven and K.D.M. Snell (eds), *Women, Work and Wages in England, 1600–1850* (Woodbridge: Boydell and Brewer, 2004): 15–46.

Horn, Pamela, 'Child workers in the pillow lace and straw plait trades of Victorian Buckinghamshire and Bedfordshire', *Historical Journal*, 17 (1974): 779–96.

——, 'The traffic in children and the textile mills, 1780–1916', *Genealogists' Magazine*, 24/5 (1993): 353–70.

Horrell, Sara and Jane Humphries, 'Child labour and British industrialisation' in M. Lavalette (ed.), *A Thing of the Past? Child Labour in Britain in the Nineteenth and Twentieth Centuries* (Liverpool: Liverpool University Press, 1999), pp. 76–100.

——, '"The exploitation of little children": child labour and the family economy in the industrial revolution', *Explorations in Economic History*, 32/4 (1995): 485–516.

——, 'Old questions, new data and alternative perspectives: families living standards in the industrial revolution', *Journal of Economic History*, 54/2 (1992): 849–80.

——, 'The origins and expansion of the male breadwinner family: the case of nineteenth century Britain', *International Review of Social History*, 42 (1997): 25–64.

Horrell, Sara, Jane Humphries and Hans-Joachim Voth, 'Destined for deprivation: human capital formation and intergenerational poverty in nineteenth century England', *Explorations in Economic History*, 38/3 (2001): 339–65.

——, 'Stature and relative deprivation: fatherless children in early industrial Britain', *Continuity and Change*, 13/1 (1998): 73–115.

Huberman, Michael, 'How did labour markets work in Lancashire? More evidence on prices and quantities in cotton spinning, 1822–1852', *Explorations in Economic History*, 28/1 (1991): 87–120.

Hudson, Pat, 'A new history from below: computers and the maturing of local and regional history', *The Local Historian*, 25 (1995): 209–222.

Humphries, Jane, 'Enclosures, common rights, and women: the proletarianisation of families in the later eighteenth and early nineteenth centuries', *Journal of Economic History*, 50/1 (1990): 17–42.

——, 'Female-headed households in early industrial Britain: the vanguard of the proletariat?', *Labour History Review*, 63/1 (1998): 31–65.

——, 'Short stature among coal-mining children: a comment', *Economic History Review*, 50/3 (1997): 531–7.

——, '"The most free from objection ...". The sexual division of labour and women's work in nineteenth century England', *Journal of Economic History*, 47/4 (1987): 929–49.

Hunt, E.H. and F.W. Botham, 'Wages in Britain during the industrial revolution', *Economic History Review*, 40/3 (1987): 380–99.

Innes, Joanna, 'The distinctiveness of the English poor laws, 1750–1850', in Donald Winch and Patrick O'Brien (eds), *The Political Economy of British Historical Experience, 1688–1914* (Oxford: Oxford University Press 2002): 381–407.

——, 'Parliament and the shaping of eighteenth-century English social policy', *Transactions of the Royal Historical Society*. 5th series, 40 (1990): 63–92.

——, 'Origins of the factory acts: the Health and Morals of Apprenticeship Act, 1802', in Norma Landau (ed.), *Law, Crime and English Society, 1660–1830* (Cambridge: Cambridge University Press, 2002), pp. 230–55.

Jenkins, David T., 'The cotton industry in Yorkshire 1780–1900', *Textile History*, 10 (1979): 75–95.

Jones, S.R.H., 'Technology, transaction costs and the transition to factory production in the British silk industry, 1700–1870', *Journal of Economic History*, 47/1 (1987): 71–95.

Jordanova, Ludmilla, 'Children in history: concepts of nature and society', in Geoffrey Scarre (ed.), *Children, Parents and Politics* (Cambridge: Cambridge University Press, 1989): 3–24.

——, 'Conceptualising childhood in the eighteenth century: the problem of child labour', *British Journal for Eighteenth Century Studies*, 10/2 (1987): 189–99.

——, 'New worlds for children in the eighteenth century: problems of historical interpretation', *History of the Human Sciences*, 3/1 (1990): 69–83.

Kent, D., '"Gone for a soldier": family breakdown and the demography of desertion in a London parish 1750–1791', *Local Population Studies*, 45 (1990): 27–42.
Kidd, Alan J., 'Historians or polemicists? How the Webbs wrote their history of the English poor laws' *Economic History Review*, 40/3 (1987): 400–417.
King, Steve, 'Reconstructing lives: the poor, the poor law and welfare in Calverley, 1650–1820', *Social History*, 22/3 (1997): 318–38.
——, 'Poor relief and English economic development reappraised', *Economic History Review*, 50/2 (1997): 360–68.
——, 'Power, representation and the self: problems with sources for record linkage', *Local Historian*, 27 (1997): 1–11.
Kirby, Peter, 'Causes of short stature among coal mining children, 1823–1850', *Economic History Review*, 48/4 (1995): 687–99.
——, 'The viability of child labour and the Mines Act of 1842', University of Sunderland, School of Social and International Studies, Occasional Papers no. 2, 1996.
Landau, Norma, 'The eighteenth-century context of the Laws of Settlement', *Continuity and Change*, 6/3 (1991): 417–39.
——, 'The laws of settlement and the surveillance of immigration in eighteenth century Kent', *Continuity and Change*, 3/3 (1988): 391–420.
Lane, Joan, 'Apprenticeship in Warwickshire cotton mills, 1790–1830', *Textile History*, 10 (1979): 161–74.
Lane, Penelope, 'Work on the margins: poor women and the informal economy of eighteenth and nineteenth century Leicestershire', *Midland History*, 22 (1997): 85–99.
Levene, Alysa, 'Pauper apprenticeship and the Old Poor Law in London: feeding the industrial economy', forthcoming.
Levine, David, 'Industrialisation and the proletarian family in England', *Past and Present* 107 (1985): 204–226.
——, 'The demographic implications of rural industrialization: a family reconstitution study of Shepshed, Leicestershire, 1600–1851', in Pat Thane and A. Sutcliffe (eds), *Essays in Social History*, vol. 2 (Oxford: Oxford University Press, 1986): 1–22.
Levine-Clark, Marjorie, 'Engendering relief: women, able-bodiedness and the New Poor Law in early Victorian England', *Journal of Women's History*, 11/4 (2000): 107–130.
Lindert, Peter H., 'English living standards, population growth and Wrigley-Schofield', *Explorations in Economic History*, 20/2 (1983): 131–55.
——, 'English occupations 1670–1811', *Journal of Economic History*, 40/4 (1980): 685–712.
Lindert, Peter H. and Jeffrey G. Williamson, 'Revising England's social tables, 1688–1812', *Explorations in Economic History*, 19/4 (1982): 385–408.
Lindsay, Jean, 'An early industrial community. The Evans' cotton mill at Darley Abbey, Derbyshire, 1783–1810', *Business History Review*, 34/5 (1960): 277–301.
Lyons, John, 'Family response to economic decline. Handloom weavers in early nineteenth-century Lancashire', *Research in Economic History*, 12 (1989): 45–91.

McCloskey, D.N., 'New perspectives on the Old Poor Law', *Explorations in Economic History*, 10/4 (1973): 419–36.

MacKenzie, M.H., 'Cressbrook and Litton mills, 1779–1835. Part 1', *Derbyshire Archaeological Journal*, 88 (1968):1–25.

——, 'Cressbrook Mill 1810–35', *Derbyshire Archaeological Journal*, 90 (1970): 60–71.

——, 'Cressbrook and Litton mills: a reply', *Derbyshire Archaeological Journal*, 90 (1970): 56–9.

Marglin, Stephen A., 'What do bosses do? The origins and functions of hierarchy in capitalist production', *The Review of Radical Political Economics*, 6/2 (1974): 60–112.

Marvel, H.P., 'Factory regulation: a reinterpretation of early English experience', *Journal of Law and Economics*, 20/2 (1977): 379–402.

Mathias, Peter, 'Labour and the process of industrialisation in the first phases of British industrialisation', in Peter Mathias and John A. Davis (eds), *The Nature of Industrialisation*, vol. 3, *Enterprise and Labour: From the Eighteenth Century to the Present* (Oxford: Blackwell, 1996), pp. 3–47.

Medick, Hans, 'The protoindustrial family economy: the structural function of household and family during the transition from peasant society to industrial capitalism', in Pat Thane and Anthony Sutcliffe (eds), *Essays in Social History*, vol. 2 (Oxford: Clarendon, 1986): 23–52.

——, 'The proto-industrial family economy', in Peter Kriedte, Hans Medick and Jurgen Schlumbohm, *Industrialisation before Industrialisation: Rural Industry in the Genesis of Capitalism*, (Cambridge: Cambridge University Press, 1981), pp. 38–73.

Minge-Kalman, Wanda, 'The industrial revolution and the European family. The institutionalisation of 'childhood' as a market for family labor', *Comparative Studies in Society and History*, 20 (1978): 454–68.

Mitch, David F. 'The role of human capital in the first industrial revolution' in Joel Mokyr (ed.), *The British Industrial Revolution: An Economic Perspective* (Boulder, Oxford: Westview Press, 1993): 267–307.

Mitchell, Sebastian, '"But cast their eyes on these little wretched beings": the innocence and experience of children in the late eighteenth century', *New Formations*, 42 (Winter 2001): 115–30.

Morris, Morris David, 'The recruitment of an industrial labor force in India, with British and American comparisons', *Comparative Studies in Society and History*, 2/3 (1960): 305–328.

Murray, John E. and Ruth Wallis Herndon, 'Markets for children in Early America: a political economy of pauper apprenticeship', *Journal of Economic History*, 62/2 (2002): 356–82.

Musson, A.E., 'Robert Blincoe and the early factory system', in A.E. Musson, *Trade Union and Social History* (London: Cass, 1974): 195–206.

Nardinelli, Clark, 'Child Labor and the Factory Acts', *Journal of Economic History*, 40/4 (1980): 739–55.

——, 'Corporal Punishment and children's wages in nineteenth century Britain', *Explorations in Economic History*, 19/3 (1982): 283–95.

——, 'The successful prosecution of the Factory Acts: a suggested explanation', *Economic History Review*, 38/3 (1985): 428–30.
——, 'Were children exploited during the industrial revolution?', *Research in Economic History*, 11 (1988): 243–76.
Neff, Charlotte, 'Pauper apprenticeship in early nineteenth century Ontario', *Journal of Family History*, 21/2 (1996): 144–71.
Nelson, Claudia, 'Sex and the single boy: ideals of manliness and sexuality in Victorian literature for boys', *Victorian Studies*, 32 (1989): 525–50.
Nicholas, Stephen and Deborah Oxley, 'The living standards of women during the industrial revolution, 1795–1820', *Economic History Review*, 46/4 (1993): 723–49.
Peacock, A.E., 'Factory Act prosecutions: a hidden consensus?', *Economic History Review*, 38/3 (1985): 431–36.
——. 'The successful prosecution of the Factory Acts', *Economic History Review*, 37/2 (1984): 197–210.
Plumb, J.H., ' The new world of children in eighteenth century England', *Past and Present*, 67 (1975): 64–95.
Pollard, Sidney, 'Factory discipline in the industrial revolution', *Economic History Review*, 16/2 (1963): 254–71.
Pooley, C.G. and J. Turnbull, 'Migration and mobility in Britain from the eighteenth to the twentieth centuries', *Local Population Studies*, 57 (1996): 50–71.
Rimmer, W.G., 'Castle Foregate Flax Mill, Shrewsbury (1797–1886)', *Transactions of the Shropshire Archaeological Society*, 56 (1957–60): 49–68.
Robson, Catherine, 'The Ideal Girl in Industrial England', *Journal of Victorian Culture*, 3/2 (1998):197–233.
Rose, Mary B., 'Social policy and business: parish apprentices and the early factory system 1750–1834', *Business History*, 31/4 (1989): 5–32.
Rose, Michael E., 'Settlement, removal and the new poor law', in Derek Fraser (ed.), *The New Poor Law in the Nineteenth Century* (Basingstoke: Macmillan, 1976): 25–44.
Rose, Sonya O., 'Gender antagonism and class conflict: exclusionary strategies of male trade unionists in nineteenth century Britain', *Social History*, 13 (1988): 191–208.
——, 'Protective labour legislation in nineteenth-century Britain: Gender, class and the Liberal state', in Laura L. Frader and Sonya O. Rose (eds), *Gender and Class in Modern Europe* (Ithaca, NY: Cornell University Press, 1996), pp. 193–211.
Rothschild, Emma, 'An infinity of girls: the political rights of children in historical perspective', Centre for History and Economics, discussion paper (May 2000).
Rushton, Peter, '"The matter in variance": adolescents and domestic conflict in the pre-industrial economy of north east England, 1600–1800', *Journal of Social History*, 25 (1991): 89–107.
Ryden, Goran, 'Iron production and the household as a production unit in nineteenth-century Sweden', *Continuity and Change*, 10/1 (1995): 69–104.
Saito, O., 'Labour supply behaviour of the poor in the English industrial revolution', *Journal of European Economic History*, 10/3 (1981): 633–52.

Sanderson, Michael, 'Education and the factory in industrial Lancashire, 1780–1840', *Economic History Review*, 20/2 (1967): 266–79.

Scholliers, Peter, 'Grown-ups, boys and girls in the Ghent cotton industry: the Voortman mills, 1835–1914', *Social History*, 20 (1995): 201–218.

Shannon, Issy, 'The orphans of Luddenden Dean', *Milltown Memories*, 12 (Summer 2005): 11–12.

Sharpe, Pamela, 'Poor children as apprentices in Colyton 1598–1830', *Continuity and Change*, 6 (1991): 253–70.

Simonton, Deborah, 'Apprenticeship: training and gender in eighteenth century England' in Maxine Berg (ed.), *Markets and Manufacture in Early Industrial Europe* (London: Routledge, 1991), pp. 227–58.

Smail, John, 'Manufacturer or artisan? The relationship between economic and cultural change in the early stages of the eighteenth century industrialisation', *Journal of Social History*, 25/4 (1992): 791–814.

Snell, K.D.M., 'The apprenticeship system in British history: the fragmentation of a cultural institution', *History of Education*, 25/4 (1996): 303–321.

——, 'The Sunday School movement in England and Wales: child labour, denominational control and working class culture', *Past and Present*, 164 (1999): 122–68.

—— and Millar, J., 'Lone-parent families and the Welfare state: past and present.', *Continuity and Change*, 2/3 (1987): 387–422.

Solar, Peter, 'Poor relief and English economic development. A renewed plea for comparative history', *Economic History Review*, 50/2 (1997): 369–74.

Spenceley, G.F.R., 'The health and disciplining of children in the pillow lace industry in the nineteenth century', *Textile History*, 7 (1976): 154–71.

Stobart, J., 'An eighteenth century revolution? Investigating urban growth in north-west England, 1664–1801', *Urban History*, 23 (1996): 26–47.

Tadmor, Naomi, 'The concept of the household family in eighteenth century England', *Past and Present*, 151 (1996): 111–40.

Taylor, James S., 'A different kind of Speenhamland: non resident relief in the industrial revolution', *Journal of British Studies*, 30 (1991): 183–208.

Thane, Pat,'Childhood in history', in Michael King (ed.), *Childhood, Welfare and Justice: A Critical Examination of Children in the Legal and Childcare Systems* (London: Batsford, 1981), pp. 6–25.

Thomas, E.G., 'Pauper apprenticeship', *The Local Historian*, 14 (August 1981): 400–406.

Thompson, Kathryn M., 'Apprenticeship and the New Poor Law: a Leicester example', *The Local Historian*, 19 (1989): 51–8.

Tuttle, Carolyn, 'A revival of the pessimist view: child labour and the industrial revolution', *Research in Economic History*, 18 (1998): 53–82.

Walker, Kenneth O., 'The Classical Economists and the Factory Acts', *Journal of Economic History*, 1 (1941): 168–77.

Wall, Richard, 'The age at leaving home', *Journal of Family History*, 3/2 (1978): 181–202.

——, 'Leaving home and the process of household formation in pre-industrial England', *Continuity and Change*, 2/1 (1987): 77–102.

Whipp, Richard, 'Labour markets and communities: an historical view', *The Sociological Review*, 33 (1985): 768–91.

—— and M. Grieco, 'Family and workplace: the social organisation of work', Warwick Economic Papers, 239 (1983).

Winstanley, Michael, 'The factory workforce' in Mary B. Rose (ed.), *The Lancashire Cotton Industry: A History since 1700* (Preston: Lancashire County Books, 1996), pp. 121–53.

Woodward, Donald, 'The determination of wage rates in the early modern north of England', *Economic History Review*, 47/1 (1994): 22–43.

Wright, H., 'Sowerby Parish Apprentices', *Transactions of the Halifax Antiquarian Society* (1934): 57–76.

Unpublished Theses

Anderson, Philip W., 'The Leeds workhouse under the old Poor Law, 1726–1844', University of Leeds MPhil, 1977.

Capper, T.E.H., 'The rise and decline of the industrial colonies at Backbarrow, Cark-in-Cartmel and Lowood between the eighteenth and the twentieth centuries', University of Lancaster MA, 1969.

Evans, Clare, 'The separation of work and home? The case of the Lancashire textiles 1825–1865', University of Manchester PhD, 1990.

Ferguson, I.D.B., 'Fewston Mill', University of Leeds BA Dissertation, Folk Life Studies, 1967.

Knox, W.W., 'British apprenticeship 1800–1914', University of Edinburgh PhD, 1980.

Moore, Sian, 'Women, industrialisation and politics', University of Essex PhD, 1988.

Randall, Adrian R., 'Labour and the Industrial Revolution in the West of England woollen industry', University of Birmingham PhD, 1979.

Shutt, Graham, 'Wharfedale water mills', University of Leeds MPhil, 1979.

Unpublished Typescript

Newbold, Dorothy Hester Helena, 'The Poor Law. St Mary Newington, 1790–1834 n.d.' [SLHL].

Index

absconders 115, 123, 124, 132, 183, 201, 210
    returning 115, 124
absconding 8, 39, 122, 124, 160, 179, 181, 182, 199, 206, 209, 228
    costs of 124
    gender differences in 160
abuse 19, 25, 27, 31, 50, 51, 52, 107, 175–86, 221, 236, 248, 250, 253, 254
    physical 25, 175–86, 221, 250, 258
    sexual 13, 176, 185, 186, 255
accidents, mill 210
Act of 1691 23
Act of 1778 19, 304
Act of 1802 (Health and Morals of Apprentices) 11, 47, 48, 50, 51, 53, 115, 140, 170, 171, 172, 173, 182, 186, 187, 211, 234, 235, 240, 242, 244, 245, 252, 254, 255, 256, 257, 258
Act of 1802 (register of apprentices) 49
Act of 1816 51, 52, 103, 231
Acts of Parliament 11, 215
advertisements 6, 35
    newspapers 35, 36, 124, 157
agents 8, 11, 34, 37, 38, 39, 40, 44, 95, 114, 116, 123, 157, 190, 191, 192, 201, 232, 233
Aikin, John 131
Ainsworth, David 60, 61, 68
Akers and Beever 92, 96
Akroyd, J 103, 299
Alder Mills 83, 273
Aldermanbury 38
Alfreton parish 277, 293
Almondbury 69
Alrewas 84, 107
Andrew, Thomas 68, 92, 154, 265
Appleby 84, 277
apprentice children (see also under parish apprentice) 40, 47, 124, 145, 228, 237, 255
apprentice house 27, 40, 104, 108, 110, 119, 127, 138, 171, 186, 188, 254, 265, 266

apprenticeship, fictive 129, 137
apprenticeship, 'real' 129, 222
apprenticeship system 87, 113, 126, 139, 216, 261, 262
apprenticeships, trade 40, 42, 129
    traditional 26, 33, 40, 53, 78, 88, 261
arithmetic (*see also* numeracy) 48, 140, 165
Arkwright, Richard 6, 34, 156, 185
Arnold Parish 41, 63, 70, 71, 73, 80, 84, 86, 88, 92, 123, 231, 250, 270
Ashby 84, 277
Ashby de la Zouch 104
Ashton, Samuel 45, 46, 64, 67, 92, 97, 105, 106, 109, 154, 240, 243, 244, 265
Aspin, Chris 131
assault 185
Atherton, Peter (see also Harrison and Atherton) 59, 61, 62, 66
autobiography 131, 200, 209, 232

Backbarrow 2, 36, 38, 40, 41, 59–61, 68, 92, 96, 105, 107, 130, 138, 141, 147, 159, 161, 164, 166, 167, 171, 172, 178, 186, 188, 196, 205, 207, 228, 229, 240, 244, 251, 266
Bakewell 66 185
Bank mill, Salford 88, 96, 265
bankruptcy 79, 106, 195, 196, 221, 247, 250, 258, 259, 276
Barnsley, Joshua 38
bastardy 172
beating 178–84, 211, 242, 248
beds 145, 246, 257
Bedworth parish 158, 275, 278
Benyon and Benyon 81, 85, 92, 99, 154, 157, 267
Benyon's linen factory 85
Bermondsey lace factory 225
Bermondsey parish 57
Bernard, Thomas 47
Bible 116, 141
Biddulph, parish 117
    Vicar of 37
Bill of 1811 51, 52

Birch, John 59, 60, 61, 92, 96, 105, 106, 107, 154, 251, 266
Birmingham 149, 157, 158, 159, 169, 203, 206, 207, 209, 210, 212, 217, 219, 220, 221, 225, 226, 246, 253, 259, 263, 267, 271, 277, 282, 283, 284, 288
Birmingham Guardians 133, 136, 159, 180, 181, 206, 209, 225, 226, 243, 246, 247, 251, 253
Birmingham workhouse 35, 98,
Birstall 67
birth parish 58, 95, 196, 203, 205, 206, 236, 238, 261
birth rate 18
birth, place of 259
Blackwall, Robert 71, 270
bleaching 127, 137
Blincoe, Robert 64, 107, 124, 132, 144, 145, 147, 149, 183, 184, 186, 188, 192, 201, 209, 212, 252, 264
Blymhill 82
board and lodging 119, 120, 128, 161, 162
bobbin doffers 131, 132
Bolton 88, 136
books, for apprentices 141, 164, 210, 211, 224
Bott, John 62, 74, 92, 99, 158, 159, 161, 181, 243, 246, 267
Bowcock Charity 79
Bradford 79, 288
breakfast 191, 192, 205, 251, 257
Brighton 217, 219, 220, 251, 266
Bristol Corporation 85, 86, 87, 89, 96, 97, 98, 110, 120, 217, 219, 220, 221, 233, 234, 268, 270, 271, 272, 281, 289
Bristol Guardians 233
Bristol workhouse 234
Bromley, Rev. William 140, 223
Bromsgrove factory 131
Broster, Joseph 68
Buckinghamshire 100
Buckley, James 65
Burley mill 44, 180, 225, 254
Burley-in-Wharfedale 2, 38, 64, 70, 71, 96, 109, 190, 207, 209, 240, 247, 249, 279
Burn, Dr Richard 24, 25
Burton (on Trent) 84, 92, 149, 271
Bury St Edmunds 88, 96, 265

Bury, Jeremiah 38, 67, 71, 92, 97, 105, 154, 179, 185, 240, 259, 268
business difficulties 108, 115, 248, 249, 250, 260
business failure 106, 195, 196, 232, 247, 259, 260, 262
business performance 239, 246, 247, 248, 255
business records 7, 11, 142
business success 97, 98, 99, 107, 109, 110, 111, 121, 149, 239, 243, 255, 259, 260

Calder Valley 104
calico printers 68, 71, 74, 75, 83, 92, 265, 277
calico weaving 71, 72, 76, 80, 83, 93, 98
Calrow, William 68, 92, 106, 154, 268
Calverley-cum-Farsley 30, 79
Calvert I&C 104
Canewdon, Essex 217, 219, 220, 231
Capitalism 10, 106, 175, 195
carding 21, 131, 133, 137
care (*see under* parish apprentices)
Carleton 79
Cartmel[l] 27, 59, 60, 68, 161, 229, 240, 243, 266
Castleton 70, 71, 99, 231, 270
Catechism 22, 116, 223
centralised production 1, 3
chalk dust 144
Chambers, Mr 103
Chapman, Stanley 123
charity 16, 79, 231
chastisement (see also beating, punishment) 179, 182, 183, 211
Chatham, Kent 88, 96, 100, 217, 219, 220, 229, 272
Chavat and Co 62
Chelmsford apprentices 81, 114, 116
Chelmsford parish 27, 38, 81, 96, 114, 116, 181, 217, 219, 220, 221, 230, 273
Chelmsford overseers 27, 211
Cheshire 7, 74, 75, 92, 93, 94, 95, 107, 166, 167, 196, 269, 275
child labour 5, 142, 145, 146, 151, 175, 176, 247
 abuse of 175, 186
 as independent worker 146
 attitudes to 4, 5, 9, 10
 demand for 6, 34, 78, 85, 95, 98, 130

'free' 7, 247
institutional 98
supply of, 95, 98, 102, 125, 141
child poverty 22, 73
childbirth 142, 169
childhood 3, 145, 146, 193, 200
children
    abused 10, 233, 260
    illegitimate 19, 172
    nimble fingers of 131, 178
    pauper 8, 18, 19, 25, 26, 27, 28, 29, 30, 47, 81, 87, 88, 130, 227, 233, 264
    poor 7, 8, 13, 19, 22, 25, 33, 35, 38, 51, 55, 58, 60, 63, 71, 73, 78, 82, 83, 85, 87, 88, 89, 95, 97, 98, 99, 100, 101, 106, 108, 111, 18, 128, 139, 149, 152, 200, 206, 215, 216, 224, 227, 231, 237, 238, 246, 253, 262, 280, 289
    voices of 12, 199–214, 221
    workhouse 4, 22, 34, 35, 36, 44, 55, 59, 60, 98, 99, 104, 110, 117, 118, 126, 157, 177, 180, 201, 237, 269
Chingford, Essex 77, 93, 100, 241, 257, 280
Chorlton 96
Christie, Lorenzo 87, 103, 231
Church Broughton parish 80
Church of England 116, 141
Churchill, Benjamin 74, 86, 92, 98, 154, 162, 240, 268
Churchwardens 18, 25, 39, 42, 49, 56, 75, 185, 215, 247
City of London 38, 52, 217, 220, 288
Clapham parish 78, 217, 219
Clayton and Walshman 6, 105
cleaners 131
cleaning 126, 131, 132, 137, 166, 188, 256
cleanliness 5, 48, 49, 104, 248, 253, 255, 265
Clegg, Benjamin 78, 92, 154, 240
Clegg, John 65
clergyman 49, 116, 140, 141, 164, 202, 246, 254, 258
Clitheroe 41, 65, 93, 115, 273
cloaths 42, 117, 124, 167
clothing 23, 48, 103, 104, 114, 116, 117, 119, 120, 121, 126, 127, 194, 206, 242, 253, 254, 258
clothing allowance 42, 118, 119
Coggeshall 81

Colbeck, Ellis and Wilks 43, 137, 154, 182, 257, 269
Coleshill 28, 82, 83, 274
Collier, James 65
collusion 180, 238
    between employers and parish 11, 180, 194, 238, 240
Collyer, Edward 68
Colne, Lancs 60, 72, 93, 273
Colquhoun, Patrick 5
combing 108, 131
compassion 217
complaints
    about apprenticeship system 25, 39, 43, 47, 107, 116, 180, 181, 185, 189, 236, 242, 250, 251
    by apprentices 26, 127, 141, 161, 181, 182, 183, 192, 199, 200, 201, 202, 203, 204, 205, 206, 207, 208, 209, 211, 212, 213, 218, 224, 248, 249, 250, 252, 253, 257, 259, 262, 263
compulsion 13, 31, 176, 177, 178, 182, 218, 221, 227, 232, 264
Congleton 62, 94, 96, 109, 239, 282
consent 28, 37, 44, 177, 210, 227, 230, 235, 237
control (of labour) 7, 12, 113, 124, 125, 126, 129, 173, 178, 180
Cooke and Kilner 71
cooking 166, 167
Cooper and Matchett 74, 92, 98, 109, 110, 155, 241,169
cordwainer 79
corporal punishment 13, 176, 178, 179, 213
correspondence between parish and firm 11, 95, 117, 133, 136, 147, 161, 166, 209, 216
cost containment 116, 118, 176, 248, 260
costs of parish apprentices 13, 42, 103, 107, 111, 113–28
costs and benefits of parish apprentices 113–28
cotton bleaching 127
cotton dust 144
cotton industry 1, 108, 261
cotton particles 144
cotton picking 21, 132, 133
cotton spinners 6, 67, 68, 70, 73, 83, 109, 265, 266, 267, 269, 274, 278, 282, 290, 291
cotton trade 53, 89

cotton weaver 65, 67, 68, 71, 84, 93, 94, 276, 277, 291
Courtauld's silk mill, Braintree 222
Coventry 83, 99, 217, 219, 220, 267
Coventry silk manufacturers 83
Cowpe, Hollins, Oldknow 92, 98, 105, 106, 155, 241, 269
Cowpe, John 61
Cragg works, Prestbury 66, 75
Cresswell, Nicholas 70, 92, 99, 155, 157, 241, 270
Cromford 2, 6, 131
crooked legs (see also deformity) 136
cruelty 25, 26, 182, 184, 185, 186, 211, 222, 237, 254, 259, 263
cruelty, apprentices' complaints of 182, 211, 222
Cuckney 45, 46, 57, 66, 70, 73, 75, 77, 80, 81, 84, 93, 94, 97, 99, 123, 133, 138, 157, 160, 162, 171, 189, 195, 202, 206, 212, 219, 221, 230, 231, 242, 248, 249, 274, 285, 288

Dale Abbey parish 80
danger 6, 145, 188, 250
Darley Abbey 241
Dartford, Kent 70, 94, 291
Davison and Hawksley 41, 45, 63, 70, 71, 73, 74, 84, 88, 98, 106, 108, 123, 127, 155, 185, 193, 195, 205, 231, 236, 241, 243, 250, 259, 270
death rate 18, 123
Defoe, Daniel 4
deformity 135, 169, 188
Denby parish 80, 277
dependency ratio 3, 7, 18
Derby 22
Derbyshire 7, 12, 24, 62, 71, 72, 74, 75, 80, 83, 87, 92, 93, 94, 95, 97, 98, 99, 103, 108, 110, 126, 148, 149, 217, 220, 231, 235, 269, 277, 281, 286, 288, 289, 291
Dicken and Finlow 84, 92, 99, 149, 155, 157, 158, 159, 209, 212, 241, 243, 246, 271
diet 122, 202, 203, 29, 242, 248, 260, 262
   apprentices' complaints about 191, 192, 204, 206, 248, 252, 255
   bland 191, 193, 235, 253
   composition of 191, 204, 205

   inadequate 13, 123, 176, 191, 192, 193, 204, 205, 250, 251, 254, 258
   monotony of 192, 193, 253, 258
   quality of 170, 192, 202, 204
dietary deficiency 192, 193, 225, 251
dietary deprivation 190, 193
dinner 172, 188, 191, 192, 193, 205, 212, 256, 257
Directors of the Poor 39, 41, 44, 56, 136, 139, 183
dirtiness 193, 206, 251, 253
disability 30, 188
disciplinary practices 161
discipline 1, 3, 7, 16, 49, 50, 113, 125, 126, 142, 143, 145, 175, 177, 178, 180, 182, 183, 194, 197, 211, 213, 242, 258
disposable labour (see also expendability) 8, 102, 114, 124, 146, 158
disposal of children 12, 26, 33, 89, 117, 237, 262, 263
dissatisfaction of children 204, 205, 209, 210, 212, 213
Dixon, Thomas 67
Dodenhoff, Clement 149, 196
domestic production 1, 2, 5
domestic service 33, 87, 103, 129, 165, 166, 168
domestic skills 167, 173, 208, 224, 229
domestic trades 151
domestication 142
domesticity 165, 166, 167, 168, 173, 229
Doncaster 88, 98, 217, 219, 220, 221, 231, 259, 270, 287
Douglas, John 38, 43, 62, 66, 230
Douglas, William (see also Holywell and Pendleton) 27, 36, 37, 38, 43, 59, 61, 63, 64, 65, 66, 69, 75, 76, 81, 88, 93, 96, 105, 106, 109, 114, 116, 122, 131, 32, 133, 137, 147, 148, 152, 155, 162, 168, 170, 181, 182, 190, 191, 203, 204, 21, 224, 228, 258, 272
drawers 122, 163
dyeing 137

Ealing 21
earnings of children 4, 122, 123, 163, 164
East midlands 80
Eccles 27, 66
economic conditions 17, 78, 106, 250

economic structure 56, 70, 126
Edale cotton mill 87, 92, 157, 270
Eden, Frederick 5, 6
Edgbaston 84, 85, 267
Edmonton parish 57, 212, 286, 287
education 25
    basic 48, 115, 141
    complaints of efficiency of 141, 207,
        209, 210, 211, 213, 251, 254, 257
    costs 114, 115, 116, 123, 126
    provision 39, 48, 115, 123, 126, 140,
        141, 229, 242, 246, 248, 251, 254,
        258, 260, 262
efficiency of parish apprentice 121
Elizabethan Poor Law 17, 22, 215
Ellis, Needham 61, 71, 75, 93, 99, 107, 155,
    167, 195, 241, 245, 252, 280
Elmton parish 24, 286
emetics 144
emoluments 163, 189
employability of apprentices 136, 139, 140
employment 6, 7, 8, 53, 56, 124, 248, 256
    of apprentices 92, 106, 111, 133, 134,
        135, 241
    of children 8, 10, 15, 21, 22, 35, 92,
        133, 158, 203
    factory 6, 48, 59, 133–5, 141, 142, 143,
        146, 149, 169, 187, 261
    gender 151–73, 246
    at night 190, 234
    opportunities after apprenticeship 13,
        21, 43, 111, 124, 126, 129, 130, 138,
        139, 141, 142, 143, 146, 147, 149,
        159, 160, 163, 164, 165, 166, 168,
        221, 224, 255, 264
Emscote mill 28, 157, 245, 256
England, south of 34, 37, 58, 99
enterprise(s) 12, 33, 46, 50, 52, 56, 61, 63,
    73, 79, 83, 90, 91–112, 114, 119,
    120, 123, 127, 141, 148, 149, 154,
    161, 170, 172, 176, 178, 182, 185,
    189, 190, 191, 195, 196, 202, 211,
    222, 233, 240, 246–50, 253, 257,
    264
entrepreneur 15, 95, 108, 177, 227
Epsom 217, 219, 279
Essex 12, 38, 68, 77, 78, 81, 89, 93, 96, 97,
    100, 217, 220, 230, 257, 274, 280,
    287
Euxton, Lancs 93, 275
Evans, Darley Abbey 241, 243, 244

expendability 8, 102, 114, 124, 147, 158
expenses 114, 115, 116, 120, 124, 126, 128
experimental methods 3, 106, 114, 125, 128,
    129, 175, 178
experimentation 13, 125, 136, 173, 176
exploitation 5, 10, 13, 175–97, 204, 210,
    212, 213, 238, 247, 250, 253

Factories Regulation Act 1819 53
factories
    rural 2, 7, 34, 96, 106, 125, 159, 209
    urban 2, 59, 96
factory
    atmosphere 144
    conditions 197, 203, 224, 231, 232, 235,
        262
    legislation, and Poor Law 48, 51
    longevity 109, 110, 255
    management 13, 119, 149, 195, 239
    masters 7, 38, 40, 47, 197, 239, 262,
        263, 264
        bankruptcy of 195
        character of 108, 115, 179, 197, 223,
            239
        cruelty of 179, 184, 186, 197, 211,
            233, 263–4
        propriety of 15, 25, 139, 186
        supply of 8, 29–30, 36
    noise 145
    owners, character of 11, 48, 50, 51, 114,
        119, 159, 204, 234, 235
    proprietors, parish pre-binding screening
        of 43, 44, 95, 116, 133, 138–40, 147
        163, 219, 222, 225, 227, 230, 232,
        234, 256, 262
    regime 144, 197, 262
    visitors 11, 126, 180, 183, 200, 211
    visits 132, 140, 204, 216, 228
    worker, requirements of 13, 123, 128,
        130, 140, 143, 146, 160, 167, 176,
        261
family
    economy 10, 151
    separation 207
    visits to factories 236
fatherless families 19
Fazeley 28, 82, 83, 84, 283
fees 40, 41
Felkin, William 26
female apprentices 103, 142, 148, 156, 168
female puberty, issues of 151, 153, 168

Fewston 70, 73, 87, 96, 137, 231, 244, 257, 269
fibres 131, 137, 144
Fielding, Sir John 24, 25
fines 29, 30, 49, 52, 178, 185
fine income 29, 30, 119
Firm failure, cost to ratepayers of 79
fish oil 145
fishing trade 68, 231
Fitz, Shropshire 267
flax dressing 43, 136, 137
flax spinning 87, 110
food 103, 104, 116, 122, 126, 127, 176, 188, 190, 194, 196, 204, 229, 251
   complaints about 192–3, 204–7, 213, 249
   monotony of 191, 205, 252
   quality of 190–93, 203–7, 246, 248, 251–2
   quantity of 190–93, 203–7, 213, 224, 237, 246, 251–2, 258
Foremark parish 80, 277
Foundlers 219
Foundling Hospital 26, 41, 99, 103, 118, 138, 217, 218, 219, 221, 226, 248, 281–2, 288
Fowler brothers 83, 93, 99, 155, 273
frames 26, 132, 144
framework knitting 82, 83
French, Philip 38–9
fresh air 145

Galbi, Douglas 143, 145, 146, 154
Garnett and Horsfall 39
Garnett, Jeremiah 65, 93, 155, 173
Garnett, Thomas 41, 115
Garth, William 60, 93, 97, 155, 273
Gauxholme mill 62, 277
Geary and Ranyard 72
gender
   constructs 165
   differences 151–2
   division of labour 9, 10, 13, 78, 114, 151–4, 160, 164, 173
   identity 10, 165
   inequality 151–2, 161, 173
   and parish apprenticeship 103, 155–73
   gender pay 161
   preference 30, 154, 158
   segregated sleeping accommodation 126, 170, 172
   socialisation 142, 153, 160, 166, 173
gendered workers 142, 153, 160
gendering of education 164
gendering of trades 9, 78
geographical distribution of apprentices 95
George, Dorothy 23, 223
girl preference (by employers) 103, 155, 156, 158, 159, 160, 173, 246, 271, 277
girls
   cheerful 156, 160, 166, 189
   healthy 35, 117, 157
Gisborne, Thomas 6
Glasgow 28, 37, 45, 60, 61, 93, 154, 239, 280
Glossop 64, 93, 157, 278
glove making 21, 86
Gnosall parish 24, 82
Gorton and Thompson 75, 99, 124, 155, 157, 162, 202, 241, 243, 274
Gorton, Richard 66
Gorton, Thomas 38, 39, 40, 116
Gosport 96, 265
government 11
Greenholme mill 109
Greg, Samuel 37, 93, 105, 106, 109, 117, 127, 132, 160, 171, 188, 210, 241, 243
Guardians of the Poor 18, 49, 215
guild 151

Haigh, John 43, 93
Haigh, Samuel 107
Haigh, Thomas 107
hair picking 21
Halifax 78, 79, 96, 104, 289
Halstead parish 81, 217, 220, 221, 230, 274
Hampstead 21, 217
   Board of Guardians 21
Hancox and Wakefield 84, 130, 263
handspinning 131
Hanging Bridge mill 104
Hanway, Jonas 19
Hanway's Act 1767 19, 41
Hanwell parish 81, 217, 219, 220, 227, 288
Harding, Charles 67, 83, 93, 99, 155, 158. 274
Hardnumm, Norris and Co 93, 155, 275
Harrison and Atherton 62, 92, 154, 157, 266
Harrison and Leyland 93, 155, 241, 243, 244, 275

Harrison, William 69
Haslam, Thomas 46, 64, 67, 93, 97, 155, 275
Hawksworth, Thomas 80
Haywood and Palfreyman 38, 46, 74, 75, 76, 93, 96, 107, 116, 137, 155, 157, 195, 202, 207, 210, 241, 243, 258, 275
Head, John 67, 93, 155, 276
health 37, 45, 48, 134, 203, 208, 228, 229, 242, 246–58
    damage to 6, 13, 22, 135, 144, 145, 176, 181, 188, 190, 205
    gender differential of 159–60, 169
    implications of night work 50, 189
healthy 5, 35, 117, 123, 157, 158, 173, 190, 246
heat of factories 144
heating in factories 256
Heaton Norris, Stockport 71, 268
Heptonstall 79
Hereford 86, 97, 217, 220, 287
Herefordshire 12, 29, 85, 86
Hertfordshire 89, 100, 147, 272, 283
Hey, William 50, 249
Heywood, Colin 146, 151
Hides, Andrew 184
Hind mill 84
Hodgkinson, R&G 71, 93, 155, 276
Hodgson, Isaac 65, 93, 97, 106, 108, 133, 149, 155, 241, 255, 276
Hodgson, John 66
Holbeck 121
Hollins and Co 62, 105, 106
Holt Town, Manchester 66, 74, 75, 76
Holt, David 74, 75, 76, 93, 96, 109, 132, 133, 140, 155, 241, 255, 276
Holywell (Douglas) 38, 39, 43, 59, 61, 63, 65, 66, 75, 76, 86, 93, 105, 109, 123, 135, 147, 148, 155, 169, 170, 182, 190, 191, 202, 228, 240, 243, 257
Holywell Twist Company 39, 96, 147, 161, 271
home, parish apprentice concept of 195, 199, 205, 206, 207, 209, 224, 238
homesickness 202, 204, 206, 207, 208, 209, 210, 213, 253
Hope-under-Dinmore 29
Hornsey parish 57
Horrell, Sara 151, 177–8
Hounslow 44, 64, 74, 75, 78, 257, 284

Hounslow flax mills 44, 64, 74, 75, 94, 100, 171, 285
hours
    long 13, 59, 126, 135, 144, 149, 176, 179, 181, 187, 189, 194, 196, 212, 248, 252, 254, 258
    of work 13, 176, 187, 188, 204, 206, 211, 229, 242, 245, 251, 253, 254, 255, 258, 262
House of Industry 19, 88, 267, 278
House of Lords Committee
    (1818) 134, 159, 169, 181, 256
    (1819) 134, 159, 169, 181. 256, 275, 289
household work 166–7
housewifery 78, 79, 129
Hudson, John Edward 62, 93, 155, 277
Hull 64, 87, 96, 99, 102, 217, 219, 220, 231, 269, 270
    Guardians 104
    workhouse 104
Hulse, Joseph 80, 93, 98, 106, 155, 277
humanitarian 16, 178, 197
Humanitarianism 16
Humphries, Jane 151, 178
hunger 188, 192, 204

illegitimacy 170
ill health 30
illness 48, 210
ill-treatment 183, 233, 236
indentures 24, 25, 27, 28, 29, 38, 41–5, 56, 76, 85, 87, 122, 136–7, 140, 213, 217, 226, 253, 263
    execution of 27, 40, 43, 44, 64, 232, 263
    expiration of 228
    signing of 44, 139, 176–7, 217, 226, 233
independent workers 130, 131
industrial
    schools 104
    system 9, 12
    training 140
industrialisation 4, 8, 9, 13, 55, 59, 128, 143, 151, 175, 261
Ingersley mills 68
injury 48, 145, 188
Innes, Joanna 47, 55
inspection 22, 47, 50, 51, 132, 133, 134, 167, 172, 173, 180, 209, 218, 221, 224–5, 228–37, 245, 251, 253, 256, 263

Inspectors 11, 134, 184, 245, 255
intercourse (improper) 172, 246
interviews with parish apprentices 132, 168, 199–200, 205, 208, 213, 228
iron trades 26
Islington 78, 100, 217, 219, 220, 222
Iver, Bucks 69, 93, 100, 279

Jackson, Charles 70
Jewsbury, Thomas 80, 83, 84, 93, 98, 108, 133, 149, 155, 157, 159, 161, 172, 203, 241, 243, 244, 246, 277, 294
Johnson, Mr 39, 123, 190
Jordanova, Ludmilla 200
Justice of the Peace 29, 49, 52, 215, 234

Keighley 6, 79, 96, 105
Kent 12, 70, 78, 88, 89, 94, 100, 217, 220, 229, 272, 291
Kenyon, Lord 215, 234
Kershaw, Ottiwell 65
Kidderminster
　carpet weaving 81
　carpet weavers 82, 83, 85
King, Steve 17
Kingsbury parish 83, 273, 277
Kirk mill, Chipping, Preston 62, 92, 241, 243, 244, 266

labour
　'free' 7, 53, 97, 102, 109, 119, 120, 124
　　cheap 127
　　gender of 151–73
　　hours of 133, 179, 189, 194, 254
　　intensification of 13, 123, 125, 175, 176, 187, 247
　　quality of 95, 123, 139
　　redistribution of 56
　　renewal 7
　　supervision of 128, 129, 145, 197, 226
　　unpaid 7, 111, 212
　force
　　controlled 113, 126
　　disciplined 113, 126, 129, 143
　　docile 113, 128
　　gender composition of 114
　　industrial 9–10, 13, 15, 48, 52, 55, 57, 59, 98, 125, 261, 164
　　youthful 7, 20, 55, 95, 103, 264

market 8, 13, 15, 21, 57, 58, 89, 95–6, 106, 111, 113, 125, 146, 177, 264
　flexible 13, 106, 125, 264
productivity 130
retention 147–8, 219, 242, 247, 258
supply 34, 128, 148
turnover 7, 123
lace
　factory 22, 225
　manufacturer 22
Lambert, Messrs 46, 64, 93, 99, 107, 155, 192, 195, 237, 241, 243, 254, 278
Lambeth parish 69, 71, 99, 100, 225, 247
Lancashire 7, 12, 33, 39, 46, 61, 64, 80, 85, 87, 88, 89, 92, 93, 94, 95, 100, 116, 167, 177, 180 205, 275
Lane, Joan 179
language of parish apprentices 13, 173, 199
Lavalette, Michael 175
Lecky, Hugh 71
Leeds 29, 30, 50, 78, 96, 180, 217, 219, 220, 221, 222, 249, 279
　Poor Law 249
　workhouse 180, 205, 222
Lees, James 67
Lees, Lynn Hollen 16, 152
legislation 33–53, 113, 126, 140, 215, 221, 225
Leicester 72, 74, 78, 102, 103, 104, 110, 157, 269, 288
Leicestershire 80, 92, 95
letters from apprentices 147, 199, 203, 228
liking 38, 45, 177, 218, 223, 226
Lincoln 87
Lincolnshire 12, 287–8
linen 1, 12, 42, 76, 80, 81, 92, 93, 172, 261, 267, 275, 278
　factory 76, 81, 85, 92, 93, 99
　yarn 137
literacy 115, 129, 140, 141, 164, 210
litigation 128
Litton mill, 71, 73, 74, 75, 86, 99, 105, 147, 162, 167, 173, 184, 186, 188, 192, 195, 196, 211, 212, 224, 241, 245, 251, 252, 280
Liverpool 21, 80, 89, 96, 97, 98 102, 104, 110, 265, 266, 269, 276, 281, 289
Liverpool workhouse 110
local support systems 219
Locke, John 4

lodging 103, 119 120, 128, 161, 162, 171, 172, 203, 206, 251, 252, 256
lodgings 170, 204
London parishes 12, 19, 22, 26, 28, 33, 35, 38, 41, 43, 49, 52, 55–61, 73, 77, 78, 88, 89, 95, 96, 97–100, 107, 110, 120, 133, 157, 158, 161, 168, 202, 209, 212, 217, 220, 223, 227, 231, 233, 249, 252, 255, 257, 286
long hours, apprentices' complaints of 248, 252
Lowdham mill 46, 93, 107, 184, 188, 192, 195, 209, 236, 237, 241, 254, 278
Luddenden Dean 104

machine minders 30, 130–31
machinery 127, 145, 192
   automatic 192
   cleaning 132, 141, 188, 156
   oiling of 132, 188
   unguarded 145
machines 3, 21, 127, 130–35, 145, 188, 256
Madeley parish 82
magistrates (role in apprenticeship system) 13, 18, 20, 42, 44, 47, 51, 54, 185, 196, 197, 215, 225–6, 234–5, 237, 239, 247
   factory inspections 49, 51, 132, 185, 234–5, 237, 239, 247, 255
male apprentices 148–9, 157
Malthus, Thomas 16
Malthusian Trap 3
management of apprentices 138, 194
Manchester 2, 36, 38, 65, 66, 68, 71, 74, 75, 76, 79, 93, 94, 96, 107, 116, 122, 126, 133, 135, 146, 154, 159, 163, 168, 169, 184, 217, 220, 222, 234, 241, 243, 244, 247, 250, 256, 265, 276, 291
   magistrates 234
   Poor House 135
Mansfield 80, 84, 92, 97, 130, 133, 134, 135, 219, 241, 263, 269, 285–6
Marlow, William 65
Marquis de Bombelles 131
marriage 18, 142
mariners 68
Marsden 69, 71–2, 77, 81, 93, 96, 105, 107, 133, 157, 171, 182, 188, 194, 196, 203, 208, 211, 231, 236, 241, 253, 274, 279,

Marshall Edward 24
Marshall, John 121, 243
Marshall, Hutton and Hives 81, 93, 99, 137, 155, 241, 278
Marshall's Shrewsbury linen factory 81, 85, 99, 179, 243
Marsland and Kelsall 64, 93, 155, 157, 278
Mason, Nathaniel 69, 93, 100, 155, 157, 279
Matlock, Derbyshire 94, 109, 291
Mayfield 103–4
McConnell, Henry 110
McConnell, James 126–7
McGarrick, John 65
meal breaks 188, 205, 212, 256
meals, irregularity of 192, 205–206
Measham 80, 83, 84, 93, 98, 133, 161, 172, 203, 277
medical
   evidence 50, 135, 159
   men 144, 256
   officers 45
   opinion 134, 169
medicine 251
Melborne parish 80
Mellor 6, 65, 94, 202, 219, 233, 241, 245, 282
Merryweather and Whitaker 46, 62, 96, 105–106, 148, 180, 196, 222, 247, 249, 279
Merryweather, George 37, 38, 39, 44, 50, 64, 67, 70–74, 77–8, 93, 115, 159, 166, 172, 184–5, 189–90, 193–4, 202, 205, 207, 209, 222, 234, 241, 243–4, 247, 249–50, 254
Metropolis 55, 97, 99, 185
Meyer, Joseph 56
Middleton, Lancs 64, 67, 265
Midlands, the 26, 38, 52, 71, 78, 80, 81, 82, 85, 86, 88, 89, 95, 96, 97, 99, 109–10, 124, 142, 153, 158, 159, 226, 227, 232, 253, 262
migrants 24
migration 106
mill inspection (see under inspection)
mills
   rural 2, 7, 58, 96
   isolated 2, 34, 58, 91, 95, 96, 194
Mitchell and Co. (including Mitchell and Holt) 66, 76, 96, 109, 115, 122, 123, 137, 157, 163, 164, 183, 202, 223, 224, 256, 277
Monteith and Bogle 28, 45, 60, 61

moral
   control 129, 186
   effects of children's factory work 5, 6, 22, 187
   standards 4, 158
   teaching 141, 254, 256
morality 170, 173, 186
morals, children's 22, 48, 115, 168, 172, 230, 246, 248, 251, 254
Morley, John 77, 93, 155, 241, 257, 280
Morley, Mr 100, 120, 230, 243, 257
Moss, John 138, 188, 266
Muggeridge, Richard 201
mule spinners 122, 163
mule spinning 2, 122, 131, 132, 136, 144, 163, 189
Mulverton, Warwickshire 63
Murgatroyd, William Henry 104
muslin 21, 71, 166
mutilations 145

Nantwich cotton mill 84, 92, 99, 120, 124, 154, 159, 161, 181, 209, 226, 240, 243, 267
Napoleonic Wars 18, 102, 103, 106, 108
Nardinelli, Clark 176
Navy 103
Needham, Smith and Heywood 61
neglect 216, 219, 239–60
neglectful parishes 173, 231, 239–60, 262, 263
neglectful practices 13
neglectful proprietors 108, 173, 195, 233, 239–60, 262, 263
negligence 219, 220–1, 225, 228, 230, 232, 242
negligence
   of factory owners 225–42
   of parish 219–32
   rating 225, 229
networks 1, 234, 235, 249
New Lanark 131
Newcastle 68
newspaper advertisements (see under advertisements)
newspapers 6, 35, 36
Newton, James 60
Newton, Messrs 281
night work 48, 50, 190, 195, 242, 244, 255–6

night working 51, 125, 187, 189–90, 194, 221, 242, 249, 253, 258
Noaille, Peter 157
Noble, James 157
north of England 38, 52, 78, 96
Nottingham 22, 36, 37, 63, 64, 71, 73, 74, 80, 86, 88, 98, 231, 236, 278
Nottinghamshire 12, 41, 45, 75, 80, 92–5, 97–9, 127, 217, 219, 227, 269–70, 284, 286–8
numeracy 115, 129, 140, 164, 165
Nuneaton 83, 277, 283
nutrition 191, 193

oakum picking 21
obedience 104, 121, 166
officialdom 15, 19
old Poor Law 15, 17, 18, 25, 33
Oldham 65, 78, 79, 80, 92, 132
Oldknow, Samuel 6, 41, 65, 94, 106, 155, 156, 219, 233, 241, 243, 245, 282
Ombersley parish 42, 85
Operatives 34
organisational change 106
organisational forms 13, 95
Ormskirk, Lancs 67
orphans 19, 104, 207, 235
Oswestry Guardians 36
Otley 38, 44, 67, 70, 72, 73, 76, 78, 93, 96, 222, 249
outputs 11
out-relief, loss of 23, 227, 231
outworkers 96
overlookers 97, 105, 130, 148, 166, 179, 184–6, 192, 201, 246
Overseers of the Poor 25, 27, 28, 49, 52, 56, 87, 88, 116, 117, 166, 200, 215, 217, 224, 226, 239, 258
overtime work 189, 193, 211
Overwork 123, 135–6, 187–9, 225, 250, 255
Owen, Robert Dale 131
Oxfordshire 28, 87, 99, 218, 236

paper trail 263
Papplewick 84, 94, 98, 109, 127, 128, 284
Papplewick cotton mill 98, 109, 127, 284
parental approval of binding 177, 218, 223, 225, 230
parental opposition to binding 81, 177, 182, 194, 221, 227, 231, 232, 233, 235–6

Index   335

parents 5, 7, 33, 52–3, 55, 103, 121, 125,
    177–8, 182, 194, 202, 207–8, 215,
    223, 225, 227, 230–1, 233, 234–5,
    238, 248
parish and firm interaction 36, 95
parish apprentices
  abuse of (see also under abuse) 27,
      175–97
  age distribution 45, 46
  appearance of 160, 169, 187, 193, 202,
      203, 206, 228, 248, 257
  benefits of 113–28
  binding of 11, 24, 26–8, 33, 37, 41,
      43–4, 46, 51, 52, 54, 58, 60, 73,
      78, 85, 87, 95, 101–2, 116–7, 133,
      138–40, 147, 151–3, 163, 173, 176,
      192, 212–3, 216, 225, 227, 231, 232,
      235, 237, 256, 258, 262–3
  care of 11, 13, 15, 19, 25, 44, 63, 88,
      103, 104, 115, 120, 138, 171, 172,
      177, 182, 187, 202, 215, 217, 221,
      227, 231, 233, 234, 235, 237, 248,
      250, 251, 252, 256, 257, 259, 263
  cost of 113–28
  distribution of 55–90
  economic contribution of 91–111
  expiry of term 7–8, 41–2, 114, 122, 139,
      141, 146, 147, 148, 149, 153, 158–9,
      161, 162, 163, 168, 212, 238, 242,
      246, 259
  gender of 103, 151–73
  group binding of 45, 60, 64, 69, 71, 73,
      74, 81, 82, 83, 86, 88, 89, 91, 96,
      98, 99, 103, 104, 106, 118, 156, 217,
      219, 220, 228, 231, 232, 252, 283
  health of (see under health)
  height of 157, 193
  indentures (see under indentures)
  independent workers 13, 130, 199, 261
  length of term 39, 41, 121, 212
  long distance binding of 52, 58, 61, 63,
      80, 81, 88, 91, 95, 111, 261
  maintenance costs of 113–28
  marginal cost of 121
  measurement of value 137–43, 264
  as proportion of total labour 104–6
  protection of (see under protection,
      protective)
  register 25, 57
  re-binding 60
  regulation 11, 47, 171, 230, 234, 256

  return to parish 11, 30, 45, 118, 177,
      183, 195, 199, 202, 205, 207, 226
  supervision by clergymen 116, 141, 226
  term 8, 13, 20, 24, 28, 39, 42, 45, 121–2,
      139, 140, 148–9, 162, 222, 255, 262
  testimony of 152, 170, 182, 224, 234,
      256
  traffic in 26, 88, 110
  treatment of 247
  upkeep of 107, 119, 120, 121
  use of 91–111
  value of 91, 114, 121, 128
  voices of 199–213
  wastage rate 118, 123
parish apprentices' concept of 'home' 199,
    206–7, 209, 238
parish apprenticeship system (factory) 8,
    12, 13, 26–7, 33–54, 55–8, 71, 73,
    78, 87, 88–9, 100, 102–4, 113–4,
    118–9, 121, 123, 126, 129–30, 139,
    176, 200, 216, 221, 223, 227–8, 237,
    261–2
  Emergence of 12, 26
  decline of 227
  economics of 40, 42, 129
  gender and 103, 153, 154, 165, 173
parish apprenticeship
  concern about 236, 237
  extent of 33, 55–90
  gains from 113–28
  long term outcomes of (see under
      employment opportunities)
parish communication with parents
parish examinations 142, 199
parish meetings, minutes of 216, 228
parish officers 17, 25, 27, 28, 34, 38, 52,
    88, 122, 124, 132–3, 139, 140, 142,
    147, 167, 171, 177, 178, 182–4, 201,
    204–7, 215, 217, 223, 228, 229, 234
parish records 15, 56, 57, 82, 83, 87, 200,
    227
parish reports 182, 186, 239, 242, 251
parliamentary committees 109, 134, 144,
    148, 159
parochial officers 18, 185
patrons 22
Pattingham 82
Pattison, James 94, 96, 156, 239, 241, 282
Pattison, Nathaniel 62
pauperism 15, 16
pay 7, 124–5

differentials 160, 162, 167, 168
  equal 163
  gender gap 161
Pearce William 71
Peel, Robert 37, 61, 68, 94, 124, 172, 239, 253, 283
Peel, Yates and Co 72, 84, 282
Peel's Lancashire mills 172, 180, 189, 206, 226, 253
Pendleton (Douglas) 27, 38, 43, 59–66, 69, 75, 76, 81, 88, 93, 96, 109, 114, 116, 122, 132–3, 137, 147, 148, 155, 162, 168, 170, 181, 189, 191, 203, 211, 230, 240, 243, 257, 272
Pennant, Thomas 170
Pepall, William 116
petitions 50
Philanthropic Society 5
Picking 21, 132–3
piecers 131
piecing 132
Pitt, William 4
placements for parish apprentices 20, 26, 28, 33, 35–6, 51, 58, 73, 81, 85, 86, 117, 128–9, 139, 153, 158, 195, 219
placements, suitability of 20, 33, 35–6, 225, 232, 234, 262
Plagiarism (in factory reports) 240
Plant, John 38, 114, 191
Pleasley 105, 126, 133, 269
pocket money 162, 189
Pollard, Sidney 178
Pontefract 6
poor children
  demand for 33, 35, 55, 78, 85, 95, 101, 106, 128
  supply of 7, 8, 33, 35, 55, 73, 78, 85, 88, 95, 101, 128
Poor Law
  administration 31
  legislation 51
  officials 13, 29, 30, 133, 152, 178, 209, 215, 222, 238, 239, 246, 251, 261, 264
  system 15–31
Poor rate 16, 18
Poor relief 15, 16, 17, 23, 31, 126
Poor relief crisis 31
population 3, 18, 141
  centres 96
  pressure 110

Post-binding enquiries 140
poverty 7, 12, 15, 17, 18, 22, 31, 58, 78, 200
Poynter, J R 17
prayer books 141
prayers 141, 208, 258
pre-binding inspection 230
preferential sorting 148, 154
pregnancy 170
premium 19, 20, 23, 24, 25, 30, 34, 35, 40, 41, 42, 44, 108, 117, 118, 119, 120, 121, 123
  installments of 19, 42, 114, 118, 223
Prestwich 65, 80
printing 137
privies 250
productivity 1, 3, 121–2, 125, 127, 130, 168
profits 11, 40, 120
profitability 98, 108, 111, 127, 129, 130, 131, 176, 189
promiscuity 173, 256
protection of parish apprentices 215–38, 239
  by community 216, 236, 250
  by parents 235
protection
  formal mechanisms of 216
  informal mechanisms of 216, 228, 235
  ratings 219
protective measures 13, 116, 216, 217, 229, 237
protective parishes 115, 179, 225, 226, 239, 259
proto-industry 2
puberty 146, 151, 153, 160, 164, 168, 169
punishment 179, 180, 181, 184, 201, 254
  corporal 13, 176, 178, 179, 213
punishments 179

Quarry Bank 37, 119
Quarter Sessions 18, 49, 235, 255, 281, 282

Radcliffe Bridge 94, 172, 206, 253, 282
Rainey, Mr 38
Rainow, Macclesfield 68, 77, 268
Ratcliffe Bridge 84
rate payments 16, 27
ratepayers 15, 16, 29, 30, 107
reading 48, 141, 165
reassignment 30, 40, 52, 84, 98, 101, 195–6, 247, 254, 263, 266, 270, 271, 276, 283
record-keeping 102

recreation 98, 173, 242, 246, 248, 257
Rector 18, 221
Redford, Arthur 6, 27
regulation 11, 34, 47, 125, 171, 234, 256
relationship between parish and factory
    owner 11, 27, 33, 36–7, 95, 99, 106, 111, 117, 140, 176, 180, 218, 239, 260
religion 248
    instruction in 48, 115–16, 140, 141, 142, 164, 244, 246, 247, 256
Report from the Committee on Parish Apprentices, 1815 56, 57
reporting, frequency of 49, 224, 231, 246
reports
    of inspections 49, 51, 221, 224, 226, 246
    of parish visitors 221, 224, 226, 246
Repton parish 80
retention intentions 219
retention rate 147, 148, 156, 242, 247, 258
rewards 124, 179, 180
ribbon weaving 82, 83, 227
Rickmansworth 75, 78, 89, 94, 100, 121, 161, 182, 190, 211, 241, 243, 258, 285
River Leen 127
Robinson, Mr 38, 157
Robinson of Papplewick 84, 94, 98, 109, 127–8, 156, 284
rollers 131, 144, 184
Romilly, Sir Samuel 33, 34
Rose, Mary 34
rovers 122, 163
roving 133, 137
Royal Military Asylum (RMA) 98, 99, 103, 110, 281, 282
Royds, Toplis and Toplis 70, 77
Royston parish 147, 272
runaway apprentices 76, 122, 124, 132, 160, 171, 180, 205–6, 209, 228, 242, 289
running away 27, 160, 183, 203, 209
Rushworth, John 72

sadistic acts 179, 184
St Anne parish Soho 39, 42, 43, 73, 76, 218, 219, 220
St Barts the Great parish 100, 284
St Botolph Aldergate parish 76, 227, 268, 275, 276
St Botolph parish 73, 277
St Botolph without Aldersgate parish 77. 227, 268

St Clement Danes parish, Westminster 40, 42, 45, 59, 60–61, 96, 118, 147, 157, 161, 166–7, 183, 190, 205, 207, 218, 219, 220, 221, 228, 251, 266, 269, 271, 272, 273, 274, 280, 281, 290
St Clements parish, Oxford 28, 108, 217, 220, 251, 285
St Dunstan in the West parish 28, 295
St George in the East parish 71
St George parish, Edgbaston 84, 85, 267, 293
St George the Martyr parish, Southwark 71, 72, 147, 166, 179, 218, 219, 220, 221, 231, 266, 268, 269, 270, 271, 276, 280, 281, 282, 289
St George parish, Hanover Square 26, 39, 73, 74, 115, 218, 219, 220, 221, 249, 256, 267, 268, 269, 270, 271, 276, 280, 281, 284
St Giles in the Fields parish 60, 61, 63, 118, 158, 218, 220
St Giles workhouse 59
St Giles, Middlesex 28
St James parish Piccadilly 35, 38, 42, 46, 73, 75, 99, 100, 115–16, 122–4, 137, 140, 141, 146, 147, 152, 157, 161, 162, 163, 164, 167, 173, 182, 183, 189, 195, 202–203, 207, 210, 211, 218, 219, 220, 221, 222, 223, 224, 225, 256, 258, 259, 272–3, 272, 275, 276, 277, 280, 281, 284, 285
St Leonard parish Shoreditch 28, 43, 46, 71, 73, 118, 218, 219, 220, 271
St Luke parish Finsbury 138, 218, 219, 220
St Luke parish Chelsea 36, 37, 41, 45, 60, 63, 95, 117, 193, 205, 218, 219, 220
St Margaret and St John parish Westminster 43, 73, 77, 205, 206, 208, 218, 219, 220, 221, 236, 238, 270, 274, 279, 280, 288, 289
St Martin in the Fields parish 21, 42, 45, 60, 65, 108, 149, 158, 218, 219, 220, 221, 257, 265, 266, 268, 271, 272, 273, 274, 275, 276, 277, 279, 280, 283, 284, 290, 291
St Mary Newington parish 28, 38, 44, 73, 76, 148, 177, 218, 219, 220, 225, 247, 259
St Marylebone parish 22, 57, 98, 284, 288
St Olave parish, Southwark 118

St Pancras Directors of the Poor 39, 139, 183
St Pancras parish 38, 39, 41, 42, 43, 44, 46, 60, 63, 64, 99, 115, 116, 136, 139, 171, 177, 183, 201, 218, 219, 220, 221, 232, 233, 236, 237, 254, 263, 265, 272, 273, 274, 275–6, 278, 279, 281, 282, 284
St Paul parish, Covent Garden 73, 75, 218, 219, 220, 275, 276, 280, 281
St Sepulchre parish 100
scavengers 131, 132
scavenging 132, 145
School of Industry 5, 10, 20, 21, 35
schoolmaster 141
science 165
Scotland 95, 159, 163, 168
Sculwater parish 87, 269
scutchers 148
Seccombe, Wally 121, 175, 176
seduction 172
segregation 48, 126, 158, 170–73, 186
Select Committee 1816 56, 59, 109, 135, 138, 147, 169, 185, 186, 256, 258, 264, 266
Select Committees 11, 56, 59, 109, 135, 138, 147, 169, 185, 186, 187, 246, 247, 256, 258, 264, 266
sense of exploitation by apprentice 204, 210, 212
serge weaver 79
servants 24, 50, 105, 121, 168, 265
settlement 23–8, 95, 104, 263
settlement examinations 7, 79, 147, 168, 200, 212, 213, 264
Sevenoaks 157
Sewardstone 120, 230, 257, 280
Sewell and McMurdo 64, 74, 94, 110, 156, 257, 284
Sewell, Mr 44
sex ratio 38, 158
sex of worker 21, 151–8, 169, 170, 186, 265–91
sexes
    mingling of 6, 35, 157, 164, 170, 173, 256
    separation of 164, 170–72
sexual
    abuse 13, 176, 185, 186, 255
    exploitation 185, 186
    impropriety 170

sexuality 170
Sheepshead, Leics 74, 86, 268
Sheffield 2, 51, 62, 66, 67, 69, 73, 94, 97, 105, 108, 123, 184, 205, 228, 242, 245, 254, 290
Shrewsbury 21, 81, 85, 92, 93, 99, 137, 157, 179, 218, 219, 220, 240, 267
Shrewsbury workhouse 21
Shrewsbury House of Industry 267, 278
Shropshire 81, 95, 267, 298
Shustoke parish 83, 277, 278
Shute, Thomas Rock 94, 156, 284
siblings 207
sickness 118, 160, 251, 254
silk 12, 26, 58, 83, 95, 108, 157, 239, 261
silk mills 22, 81, 89, 96, 98, 100, 109, 118, 120, 211, 222, 230, 257, 280
    Berkshire 100
    Hertfordshire 89, 100, 120, 211, 230, 257
Singleton, John and William 67, 94, 97, 106, 156, 284
skill 5, 9, 13, 21, 22, 43, 129–31, 136, 138, 140–2, 145, 146, 149, 151–2, 158, 166–7, 208, 210, 224, 261
    gender distinctions in 142, 151–2, 158, 166–7, 208, 224
skills
    specialist 130, 261
    transferable 13, 129, 130, 139–42, 149
Skipton in Craven 6
sleeping
    accommodation 48, 170, 173, 253, 262
    rooms 246
Smart, Benjamin 28, 36, 42, 63, 87, 94, 99, 108, 117, 156, 157, 241, 245, 284, 285
Smell 145
Smelser, Neil 119
Snell, K. D. M. 23, 129, 141
social control, 129
social mobility, 149
socialisation 142, 144, 153, 165–7, 173
Society for Bettering the Condition of the Poor 5, 47, 201, 250
soldiers 103
South Shields 68
Southampton 99, 103, 110, 281–2
Southwark 118, 166, 219, 220, 221, 231, 268, 269, 270, 276, 280, 281, 282, 288, 289

Southwell 62
spelling 22
spindles 79, 131, 145
Staffordshire 12, 26, 28, 63, 80, 81, 82, 92, 93, 94, 95, 103, 149, 218, 219, 253
statutes 18, 48
steam power 2, 133, 144
Stock, William 233
Stockport 56, 67, 71, 72, 92, 97, 105, 141, 157, 165, 166, 179, 185, 219, 265, 268, 269
stoicism of parish apprentices 182, 195, 199, 201, 208
strapped 132, 180, 183, 184, 201, 254
Strutt, Messrs 75, 94, 100, 156, 161, 182, 190, 211, 224, 241, 243, 258–9, 285
Styal 2, 81, 82, 93, 96, 102, 105, 109, 132, 148, 171, 188, 203, 210, 244
subsistence costs 122
Suffolk 12, 88, 218, 219, 220
Summerseat 84, 94, 172, 206, 282–3
Sunday School 115, 141, 159
Superintendent 131, 135, 171, 182, 248, 266
supervision 3, 129, 145, 197, 226
    costs of 125, 128
supper 191–2, 205
surgeon 50, 59, 134, 135, 159, 169
Sutton in Ashfield, Notts 24, 286
sweepers 131

Tamworth 67, 68, 80, 82, 83, 93, 94, 99, 273, 274, 283, 291
Taplow, Bucks 71
tasks 3, 9, 13, 130–32, 136, 142, 153, 154, 166
    gendering of 153–4, 160, 164, 166–7, 173
taxpayers 24
technical change 106, 127, 158, 159, 250
technology 1, 2, 9, 12, 114, 127, 130, 131, 136, 178
testimony 59, 133, 135, 138, 144, 147, 152, 160, 170, 182, 185, 190, 224, 234, 236, 256
Tettenhall 82
textile manufacturers 8, 85, 113, 148, 156
textile production 2, 6, 12, 13, 82, 91, 92, 129, 130, 151
textiles 58, 91, 111, 152
Thaxted 81
Thompson, E P 143, 175

Thompsons, Thorner 78, 222
Tideswell 61, 71–2, 74, 93, 162, 280
Tissington 92, 98, 109, 269
Toplis and Co. 45, 57, 70, 73, 77, 80, 81, 84, 86, 94, 97–9, 105–107, 123, 138, 156, 160, 162, 166, 172, 177, 188–9, 191, 193, 195, 203, 206, 208, 212, 219, 221, 230–34, 241, 243, 247–9, 262, 270–271, 276, 285
Toplis, John 97, 219, 227
Toplis, William 37, 46, 219, 276, 289
Tottenham parish 57, 287
training 7, 13, 20, 21, 23, 37, 129, 130, 136, 139–40, 146, 235, 242, 243, 259, 262
    programme 136–7, 153
    formal 129, 137
    in domesticity 167, 229
    through 'experience of work' 122–3, 136–7, 142–4, 146 149, 264
transferable skills, gender-specific 152–3, 164
transportation costs 95, 106, 114, 116, 124, 128
Trollope, Frances 251
Tutbury 62, 74, 82, 84, 85, 92, 99, 149, 154, 158, 159, 161, 240, 243, 246–7, 267
twisting 131

Ure, Andrew 134, 146

Vaux, Mr 22
Vavasour, William 209, 250
ventilation 48, 49, 244, 250, 253, 256
vestry meetings 11, 44, 47
Vicar 18, 37, 247
visits of parish officers to apprentices 47, 117, 132, 140, 170, 180, 195, 199, 204, 221, 225, 226, 228, 235, 239, 246
visits, reports of 11, 74, 132, 199, 216, 218, 226, 246

wage differentials 121–2, 153, 161–3, 164,166–7
wage rates 119,121–2, 125, 126, 128, 142, 146, 161, 167, 212
Wales 95, 96
Waltham Cross 230
Walton Twist Co 94, 105, 156, 171, 241, 243, 289
Walton-le-dale, Lancs 77, 94, 171, 289
Warley 79

Warwickshire 12, 28, 36, 63, 82, 87, 95, 98, 99, 108, 218, 219, 220, 236, 273–4, 277, 284–5
washing 117, 167, 208
water frame 2, 132, 144, 158
water power 2, 124–5, 127
water spinners 96
water spinning 131–2, 136, 189
Watford 66, 94, 118, 181, 211, 227, 241, 257, 284, 290
Watson, Thomas 66, 94, 156, 241, 243, 257, 290
Webb, Beatrice 25, 34, 40
Webb, Sidney 25, 34, 40
Wednesbury 83
Weir, John 94, 196, 290
welfare of apprentices 104, 116, 119, 127, 165, 170, 173, 195–6, 204, 216, 221, 225, 229, 238, 242–3, 246, 261, 263
well-being of apprentices 132, 138, 202, 247, 259
Wells, Joseph 62, 69
Wells, Middleton 66, 94, 105, 156, 183, 228, 242–3
West House Mills 70, 72, 73, 137, 257, 269
Westbury, Shropshire 267
whipping (*see also* beating, corporal punishment)
Whitaker, John 38, 94, 242, 243, 247
Whitby 64, 68
Whitelegg, James 68, 94, 97, 106, 156, 291
whitewashing 49, 126, 244, 257
Whitham 81
Wigan 67, 94, 149, 284
Wildboar Clough 38, 74, 75, 76, 96, 140, 195, 202, 210, 223, 275
Wild, John 65
Wilks and Jewsbury 83
Willcock, William 28, 82, 83
Willenhall 83
Wilsden 79
Winster 98, 269, 291
Witney, Oxon 87, 218, 220, 236
Wokingham, Berks 94, 290
Wolfenden, Joseph 65
Wolverhampton metal trades 81
Wood, Kinder 59
Woodford parish 177, 230, 280, 287
Woollan, Charles 94, 156, 291
Woolley and McQueen 94, 156, 157, 242, 245

Worcester St John parish 85
Worcestershire 12, 26, 42, 51, 85, 218, 219, 220
work
  apprentice experience of 176
  as amusement 135
  children's (*see under* children)
  conditions of 178, 188
  ease of 133–4
  factory 5, 45, 129, 134, 135, 136, 143, 144, 146, 149, 154, 168, 169
  farm 37
  habit of 4, 5, 20, 22, 144, 187
  hours of 13, 176, 187, 188, 204, 206, 211, 229, 242, 245, 251, 253–5, 258, 262
  intensity of 135
  'lightness' of 134, 200
  monotony of , 3, 133
  nature of 2, 26, 129–49, 188, 193, 262
  regularity of 144, 189
  routine 143, 180
  skilled 129
  discipline 142, 178, 262
  identity 10, 167–8, 173
Workers, independent 131
  youthful 10, 97, 114, 125, 152–3, 200, 213, 262
workforce 8, 9, 12, 35, 99, 104, 124–5, 130, 151, 258
workhouse 140–41, 143, 157, 177, 180, 190, 196, 201, 205, 207–208, 212, 223, 225, 234, 237, 255, 262
Workman, Brummell and Hall 70, 94, 100, 156, 157, 291
workshop 1, 10, 21, 26, 249
Worksop 71, 93, 276, 286
worsted 1, 6, 12, 45, 58, 63, 67, 70–74, 77, 79, 84, 86, 88, 92–5, 97–8, 108, 138, 231, 261, 270, 276
  spinning 79, 138
writing (*see also* literacy) 48, 165
writing materials 224

Yates, Thomas 68, 72, 94, 156, 291
Yorkshire 4, 7, 12, 37, 50, 67, 71, 72, 74, 89, 95, 96, 205, 276
Yorkshire spinners 50